Computer Science: A First Course

NEW YORK   LONDON   SYDNEY   TORONTO

COMPUTER SCIENCE
A First Course

A. I. Forsythe

T. A. Keenan

E. I. Organick

W. Stenberg

SECOND EDITION

John Wiley & Sons, Inc.

Library of Congress Cataloging in Publication Data

Main entry under title:

Computer science, a first course.

  Includes index.
  1. Algorithms. 2. Electronic data processing.
I. Forsythe, Alexandra I.
QA76.C573 1975   001.6′4   74-34244
ISBN 0-471-26681-7

Printed in the United States of America

10 9 8 7 6 5 4 3 2 1

In today's world (and even more in tomorrow's) timely, accurate, and appropriate information is a prime commodity. The communication and processing of information, whether in business, science, education, or government, has become one of the world's major endeavors. Computers are indispensable in this effort and students at all levels, particularly in colleges, want to learn not only what computers are, but also what computers can and cannot do. Many of these students hope to understand how they themselves can use computers to solve problems and to process information. To help all such people reach these educational objectives, this book is designed either as a self-study guide or as a basic textbook for an introductory course in computer science.

The book has evolved over a ten-year period in parallel with the subject itself. The first printing appeared under the series title, "Algorithms, Computation and Mathematics," published by the School Mathematics Study Group program at Stanford University (1965). Later this text was extended in scope for a broader audience as *Computer Science: A First Course* (Wiley, 1969). Ten years of teaching, testing, and learning with previous versions have led us to the present edition. We hope that it is a major improvement and enrichment of our earlier efforts.

In several ways this series has served as a model for other writers. The fundamental plan has been to order and develop a carefully selected set of concepts and principles while deliberately omitting all of the special details one needs to use a particular tool. Examples of such special detail are the properties of individual computing systems and particular programming languages. We have concentrated on providing for the student a useful frame of reference in which to understand and interpret these "laboratory" details, expecting him to acquire specific information on particular systems and languages from manuals written for that purpose. Certain manuals have been designed to supplement this text and are therefore especially convenient sources of reference information, but almost any language or system manual can be used profitably as a supplement. Thus an introductory course using this text can be organized so that the (essential) laboratory part is as distinct from and complementary to the lecture-discussion part as the instructor may desire to make it.

The useful *frame of reference* mentioned above consists of two major components and one connecting theme. The two components are:

1. A classroom-tested conceptual model of a computer system. [This powerful (and extendable) abstraction is used instead of any particular computer system with its inevitable idiosyncracies.]
2. A classroom-tested simple flowchart language (including declarative annotations) that serves as a common denominator and abstraction of many widely used programming languages.

The connecting theme is the emphasis placed on operational semantics to deduce the meaning of computer algorithms. Students learn to trace the execution of flowchart algorithms by "exercising" the conceptual model, which serves as the interpreter or abstract machine.

Most early introductory computer science texts used an actual machine and an actual language as teaching vehicles—usually selecting among the most "popular" of these, for example, the IBM Systems 360 or 370 and the FORTRAN, BASIC, or COBOL languages. However, a student whose introduction to computer science is tied too closely to such *particular* tools may end up equating the tools with the science that now gives rise to them. We believe our approach avoids this pitfall with ease.

If our approach offers greater generality and thus greater educational opportunity, it is also more challenging to the teacher and more demanding of the student. More responsibility falls on the learner to apply the principles and to discover the connections between the abstract concepts and their concrete realizations as he uses and experiments with them in the laboratory.

A student who first reads this book as a one-time ("one-shot") study effort but who later becomes interested in deeper study will find that no *unlearning* is necessary. He should be able to proceed with confidence to the next course in any collegiate-level computer science curriculum. This explains our subtitle, "A First Course."

A book of this size requires a brief overview of its contents, chapter by chapter. But first, for the benefit of readers familiar with the previous edition, we list eight key improvements of this edition.

1. Greater emphasis on the connection between procedural language (high-level) constructs and their realization in actual machines. Several types of computer architecture are considered including non-von Neumann storage structures and stack machines.

2. Special emphasis on program annotation, achieved partly by the use of flowchart *legends,* an abstraction of the usual declarative information found in computer programs written in everyday programming languages.

3. A consistent effort to develop and exploit concepts of top-down problem solving and methods of structured programming.

4. A significant increase in the number and type of classroom-proven drill exercises, problems, and projects. (Many of the new ones are drawn from *Projects and Study Problems* by Forsythe, Organick, and Plummer, Wiley, 1973.)

5. A new and more extensible model for explaining the semantics of subroutines (procedures and functions) and an in-depth treatment of *recursion.*

6. An introduction to data processing fundamentals, stressing both *batch* and *on-line* processing in record-keeping systems (an entirely new chapter).

7. A deeper treatment of numerical approximation and the origin and propagation of roundoff and truncation error, in floating-point number systems.

8. Most chapters include a bird's eye view introduction to put the material into perspective for the reflective student. (See, for instance, the overview on page 1 of Chapter 1 that discusses What is Computer Science? This particular overview was drawn, in part, from the published remarks of Professor Alan J. Perlis, in *ACM SIGCSE Bulletin, Vol. 2, No. 4,* Sept.-Oct., 1970, pp. 26–29.)

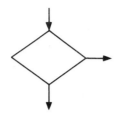

A. N. S. I. decision box

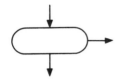

Our decision box

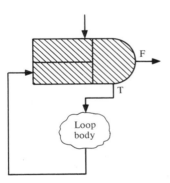

Definite iteration

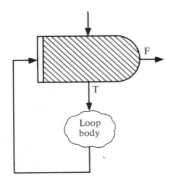

Indefinite iteration

To facilitate the construction of algorithms having both good structure and good documentation, our flowchart conventions differ in several respects from the standards adopted by the American National Standards Institute (A.N.S.I.). For example, as our decision box we have chosen a flattened oval shape of arbitrary length rather than the A.N.S.I. diamond shape. Our motivation is to encourage the student to describe each decision step in full rather than to curtail or abbreviate it, especially during initial attempts at problem decomposition. The diamond shape reenforces condensation in the sense that as one attempts to describe a decision in any detail, the enclosing diamond grows large not only horizontally, but *vertically* as well.

The ideas of structured programming lead to the conclusion that every entry into a loop and every departure from one should be carefully controlled. To help implement this control we use two special bullet-shaped flowchart boxes, one for definite iteration (a loop controlled by a counter) and the other for indefinite iteration (a loop controlled by a *while* condition). In each case the loop body "hangs" from the control structure, as shown on the left. We are convinced that these non-standard loop control boxes help the student to understand and to practice structured programming without overconstraining him.

This book is organized into thirteen chapters, the first five of which form a basic introductory unit. Three fundamental ideas of computing appear in the first chapter: the algorithm, its expression as a flowchart, and SIMPLOS, a conceptual model of a computer that can execute such algorithms. In addition the reader learns about a (widely simulated) hypothetical but realistic von Neumann-like digital computer, called SAMOS. SAMOS is especially useful for early laboratory practice.

SIMPLOS is an amplification of the conceptual model used in previous editions. Now an additional robot, the Affixer, functions as a storage and name manager, serving with the Reader and Assigner as aides to the Master Computer robot. (The Affixer plays a key role in the handling of storage environments for *procedures,* a very important topic covered in later chapters.)

The first chapter also discusses numeric and nonnumeric information representation. By the end of this chapter all the fundamentals of the flowchart language have been introduced, accompanied by appropriate discussions of assignment, branching, and looping, and with the realization of these algorithmic constructs on an actual machine.

The next two chapters not only develop more complete explanations of the fundamentals but add auxiliary concepts for computation and data organization, such as arithmetic and string expressions, conditional branching and one-dimensional array (or list) structures. Chapter 2 strongly emphasizes character string processing, treating it on a par with arithmetic processing. Chapter 3 shows several examples of the construction of an algorithm; the Euclidean algorithm example illustrates integer data, while the Newton square root algorithm shows a case with real data. The section on lists and subscripted variables extends the storage cell model developed in Chapter 1 to accommodate lists. The discussion of list operations includes notation not only for element-by-element operations but also for higher-level (APL-like) operations on entire lists.

In Chapter 4 the student's understanding of all these concepts is integrated and refined with the help of more illustrative examples and by an emphasis on looping and loop structures. Careful distinction is drawn between *definite* iteration, using the counter controlled *iteration* box, and *indefinite* iteration, using the *while* box construct. The chapter focuses on single loops and their structure. Two-dimensional arrays are introduced and used in many examples and problems. Various other types of data structures are examined (e.g., tables, jagged arrays, and linked lists). Discussion of nested loops and more difficult problems requiring more control structure is left to the next and last of the five most "basic" chapters.

Chapter 5 uses nested loops as a vehicle to introduce the concept of *stepwise decomposition* (the well-known top-down problem-solving methodology). The second section introduces parameterless procedures as part of the decomposition method. A substantial problem is then illustrated using the decomposition philosophy. The last two sections squarely face the problem of achieving program quality by explicit attention to good structure. This portion of the book constitutes an elementary treatment of structured programming. The subject is continued in Chapter 9, but the development in Chapter 5 is applied informally in all the remaining chapters. Chapter 5 ends with an example showing that "good structure" is not entirely synonymous with good algorithm.

Chapters 6 to 8 provide an informal introduction to data structures primarily as a basis for the nonnumerical applications including data processing (Chapter 10) and symbol manipulation (Chapter 13). Chapters 6 and 7 introduce the reader to the representation, scanning, and manipulation of tree structures. Certain decision processes (such as two-person games) and certain types of data (such as character strings representing arithmetic expressions) inherently possess, or are best exhibited as, tree structures.

Chapter 6 introduces and applies one tree search algorithm (depth first). The same algorithm is reapplied in Chapter 7 and is redeveloped in Chapter 9 using recursive procedures. A second tree-scanning algorithm (breadth first) is also introduced in Chapter 7, along with concepts for the storing of tree-structured data and for the pruning of such structures. Algorithms are developed to analyze the outcome of games as applications of tree search concepts.

Chapter 8 is concerned with the manipulation of (program) trees as a basis for interpreting or compiling programs by computer. We show how to express program statements as trees in either infix or postfix form and introduce concepts and methods to convert infix expressions into postfix form and to evaluate postfix expressions. A stack machine architecture, called POSTOS, is described as a device that can execute (and hence evaluate) postfix code. Finally, generalized interpreter and compiler algorithms are developed as natural extensions of the postfix evaluator algorithm. (The interpreter and compiler algorithms are reconsidered in Chapter 13 where string processing primitives are applied to streamline the algorithmic description.)

Chapters 9 to 13 focus on significant but more advanced and more technical topics, some of which will be of interest to practically every student. Majors in computer science will probably investigate all these topics more completely in later courses. Each of these five chapters deserves two or more weeks of study.

Chapter 9 develops to its full usefulness the crucially important concept of procedure, first introduced in Chapter 5. Procedures are the building blocks from which complex modular systems can be formed. The idea of a separate storage environment for each procedure unit is motivated. The sharing of global variables, the isolation of locals, and the transmission of information between environments by means of an argument-parameter matching mechanism are introduced in this chapter. The semantics of procedure entry and exit and the distinction between call by reference and call by value parameter treatments are explained by an easy extension of the cell-oriented SIMPLOS model of Chapter 1. This new extension enables the explanation of recursion to be greatly simplified. Recursive procedures are discussed at length, as is the natural equivalence between tree traversal and the execution of recursive procedures.

Chapter 10 is an in-depth introduction to some of the characteristic data structures, accessing methods, and processing common to "business data processing" (e.g., merging and sorting of sequential files, handling of variable-length records, table management (including hashing), and storage allocation strategies using linked lists and linked records). The first half of the chapter focuses on *batch*-organized record-keeping operations, and the second half focuses on *on-line* data base management operations.

Chapters 11 and 12 comprise the numerical methods portion of this book. Chapter 11 is an informal but rich introduction to the practical problems and pitfalls that arise in the representation and arithmetic processing of real numbers on real computers. It discusses the origin and propagation of error, especially in approximating real numbers using floating-point number systems. We examine how arithmetic is carried out on floating-point numbers on an actual machine in order to gain better understanding of round-off error and how to reduce it. (Chapter 11 draws heavily on the blueprint provided by the late G. E. Forsythe in the paper "Pitfalls in Computation", November 1970, *Mathematical Monthly,* and in his equally informative essay, "Solving a Quadratic Equation on A Computer", in *The Mathematical Sciences,* MIT Press, 1969.)

Chapter 12 develops four mathematical applications of computing selected from those used most often in scientific and engineering computation. These applications are: (1) finding the roots of an algebraic equation (method of bisection), (2) computing the area under a curve as required in numerical integration (trapezoidal, midpoint, and Simpson's rules), (3) solving systems of linear algebraic equations (Gauss elimination), and (4) averaging and linear regression (least squares). Neither Chapter 11 nor Chapter 12 presupposes the study of calculus. However, all students, even those who know calculus, should find that their understanding of mathematics and statistics has been strengthened through the study of this material.

Chapter 13 extends the earlier treatment of string processing by introducing powerful new flowchart primitives for string pattern match and replacement. These primitives are analogous to those found in some of the more specialized programming languages, in particular SNOBOL 4. For this reason, flowchart algorithms developed in this chapter may be mapped into SNOBOL programs with a minimum of effort. The chapter ends by applying the primitives developed here to the design of interpreter, compiler, and assembler algorithms. The simplification resulting from the use of string data structures and appropriate primitives enables the student of computer science to gain further insight into the close interdependence of algorithm, language, data representation, and computer system architecture.

There are two appendices followed by a set of answers to well over one hundred of the almost five hundred exercises in this book. Appendix A is an elementary programmer's guide for the hypothetical one-address digital computer called SAMOS. This computer is also discussed at some length in Chapter 1 and more briefly in several later chapters. Numerous exercises, especially in the early chapters, are keyed to this computer; therefore, a reading knowledge of at least the first sections of this appendix is useful to most students. Also, the text of this appendix attempts to couple the SAMOS machine constructs with the corresponding constructs of higher-level languages that are stressed in the text. This appendix is suggested as collateral reading at appropriate times in the course of studying the body of this book. However, instructors who have simulators for SAMOS find that asking students to write and test simple programs on this computer during the first week or two of the course helps the students to gain an early grasp of many basic principles.

Appendix B is a list of carefully selected readings, most of which also contain further reading lists. Our list is organized according to topics that a student may wish to pursue further after reading a particular chapter. No list of this type can be foolproof or complete, but we hope we have not omitted any important item that a reader will not discover starting from our list.

The entire book, together with laboratory exercises and experiments, may take a full year for thorough study and practice. Shorter courses using the book should cover most of the basic part (Chapters 1 to 8), and either Chapter 9, Chapter 10, Chapters 11 and 12, Chapter 13, or some combination of these chapters, depending on the orientation of the teacher or the interests of the students. These chapters are intended as advanced topics (the latter half of Chapter 9), as applications of the basic set to business data processing (Chapter 10), as

Selected Chapter Sections for a Nine- or Ten-Week Course with an Accompanying Laboratory

Chapter	Major Student Interest			
	General Education	Math/ Physical Science	Social/ Behavioral Science or Business	Computer Science
1	1 to 6	All	1 to 6	All
2	All	All	All	All
3	1,2,3,5,6	All	1,2,5,6	All
4	All	All	All	All
5	1 to 4	1,2,4	1,2,4	All
6	All	All	All	All
7	All	1,2	1,2	All
8	1 to 4	1 to 3	1,2	All
9	1 to 4	1 to 5	1,2,4	All
10	1,2	—	1 to 5	—
11	—	1,2,3,5	—	—
12	—	1,2,4	4,5	—
13	1 to 5	—	—	All
SAMOS	1 to 4	1 to 4	1 to 4	1 to 7

scientific and engineering applications (Chapters 11 and 12), or as computer science applications (Chapter 13).

According to the students' major interest the preceding table shows in greater detail several possible section sequences that can be selected from the chapters of this book for a nine-week quarter (three lecture hours per week plus laboratory). Some teachers may find a slower pace desirable. If two quarters are available, the first quarter might cover the first eight chapters, with the remainder of the text used in the second quarter. The perceptive instructor will find other paths through this text to satisfy the needs of his class.

Deciding how long to spend on the various chapters or sections is often a problem that confronts an instructor using this text for the first time. As a rough guide, each of the first eight chapters can be covered in a week or slightly longer, one or two sections per lecture. It is a good idea to proceed rapidly through the first three chapters in three or four weeks and then slow down a little in Chapters 4 and 5, especially if students require more time to complete the first few laboratory exercises and to consolidate their understanding. Chapters 6 to 8 can be covered in just over three weeks. Material selected from the later chapters can be covered at a comparable pace or may be stretched out according to the interests of the students and the amount of assigned homework and laboratory.

Objectives for the laboratory component of this course will naturally vary with the instructor and the curriculum. For example, at the University of Utah, the objective in the first quarter is for the student to become acquainted with programming in several types of languages instead of gaining expertise in one programming language. Hence the laboratory exercises are divided into three sets of experiments, each set using a different programming language. The first language, SAMOS, is the most primitive, and the third language, SNOBOL 4, is the most sophisticated, offering the highest level of semantic constructs. The second language, of intermediate level, may be any one comparable to BASIC or FORTRAN.

We have also experimented at the University of Utah with a variety of man-machine interfaces, one for each set of experiments. Thus the first set (SAMOS) runs on an interactive time shared minicomputer; the second set uses desk-top programmable calculators that directly execute a BASIC-like language;

the third set (SNOBOL 4) uses the university computer center's large-scale computer system from a remote batch terminal with an eighty-column card deck for input.

It is difficult to acknowledge everyone who supported us in preparing this edition. What began as a modest face-lift of an earlier work soon developed into another major project that could not have been completed without the help and encouragement of many individuals, including hundreds of students who agreeably accepted the chore of studying from notes that were hard to read and under almost continuous revision for a period of two years.

Special help and advice regarding portions of this manuscript were given to us by William Kahan, Robert Barnhill and John G. Herriot. We are also indebted to our coauthor and colleague R. P. Plummer who permitted us to reproduce and adapt to this edition a number of exercises and problems from *Projects and Study Problems*. Mike Milochik did the photograph in Figure 1·36, and Jerry Wray, her husband, and her daughter designed the robots. The best help of all came from Betty Organick, who patiently typed and retyped the final manuscript and provided the hospitality that made our writing sessions in Salt Lake City pleasant and productive.

A. I. Forsythe
T. A. Keenan
E. I. Organick
W. Stenberg

October, 1974

Contents

Computer Science: A First Course

Chapter

Algorithms and computers

Computers arouse curiosity in most of us. Articles in popular magazines and newspapers, current books, and TV shows heighten this curiosity, but such sources cannot be expected to present information in the carefully ordered sequences that is possible in a book like this. Whether you are drawn by curiosity alone, or economic necessity, or both, conscientious study of this book will help you to break through to a new level of understanding about computers, their uses, and their consequences.

Computer science deals with people who have problems to solve and with algorithms, the solutions to these problems. The solutions are expressed in special languages that represent stored data and communicate to machines the manipulations that are to be carried out on that data.

Each of these four elements (problem solver, algorithm, language, and machine) affects the others in interesting ways. For example, depending on its richness, a language can either limit or extend our ability to express complex plans of action effectively. And, depending on its capabilities (i.e., its architecture), a machine can execute some plans of action on certain data representations more effectively than on others. The loop of interaction closes when the problem solver changes the plan of action, the language, or the machine architecture to suit his purpose.

This book introduces all four components of this interaction. Every chapter takes you around this "four-cornered race track" and, with every circumnavigation, you gain a deeper and clearer understanding of the interplay among the four elements. You, of course, play the problem solver using a computer. To get the most out of this experience, laboratory practice is almost indispensable. But, even if you can't have actual computer experience, a careful reading of this book should illuminate the computer science scene far better and far beyond what you have previously perceived.

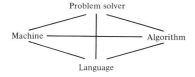

Elements of computer problem solving.

1·1
Algorithms and flowcharts

What is an algorithm? An *algorithm* is a list of instructions for carrying out some process step by step. A recipe in a cookbook is an excellent example of an algorithm. The preparation of a complicated dish is broken down into simple steps that every person experienced in cooking can understand. Another good example of an algorithm is the choreography for a classical ballet. An intricate dance is broken down into a succession of basic steps and positions of ballet. The number of these basic steps and positions is very small but, by putting them together in different ways, an endless variety of dances can be devised.

In the same way, algorithms executed by a computer can combine millions of elementary steps, such as additions and subtractions, into a complicated mathematical calculation. Also by means of algorithms, a computer can control a manufacturing process or coordinate the reservations of an airline as they are received from ticket offices all over the country. Algorithms for such large-scale processes are, of course, very complex, but they are built up from pieces, as in the example we will now consider.

If we *can* devise an algorithm for a process, we can usually do so in many different ways. Here is one algorithm for the everyday process of changing a flat tire.

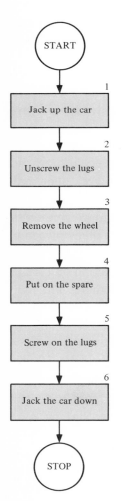

FIGURE 1·1
First flat-tire flowchart.

1. Jack up the car.

2. Unscrew the lugs.

3. Remove the wheel.

4. Put on the spare.

5. Screw on the lugs.

6. Jack the car down.

We could add many more details to this algorithm. We could include getting the materials out of the trunk, positioning the jack, removing the hubcaps, and loosening the lugs before jacking up the car, for example. For algorithms describing mechanical processes, it is generally best to decide how much detail to include. Still, the steps we have listed will be adequate to convey the idea of an algorithm. When we get to mathematical algorithms, we will have to be much more precise.

A *flowchart* is a diagram representing an algorithm. In Figure 1·1 we see a flowchart for the flat-tire algorithm.

The  and

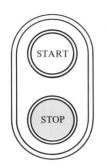

in the flowchart remind us of the buttons used to start and stop a piece of machinery. Each instruction in the flowchart is enclosed in a frame or "box." As we will soon see, the shape of the frame indicates the kind of instruction written inside. A rectangular frame indicates a command to take some action.

To carry out the task described by the flowchart, we begin at the start button and follow the arrows from box to box, executing the instructions as we come to them.

After drawing a flowchart, we always look to see whether we can improve it. For instance, in the flat-tire flowchart we neglected to check whether the spare was flat. If the spare *is* flat, we will not change the tire; we will call a garage instead. This calls for a decision between two courses of action. For this purpose we introduce a new shape of frame into our flowchart.

Inside this oval frame we will write an assertion instead of a command.

This is called a *decision box* and will have two exits, labeled T (for true) and F (for false). After checking the truth or falsity of the assertion, we choose the appropriate exit and proceed to the indicated activity. Incorporating the flowchart fragment on the left into Figure 1·1, we obtain the flowchart in Figure 1·2.

There is another instructive improvement possible. The instruction in box 2 of our flowchart actually stands for a number of repetitions of the same task. To show the additional detail we could replace box 2 by a step for each lug:

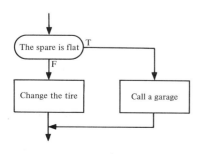

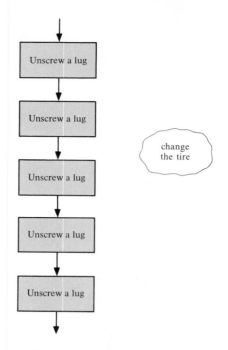

The awkwardness of this repeated instruction can be eliminated by introducing a *loop*.

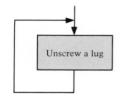

As we leave the box, we find that the arrow leads us right back to repeat the task again. However, we are caught in an endless loop, since we have provided no way to get out and go on with the next task. To correct this situation, we require another decision box, as shown on the left.

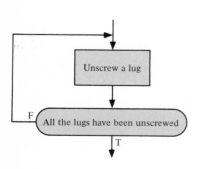

Replacing box 2 of our flowchart with this mechanism and making a similar replacement for box 5, we get the final result shown in Figure 1·3.

Now that you have followed the development of the flat-tire flowchart, try to devise one of your own. In the algorithm of the following exercise, you will probably discover some decisions and loops. There are many different ways of flow-charting this algorithm, so many different-looking flowcharts will be created.

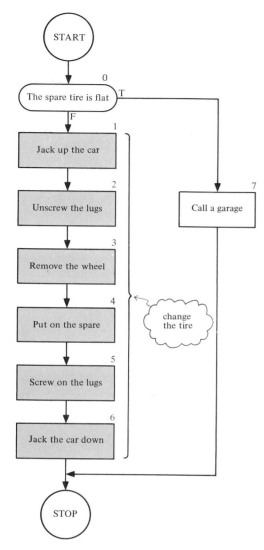

FIGURE 1·2
Second flat-tire flowchart.

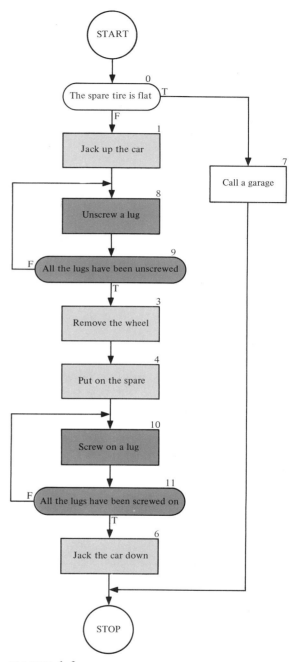

FIGURE 1·3
Final flat-tire flowchart.

1. Prepare a flowchart representing the following recipe.

Mrs. Good's Rocky Road

Ingredients:

1 cup chopped walnuts	$\frac{1}{2}$ cup evaporated milk
$\frac{1}{4}$ pound block of baker's chocolate	$\frac{1}{2}$ cup corn syrup
$\frac{1}{2}$ pound of marshmallows	1 teaspoon of vanilla
cut in halves	$\frac{1}{4}$ pound of butter
3 cups sugar	$\frac{1}{2}$ teaspoon of salt

Place milk, corn syrup, sugar, chocolate, and salt in a four-quart pan, and cook over a high flame, stirring constantly until the mixture boils. Reduce to medium flame and continue boiling and stirring until a drop of syrup forms a soft ball in a glass of cold water. Remove from the flame and allow to cool for 10 minutes. Beat in butter and vanilla until thoroughly blended. Stir in walnuts. Distribute marshmallow halves over the bottom of a 10-inch square, buttered baking pan. Pour syrup over the marshmallows. Allow to cool for 10 minutes. Cut in squares and serve.

1·2 A numerical algorithm

Now we are ready to examine an algorithm for a mathematical calculation. As a first example, we consider the problem of finding terms of the Fibonacci sequence:

$$0, 1, 1, 2, 3, 5, 8, 13, 21, 34, 55, \ldots$$

In this sequence, or list of numbers, the first two terms given are 0 and 1. After that, the terms are constructed according to the rule that each number in the list is the sum of the two preceding ones. Check that this is the case. Thus, the next term after the last one listed above is

$$34 + 55 = 89$$

Clearly, we can keep on generating the terms of the sequence, one after another, for as long as we like. But, in order to write an algorithm for the process (so that a computer could execute it, for example), we have to be much more explicit in our instructions.

Before subjecting this process to closer scrutiny, let us review a little of the interesting history of this sequence. It was introduced in 1202 A.D. by the Italian mathematician, Fibonacci, to provide a model of population growth in rabbits.

His assumptions were: (1) it takes rabbits one month from birth to reach maturity; (2) one month after reaching maturity, and every month thereafter, each pair of mature rabbits will produce another *pair* of rabbits; and (3) rabbits never die.

One senses that this model is not completely realistic. But the essence of mathematical modeling is to start with a crude model that emphasizes the important aspects of the situation and suppresses less important information. A more refined model can be developed later, profiting from the experience with the crude model. Thus we might eventually improve the Fibonacci model by obtaining more accurate figures on the birth rate, taking mortality into account, considering the limitations of food supply, the effects of predators, disease, and overcrowding, and the like.

In spite of its frivolous origins, the Fibonacci sequence has many fascinating properties and plays a role in the solution of a number of seemingly unrelated mathematical problems. There is currently a published quarterly journal entirely devoted to the properties and applications of the Fibonacci sequence.

After this long digression, let's see how the rabbit-pair population model gives rise to the Fibonacci sequence. Fibonacci starts with one pair of newborn rabbits at the beginning of month *one,* and he then lets nature take its course. This is shown in Table 1·1, which we now explain.

TABLE 1·1
Rabbit Population

Beginning of Month	1	2	3	4	5	6	7	8
Infant rabbit pairs	1	0	1	1	2	3	5	8
Mature rabbit pairs	0	1	1	2	3	5	8	13
Total rabbit pairs	1	1	2	3	5	8	13	21

Look at the arrows in the table. The number of pairs of infant rabbits in any month (after the first) is equal to the number of pairs of mature rabbits in the preceding month (condition 2 in the Fibonacci model). This explains the green arrows. In each month after the first, the number of pairs of mature rabbits will equal the total number of rabbit pairs in the preceding month (condition 1 in the Fibonacci model). This explains the gray arrows. Following the arrows, we see that, from the third month onward, the total in any month is the sum of the totals in the two preceding months. Thus the rabbit population model generates the Fibonacci sequence except for the initial zero, which can be taken as the total number of rabbits in month zero.

Eliminating the reference to rabbits, we can tabulate the calculation of the terms of the Fibonacci sequence in Table 1·2.

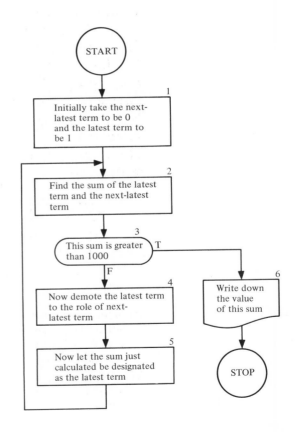

FIGURE 1·4
Flowchart for Fibonacci
sequence.

TABLE 1·2

Next Latest Term	Latest Term	Sum
0	1	0 + 1 = 1
1	1	1 + 1 = 2
1	2	1 + 2 = 3
2	3	2 + 3 = 5
3	5	3 + 5 = 8
5	8	5 + 8 = 13
8	13	8 + 13 = 21

We can see that in each step the latest term gets "demoted" to the role of next latest term and the sum becomes the new latest term.

Let's construct a flowchart for finding the first term to exceed 1000 in the Fibonacci sequence (Figure 1·4).

After going through the loop of flowchart boxes numbered 2 to 5 enough times (it happens to be 15 times), we eventually emerge from box 3 at the T exit and proceed to box 6. This box is seen to have a different shape because it calls for a different kind of activity—that of writing down our answer. The shape is chosen so as to suggest a page torn off a line printer, once the most common of computer output devices.

EXERCISES 1·2

1. (a) Suppose in the rabbit problem we had started in month one with one pair of infant rabbits and three pairs of mature rabbits. Make a table similar to Table 1·1 to show the state of the population over the first eight months.
   (b) How would you modify the flowchart of Figure 1·4 so as to generate the first term of this modified sequence greater than 1000?

2. Repeat Problem 1 with three pairs of infant rabbits and one pair of mature rabbits.

3. (a) For the Fibonacci sequence in Table 1·1, calculate from month two through month twelve the ratio, r, of the total number of

rabbits in the current month to that in the preceding month. Express each ratio as a decimal and carry out the calculation to the nearest thousandth.

(b) Express in your own words what seems to be happening to these ratios.

(c) Find the reciprocals of each of the ratios in Problem 3a.

(d) What relationship between the ratio r and its reciprocal $1/r$ seems to be becoming more and more true? Express this relationship as an equation.

(e) If this relationship held exactly, what would be the exact value of r? That is, solve the equation for r.

4. Repeat Problem 3 using:

(a) The table in Problem 1.
(b) The table in Problem 2.

1·3 SIMPLOS, a conceptual model of a computer

The algorithm of the preceding section can be expressed in much simpler notation that is, at the same time, more nearly acceptable by a computer as a set of instructions. To do this we must introduce a conceptual model of how a computer works. This conceptual model is so extraordinarily simple that we will call it the SIMPLOS computer. It is amazing, but true, that such a simple view of how a computer works is completely adequate for this entire course. We will present a more realistic picture of a computer in later sections of this chapter.

Variables

In computing work, a *variable* is a letter or a string of letters used to stand for something. For now, this "something" that a variable stands for will always be a number. (As we progress through this book, we will take an ever broadening view of the sort of thing a variable can stand for.) In the formula

$$A = L \times W$$

the letters A, L, and W are variables. In the formula

$$DIST = RATE \times TIME$$

DIST, RATE, and TIME are variables.

At any particular time, a variable will stand for one particular number, called the *value* of the variable, which may change from time to time during a computing process. The value of a variable may change millions of times during the execution of a single algorithm.

In our conceptual model of a computer we associate with

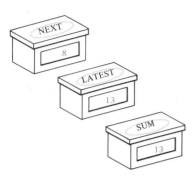

FIGURE 1·5
Storage.

each variable a *storage box*. On the top of each box there is a removable gummed sticker with the associated variable inscribed on it, and inside the box there is a strip of paper with the *present value* (or current value) of the variable written on it. The variable is a *name for the number* that currently appears inside.

Each box has a lid that may be removed when we wish to assign a new value to the variable. Each box has a window in the side so that we may read the value of a variable with no danger of altering its value. These boxes constitute the *storage* of our computer. In Figure 1·5 we see one stage in the execution of the Fibonacci sequence algorithm of the preceding section. Here NEXT stands for "next latest term" and LATEST stands for "latest term."

To summarize, the *data storage* of a computer is to be thought of as subdividable into a number of information containers or boxes. Each such storage box may be given a meaningful name (sticker), and each may be given (assigned) a value.

Some people view a computer as an electronic and mechanical system having a data storage similar to that just described, along with a number of other interconnected units or modules, each with a special set of functions that, when activated appropriately, carry out algorithms. Figure 1·6 is one way to depict the organization of such a computer system. If we were to pursue the explanation of this system according to the module view, it would be necessary to define the functions of each module and explain the significance of the arrowed lines into and out of each box. But it would also be

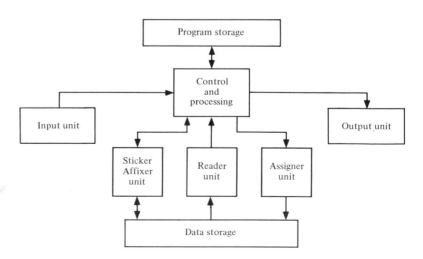

FIGURE 1·6
View of a SIMPLOS system as a set of interconnected modules.

necessary to bring the diagram to life by explaining the action sequences that occur in which each module serves the needs of the others so that the overall effect is to process information (i.e., to compute) in the desired fashion.

A second way to view a computer is to picture the active modules as robots working as a team. The actions of each robot always follow a fixed pattern, according to a set of relatively simple rules. We shall take this view in our conceptual model, SIMPLOS.

The Model and
How It Works

We visualize a computer as a number of storage boxes together with a staff of four robots—the *Master Computer* and three assistants, the *Assigner,* the *Reader,* and the *Sticker Affixer*. All these components are quartered in one room, isolated from those who will use the computer.

The Master Computer corresponds to the control and processing unit in Figure 1·6. He has a flowchart on his desk that sets forth the instructions according to which he delegates certain tasks to his assistants (Figure 1·7). "Note that the flowchart corresponds to the information kept in the *program storage* module of SIMPLOS."

FIGURE 1·7
The Master Computer and his staff.

Master Computer   Assigner   Reader   Sticker Affixer

To see how this team operates, let us suppose the computer is in the midst of executing the Fibonacci sequence algorithm of Figure 1·4. One of the instructions in this algorithm was:

2

Find the sum of the latest term and the next-latest term

In a simplified flowchart notation, this instruction will take the form:

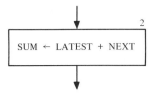

Inside this flowchart box we find an *assignment statement*. Reading this statement aloud, we would say, "Assign to SUM the value of LATEST plus NEXT," or more simply, "Assign LATEST + NEXT to SUM." The arrow pointing left is called the *assignment operator* and is to be thought of as an order or a command. Rectangular boxes in our flowchart language will always contain assignment steps and will therefore be called *assignment boxes*.

To see what takes place when the Master Computer comes to the above statement in the flowchart, let us assume that the variables LATEST and NEXT (but not SUM) have the values seen in Figure 1·5. The computation called for in the assignment statement is spelled out on the right-hand side of the arrow, so the Master Computer looks there first.

He realizes that he needs to know the values of the variables LATEST and NEXT, so he sends the Reader out to fetch copies of these values from storage.

The Reader then goes and finds the storage boxes labeled

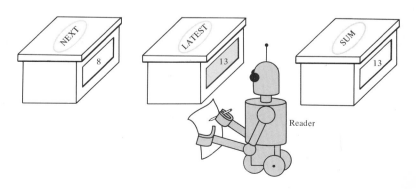

FIGURE 1·8
The Reader copying a value from storage.

LATEST and NEXT. He reads the values of these variables through the windows (Figure 1·8), jots down the values, and carries them back to the Master Computer (Figure 1·9).

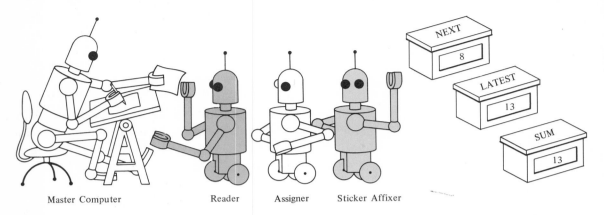

Master Computer   Reader   Assigner   Sticker Affixer

FIGURE 1·9
The Master Computer receives the copy.

The Master Computer computes the value of LATEST + NEXT using the values of these variables brought to him by the Reader:

$$8 + 13 = 21$$

What does he do with this value?

The Master Computer now looks to the left of the assignment arrow in his instruction.

SUM ← LATEST + NEXT

He sees that he must assign the computed value of LATEST + NEXT, namely, 21, to SUM so he writes "21" on a slip of paper, calls the Assigner, and instructs him to assign this value to the variable SUM.

The Assigner goes to storage, finds the box labeled SUM, and dumps out its contents (Figure 1·10). Then he places in the box the slip of paper containing the new value, closes the lid, and returns to the Master Computer for a new task.

In other words, assignment is the process of giving a value to a variable. We say that assignment is *destructive* because it displaces the former value of the variable. Reading is *nondestructive* because the process in no way alters the values of any of the variables in storage.

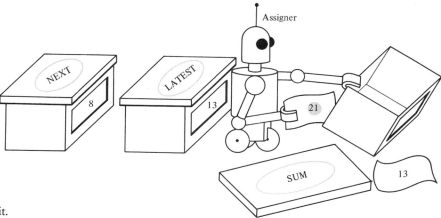

FIGURE 1·10
The Assigner emptying a
storage box and refilling it.

In Figure 1·11 we present the entire flowchart of Figure
1·4 in simplified flowchart language. The old and new flowcharts are placed side by side for easy comparison.

The translation requires very little explanation. It should
be obvious that the statement in box 1 on the left is equivalent
to the two statements in box 1 on the right. The new version
of box 2 has been discussed in detail.

We see that the two statements in boxes 4 and 5 of the
old flowchart are compressed into one box, box 4 of the new
flowchart. This is permissible whenever we have a number of
assignment statements with no other steps in between. However, it is very important to understand that these assignment
statements must be executed in order from top to bottom, not
in the opposite order and not simultaneously. The order in
which things are done may be extremely important.

You can see that the statements in box 4 involve no computation but merely change the values in certain storage boxes.
This sort of activity occurs frequently in flowcharts.

In box 6 of the flowchart we see only the word SUM.
The shape of the box (called an *output box*) tells us that the
value of the variable SUM is to be written down or displayed.
If, in some other algorithm, we wished to write down the values
of several variables, we would list these variables in an output
box separated by commas, as illustrated on the left.

We will now describe the duties of the Sticker Affixer.
We consider that the computation is begun by the transmittal
of a flowchart to the Master Computer. The first thing the
Master Computer does is to scan the flowchart, making a list

A, B, C, DIST

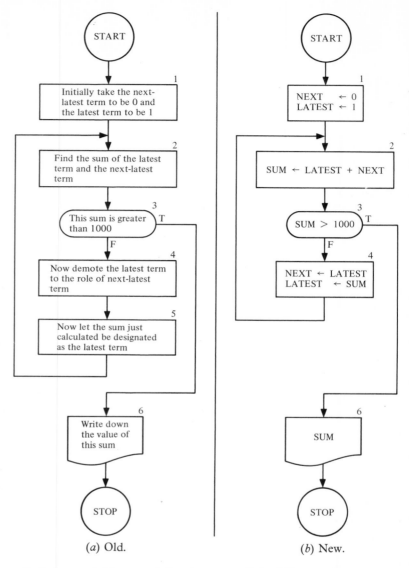

(a) Old. (b) New.

of all the variables used. In the case of the Fibonacci sequence flowchart of Figure 1·11b, this list would have the form

NEXT
LATEST
SUM

The Master Computer hands this list to the Sticker Affixer, who now springs into action. He inscribes each of these variables on a sticker, goes to a bin of unlabeled storage boxes, and slaps one of these stickers on each of three boxes (Figure 1·12).

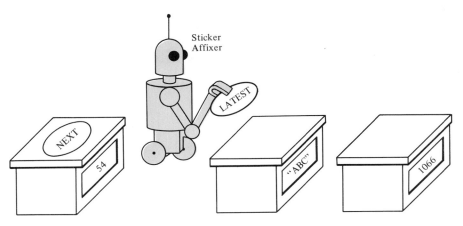

FIGURE 1·12
Sticker Affixer at work.

Now the instructions in the flowchart are executed until the

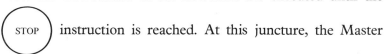 instruction is reached. At this juncture, the Master Computer directs the Affixer to unpeel all the labels and throw them into a recycle bin.

Tracing the Flowchart

To understand better what our flowchart in Figure 1·11*b* does, let us trace through it, executing the steps as the Master Computer and his assistants do them (see Table 1·3).

In this trace, for ease of reading, the values of the variables are reproduced only when assignments are made to them. In between such steps, the values of the variables do not change and therefore have the most recently recorded values. For example, in step 33, where a test is performed, the values of the variables are

$$NEXT = 55, \quad LATEST = 89, \quad SUM = 144$$

In step 34 the values are

$$NEXT = 89, \quad LATEST = 144, \quad SUM = 144$$

You can see that in step 48 in the execution of our algorithm we finally leave box 3 by the *true* exit and pass on to box 6, where we output the answer, 1597, and stop.

The utter simplicity of our conceptual model avoids and removes certain pitfalls. There is an ever-present danger of thinking of assignment as equality or substitution. (We will say

TABLE 1·3
Tracing of the Flowchart of Figure 1·11*b*

Step Number	Flowchart Box Number	Values of Variables			Test	True or False
		NEXT	LATEST	SUM		
1	1	0	1			
2	2			1		
3	3				1 > 1000	F
4	4	1	1			
5	2			2		
6	3				2 > 1000	F
7	4	1	2			
8	2			3		
9	3				3 > 1000	F
10	4	2	3			
11	2			5		
12	3				5 > 1000	F
13	4	3	5			
14	2			8		
15	3				8 > 1000	F
16	4	5	8			
17	2			13		
18	3				13 > 1000	F
19	4	8	13			
20	2			21		
21	3				21 > 1000	F
22	4	13	21			
23	2			34		
24	3				34 > 1000	F
25	4	21	34			
26	2			55		
27	3				55 > 1000	F
28	4	34	55			
29	2			89		
30	3				89 > 1000	F
31	4	55	89			
32	2			144		
33	3				144 > 1000	F
34	4	89	144			
35	2			233		
36	3				233 > 1000	F
37	4	144	233			
38	2			377		
39	3				377 > 1000	F
40	4	233	377			
41	2			610		
42	3				610 > 1000	F
43	4	377	610			
44	2			987		
45	3				987 > 1000	F
46	4	610	987			
47	2			1597		
48	3				1597 > 1000	T
49	6			1597		

more about this later.) This and other potential sources of confusion, such as the effect of a certain sequence of flowchart statements, can be cleared up by thinking in terms of the SIMPLOS model, which will always give the right answers.

In fact, an excellent way to understand these ideas of reading and assigning values to variables is to make some storage boxes and, with some friends, work through several algorithms as described in this section.

EXERCISES 1·3

1. What is the effect of changing the order of the two assignment statements in box 4 of Figure 1·11*b* so as to appear as seen below?

$$
\boxed{\begin{array}{l} \text{LATEST} \leftarrow \text{SUM} \\ \text{NEXT} \leftarrow \text{LATEST} \end{array}}
$$

Trace through the flowchart with this modification until you find the answer.

2. (a) To compare the effects of the assignment statements

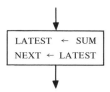

$$
\boxed{A \leftarrow B} \quad \text{and} \quad \boxed{B \leftarrow A}
$$

find the missing numbers in the table below.

Values Before Execution of Assignment		Assignment To Be Executed	Values After Execution of Assignment	
A	B		A	B
7	13	$\boxed{A \longleftarrow B}$	?	?
7	13	$\boxed{B \longleftarrow A}$	?	?

(b) In which of the two cases is it true that A = B *after* assignment?
(c) Are the effects of the two assignment statements the same or different?

3. Modify the flowchart in Figure 1·11*b* so as to carry out the algorithm of Problem 1, Exercises 1·2.

4. Modify the flowchart of Figure 1·11*b* so as to output each term of the Fibonacci sequence starting with the third (i.e., omit the initial 0, and 1).

5. Revise the flowchart of Problem 4 to calculate the ratio, r, of LATEST to NEXT (as calculated in Problem 3a, Exercises 1·2) and output this ratio (as well as LATEST) at each step.

6. Revise the flowchart of Problem 5 to calculate at each step the reciprocal of r. Add this value to the output list.

1·4
Input/output

Imagine that you are a bookkeeper in a large factory. You have records of the hourly rate of pay and the number of hours worked for each employee, and you have to calculate the week's wages. Of course, this can be done by hand, but assume there are nearly 1000 workers in the plant, so that the job would be quite tedious. Naturally you prefer to have the computer execute this task for you, but you will have to devise a flowchart to convey the instructions to the computer.

How will the hourly wages and the hours worked come into our computation? Must each new value of RATE and TIME be represented by a separate assignment box? This is certainly a possibility, but it would require thousands of flowchart boxes—a most undesirable state of affairs. This unpleasant necessity can be eliminated by using the concept of *input*.

We now introduce a new shape of frame, the *input box*, into the flowchart language. The input box has this shape to suggest a "punch card" (a frequently used input medium, but not the only one). Inside the box will appear a single variable or a list of variables separated by commas.

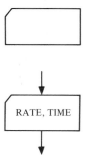

What happens in our SIMPLOS model when the Master Computer encounters such an instruction? To answer this question, we must endow the SIMPLOS model with an additional feature not previously needed (Figure 1·13). SIMPLOS has a conveyer belt (called the *input belt*) that carries slips of paper from outside the room into the environment of the computing staff. On the outside end of the belt the "user" or "programmer" (who is not a member of the computer staff) places these slips of paper, with values written on them, on the conveyer belt in the order in which he wants them to be used.

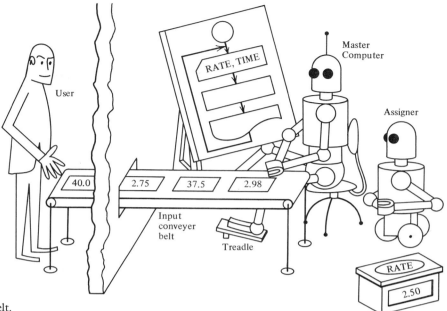

FIGURE 1·13
SIMPLOS with Input belt.

When the Master Computer comes to the input instruction he does the following.

1.   Steps on a treadle running the conveyer belt until the next slip of paper comes within reach.

2.   Remove his foot from the treadle, stopping the belt.

3.   Takes a slip of paper from the belt and hands it to the Assigner with instructions to assign the value thereon to the variable, RATE.

When the Assigner returns from this task, the Master Computer repeats the above process, but this time tells the Assigner to assign the new value to TIME. When this is done, the Master Computer follows the arrow in his flowchart to the next instruction.

We see that an input box is a command to make assignments, but this command is essentially different from that in an assignment box. In an assignment box the values to be assigned are to be found in computer storage or are computed from values already stored, whereas with an input box the values to be assigned are obtained from outside the computer. No calculation is called for in an input box. Moreover, the *values* to be input never appear in the flowchart itself. Only the *variables* to which these values are to be assigned appear in the input boxes of the flowchart.

In an actual computer (not our conceptual one) the distinction between the two kinds of assignment need not be so sharp. Assignments called for in an input box *usually* involve some mechanical motion such as transporting a punched card or other unit of recorded information past a reading station where the coded contents may be copied. But to gain speed the data often are transported into a special section of storage called an *input buffer,* well before the data are actually needed by the executing algorithm. In this case, when the input step is executed, what actually happens is that data values are simply copied at electronic speed from storage boxes of the input buffer to storage boxes of the variables that are specified in the input step of the algorithm.

Now let's see how to use the input box in our hourly rate and payroll problem. Should we input the data from all the cards before we start our calculations? If so, we would need a great many storage boxes in which to store all these data. Instead, we will calculate the wages after each data set is read. A description of our method is as follows.

1.   Input one value of RATE and one value of TIME by the process described above.

2.   Multiply the RATE by the TIME to get the WAGE.

3.   Output the values of RATE, TIME, and WAGE.

4.   Return to step 1.

In the flowchart of Figure 1·14 each of the first three steps of the above list appears in a similarly numbered box. Step 4 is represented by the arrow returning from box 3 to box 1.

You may wonder why the flowchart does not have a stop button. SIMPLOS always terminates execution of an algorithm when an input step is being executed, and the input belt contains too few values to match the variables in the input box. Execution of the payroll algorithm will therefore always halt after the last *rate, time* pair of data values has been processed and control once again reaches box 1, where it is discovered that the input belt is empty.

It will also be useful to visualize output in a similar way.

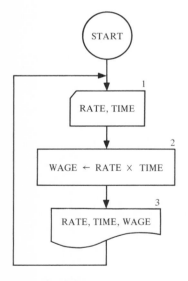

FIGURE 1·14
Payroll algorithm.

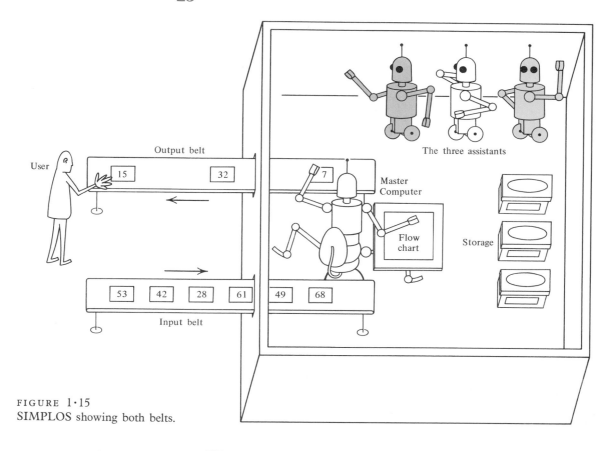

FIGURE 1·15
SIMPLOS showing both belts.

We endow SIMPLOS with a second conveyer belt, the *output belt*. This belt runs *out* instead of in and runs continuously—it needs no treadle. Each time the flowchart calls for output, the Master Computer writes the proper value on a slip of paper and drops it on the output belt, which carries the slip through the wall to the outside environment of the user. A view of this situation from the top is seen in Figure 1·15.

Records versus Streams

Our conveyer belt model of input-output suggests that data values move as a stream into and out of a computer system. Although in actual computers this is not always strictly the case, the analogy nevertheless is quite close. To pursue this idea let us consider the punched card reader, one of the most common input devices on actual computers. First, a sequence of data values is punched on cards. The cards are then placed in proper order in the *input hopper* of the card reading device.

Usually the card deck is placed face down so that the bottom (first) card in the deck is the first one to be read. Each time more input data are required, another card is drawn from the bottom of the deck and its contents are read, either electro-mechanically or photo-optically. Once read, the card is dropped into an *output stacker* and thus discarded.

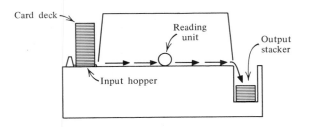

The information contained on a single punched card need not in principle be limited to one value. For example, depending on what a program is designed to expect, an 80-column card may contain up to eight 10-digit integers or up to twenty 4-digit integers.

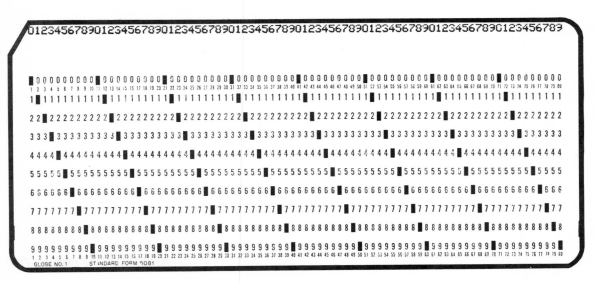

When preparing data cards one is always faced with the decision of whether to utilize their capacity fully or to punch on each only the values required for the execution of one input step in the algorithm. The latter choice, although somewhat wasteful of card space, makes the data cards easier to check.

Our payroll problem provides us with a case in point. If,

for convenience in locating data preparation errors, we restrict the contents of each card to one *rate, time* pair, then each time box 1 is executed, one and only one data card will be drawn off the input deck, read, and discarded. We could be more wasteful and punch only one data value on each card. Then successive cards would contain first a *rate* value, then a *time* value, and so on. In this case, each execution of box 1 must cause *two* data cards to be drawn from the deck and read, and the analogy between the input conveyer belt and the card reading activity is very close indeed. That is, when the Master Computer hits the foot treadle to bring in one data value, the actual computer will signal the card reader to draw off one card and read it.

The analogy is less apparent if we allow the data cards to contain more than one *rate, time* pair and if we expect the pairs to be considered in turn during successive executions of box 1. In this case, box 1 can no longer mean "read a card" but, instead, "assign respectively to *rate* and *time* values from the next data pair in the deck. If the next pair cannot both come from the current data card, then draw off another card from the deck and read it. If, on the other hand, there is at least one more data pair yet to be processed from the most recently read card, then process that data pair." This interpretation assumes that an input buffer is filled (and refilled) with data from each newly read data card and that values are assigned to *rate* and *time* by simply copying information from this buffer into the respective program variables, always remembering for future use which items in the buffer have not yet been copied.

We see, therefore, that using an input buffer guarantees that each data pair in the sequence will be processed in turn, no matter how many pairs are punched on each data card. None will be missed or skipped over. It is in this sense that the stream analogy is preserved even though the sequence of data items is grouped into arbitrary-sized *card records*.

The SIMPLOS model is a primitive machine. It has only stream-oriented input and output. After values are placed on the conveyer belt to be output and are carried to the outside environment of the user, how are they displayed? We certainly are aware that in actual computer systems all values are printed or displayed on a screen in some sort of "format" with a particular number of columns, but the only fact we are interested in with respect to SIMPLOS is that the values *are* output.

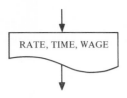

When it comes to interpreting output boxes of a flowchart, the situation is somewhat different. The output box on the left is considered to be a command to print the current values of the three variables, RATE, TIME, and WAGE *on one line*. (If the list won't fit on one print line, more lines are used.) Furthermore, if the same output box is executed again, the next set of three values will appear on a new line below the first set. If the three variables appeared in three individual boxes instead of in one single box, then each would be printed on a separate line. Thus each execution of an output box is considered to begin printing a new line.

Importance of the Conceptual Model

No doubt you have wondered why, at the very start of our study, so much attention has been given to a conceptual model of a computer and its details. Can any model, especially this one, which seems so simple and at the kindergarten level for some readers, be that important or that valuable to us? You may develop similar doubts about the value of flowcharts as you proceed further.

The model and the flowcharts we develop are *abstractions* of real machines and of real computer programs. Once we see the connection between an abstraction and the *concrete* or real thing, we can often gain more understanding of the real thing by studying and manipulating its abstract counterpart. So, high on our list of priorities should be an attempt to understand and appreciate the connections between the abstract and the concrete. For example, in the next sections of this chapter we examine how an actual computer is organized and how it works. Thereafter, it will be easier to see why the conceptual model, no matter how silly it may have first appeared, is a very useful, simplified view of a real computer. Likewise, just as soon as we try to write and test actual computer programs, we shall see that the flowchart gives us a simpler but more revealing way to think about computer programs for most purposes.

Experience has taught us that problem solving with computers is very effective if we can work first with a simplified model of a machine and a simple descriptive algorithmic language in which to express our problem solutions. Then it is comparatively easy to *map* these solutions over to programs written in some convenient programming language such as BASIC, FORTRAN, ALGOL, or COBOL, so that the programs can be executed on some real, convenient computer.

EXERCISES 1·4

1. Modify the flowchart of Figure 1·14 to provide for an overtime feature. All hours in excess of 40 are to be paid at time and a half. You will have to place a decision box somewhere in the flowchart to determine whether the worker actually put in any overtime. The formula by which his wages are computed will depend on the outcome of this test.

1·5
Actual computers

Now we are ready to examine how our conceptual model of a computer can be realized in an actual machine. For the first 25 years of modern computer history (1949 to 1974), nearly all actual machines were built following a more or less stereotyped pattern suggested by John Von Neumann (1903–1957). A prototype machine following this pattern is discussed in this and following sections. We will call it SAMOS. SAMOS is a very simple machine; that is, it is stripped down to the bare essentials. Some features of its operation are described in considerable detail, while others are glossed over. The programming of SAMOS is described briefly in Section 1·6 and in more detail in the Appendix, the purpose of which is to help the reader see a closer connection between language for expressing algorithms and machines that execute them.

It would be foolhardy to assume that SAMOS-like machines are the "be all and end all of computers," since the architecture of computers is still undergoing rapid change. For this reason, aspects of two other machines are discussed briefly in this book. One machine, called BITOS, appears later in this chapter; the other, called POSTOS, is considered in Chapter 8. Each of the three machines exhibits certain distinct characteristics for the implementation of our conceptual model, SIMPLOS.

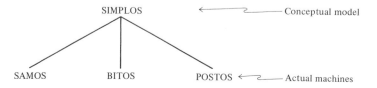

In order to study this book it is useful, although not essential, to gain a good understanding of how an actual computer works. We suggest that you read once through the material of the next two sections without attempting to master it. As you work exercises that relate to SAMOS, or have occasion to study SAMOS in the Appendix, you will no doubt come back to the next two sections for a more careful study.

1·6 SAMOS

How are all those storage boxes of SIMPLOS realized in actual practice? The storage of actual computers is built of electronic components in a variety of ways and with a variety of materials. Here we describe one way that a SAMOS storage can be built.

Core Storage

FIGURE 1·16
A magnetic core.

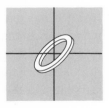

FIGURE 1·17
Where two wires cross.

SAMOS storage, packaged in a rectangular box, is an arrangement of tiny magnetic doughnuts as small as 1/40 of an inch in diameter. These doughnuts are called *cores* (Figure 1·16). The cores are laid out in 61 horizontal layers or trays called *core planes*. On each of these layers, wires are strung evenly in two directions like the lines on a sheet of graph paper. There are 100 wires in each direction. At each point where two wires cross, the wires are threaded through a core, like the thread passing through the eye of a needle (Figure 1·17). (Still other wires are threaded diagonally through each core within each plane. Their function is not important to the discussion that follows, and they are therefore ignored.)

Figure 1·18 is a picture of a core plane from an actual computer built in the mid-1960s. Since there are 100×100 crossings in each SAMOS core layer, we see that there are 10,000 cores in each core plane and hence $61 \times 10,000 = 610,000$ cores in the entire SAMOS *store* (storage).

These cores are capable of being magnetized in either the clockwise or the counterclockwise sense (Figure 1·19). Because of this a core can store information. We could think of clockwise magnetization as meaning "yes" and counterclockwise as meaning "no." We will instead think of clockwise as standing for "0" and counterclockwise for "1." In any event, the information contained in the magnetization of a core is the smallest

FIGURE 1·18
An actual core plane.
(Courtesy of IBM).

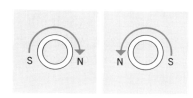

FIGURE 1·19
Magnetization of cores.

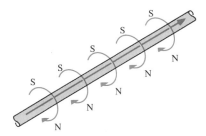

FIGURE 1·20
A magnetic field resulting from
a pulse of electric current.

unit of information and is called a *bit* of information. We see that one core can store one binary digit, 0 or 1, but a collection of cores can store a very large number of bits. We will discuss this idea later, after a digression on how the cores get their magnetism.

First, you must know that a pulse of electric current moving along a wire generates a magnetic field running around the wire, as shown in Figure 1·20. The strength of the magnetic field is strongest near the wire and dies away as we move further from the wire.

If the direction of the current is reversed, the direction of the magnetic field is also reversed (Figure 1·21).

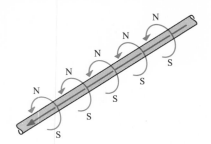

FIGURE 1·21
Reversing the direction of the
magnetic field.

Thus, when a pulse of current passes through a core, the core will become magnetized in one direction or the other, depending on the direction of the current (Figure 1·22).

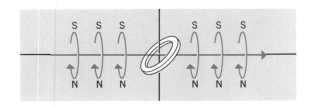

FIGURE 1·22
A core in a magnetic field.

But how can we manage to magnetize just one core instead of the whole string of cores (Figure 1·23) through which the pulse passes? The answer lies in the magnetic properties of the material from which the core is made. In this material,

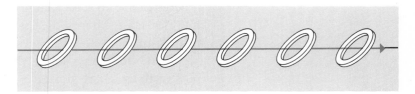

FIGURE 1·23
A row of cores in a magnetic field.

if the pulse is too weak, the direction of magnetization of the core is only *temporarily* altered, and after the pulse of current has passed by, the core merely returns to its former magnetic condition, whatever that was.

On the other hand, if the current is strong enough, the core remains magnetized in the sense established by the direction of the current, regardless of the former magnetic condition of the core. The situation is analogous to trying to throw a ball from the ground to the flat roof of a building. If you have enough power in your throw, the ball will land on the roof; otherwise it will bounce against the wall and fall back to the ground.

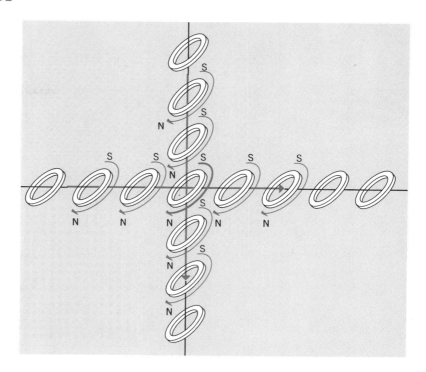

FIGURE 1·24
Doubling the magnetic field at
the wire crossing.

The strength of the pulses is carefully regulated so that one pulse is not sufficient to permanently magnetize a core, but two pulses acting simultaneously will exceed the threshold strength and result in permanent magnetization. Thus, pulses passing along two of the wires (Figure 1·24) will permanently magnetize just the one core that is located where the wires cross.

SIMPLOS and SAMOS Stores Compared

Let's leave the individual core planes and consider the entire store of the SAMOS computer, composed of the 61 core planes (Figure 1·25). Each vertical column of 61 cores constitutes a *computer word*. Thus, the storage of the computer is composed of 10,000 words. These words have addresses that are four-digit numbers from 0000 to 9999 and, like house numbers, the addresses identify the words. Each of the 10,000 dots suggested on the top of the box is the top of a vertical column of 61 cores (or a word). The method of assigning the addresses is indicated in the figure.

Each of these words corresponds to a storage box in our conceptual SIMPLOS model. For each variable in the flow-

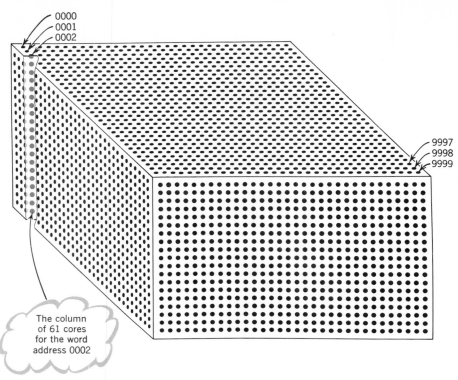

0000
0001
0002

9997
9998
9999

The column
of 61 cores
for the word
address 0002

FIGURE 1·25
Cores of one computer
word.

chart there is a SAMOS word with a definite address. The
word contains a certain pattern of bits determined by the directions of magnetization of its cores and representing the value
of that variable. "Assigning a value to a variable" is effected
by putting a certain pattern of bits into a word (Figure 1·26).

When we say "the Master Computer tells the Assigner
to assign the value 1597 to the variable SUM," what actually
takes place is this. The variable SUM is represented inside
the machine by means of its address; suppose it is 0103. Now
all the $61 \times 2 = 122$ wires passing through cores in the word
addressed 0103 are energized with pulses of current in the
proper directions so as to achieve the pattern of bits representing the number 1597. In a modern computer this assignment
process can be performed in a fraction of a microsecond; a
microsecond is a millionth of a second.

Characters

In the binary system of representation, a number such as 1597
is coded as a string of 1's and 0's, for example:

1 1 0 0 0 1 1 1 1 0 1

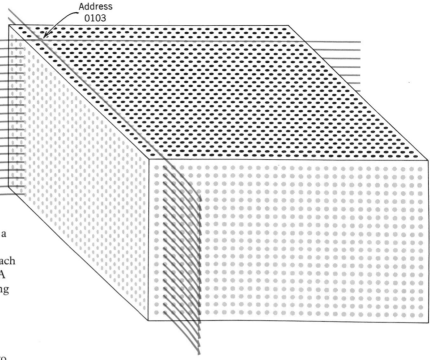

Address
0103

FIGURE 1·26
A bit pattern is assigned to a
computer word by
appropriately magnetizing each
of the cores for that word. A
core is magnetized by passing
an electronic pulse through
each of the two wires that
intersect at that core. The
diagram identifies the wire
pairs that must be selected to
assign a bit pattern for the
word at address 0103.

For SAMOS any string would be preceded by a string of zeros
to fill out all the bit positions of the word of storage. While
numbers are coded in binary form in many computers, binary
is certainly not the only choice. In a machine such as SAMOS,
for instance, computation is carried out in the decimal system,
which means that bit patterns in a word of storage must be
coded to represent decimal digits instead of binary digits.
Moreover, we want to store letters as well as decimal digits.
For this reason, we subdivide our 61-bit SAMOS words into
11 character positions as shown below.

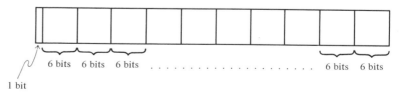

1 bit   6 bits   6 bits   6 bits .... 6 bits   6 bits

The first position (one bit only) is reserved for a code that
designates the sign, + or −. Here 0 is sufficient to represent
the + character and 1 signifies the − character. Each of the
other positions consists of six bits and can be used to store

Character	Code	Character	Code	Character	Code	Character	Code
0	00 0000					□	11 0000
1	00 0001	A	01 0001	J	10 0001		
2	00 0010	B	01 0010	K	10 0010	S	11 0010
3	00 0011	C	01 0011	L	10 0011	T	11 0011
4	00 0100	D	01 0100	M	10 0100	U	11 0100
5	00 0101	E	01 0101	N	10 0101	V	11 0101
6	00 0110	F	01 0110	O	10 0110	W	11 0110
7	00 0111	G	01 0111	P	10 0111	X	11 0111
8	00 1000	H	01 1000	Q	10 1000	Y	11 1000
9	00 1001	I	01 1001	R	10 1001	Z	11 1001

FIGURE 1·28
Detailed bit patterns for two computer words.

a digit or a letter, that is, *character,* according to the code shown in Figure 1·27.

For each group of six bits, 2^6 or 64 distinct combinations of zeros and ones are possible. In Figure 1·27 we have used up only 37 of the 64 combinations possible with a six-bit code. This leaves 27 additional combinations for other special symbols such as $+$, $\geq$, and the like. One of the 37 combinations of special interest is the blank space, □, which is coded as

$$1\ 1\ 0\ 0\ 0\ 0$$

With this code you can see that the two 61-bit computer words displayed vertically in Figure 1·28 turn out to be

+	B	U	Y	□	6	□	E	G	G	S

and

−	0	0	3	9	7	5	0	1	2	8

From now on we shall represent our SAMOS computer words as strings of 11 characters instead of strings of 61 bits. In a number of conventional computers of similar design eight instead of six bits are grouped to represent character codes, making it possible to distinguish among a considerably larger set of characters than is the case in SAMOS. This distinction, however, has absolutely no effect on the principles of character representation and manipulation that occur in ensuing chapters.

The construction of the main storage for any actual computer is of great interest mainly to computer engineers and designers. Storage components currently are built from various types of physical devices and materials, including magnetic cores, magnetic thin films, and transistor flipflops. There is considerable variety in the circuitry used to organize and utilize such components and in the methods of packaging and miniaturizing them. Their physical characteristics, such as size, speed of access for storing and retrieving information, energy requirements to operate them, and cost of fabrication, vary also. Nevertheless, schemes similar to that used in the word-organized core storage of SAMOS have been used to assemble and incorporate all of these types of storage units into conventional computer systems. You might be surprised at how much understanding of this subject you can gain with a relatively small investment of study time. (See, for example, one of the references on this topic in the reading list at the end of this book.)

SAMOS Processing Unit

Now that we have seen how the SAMOS storage is structured, we will consider how the storage is used in executing an algorithm.

Our computer has several other components besides the store. These are shown in Figure 1·29.

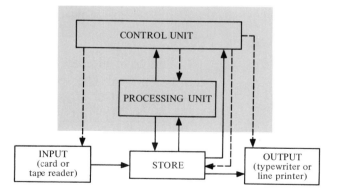

FIGURE 1·29
The principal components of SAMOS.

The solid lines indicate the directions in which values or instructions may be transferred. The dashed lines indicate the exercise of control. The control unit and the processing unit perform the duties of the "Master Computer" and his helpers.

An important part of the processing unit is the *accumulator*. This special computer word holds the result of each arithmetic operation.

Furthermore, a simple assignment such as

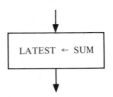

is carried out by first obtaining a copy of the value of SUM, placing it in the accumulator, and then copying the value in the accumulator into the computer word belonging to the variable LATEST. The value of SUM is unchanged in this process. Notice, however, that values to be input or output do not pass through the SAMOS accumulator but go directly into and out of storage.

When the control unit receives and interprets an *order*, some computer operation is activated. The orders are in the form of coded instructions stored in the computer; we will see about them presently.

Machine Language

Getting an algorithm into a form a machine can execute involves several translations that we can represent as follows:

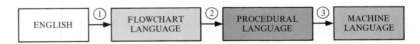

You have already had a little experience with the first translation step. The second translation step is the process of converting a flow chart into a procedural language such as FORTRAN, ALGOL, COBOL, or PL / I. You learn how to do this in your language manual. If approached properly, this translation step is quite mechanical and can be performed by a person (or by a machine) who has no idea what the algorithm is all about.

In many computers of advanced design, the third translation process can be omitted because the machine's language and the procedural language are effectively identical. When the third translation step is necessary, and it is for a computer such as SAMOS, the process is completely mechanical and is normally done by the computer itself. This process is called *compiling*.

It is not necessary right now to know how compiling is done, but it may be interesting to know the reason for doing it. Each make and style of computer has its own language—that is, its own set of instructions that it can understand. Use of a procedural language allows us to avoid a tower of Babel in which a programmer would have to learn a new language for each machine he wishes to use. A procedural language constitutes a kind of "Esperanto" that enables a programmer to communicate with many different machines in the same language. Moreover, a procedural language is generally much easier to learn to use than machine language. The programmer merely prepares, say, a FORTRAN program on punched cards and feeds it into the computer, which "compiles" a sequence of machine language instructions. This sequence, called a *machine language program,* is then placed in the computer storage. In many systems the programmer may transmit his program to the computer storage by typing it a line at a time, using a typewriter or other keyboard instrument to serve as the input device of the computer system.

Sequencing of Computer Instructions

Successive SAMOS instructions are placed in consecutively addressed storage locations starting with 0000. After the computer has executed an instruction, the control unit will always take the next instruction from the next address, unless there is a *branching* instruction providing a different address from which to take the next instruction.

To see how this works, consider the instruction taken from the Fibonacci sequence flowchart (Figure 1·11*b*), shown here in Figure 1·30.

The procedural language equivalent will not look much different. Thus, in FORTRAN this instruction would appear as

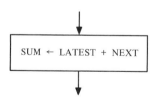

FIGURE 1·30
A flowchart box.

and in ALGOL as

and in APL as

and in BASIC as

and in COBOL as

$$\text{SUM} = \text{LATEST} + \text{NEXT}$$

$$\text{SUM} := \text{LATEST} + \text{NEXT}$$

$$\text{SUM} \leftarrow \text{LATEST} + \text{NEXT}$$

$$\text{LET} \quad \text{SUM} = \text{LATEST} + \text{NEXT}$$

$$\text{COMPUTE SUM EQUALS LATEST}$$
$$\text{PLUS NEXT}$$

+	LDA	000	0101
+	ADD	000	0100
+	STO	000	0102

FIGURE 1·31
SAMOS instructions for
Figure 1-30.

In the SAMOS machine language, a variable cannot be referred to by *name* but only by the *address* in storage associated with the variable. Suppose that NEXT, LATEST, and SUM have been given, respectively, locations 0100, 0101, and 0102. Then in the SAMOS language, the flowchart instruction translates to a sequence of three machine instructions, as shown in Figure 1·31.

These instructions have the form of 11-character words, although the first character is unimportant and the fifth, sixth, and seventh are of no interest to us here. The type of *operation* to be performed is coded using the three letters in positions two, three, and four, and the four-digit numeral at the right is the *address* associated with that operation.

The letters LDA stand for "LoaD the Accumulator." The whole instruction

    + L D A 0 0 0 0 1 0 1

means, "Make a copy of the value stored in address 0101 without altering the original, and store the copy in the accumulator." Clearly, this is the function of the Reader in our conceptual model. We will not go into the details of the electronics involved in carrying out this instruction. It is sufficient to know that when a copy of that instruction is brought to the control unit, certain switches are set by the control unit that allow a pulse current to pass through the cores of the word 0101. The magnetized cores cause a change in the current that, in turn, allows a copy to be made.

The second instruction in Figure 1·31 means, "ADD the value in the word addressed 0100 to the value already in the accumulator and place the result in the accumulator." The third instruction means, "Copy (or STOre) the value in the accumulator *into* the word addressed 0102." Executing a STO instruction is analogous to the work of the Assigner in our conceptual model. Speeds vary from machine to machine, but in modern computers, the time required to carry out such instructions is usually on the order of a millionth of a second.

A Complete SAMOS
Program

We are almost able to translate the entire flowchart for the Fibonacci sequence algorithm (repeated here in Figure 1·32) into SAMOS language. First note, however, that constants never appear explicitly in SAMOS instructions. Instead, an instruction to fetch a constant must refer to the storage address where the desired value may be found. Of course, this also applies to variables. Thus part of the compiling process involves providing storage addresses for the constants (as well as for the variables) appearing in the program. We allocate the locations 0017, 0018, and 0019 for the constants 0, 1, and 1000 appearing in the flowchart and specify the proper values for these words.

We assume that the storage locations 0100, 0101, and 0102 have been allocated for the variables NEXT, LATEST, and SUM, but that no values have been placed in these words. As execution of the SAMOS program for the Fibonacci algorithm starts, the state of storage is shown in Figure 1·33. This figure

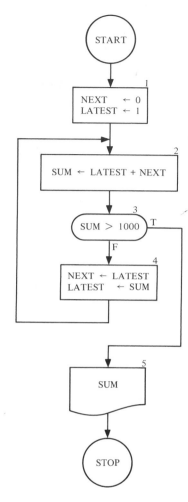

FIGURE 1·32
Fibonacci sequence algorithm.

FIGURE 1·33
Fibonacci sequence algorithm. The ± column and columns 5, 6, and 7 may be left empty on lines containing instructions.

Storage Location (Address)	± 1	Operation Code 2 3 4	5 6 7	Address 8 9 10 11	Flowchart Equivalent
0 0 0 0		L D A	0 0 0	0 0 1 7	1a NEXT ← 0
0 0 0 1		S T O	0 0 0	0 1 0 0	
0 0 0 2		L D A	0 0 0	0 0 1 8	1b LATEST ← 1
0 0 0 3		S T O	0 0 0	0 1 0 1	
0 0 0 4		L D A	0 0 0	0 1 0 1	2 SUM ← LATEST + NEXT
0 0 0 5		A D D	0 0 0	0 1 0 0	
0 0 0 6		S T O	0 0 0	0 1 0 2	
0 0 0 7		L D A	0 0 0	0 0 1 9	3 SUM > 1000 T
0 0 0 8		S U B	0 0 0	0 1 0 2	F
0 0 0 9		B M I	0 0 0	0 0 1 5	
0 0 1 0		L D A	0 0 0	0 1 0 1	4a NEXT ← LATEST
0 0 1 1		S T O	0 0 0	0 1 0 0	
0 0 1 2		L D A	0 0 0	0 1 0 2	4b LATEST ← SUM
0 0 1 3		S T O	0 0 0	0 1 0 1	
0 0 1 4		B R U	0 0 0	0 0 0 4	Arrow from flowchart box 4 to box 2
0 0 1 5		W W D	0 0 0	0 1 0 2	5 SUM
0 0 1 6		H L T	0 0 0	0 0 0 0	STOP
0 0 1 7	+	0 0 0	0 0 0	0 0 0 0	The constant 0
0 0 1 8	+	0 0 0	0 0 0	0 0 0 1	The constant 1
0 0 1 9	+	0 0 0	0 0 0	1 0 0 0	The constant 1000
0 1 0 0					The variable NEXT
0 1 0 1					The variable LATEST
0 1 0 2					The variable SUM

also illustrates a "coding form" on which one might have written the SAMOS program (gray-colored information). You will notice several new SAMOS operations not previously seen. These are explained in the following discussion.

Discussion

The instructions in storage addresses 0004, 0005, and 0006 have already been discussed. Before looking at the other instructions, remember that the variables are in storage locations 0100 through 0102.

From previous discussions you should see that the instruction found at 0000 will, when executed, copy the value in 0017 (i.e., the number 0) into the accumulator. Next, the instruction in 0001 copies the value in the accumulator into the word at address 0100. Together these steps are equivalent to assigning 0 to the variable NEXT. Similarly, the instructions in addresses 0002 and 0003 are equivalent to assigning the value 1 to the variable LATEST.

Remember that the control unit executes the instructions in order until it comes to a branching instruction. The first branching instruction is found in address 0009, reading

	B	M	I	0	0	0	0	0	1	5

The code BMI stands for "Branch on a MInus." The whole instruction means, "If the value in the accumulator is negative, go to address 0015 for the next instruction; otherwise, go on as usual to the next numbered address (0010)." We will see shortly that the value in the accumulator at this time is just

$$1000 - SUM$$

so that the value in the accumulator will be negative only in the case that

$$SUM > 1000$$

is true. In this case, the branching instruction sends us to address 0015, where we see the instruction

	W	W	D	0	0	0	0	1	0	2

which means, "Write the WorD in address 0102." This amounts to printing out the value of SUM.

Now why is it that when the instruction in address 0009 is reached, the number in the accumulator is

$$1000 - \text{SUM}$$

Well, on looking at the instruction in address 0007, we see that it instructs us to load the accumulator with the contents of address 0019, that is, to put the number 1000 in the accumulator. The next instruction, the one in 0008, tells us to "subtract the contents of address 0102 from the accumulator and put the result in the accumulator." Since the contents of 0102 are just the value of SUM, this amounts to the placing of

$$1000 - \text{SUM}$$

in the accumulator.

You should be able to verify for yourself that the instructions in addresses 0010 through 0013 accomplish the assignments indicated in the right-hand column of Figure 1·33.

The instruction in address 0014 needs to be described.

	B	R	U	0	0	0	0	0	0	4

BRU stands for "BRanch Unconditionally." The meaning of the entire instruction is, "Go back to address 0004 for the next instruction and continue in order from there." You can see that this corresponds to the arrow from flowchart box 4 leading back to flowchart box 2, where we repeat the summing step.

The instruction in 0016, of course, stands for HaLT and amounts to stopping the computing process.

You can best understand all this by tracing through the SAMOS program by hand, keeping a record of the following details.

1. Which instruction is being executed.

2. The value in the accumulator.

3. The values in the addresses 0100, 0101, and 0102 (the values of NEXT, LATEST, and SUM).

Notice that the instructions in addresses 0000 through 0016 are never altered, nor are the contents of the locations 0017 through 0019 (the constants 0, 1, and 1000).

EXERCISES 1·6

1. Construct a list of SAMOS instructions for the flowchart in Figure 1·14. You will need two additional types of instructions. The first is

	OPERATION						ADDRESS			
1	2	3	4	5	6	7	8	9	10	11
	R	W	D	0	0	0	1	0	0	5

which is an instruction to read a value from a card into the computer word addressed 1005.

The second is

	M	P	Y	0	0	0	1	0	2	3

which is an instruction to multiply the value in the accumulator by the value in address 1023 and put the result in the accumulator. (Of course, in the address part of these instructions, we may put any address we wish.)

2. This question relates to the flowchart fragment and proposed SAMOS translation of it shown below. For each of your answers the assumed objective is to make the proposed SAMOS fragment consistent with the given flowchart fragment.

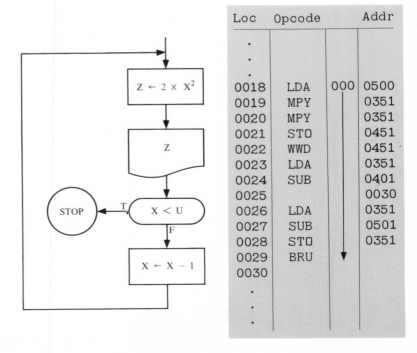

Loc	Opcode		Addr
.			
.			
.			
0018	LDA	000	0500
0019	MPY		0351
0020	MPY		0351
0021	STO		0451
0022	WWD		0451
0023	LDA		0351
0024	SUB		0401
0025			0030
0026	LDA		0351
0027	SUB		0501
0028	STO		0351
0029	BRU		
0030			
.			
.			
.			

Flowchart: $Z \leftarrow 2 \times X^2$ → Z → $X < U$ (T → STOP; F → $X \leftarrow X - 1$)

(a) With what memory location must the variable X be associated?
(b) What operand address is needed for the BRU instruction that is shown at location 0029?
(c) What should be the operation code for the instruction at location 0025?
(d) What operation code is needed for the instruction located at 0030?

3. This question relates to the flowchart fragment and proposed SAMOS translation of it shown below. For each of your answers, assume the objective is to make the proposed SAMOS fragment consistent with the given flowchart fragment.

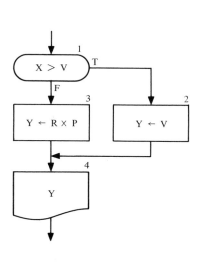

Loc	Opcode		Addr
.			
.			
.			
0017	LDA	000	0100
0018	SUB	000	0200
0019	BMI	000	0024
0020	LDA	000	0105
0021	MPY	000	0107
0022	STO	000	
0023	BRU	000	
0024	LDA	000	0100
0025	STO	000	0201
0026	WWD	000	0201
.			
.			
.			

(a) With what location must the variable X be associated?
(b) What is the operand address that should be filled in for the BRU instruction shown at location 0023?
(c) What should be the value of the address field for the STO instruction at location 0022?
(d) If at location 0022 the STO were replaced by a BRU operation code, what then would be the appropriate value for the address field?

4. This question relates to the following SAMOS program and the four data cards displayed to the right of it; you are to assume that the given SAMOS program executes with the data cards shown. The DIV (divide) instruction produces an *integer* quotient (see Appendix A).

0000	RWD	000	0012
0001	RWD	000	0013
0002	LDA	000	0012
0003	DIV	000	0013
0004	MPY	000	0013
0005	STO	000	0014
0006	LDA	000	0012
0007	SUB	000	0014
0008	STO	000	0014
0009	WWD	000	0014
0010	BRU	000	0000
0011	HLT	000	0000

SAMOS program

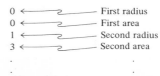

Data cards

(a) Which of the following is a *false* statement?
    (1) The instruction at 0011 will never be reached.
    (2) Only two values will be printed.
    (3) All four data cards will be read.
    (4) The first value printed will be 3.
    (5) Three values will be printed.

(b) Which of the following is a *true* statement?
    (1) The program will halt whenever the result of a division is zero.
    (2) The instruction at 0011 would be executed using the given set of data if the instruction at 0010 were revised to BMI 000 0000.
    (3) This program inputs two numbers, selects the larger, and prints its value.
    (4) All three of the above statements are false.

Problems 5 through 7. The following three problems involve programs to be written in SAMOS machine language and run on a computer using a SAMOS simulator. If you do not have a computer available, your final result will be a SAMOS coding form showing your program.

5. Draw a flowchart and write and run a SAMOS program to find the areas (to the nearest integer) of circles with each of the following radii: 0, 1, 2, 3, . . . , 10, 11, 12. Use $\pi = 22/7$. The output is to consist of each radius value followed by the associated area, that is,

0 ←————— First radius
0 ←————— First area
1 ←————— Second radius
3 ←————— Second area
    .
    .
    .

This SAMOS program should not execute any *input* steps. Storage locations will be required for instructions and for all constants, including 22, 7, the current radius, 1 (to increment the radius to the next value), and a number (11, 12, or 13, depending on your particular flow chart) to test against to determine when to branch to *halt*.

Question Will SAMOS give the same result when you compute $(22 / 7) \times r^2$ as when you compute $(22 \times r^2) / 7$? If not, which gives a better result? Why?

6. Draw a flowchart and write and run a SAMOS program to do the following:

For the values from 1 to 10 inclusive (i.e., $1 \leq X \leq 10$), evaluate the following mathematical expression:

$$F = 5X^2 + 10X + 6$$

Print out the value for X and F after each evaluation.

Example The first value of X will be 1. For this value,

$$F = 5(1) + 10(1) + 6$$
$$F = 5 + 10 + 6 = 21$$

Thus the numbers 1 and 21 will be printed out, and F will then be evaluated for $X = 2, 3, \ldots , 10$. The complete output will consist of 20 numbers:

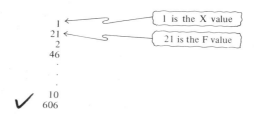

Note Additional Information for Problem 6

1. No data cards will be needed for this program.
2. The values from 1 to 10 need not all be stored at the beginning of the program.
3. You must include some way to terminate your program after the final value has been processed and printed.

7. Draw a flowchart using variables C, X, TALLY, SUM, and AVG, and write and run a SAMOS program to do the following:

(a) Read a value for the variable C.
(b) Read a value for the variable X.
(c) Check to see whether X equals 9999. If X does not equal 9999 then check whether X equals C. If X equals C, then return to

step (b). If X does not equal C, then add one to a counter called TALLY and add X to the variable SUM and then return to step (b).

　　If X equals 9999, then no more data cards are to be read. At this point print out the values of TALLY and SUM. Compute AVG, the quotient of SUM and TALLY (AVG = SUM/TALLY). Print the value of AVG.

Note   Additional Information for Problem 7
1. In your flowchart the average will be a variable AVG. The variable TALLY will hold a count of how many values of X are *not* equal to C. The assignment

$$\text{TALLY} \leftarrow \text{TALLY} + 1$$

will be needed. The sum of the values of X not equal to C will be called SUM. What should be the initial values of TALLY and SUM?

2. The value 9999 is called a *sentinel* value. Its purpose is to indicate that all the values of X have been read and processed. (In computer language a sentinel value is said to represent the end of file, i.e., the end of data.) Therefore, your data deck will consist of a value for C, the given values for X, and the value 9999. (See Section 2 · 2 for additional discussion of sentinels.)

3. In SAMOS the only conditional branch instruction is BMI (Branch On Minus). The programmer faces a problem when he needs to check whether the values of two variables are equal or whether the value of a variable is equal to some constant value. The following is one method of determining whether the values of the variables A and B are equal. First, subtract the value of B from the value of A and, if the result is not negative, subtract the value of A from the value of B. If this result is not negative, we can conclude that the values of A and B are equal.

Examples
(a) A = 6 and B = 9
　　A − B = 6 − 9 = −3
　　Result: A ≠ B since A − B is a negative number.
(b) A = 5 and B = 5
　　A − B = 5 − 5 = 0
　　B − A = 5 − 5 = 0
　　Result: A = B since neither subtraction produced a negative number.
(c) A = 4 and B = 3
　　A − B = 4 − 3 = 1
　　B − A = 3 − 4 = −1
　　Result: A ≠ B since B − A is a negative number.

4. The data for Problem 7 are as follows:

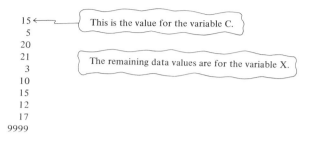

```
15 ←          This is the value for the variable C.
 5
20
21            The remaining data values are for the variable X.
 3
10
15
12
17
9999
```

1·7
BITOS

Most of the storage capacity of a 61-bit SAMOS word goes unused when a small integer, for instance, 2, is represented. Conversely, even though a number is known to very great precision, a 61-bit word has a fixed capacity to represent digits. Character strings, such as names and addresses, for instance, vary greatly in length. In general, information comes in many sizes and lengths, and it would be exceedingly convenient to have computer storage responsive to this fact.

The SAMOS language is heavily influenced (i.e., constrained) by its *word-organized* storage system. We briefly mention here another kind of computer storage called BITOS (BIT-Organized SAMOS), whose storage is structured in a more flexible and natural way—natural for the processing of different types of information. The BITOS storage is best thought of as a single sequence of bits instead of a single sequence of words that are, in turn, sequences of bits. For example, a BITOS store roughly equivalent to the SAMOS store contains 610,000 bits whose addresses are 0 through 609,999 respectively. To fetch a unit of information of some known length, one must specify the "bit address" of the beginning of the desired information unit together with its "bit length." Thus,

op code	address	length
LDA	24972	39

is the way one might write out a BITOS instruction to load the accumulator with a data value 39 bits long beginning at bit location 24972.

The information containers in a BITOS machine resemble the storage boxes of the conceptual model SIMPLOS in that the capacity of the containers is arbitrary.

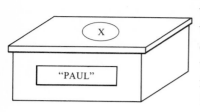

There is a second important way in which the containers of SIMPLOS and BITOS resemble one another. In both cases, values stored in these containers are *self-describing*. Note that the SIMPLOS Reader is able to deduce that a storage box contains a character string value as opposed, say, to a numerical value, because he is able to see the quotation marks. The fetching mechanism of BITOS can convey the same type of information to its processing unit because the data object in each container consists of two parts: a code that describes the type or nature of the value and the data value itself. For example, suppose the container associated with X is located at bit address 3901, and suppose character coding for the BITOS store employs the same 6-bit representation used in SAMOS. We might expect to see at that location:

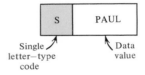

where the type code S stands for *string*. Then, to represent a string of 4 characters would require 24 bits for the string itself and 6 more bits (for the letter S) to identify the 24 bits as a string. For a string of 91 characters, 546 bits are needed for the string and 6 more for the type code—or 552 bits in all. If a nonnegative integer variable, AGE, never requires more than three digits we can picture the corresponding BITOS container as

I	0	5	2

for a data value of 52. Here the type code I denotes *integer*.

To recapitulate, in BITOS one defines the size of the container to fit the need. That is, the store is divided up into containers that reflect their actual use. Every reference to a container consists of the bit address of the container and its length. The container itself holds as part of the data object a code that makes the remainder of the information *in* the container self-describing. Each time a new container is needed, a section of the store large enough to hold the required number of bits is "partitioned" for this purpose. When this container is no longer needed, that section of store and others like it are repartitioned, that is, reused, typically in different container sizes, to suit new needs. To make an analogy with SIMPLOS, imagine that all storage boxes are constructed to fit dimensions of the data values they are to contain. (The Affixer who pastes the sticker on the storage box can also adjust the size of the box if necessary.)

1·8
Floating-point
representation

Only a few of the ideas about SAMOS and BITOS need to be remembered. One of the important ideas is the sequential manner in which the computer works, that is, the step-by-step way in which the computer performs its tasks. The order in which the tasks are performed is just as important as what is accomplished.

Another property of computers that we must understand is the *finite word length*. We have seen that SAMOS words consist of 10 characters and a sign, so that the largest number representable in this coding system is

$$+9,999,999,999$$

a rather large number, but still finite. Although BITOS store may use very "long" containers, they are still finite, so the limitation on what can be represented, although less constricting, still exists in principle. From a practical viewpoint, integer containers, whether in a SAMOS-like or in a BITOS-like store, are sometimes very unsuitable. Consider a variable that, from time to time, has various values assigned to it, sometimes very small integers and at other times very large integers. The storage container for such a variable cannot always be used efficiently if it must be large enough for the largest possible integer value that will be assigned to it.

To cover this situation there are other ways of coding numbers that not only solve this problem but also allow us to work with real numbers as well as integers. One of the most common of these alternate codings is *floating-point* form, which is related to the so-called "scientific notation."

To see how this works, recall that any decimal numeral such as

$$- 382.519$$

can be expressed as

$$-.382519 \times 10^3$$

in which there is a decimal point (just after the sign, if any) followed by a string of digits (the first not zero) and multiplied by a suitable power of 10. We can code numbers in this way by reserving three character positions for the exponent. The result is shown in Figure 1·34 for -382.519.

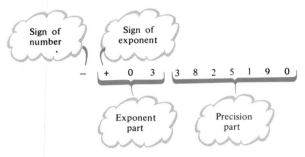

FIGURE 1·34
Anatomy of a floating-point number for a fixed-word size store.

Some examples of how to code numbers including integers in this system are given in Figure 1 · 35. In this figure, we see that the 8-digit representation of π, as given in the first column of the third entry, has to be chopped to 7 digits of precision because of space requirements. The same holds true for $1/3$ and $11/7$ at the bottom of the table. Thus we see that in a computer even a simple fraction such as $1/3$ cannot be represented exactly, but only to a close approximation. This characteristic of "finite word length" presents important prob-

Number	Floating-Point Form	Coding of Floating-Point Form
4	$.4 \times 10^1$	+ + 0 1 4 0 0 0 0 0 0
-999999000	$-.999999 \times 10^9$	− + 0 9 9 9 9 9 9 9 0
3.1415926	$.31415926 \times 10^1$	+ + 0 1 3 1 4 1 5 9 2
-273.14	$-.27314 \times 10^3$	− + 0 3 2 7 3 1 4 0 0
.0008761	$.8761 \times 10^{-3}$	+ − 0 3 8 7 6 1 0 0 0
.73	$.73 \times 10^0$	+ + 0 0 7 3 0 0 0 0 0
$\frac{1}{3}$	$.333333333 \times 10^0$	+ + 0 0 3 3 3 3 3 3 3
$\frac{11}{7}$	$.157142857 \times 10^1$	+ + 0 1 1 5 7 1 4 2 8

FIGURE 1·35
Floating-point coding of numbers in a fixed word-sized store.

lems that will be discussed in various places in this text, especially Chapter 11.

In floating-point form we can represent large numbers, but for computers such as SAMOS with fixed-word size stores the price we pay is giving up three places of precision. Were SAMOS to use floating-point numbers, the largest number representable in floating-point form would be:

which represents the number

999,999,900,000,000,000,000,000,000
000,000,000,000,000,000,000,000,000
000,000,000,000,000,000,000,000,000
000,000,000,000,000,000

Similarly, there is a smallest positive number that could be represented:

.000 000 000 000 000 000 000 000 000
000 000 000 000 000 000 000 000 000
000 000 000 000 000 000 000 000 000
000 000 000 000 000 000 1

which is very small, indeed.

Coding in floating-point form for a BITOS-like machine could be quite similar to the scheme shown in Figure 1·35. On the other hand, since the size of the container may be chosen to fit the particular "needs" of a given variable, the size of the precision part could easily be permitted to vary as required. For that matter, the size of the exponent part could also be expanded or contracted to fit the need.

In summary, both SAMOS-like and BITOS-like machines are often built to operate on numbers coded in floating-point form. However, in our discussions of SAMOS, in particular in the description given in the Appendix, the machine is initially described as if it were not capable of dealing with numbers coded in floating-point form, but only with numbers coded as integers.

EXERCISE 1·8

1. Several million pocket-sized electronic calculators are now being produced annually. They are becoming relatively accessible to the average student. Many of these calculators, such as the one shown in Figure 1 · 36, use floating point arithmetic.

FIGURE 1·36
A popular hand-held calculator.

(a) Locate an electronic calculator and compare the method it uses to represent floating-point numbers with the method used in SAMOS.

(b) Which form do you prefer and why?

(c) Run several simple computations on the pocket calculator, such as

$$a + b, \text{ to obtain } c$$

or

$$a \times b, \text{ to obtain } d, \text{ etc.}$$

where a and b are keyed in manually as real numbers in ordinary decimal notation, for example, -382.519. Determine under what conditions results c and d are displayed in floating-point form.

Chapter 2

The flowchart language

In Chapter 1 we described a flowchart as a diagram for representing an algorithm. We may also view flowcharts as constituting a *language* for expressing algorithms. Today our algorithms must still be translated into a procedural language before a computer can understand them, but the day may not be far off when algorithms in the flowchart language can be communicated directly to a machine.

Fortunately, the vocabulary and structure of the flowchart language are much simpler than in Latin or French. Indeed, these rules can be learned in half an hour or less. What is more difficult is learning to use the language as an effective tool to express ideas. That will come only with practice.

Additional structures will be added to the language in later chapters to streamline and simplify it. However, the components introduced in Chapter 1 already constitute a "basic flowchart" language in which any algorithm may be expressed, even though somewhat inelegantly. This section discusses these components in more detail.

The flowchart components presented in Chapter 1 were:

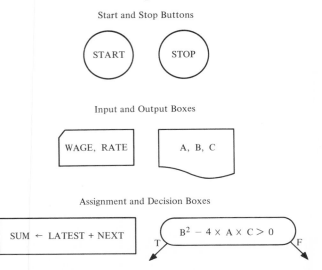

We start with a discussion of the assignment box.

The Assignment Box

The assignment instruction appearing inside an assignment box has the form

$$\boxed{\text{variable} \leftarrow \text{expression}}$$

The expression appearing on the right-hand side of the arrow may be a simple numerical or string value as in

$$\boxed{\text{K} \leftarrow 35.29} \quad \text{or} \quad \boxed{\text{C} \leftarrow \text{``FLOWCHART''}}$$

or a value represented by a single variable, as in

$$\boxed{\text{A} \leftarrow \text{B}}$$

or the expression on the right may be more complicated, as in

$$\boxed{\text{D} \leftarrow \text{B}^2 - 4 \times \text{A} \times \text{C}}$$

We cannot assign a value to an expression and thus, such an assignment instruction as

$$\boxed{\text{B}^2 - 4 \times \text{A} \times \text{C} \leftarrow 5}$$

is invalid. (To what storage box should the value 5 be assigned? Since there is no storage box with the sticker $B^2 - 4 \times A \times C$, the Assigner has no place to put the value 5.)

When numerals or explicit (quoted) values of strings appear in the expressions of flowchart boxes, we will refer to them as *literals* or *constants*. Thus, 35.29 and "FLOWCHART" are both literals. The former is a numerical constant. The latter is a string constant. We must remember that assignment is destructive, that is, each time a new value is assigned to a variable, the former value of that variable is destroyed and is no longer recoverable from the computer storage.

To carry out an assignment instruction requires a number of steps.

Rules for Evaluating
an Assignment Box

> 1. Fetch from storage the current values of any variables appearing on the right-hand side of the arrow (the work of the Reader).
> 2. If the expression on the right-hand side of the arrow is more complicated than a simple constant or a single variable, evaluate this expression (the work of the Master Computer).
> 3. Assign the value of this expression to the variable on the left-hand side of the arrow (the work of the Assigner).

$$N \leftarrow N + 1$$

$$N \leftarrow \boxed{N} + 1$$

It is important to think of assignment as "the act of giving a value to a variable" and not as meaning "equals." To see why this is true, consider the instruction on the left. Surely this should not be interpreted as meaning $N = N + 1$, which is nonsense. To see what this does mean, think in terms of our conceptual model, SIMPLOS. First, the Master Computer looks on the right-hand side of the arrow and sees the variable N. He sends the Reader to fetch the value of this variable and adds 1 to it. Now he looks at the left side of the arrow and finds that N appears here as well. So he sends the Assigner to assign the computed value as the new value of N. Thus, for example, if the value of N was 7 before the execution of the instruction, then the value of N will be 8 after the execution.

$$A \leftarrow B \quad \text{and} \quad B \leftarrow A$$

On the other hand, while the instructions on the left have quite different effects, they both result in A and B having the same value.

Variables and Expressions

As mentioned in Chapter 1, in computing work as in mathematics we have considerable leeway in the symbols we may use as variables. The following is a complete list of symbols that may be used as variables. These are single letters such as

A, B, K, N, O, X, Z

or descriptive combinations of letters such as

DIST, AREA, LENGTH, UGH

or sequences of letters and digits commencing with a letter such as

A3, ANY6, Y365, R5C6

There are two principal reasons for enlarging our list of variables to include these combinations. First, the list of symbols available to computers unfortunately is often limited to uppercase Roman letters. There are no Greek letters and often no lowercase letters. We just do not have enough single letters in the alphabet to fill our needs for variables. Second, choosing a descriptive combination of letters as a variable is often helpful in reminding us how the variable is used.

We take a special attitude toward such unbroken combinations of letters and digits starting with a letter. We regard them as connected together forming one brand new symbol, somewhat like handwriting.

DIST *list*
R5C6 *R5C6*

From this point of view, the variable XN is *not* considered to contain either of the variables X or N but, instead, to be a brand new single symbol. In other words, we insist no variable is to be considered part of another variable.

Following the SIMPLOS model of a computer introduced in Section 1 · 3, we think of each variable as having a container associated with it, with the value of the variable "residing" inside the container (Figure 2 · 1). At any time the variable

FIGURE 2·1

is considered to be a name for the value that resides in its container. The value may be a number or a string.

The expression appearing on the right of an assignment arrow may be an arithmetic expression or a string expression. Arithmetic expressions are written in the usual mathematical notation with one exception. We cannot write

AB

to denote the product of A and B, since the symbol AB denotes a single variable. Therefore, the multiplication operator must always appear explicitly and the product of A and B must be written as

$$A \times B$$

Similarly, instead of 3Y, we write

$$3 \times Y$$

The familiar expression $B^2 - 4AC$ will now be written as

$$B^2 - 4 \times A \times C$$

In the text we shall generally use $\times$ instead of $\cdot$ to denote multiplication and $/$ instead of $\div$ to denote division. Thus $A \div B$ will usually appear as A/B.

We will say more about arithmetic expressions in a later section.

String expressions are sequences of string operands and string operators. Probably the most common string operation is *concatenation*. We will use the operator symbol $\|$ (a pair of vertical bars) to denote it. For example, the string expression $A \| B$ means: form a new string consisting of a copy of the value of A followed by a copy of the value of B. If A has the value "CRAB" and B has the value "APPLE" then $A \| B$ has the value "CRABAPPLE". If we make the assignment

$$U \leftarrow A \| B$$

then U will have the value "CRABAPPLE". We will say more about string expressions in Section $2 \cdot 3$.

The Decision Box

The contents of a decision box usually have the form of an assertion that a certain relation holds between the current values of two expressions, as in Figure $2 \cdot 2$. Any one from the following list of relations may replace ">" in Figure $2 \cdot 2$.

$$=, \ \neq, \ <, \ \geq, \ \leq$$

Either or both expressions in a decision box may have the form of a constant or a single variable but, of course, more compli-

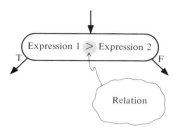

FIGURE 2·2

cated expressions are also permitted. Examples of valid decision boxes are shown in Figure 2 · 3.

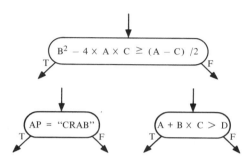

FIGURE 2·3

There are four steps in the execution of a decision box.

Rules for Evaluating
a Decision Box

> 1. Read (or look up) the values of the variables appearing in the box.
> 2. Evaluate (if necessary) the expressions on both sides of the relation using the values of the variables found in step 1.
> 3. Test the truth or falsity of the assertion appearing in the decision box.
> 4. Choose the appropriate exit path from the box depending on the result of the test in step 3.

Both reading from storage and evaluation are involved in the execution of a decision box, but assignment to storage is not.

Input and Output Boxes

The contents of input and output boxes take the form of a list of items separated by commas. On input these items must be variables. On output the items may be variables, constants, or expressions.

The *input* box is an instruction to read the required values from some data list. This list may already be in a storage buffer, or it may be read from some input medium such as tape or punch cards. As each value is read, it is assigned to the indicated variable. If the input is from tape, the tape advances as the reading is accomplished so that no values are inadvertantly reread. If the input is from punch cards, the card to be read moves under the sensing fingers of the reading device, is read, and then is stacked with other cards that have already been processed.

The assignment instruction implied in an input box typically receives its values from *outside* the computer. Apart from invoking the input mechanism, the principal action of the input box is carried out by the Assigner. Therefore, we say that *input is destructive of former values* of the input variables.

The *output* box is an instruction to print the values of the listed items, in the order given, by means of a line printer, typewriter, or other output device. If the individual item is a variable, the Reader obtains a copy of its value from storage, and this is then displayed. If the item is an expression, the Reader fetches the indicated values from storage, the Master Computer performs the evaluation, and the resulting value is displayed.

The work of the Reader is involved, but that of the Assigner is not. Thus, *output is nondestructive,* as no variables have their values changed in the process.

EXERCISES 2·1

1. Which, if any, of the following flowchart boxes is (are) invalid and why?

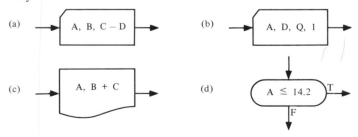

2. Discuss the advantages and disadvantages of using a flowchart instead of the English language to describe the steps of an algorithm.

3. Evaluate the truth or falsity of assertions a, b, and c relating to the following flowchart. (For parts a, b, c, and d of this question the data set read in as a result of executing box 1 is "F", "L", "O", "W", "1", 0.)

(a) Execution will reach box 5 only once for the given set of data.

(b) Execution will reach box 6 for the given set of data.

(c) If the value 6 were supplied in place of the zero in the given data set, box 2 would be executed six times.

(d) Which of the outputs given below represents that produced with the given data set?

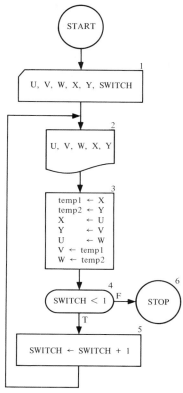

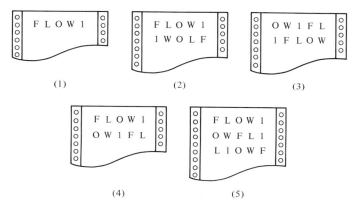

For parts e and f of this question assume that *any* set of data may be input at box 1 of the given flowchart.

(e) Box 2 is always executed twice for any set of data that is input at box 1.

(f) Only 0 or 1 is acceptable as a data value for the variable SWITCH.

4. Two assignment instructions appear in a single assignment box, as shown below. Give a general criterion under which these instructions may be interchanged without changing their net effect.

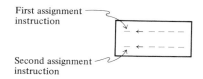

First assignment instruction

Second assignment instruction

Hint Consider the following five cases before you give your answer.

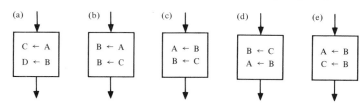

2·2
Counters and sentinels

Each year a nationwide advanced placement examination in mathematics is given to high school students wishing to receive college credit for college level math courses taken in high school. After the exam is graded, the grades are subjected to a lot of statistical analysis, such as computing the average grade. Since 10,000 to 20,000 students take the exam, no one is anxious to do this work by hand. Let's write an algorithm so a computer can do the job. If we suppose that the grades are punched on cards we will need an instruction similar to the one on the left to read grades into the computer storage.

To average a list of numbers, one must first find the sum of all the entries in the list and then divide this sum by the number of entries. Thus we will need a variable N, to keep a count of the number of grades read from the cards, and a variable SUM, to keep a running total of these grades as they are received.

Each time a grade is input we will increase or increment the value of N by 1. (The effect of this instruction has already been seen in the preceding section.) We will also want to increase the cumulative sum by the amount of the grade just read from the card. The flowchart box

$$SUM \leftarrow SUM + GRADE$$

clearly produces a new value of SUM by adding the last grade to the former sum—just what we want. We repeat these operations over and over, obtaining a loop, as shown in Figure 2·4.

Let's see what happens to N the first time through this loop. The Master Computer first reads the value of N on the right side of the arrow—but N has not yet been given a value! This brings out an important point in computer algorithms. The first occurrence of a variable in a flowchart must be for the purpose of assigning a value to it, either in an assignment box or in an input box. Accordingly, if a variable is to be assigned a new value, calculated in terms of the former value of the same variable, then this variable must previously have been given a "starting value" or "initial value." In the example above, this observation applies to SUM as well as to N. For both these variables the correct value, before any cards are

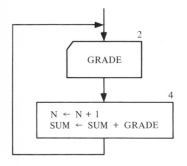

FIGURE 2·4
First attempt.

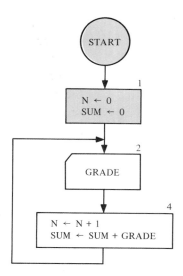

FIGURE 2·5
Second attempt.

read, is zero. Thus we have the improvement shown in Figure 2·5.

Remember that after this loop has been traversed for all the data cards, we want to compute the average grade:

How can we get to this instruction? You might suggest that we do this when we run out of cards. Unfortunately, when a computer is instructed to read data and finds no data left, the control of the machine is usually taken away from the present user and turned over to the next person waiting to run a program. The moral of this story is that unless we are content to lose control of the machine when the input data are exhausted, we must provide an exit from our loop. How can we do that in this case? We could of course, count the number of cards and find that there are, say, 17,368 and handle the problem as shown in Figure 2·6a, or we can employ the strategy (explained below) shown in Figure 2·6b and avoid counting the cards by hand.

The sentinel method shown in Figure 2·6b is used very frequently and works like this. Suppose that the maximum normal examination grade is 150. We prepare a special card with a much greater value for the grade, say 999, and put this card at the end of our stack. Now all the legitimate grades will pass straight through the test in box 3, but when the "phony" card is reached, the test in box 3 will fail and the average will be computed. Since the test (box 3) was placed before box 4 instead of after it, this "grade" will not be included in the count, nor will it be added into our SUM.

In comparing the two types of loop control illustrated in Figure 2·6 we see that in each case a decision box plays the central role in achieving escape from the loop. To emphasize the structure of the loop, we will usually flowchart the escape as the *false* exit from the controlling decision box. That is, as long as the condition in this box is *true,* looping continues. Escape will occur when the test condition becomes false.

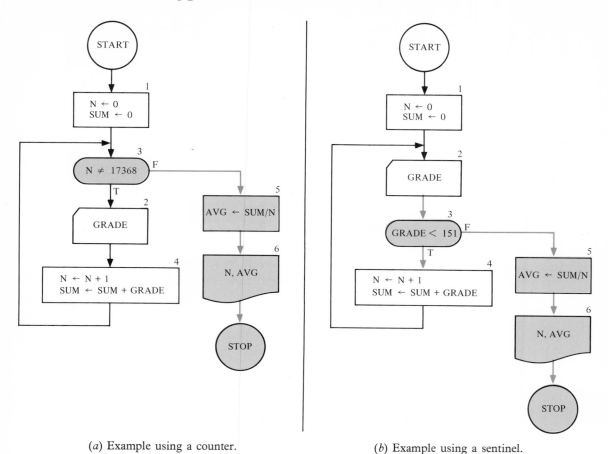

(*a*) Example using a counter.   (*b*) Example using a sentinel.

FIGURE 2·6
Two types of loop control

EXERCISES 2·2,
SET A

1. With a countercontrolled loop, repetition of a given computation will stop after the desired number of transits through the loop. Each of the following flowchart loops written by students either is, or is intended to be properly countercontrolled. For each flowchart on the next two pages, identify the answer that best indicates the number of loop transits that will occur when the given flowchart is executed (i.e., the number of times the output box will be executed).

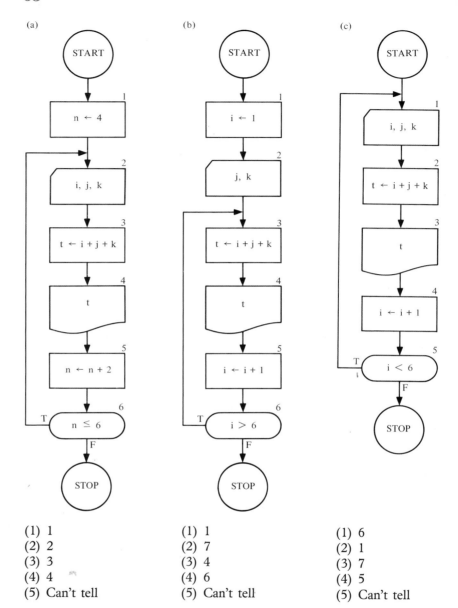

(a)

(1) 1
(2) 2
(3) 3
(4) 4
(5) Can't tell

(b)

(1) 1
(2) 7
(3) 4
(4) 6
(5) Can't tell

(c)

(1) 6
(2) 1
(3) 7
(4) 5
(5) Can't tell

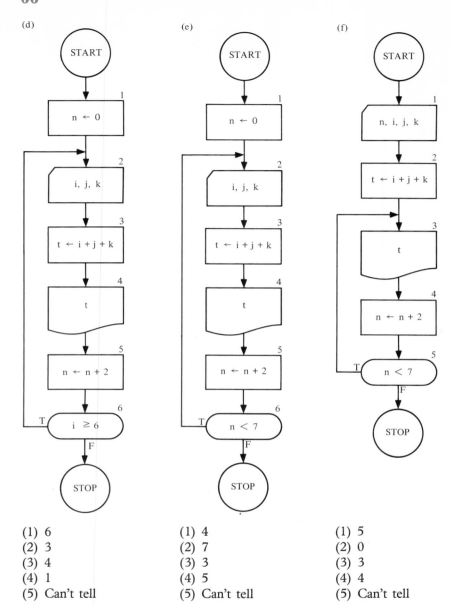

(d)

(1) 6
(2) 3
(3) 4
(4) 1
(5) Can't tell

(e)

(1) 4
(2) 7
(3) 3
(4) 5
(5) Can't tell

(f)

(1) 5
(2) 0
(3) 3
(4) 4
(5) Can't tell

2. Trace the flowchart below using the data supplied. Then determine the truth or falsity of each of the assertions a through d.

Assertions

(a) The second printed value (at box 6) is 7.
(b) Box 9 will be executed 4 times.
(c) The last value given for A3 will not be input.
(d) The variable n serves as a counter for control of the loop in this algorithm.

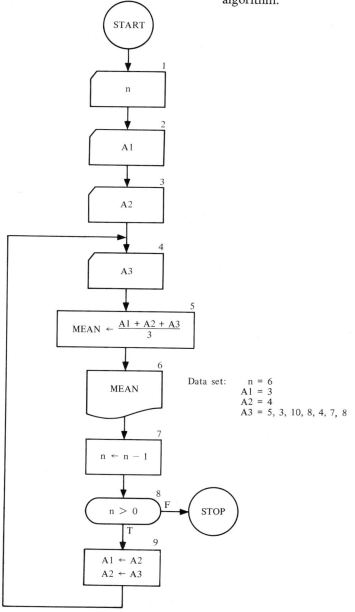

Data set: n = 6
A1 = 3
A2 = 4
A3 = 5, 3, 10, 8, 4, 7, 8

3. This question relates to the flowchart and to an incomplete SAMOS translation of it shown below.

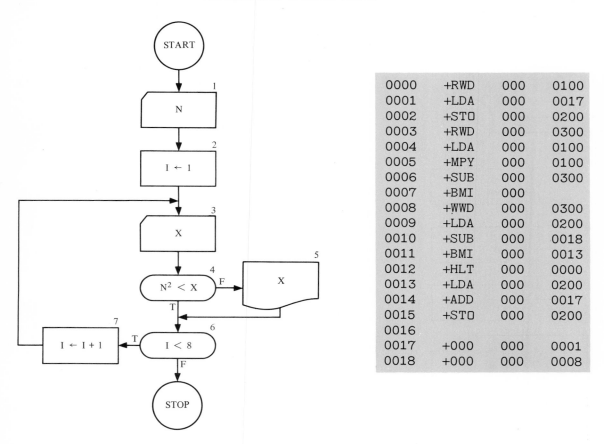

0000	+RWD	000	0100
0001	+LDA	000	0017
0002	+STO	000	0200
0003	+RWD	000	0300
0004	+LDA	000	0100
0005	+MPY	000	0100
0006	+SUB	000	0300
0007	+BMI	000	
0008	+WWD	000	0300
0009	+LDA	000	0200
0010	+SUB	000	0018
0011	+BMI	000	0013
0012	+HLT	000	0000
0013	+LDA	000	0200
0014	+ADD	000	0017
0015	+STO	000	0200
0016			
0017	+000	000	0001
0018	+000	000	0008

(a) Suppose the data cards supplied for this program contained the following values, in order:

   2, 1, 6, 14, 7, 3, 2, 4, 5

What values would be printed by the program when the flowchart is executed?

(b) What should be the address field for the SAMOS instruction at location 0007?

(c) What should be the SAMOS instruction at location 0016?

4. A teacher assigned a class of students the problem of constructing a flowchart as follows. The input consists of the lengths and widths of several rectangles. The purpose is to produce a list with consecutively numbered lines giving the length, L, the width, W, and the area, A, of only those rectangles with a perimeter greater than 12. The eight flowcharts shown in Figure 2·7 were turned in by students as solutions to the problem. Your job is the following.

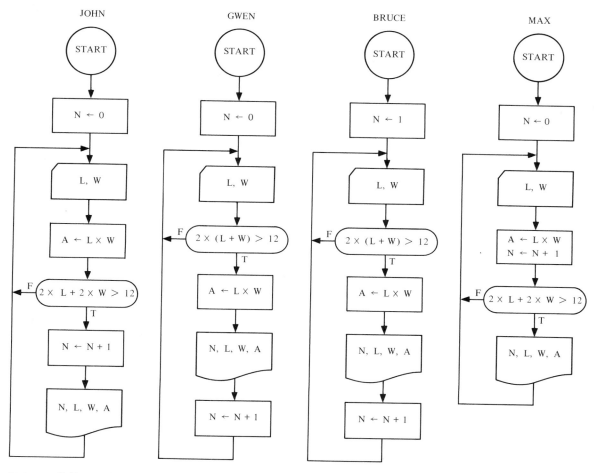

FIGURE 2·7, part 1

(a) Tell which of the solutions are correct and which are incorrect. (For our purposes a correct solution is one that produces the required output. It may not be the most efficient solution, however.)

(b) For those that are incorrect, in what way will the answers produced be wrong?

(c) Study those that are correct for efficiency, and construct one flowchart using the most efficient features of each. (Of two programs, the one requiring the smaller number of calculations is the more efficient.)

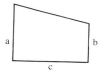

5. On pages 71 and 72 are five flowcharts constructed by students as solutions to the following problem. As input you are given values of the base c and sides a and b of several trapezoids. (Assume a > b.) Produce a list with lines numbered consecutively (beginning with 1)

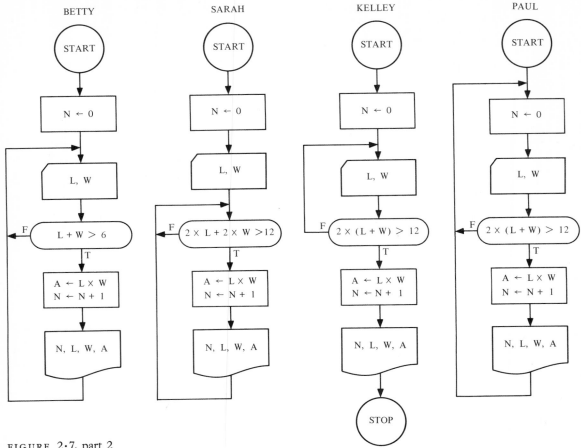

FIGURE 2·7, part 2

giving values for a, b, c, and the area, T, of only those trapezoids whose average height, (a + b)/2, is at least twice the base c.

(a) Tell which of the student solutions are correct and which incorrect. (A correct solution is one that produces the required output, although not necessarily the most efficient solution.)

(b) Construct a correct flowchart using the most efficient features found among the five solutions. (Of two programs, the one requiring the smaller number of calculations is the more efficient.)

6. Construct a flowchart for an algorithm that will accept and process, one at a time, a set of 100 values, compute the sum of those values that are positive, ignore those that are zero, and count those that are negative. When all 100 values have been processed, the sum of the positive values and the count of the negative values should be printed out.

7. Flowchart an algorithm to compute and print a student's grade point average. Make the following assumptions.

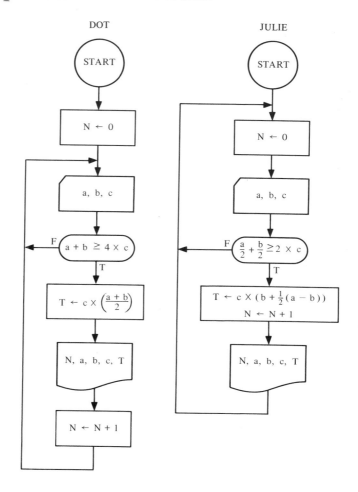

(a) It is not known in advance how many courses the student has taken. Thus you will have to invent a signal for the end of the data.

(b) Each input card contains a course grade in the form of a letter grade (A, B, C, D, or F) and the number of hours credit given for the course.

(c) Grade points earned for a course equal the number of course credit hours multiplied by

4 for a grade of A
3 for a grade of B
2 for a grade of C
1 for a grade of D
0 for a grade of F

(d) Grade point average is the sum of the grade points earned in all courses divided by the total number of hours.

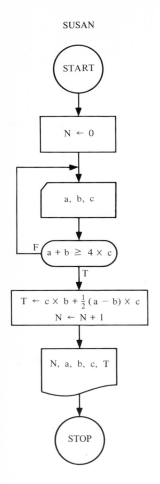

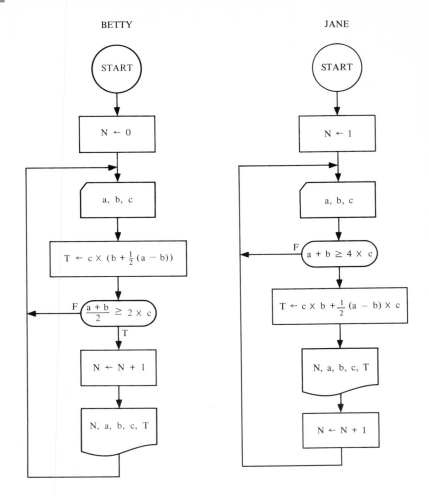

8. (a) Draw a flowchart that accomplishes the following.
   (1) Input four distinct characters.
   (2) Output the four characters.
   (3) Reorder the four characters so that the second character becomes the first, the third character becomes the second, the fourth becomes the third and the first becomes the last, that is, "rotate" the characters one position to the left.
   (4) Output the four characters in their new order.
   (5) Repeat steps 3 and 4 two more times.
       Example If the four characters "S", "V", "P", and "R" were read in, the output would be as shown on the left.

   (b) Indicate what types of changes, if any, would be necessary to increase the number of input characters and to produce the correspondingly larger and longer output.
       Note. Do not use more than one input and one output box in part a or part b.

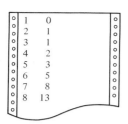

FIGURE 2·8

9. Modify the Fibonacci sequence flowchart (Figure 1·11*b*) so as to print out all terms of the Fibonacci sequence that are less than 10 million. Also include the feature of having the lines of output consecutively numbered, as in Figure 2·8.

10. According to U.S. Postal regulations, no box may be mailed if its length plus its girth exceeds 72 inches. (The girth is the length of the shortest string that will go all the way around the box.) A manufacturer has a large number of boxes that he wishes to mail. For each box he has a punch card with an ID number for the box and the three dimensions (the longest first) punched on it. Construct a flowchart to read these cards and print out the ID number and the length plus girth of each box *failing* to meet postal regulations.

Search for a Substring

Suppose we want to know whether the letter "P" occurs, at least once, somewhere in the string that is currently assigned to the variable TREENAME. Will the following

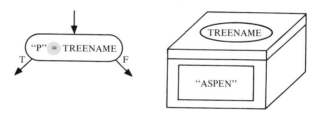

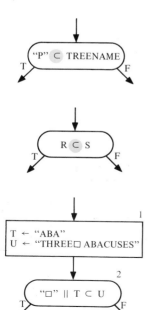

help us find out? Unfortunately, this test gives a *false* response, even though a "P" does appear in "ASPEN", the value of TREENAME. The other relations, $\neq$, $<$, $\leq$, $\geq$, and $>$, are of no more help to us. What we need is a different type of relation that we will call the *inclusion* relation and denote by the symbol, "$\subset$". To ask if the letter "P" occurs in the value currently assigned to TREENAME, we use the first decision box on the left. In general, the second figure on the left is a decision box that evaluates the assertion: "A copy of the value of R can be found as a substring in the value of S." With this definition, for instance, the assignments in box 1 on the left result in a *true* assertion in box 2. This is because there is at least one instance of the substring "□ABA" in the value of U.

In this chapter we will use the inclusion relation along with several other string processing "primitives" to develop useful string processing algorithms. Examples of several other string operators and relations will be introduced and applied in Chapter 13. Here we give a very simple but still illustrative example of the use of "⊂".

Scenario

The Texas Dry Ice Company of Waxahatchie was interested in changing its trademark. To save thousands of dollars of research, one member of the board suggested the name "The Texxon Co.," guessing that the proposed name would not conflict with existing trademarks because of its double "x." As an initial test it was decided to search the Dallas phone book to see if there were any names containing "xx". The Dry Ice Company was able to obtain a "tape" from the Dallas phone company containing a list of all the names in their metropolitan directory. The flowchart algorithm was simple to design after it was learned that the last name on the tape from the phone company was a sentinel whose value was "ZZZZ". The flowchart is shown in Figure 2·9.

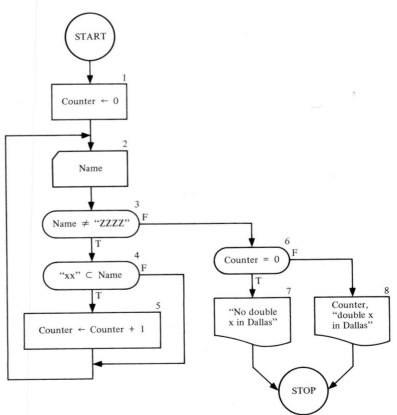

FIGURE 2·9
A sentinel-controlled loop for counting occurrences of "xx" in names.

1. How would you generalize the algorithm of Figure 2·9 to handle similar telephone name tapes from other cities where the sentinels may have different values?

2. How would you generalize the algorithm of Figure 2·9 to handle various other suggested trademarks whose basis for uniqueness is some other unusual substring? Thus The Texzon Co. might be another one of many other suggestions.

2·3
Expressions

As seen in earlier sections, the basic calculations executed by a computer consist of the evaluation of arithmetic and string expressions found in assignment boxes, output boxes, and decision boxes. As an example of an arithmetic expression, consider

$$\frac{-b + \sqrt{b^2 - 4ac}}{2a}$$

which is familiar from the quadratic formula. This ordinary mathematical notation might be acceptable in informal flowchart language, but it is not at all satisfactory for a procedural language such as FORTRAN or ALGOL. In such procedural languages expressions must be written in a form that can be read by a machine. To make this expression machine readable, several alterations are necessary, as discussed below. The various programming languages will handle these problems differently. The solutions we propose are merely possibilities.

Considerations for Machine Readability

1. We have already observed that conventions regarding variables make it impossible to use juxtaposition to represent multiplication. Thus, "4ac" must be written as "$4 \times a \times c$" if a and c are both variables. Some languages use symbols other than $\times$ for the multiplication operator. The important idea here is that the multiplication operator must appear explicitly.

2. The use of special symbols to represent particular functions complicates the process of machine reading. Thus such suggestive letters as SQRT could replace $\sqrt{\quad}$ and we could write

$$\text{SQRT } (b^2 - 4 \times a \times c) \quad \text{for} \quad \sqrt{b^2 - 4 \times a \times c}$$

Similarly, instead of $|R|$ we could write ABS(R), especially in a language whose alphabet does not contain the vertical bar.

How would the computer know that SQRT and ABS denote functions and not variables? The reason is that they are followed by left parentheses. Therefore enclose function arguments in parentheses and write, for example, SIN(X) rather than SIN X. Of course, some functions take more than one argument. Thus MIN(A,B) could be a function yielding the minimum of the two arguments, A and B. For such functions the arguments are separated by commas.

3.   Many procedural languages do not have lowercase letters in their character sets. For these, the variables a, b, and c would have to be replaced by other variables, most likely A, B, and C.

4.   In order to be read by a typical computer, an arithmetic expression must be written as a *linear* string of symbols. Off the line notations, such as B^2, are unacceptable. Thus an operator, such as $\uparrow$, is introduced to represent exponentiation, and we write B↑2 instead of B^2.

Also, the division by 2a was represented above by an off the line notation. We have to give up "fraction" notation and use an operator such as the slash (/) for division when we need machine readability.

With all these changes made, our quadratic formula expression has the form

$$(- B + SQRT(B{\uparrow}2 - 4 \times A \times C))/(2 \times A)$$

Although the changes were slight, the combination of all the changes produces an expression that looks quite foreign. It is difficult to recognize it at first glance as the quadratic formula.

Notice that when we shifted from fraction notation to slash notation for division, two additional pairs of parentheses had to be included, one pair embracing the numerator of the fraction and one pair embracing the denominator. Were either pair of parentheses omitted, the expression would not be evaluated correctly. For example, if the parentheses around $2 \times A$ were omitted, then the resulting expression would have the meaning of

$$\frac{- B + \sqrt{B^2 - 4AC}}{2} \times A$$

Good advice concerning parentheses is, "If in doubt whether parentheses are necessary, put them in." Whether parentheses are necessary or not can be decided by consulting the precedence rules for performing operations in the absence of parentheses. These rules conform with the usual mathematical conventions in this regard (where such conventions exist). For example, in evaluating the expression

$$A + B \times C$$

with the values of the variables being $A = 5, B = 3, C = 2$, multiplication takes precedence over addition and we first multiply B times C and then add A to the result. Thus,

$$A + B \times C = A + 3 \times 2 = A + 6 = 5 + 6 = 11$$

If we want A and B to be added first, we must include the parentheses, thus,

$$(A + B) \times C$$

In evaluating this expression, we obtain

$$(A + B) \times C = (5 + 3) \times C = 8 \times C = 8 \times 2 = 16$$

The complete table of precedence levels for arithmetic operations is found in Table 2·1.

TABLE 2·1
Precedence Levels for Evaluating Parenthesis-Free Arithmetic Expressions

Level	Operation Name	Operator Symbol
Highest	Exponentiation	↑
Next	Multiplication	$\times$
	Division	/
	Taking the negative	$-$ (unary)
Lowest	Addition	$+$
	Subtraction	$-$ (binary)

The Minus Sign

Before showing how the table works, we must explain the two occurrences of the minus sign. There are actually three ways in which the minus sign is used in mathematics.

1. To indicate the binary operation of subtraction, as in

$$X - 5$$

2. To indicate the unary operation of taking the negative, as in

$$- X$$

3. As part of the name of a negative number as in

$$- 5$$

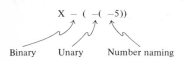

X − (−(−5))

Binary   Unary   Number naming

In the expression on the left, the minus is seen in all three roles. The three uses of minus are all handled differently by the computer. Why doesn't this lead to confusion? Only because the role of the minus can always be determined from the way it occurs in the expression. A minus is binary unless it occurs at the beginning of the expression or immediately after a left parenthesis. If the minus occurs in one of these positions, then it is number naming if the next symbol is a digit or a decimal point, and unary otherwise.

The Evaluation Process Using the Precedence Table 2·1

This illustration shows how evaluation of arithmetic expressions can be a mechanical process performable by a machine.

To see how a computer could evaluate an expression using the precedence table, cast yourself in the role of the Master Computer. First you scan the expression for operators of the highest level. But how do you scan? For correct interpretation, mathematical notation is quite dependent on our style of *left-to-right reading* and, for instance, an expression such as A − B − C would be evaluated incorrectly as A − (B − C) *if it were scanned right to left*. Therefore you first scan the expression from left to right for operators of the highest level. When you find an operator of this level, perform the operation indicated and resume scanning at the point where you left off. When all operations of the highest level have been performed, repeat the left-to-right scan for operators of the next level, and so forth. [Actual computers are usually equipped with special facilities (interpreters and compilers) that obtain equivalent results without all this repeated scanning. In Chapters 8 and 13 you will see how this can be accomplished.]

Here is an example to show how the evaluation scheme described above works out.

Example The expression is

$$-A \times L - G \times O{\uparrow}R / I + T / H \times M$$

Here we tabulate the values of the variables:

A	L	G	O	R	I	T	H	M
5	6	8	2	3	4	6	2	7

Table 2·2 shows the step-by-step evaluation process. Little triangular marks (▲) are used to indicate the operator to be dealt with next. The colored horizontal line after step 1 in the table indicates completion of operations of the highest level of precedence. The colored line after step 7 indicates completion of operations of the next level. Notice that in step 2, $-A$ evaluates to -5 and, while the minus sign of $-A$ is unary, that of -5 is number naming.

The scanning procedure is the heart of the evaluation process. To complete the description we need to know what to do with expressions containing parentheses. The part of an expression included between a pair of parentheses is called a *subexpression*. For example, in

$$(A \times C - D) \times E$$

TABLE 2·2
Display of Step-by-Step
Evaluation of Arithmetic
Expression

Step	Action	Expression After Step
0	Initial expression	$-A \times L - G \times O{\uparrow}R / I + T / H \times M$
1	Compute O↑R	$-A \times L - G \times 8 / I + T / H \times M$
2	Compute $-A$	$-5 \times L - G \times 8 / I + T / H \times M$
3	Compute $-5 \times L$	$-30 - G \times 8 / I + T / H \times M$
4	Compute $G \times 8$	$-30 - 64 / I + T / H \times M$
5	Compute $64 / I$	$-30 - 16 + T / H \times M$
6	Compute T / H	$-30 - 16 + 3 \times M$
7	Compute $3 \times M$	$-30 - 16 + 21$
8	Compute $-30 - 16$	$-46 + 21$
9	Compute $-46 + 21$	-25

we see that

$$A \times C - D$$

is a subexpression. General rules for evaluating subexpressions are given in Table 2·3.

(*Note.* Parentheses surrounding a constant should be deleted if possible. Undeletable parentheses surrounding a negative constant but not preceded by a function name should be ignored.)

1. Scan the expression from left to right for the first right parenthesis ")".
2. Evaluate the subexpression ending with this right parenthesis according to the correct rule for parenthesis-free expressions (Table 2·1 for arithmetic expressions).
3. If this subexpression is a constant, see whether it is preceded by a function name and, if so, compute the indicated functional value.
4. Return to step 1.

If the Table 2·1 and Table 2·2 rules are followed with left to right scanning, there is only one place where the order of evaluation of arithmetic expressions is not in conformity with usual mathematical conventions. The rules we have given evaluate

$$A \uparrow B \uparrow C \qquad \text{in the order} \qquad (A \uparrow B) \uparrow C$$

In mathematics, however, the convention is that

$$A \uparrow B \uparrow C \qquad \text{means} \qquad A \uparrow (B \uparrow C)$$

If you are aware of this discrepancy, you can always force your intent by use of parentheses.

Not all evaluation schemes involve precedence levels for operators. We could simply agree to scan from left to right (or visa versa) evaluating every operation as it occurs. The language APL, for example, uses a right to left scan without precedence levels. Such a scheme is certainly less complicated to implement. On the other hand, it results in an evaluation order that often differs from usual mathematical conventions. For instance, in APL, $A \times B + C$ is evaluated as $A \times (B + C)$, and $A - B - C$ is evaluated as $A - (B - C)$.

Other String Operations

Most of the information computers process has the form of character strings and much less, proportionately, the form of numbers for computation. We have not defined arithmetic operations, such as multiplication, for character strings such as "ABEL" and "BAKER". We have, however, defined string operators and relations for concatenation, ||, and for inclusion, ⊂ (and we will define others as we need them.) We might like to concatenate "ABEL" with "BAKER" and also with "571 GREEN STREET" to make a single string, S.

$$S \leftarrow \text{"ABEL"} \,\|\, \text{"□BAKER"} \,\|\, \text{"□571□GREEN□STREET"}$$

The value of S is then the string constant,

"ABEL□BAKER□571□GREEN□STREET".

We need two more string operations if we want to edit strings, one to determine the length of a given string, the other to extract copies of selected pieces or *substrings* of the given string. The former is achieved with the length function LENSTR, the latter with the substring operation SUBSTR. Several illustrations will show how these functions allow us to express various text editing operations. The use of the length function is very simple. Thus the execution of the first box on the left assigns the value 6 to the variable LEN, while executing the second box on the left assigns the value 27 to LENS, assuming S has the string value assigned to it in the above example.

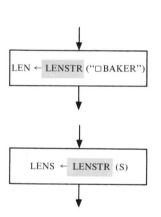

To extract a copy of part of a string, for example the first 13 characters of S, we use the function SUBSTR. Thus

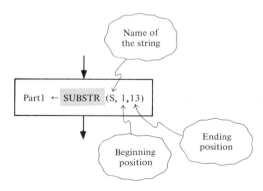

Here we see that the function SUBSTR has three arguments. The first argument is the name of the string from which a substring is to be copied. The next two arguments hold values

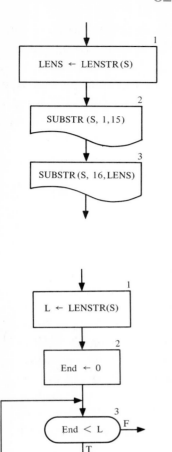

for the beginning and ending positions of the substring, a copy of which is to be assigned to Part1.

We will adopt the convention that if the ending position is less than the beginning position, the value of the substring function is null, that is, the value of SUBSTR(S, 13, 1) is null.

The flowchart fragment on the left might be used to print out the string S on display lines whose maximum width is 15 characters.

When executed, this fragment will create the following display.

Execution of box 2 causes the first 15 characters of S to be printed on one line. Execution of box 3 causes the remaining characters of S from positions 16 through LENS, inclusive, to be printed.

While this display may not be a desirable way to break up a person's address, it is an initial attempt that we can improve later when we gain more experience with text editing operations (see Chapter 13). A more realistic approach to displaying long strings on lines of fixed width must take into account the possibility that the string length may actually exceed the width of two lines or three lines. In fact, we may not even know how many lines will be printed. In such cases, a program loop is required to print a line of up to (in this example) 15 characters, followed by another and another until the last line is printed. The logic for this print control is illustrated in Figure 2·10.

The variable End is the controlling variable. Whenever box 3 is executed, the value of End represents the number of

FIGURE 2·10
Printing out parts of a long string under program control.

characters of S already printed. End is initialized to 0 in box 2 and is either increased by 15 or set to the value of L before each use of the SUBSTR function in box 8. In box 8 the variable End also denotes the end of the substring to be printed. The variable Begin is not given an initial value in box 2 but is set repeatedly to one more than the value of End, so that when used as the second argument of SUBSTR in box 8, its value always represents the beginning of the wanted substring of S.

To recapitulate, our discussion of string operations has called attention to a string operator, concatenation ($\|$), a string relation, inclusion ($\subset$), and two additional string operations, length (LENSTR) and substring (SUBSTR). Of these four only the inclusion relation is not basic. Without inclusion we could still accomplish the equivalent testing for or editing of a substring by algorithms utilizing the other three operations, but things would get fairly disorganized. Working the next exercises should convince you that this observation is correct.

EXERCISES 2·3,
SET A

1. Suppose at a certain point in an algorithm you are developing, a printout is required in box 10 or box 20, depending on the result of a given test x < y in box 5.

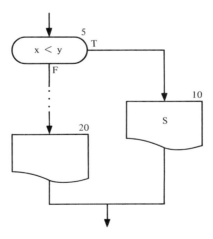

The printout in box 10 is the entire value of the string S. The printout in box 20 is the string formed by concatenating the three *unshaded* parts of S as shown in this diagram.

The string S
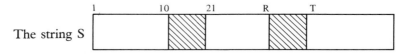

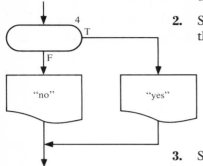

Complete the details on the *false* side of the box 5 test to accomplish the indicated task.

2. Show the details of decision box 4 on the left which tests whether the 14th character of a given string T is the letter "P".

3. Show flowchart details similar to those required in the preceding exercise for determining whether the nth character of a given string T is the letter "P", where

    (a) The length of T is known to be greater than n.
    (b) The length of T may not be as large as n and hence three different printouts are required.

4. Without using the inclusion relation, ⊂, develop a flowchart fragment to determine whether a substring "XY" occurs in positions 14 and 15 of the string S.

5. Describe an algorithm without using the inclusion relation, ⊂, that when executed will determine whether the substring "XY" occurs anywhere in the string S.

Printing Patterns

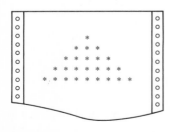

FIGURE 2·11

Line printers and typewriters usually have 10 characters to the inch horizontally and 6 lines to the inch vertically. Unfortunately, the two scales are not equal; for printing patterns we would prefer the same scale both ways. However, let us try to flowchart an algorithm to read in one character value, C, and one integer value, n, and print out a symmetric triangle using the character value. The triangle should be i lines high and $2 \times n - 1$ characters wide at the base, as shown in Figure 2·11 for the character value C = "*" and the integer value n = 5.

Using the concatenation operator introduced in Section 2·1 and the substring operator introduced in this section, it is not difficult to design a flowchart to produce this pattern, as we see in Figure 2·12. The triangular pattern consists of

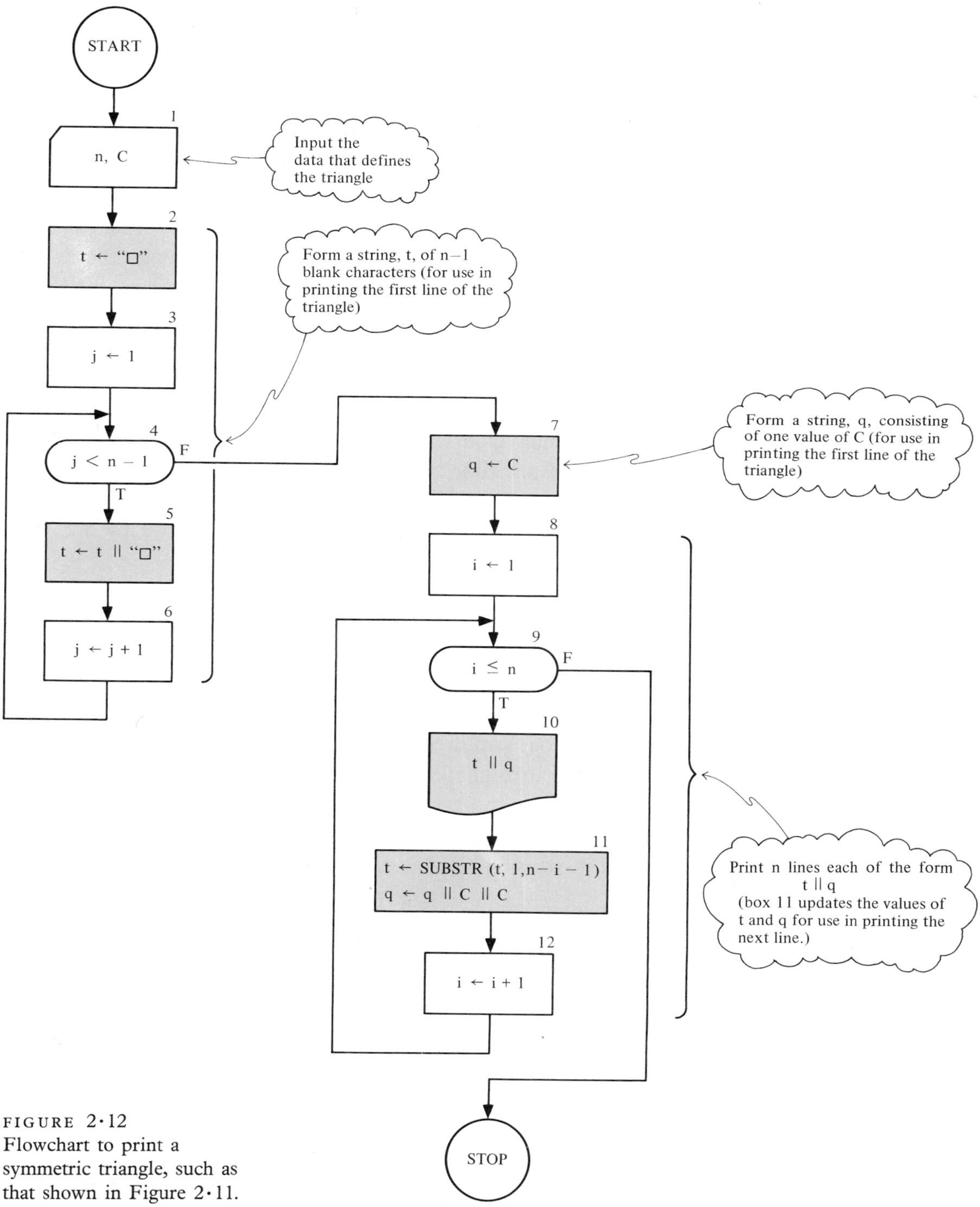

FIGURE 2·12
Flowchart to print a
symmetric triangle, such as
that shown in Figure 2·11.

n lines such that each line, for example the ith line, has the form

$$t \parallel q,$$

where t is a string of $n - i$ blank characters and q is a string of $2 \times i - 1$ characters, each having the value of C.

The heart of the algorithm, boxes 8 through 12, is a loop to print these n lines. When the loop is entered, t has already been initialized to a string of $n - 1$ blanks through the execution of boxes 2 through 6, and q has already been initialized to a string of one value of C. Thus t and q are ready to be used in printing the top line the first time box 10 is executed. Then t and q are updated in box 11. One blank is removed from t and two values of C are appended to q. The removal of one blank from t is achieved by applying the SUBSTR function. Each time box 11 is entered, the length of t is $n - i$, so by "extracting" a substring from positions 1 through $n - i - 1$, we get a new string of blanks shorter by one, and we use this string to update t.

Notice that it is absolutely necessary to print the (decreasing) string of blanks *preceding* the triangle characters on each line in order to position the triangle characters, but there is no need to print any blank characters afterward.

Using the concatenation operator, many interesting patterns can be "captured" in flowcharts and printed on an output device. You might like to study the pattern in an oriental or a Navajo rug and try to design a flowchart to reproduce some part of it. The following exercise set suggests some easy patterns to start on.

EXERCISES 2·3, SET B

1. Using the concatenation operator but not the substring function, construct an algorithm to print a block letter "C" two inches wide (i.e., 20 characters) and two inches high (i.e., 12 lines). Print the block C with the character "C" as shown on the next page.

2. (a) Using the concatenation operator but not the substring function, construct an algorithm to print a chessboard pattern similar to that shown on the next page. Read in the two single character values as data.

   (b) *Challenge.* Change the algorithm so as to add a frame to the printed chess board, that is, line segments enclosing the board.

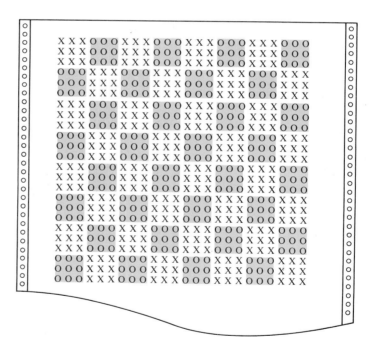

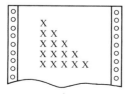

3. Flowchart an algorithm to read in one character value, C, and one integer value, i, and print out an isosceles right triangle using the character value of the variable C. The triangle should be i characters wide and i lines high, as shown on the left for the character "X", and the integer 5.

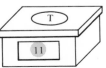

4. Flowchart an algorithm to print a diamond R characters wide at its maximum (or middle). Read in the (odd) value for R as data and also the value for S, the character in which the diamond is to be printed. The figure on the left indicates the desired output when R = 7 and S = "K".

Evaluation of String Expressions

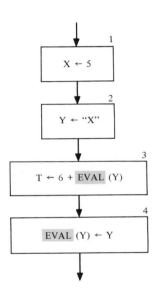

Although we have not defined arithmetic operations on strings, we might find it useful to be able to signal the computer that we wish to shift our point of view and, instead of considering "6 × Y" as a string, we wish to consider it as a numerical expression and evaluate it. To achieve this we define another string function, EVAL. Thus if Y has been assigned the value 5, EVAL ("6 × Y") = 30 and EVAL ("Y^2 − 10 × Y + 4") = −21.

We see that the EVAL function merely acts to remove the quote marks that surround its argument. That is,

EVAL ("Y^2 − 10 × Y + 4")

evaluates to

Y^2 − 10 × Y + 4

To see this function in more interesting contexts, consider the uses of EVAL in boxes 3 and 4 on the left. Executing the first two boxes has the effect of assigning values to X and Y.

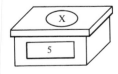 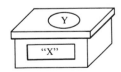

To interpret box 3, the Master Computer sends the Reader to retrieve the value of Y, which is "X". Then the Master Computer computes EVAL ("X"), which is simply X. So the expression 6 + X = 6 + 5 is then evaluated and this sum is assigned to T.

Now box 4 is interpreted by first fetching the value of Y, which is "X", and then assigning it to the variable that EVAL (Y) stands for. The process of evaluating EVAL (Y) is the same as before; that is, EVAL (Y) evaluates to EVAL

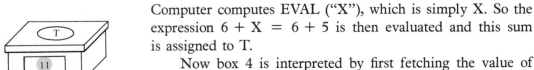

("X"), which evaluates to X. So the effect of executing box 4 is to assign "X" to the variable X.

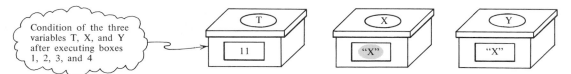

Condition of the three variables T, X, and Y after executing boxes 1, 2, 3, and 4

EVAL can be applied to any string expression for which it makes sense. Study the use of EVAL in the following flowcharts, which also illustrate the difference between assignment and substitution. We will find important uses for EVAL in some of the later chapters of this book (Chapters 8 and 13).

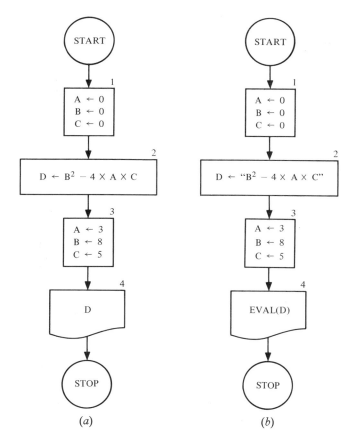

In the first flowchart, (*a*), the output value of D will be 0, because A, B, and C all had value 0 when D was computed in box 2. In the second flowchart (*b*), the evaluation takes place in the output box 4 and thus the value 4 will be output.

**Reading Expressions
into Computer Storage**

Once an arithmetic expression such as

$$\frac{-b + \sqrt{b^2 - 4ac}}{2a}$$

has been properly represented as a string of characters, such as

$$(- B + SQRT(B{\uparrow}2 - 4 \times A \times C))/(2 \times A)$$

it can be read from a data card or typed at a computer terminal and stored in the computer ready to be broken down into a list of machine-language instructions. In the case of cards, most available key punches do not have keys for the ↑ and × characters, so a "transliteration" is generally used. For example, on the key punch the ↑ character is usually represented by ** (double asterisk obtained using two key strokes) and the × symbol by * (single asterisk).

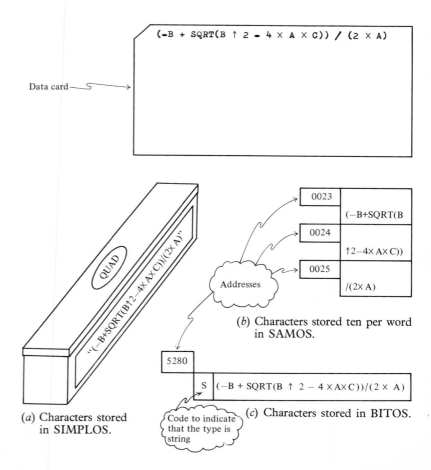

Data card

0023

(−B+SQRT(B

0024

↑2−4×A×C))

0025

/(2×A)

Addresses

(b) Characters stored ten per word in SAMOS.

QUAD

"(−B+SQRT(B↑2−4×A×C))/(2×A)"

5280

S   (−B + SQRT(B ↑ 2 − 4 ×A×C))/(2 × A)

Code to indicate that the type is string

(c) Characters stored in BITOS.

(a) Characters stored in SIMPLOS.

FIGURE 2·13
An expression in storage after input from a data card.

Computers store a string of symbols such as the one shown above in many different arrangements. In our conceptual model SIMPLOS, a storage box is constructed to order and the whole string fits in, as shown in Figure 2 · 13*a*. In SAMOS each word holds 10 characters and the expression can be stored as in Figure 2 · 13*b*. The three locations 0023, 0024, and 0025 are considered to be stuck together to form one unit whose starting address is 0023. A BITOS cell, as shown in Figure 2 · 13*c*, can be long enough to hold the whole string.

When we speak of the computer scanning an expression, we will mean that the expression, originally punched on a card or transmitted by some other input medium, is examined one character at a time from its location in storage.

EXERCISES 2 · 3, SET C

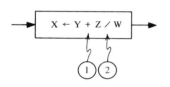

Correct order: ② , ①

1. In parts a through d below, you are given an assignment box from a flowchart. Your job is to use the rules of precedence (as shown in Table 2 · 1) to determine the order in which the arithmetic operations are carried out when the box is executed. For easy reference, an identifying number has been placed below each operator. A worked example is shown on the left.

(a)

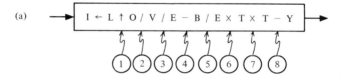

(b)

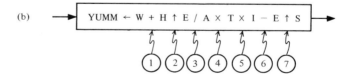

(c)

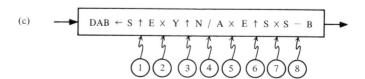

(d)

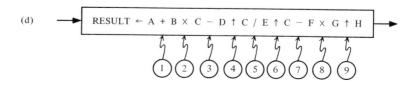

2. Select, if possible, the flowchart box that will assign to K the value of

$$\frac{(A - C)^2 - D + C}{A + B^2}$$

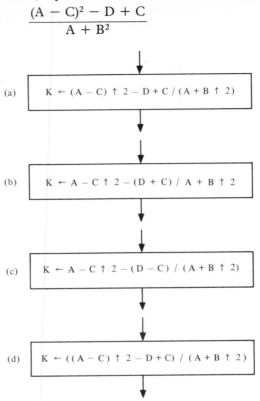

(a) $K \leftarrow (A - C) \uparrow 2 - D + C / (A + B \uparrow 2)$

(b) $K \leftarrow A - C \uparrow 2 - (D + C) / A + B \uparrow 2$

(c) $K \leftarrow A - C \uparrow 2 - (D - C) / (A + B \uparrow 2)$

(d) $K \leftarrow ((A - C) \uparrow 2 - D + C) / (A + B \uparrow 2)$

3. In parts a and b below you are to determine what value will be assigned to A by executing the given flowchart assignment box, assuming that the other variables that appear in the expression to the right of the assignment arrow have the values:

$$B = 4 \qquad D = 2$$
$$C = 12 \qquad E = -4$$

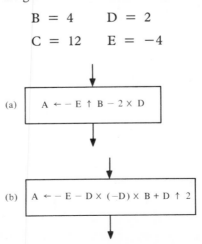

(a) $A \leftarrow - E \uparrow B - 2 \times D$

(b) $A \leftarrow - E - D \times (-D) \times B + D \uparrow 2$

4. The flowchart below follows all of our flowcharting conventions, but would cause an error message if converted to a computer language and executed. Explain what is wrong.

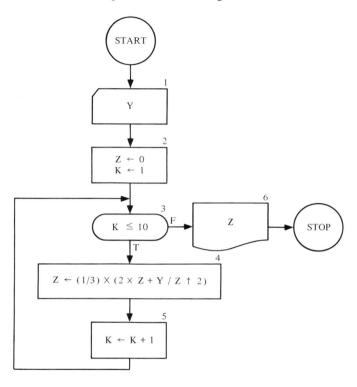

2·4 Rounding

You already know several different ways of representing numbers. For example, if asked to express the quotient of 125 and 8, you could write the answer in any of these forms.

$$\frac{125}{8} \qquad 15\tfrac{5}{8} \qquad 15.625 \qquad .15625 \times 10^2$$

Fraction   Mixed number   Decimal   Floating point

All these answers are equally correct; which form you choose depends on the use to which you intend to put your answer. Generally, however, only the third or fourth form could be easily represented in a computer such as SAMOS. For our discussion here, we will use the decimal form to represent such numbers. We will not make any distinction here between decimal form and the floating point notation used in computers.

If we replace the problem discussed above by that of

finding the quotient of 125 and 7, we would have

$$\frac{125}{7} \qquad\qquad 17\tfrac{6}{7} \qquad\qquad 17.8571428$$

Fraction   Mixed number   Decimal

Here, the first two forms are exact representations of the quotient, but the decimal form (the one used by the computer) is only approximate. The reason is that the process of grinding out successive digits in the quotient cannot be allowed to go on forever and must eventually be terminated.

$$17.\,8\;5\;7\;1\;4\;2\;8\;5\;7\;1$$
$$7\,\overline{\big)\,1\;2^55.^60^40^50^10^30^20^60^40^50^10}$$

The same holds true for the computer. In a word-organized computer such as SAMOS, the number of digits carried in the quotient of a division depends on its "word length."

In a BITOS-type machine the user may choose how many digits of precision are to be carried. In either case some *rounding* must be done before the quotient of 125 / 7 can be assigned to a variable, or output. You may feel that seven digits of precision, 17.85714, is close enough to 125 / 7 "for all practical purposes," but there are some dangers inherent in this attitude, as will appear in Chapter 11. In that chapter it will also be seen that rounding may occur in connection with all arithmetic operations, not only with division.

What You Used To Know About Rounding

We are all inclined to think of rounding as a sort of anomaly—something to apologize for—certainly not a mathematical process. And yet there is a large class of problems in which rounding is absolutely necessary in order to get the correct answers! For an example of such a problem, let us return to the fourth grade level.

Problem A playground director found a sack containing 125 marbles in his desk and decided to distribute them equally among the eight boys on the playground. How many marbles did each boy get?

In order to solve this problem, you first divide 125 by 8, obtaining

$$15\tfrac{5}{8} \qquad \text{or} \qquad 15.625$$

You know that this is not yet the right answer, since the playground director will not smash up any marbles into eighths in order to distribute them in this way. What he will do is to "round off" the number $15\frac{5}{8}$ obtained by division and give each boy 15 marbles. The 5 leftover marbles he will put quietly in his pocket. At the fourth-grade level, we had no difficulty in finding the answer 15, since the method of "integer division" we used in those days gave this answer directly.

We then said that "each boy gets 15 marbles with 5 left over."

From the fourth-grade viewpoint, this "integer division" process for dividing N by D consisted of finding integers Q and R so that

$$N \;=\; D \times Q + R \qquad \text{with} \qquad R < D$$

This is the division algorithm of elementary school arithmetic. The method of finding Q and R is one of repeated subtraction and is easily flowcharted.

The process by which the playground director got the answer 15 from the quotient 15.625 can be viewed as being performed by a mathematical function, CHOP (Figure 2·14). We may think of CHOP as a machine that accepts real numbers as input and outputs whole numbers. (In everyday computing CHOP is often called *truncate*.) In functional notation, the fact represented in this picture may be expressed as

$$\text{CHOP}\,(15.625) \;=\; 15$$

To understand the behavior of CHOP, note that every real number is composed of a whole number part and a fractional part. When a number is put into the input hopper of the function, CHOP, the fractional part is lopped off and the whole number part is returned as the output value. Thus,

$$
\begin{array}{ll}
\text{CHOP}\,(-17.68) = -17 & \text{CHOP}\,(\pi) = 3 \\[4pt]
\text{CHOP}\,(7\frac{3}{4}) = 7 & \text{CHOP}\,(-\frac{14}{3}) = -4 \\[4pt]
\text{CHOP}\,(29) = 29 & \text{CHOP}\,(-537) = -537
\end{array}
$$

There are several reasonable integer rounding processes, and the CHOP function carries out one of them.

Now we can see that Q and R in the division algorithm

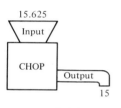

FIGURE 2·14

can be expressed in the form

$$Q = \text{CHOP}\left(\frac{N}{D}\right) \qquad R = N - D \times \text{CHOP}\left(\frac{N}{D}\right)$$

Frequently, in flowcharting, we will wish to make such tests as

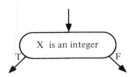

The CHOP function enables us to rewrite this test as

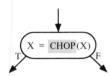

The assertion in this box is true only in the case that X has an integer value.

This same CHOP function can be used in rounding to a certain number of decimal places. For example, if we wish to round

23.84627

to two decimal places to get

23.84

this can be accomplished in the following way.

1. Multiply the number to be rounded by 100.

    $100 \times 23.84627 = 2384.627$

2. Apply the function CHOP to the result.

    $\text{CHOP}(2384.627) = 2384$

3. Divide this result by 100.

    $$\frac{2384}{100} = 23.84$$

This is called "rounding by chopping to two decimal places" and is described by the expression

$\text{CHOP}(100 \times X) / 100$

Similarly, chopping X to three decimal places is accomplished by

$$CHOP(1000 \times X) / 1000$$

Fifth-Grade Rounding

In the fifth grade, in work on measurement, you were often asked to round your measurements to "the nearest whole number of inches." Thus a measurement of $15\frac{5}{8}$ would be rounded to 16, not 15, inches.

There is another integer rounding function called ROUND, which does this job for us. The effect of ROUND can be defined in terms of CHOP. That is (for positive values of X),

$$ROUND(X) = CHOP(X + .5)$$

For example,

$$ROUND\,(15.625) = CHOP\,(15.625 + .5) =$$
$$CHOP\,(16.125) = 16$$

If the value of X is negative, then we must subtract .5 before applying CHOP. The flowchart in Figure 2·15 covers both cases. The output value of Y is ROUND(X).

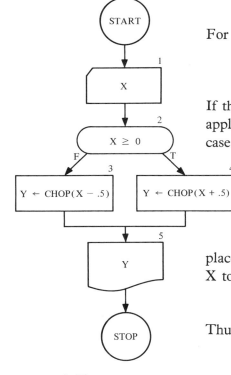

FIGURE 2·15
The meaning of ROUND(X).

One can also ROUND to a given number of decimal places as we did with CHOP. The formula for ROUNDing X to the nearest thousandth is

$$ROUND(1000 \times X) / 1000$$

Thus, 17.68479 ROUNDed to three decimal places is

$$ROUND\,(1000 \times 17.68479) / 1000$$
$$= ROUND\,(17684.79) / 1000$$
$$= 17685 / 1000$$
$$= 17.685$$

A Final Remark

We must be aware that all computer calculations in word-organized machines are rounded by chopping or by some other method to produce results that will fit into a computer word. From a mathematical viewpoint, it is convenient to consider that the computer makes the exact calculation followed by the application of some rounding function.

In our flowchart language we normally will not take the effect of rounding into account; we will act as though all calculations are exact. Before translating flowcharts into programming languages however, it is often necessary to replace decision boxes such as

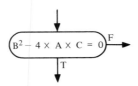

by approximate forms such as

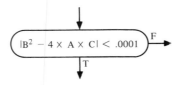

In Chapter 11 the effect of rounding on computer calculations will be considered in much more detail.

EXERCISES 2·4

1. Parts a through f of this question relate to the flowchart below, and parts g through i relate to the incomplete SAMOS translation also given below. Remember that DIV means integer division.

(a) True or false: For every execution of box 1, box 6 is executed four times.

(b) If 6 pairs of values (a pair being a value for N and a value for L) are supplied as input data, the number of values printed by the program would be:
   (1) Dependent on the actual data supplied.
   (2) Exactly 18.
   (3) At least 24.
   (4) No values will ever be printed.
   (5) Exactly 3.

(c) Suppose the data cards supplied for this program contained the following values in order:

$$791, 323, -792, 324$$

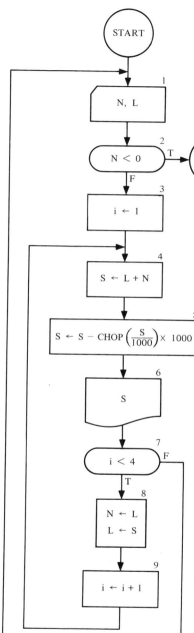

Location	Instruction		Remarks
0000	RWD	000 0200	N
0001	RWD	000 0201	L
0002	LDA	000 0200	
0003	BMI	000	
0004	LDA	000	1
0005	STO	000 0203	i
0006	LDA	000 0201	
0007	ADD	000 0200	
0008	STO	000 0202	S
0009	LDA	000 0202	
0010	DIV		
0011	MPY		
0012	STO	000 0400	temp
0013	LDA	000 0202	S
0014	SUB	000 0400	
0015	STO	000 0202	
0016	WWD	000 0202	
0017	LDA	000 0203	
0018	SUB	000	4
0019	BMI	000 0021	
0020			
0021	LDA	000 0201	
0022	STO	000 0200	
0023	LDA	000 0202	
0024	STO	000 0201	

Which of the following sets of values would be printed by the program:

(1) 114, 437, 760, 197.
(2) 114, 905, 696.
(3) 1114, 437, 551, 988.
(4) 114, 437, 551, 988.
(5) 1114, 905, 696, 601, 988.

(d) True or false: The inner loop of the flowchart, that is, flowchart boxes 4 through 9, constitutes a countercontrolled loop.

(e) True or false: The outer loop of the flowchart, that is, boxes 1 through 7, is sentinel-controlled if negative values of N are regarded as otherwise inadmissable values.

(f) How can flowchart boxes 4 and 5 be combined into a box with a single assignment step without significantly affecting the program or the results it produces?

(g) At what locations are the SAMOS instructions that correspond to flowchart box 4?

(h) Select the correct answer:
The SAMOS instruction at location 0020 should be:

(1) BMI   000   0000
(2) HLT   000   0000
(3) BRU   000   0000
(4) STO   000   0203
(5) None of the above.

(i) What decision must be made before the SAMOS instruction at location 0010 can be completed?

2. For each of the following five flowchart assignment boxes* there is given a set of current values for the variables involved prior to execution of the assignment step. Your job is to determine the value assigned to T in each box.

		Current Values of the Variables
(a)	$T \leftarrow I/J + K$	$I = 17$ $J = 4$ $K = 7$
(b)	$T \leftarrow CHOP\left(\dfrac{I - J}{T}\right)$	$I = 12$ $J = 6.6$ $T = 4.5$
(c)	$T \leftarrow CHOP\ (I/J + K)$	$I = 12$ $J = 7$ $K = -4$
(d)	$T \leftarrow N - CHOP\left(\dfrac{N}{D}\right) \times D$	$N = 17$ $D = 4$
(e)	$T \leftarrow N/3 - CHOP\left(\dfrac{N/3}{D}\right) \times D$	$N = 4$ $D = 7$

3. In parts a, b, and c below, you are given initial values for a set of variables that appear in an associated sequence of flowchart boxes, and you are to designate the values for the same or other variables after executing that flowchart sequence.

(a) Initial values: $P = 7, T = 4$

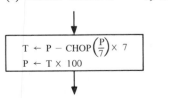

$$T \leftarrow P - CHOP\left(\frac{P}{7}\right) \times 7$$
$$P \leftarrow T \times 100$$

What are the resulting values for T and P?

*Reminder These are flowchart assignment steps, not statements in a programming language such as ALGOL or FORTRAN.

(b) Initial values: S = 4, M = 21

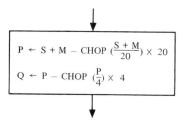

$$P \leftarrow S + M - CHOP \left(\frac{S + M}{20}\right) \times 20$$

$$Q \leftarrow P - CHOP \left(\frac{P}{4}\right) \times 4$$

What are the resulting values for P and Q?

(c) Given the accompanying flowchart fragment and the following four values for x:

(1) x = − 14.9. (3) x = 14.4.
(2) x = − 12.1. (4) x = 14.

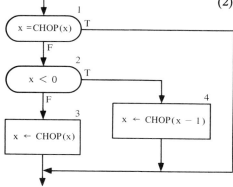

What is the resulting value of x in each of the four cases?

4. The effect of executing the flowchart fragment given in part c of the preceding question is equivalent to the application of a well-known integer-rounding function. What is that function?

5. In parts a and b below you are given logical expressions in flowchart notation. Your job is to evaluate the truth or falsity of these expressions, assuming the given values for the variables.

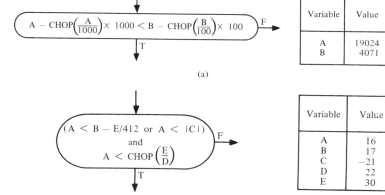

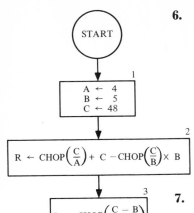

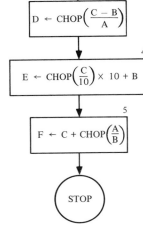

6. Trace through the execution of the flowchart given on the left and complete the following statements:

(a) After box 2 is executed, R has the value _____.
(b) After box 3 is executed, D has the value _____.
(c) After box 4 is executed, E has the value _____.
(d) When STOP is reached, F has the value _____.

7. In parts a through e below what value (or values) will be output by the given flowchart?

(a)

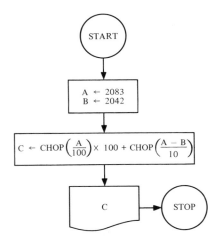

(b)

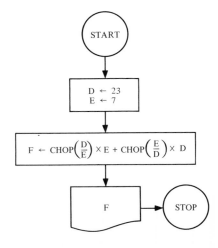

(c)

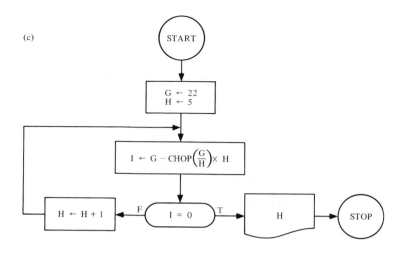

(d)

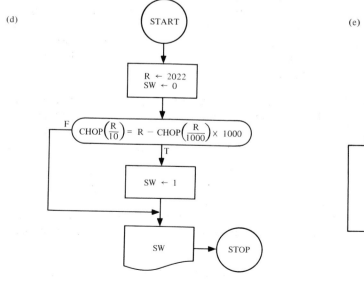

(e)

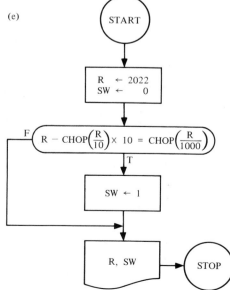

8. Draw a flowchart that inputs a set of 100 data values and outputs all the even values except those that are multiples of 10. Be sure that your flowchart inputs exactly 100 values.

9. A and B are four-digit positive integers. You are given an incomplete flowchart in Figure 2 · 16.

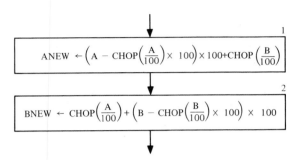

FIGURE 2·16

(a) If the value of A is 1468 and the value of B is 2357, then what is the value of ANEW after executing box 1?
(b) For the same values of A and B, what is the value of BNEW after executing box 2?

10. Draw a flowchart that describes the following process. A series of integer data values are input, one value at a time. The computer prints a two-digit number that consists of the lowest-order (rightmost) two digits of each input value. A series of positive integers is available as data, one data value per input record (i.e., one value per data card).

11. Draw a flowchart that describes the following process. Values are read two at a time. A new number consisting of the high-order (leftmost) two digits of the first number and the low-order two digits of the second number is formed and printed. The process is repeated for the next pair of numbers, and so forth. A series of four-digit positive integers is available as data.

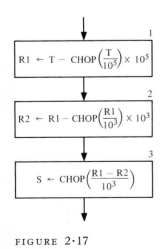

12. Study the sequence of flowchart boxes in Figure 2 · 17. These boxes are intended to represent a series of computations involving only integers (i.e., no reals). Assume that prior to executing box 1, the value of T is that of an eight-digit positive integer.

(a) What is the maximum value of R1 after executing box 1?
(b) What is the maximum value of S after executing box 3?
(c) Someone observes that the effect of executing boxes 1 through 3 is that of an "extraction" process, that is, that the value assigned to S is an "extract" of T. Explain what specific extraction process is performed.

FIGURE 2·17

13. Determine the values of ROUND(x) when x is an odd multiple of 1 / 2.

14. A camp director wishes to divide his boys into nine-man baseball teams. Construct a formula that uses one of the rounding functions, CHOP or ROUND, on NBOY, the number of boys, and evaluates to the number of full teams. No boy is to be on more than one team.

15. It costs 13 cents an ounce to send an airmail letter. Draw flowchart steps to represent evaluating the cost of sending an airmail letter as a function of the (real) variable WT. Use either CHOP or ROUND.

16. A game wheel shown in Figure 2 · 18 is divided into five equal sectors, numbered consecutively from zero in a clockwise manner as shown. There is a spinner that rotates on a shaft mounted at the center of the wheel.

Let S be the sector pointed to by the spinner at rest. We now flick the spinner with our fingers in a clockwise direction. It spins through M sectors and comes to rest *inside* a sector, that is, not on a line.

(a) Write a formula that uses one of the rounding functions to give you the new sector number NEWS in terms of the original rest position S and the spin span M.

(b) Generalize the formula developed in part a of this problem to the case of a game wheel having K sectors numbered consecutively from zero.

(c) Draw the flowchart steps needed to arrive at the sector number NEWS computed in part a so that it would be applicable for spins in either the clockwise or the counterclockwise directions.

17. The carnival wheel shown in Figure 2 · 19 has 32 painted sectors numbered clockwise, s = 0, 1, 2, . . . , 31. The sectors are divided into 8 groups, 4 sectors per group. In each group, the sectors are painted gray, white, light green, and dark green (g, w, lg, and dg) going clockwise.

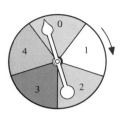

FIGURE 2·18

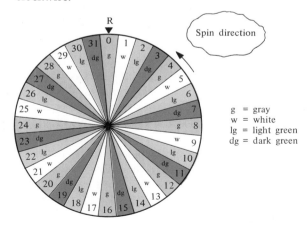

g = gray
w = white
lg = light green
dg = dark green

FIGURE 2·19

When the wheel is spun (always counterclockwise) and comes to rest, the color of the sector opposite the fixed pointer, R, tells you how the game comes out.

Suppose the rule is:

Player loses 30 points for gray
Player loses 10 points for white
Player wins 10 points for light green
Player wins 30 points for dark green

Also suppose that, before any one spin, the wheel is considered to be at rest with sector number s opposite the ratchet R. We now imagine that the wheel is spun a distance of m sector positions. How many points p will be won or lost for each data pair s and m? How can we develop a simple algorithm that simulates repeated plays at the wheel?

Hint   Your flowchart should show a loop beginning with the input of s and m, then one or more assignment boxes to compute p, an output statement to print p, and a return to the input step. One way to compute p is first to compute the new sector number s after the spin in terms of the given (or old) s, and m. Then we can compute the position k (= 0, 1, 2, or 3) within the group—corresponding to gray, white, light green, or dark green, respectively. Actually, it is simpler to compute k directly from m and the old s without first computing the new s. To simulate repeated spins, return to the input step after printing p. What changes must be made in your flowchart if after the initial input of s and m we calculate and use the new s as our new starting point and only input new values for m?

18.   What changes are needed in your solution to Exercise 16 if the wheel's sectors were labeled 1, 2, 3, 4, and 5 instead of 0, 1, 2, 3, and 4?

PAILS OF
WATER EXERCISES

1.   Suppose you are at a river with two pails, a five-quart pail and a nine-quart pail (no single quart markings on the sides). You can measure out four quarts by filling the five-quart pail from the nine-quart pail and emptying the five-quart pail back into the river.

(a)   Your task is to make a flowchart to output *all* numbers of quarts that can be measured by such back and forth pouring. You need only one variable, T, which keeps a record of the total amount of water in the two pails. The value of T is altered each time water is dipped out of the river or poured back, but not when water is transferred from pail to pail. When T is less than 5, you fill the nine-quart pail, thus increasing T by 9, while if T is greater than or equal to 5, you empty the five-quart pail, thus decreasing T by 5. Output every value of T that is computed. Don't forget to initialize T with the value 0. Stop when the value of T returns to 0. The flowchart structure is indicated in Figure 2 · 20. All you have to do is fill in the boxes.

(b)   Make a partial trace of your completed flowchart, just listing the values of T in the order in which they are output.

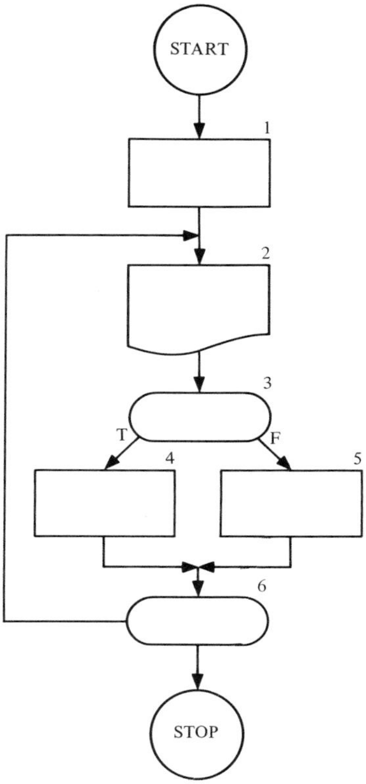

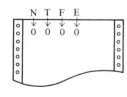

FIGURE 2·20

FIGURE 2·21

2. Modify the flowchart of Problem 1 to output with each value of T, the number of fillings of the nine-quart pail and emptyings of the five-quart pail required to get this value of T. You will have to introduce two new variables, such as F and E. Be sure to initialize them.

3. Modify the flowchart of Problem 2 so that it will work with any whole number of quart capacities (A and B) for the two pails. Fill the A-quart pail and empty the B-quart pail. Be sure to provide for the input of A and B. Also introduce a variable N that numbers the lines of output starting with 0 so that the first line of output will have the form that is shown in Figure 2 · 21.

4. Trace the flowchart of Problem 3 (just giving the lines of output) for the following pairs of input values of A and B.

(a) $A = 7, B = 10$
(b) $A = 10, B = 7$
(c) $A = 54, B = 36$

5. In connection with Problem 4, explain why the following relations always hold.

(a) $N = F + E$
(b) $T = F \times A - E \times B$

Chapter 3

Constructing algorithms

3·1
Problem solving—
some simple examples

The construction of algorithms and their flowcharts is essentially a problem-solving process. It is not adequate merely to present the straightforward development of an elegant flowchart. We must instead show how the final solution was evolved by its creator. You must see how we choose a place to start on a problem. You must see some of the false starts and oversights, some of the awkward algorithms we obtain on our first attempts. Above all, you must learn that in constructing algorithms, we first attempt to get some kind of a solution to the problem. Then we look at our solution critically, and try to improve it. In this chapter we will solve a number of simple problems to prepare ourselves for the more powerful problem solving techniques and methodologies to be introduced in subsequent chapters.

Finding the Largest of Several Numbers

Let us look at the problem of finding the largest of several numbers, each punched on a separate data card. This problem, although simple in itself, forms a part of many other algorithms and is, in fact, the simplest of a whole genre called "search algorithms." It is natural to begin with the case of just two numbers, although the solution is trivial. The flowchart (Figure 3·1) is self-explanatory.

Now let us jump to the case of finding the largest value in a stack of cards. Here is an instance in which the flowchart for the simplest case might mislead us. Looking at the flowchart of Figure 3·1, we might decide that the way to solve the problem is to read in all the cards, assigning each to a separate variable A, B, C, D, E, F, and so forth, and then to flowchart a complicated pattern of tests to find the largest value. If you pursued this method you would find that it required more flowchart boxes than data values, and you would probably decide that it would be easier to carry out the process by hand.

This is an example where common sense is a better guide to the solution than examining the flowchart of a simpler case. Let us describe how you would carry out this process of finding the largest value in a stack of cards by hand (Figure 3·2). You

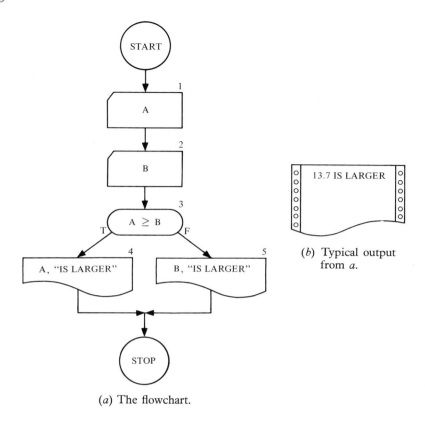

(b) Typical output from a.

FIGURE 3·1
Finding the larger of two
numbers.

(a) The flowchart.

would sit down with the pile of cards face up in front of you and remove the top card from the deck and hold it in your left hand. Next you would run through the pile, repeatedly picking up the top card and comparing it with that in your left hand. If the top card is larger it replaces the card in your

FIGURE 3·2
Searching by hand.

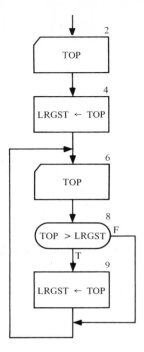

FIGURE 3·3
First sketch of finding the
largest.

left hand, otherwise it goes in a discard pile. In either event
you resume the search with the new top card. In this way the
number in your left hand is always the largest found so far
and, when the pile is exhausted, it is the largest of all.

This is the process we wish to flowchart. You may protest
that the computer has no left hand. Well we can, in effect,

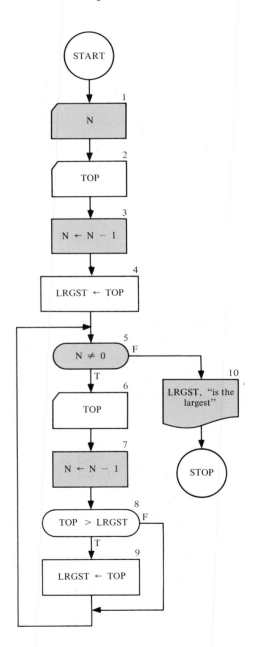

FIGURE 3·4
Finding the largest of N data
values.

give the computer a left hand by creating an "auxiliary variable." We will introduce a variable LRGST (standing for "the largest number found so far"), which plays the role of the number in your left hand.

Now we can see that the incomplete flowchart in Figure 3·3 follows the process described in words above. We see that boxes 2 and 4 initially place the top card in the left hand. The loop of boxes 6, 8, and 9 repeatedly selects a new top card (box 6), compares it with the left-hand card (box 8), and places it in the left hand if the top card is the larger (box 9). The role of the discard pile is played by the "reassignments" to the variables TOP and LRGST in boxes 6 and 9.

In order to be complete, the flowchart in Figure 3·3 needs a stopping mechanism and a provision for output of the final answer. We will suppose that we know the number of cards in the deck initially and will accordingly use a counter, N, to tell us how many cards are left. The initial value of N will have to be input, tested before each subsequent input from the deck to determine whether any cards are left, and it will have to be decremented after each card is read. These features are all seen in the final version of the flowchart in Figure 3·4.

Two lessons should have been learned from studying this algorithm.

1. The value of using common sense to find an algorithm.
2. The value of "auxiliary variables," which we can invent whenever we need them.

Tallying Grades

The final flowchart of this section (Figure 3·5) shows how a computer may be used to tally data read from cards. Recall Section 2·2, which dealt with the analysis of grade results from the advanced placement examination. Another type of analysis we could perform is to tabulate the number of grades falling in the high range ($100 \leq$ GRADE ≤ 150), the middle range ($50 \leq$ GRADE < 100), and the low range (GRADE < 50). The variables HIGH, MID, and LOW are counting or "tallying" variables. For each input value of GRADE, one of the three counters clicks up one notch. Another variable, N, keeps a count of the number of grades read. Again we put a card

with an impossible grade (anything greater than 150) at the
end of the stack. The test in box 3 will alert us to stop tallying

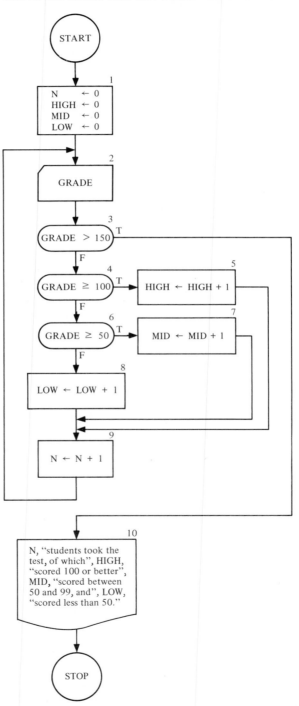

FIGURE 3·5
Tallying by computer.

when this card is reached. Notice how the printing in box 10 identifies the output.

1. Modify your postal regulation flowchart of Exercises 2·2, Set A, Problem 10, to handle the case when the dimensions of the box are not punched on the data cards in any particular order (i.e., longest not necessarily first).

   Hint In both problems, you can imagine the flowchart begins with an input step of the form

   where L1, L2, and L3 represent the measured lengths of the three sides. In the original problem, the L1 was known in advance to be the largest, so the girth was $2 \times (L2 + L3)$. In this problem the girth is

   $$2 \times (L1 + L2 + L3 - x)$$

   where x is the largest of L1, L2, and L3.

2. Draw a flowchart to input values of b and c, output both values immediately, and then perform the following.

   (a) If $b = 0$ and $c \neq 0$, output "bx + c = 0 has no root."
   (b) If $b = 0$ and $c = 0$, output "Every real number satisfies bx + c = 0."
   (c) If $b \neq 0$, compute the root of the equation $bx + c = 0$. Output "The root of bx + c = 0 is," followed by the root.
   (d) Finally, return to the input step for more data.

3. Flowchart an algorithm that, when given the heights of a group of people, as input, determines which height is nearest to 5 feet, 10.5 inches. The details of the data are as follows.

   (a) Each data card contains one person's height expressed as two numbers—the first being feet and the second, inches.
   (b) You are not told how many heights will be considered, but a card with 0 feet, 0 inches will be placed at the end of the data.

   Hints
   (1) Should the heights be converted to inches when they are read in or may they be left in their feet-inches form? In considering this question, try to see what effect this decision on internal data handling has on the complexity of the algorithm.

(2) Don't forget to consider the possibility that a height may be exactly 5 feet, 10.5 inches.

EXERCISES 3·1, SET B

In the tallying problem (Figure 3·5) we saw how a computer might examine and tally a series of values, T, input from data cards. There are many similar things to do with a series of input values. For example, we may wish to sum all the values of T, or sum the squares of T, or sum the absolute values of T, and so forth. In the following exercises, develop a flowchart for the described operation on a series of input values for T. Always print some appropriate message that identifies the numerical result that is also to be printed. The basic ingredients for the desired flowcharts can be found by restudying Figure 3·5.

1. Sum the cubes of 100 values of T. Call this SUMCUB.

2. Without reading the input values more than once, develop all three sums: SUMALL, SUMCUB, and SUMNEG (the sum of the negative values).

3. For each of the 100 values that are input, print the cumulative sum to that point. Call it CUMSUM. Thus, after reading the fifth value for T, print the sum of the first five values. After the sixth value of T has been read, print the sum of the first six items, and so on.

4. Think of the 100 input values mentioned in the preceding exercises as representing the plays of a game that has two players. If an input value is ≥ 0, it means player A has won that play, whereas if it is negative, player B has won that play. Now suppose the game is scored as follows (like badminton or volleyball). Player A begins by serving. If the server wins a play, a point is added to his score. If the server loses a play, the other player becomes server and the score does not change. Prepare a flowchart to print which player wins and the score after 100 plays.

5. Somewhere there is an island where only rabbits and wolves can live. Rabbits are the more prolific, having a constant birth rate of 0.2 per month; that is, if there are R rabbits at the beginning of the month, $0.2 \times R$ offspring will be born during that month. Rabbits die from starvation or are eaten by wolves. The starvation rate is $.00002 \times R$ per month; that is, if there are R rabbits at the beginning of the month, $(.00002 \times R) \times R$ will die of starvation during the month. If there were no wolves to worry about, the rabbit population would simply increase by $.2 \times R$ every month from births and decrease by $.00002 \times R^2$ from starvation. Equating these two population changes and solving for R, we find:

$$.2 \times R = .00002 \times R^2$$
$$R = 10,000$$
$$R = 0$$

The solution R = 0 is not interesting, but the solution R = 10,000 indicates that when there are 10,000 rabbits, the births and deaths equal one another and the population stabilizes—if there are no wolves.

However, when the island has a full population of rabbits, each wolf eats one rabbit a day and proportionately less when rabbits are fewer. Using R / 10000 as a "rabbit density" and W as the number of wolves, then W × R / 10000 is the number of rabbits eaten per day by wolves. Assuming 30 days per month, 30 × W × R / 10000 rabbits are eaten per month.

Wolves have a constant birthrate of 0.1 per month, just half that for the rabbits. Also, the starvation death rate for wolves is greater than for the rabbits. When the rabbit population is at its maximum of 10,000, the starvation rate for the wolves is 0.2 per month, but the rate doubles when the number of rabbits is halved. Thus we know the wolf starvation rate is equal to some constant C, divided by R, and when R = 10,000, C / R = 0.02. Solving for C, we find C = 200 or the wolf starvation rate is 200 / R per month. The following table summarizes all the given information.

	Births per Month	Deaths per Month
Rabbits	0.2 × R	.00002 × R² + 30 × W × R / 10000
Wolves	0.1 × W	200 / R × W

Suppose the island begins with a population of 100 rabbits and no wolves. After 100 months a pack of 20 wolves arrives on an ice floe. After 200 more months an earthquake reduces the island to rubble. Calculate and print the number of rabbits and the number of wolves at the end of each of the 300 months of the population study.

3·2
The Euclidean algorithm

The Euclidean algorithm, is found in the fifth book of Euclid, dating back at least to 300 B.C. This algorithm is a method for finding the greatest common divisor of two whole numbers. It plays a central role in mathematics and thus deserves our study.

Review

You have often used common divisors, also called "common factors," in simplifying fractions. Consider the problem of simplifying

$$\frac{54}{72}$$

One way of doing this is to cancel out prime factors one at a time.

$$\frac{54}{72} = \frac{2 \times 27}{2 \times 36} = \frac{27}{36} = \frac{3 \times 9}{3 \times 12} = \frac{9}{12}$$

$$= \frac{3 \times 3}{3 \times 4} = \frac{3}{4}$$

Another way would be to determine that 18 is the greatest common divisor (GDC) of 54 and 72, and divide it out all at once.

$$\frac{54}{72} = \frac{3 \times 18}{4 \times 18} = \frac{3}{4}$$

One way of defining the GCD of two numbers, say 54 and 72, is first to consider the sets of divisors of each number:

S = set of divisors of 54 = (1,2,3,6,9,18,27,54)
T = set of divisors of 72 = (1,2,3,4,6,8,9,12,18,24,36,72)

The intersection of the two sets

S ∩ T = (1,2,3,6,9,18)

is the set of common factors of the two numbers. The greatest number of this set of common factors is the greatest common divisor.

One way of finding this greatest common divisor is to factor each number completely.

54 = 2 × 3 × 3 × 3
72 = 2 × 2 × 2 × 3 × 3

Then, by taking as many factors of each kind as are common to both these factorizations (here one 2 and two 3's), we form the factorization of the GCD.

GCD = 2 × 3 × 3

However, in case the given numbers are very large, finding their factorizations can be very difficult. The Euclidean algorithm is a technique for finding the GCD without finding these complete factorizations.

Developing the Algorithm

In the equation

$$364 = 245 + 119$$

suppose we know that two of the numbers (say 364 and 245) have 7 as a common divisor. Then we can be sure that the third number is also divisible by 7. This is a simple consequence of the distributive property, since writing 364 as 7×52 and 245 as 7×35, we have

$$119 = 364 - 245 = 7 \times 52 - 7 \times 35$$
$$= 7 \times (52 - 35)$$

In general, suppose that three integers, A, B, and C, are so related that one can be expressed as the sum of the other two. That is,

$$A = B + C$$

or equivalently,

$$C = A - B$$

Then any number that is a common divisor of two of these integers is also a divisor of the third.* Thus any pair selected from these three numbers will have the same set of common divisors as any other pair.

Let's see how this statement helps us in looking for the GCD of two numbers, say 943 and 437. Now

$$943 - 437 = 506$$

According to our statement, the pair

$$506, 437$$

will have the same set of common divisors as the pair

$$943, 437$$

Thus our problem can now be replaced by that of finding the greatest common divisor of 506 and 437, which is simpler than the given problem because one of the numbers is smaller. Repeating this process,

$$506 - 437 = 69$$

---

*The verification is the same as for the preceding example. If $A = D \times M$ and $C = D \times N$, then $B = A - C = D \times M - D \times N = D \times (M - N)$.

Again, if we now consider the pair

437, 69

the set of common divisors is again unaltered. A third application yields

368, 69

This process is quite clearly algorithmic.

Constructing the Flowchart

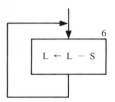

FIGURE 3·6
Endless loop.

TABLE 3·1
Trace of Figure 3·6

The basic step consists of replacing the larger of the two numbers by the difference between the larger and the smaller. In flowchart terms, letting L represent the larger and S the smaller, we have one basic assignment step that is repeated over and over, as given in Figure 3·6.

Of course, we have to provide a way out of this loop. But first, let's trace it with the example considered above (Table 3·1); that is, we enter the loop with $L = 943$ and $S = 437$.

Beginning with step 3, L is assigned negative values and will take on larger and larger negative values as the process

Step	Flowchart Box	Values of Variables	
		L	S
Start		943	437
1	6	506	437
2	6	69	437
3	6	− 368	437
4	6	− 805	437

continues. What went wrong is that after step 2, L was no longer the larger number of the pair (L,S). This can be rectified by interchanging the values of L and S before resuming the subtraction process. This requires testing $L < S$, as shown in Figure 3·7.

The interchanging seen in the cloud following the decision box in Figure 3·7 will occur in many other algorithms throughout the book. How are we to implement this idea in our flowchart vocabulary? The first idea that comes to us is:

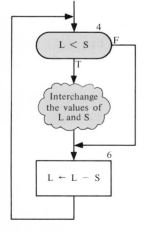

FIGURE 3·7

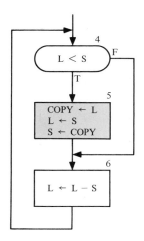

FIGURE 3·8
Closing in on Euclid's
algorithm.

But it doesn't work, since after the first assignment, L and S will have the same value, so that the second assignment has no effect.

It is equally ineffective to write the same two assignment statements in the reverse order. What can be done? This impasse illustrates an important consequence of the destructive nature of assignment. We can state the principle this way:

> Assigning a new value to a variable destroys all record of the old value, *unless we have made a copy of the old value prior to the assignment.*

Applying this principle to the problem at hand, we introduce a variable COPY and implement the cloud in Figure 3·7, as shown in Figure 3·8. Thus again we are using the "auxiliary variable" concept introduced in Section 3·1.)

Let's trace this flowchart with the same initial values of L and S as before (Table 3·2). A study of Table 3·2 shows that upon completing step 26, the repeated execution of box 6 will have reduced the value of L to zero. From this point on, execution will begin to cycle through boxes 4 and 6 over and over without changing the values of any variables.

We must be done, but what is our answer? Since we have not altered our set of common divisors at any point in the process, the set of common divisors of 23 and 0 must be the same as the set of common divisors of 943 and 437. But what are the common divisors of 23 and 0? Every integer is a divisor of 0. Thus, for any value of N, the common divisors of N and 0 are simply the divisors of N, and the largest of these is of course N itself, so that the greatest common divisor of N and 0 is N. In particular the common divisors of 23 and 0 are the divisors of 23 (which are 1 and 23), and the greatest of these is 23. Thus we can output 23 (the final value of L) as the GCD. The complete flowchart is seen in Figure 3·10.

Inspecting the structure of the final algorithm, we can once again observe the two distinct roles of the decision box in our algorithms. One role, played here by box 3, controls the escape from a loop. The other role, played by box 4, selects among alternative action paths.

By studying the trace (Table 3·2) of the Euclidean algorithm, we see that the value of L was reduced by 437 two times, then reduced by 69 six times, and finally reduced by 23 three

TABLE 3·2
Trace of Figure 3·8

Step	Flowchart Box	L	S	COPY	Test	T or F
Start		943	437			
1	4				943 < 437	F
2	6	506				
3	6				506 < 437	F
4	6	69				
5	4				69 < 437	T
6	5	437	69	69		
7	6	368				
8	4				368 < 69	F
9	6	299				
10	4				299 < 69	F
11	6	230				
12	4				230 < 69	F
13	6	161				
14	4				161 < 69	F
15	6	92				
16	4				92 < 69	F
17	6	23				
18	4				23 < 69	T
19	5	69	23	23		
20	6	46				
21	4				46 < 23	F
22	6	23				
23	4				23 < 23	F
24	6	0				
25	4				0 < 23	T
26	5	23	0	0		
27	6	23				
28	4				23 < 0	F
29	6	23				

times. Much needless repetition can be eliminated. For example, the six subtractions of 69 can be all performed at once as

$$437 - 6 \times 69 = 23$$

The values 6 and 23 are the result of applying the division algorithm of arithmetic (mentioned in Section 2·4):

$$
\begin{array}{r}
6 \longleftarrow \text{Quotient} \\
S \longrightarrow 69\overline{)437} \\
L \longrightarrow 414 \\
\hline
23 \longleftarrow \text{Remainder}
\end{array}
$$

In general, then, we can introduce variables Q and R as the quotient and remainder on dividing L by S. According to the

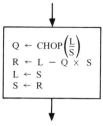

$$Q \leftarrow \text{CHOP}\left(\frac{L}{S}\right)$$
$$R \leftarrow L - Q \times S$$
$$L \leftarrow S$$
$$S \leftarrow R$$

FIGURE 3·9

division algorithm, the remainder, R, will always be less than the divisor, S.

These computations are represented in flowchart language by the first two assignments of Figure 3·9, which accomplish at once all the subtractions using the same value of S. The present value of S becomes the next value of L and the present value of R becomes the next value of S. No test of $L < S$ is necessary, since, as was remarked above, the division algorithm assures us that the new value of L will always be greater than the new value of S. When the value of S becomes zero, then the value of L is the GCD. Our final flowchart appears in Figure 3·11.

Comparing a trace of Figure 3·11 with the trace (Table 3·2) of Figure 3·10 will make the saving evident. The same input values of A and B are used for easy comparison. Table 3·3 gives the new trace.

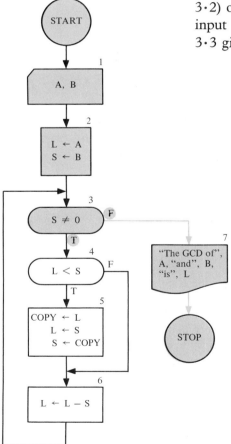

FIGURE 3·10
Euclidean algorithm
(subtraction form).

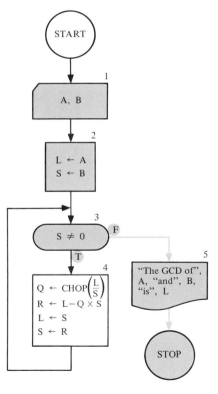

FIGURE 3·11
Final Euclidean algorithm
(using division).

TABLE 3·3
Trace of Figure 3·11

| | Flowchart | Values of Variables | | | | | | | |
Step	Box	A	B	Q	R	L	S	Test	T or F
1	1	943	437						
2	2					943	437		
3	3							437 ≠ 0	T
4	4			2	69	437	69		
5	3							69 ≠ 0	T
6	4			6	23	69	23		
7	3							23 ≠ 0	T
8	4			3	0	23	0	0 ≠ 0	F
9	5	943	437			23			

Using hand computation on this problem without following the flowchart, we have

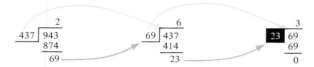

Thus the algorithm is a succession of division problems in which the divisor of one is promoted to dividend of the next and the remainder is promoted to divisor. When the remainder finally becomes zero, the divisor is the GCD.

EXERCISES 3·2

1. Fill out a trace like that of Table 3·3 for the Euclidean algorithm (Figure 3·11) using the values given below.

(a) A = 177, B = 379
(b) A = 4465, B = 3363

2. Draw a flowchart to print the three right-most digits of each of 100 terms of the Fibonacci sequence beginning with the seventeenth term. Make guesses at how many of these 100 numbers will be even, how many greater than 500, and how many between 300 and 400. Save these guesses to see how they compare with results when you run the program on a computer. (*Hint.* Use the CHOP function.)

> In Exercises 3·1, Set B, a series of 100 values of T were input from data cards. In the following two exercises develop a flowchart for the described operation on this same series of input values of T. Always print some appropriate message identifying the numerical result printed.

3. For each input value after the first, print the two most recently input values of T and their sum. Call this sum TWOSUM.

4. For each input value after the Kth (where the value of K is itself supplied as data and where $3 \leq K \leq 100$), print out the average of either the most recent three values or, if the most recent value is lower than its predecessor, print the average of the preceding two values (omitting the most recent one from this average).

5. Prepare a flowchart to calculate and print the first 15 rows of a table according to the following rules.

   (a) The table is to have four columns called N, A, B, C.
   (b) The values in the first row of the table are 0, 1, 1, 1.
   (c) The value of N is one greater than its value in the preceding row.
   (d) The value of A is one greater than its value in the preceding row.
   (e) The value of B is one greater than the sum of the values of A, to and including the preceding row.
   (f) The value of C is one greater than the sum of the values of B, to and including the preceding row.

6. A high school student in Minneapolis pointed out that the interchange feature

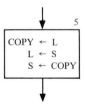

could as well be obtained by

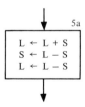

thus eliminating the need for the copy variable. We agree that this is interesting and ingenious, but it is not very good programming because it is confusing. We gladly pay the price of one cell of storage for greater clarity.

   (a) Check that box 5a really does perform the interchange by tracing the following.
      (1) When the initial values of L and S are 19 and 7.
      (2) When the initial values of L and S are -61 and 53.
   (b) Show that box 5a always performs the interchange by tracing with the initial values of L and S being a and b.
   (c) Show, using a trace as in part b, what would happen if the assignment statements in box 5a were written in the reverse order.

7. Suppose that we want to move the values of three variables in the circular pattern

or by the table given below

	A	B	C
Initial values	3	7	11
Final values	11	3	7

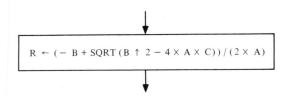

Show how this can be accomplished using one copy available.

3.3
The square
root algorithm

Most computer languages have a square root function as one of the so-called "library" functions. Thus, for example, the assignment statement

$$R \leftarrow (-B + SQRT(B \uparrow 2 - 4 \times A \times C))/(2 \times A)$$

translates into the BASIC language as

$$LET\ R = (-B + SQR(B \uparrow 2 - 4 * A * C))/(2 * A)$$

When the value of $B \uparrow 2 - 4 * A * C$ has been calculated, the library square root function, SQR, is automatically invoked to calculate the square root of this value.

Consequently there is no real need for us to develop our own square root algorithm. However, much can be learned from a study of this particular algorithm, so we will develop it here.

Of course, we cannot find all square roots *exactly* because of the finite length of computer words. We will have to settle for finding square roots to within a prescribed error tolerance.

What we will do, in effect, is to find a sequence of intervals

$$[G_1, H_1], [G_2, H_2], [G_3, H_3], \ldots$$

each one containing the desired square root, $\sqrt{A}$, with the interval lengths shrinking so as to eventually become less than any preassigned error bound, ERR. When the length $|G_n - H_n|$ is less than ERR, then both G_n and H_n approximate $\sqrt{A}$, with error less than ERR, as illustrated in Figure 3·12.

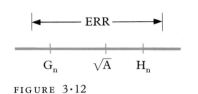

FIGURE 3·12

Let us start off by making an arbitrary guess, G_1, for the approximate value of $\sqrt{A}$. Then we let $H_1 = A/G_1$ so that

$$G_1 \times H_1 = A = \sqrt{A} \times \sqrt{A}$$

Now we cannot have $\sqrt{A}$ greater than both G_1 and H_1, for then we would have $A = G_1 \times H_1 < \sqrt{A} \times \sqrt{A} = A$ contrary to the definition of H_1. In the same way we see that $\sqrt{A}$ cannot be less than both G_1 and H_1. Therefore we have $\sqrt{A}$ bracketed between G_1 and H_1.

The next step is to choose G_2 as the midpoint of the interval $[G_1, H_1]$.

That is,

$$G_2 = \frac{G_1 + H_1}{2}$$

Now we define H_2 by

$$H_2 = A/G_2$$

so that

$$G_2 \times H_2 = A = G_1 \times H_1$$

The further development of the algorithm rests on one simple mathematical observation: if two pairs of positive numbers (C,D) and (X,Y) have the same product

$$C \times D = X \times Y$$

and if X is selected so that $C < X < D$, then it also holds that $C < Y < D$. This is quite obvious, for if X is greater than one factor, C, then in order that $X \times Y = C \times D$, we must have Y less than the other factor D in compensation. Similarly, if $X < D$, then again we must have $Y > C$ so that the product $X \times Y$ is the same as the product $C \times D$.

Armed with that observation we can continue. Since G_2 lies between G_1 and H_1, and since the two pairs (G_1, H_1) and (G_2, H_2) have the same product, we see that H_2 also lies between G_1 and H_1. Moreover, $\sqrt{A}$ lies between G_2 and H_2 by the same reasoning used in showing that $\sqrt{A}$ lies between G_1 and H_1. Thus we have the following configuration.

Now we have a smaller interval containing $\sqrt{A}$. Not only is the length of the interval $[H_2, G_2]$ less than that of $[G_1, H_1]$, but the interval $[G_2, H_2]$ is less than *half* as long as $[G_1, H_1]$, that is,

$$|G_2 - H_2| < \frac{1}{2}|G_1 - H_1|$$

This is an obvious consequence of the fact that G_2 is the midpoint of $[G_1, H_1]$ so that the interval joining G_2 and H_2 must lie entirely in the left half or entirely in the right half of $[G_1, H_1]$.

Now we may let G_2 and H_2 play the roles of G_1 and H_1 and define

$$G_3 = \frac{G_2 + H_2}{2} \qquad H_3 = A/G_2$$

to obtain an interval containing $\sqrt{A}$ and less than half as long as $[G_2, H_2]$. And, in general, we may let

$$(1) \qquad G_n = \frac{G_{n-1} + H_{n-1}}{2}, \qquad H_n = A/G_n$$

For the sequence of intervals so constructed we have:

$$|G_2 - H_2| < \frac{1}{2}|G_1 - H_1|$$

$$|G_3 - H_3| < \frac{1}{2}|G_2 - H_2| < \frac{1}{4}|G_1 - H_1|$$

$$|G_4 - H_4| < \frac{1}{2}|G_3 - H_3| < \frac{1}{8}|G_1 - H_1|$$

$$\ldots\ldots\ldots$$

$$|G_n - H_n| < \frac{1}{2}|G_{n-1} - H_{n-1}| < \frac{1}{2^{n-1}}|G_1 - H_1|$$

We can see that by taking n sufficiently large we can make

$$\frac{1}{2^{n-1}}|G_1 - H_1| \qquad \text{and hence} \qquad |G_n - H_n|$$

less than any prescribed error bound.

The construction of the flowchart is now quite apparent. We shall think of G_1, G_2, G_3, . . . and H_1, H_2, H_3, . . . as successive values of the two variables G and H. The heart of the algorithm is the assignment of new values to G and H. Formulas 1 show that this will be achieved by the assignments

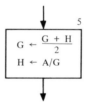

These assignments must be executed in the indicated order or else auxiliary copy variables will be required, since by Formulas 1 we see that the new value of H is defined in terms of the new value of G. The basic idea is now to repeat box 5 over and over again as suggested on the left. There are no further fundamental ideas; all that is left are the following minor details.

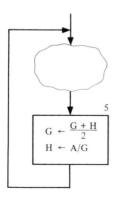

1.   Inputting the value of A whose square root we wish to find.

2.   Providing for output.

3.   Supplying a "loop control" or "stopping mechanism."

4.   Assigning initial values to G and H. (Note that G cannot get its initial value in box 5 as there would be no "old values" of G and H in terms of which to define the new value of G.)

The nature of the stopping mechanism is suggested by the foregoing discussion. We wish to stop whenever $|\,G - H\,|$ is less than some prescribed error bound. (Then, since $\sqrt{A}$ lies between G and H, both $|\,G - \sqrt{A}\,|$ and $|\,H - \sqrt{A}\,|$ will be less than the prescribed error bound.) This control can be realized by either of the decision boxes

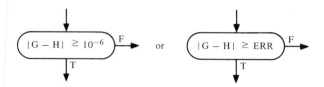

depending on whether we wish to write the error bound into the program as a constant or to input its value along with that of A. According to this choice, the input (item 1 above) will have the form

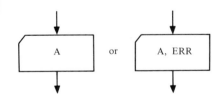

The initial value of G (item 4 above) can be chosen quite arbitrarily, subject to the restriction that it be positive. Since most people agree that 1 is the most "natural" positive number, let us initialize G and H by

Before discussing output, let us "attach" the pieces already developed to the flowchart box 5. It is clear that the input and initialization boxes must be placed outside the loop and preceding it, with initialization following input (as the initialization of H uses the value of A.) The loop controlling condition box must, of course, occur inside the loop, and it is considered good flowcharting practice to put such controlling mechanisms at the head of the loop. These remarks lead us to the two alternatives shown in Figure 3·13.

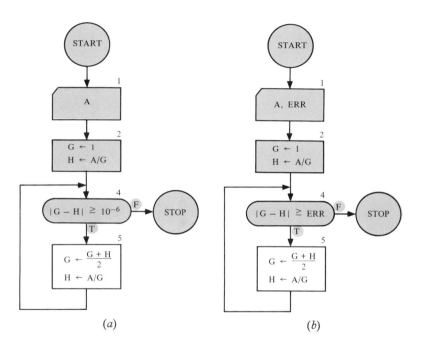

FIGURE 3·13

(a)   (b)

The question of where to place the output box depends on what we want to get out of this program. If we are only interested in knowing the final answer, the best approximation of $\sqrt{A}$, we will place an output box of the form

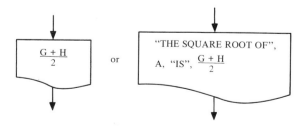

outside the loop just before the STOP. If, on the other hand, we are interested in seeing the way in which the sequences of values of G and H "home in on" or "converge to" the value of $\sqrt{A}$, then we will place an output box of the form

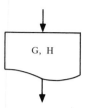

inside the loop immediately after box 5. If we want to print out the initial values of G and H as well, then we must put a second identical output box after box 2, but before the beginning of the loop. These alternatives are illustrated in Figure 3·14a and 3·14b. The flowchart in Figure 3·14a suits the person who only wants the answer and nothing else, whereas Figure 3·14b is designed for the person who wants to maintain control of the precision by supplying the value of ERR, and to observe the behavior of the sequence of values of G and H.

Before leaving this subject we would like to point out a difference between "word-organized" machines such as SAMOS and "bit-organized" machines such as BITOS.

In a bit-organized machine we can obtain to all intents and purposes as much precision as we desire, and there is no problem in implementing either of the flowcharts in Figure 3·14. However, in a word-organized machine we have only a fixed number of digits of precision, regardless of whether they come before or after the decimal point. If our machine were to provide seven digits of precision, then it would indeed be possible to calculate $\sqrt{2}$ as 1.414214 with error $< 10^{-6}$. However, if we wish to calculate $\sqrt{2,000,000}$, then the restriction of 7 digits of precision would limit us to 1414.214, and we are only able to conclude that the error in this result is less than 10^{-3}. Thus we can see that when using word-organized machines to approximate numbers, we cannot actually divorce the error tolerance from the size of the number being approximated. Chapter 11 pursues this subject in greater depth.

EXERCISES 3·3

1. (a) Write a program for the flowchart of Figure 3·14b and run it on your computer using as values of A, 2, .02, 200, 2000, 2000000.

    Reread the last several paragraphs of this section concerning error tolerance.

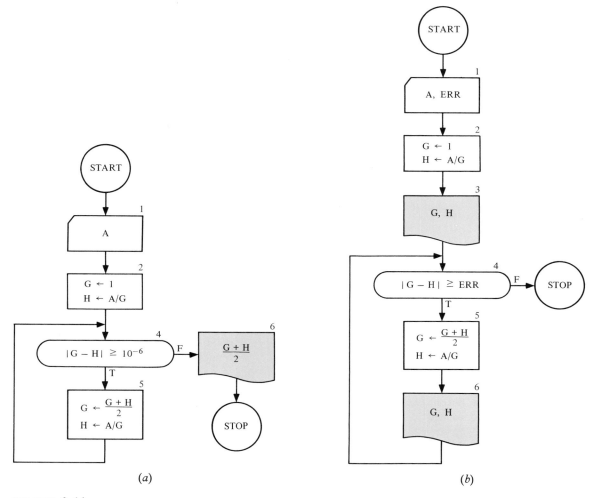

FIGURE 3·14
Two versions of the final
square root flowchart.

(b) Describe your observations concerning the speeds with which the
sequences of values of G and H "zero in" on the value of $\sqrt{A}$
for the values of A given in part a.

2. Modify (or adapt) the flowchart in Figure 3·14a for use in printing
out a table of square roots of the integers from 1 to 100, the output
having the form

```
1        1.000000
2        1.414214
3        1.732051
```

3·4
Shorthand notation for multiple decision steps

Sometimes we encounter in a flowchart a series of simple decision boxes such as the following.

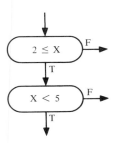

It is often convenient, for condensation of the flowchart and for seeing the overall picture, to replace such a series of boxes with a single box. Thus Figure 3·15a can be replaced by either Figure 3·15b or 3.15c.

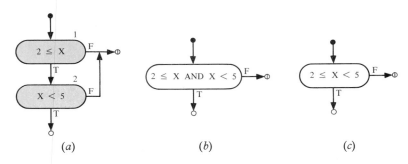

FIGURE 3·15
Set of simple decision boxes and two compound equivalents.

On the other hand there are situations in which we would like to go in the other direction and replace a box containing a more complicated or *compound* condition with an equivalent set of simple conditions. Thus the compound condition of Figure 3·16a can be replaced by the set of simple conditions in Figure 3·16b.

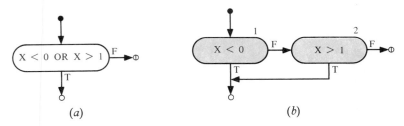

FIGURE 3·16
Compound condition and an equivalent set of simple conditions.

The set of conditions can, of course, be considerably more complicated. For example, if we want to know when both X and Y are positive or Z is zero, we can draw the compound box or its decomposition, as in Figure 3·17. Notice that the decomposition in Figure 3·17 can be accomplished in two stages, first *b* and then *c*.

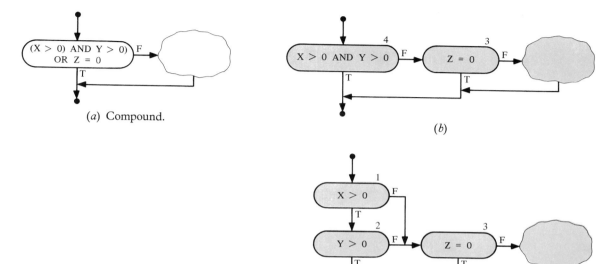

(*a*) Compound.

(*b*)

FIGURE 3·17
Composition of decision boxes.

(*c*) Combination of simple decisions.

A compound decision box may be regarded as shorthand for a combination of simple decision boxes. There is another type of shorthand associated with decision boxes that can be extremely helpful. This shorthand technique is called "multiple branching."

To indicate multiple branching, we will draw compound decision boxes with several exits. Each exit must be clearly labeled to show what condition causes its use. For example,

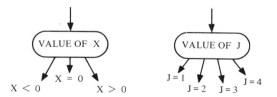

Two important warnings are in order.

1. *The conditions on the exits must not be overlapping.* If one exit were labeled "3 < X < 7" and another were labeled "5 ≤ X < 10", and if we come into this box with a value

of X between 5 and 7, we will not know which branch to take on leaving.

2. *All possibilities must be exhausted.* If the conditions on the exits were "X ≤ 3", "6 ≤ X < 9", and "9 ≤ X", and if we come into the box with a value of X between 3 and 6, we will have no way to get out.

Any box indicating a multiple branch of n ways can be broken down into a chain of n − 1, 2-way branches. Thus the 4-way branch on the value of J may be viewed in more detail as the chain of three 2-way branches (Figure 3·18*a*).

An example of the usefulness of multiple branching is provided by the example in Section 3·1 of tallying test grades as flowcharted in Figure 3·5. The way in which this same problem might have been handled with multiple branching is shown in Figure 3·18*b*.

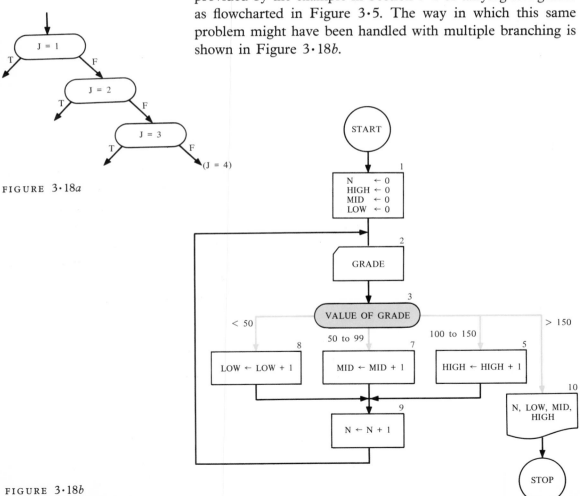

FIGURE 3·18*a*

FIGURE 3·18*b*
Use of a four-way branch.

EXERCISES 3·4

In Problems 1 to 3 you are given a word statement of a decision rule together with a proposed flowchart equivalent. The meaning of the variables used in the flowchart is self-explanatory. Your job is to decide whether each flowchart is or is not logically equivalent to the associated word statement and, if not, correct the flowchart so it *is* logically equivalent.

1. If X exceeds Y and either F is less than 2 or G equals 4 or both, then execute box 12; otherwise do not execute box 12.

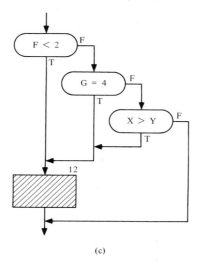

(c)

2. If X exceeds 4 while Y is less than 5 or X is less than 5 while Y is greater than 4, then print the value of Y; otherwise print the value of X and in either case then proceed to box 20.

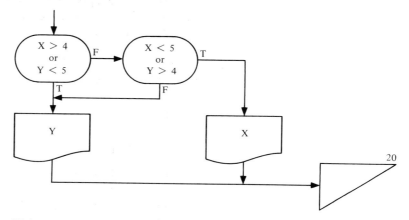

3. This rule is for a person who is over 65, married, and filing a joint (income tax) return. He pays no tax if his income is less than $2900, or if his income is less than $3500 in case the spouse is also over 65.

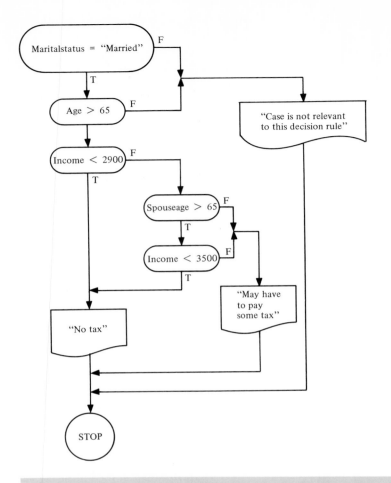

In Problems 4 to 8 you are given a word statement of a decision rule and proposed flowchart equivalents. Decide which, if any, of the given flowcharts is logically equivalent to the associated word statement.

4. If Y is less than 4 or Y is greater than 100, then do not execute box 2; otherwise execute box 2.

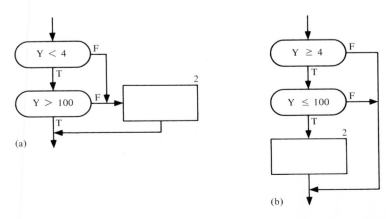

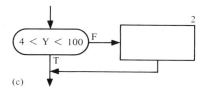

(c)

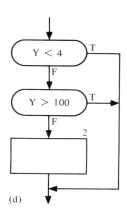

(d)

5. If gross pay is less than $8400 and number of dependents exceeds 6, or if sick days are greater than 30, then do not execute box 26; otherwise execute box 26.

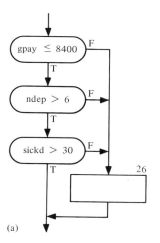

(a)

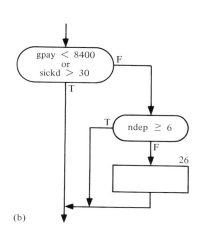

(b)

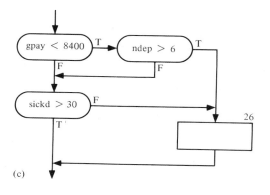

(c)

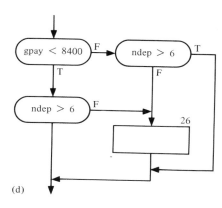

(d)

6. If A is greater than B, but the rightmost digit of A is not greater than the rightmost digit of B, then execute box 8. Otherwise, do not.

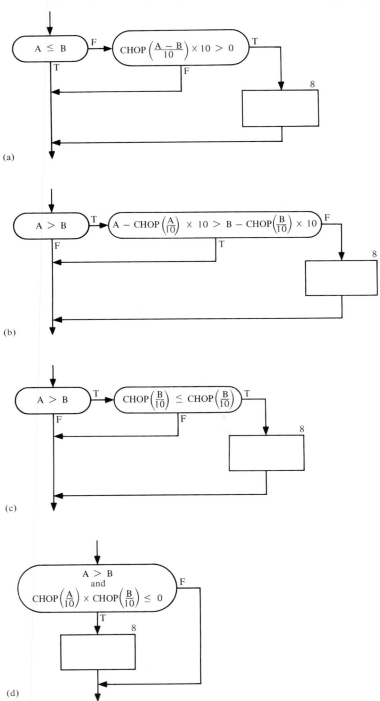

(a)

(b)

(c)

(d)

7. If X is less than Y but Y is not less than Z, execute box 8. Otherwise, execute box 9 if X − Z is less than zero and box 10 if X − Z is greater than or equal to zero.

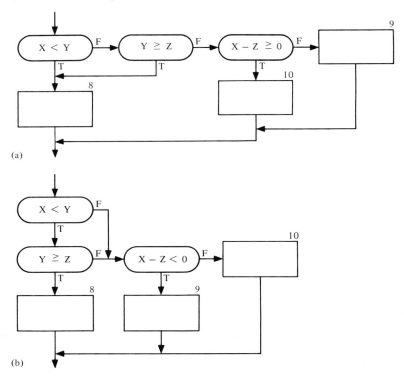

(a)

(b)

8. If both X and Y are greater than Z, then execute box 20; otherwise execute box 42 if either X or Y is greater than Z, and execute box 8 if neither is greater than Z.

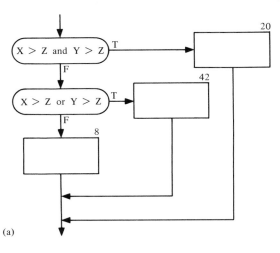

(a)

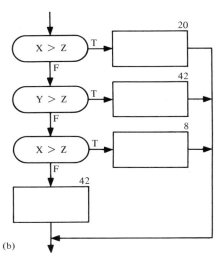

(b)

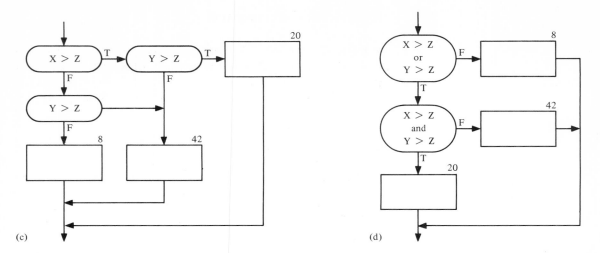

(c)

(d)

9. You are given a flowchart fragment and sets of values for some or all of the variables involved. Trace through the flowchart and determine what transfer of control results from each set of values.

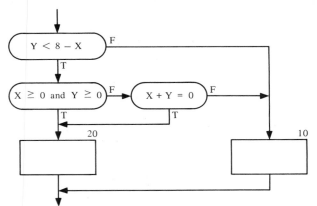

Set *a* values: X = 1
                  Y = 4
Is box 10 or box 20 executed?

Set *b* values: X = 6
                  Y = −6
Is box 10 or 20 executed?

10. True or false: The two constructions given below are equivalent.

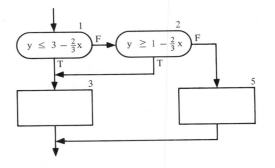

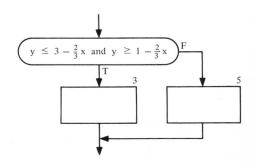

11. A mathematics professor desires an algorithm that, when given two positive numbers A and B such that A $<$ B, will either find an integer C such that A $\leq$ C^2 and C^3 $\leq$ B, or report that no such number exists. If more than one C exists, it does not matter which is selected. Here are two strategies that might be followed.

  (a) Test the values C $=$ 1, 2, 3, . . . until an acceptable value is found or it is certain that none can be found.
  (b) Compute an acceptable value of C directly (if one exists) by determining whether the largest value of C such that C^3 $\leq$ B is large enough so that C^2 $\geq$ A.
  (1) Draw flowcharts for each of the strategies a and b. Your flowcharts should indicate results by printing messages and values.
  (2) Which flowchart would you suggest the professor use? Why?

12. Shown below is an incomplete flowchart for an algorithm designed to read a set of positive numbers from cards and determine whether there are more values in the range 20–29 (inclusive) than there are in the range 70–79 (inclusive). It is not known how many cards must be read, but the end of the data will be signaled by a card containing a negative number. In parts a and b below you are to determine how to complete the flowchart correctly. Note the effect of the CHOP function in box 4.

(a) Boxes 5 and 7 should be completed to read:

(b) Box 11 should be completed to read:

	5	7		11
1.	X = 0	X > 0	1.	TWEN < SEV
2.	X = 20	X = 70	2.	TWEN = SEV
3.	X = 2	X = 7	3.	70 < 20
4.	X < 30	X < 80	4.	TWEN = 0
5.	None of the above		5.	None of the above.

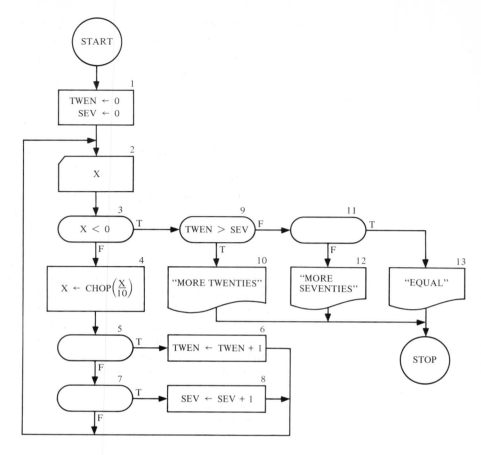

13. Draw a flowchart for an algorithm that reads (i.e., inputs) a stream of characters of the English alphabet from cards, one character per card, and

(a) Determines whether there are more J's than E's in the stream.
(b) Determines the fraction of vowels (A, E, I, O, and U) in the stream, where

Fraction of vowels $=$

$$\frac{\text{No. of A's} + \text{No. of E's} + \ldots + \text{No. of U's}}{\text{Total number of letters in the stream}}$$

It is not known how many cards must be read, but the end of the data set will be signaled by a card containing the nonletter character zero.

In Problems 14 and 15, box 20 will be executed for certain x,y pairs. These pairs define a region in the x-y plane. Your job is to draw the graph of this region.

14.

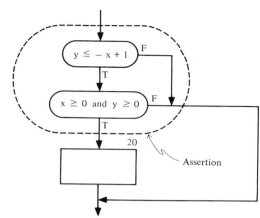

Assertion

15.

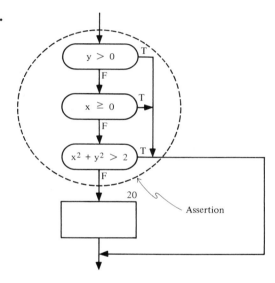

Assertion

16. Draw a flowchart that computes and prints the numbers 1, 2, 3, or 4 as a message to indicate in which quadrant a point P lies. The coordinates (xl,yl) of P are given. You must decide how to handle the cases when P lies on one or both axes.

17. We return to the carnival wheel problem (Problem 17, Section 2·4). We now suppose the point rule is modified. Recall that p, the number of points won or lost, was originally a straight-line function of k, the position number in the repeated group of four sectors. We now want a new point rule where p is an arbitrary function of k. For example,

k	Old Point Rule	New Point Rule
0	Lose 30	Lose 20
1	Lose 10	Lose 30
2	Win 10	Win 0
3	Win 30	Win 50

Draw a revised flowchart to show p as a function of the same data pair s and m but with the new point rule given above. (s is the sector position of the wheel at rest, and m is the number of sector positions the wheel is spun.)

3·5
Interpreting relational expressions

We pause briefly to look in a more formal way at what we have been writing inside an oval decision box and to see how it is interpreted. When the lines emanating from the oval are marked *true* (or T) and *false* (or F), we have been referring to what appears inside as an *assertion*.

Here is a review of the method for determining whether the assertion is true or false, originally given in Section 2·1.

> We look up the current values of the variables and evaluate the expression on each side of the relation symbol. Then we determine whether the relation in question holds between the values obtained.

It follows, for example, that the relational expression

$$X^2 + 2 \times X + 1 < 2 \times A \times B$$

will be read as though parentheses were inserted as follows:

$$(X^2 + 2 \times X \times 1) < (2 \times A \times B)$$

We can convey the same idea by saying that in reading expressions having no parentheses, relational symbols have a lower precedence than the operators. We can expand the precedence table (Table 2·1) to include fourth-level arithmetic and string relational symbols, as shown in Table 3·4.

TABLE 3·4
Precedence Levels for Relational Expressions

Levels		Arithmetic Symbol	String Symbol
High	First	$\uparrow$	
	Second	$\times$, $/$, $-$ (unary)	$\|$
	Third	$+$, $-$ (binary)	
Low	Fourth	$<$, $>$, $\leq$, $\geq$, $=$, $\neq$	$<$, $>$, $\leq$, $\geq$, $=$, $\neq$, $\subset$

We note in passing that since the SAMOS repertoire of commands includes only a "branch on minus" command, a condition such as $A < B$ must be reexpressed as

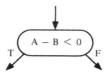

after which it can be coded in SAMOS in the form:

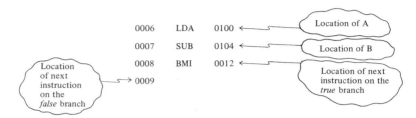

We conclude with a few words about how to establish order relations such as $>$ (greater than) between two strings. Recall for a moment the SAMOS computer and Figure 1·27, giving the character code for digits and letters. This code imposes an order on the individual characters. This order agrees with numerical order if one is comparing two strings of the same length composed of numerals alone, and with *lexicographic* or dictionary order for same-length strings composed of letters alone. But *all* strings of the same length are ordered by the code into a unique ordering.

If two strings are of unequal length, let us think of them as compared, character by character from the beginning, until one of two eventualities occurs. Either at some stage the character in one string will be "greater" (have a higher code) than that of the other, in which case the order of the entire strings is established, or the strings agree in every character until one string is exhausted. In that case, the "surviving" string is greater. For example, the following are true assertions.

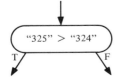
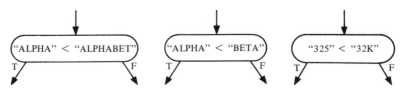

The SAMOS appendix (Section A·5) discusses part of the problem of implementing such decision boxes in a word-organized machine.

3·6
List variables
and subscripts

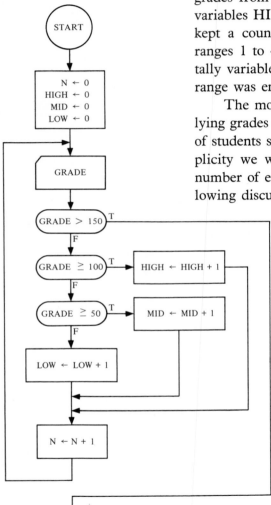

FIGURE 3·19

In Section 3·1 we studied a flowchart for tallying grades. We repeat the flowchart in Figure 3·19 for easy reference because we want to modify it.

Recall that the examination under discussion allowed grades from 1 to 150. (Scores of zero are unthinkable!) The variables HIGH, MID, and LOW were "tally" variables that kept a count, respectively, of the number of grades in the ranges 1 to 49, 50 to 99, and 100 to 150. The value of each tally variable was incremented by 1 every time a grade in its range was encountered.

The modification we wish to make is that instead of tallying grades in these three ranges we wish to tally the number of students scoring each of the 150 possible grades. (For simplicity we will omit the variable N, which counts the total number of examinees, as that feature is extraneous in the following discussion.)

Conceptually this problem offers no difficulty. The only difference is that we need 150 tally variables instead of just 3. Accordingly, it will be convenient to invent descriptive names for these variables. One possibility for these names is:

NUM1, NUM2, NUM3, . . . , NUM149, NUM150

where, for example, NUM87 denotes the number of students scoring 87 points on the exam. Equipped with this notation we can now draw the flowchart as shown in Figure 3·20, which is simple enough to understand, although it presents us with a most unpleasant prospect. We have 150 initializations in box 1! From boxes 3 to 302 there are 150 decision boxes and 150 assignment statements, and finally there are 150 output boxes. To write this program 452 flowchart boxes will be required. This is a formidable task. We can take solace only in the fact that there aren't 1000 possible scores instead of just 150. Every reader must suspect that there is a way of avoiding such absurdities. Let's try to find the way.

To this end let's consider what's going on in the flowchart of Figure 3·20. The value of GRADE input in box 2 tells us which tally variable we wish to increment. Thus, if the value of GRADE were 73, we would want to make the assignment

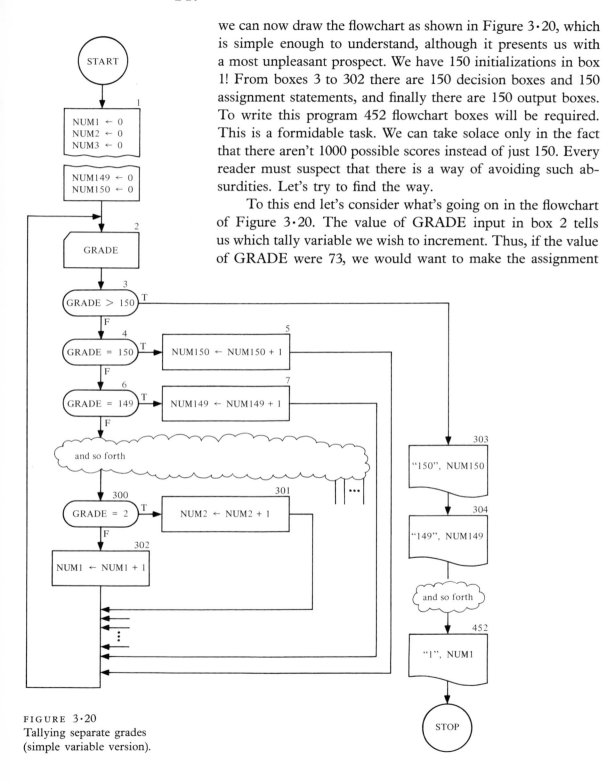

FIGURE 3·20
Tallying separate grades
(simple variable version).

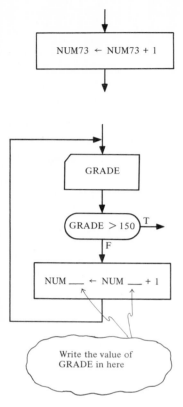

FIGURE 3·21

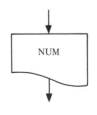

shown on the left. If only we had a flowchart feature that enabled us to determine the *name* of one variable on the basis of the *value* of another variable, then the portion of the flowchart from box 2 to box 302 could be replaced by the fragment in Figure 3·21. We would need only 1 assignment box instead of 150, and we would need no decision boxes at all.

Unfortunately, in Chapter 2 we were told that decomposition of variables is not allowed; each name is considered as a single unit and cannot be subdivided. But now we are going to introduce a new kind of variable, the *list variable* (or subscripted variable), which is, in a way, equivalent to this desired "name modification." We will describe how this works in the case at hand.

We are going to replace all of the variables NUM1, NUM2, NUM3, . . . , NUM150 by a single list variable, NUM. The storage box for NUM is quite different from the storage boxes for simple variables in that NUM is divided into 150 compartments (or components), each compartment being indexed by an integer from 1 to 150, as illustrated in Figure 3·22.

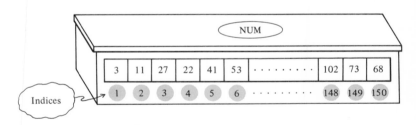

FIGURE 3·22

The value of NUM shown is the whole list of 150 numbers:

3, 11, 27, 22, 41, 53, . . . , 102, 73, 68

That list would be printed out on execution of the output box given on the left when the value of NUM was as illustrated in Figure 3·22.

But, in addition to being able to access the whole list (for either reading or assignment), *we can access each compartment separately*. This is done by attaching an integer subscript to NUM, as in NUM_5 or NUM_{149}. In the illustration above the value of NUM_5 is 41 and the value of NUM_{149} is 73. The assignment step

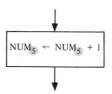

will increment the value of NUM_5 by 1 (to give 42 in the illustrated case) and leave all the other compartments of the storage box unchanged.

Now we are about to see what advantage NUM_5 and NUM_{149} have over their earlier counterparts NUM5 and NUM149. The advantage is that we can now write variables (or even expressions) in the subscripts as, for example, in

$$NUM_K$$

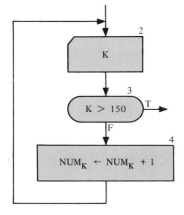

FIGURE 3·23

But what can this mean? Evidently it designates some component of the list variable NUM, but which one? In looking at the storage box for NUM we see the indices 1, 2, 3, . . . , 150, but we see no index K. The whole advantage of this notation is that NUM_K can designate different components at different stages in the execution of a program. More precisely, at any stage in the execution of a program, the component designated by NUM_K is determined by evaluating K, which must be an integer between 1 and 150.

Look, for example, at Figure 3·23. Suppose that on a particular transit of the loop the value of K input in box 2 is 149. On reaching box 4 the statement appearing there is interpreted as

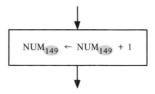

that is, increment the value in the 149th compartment of NUM by 1. (In Figure 3·22 this results in replacing the value 73 by 74.) On the next transit of the loop the input value of K might be 5. Then the assignment carried out on the next

execution of box 4 will be

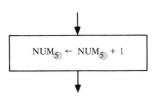

[In terms of the SIMPLOS model, note that finding the value of NUM_K on the right side of the assignment arrow requires two trips of the Reader. First, he must find the value of K (say it turns out to be 5), then he must make another trip to find NUM_5. The occurrence of NUM_K on the left of the arrow requires a trip of the Reader to find the value of K (still equal to 5) and then a trip of the Assigner to put the value computed by the Master Computer in the 5th compartment of NUM.]

Now it is easy to see that the flowchart in Figure 3·23 accomplishes what we were attempting in Figure 3·21: updating the proper counter each time a grade is read. (We replaced the variable GRADE by K only in the interest of easier reading; there would certainly have been nothing wrong with writing NUM_{GRADE}.)

We can now replace the cumbersome flowchart of Figure 3·20 by that in Figure 3·24. We see that the 452 separate flowchart boxes have been reduced to 8. The initialization of the components of NUM in the loop of boxes 1a, 1b, 1c, 1d, is self-explanatory. Now that we have more than one kind of variable we will include a "legend" with the flowchart to tell

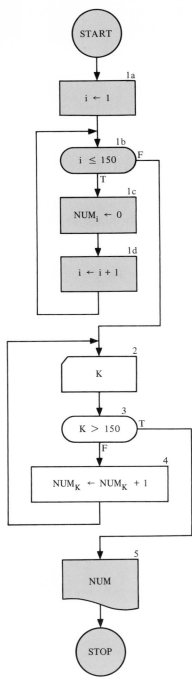

FIGURE 3·24
Flowchart and *legend* for tallying grades (subscripted variable version).

Legend	
Variable	Description
i, K	Integer
NUM	List of 150 integer components

whether the variables are simple or list variables and what kinds of values (integer, real, string) the variables (or their components) can have.

We remark that the contents of the compartments of a list variable are not restricted to integers. Ordinarily, however, every element of a list will be a value of the same type; for example, every element is a real number, or every element is a string, as illustrated in Figure 3·25.

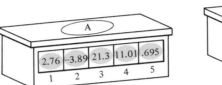 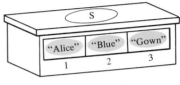

FIGURE 3·25

It was mentioned earlier that expressions may appear in subscripts. Thus such subscript expressions as

$$A_{N+3} \qquad B_{2\times J\times K-I} \qquad C_{NUM_K} \qquad D_{CHOP(X)}$$

are entirely permissible in flowcharts. The component designated is found by evaluating the subscript expression (which value must, of course, be an integer in the range of permissible indices as designated in the legend). Some programming languages (or local implementations of them) place limits on the complexity of expressions appearing in subscripts. For example, the subscripted subscript in C_{NUM_K} is frequently disallowed. (Here the value of K determines the desired component of NUM, and the value of this component determines the component of C to be referenced.)

Now that we know about list variables and how to refer to individual list elements, we want to consider how to input and output entire lists or portions of lists in the flowchart language. The simplest notations for input and output are

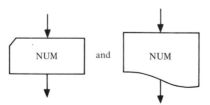 and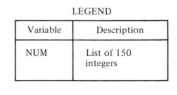

LEGEND	
Variable	Description
NUM	List of 150 integers

which, respectively, input a value to each component of NUM in order, and output the value of NUM (or, what is the same thing, the list of values of the components of NUM in order.) An optional notation for accomplishing the same results is seen in the examples

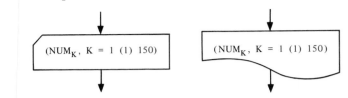

which we explain below.

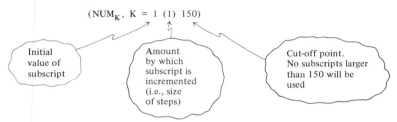

The advantage of this latter notation lies in its flexibility, which often eliminates the necessity of writing a loop. For example, the input and output boxes

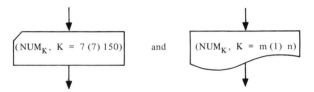

mean respectively; input values only to those components of NUM whose indices (or subscripts) are multiples of 7; output only the values of the components of NUM from the mth through the nth inclusive. (Which these are depends, of course, on the values of m and n.)

Also permissible is the notation

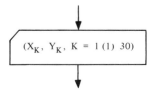

which is an instruction to input values in the order X_1, Y_1, X_2, Y_2, X_3, Y_3, and so forth through X_{30}, Y_{30}.

We now know how to represent and use list variables in any flowchart algorithm to be executed on a SIMPLOS machine. Can we guess from this study how lists can be represented in a machine such as SAMOS? Since its basic unit of storage is a *word*, it is natural to consider grouping adjacent SAMOS storage words to form "super" words for list variables. For example, the 5-element list A of Figure 3·25 might be represented as a block of 5 storage words, say, at addresses 0105 through 0109 inclusive. Then a reference to any element of A would be achieved by using its proper address in the block of storage, for example, 0105 for A_1, 0106 for A_2, and so on. As another example, the 3-element list of strings, S, of Figure 3·25 might be represented using a block of three SAMOS words, each able to contain a string of up to 10 characters.

EXERCISES 3·6,
SET A

1. When we revised the carnival wheel problem in Problem 17, Section 3·4, we could have employed a multiway decision box to model the new point rule. In Figure 3·26a you can see one way to achieve that objective.

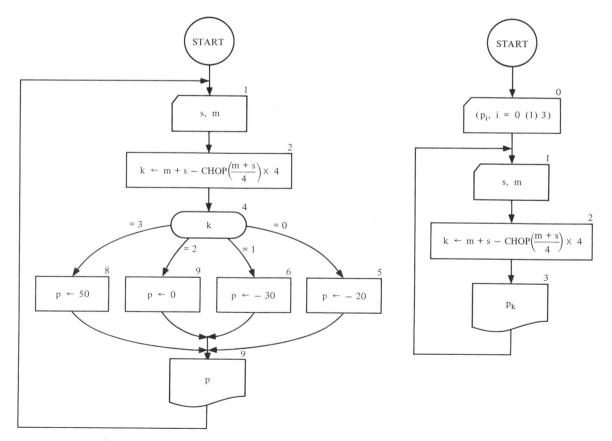

(a) Carnival wheel with a multiway decision step.

(b) Carnival wheel with subscripts.

FIGURE 3·26

A student now proposes an alternative solution, shown in Figure 3·26b. He claims it is simpler, equivalent, and an inherently more general solution. Study these two flowcharts carefully and answer the two questions given below.

(a) Under what circumstances are the flowcharts equivalent?
(b) In what sense can Figure 3·26b be construed to be more general than Figure 3·26a?

2. The algorithm for finding the largest of N data values that was illustrated in Figure 3·4 requires that no more than two of the N data values need be held in storage at any one time. In many situations we have a list of N values that is already held in storage, and the problem is to find the largest. Sometimes we not only want to obtain a copy of the largest value, but we also want to determine *where* (at what index) that value is found.

(a) Develop a flowchart fragment that when executed finds and prints the largest data value in a list A of N real elements, where the value of N and of the list A are already held in storage.
(b) Modify the flowchart fragment that was developed in part a to print not only the largest value but also the "location," that is, the *index*, of the selected list element. If the largest value occurs more than once in the list, print the index of the *first* such largest value, that is, the one having the smaller or smallest index.

3. The flowchart in Figure 3·27 is an algorithm that accomplishes the following three steps.

Inputs a number c.
Inputs 100 numbers $b_1, b_2, \ldots, b_{100}$.
Determines and prints a list of the b_i that satisfy the relation $b_i \geq c$.

Study the flowchart carefully and answer the following questions.

(a) How many times is box 6 executed?
(b) How many times is box 8 executed?
(c) Under what circumstance will box 10 be executed? The remark is made that ANY is a "switch variable"; that is, it is used like railroaders use a rail switch. Explain.
(d) Is it really necessary for there to be more than one value of b in memory at any given time in order to achieve the same output objectives for this program? Another way of asking this question is, "Are subscripts really necessary in this algorithm?" If your answer is no, redraw the flowchart accordingly, putting a check mark next to each box you change.
(e) How would you modify either Figure 3·27 or your modified version, resulting from part d, to generalize the flowchart, so that instead of reading 100 elements for b we read any given number n of them?

4. An investor who wishes to take an "algorithmic" approach to stock-market purchases has come up with the following set of buy/sell rules.

(a) If a stock goes up for two consecutive weeks, buy 100 shares (even if the stock is already owned).

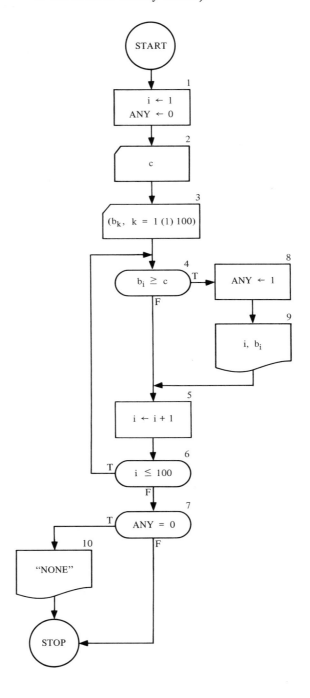

FIGURE 3·27
An algorithm to study.

(b) If a stock that is owned goes down for two consecutive weeks, sell all shares owned.

To test this strategy, he has assembled a data deck of 52 weekly prices for a certain stock. Your job is to construct a flowchart that will calculate his net profit or loss at the end of the 52 weeks, assuming money for purchases is always available. Profits or losses will occur when the stock is sold and, since 100 shares are always purchased, the profit (on any 100 shares) will be equal to 100 × (selling price— buying price). (A negative profit is thus a loss.) If the stock is bought several times before it is sold, then it will be necessary to keep a record of each buying price so that profits or losses may be correctly computed at selling time. (Will a subscripted variable be useful?) If the stock is owned at the end of the 52nd week, assume that it is then sold and figure in the resulting profit or loss. It will probably be useful to let some variable, perhaps OWN, indicate whether or not the stock is currently owned.

5. Draw a flowchart to input n and a vector (list) $a_0, a_1, \ldots, a_n$. The a's are considered to be coefficients of the polynomial

$$a_0 + a_1x + a_2x^2 + \ldots + a_nx^n$$

and n is its apparent degree. However, some or all of the coefficients may be zero. Construct a flowchart to determine the actual degree, m, of the polynomial. Of course, it is true that $m \leq n$ and m can be determined by searching the set of coefficients for the nonzero element with the highest subscript. Output m and the coefficients from a_0 through a_m inclusive. If all the coefficients are zero, do not print any coefficients, but let the printed value of m be -1.

6. Prepare a flowchart solution to the problem that follows. Be sure to include a legend for the variables. Give some thought to the selection of variables and use meaningful names.

At University X in course Y there are two midterm exams and one final exam. Each exam has a maximum score of 100 and a minimum of 0. For each student, the final course grade is computed as a weighted average of the exam scores so that the final counts twice as much as a midterm. Thus the term grade will also be a number in the range 0 to 100, inclusive.

Each student has an individual student code number, from 001 to 100. A deck of data cards has been prepared to use in processing the grades. The cards contain a series (stream) of 12-digit numbers such as the following.

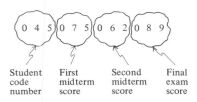

0 4 5 0 7 5 0 6 2 0 8 9   0 3 4 0 3 0 0 5 0 0 6 0

| Student code number | First midterm score | Second midterm score | Final exam score |

The first three digits of each 12-digit number are a student code number. The second group of 3 digits is the score on the first midterm, the third group of 3 digits is the second midterm score, and the last three digits are the final exam score. Some students failed to take any exams and thus had no data card containing their code number.

The execution of your flowchart should cause the data deck to be read, final grades to be computed when possible, and a class roster to be printed. Input is *not* ordered by student number. The class roster is to be ordered by student code number and should list the final grades, somewhat as follows.

STUDENT CODE NUMBER	GRADE
001	96
002	70
003	NO SCORES FOUND
004	85
.	.
.	.
.	.
.	.
100	75

An identifying heading is to be printed somewhere above each column. If no scores are found for some code numbers, the message "NO SCORES FOUND" is to be printed in place of a final grade. A sentinel card containing 0 (zero) will be placed at the end of the deck, since there may not be exactly 100 cards.

Start by thinking over the problem until you completely understand what is given and what is required. Your flowchart must separate the 12-digit input into 4 groups of 3 digits. You may want to review Sections 2·4 and 3·6.

In this book we discuss several methods of sorting. Each is based on discovering adjacent pairs of elements in a list that are "out of order" and then interchanging these elements. One such method, in fact, is discussed in the following section. Do not solve this problem by sorting because there is a much easier way to do it.

Sorting Example   One can order a collection of objects, such as numbers, by taking each element of the collection, one at a time, and putting it into the position *where it belongs*. People do this when sorting poker chips into a poker chip holder, silverware into the kitchen drawer, hand tools onto a tool rack, coins and bills into the cash register drawer, and letters into the proper post-office boxes. In each case the method of ordering depends on the fact that the nature of the objects examined provides positive information concerning the slot, bucket, rack, position, or cubbyhole where that element must go. We have already seen an application of this principle in the grade-tallying method of Figure 3·24, where grades of like value were tallied in the appropriate bucket.

Unfortunately, for many other problems that require sorting, this approach, often called "bucket sorting," is impractical. In these cases, because we do not know in advance exactly which buckets will be needed as receptacles for the objects in the list, too many buckets must be provided. For example, using a bucket-sorting method to create an alphabetical ordering of all six-letter words in the Bible would require an ordered group of 26^6 (over 100 million) buckets (storage cells), even though there are only a few thousand such words in the Bible.

Fortunately, there are other methods of sorting that, although they require more work (i.e., more algorithmic steps to sort a given list of n elements), require the minimum number of buckets or storage cells, that is, only n of them. Now we will develop one such algorithm for sorting and, later, some better sorting algorithms of this type.

In sorting, the problem is this. If we input a set of numbers

we should output

Consider an input list variable A whose value is

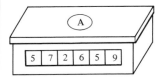

We scan the element values from left to right until we encounter the first place where the values decrease. (If there is no such decrease, then the values are already in increasing order.) In the above example, we find this first decrease when going from A_2 to A_3. Interchange these values.

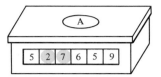

What next? We seem to have made some progress, so let's treat this list as though it were new, that is, go back to the beginning and scan from left to right, and so forth.

This seems almost too simple to work. Nevertheless, we observe that as long as the list is not in increasing order, there will always be another interchange to do. Each interchange affects the relative order of just one pair of values, and each pair will be interchanged only once. Since there are only finitely many such pairs, the algorithm must terminate. Perhaps you would like to try the process with some playing cards.

Next, we flowchart this algorithm. The basic idea is the interchange of A_K and A_{K+1}, which we know to represent as box 5 of Figure 3·28.

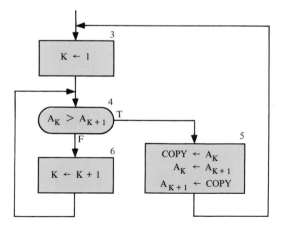

FIGURE 3·28
Skeleton of an abominable sort.

We execute this interchange only if $A_K > A_{K+1}$. Thus, if the condition in box 4 is false, we go to the next position in the list, that is, increment K and repeat the test (i.e., return to the decision box). On emerging from the interchange box, we set K back to 1 and start over. We now have the skeleton given in Figure 3·28.

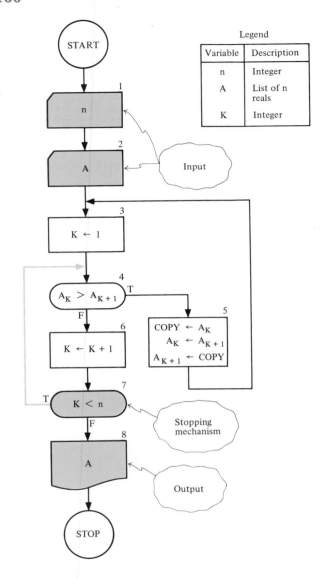

FIGURE 3·29
Abominable sort.

This skeleton still lacks a stopping mechanism as well as steps for input and output. We should also decide on how large a list of numbers the flowchart should be set up to handle. One time we may want to sort 13 numbers, another time 200, or perhaps 1000. Why not let the variable n denote the length of the list? This is all put together in Figure 3·29.

EXERCISES 3·6,
SET B

This group of problems concerns the sorting algorithm given in Figure 3·29.

1. Suppose you want to test the algorithm by determining whether the list

$$7 \quad 2 \quad -5 \quad 4$$

will be properly sorted in ascending order, that is

$$-5 \quad 2 \quad 4 \quad 7$$

(a) What are the values of the input data at boxes 1 and 2?
(b) With these input data, trace through the algorithm beginning at box 3, showing the box numbers in the sequence they are actually executed until box 8 is reached. Use a table such as the one given here. It is partially filled for this problem to help you get started.

Step Number \ Box	3	4	5	6	7	8	Assigned Value of K
1	√						1
2		√					
3			√				
4	√						1
5		√					
6				√			2
7							
8							
9							

Scratch Pad for a Vector

1	2
2	7
3	− 5
4	4

(c) After the input step, how many flowchart boxes are executed in total before the (STOP) is reached?

(d) How many times is box 4 reached?

2. By now you should be thoroughly convinced this algorithm will work every time. Suppose the values to be sorted are

$$-9 \quad 5 \quad 9 \quad 12$$

That is, they are already in ascending order. How many times will box 4 be executed before box 8 is reached?

3. What if the input values are already sorted, but in opposite order, say,

    12   9   5   − 9

    How many executions of box 4?

Final Notes   Save your results for Exercises 1, 2, and 3. In Chapter 5 we will look at another sorting algorithm, and we will wish to compare these saved results with corresponding results of that new and much better algorithm.

In spite of the fact that we now know the sorting algorithm works, there is still something inherently "fishy" about it. Ideally, the structure of an algorithm as seen from its flowchart should help us to see what goes on when the algorithm is executed. In this algorithm, however, the structure seems, if anything, to hinder our understanding. Why is this? Attention will be focused at length on this point in Chap. 5. For the present just observe that the loop consisting of boxes 4, 6, and 7, and the loop of boxes 3, 4, and 5 are neither totally separate nor totally "nested" (one loop inside the other). Instead, the loops intersect at (i.e., they share) box 4. More practice in constructing and comprehending algorithms will convince you that loops that "straddle" one another in this way result in structures that are difficult to understand. The fact that such structures can be avoided is one of the important ideas discussed in Chapter 5.

EXERCISES 3·6,
SET C

1. Suppose the data set for use with the flowchart at the top of the next page consists of the following values.

    1, 2, 3, 4, 5, 6, 7, 8

    (a) After the first execution of box 3, the values in the A and B lists are (choose one):

    (1) A: 1, 2, 3, 4   (4) A: 8, 2, 3, 4
         B: 5, 6, 7, 8   B: 5, 6, 7, 1
    (2) A: 1, 2, 3, 5   (5) A: 8, 2, 3, 5
         B: 4, 6, 7, 8   B: 1, 6, 7, 4
    (3) A: 5, 2, 3, 4
         B: 1, 6, 7, 8

    (b) The values that are output will be (in order) (choose one):

    (1) 8, 7, 6, 5, 4, 3, 2, 1   (4) 6, 5, 3, 4, 1, 2, 7, 8
    (2) 1, 2, 3, 4, 5, 6, 7, 8   (5) None of the above
    (3) 5, 6, 7, 8, 1, 2, 3, 4

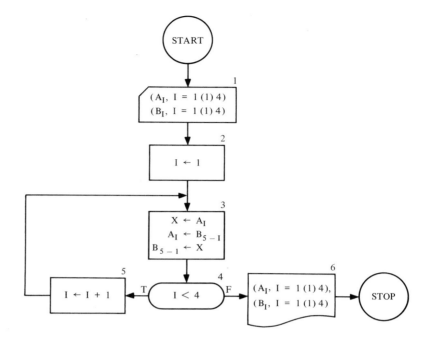

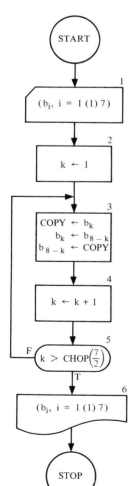

2. Suppose the values input at box 1 of the flowchart given on the left are:

$$b_1 = 2, b_2 = 3$$
$$b_3 = 4, b_4 = 5$$
$$b_5 = 6, b_6 = 7$$
$$b_7 = 8$$

What values are output at box 6?

3. Suppose the input data for the flowchart at the top of the next page consists of the following values.

$$1, 2, 3, 4, 5, 6, 7, 8$$

(a) True or false: After the first execution of box 7, the values in the list C are undefined except for the value of C_1.

(b) True or false: After the last execution of box 7, the values of the elements of the list B are 5, 6, 7, and 8.

(c) The values output upon execution of boxes 9 and 10 will be (in order) (choose one):

(1) 10, 1, 2, 3, 4   (4) 18, 1, 2, 3, 4
(2) 26, 5, 6, 7, 8   (5) None of these.
(3) 10, 5, 6, 7, 8

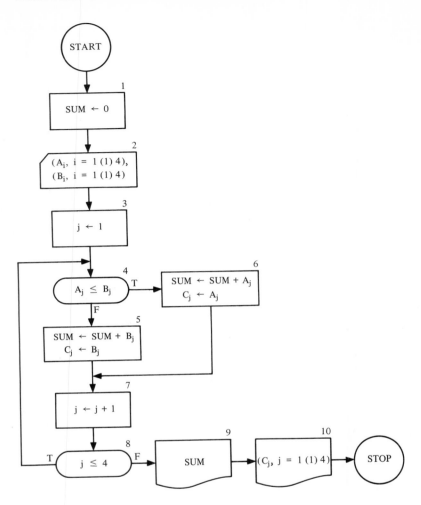

EXERCISES 3·6,
SET D

1. There are 101 members in a youth symphony orchestra about to make a concert tour. A reporter asks the conductor, "What is the *median* age of your members?" The conductor answers, "I don't know, but here is an alphabetical list of the players' names and ages."

(a) For the purposes of this problem we will define the median of an ordered set of numbers to be the "middle" one of the set; in other words, there are as many preceding it as following it. For example, in the set

   3, 7, 24, 35, 67, 81, 97

the median is 35.

   Draw a flowchart to find the median age of the players from the list of ages provided, which cannot be assumed to be in numerical order.

(b) The definition of the median given above does not work if the number of items is even. For example, there is no "middle" number in the sequence

4, 17, 31, 43, 57, 68

In this case the median could be defined to be the mean of the two numbers adjacent to the "split"—in the above case $(31 + 43)/2 = 37$.

Develop an expression that will determine the median of an ordered set of n numbers $a_1, a_2, \ldots, a_n$. Your answer should be one expression that gives the correct answer, for n either odd or even. (*Hint.* You will find the CHOP function useful.)

(c) Prepare a flowchart similar to the one prepared in part a, but designed to work for an orchestra containing an arbitrary number of players, and to produce not only the median age, but also the ages of the oldest and youngest players.

2. Study the flowchart on the left and answer parts a and b.

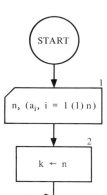
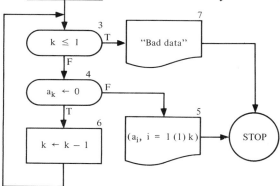

(a) Suppose the data set that is input as a result of executing box 1 in the flowchart is

6, 19, 2.1, − 4.1, 0, 4.4, 16.7

Which of the following will be the value assigned to the variable k at the time execution of the above algorithm reaches box 8?
(1) 0
(2) 6
(3) − 1
(4) 4
(5) 5

(b) If the data set input as a result of executing box 1 is

5, 4, 0, 4, 0, 0

which of the following represents the output produced by the algorithm?
(1) 4, 0, 4
(2) "Bad data"

(3) 3, 4, 0, 4, 0, 0
(4) 3, 3, 0, 4
(5) 2, 4, 0, 4

3. Suppose that execution of box 1 of the flowchart below results in the following value assignments.

$$a_1 = 1, a_2 = 2, a_3 = 3, a_4 = 4, \ldots, a_{10} = 10$$
$$b_1 = 0, b_2 = 1, b_3 = 2, b_4 = 3, \ldots, b_{10} = 9$$

What values will be output at box 6?

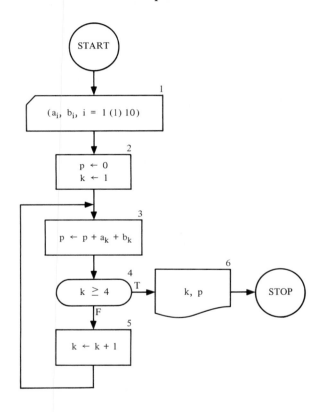

4. Assume the flowchart on the next page is executed using the following input data set.

    8, 3, 6, 12, 10, 22, 7, 3, 9

    (a) How many times will box 8 be executed?
    (b) How many times will box 5 be executed?
    (c) Show all the values that will be printed. Assume each execution of box 6 or box 10 causes printing on a new line (with three values printed on a line when box 6 is executed and one value printed on a line when box 10 is executed).

(d) Are subscripts really necessary in this algorithm? If your answer is no, redraw the flowchart to eliminate subscripts, putting a check mark next to each flowchart box you change.

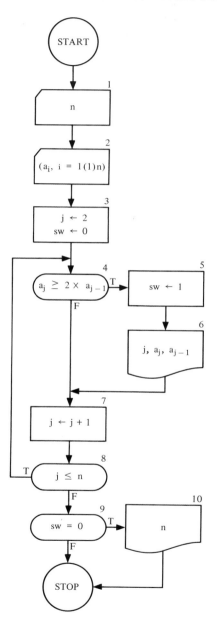

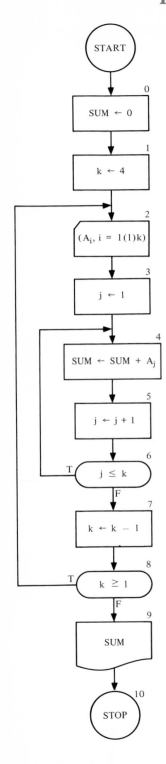

5. Study the flowchart shown on the left and determine whether each of the assertions a through e is true or false.

(a) Each time box 2 is executed, 4 items are to be read from the input stream.

(b) Box 3 is executed once for every item that is summed.

(c) Box 5 is executed once for every item that is summed.

(d) Box 8 will be executed four times.

(e) If execution reaches box 10, then 10 items will have been read from the input stream and summed.

4·1
Introduction

Chapters 1 to 3 have provided you with most of the basic concepts you need to construct computer algorithms for problem solving. So far we have not tried to solve many problems. But now we are ready to tackle a wide variety of elementary problems. In this chapter we will do just that, but several more conceptual tools are needed to make the job easier. First, because most algorithms of interest involve looping, we must become more conscious of loop structures and how to use them to organize algorithms, thus making the job of problem solving easier. For this purpose we will study the most common types of looping patterns and learn to recognize and use these patterns in a systematic way. Two new flowchart boxes will be introduced in Section 4·1 to provide the notational tools for expressing loop structures.

Second, because many, if not most, interesting algorithms become simpler if data are represented by structured variables such as lists, we will carry the concept of list variable one step further to that of *arrays* and *tables* of data elements. You will see that in some sense an array is similar to a *list of lists*.

This chapter will be helpful to you in direct proportion to the amount of study time you invest in it. There are many exercises and problems here, and you should try to work many of them. More than ever, your learning process must now become a *by-doing* experience if you are to appreciate the significance of the principles and tools presented.

The Control of Loops

Let us begin by putting down side by side in Figure 4·1 two different flowcharts for the Fibonacci sequence problem of Section 1·2. Remember that the Fibonacci sequence

$$1, 1, 2, 3, 5, 8, 13, 21, 34, \ldots$$

has the property that each term (after the two 1's) is the sum of its two immediate predecessors.

The flowchart in Figure 4·1a represents an algorithm for

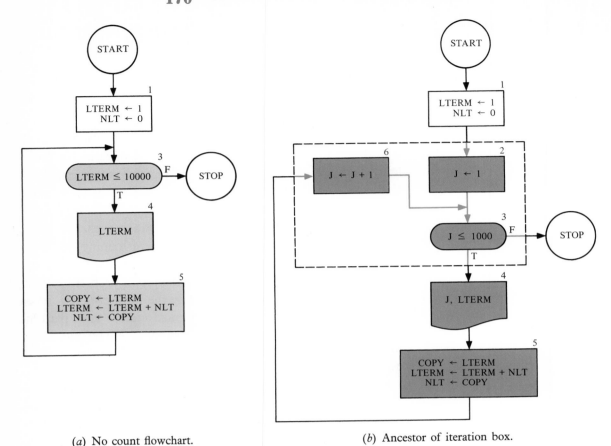

(a) No count flowchart.

(b) Ancestor of iteration box.

FIGURE 4·1
Two flowcharts for the
Fibonacci sequence.

computing and printing in order all of terms of the Fibonacci
sequence that are not greater than 10,000. The flowchart in
Figure 4·1b represents an algorithm for computing and printing a numbered list of the first 1000 terms of the Fibonacci
sequence.

We can see that box 5 is exactly the same in each flowchart. This box contains the fundamental computation in this
algorithm.

Each flowchart has a loop, that is, boxes 3, 4, and 5 in
the first flowchart and boxes 3, 4, 5, and 6 in the second. Each
loop is equipped with an absolutely certain exit. In Figure 4·1a
we exit or *branch out* of the loop as soon as the variable
LTERM exceeds 10,000. In Figure 4·1b we exit when J exceeds 1000, so that the loop will be executed 1000 times. (*Question.* Can this algorithm be executed to completion on a
SAMOS computer? Will it work on a BITOS computer?)

In Figure 4·1a it is not at all clear how many times the loop will be executed, but as long as LTERM is less than or equal to 10,000, the looping will continue.

The situation of *a loop controlled by a condition* instead of by a counter occurs so often that it is convenient to name it the *while* loop and put it in a special loop-controlling, bullet-shaped *while box,* as shown in Figure 4·2a. In Figure 4·3a we redraw Figure 4·1a incorporating a while box. In Figure 4·3b we redraw the Euclidean algorithm of Figure 3·11, adding a while box. In each case the number of transits through the loop is indefinite. That is, before entering the loop we do not generally know how many times the loop computation will be repeated. We will therefore refer to such looping as *indefinite iteration.*

You may wonder at first what is gained from a while box. To understand this point we must state exactly what we will mean by it. Referring to Figure 4·2a, we enter the while box and test the condition stated there. If the condition is satisfied we do the computation that the condition controls. Then we loop back and test the condition again. The looping continues until the condition is *no longer* satisfied. Presumably within the loop something happens that alters the values tested by the controlling condition; otherwise we might be in a perpetual loop!

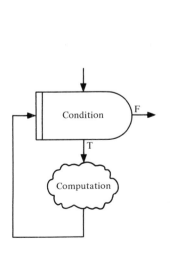

FIGURE 4·2
The *while* Box.

(a)

(b) While loop structure viewed as a single step.

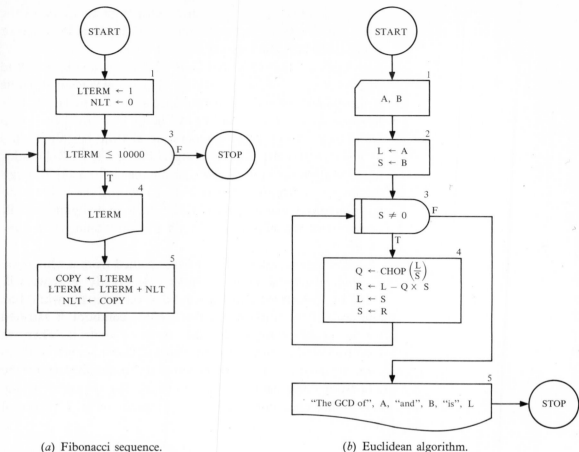

(a) Fibonacci sequence.

(b) Euclidean algorithm.

FIGURE 4·3
Familiar flowcharts with while
box.

The entire loop structure of Figure 4·2a should be
thought of as if it were a single step in the algorithm in the
sense that it has just one entry point and just one exit point.
This important concept is suggested in Figure 4·2b.

Now let's look at a third example of indefinite iteration.
Suppose we have a stack of cards each containing two pieces
of information: the name of a person (last name first) followed
by his address. Our task is to find the address of John Jones.
(Assume for the moment that John Jones' card *is* in the deck.)
The core of the testing process is as follows.

We read a name and test to see if it is the one we are
looking for. If it is not, we keep reading cards until we do
come to "JONES, JOHN." Then we output his name and
address (Figure 4·4a).

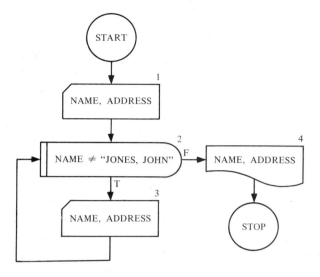

FIGURE 4·4a

We have assumed, however, that the JOHN JONES card is actually present in the deck. What if it isn't? We had better place a sentinal card at the end of the deck, that is, a card with a distinctive name and address that we will recognize as the "end of the deck" marker. We might use "ENDLIST". Then the while condition in box 2 of Figure 4·4a becomes a compound one, such as

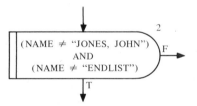

Now we either find what we want or we can see from the output "ENDLIST", produced in box 4, that the name we sought was not in the deck. But detecting that the name card is missing from the deck is not always so easy. Suppose we are not going to output John Jones' name and address, but want to add it to a list of potential contributors to a campaign fund. Now when we exit from while box 2 on the *false* side we want to distinguish which of the two conditions was violated. Otherwise we may have "ENDLIST" scattered many times throughout our list of contributors, inflating the number of names but not the potential donations. We can solve this problem, if we like, by a second test, as shown in box 5 of Figure 4·4b.

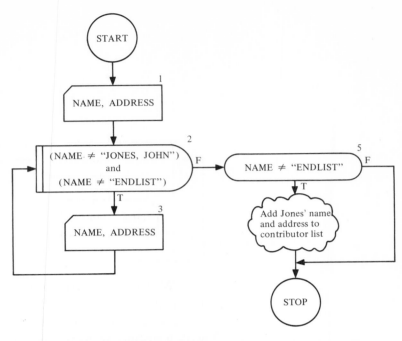

FIGURE 4·4*b*

Now let's turn our attention back to Figure 4·1*b*. We can tell the exact number of times the loop will be executed because that loop is *controlled by a counter*. The variable J works exactly like a counter (Figure 4·5).

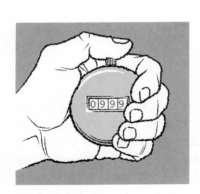

FIGURE 4·5
The variable J.

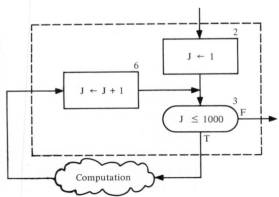

FIGURE 4·6

In Figure 4·6 we repeat flowchart boxes 2, 3, and 6 from Figure 4·1*b* because these are the actions on which we want to focus. The variable J is incremented by one in box 6 each time we pass through the loop. Furthermore, box 2 in this figure sets the counter to 1 at the start. Thus, when box 3 is executed, the value of J gives us one more than the number of transits that have been made through the loop.

In addition to acting as a counter, J has one additional duty; it controls the exit switch. This controlling or switching duty of the variable J can be seen in box 3 of Figure 4·6 or in the flowchart it came from, Figure 4·1*b*, where a comparison is made to determine when to exit from the loop. The variable J then has both counting and switching duties. You can conceive of J as a switchman who has been given the instructions, "Let the first 1000 through and then throw the switch."

The situation represented in Figure 4·6 (initialization, test, and incrementation of a loop variable) occurs so often that we find it expedient to introduce a special box to combine all three actions and also call attention to the *definite* nature of the iteration. The three-compartment box of Figure 4·7*a*

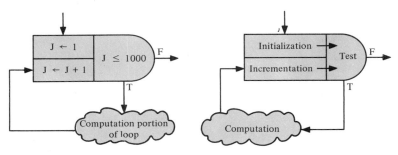

(*a*) Birth of the iteration box.   (*b*) Iteration box flow.

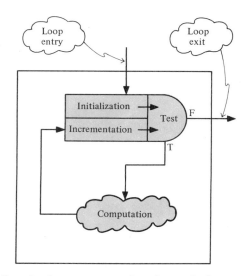

(*c*) Iterative loop structure viewed as a single step.

FIGURE 4·7

shows our shorthand, which we call the *iteration box*. It can be used whenever a counter controls the exit from a loop. Such a loop is called a *definite iteration* when the number of transits through the loop is independent of what happens within the computation portion of the loop. Definite iteration is guaranteed when the control counter, its increment, and its limit are not changed inside the loop.

Figure 4·7b shows the internal flow in the iteration box. The exits from the initialization and incrementation compartments lead directly into the test compartment. Figure 4·7c again stresses the importance of viewing the loop structure as if it were a single step in the flowchart, having one entry and one exit.

Incorporating the iteration box into Figure 4·1b, we have Figure 4·8a.

To emphasize the distinction between definite and indefinite iteration, we present still another flowchart (Figure 4·8b)

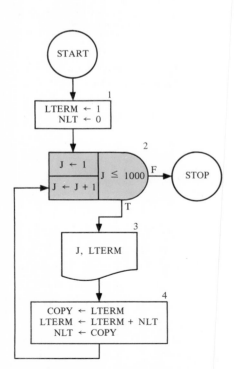

(a) Fibonacci sequence algorithm with an iteration box.

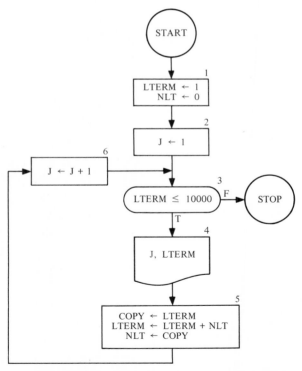

(b) Fibonacci sequence with a noncontrolling counter.

FIGURE 4·8

in which a counter has been added to Figure 4·1a merely to print out a numbered list. Note that the variable J in Figure 4·8b has the same counting duty as the variable J in Figure 4·1b, but it does *not* control the exit switch.

Now that we have an iteration box, what have we gained? A great deal in terms of assistance in organizing flowchart loops controlled by a counter. When we draw the box we are agreeing to outlaw any branching into the computation portion of the loop from other parts of the program. The box collects together the vital information on a countercontrolled loop: the initialization (which may be any integer-valued expression), the incrementation, and the test (based on the value of the counter variable). With the control taken care of, we are able to turn our whole attention to the computation controlled by the loop.

The Use of Iteration Boxes   We will now exhibit additional examples to illustrate the iteration box. To make what we wish to emphasize stand out, we may present only fragments of flowcharts. Consider the task: given a list of N numbers, print out these numbers and their cubes, thus in effect constructing a table of cubes.

Suppose the list is already stored in compartments of a list variable, X. We will run through the indices, selecting from storage the values of the X_J, and making the desired computations. This suggests the use of an iteration box with the loop variable doing the *running*, as shown in Figure 4·9a. In Figure 4·9b the same computation is performed with the data stored on cards instead of in the machine.

Notice that in Figure 4·9b the loop variable is nowhere to be seen in the computation portion of the loop. Figure 4·9a shows a common occurrence, a loop variable going click, click, click through the indices of a list.

We see this again in our next two examples: adding up a list of numbers already in storage, and finding for a list of numbers in storage the maximum of their absolute values. These are flowcharted in Figure 4·10.

There is a fundamental difference between the algorithms of Figure 4·10 and those of Figure 4·9. In any transit of the loops of Figure 4·9, no use is made of calculations from previous transits, while that is certainly not the case in Figure 4·10. Figure 4·11a is a variation of Figure 4·10b and finds not only

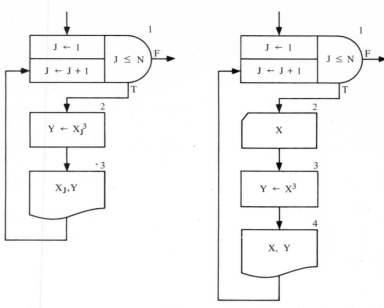

FIGURE 4·9
Making a table of cubes.

(a) From internally stored data.

(b) From external data.

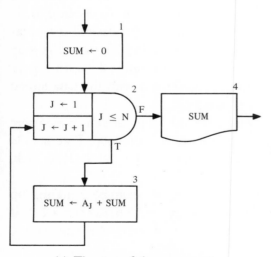

(a) The sum of the components
of a list.

FIGURE 4·10
Iteration boxes in list
calculations.

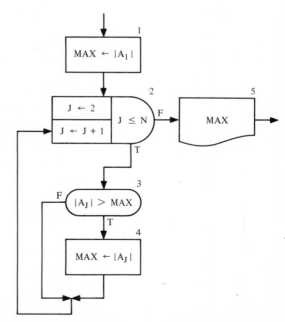

(b) The maximum of the absolute values
of the components of a list.

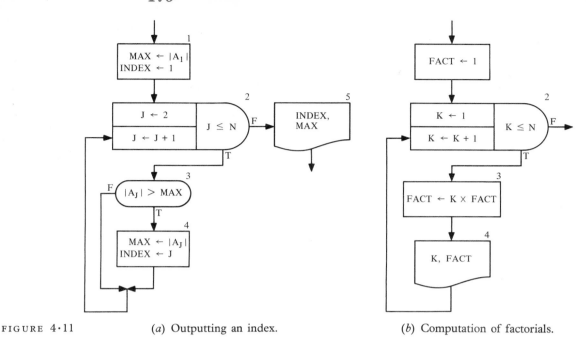

FIGURE 4·11   (a) Outputting an index.   (b) Computation of factorials.

the maximum value but also the value of the index J at which the maximum was found. Figure 4·11b shows a calculation of factorials.

Integer Factors of an Integer

Consider the problem of finding all the integer "cofactors" of a given integer N. The cofactors of an integer N are pairs of factors, such that the product of each pair is the number N itself. For example, a listing of all the cofactors of 20 is:

    1, 20
    2, 10
    4, 5

The cofactors of 25 are:

    1, 25
    5, 5

If N is large, the task of finding all these factors is tedious and we will be delighted therefore to have a computer do the job for us. The word statement of the algorithm to solve this problem is very simple: Go through the integers 1, 2, 3, 4, and so forth, checking each one to determine whether it is a

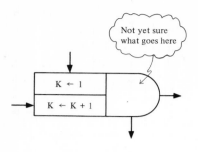

divisor of N and, if it is, write it down along with its cofactor.

Since, for each integer, we must check whether it divides N, we have a repetitive process, a loop, and our loop seems to involve a counter. Now we draw the iteration box, noting that we are not yet sure what to put inside.

Of what does the calculation consist? Of determining whether K is a divisor of N. For K to be a divisor of N means that N/K is an integer or, equivalently, CHOP(N/K) = N/K. Thus

is equivalent to

Now we come to the important question of when to stop the computation. We could let K go all the way to N; that is, we could put $K \leq N$ in the empty space in the test compartment of the iteration box. Then, if N were a million, we

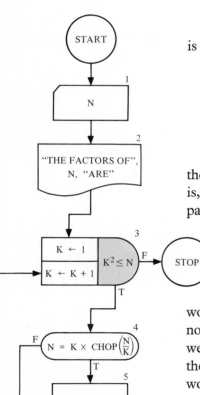

would have to go through the loop a million times. However, notice that whenever we find one integer factor of N, say K, we have, in effect, also found its cofactor N/K. Moreover, these two factors cannot both be less than $\sqrt{N}$, or else we would have

$$N = K \times (N / K) < \sqrt{N} \times \sqrt{N} = N$$

which is a contradiction. By the same reasoning, K and N/K are not both greater than $\sqrt{N}$. Thus, whenever we express N as the product of two factors, one of these factors is $\leq \sqrt{N}$ and the other is $\geq \sqrt{N}$. This means that we only need to go as far as $K \leq \sqrt{N}$ in our search for factors if, in our output

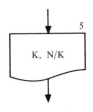

step, we print the cofactor, that is, the value of N / K, along with each factor, K, as shown on the left.

Before we complete the algorithm we want to make one last observation. The condition K $\leq \sqrt{N}$ involves a computation of $\sqrt{N}$ and, in an actual machine, this computation usually includes an approximation. The particular approximation (CHOP or ROUND or some other rounding function) is hidden in the square root algorithm. We can easily avoid this approximation if we rephase the condition as

$$K^2 \leq N$$

The complete flowchart is shown in Figure 4·12.

Notice that when N is a perfect square, like 25, the cofactor algorithm prints a duplicate of the factor N. How should the flowchart in Figure 4·12 be modified to print all the factors of N, but no duplicates?

EXERCISES 4·1,
SET A

1. With the aid of a while box, draw a flowchart to describe the following process. Given a list of positive integers (B_i, i = 1(1)n), search the list from B_1 *forward* to B_n and locate and print the value of the first element B_j, that is at least twice the value of its immediate predecessor, B_{j-1}. If no such element is found, print "none".

2. With the aid of a while box, draw a flowchart to describe the following process. Given a list of integers (B_i, i = 1(1)n), search every other element of the list *backward* from B_n, that is, B_n, B_{n-2}, B_{n-4}, · · · , down to B_1 if n is odd or down to B_2 if n is even. If an element B_j is found whose magnitude is more than twice its scanned predecessor B_{j+2}, print out the values of j, B_j, and B_{j+2}; otherwise print "none can be found".

3. A student has presented to you the algorithm whose flowchart is given on the left.

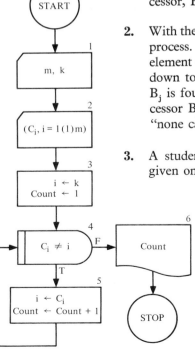

(a) Will execution reach box 6 if the flowchart is executed using the data set: m = 9, k = 1, $(C_i, i = 1(1)m) = 5,6,7,8,3,2,4,1,9$? If not, why not, and if so, what value is printed when box 6 is executed?

(b) If you have done part a, you have probably now guessed what the student was trying to accomplish with his algorithm.

Show what change should be made to the test in box 3 to guarantee, for any consistent data sets supplied, that box 6 will always be reached, and when executed will print out the number of elements in the list C that have been "visited." Test your hypothesis by trying all possible values of k from 1 to 9 keeping the other values of the given data set the same.

(c) Show what further modifications in the student's algorithm are required to indicate whether or not the printed value of Count (box 6) represents a "cycle."

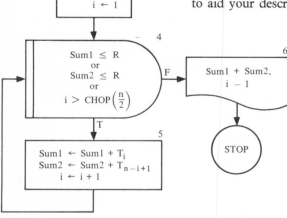

4. With the aid of a while box draw a flowchart that describes the following process. Given a list of integers $(T_i, i = 1(1)n)$, scan the list, element by element, from $T_n, T_{n-1}, \ldots$, summing the integers encountered until the sum thus developed exceeds a given value R. (If the sum never exceeds R in the process then the entire list should be summed.) Print out the index of the last element included in the sum.

5. Describe in simple terms, in English, what execution of the following flowchart accomplishes. You may use a diagram, say, of the list T to aid your description.

1. You are given a flowchart and an input data sequence. Your job is to determine what values will be output.

Input data sequence: 7, 1, 2, 3, 4, 5, 6, 7, 8, 9.

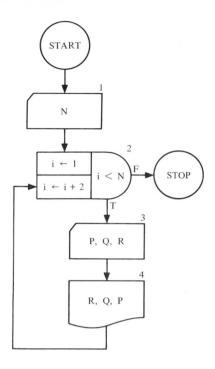

2. Given the following flowchart and input data sequence, what values will be output?

Input data sequence: 8, 1, 9, 8, 2, 3, 7, 6, 4.

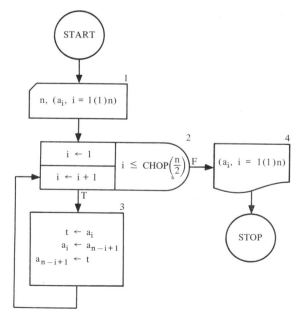

3. Consider two lists p and q each of length n relating to an inventory of n types of commodities. Elements of the p list contain *unit prices* (i.e., p_i is the unit price of the ith commodity). Elements of the q list contain *quantities* (i.e., q_i is the number of units of the ith commodity on hand). The value of the entire inventory is

$$Value = \sum_{i=1}^{n} p_i \times q_i = p_1 \times q_1 + p_2 \times q_2 + \ldots + p_n \times q_n$$

Which of the flowchart fragments given below is equivalent to the above statement?

(a)

(b)

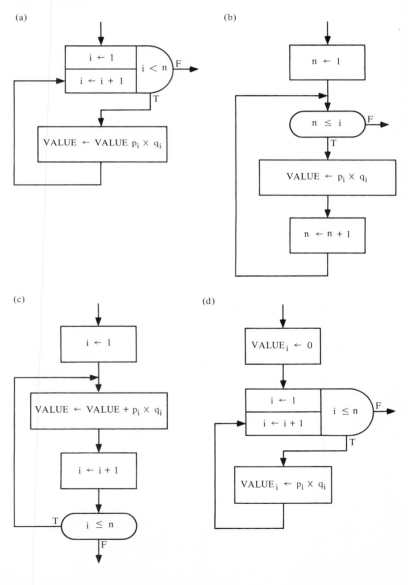

(c)

(d)

(e)

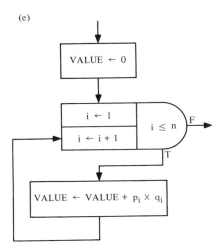

4. Revise the flowchart shown below so that an iteration box governs the loop that is controlled by the counter K.

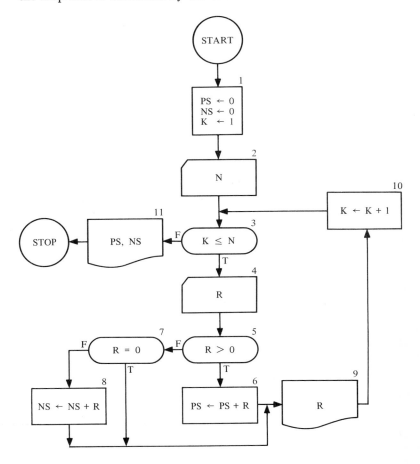

5. Draw a flowchart fragment that:

(a) Assumes the variable n and the list $(a_i, i = 1(1)n)$ have already been assigned values.

(b) Prints out the message "YES" if all the elements $(a_i, i = 1(1)n)$ are equal, and prints "NO" otherwise. Use an iteration box in your flowchart.

6. Shown below are two flowchart sequences in which the contents of the two clouds are assumed to be identical. Under what circumstances will these two flowcharts fail to be equivalent?

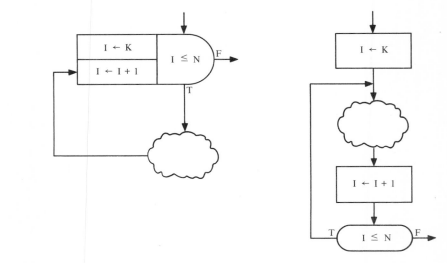

7. Using some form of loop control box, write a complete algorithm that does all the following.

(a) Inputs M numerical values for a list VEC. (These input values are already arranged in nonascending numerical order.)

(b) Searches, beginning at VEC_1, for a pair of duplicate values.

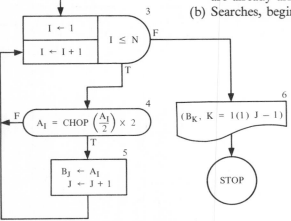

FIGURE 4·13

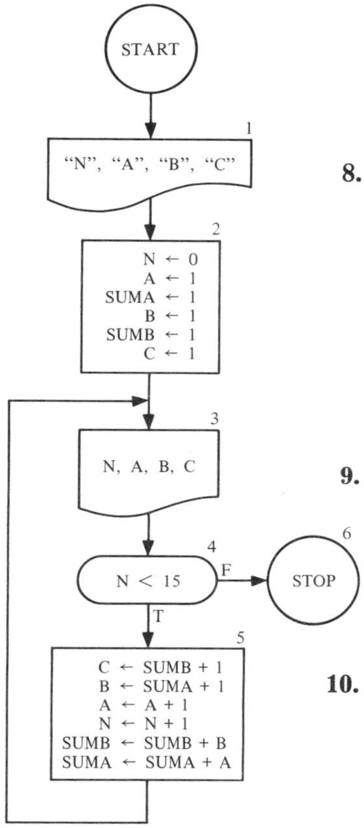
START
1
"N", "A", "B", "C"
2
N ← 0
A ← 1
SUMA ← 1
B ← 1
SUMB ← 1
C ← 1
3
N, A, B, C
4
N < 15
F
T
6
STOP
5
C ← SUMB + 1
B ← SUMA + 1
A ← A + 1
N ← N + 1
SUMB ← SUMB + B
SUMA ← SUMA + A

FIGURE 4·14

(c) If a pair of duplicate values is found, prints out the duplicated value and the index value of the first element of the duplicate pair and stops.
(d) If no pair of duplicates is found, prints out an appropriate message and stops.

8. You are given a flowchart in Figure 4·13.

(a) What, in simple terms, does this algorithm do? Give a clear description.
(b) Suppose the following six input values are assigned to the A list at box 1.

3, − 4, 6, 6, 7, 12

What values, if any, will be printed when box 6 is executed?

9. Study the flowchart in Figure 4·14 and answer the following questions.

(a) Show what is printed on the first five lines of the output from this algorithm.
(b) Redraw this flowchart using an iteration box.

10. A toy distributor has purchased 10,000 small toys packaged in rectangular boxes of varying size. He intends to put the boxes into plastic spheres and resell them as surprise packages. However, he needs to know how many spheres of each diameter (4, 6, 8, 10, and 12 inches) he will need. Since the diagonal

$$D = \sqrt{A^2 + B^2 + C^2}$$

of a rectangular box having sides A, B, and C is its largest measurement, the distributor needs to calculate the diagonal lengths of the boxes. Then he must determine the number of boxes whose diagonals are 4 inches or less, the number whose diagonals are between 4 and 6 inches, and so on. The distributor decides to calculate D for each of the 10,000 boxes. Each box has an identification number, ID, and a set of measurements A, B, and C. Your job is to draw a flowchart to produce a printed table, each line having five entries, that is, the input values (ID, A, B, and C), and the computed value, D. Each line of the printed table is to correspond to one packaged toy. Use an iteration box. Only four flowchart boxes are needed—not counting START and STOP boxes.

11. This is an extension of Problem 10. Assume the toy distributor realizes there is an easier way to tally the required number of plastic spheres of each diameter than to scan the 10,000-line computer-produced table by eye. Modify the flowchart prepared in Problem 10 so that instead of printing the long table, the algorithm tallies the number of spheres of each size needed, and prints these tallies after processing the 10,000 data sets.

12. In Figure 4·8a we studied a way to generate the terms of the Fibonacci sequence. Now you are to flowchart a related algorithm; generate both the Fibonacci sequence and its sum sequence. Let F_J be the Jth term of the Fibonacci sequence. Thus, F_3 is 2, F_4 is 3, F_5 is 5, and so forth. Let S_J be the sum of all terms of the Fibonacci sequence up to and including the Jth term. Thus

$$S_5 = 1 + 1 + 2 + 3 + 5 = 12$$
$$S_6 = 1 + 1 + 2 + 3 + 5 + 8 = 20, \text{ etc.}$$

Each term of the S sequence is a cumulative sum. Your flowchart should generate pairs of values of these two sequences and print the pairs as they are generated. The first pair to be printed is F_3, S_1, the second is F_4, S_2, and so forth. The algorithm should terminate after printing 60 such pairs.

As an added challenge, see if you can construct the flowchart without using subscripts.

13. Recall Figure 3·26b, which was an algorithm for computing the points won or lost in one spin of the carnival wheel (i.e., for one data pair s and m). This algorithm allowed us to have an arbitrary point rule by input of four values into list elements p_1, p_2, p_3, p_4.

Now suppose we are interested in determining our score after a large number of spins, say N. To represent the first spin, an arbitrarily chosen data pair s, m is needed. Each successive spin can be represented by another value of m. For the moment we won't concern ourselves with where these data values come from. Your job is to revise the flowchart in Figure 3·26b so that it now does the following:

(a) Inputs values of p_i for a 4-point rule.
(b) Determines a point value for each of N spins, given a value for s, and N successive values for m and, instead of printing these values, forms their sum (in SUM).
(c) After the N spins have been "processed," prints N and SUM using appropriate literals to explain the significance of the values that are printed. For example, "After 35 spins your score is 552 points."

EXERCISES 4·1, SET C

1. Construct a flowchart to calculate and output a table of four columns. The first column is to contain the integers from 1 to 100. The second column is to contain the squares of the corresponding integers in the first column. The third and fourth columns are to contain the cubes and fourth powers of the integers in the first column. For example, the second line of output should be

2   4   8   16

In Problems 2, 3, and 4 you are given a flowchart fragment on the left panel that exhibits a counter-controlled loop. On the right panel are several alternative flowchart fragments that include the use of iteration boxes, presumably to achieve the same net effect. At most, one of the alternatives is equivalent to the diagram on the left panel.

You are asked to select the one (if any) that does in fact achieve the same net effect.

2.

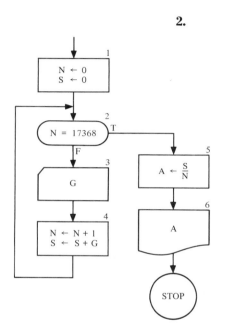

Alternative a

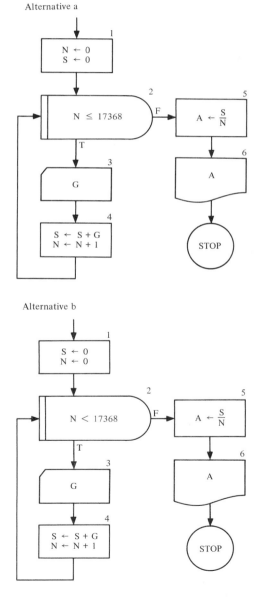

3. (See the directions preceding Problem 2.)

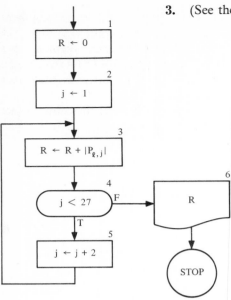

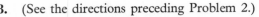

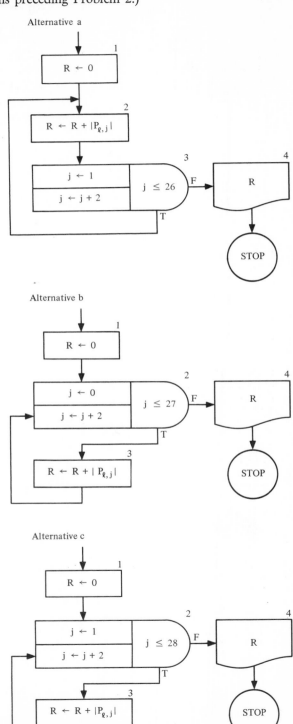

4. (See the directions preceding Problem 2.)

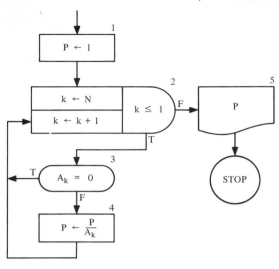

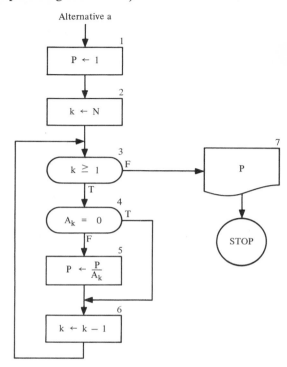

Alternative a

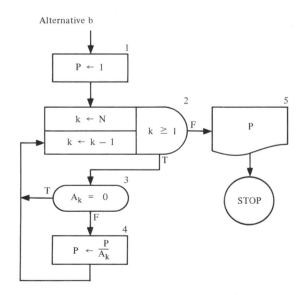

Alternative b

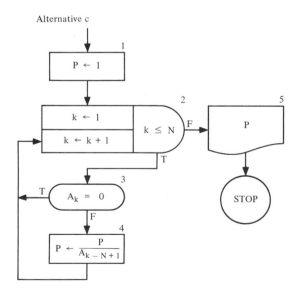

Alternative c

> In Problems 5 to 11 you have in storage two lists of N numbers each. One list is called P, the other Q. For each problem in this set your job is to convert the word statement to an equivalent partial flowchart. You should find the iteration box helpful. You may wish first to flowchart the computation part of the loop, then hang it from the proper iteration box and, finally, precede the iteration box, if appropriate, by an initializing box.

5. Think of the Ith value of P and the Ith value of Q as the pair P_I, Q_I. Interchange the values in every such pair.

6. Modify the flowchart drawn for Problem 5 so that only even-indexed pairs are interchanged. Does it matter whether N is even or odd?

7. Modify the flowchart drawn for Problem 5, assuming you wished to interchange only every third pair of values beginning with the fifth pair.

8. Move the first CHOP(N / 2) elements of the list P to the list Q. See picture (Figure 4·15).

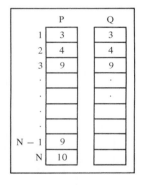

FIGURE 4·15
Moving elements of a list.

(a) Picture of storage before move.

(b) Picture of storage after move.

9. Move the last CHOP(N / 2) elements of the list P to the first CHOP(N / 2) positions of list Q. Assume N is even. *Hint.* What is the index of the first element of P that is to be moved?

10. Same as Problem 9—but don't assume N is even.

11. Let each of the last K elements of the N-element list P be "shifted" or moved two positions in storage to make room for the later insertion of two new values at positions N − K + 1 and N − K + 2 (see Figure 4·16).

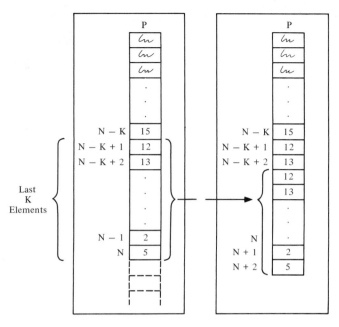

FIGURE 4·16
Shifting elements of a list.

(a) Picture of storage
before move.

(b) Picture of storage
after move.

12. You have already stored 100 input values for elements P_1, P_2, . . . , P_{100}.

(a) Form the sum of their cubes (in SUMCUB).
(b) Form the sum of the negative values (in SUMNEG).
(c) Form the sums SUMCUB, SUMNEG, and SUMBIG (where SUMBIG is the sum of the absolute values greater than 50.)

13. This question refers to the flowchart on the next page.

Suppose the sequence of data values available is

2, 3, 1, 2, 3, 3, 4, 8, 6, 5, 4, 0

Trace through the flowchart and answer the following questions. (Remember to match input values carefully with variables in the flowchart.)

(a) When the *false* exit is taken from box 7 for the first time, what are the current values of N and S?
(b) For the given data how many times will box 8 be executed?
(c) For the given data how many times will box 9 be executed?
(d) What value will be printed when box 4 is executed?

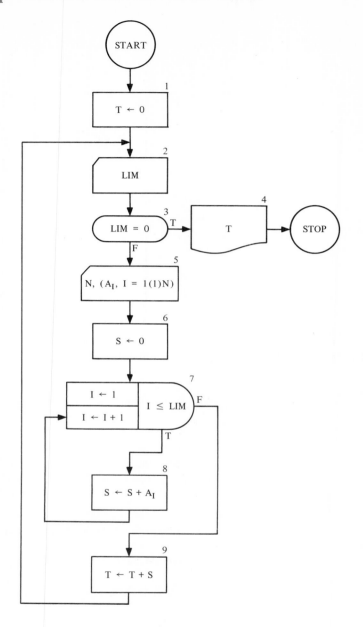

14. Trace the flowchart on the next page with the accompanying input data sequence and answer questions a through d.

    Input data: 6, 17.4, 13.2, 18.7, − 9.7, 2.4, 3.9, 3.9, 2.4, 3.3, 3.3, 9.1, 9.2.

    (a) How many times is box 5 executed?
    (b) How many times is box 4 executed?

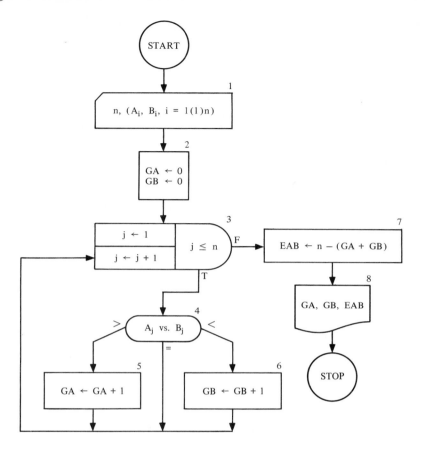

(c) If box 3 were replaced by

what values would be printed when box 8 is executed?

(d) If box 1 were replaced by

and if box 3 were replaced by

and if box 4 were replaced by

what would be the change, if any, in the values printed when box 8 is executed?

15. Shown below is an incomplete flowchart for an algorithm that reads N and a list A of length N, none of whose elements is zero. If A_1 is greater than A_2, but A_{N-1} and A_N have different signs, then the algorithm prints the sum of all the elements of A and stops. Otherwise, the algorithm prints the product of all the elements of A and stops.

(a) Complete the flowchart by specifying the contents of boxes 3, 10, and 11.

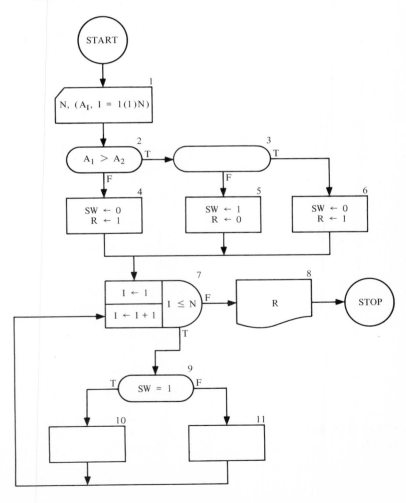

(b) Select the most meaningful of the five given responses to the following.

   This algorithm could be rewritten so that the variable SW need not be tested N times (at box 9). This revision can be accomplished by (choose one):

(1) Replacing the iteration box with an equivalent sequence of initialization, test, and incrementation boxes.
(2) Combining boxes 2 and 3 into a single box to eliminate the *true* exit from box 3.
(3) Using two iteration boxes, one for a sum-forming loop and one for a product-forming loop and directing flow to the appropriate loop after correctly setting the initial value of R in boxes 4, 5, or 6.
(4) Removing box 10 and altering box 7 to read

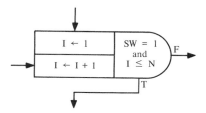

(5) None of the above.

> In each of the following three exercises, remember to use *while* boxes where they seem appropriate, and assume there are N values currently assigned to the list P in storage.

16. Search the list in the forward direction, that is, P_1, P_2, P_3, and so forth, for the first value greater than 50 in absolute value, assigning this value to W and 1 to ANY. If no such value is found, assign 0 to ANY. In either case, now proceed to the same point in the flowchart.

17. Search the list in the backward direction, that is, P_N, P_{N-1}, P_{N-2}, and so forth, for the first value greater than 50 in absolute value, assigning this value to W. If no such value is found, assign 50 to W. In either case, now proceed to a common point in the flowchart.

18. Search the N elements of the P list for the nonzero element of largest absolute value less than $|M|$. Assume the value of M has already been stored. Assign the value of the list element found in this search to T. If no such value is found, print the message "NONE" and stop.

EXERCISES 4·1, SET D

*1. Develop an algorithm to test the first 500 integers and output only those that are *perfect*. A perfect number is one that is equal to the

* *Note.* An interesting article on perfect numbers appeared in the Mathematical Games section of the *Scientific American, 218* (3), pp. 121–126 (March 1968).

sum of all its factors. The smallest perfect number is $6 = 1 + 2 + 3$. (By definition, the number 1 is excluded from the perfect numbers.)

2. Given a list X of N values, that is, $X_1, X_2, \ldots, X_N$, and given a value of A:

   (a) Draw a flowchart for the computation of NUM defined mathematically as an N-term product:

   $$NUM = (X_1 - A) \times (X_2 - A) \times (X_3 - A) \times \ldots \times (X_N - A)$$

   Show input and output of all required data and results.

   (b) Same as part a except that NUM has the Kth term of the N terms omitted.

3. Study the two flowcharts given in Figure 4·17 to evaluate polynomials of 3rd degree and answer the following questions.

   (a) Are the two flowcharts equivalent in net effect? Explain.
   (b) What changes are needed in each flowchart to permit the evaluation of polynomials of any degree, N?
   (c) Which flowchart is more efficient (fewest computations)? Explain.

4. In Problem 13, Exercise 4·1, Set B, you were asked to spin the carnival wheel N times. Here we wish to develop more seriously the concept of simulating the play of a game for the purpose of predicting, with the aid of a computer, something about its outcome. It is a "spinning wheel game." Imagine you are given as input a value for s, the starting position, and an inexhaustible supply of values for the spin span, m.

   These data are somehow representative of what a person might actually experience if he were to take repeated turns at spinning the wheel with no other player intervening. We will say that a "game" consists of a series of spins for a given player and terminates whenever the absolute value of his score, |SUM|, exceeds some given critical value, CV. We will say that the "length" of the game is the number of spins in the series. The question we really want to ask is, "How many turns 'on the average' can a player be 'expected' to take before $CV \leq |SUM|$ is true?"

   In this exercise you are preparing the groundwork to answer the question later. Your job now is to draw a flowchart that simulates one complete game. Below are some guidelines—to be consulted only after you have experimented with a plan of your own.

   (a) As before, first input the four values constituting the "point rule" to be used.
   (b) Next input a value for CV, the critical value.
   (c) Then input a value of s and a series of values of m.
   (d) After each value of m is input, the new value for the net winnings (SUM) is computed and a counter L of the number of spins is updated.

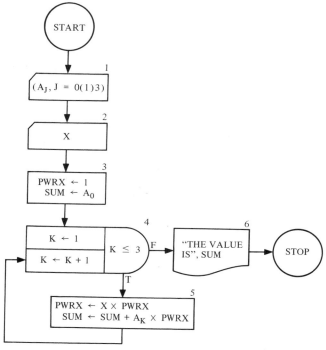

(*a*) Evaluation of polynomial, everyday method.

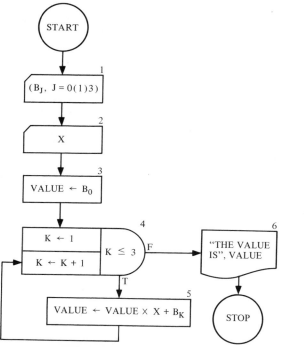

FIGURE 4·17 (*b*) Evaluation of polynomial, Sunday method.

(e) Whenever the absolute value of SUM exceeds CV, we print the values of L, CV, and SUM and then stop.

(f) For insurance against an endless loop, we print out an error message and stop if L ever exceeds 1000. Remember to use an iteration box where you think it can help to keep the flowchart simple in structure.

5. To simulate an actual game such as that in the preceding problem, an element of chance must somehow be introduced. For example, the data value for s and the series of values for m should be selected at random.

(a) Investigate how random numbers may be generated. You might ask your instructor for a literature reference on random numbers. If available, see for example Section 9·8, "Random Number Generators," in Dorn and Greenberg, *Mathematics and Computing*, pp. 474–484 (Wiley, 1967).

(b) Show how you would modify the structure of the algorithm so that the data values are generated as pseudo random numbers within the algorithm instead of being supplied as input data.

(c) Consider how you would develop an answer to the question raised in the preceding exercise, that is, how many turns on the average can a player be expected to take before his score reaches a critical value?

EXERCISES 4·1,
SET E

Problem Set on Intersection, Union, and Merge. Here we focus on a group of operations that are of fundamental importance in the real world of information processing (on or off the computer). In each of the following four problems, A is an m-element list of numbers and B is an n-element list of numbers. Moreover, *values in each list are already sorted in numerically ascending order.* Algorithms for intersection, union, and merge have certain structural similarities. The descriptive flowchart given below will be helpful as a guide in detailing the flowcharts for each of the next four problems.

1. *Intersection.* Given the two lists A and B, develop a detailed flowchart algorithm that forms a new list Int whose elements comprise the *inter-*

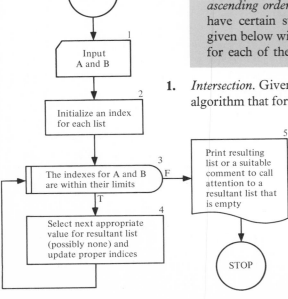

section of the sets defined by A and B. We assume here that no duplicate values occur within either list. By *intersection* we mean that Int is to contain copies of those values that are *common* to both A and B. Values placed in Int should be in ascending numerical order. Note that the maximum number of components that can occur in the intersection list Int is limited to the minimum of m and n, the dimensions of A and B, respectively.

2. *Union.* Given the two lists A and B, develop a flowchart algorithm that forms a new list U whose elements comprise the *union* of the sets defined by A and B. We assume here that no duplicate values occur within either list. By *union,* of course, we mean that U is to contain one copy of each distinct value found in the course of scanning all of A and all of B. Values placed in U should be in ascending numerical order. Note that the union U will contain at most m + n elements.

3. *Merge.* Given the two sorted lists A and B, develop a flowchart algorithm that forms a new list W composed of the combined values, still sorted, of A and B. Thus, if

$$A = \{1, 2, 4, 5, 10\}$$
and
$$B = \{2, 6, 10, 12\}$$
then
$$W = \{1, 2, 2, 4, 5, 6, 10, 10, 12\}$$

(a) In your first approach assume that no duplicates occur within either list.
(b) Now decide what changes, if any, are required for consideration of the case where duplicate values may occur within A and/or B.

4. *Union and Intersection at the Same Time.* In cases where we want both the union U and the intersection Int for the same list pair A,B, certain economy can be gained by combining parts of the algorithms for Problems 1 and 2 to form a single algorithm that develops both U and Int while making one scan of A and B. Develop the detailed flowchart for this double-purpose algorithm.

4·2 Table lookup

Now we begin an algorithmic investigation into the subject of table lookup, the looking up of values of a tabulated function, as when we "go to the tables" to find the value of sin (.3217) or of $\sqrt{147.62}$.

Example 1. Table lookup by matching

Suppose we have a function, F, and as in common mathematical notation, we write

$$Y = F(X)$$

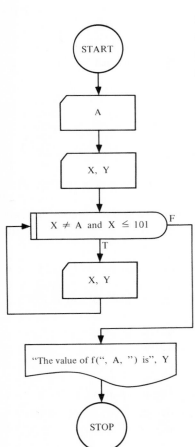

The function can be defined by a set of values punched on a stack of cards, where each card is punched with a value of the variable X and the corresponding value of Y. The box on the left panel means that each card represents an ordered pair of numbers (X,Y), related by Y = F(X). No two cards then can have the same value of X punched on them unless the values of Y are also the same. This is what is meant by saying that "Y is a function of X." The stack of cards can be regarded as a table of values of the function, F. (Let us place a card at the end of the stack containing "far out" values of X and Y to act as a sentinel.)

To look up the functional value of a certain number A, one method is to go through the cards comparing this number with the value of X on each card and, when equality is found, to print the corresponding value of Y. Figure 4·18 is a flowchart for this process.

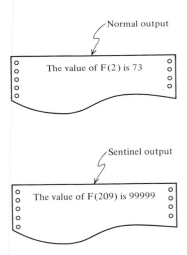

FIGURE 4·18
Primitive table lookup.

Now, instead of using the table on cards, suppose we want to read the data into storage before using it. To execute the input steps that read a whole table into storage, list variables will be needed, so now we suppose we have a stack of cards with value pairs, X_K, Y_K, punched on each, and with X_K and Y_K satisfying

$$Y_K = F(X_K), \text{ for K from 1 to N}$$

Notice that the subscript changes each time a card is read, so data from different cards go into different compartments of the storage boxes. If 1000 cards are to be read, then two storage boxes, each with 1000 compartments, must be made available to receive the data.

Once the table has been read in, the value of A is input for which F(A) is sought. The value of A is compared with each of the X_i until an equality condition is found. At this point the value of F(A), which is equal to Y_i, is printed out. The flowchart is seen in Figure 4·19.

Note that we could have drawn the Figure 4·19 algorithm to loop back for more values of A instead of stopping.

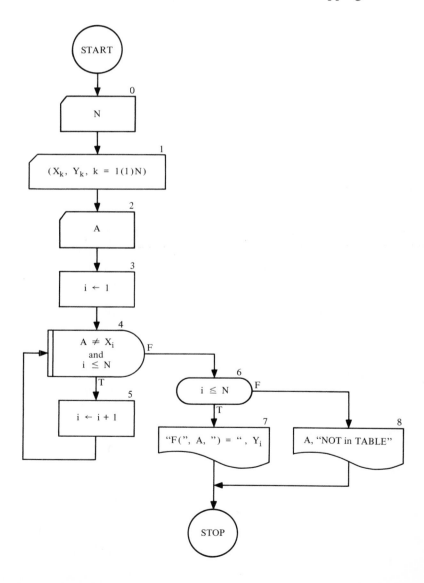

FIGURE 4·19
Lookup from an internally
stored table.

1. (a) You are given an ordered table of values of X and sin X. Your job is to construct a flowchart to: (1) read these values into the computer, (2) then read a value of A that may or may not match some value of X in the table, and then (3) print the corresponding value of sin X if possible. If A does not match any value of X in the table, print a suitable message in the case that A is outside the domain covered by the table but, if A is between two values of X, print the two bracketing values of X and the corresponding values of sin X. *Hint.* Figure 4·20a should help you.

(b) Study Figure 4·20b and then expand your flowchart to include a computation of Y_{INT}, the linear interpolation of sin A from the bracketing values of sin X that are found in the table.

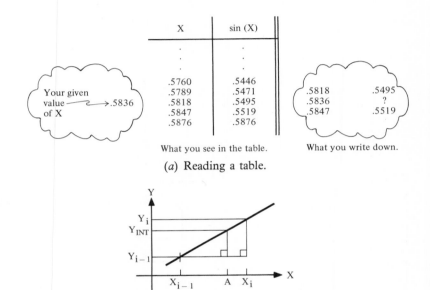

(*a*) Reading a table.

(*b*) Illustration of straight-line interpolation.

FIGURE 4·20

Example 2.
Table lookup:
Bisection method

And now we ask the familiar question: Can we improve on the algorithm of Figure 4·19? Let's compare the algorithm with what we do in real life when dealing with tables whose entries are *ordered*. In the algorithm we took a value of A and started at the beginning of the table and compared with each entry. Is this what we would really do? Take the analogy of a telephone book where the entries are ordered alphabetically. We want to find the number of Tom Spumoni. Do we start at the beginning and compare Spumoni with each entry? Certainly not! We probably split the book in the middle and check to see which "half" the name is in. Then we split that "half" and so on. Just as this is a faster way for us to look things up, so it is for a computer.

Figure 4·21 flowcharts an improved algorithm based on the telephone book lookup. We use two auxiliary variables, LOW and HIGH, to indicate the lower and upper indices of the part of the table that we are currently searching.

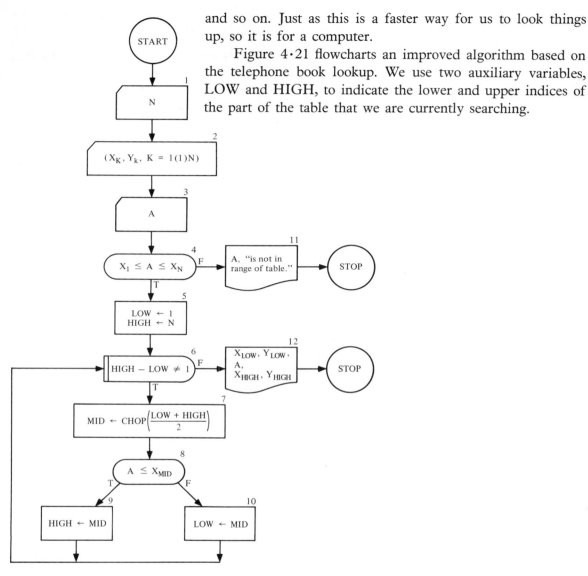

FIGURE 4·21
Bisection Table Lookup with ordered data.

On each loop transit the midpoint of LOW and HIGH is found in box 7. Then a test is made in box 8 to see whether $A \leq X_{MID}$. If so, MID becomes the new HIGH (box 9) and, if not, MID becomes the new LOW (box 10). Box 4 determines at the outset whether A is in the range of the table. Box 6 is the stopping mechanism. When HIGH − LOW = 1, we know that A is bracketed between two table entries with consecutive subscripts, that is

$$X_{LOW} \leq A \leq X_{HIGH}$$

The computation portion of the loop (boxes 6 to 10) exhibits the "bisection technique." Study this computation until you are sure you understand it. The idea occurs over and over

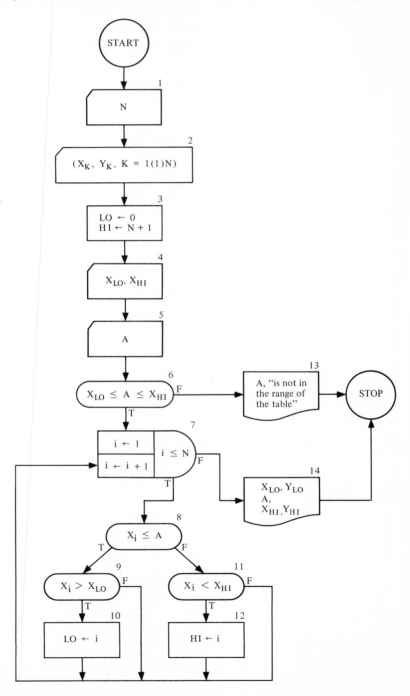

FIGURE 4·22
Lookup in an unsorted table.

again in computing and often represents maximum efficiency. Bisection will be seen again in Chapter 12.

It is interesting to compare the efficiency of the algorithms in Figures 4·19 and 4·21. The loop of Figure 4·19 (boxes 4 and 5) will be passed through $N/2$ times, on the average. The loop in Figure 4·21 will be executed a number of times equal to or one less than the number of digits required to express N in the binary system. For example, if N is 1,000,000, Figure 4·21 requires 19 or 20 transits, since $2^{19} < 10^6 < 2^{20}$, while Figure 4·19 requires 500,000 transits, on the average.

EXERCISES 4·2,
SET B

1. Add to the algorithm in Figure 4·21 the feature that if an exact match is found, a message such as

   "F(24.2) is 39.25 on the nose"

   is printed.

   Your job in this exercise is to redraw Figure 4·21, or whatever portion is necessary, with the "on-the-nose" feature added.

2. We are given an *unsorted* table of values $(X_K, Y_K, K = 1(1)N)$. Among the values of X, the minimum value and maximum value of X are known and given. We want to do many lookups in this table. Two options are open: (i) sort the table first and then do the bisection lookups or (ii) develop a new flowchart for searches of the unsorted table. Figure 4·22 is one solution to the second alternative. Here the known minimum and maximum values of X are input in box 4.

   Study Figure 4·22 and answer the following questions.

   (a) Is option i or ii better for a table with a small number of entries? Which is better for a large table?
   (b) Suppose A is equal to X_{LO}, that is, A equals the given minimum value of X. Under what circumstances will the *true* exit be taken from box 8 the first time box 8 is executed?
   (c) Someone paraphrased the action of Figure 4·22 by saying it "clamps a vice" on the value of A. Explain why you agree or disagree with this comment.
   (d) How many entries of the table must be tested before we know we have found the closest values in the table?

4·3
Double subscripts

Once you have mastered the use of subscripted variables in computing, you will find that double subscripts offer very little additional difficulty.

In mathematics, data are often presented in a *rectangular*

array or matrix of rows and columns, as illustrated in Figure 4·23*a*.

	5	2	7	1
	9	−4	0	2
	6	7	3	−2

Row \ Column	1	2	3	4
1	5	2	7	1
2	9	−4	0	2
3	6	7	3	−2

FIGURE 4·23

(*a*) Matrix.   (*b*) The matrix as a table.

One way in which such a matrix might occur is as the "coefficient matrix" of a system of equations.

$$5W + 2X + 7Y = 1$$
$$9W - 4X + 0Y = 2$$
$$6W + 7X - 3Y = -2$$

This matrix has three rows and four columns. The individual numbers appearing in the array are called "entries." In Figure 4·23*b* we see that a matrix is essentially a "table." Other types of tables are suggested in Figure 4·24.

Some arrays are nonrectangular as, for instance, the shoe price table in Figure 4·24 where some shoe styles are not made in certain sizes. Unless we qualify the nature of the irregularity we will henceforth assume that the term *array* means rectangular array and is synonymous with *matrix*. (In some later chapters we will be interested in irregular arrays.)

A table is an array in which each column of data may contain a different type of information. For example, a hotel directory may be expressed as a table (Figure 4·24*d*). Each row contains information on one guest. The information is blocked off into three parts, name, hometown, and room number, each part going into a separate column. The thing to note is that the type of information, for example, string, integer, or real, may differ from column to column of a table.

Tables are also useful for storing lists whose elements are ordered not by an index but by information within the elements themselves. Such lists are called *linked lists,* since each element (except the last one) contains a link or pointer that denotes the successor element. For example, the table in Figure 4·24*e* is a linked list of 8 alphabetically ordered names. To see this,

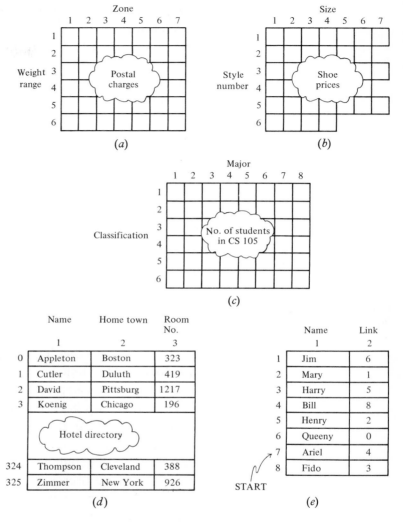

FIGURE 4·24

Examples of arrays and tables.

start at row 7 and proceed from row to row as indicated by the links and write down the names you see. For example, Ariel's link is 4, so go to row 4, giving Bill with its link 8, which locates Fido, and so forth. Extensive use is made of linked lists (also called chains) in many data processing applications. (See Section 10·6, e.g.)

Double subscripts make their appearance when we need notation to talk about entries in a matrix. We use a variable with two subscripts

$$A_{I,J}$$

to indicate the entry in the I row and the J column. *The row is always given first and the column second.* Thus, if we let A represent the matrix tabulated in Figure 4·23b then the value of $A_{2,3}$ is 0 while that of $A_{3,2}$ is 7.

As in the case of singly subscripted variables, we consider that there is a storage box associated with the 12 variables $A_{1,1}$, $A_{1,2}$ and so forth, as suggested in Figure 4·25. If we wish to

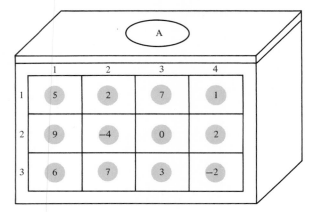

FIGURE 4·25
Storage box for a 3 × 4 matrix.

input a table into this box, we can indicate this action in a flowchart by the input box in Figure 4·26a or Figure 4·26b. These two input statements are simply extensions to matrices of the notation we have already used for lists (see p. 152). It is *essential* that a variable legend accompany the simple statement to input A, as in Figure 4·26a, because the number of elements and the number of dimensions is not otherwise known. Note that because the order in which the elements are to be supplied as input values is not specified in Figure 4·26a, a *standard order* is always assumed for this input notation. The

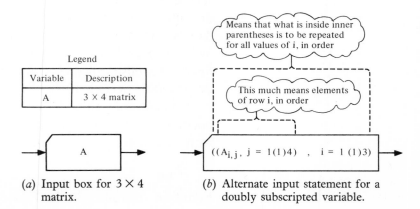

FIGURE 4·26

(a) Input box for 3 × 4 matrix.

(b) Alternate input statement for a doubly subscripted variable.

standard order is row 1, left to right, then row 2, left to right, and so forth.

The alternate notation of Figure 4·26*b* is important because it allows us to specify *subsets* of matrix elements in a particular ordered way. Thus the way the parentheses are used in Figure 4·26*b* indicates that each row is read in completely (left to right) before any of the next row is read.

Example.
Matrix solitaire

Suppose we want to play a game based on the following matrix.

$$
\begin{array}{cccccc}
6 & 2 & 5 & 4 & 3 & 1 \\
9 & 0 & 8 & 3 & 2 & 6 \\
1 & 8 & 5 & 4 & 1 & 1 \\
8 & 3 & 7 & 3 & 6 & 3 \\
5 & 5 & 4 & 8 & 1 & 2 \\
3 & 2 & 1 & 6 & 4 & 8 \\
\end{array}
$$

We have two dice, one red and one chartreuse. We roll the dice and let R denote the number on the *r*ed die and C that on the *c*hartreuse die. The score is initially zero. Now we increase our score by the sum of the entries in the Rth row, and we deduct from our score the sum of the entries in the Cth column. An overall flowchart for one play of the game is shown in Figure 4·27.

An obvious solution specific to the given problem is shown in Figure 4·28. It makes sensible use of double subscripts and leads to a simple program. But it has the great disadvantage of lack of generality, which is not the case with Figure 4·29.

Notice that in principle this game could also be played using larger matrices, say, 8 × 8 or 10 × 10. Of course, for each new size we would need either dice with more faces, such as octahedrons, or some other device for generating pairs of numbers. To generalize Figure 4·29 for any size array we need change only the 6's (where they appear in boxes 1, 4, and 6) to N's and add a box 0 to the flowchart at the start to read in this value of N—which could vary from game to game. Such generalization is not possible with the approach used in Figure 4·28. In short, while producing a shorter program, Figure 4·28 captures less of the spirit of our algorithmic method.

Often the best way to represent a data structure for a particular problem does not occur to us the first time around.

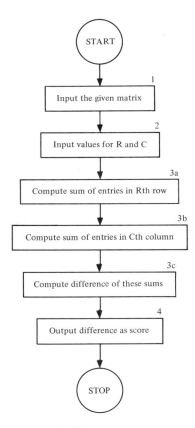

FIGURE 4·27
First flowchart for play of solitaire game.

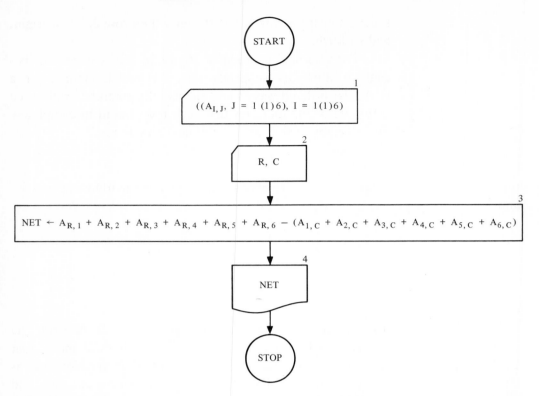

FIGURE 4·28
Less instructive solution for
play of solitaire game.

This is certainly true in the case of our game of matrix solitaire.
Notice that if the matrix remains fixed during all plays of one
game, the complete matrix need not be kept in storage. We
could just as well store only the row sums and the column
sums as two separate lists, if we are willing to compute these
sums in advance as a separate task. Thus, in our example, if
ROWS were assigned the list (21, 28, 20, 30, 25, 24) and if
COLS were assigned the list (32, 20, 30, 28, 19, 21), then boxes
3 to 8 inclusive in Figure 4·29 could be replaced by

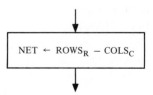

drastically reducing the complexity of this algorithm and the
computation time required.

There is another shorthand notation involving matrices
that we introduce at this point. Suppose we still have the 6×6

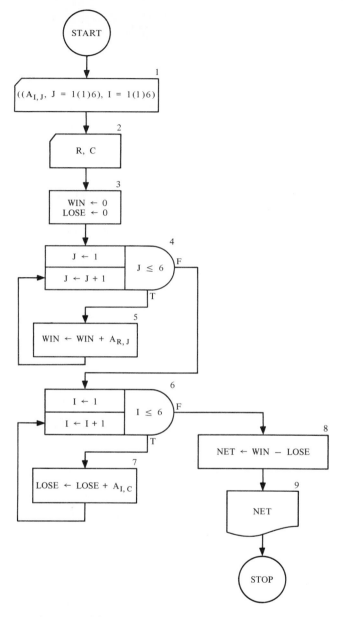

FIGURE 4·29
More instructive solution for
play of solitaire game.

matrix or table P introduced earlier in this section for the
matrix solitaire game.

$$P = \begin{bmatrix} 6 & 2 & 5 & 4 & 3 & 1 \\ 9 & 0 & 8 & 3 & 2 & 6 \\ 1 & 8 & 5 & 4 & 1 & 1 \\ 8 & 3 & 7 & 3 & 6 & 3 \\ 5 & 5 & 4 & 8 & 1 & 2 \\ 3 & 2 & 1 & 6 & 4 & 8 \end{bmatrix}$$

Legend

Variable	Description
P	6 × 6 matrix
A	Six-element list

We would like to assign the elements of the second row of the matrix P to be the six elements of a list A. At present we can do this with the flowchart loop on the left.

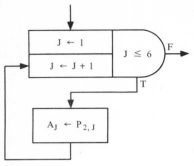

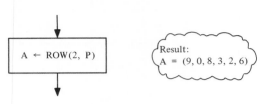

We would, however, like to be able to shorten this representation to the flowchart box on the right. Here the expression "ROW(2, P)" is to be read as, "row 2 of the array called P." Likewise we would like to be able to assign the entire kth column of P to the list A by the flowchart box

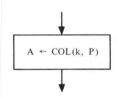

(read "COL(k, P)" as, "column k of the array called P.") If k has the value 6, the following two representations are equivalent.

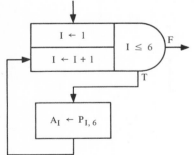

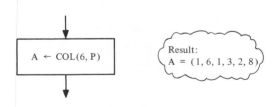

The situation may also be reversed. We may want to assign the values of the list A = (2, 5, 4, 8, 9, 1) to the second row of the matrix P. This will convert P to the following P'.

$$P' = \begin{bmatrix} 6 & 2 & 5 & 4 & 3 & 1 \\ 2 & 5 & 4 & 8 & 9 & 1 \\ 1 & 8 & 5 & 4 & 1 & 1 \\ 8 & 3 & 7 & 3 & 6 & 3 \\ 5 & 5 & 4 & 8 & 1 & 2 \\ 3 & 2 & 1 & 6 & 4 & 8 \end{bmatrix}$$

We can do this at present by the following loop on the left, but

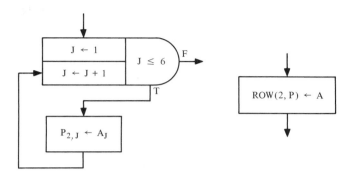

we would also like to be able to use the flowchart box on the right. Let us also agree on the equivalence of the following.

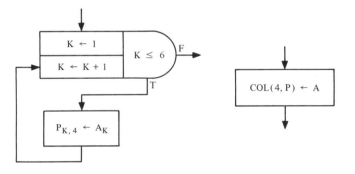

In all four cases the single flowchart box can be considered to be a *higher-level expression* than that of the corresponding loop.

EXERCISES 4·3

1. Trace the flowchart shown on the next page using the following input data values.

3, 0, 7, − 4, 1, − 3,
0, 4, 1, 6, 1, − 4,
0, − 3, 5

(a) What is the first value printed (choose one)?

(1) 5
(2) − 4
(3) 14
(4) 10
(5) 7

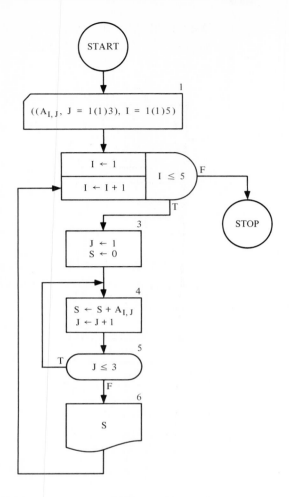

(b) How many values will be printed before the algorithm stops (choose one)?

(1) 3
(2) 5
(3) 15
(4) 1
(5) None of the above

(c) What does this algorithm do (choose one)?

(1) Sums all the elements of the array, A, and prints this sum.
(2) Sums each column of the array and prints these sums.
(3) Sums the diagonal elements of the array and prints this sum.
(4) Sums each row of the array and prints these sums.
(5) None of the above.

2. Assume that the execution of box 1 of the flowchart below results in the following values in the matrix A.

4	2	2	2	7
2	3	6	5	5
5	8	4	5	2
5	2	2	9	3
1	6	5	7	6

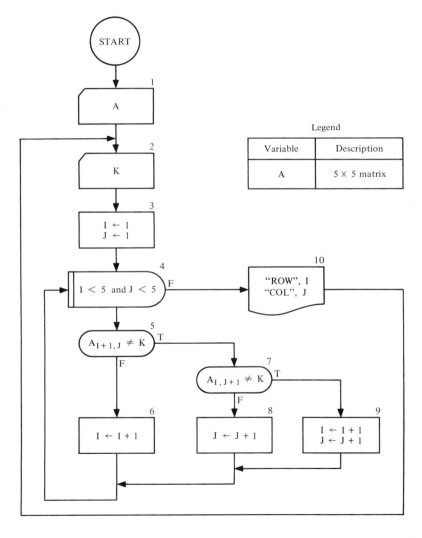

Legend

Variable	Description
A	5 × 5 matrix

(a) Suppose the first execution of box 2 assigns the value 2 to K. Then the result printed at box 10 for that value of K will be

(choose one):
(1) ROW 5 COL 3.
(2) ROW 2 COL 5.
(3) ROW 3 COL 5.
(4) ROW 5 COL 4.
(5) None of the above.

(b) Suppose the second execution of box 2 assigns the value 5 to K. Then the result printed at box 10 for that value of K will be

(1) ROW 5 COL 3.
(2) ROW 5 COL 2.
(3) ROW 4 COL 5.
(4) ROW 2 COL 5.
(5) None of the above.

3. Trace through the flowchart below and determine what values will be output. Assume the data values available for input are: 1, 2, 3, 5, 6, 7, 9, 10, 11.

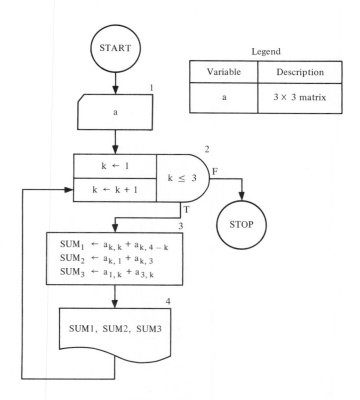

4. Trace through the flowchart on the next page and determine what value will be output.

Data values: 1, 2, 3, 4, 5, 6, 7, 8, 8, 7, 6, 5, 4, 3, 2, 1.

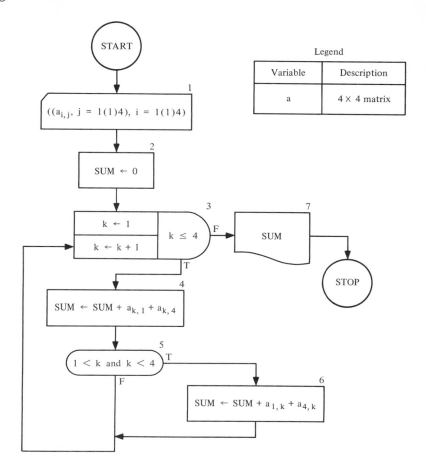

5. Using a 5 row by 25 column array A of single character strings, draw a flowchart to print the block letters C I O as shown below. These block letters are separated by a width of 5 space characters. The input values are simply the characters "C", "I", and "O".

```
C C C C C        I I I I I        O O O O O
C                     I           O         O
C                     I           O         O
C                     I           O         O
C C C C C        I I I I I        O O O O O
```

In each of the following five problems, assume that all the variables or matrix entries mentioned have already been assigned initial values. Your job is to flowchart the action described. (These are elementary operations often performed on matrices. They are usually pieces of larger problems.)

Example The matrix P has 22 rows and 27 columns. Find the sum of the absolute values of all entries in row L, where L has already been assigned a value.

One Solution

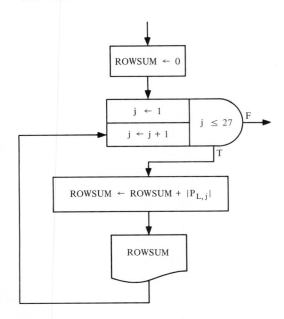

6. For the same matrix P, find the sum of all but one of the entries in the Kth column. The exception is the entry in row 12 of that column. Call the sum being generated COLSUM.

7. For the same matrix P, add to each entry in row L the value of the corresponding entry (same column) of row M. As an actual example with a much smaller matrix Q, we would have:

	Before						After				
	3	4	2	5	−4		3	4	2	5	−4
Row L	3	9	1	2	−4	→	4	10	3	5	−2
Row M	1	1	2	3	2		1	1	2	3	2

8. For the same matrix P, add to each entry in row L, *except in the Kth* entry, two times the corresponding value of the Mth row.

9. For the same matrix P, interchange row L with row M.

10. For the same matrix P, find the entry in row L having the largest magnitude. Divide every entry in row L by the entry of largest magnitude, assuming it exceeds zero.

11. In the text just preceding this set of exercises we discussed conventions for higher-level expressions. For example, where A is a list and

P is a matrix of compatible dimensions, it was agreed that the assignment notation

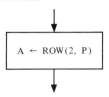

$$A \leftarrow ROW(2, \ P)$$

will mean: assign values of the second row of P to A.

(a) If you have not already done so, simplify your solution to Exercise 9 by employing a higher-level expression.
(b) None of Problems 6, 7, 8 and 10 can be simplified using higher-level expressions without further extension to our flowchart language conventions. Show (define) possible extensions to the flowchart language such that all explicit loops can be eliminated from flowchart solutions for those four exercises. (Some programming languages, among them APL, employ such conventions. You might wish to consult a manual or primer for such a language and compare the conventions you have chosen with those selected in that language. (See *Concepts of Programming Languages,* by Mark Elson, Chicago: Science Research Associates, 1973, 333 pp.)

> In the following two problems assume that all entries of a matrix Q are stored in memory. Q has M rows and N columns. Be sure to use *while* boxes where they seem appropriate.

12. Search the Lth row of Q for the smallest value. Assign this value to SMALL.

13. Search the Rth column backward (i.e., from bottom to top) for the first entry, if any, that is at least as large as the current value of T. Assign the row value for this entry to ROW and the value itself to BIG. If no such value is found, assign the value zero to ROW.

14. Study the flowchart in Figure 4·30, which has the effect of assigning values to certain elements of the array C modeled as the 8 × 8 checkerboard.

(a) What is the *range* in values that can possibly be assigned to k in box 3? Assume that the data value for r can be any five-digit integer. All data are to be integers.
(b) If 3 is the value computed for k in box 3, what values will be assigned for s during the repeated execution of box 7?
(c) Place in the squares of C the values that are assigned to the corresponding array elements as a result of executing the flowchart, using the given set of data.
(d) Is there any chess piece that you know of that could move from (u,v) to the positions into which values have been placed in one move? If so, which one?

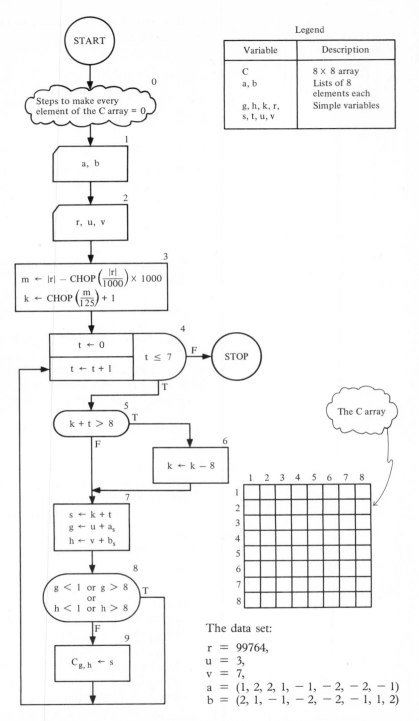

Legend	
Variable	Description
C	8 × 8 array
a, b	Lists of 8 elements each
g, h, k, r, s, t, u, v	Simple variables

The data set:

r = 99764,
u = 3,
v = 7,
a = (1, 2, 2, 1, − 1, − 2, − 2, − 1)
b = (2, 1, − 1, − 2, − 2, − 1, 1, 2)

FIGURE 4·30

15. Consider the flowchart fragment given below consisting of boxes 11 through 16 as one single, two-way decision step, leading either to the execution of box 20 or to the execution of box 30. Which of

the following sentences correctly expresses in a verbal form the essense of that single decision step?

(a) If the largest value in the matrix MAT is less than r, then execute box 20; otherwise execute box 30.
(b) If the largest value in column k of the matrix is less than item r, then execute box 30; otherwise execute box 20.
(c) If, after searching columns m through n inclusive along row k of the matrix MAT, one finds a value that is less than r, then execute box 20; otherwise execute box 30.
(d) If the largest value in the set $(MAT_{k,j}, j = m(1)n)$ is less than r, then execute box 20; otherwise execute box 30.
(e) None of the above.

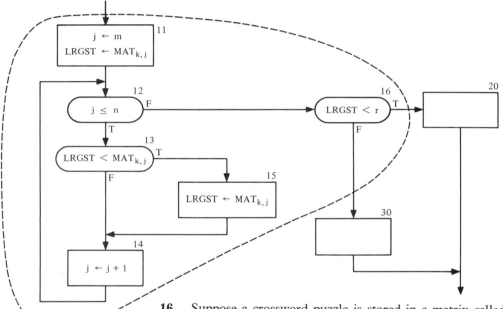

16. Suppose a crossword puzzle is stored in a matrix called CWP, each element of the puzzle being a single character or a blank (which represents a black square). The following is a matrix representation of one possible puzzle. Here, a 9×9 matrix was required.

	1	2	3	4	5	6	7	8	9
1		P	U	P		A	B	E	
2	F		P	L	A	C	E		L
3	O	N		A	R	T		C	O
4	R	E		N	E	O		R	A
5	M	E	R	E		R	O	A	N
6	I	D	E	S		S		N	E
7	N	Y	E	·	A		H	E	R
8	S		L	A	T	H	E		S
9		A	S	S		O	N	E	

Boxes 3 through 9 of the accompanying flowchart represent the steps required to probe (interrogate) the puzzle to determine whether a "horizontal" word beginning at row r in column c has a first letter matching the (single) character value of the input variable ch. Some boxes of the flowchart are incomplete.

Study the flowchart below and determine whether assertions a through d are true or false.

(a) The flowchart boxes 1 and 2 are to input, respectively, the completed crossword puzzle and the data that identify the probe.

(b) Box 3 checks the validity of the column value, c, but there is no corresponding check for the validity of the row value r.

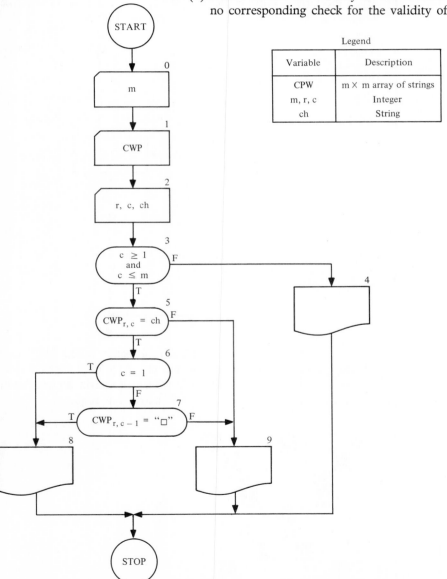

Legend

Variable	Description
CPW	m × m array of strings
m, r, c	Integer
ch	String

(c) Assume that the given puzzle has been input at box 1. Furthermore, assume that the data values 3, 5, "R" have been input at box 2. The flow of control will eventually reach box 8.

(d) If the algorithm is to be modified so it can be used for a probe for vertical words starting with the letter value of ch, the following change would be sufficient.

replace box 5 with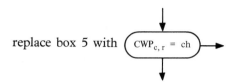

17. Assume that values for an $N \times N$ matrix P have already been assigned in storage. Draw a flowchart fragment (don't worry about input or output) to carry out each of the steps described below (in order).

Step 1 Replace each element of the main diagonal of P (from the upper left to lower right corners) by the square of its value.

Step 2 Add the largest element of the first row to each element of the last row, letting the results become new values of the last row.

Example

1 4 2		1 4 2	
3 9 5	becomes	3 9 5	in Step 2
3 4 25		7 8 29	

because 4 is added to each element of the last row. Your algorithm must, of course, determine the value of the largest first-row element before the addition can be done.

Chapter 5

Stepwise decomposition

In this chapter we continue to concentrate on how to think about complex algorithms in more and more simple terms. The while and iteration boxes helped us to get started. Here we will exploit further these loop control boxes for cases in which looping occurs not only in different parts of the same flowchart, but also in the same part when the loops are nested within one another. In addition we will examine ways of decomposing the complex steps of an algorithm into successively simpler and more elementary constituents. We will do this with the aid of a new notational device (flowchart entity) called the *procedure*. Finally we will examine stepwise decomposition as a *discipline* that increases the clarity and correctness of algorithms, thus raising the quality and economic value of the algorithms we construct.

5·1
Nested loops

The term "nested loop" refers to algorithms that have, like the silhouette shown in Figure 5·1, a loop within a loop. In this silhouette, boxes 10 and 11 form a loop *inside* the loop controlled by box 6.

You have already seen numerous examples of nested loops of a somewhat trivial kind in which the "return" on the "outer" loop merely involved coming back for more data. It is quite possible to construct valid algorithms containing nested loops without being conscious of the existence of this nesting. But when both the inner and outer loops are controlled by while or iteration boxes, we more easily observe that the inner loop is simply a component (part or all) of the computation portion of the outer loop.

A simple illustration of nested loops is the solution to the following problem. You will recognize this problem as a type often encountered in algebra courses (and puzzle books).

Stickler Find all the numbers in the range 000 through 999 that are equal to the sum of the cubes of their digits.

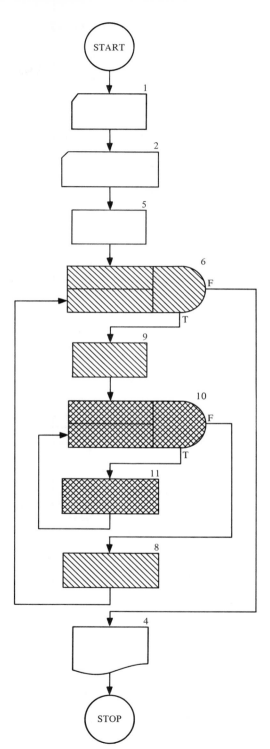

FIGURE 5·1
Silhouette of a nested loop.

This problem emphasizes the power of a computer because, although possible, it appears to be extremely tedious to solve by hand calculation. However, it is a trivial problem for a computer, and the algorithm is surprisingly easy to write.

If we represent the digits of the number by H, T, and U, then the problem is to find and print out all the triples of digits (H, T, U) that satisfy the condition

$$100 \times H + 10 \times T + U = H^3 + T^3 + U^3$$

This is, in fact, the only computation performed in this algorithm. The rest of the program merely makes the proper values of H, T, and U available for this test. The process of producing these values involves nested loops. When a value is assigned to H in Figure 5·2, we then let T "run through" the digits from 0 to 9 and, when values are assigned to both

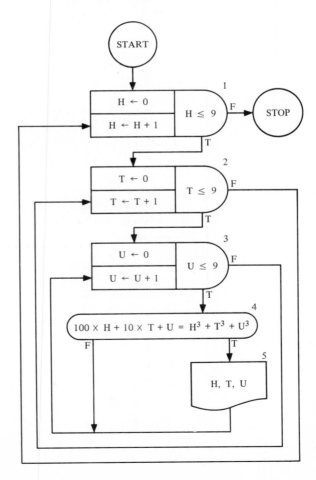

FIGURE 5·2
Flowchart for the stickler.

H and T, we then let U "run through" the digits from 0 to 9. This process of counting resembles the odometer on a car, where we consider each rotating wheel of the odometer as a variable and the value displayed as the value of that variable.

The stickler does not require any ingenuity—merely brute force. The 1000 computations required in the algorithm would probably take all day by hand, but a fast computer would complete the calculation in less than a second.

EXERCISES 5·1, SET A

Reexamine Figure 5·2 and answer the following questions.

1. How many multiplications are required from

2. How many different values of H^3 are computed from

3. How many different values of T^3 are computed from

4. Revise the algorithm so that the same value of H^3 is never recomputed and the same value of T^3 is not recomputed more than 10 times.

5. How would you revise the algorithm so that no value of H^3, T^3, or U^3 is ever computed a second time? *Hint*. Compute all values 0^3, 1^3, 2^3, . . . , 9^3 and store them in a separate list CUBE having 10 elements.

6. See if you can reduce the total number of multiplications to 120 by using no more than nine different boxes in the flowchart.

Nested loops develop naturally out of the systematic processing of the entries in a matrix. Suppose we wish to find the sum of all entries in a matrix having M rows and N columns, as in Figure 5·3.

We will input the dimensions of the matrix (box 1), input all the matrix values (box 2), and then compute the desired

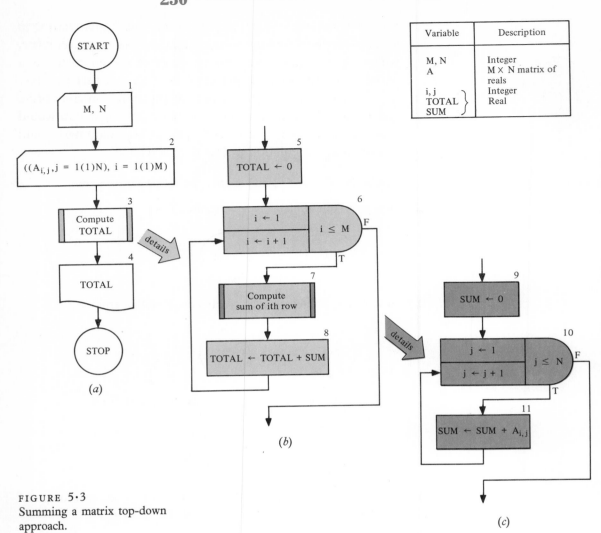

Variable	Description
M, N	Integer
A	M × N matrix of reals
i, j	Integer
TOTAL }	Real
SUM	

FIGURE 5·3
Summing a matrix top-down approach.

value of TOTAL (box 3), and output the result (box 4). The *second* level of detail (Figure 5·3b) explains what is meant by "Compute TOTAL". Here we see that TOTAL is obtained as the sum of M individual row sums. The variable SUM is used in computing each row sum at the *third* level of detail (Figure 5·3c). Here we see that SUM is first set to zero and then built up term by term using all the elements $A_{i,1}, A_{i,2}, \ldots, A_{i,N}$, inclusive. The column designation, j, is used as a loop control counter. We are free to put it all together by combining the three levels of detail into one flowchart, as is suggested in the silhouette given in Figure 5·1, but it can be argued that such an exercise provides little, if any, further understanding or insight. The top-down progression to successive levels of greater detail is what we mean by *stepwise decomposition*.

EXERCISES 5·1, SET B

In the following six exercises, you are to draw a flowchart equivalent to each word problem. Nested loops are involved, so you should find while and/or iteration boxes helpful. Use the stepwise decomposition method of Figure 5·3 if it seems appropriate. Assume that the matrix P, having M rows and N columns, is already in storage.

1. Write a flowchart to clear the matrix P; that is, set every element to zero, row by row.

2. Search P for the element of largest absolute value. Assign this element to BIG and print the value of BIG. *Hint.* Start by assuming that the entry of largest magnitude is zero.

3. Search P for the element of largest value (not absolute value), assigning it to LARGE. Print the value of LARGE and the row number, ROW, and column number, COL, where this value was found. *Hint.* Start by assuming the largest value is $P_{1,1}$.

4. Search for the algebraically least nonzero element in odd-numbered rows and even-numbered columns and assign its value to LEAST. While conducting this search, keep a tally of the number of zeros found, ZTALY, and then print values for LEAST and ZTALY. If all elements are zero, the value printed for LEAST should be zero.

5. Add a multiple, T, of the first-row entries to the entries of all other rows of P. For example, if T = 2, we show the action on a 4-row by 4-column matrix P.

$$
\text{Before action} \begin{cases} 1\ 2\ 1\ 1 \\ 3\ 4\ 2\ 5 \\ 1\ 2\ 1\ 2 \\ 3\ 1\ 3\ 2 \end{cases} \quad \begin{array}{l} \text{After adding} \\ 2 \times \text{row 1 to} \\ \text{each of the} \\ \text{other rows} \end{array} \begin{cases} 1\ 2\ 1\ 1 \\ 5\ 8\ 4\ 7 \\ 3\ 6\ 3\ 4 \\ 5\ 5\ 5\ 4 \end{cases}
$$

6. Determine the minimum value in each column, MIN, of the matrix P and print it out with its row and column identification, ROW and COL. If there is more than one occurrence of the minimum value, report the last one found. For the 4×4 array shown in the preceding exercise in the "before" state, the correct output for this exercise would be:

MIN	ROW	COL
1	3	1
1	4	2
1	3	3
1	1	4

A matrix that has the same number of rows and columns is called a *square matrix*. In the next three exercises we will assume that P is square (M rows and M columns). The *main diagonal* of a square matrix is the set of entries having equal row and column subscripts, that is, $P_{1,1}$, $P_{2,2}$, $P_{3,3}$, and so forth. The ith element on the main diagonal can therefore be referred to as $P_{i,i}$.

7. Assign to SUM1 the sum of all entries that lie to the *left* of the main diagonal of the square matrix P, accumulating the terms row by row. *Hint.* Make yourself a picture of the triangular group of entries that fall in the category to be summed. What is the first row involved? What is the last column involved? For those elements of any row, i, lying to the left of the main diagonal, what is the column subscript of the rightmost entry?

8. Form the sum of all entries that are situated to the *right* of the main diagonal of P, accumulating the terms row by row. (See Problem 7.)

9. The "triangle" to the left of the main diagonal that you worked with in Problem 7 is often called the "lower triangle," and the one to the right of the main diagonal is often called the "upper triangle." In this exercise we wish to search the upper triangle column by column, starting from the *last* column. We will search each column from top to bottom for the first entry that is at least twice as large in absolute value as its immediate predecessor in the same column. An entry that exhibits this increased magnitude will be termed a PIG.

   A PIG can occur in any but the leftmost column of the upper triangle. Print all values of PIG as they are discovered, along with their row and column subscripts I and J. If no PIG is found, print "NONE". What is the smallest matrix that can have a PIG? (*Answer.* 3×3.) *Hint.* Can the top element of a column be a PIG? What is the row subscript for the bottommost element in the Jth column?

EXERCISES 5·1, SET C

1. Study the flowchart in Figure 5·4 and answer the following questions.

   (a) Give, in your own words, a summary of what this algorithm is designed to accomplish.
   (b) If a 4-row by 17-column matrix is input as a result of executing box 1, how many times will the false exit from box 4 be taken?
   (c) Referring to the same 4×17 matrix, how many times will box 5 be executed?
   (d) Assume that the following A array is input at box 1.

3	4	6	− 2	1	9
2	5	6	1	7	1
8	15	1	2	9	8
6	1	8	3	4	7

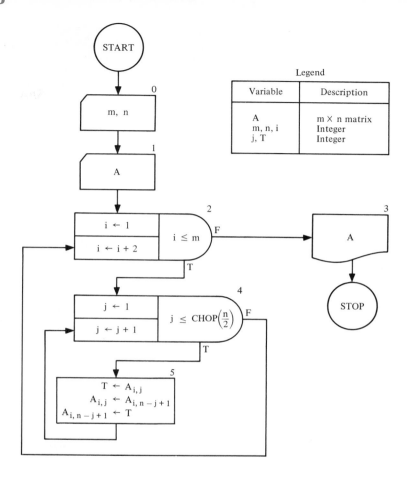

FIGURE 5·4

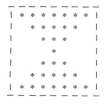

Show the array that is printed as a result of executing box 3.

2. A chessboard can be thought of as an 8 × 8 character pattern. Construct a flowchart to read in two integers (M, N) as the position of a chess Queen and print out a pattern that has a "Q" where the Queen is, asterisks (*) in the positions within the scope of the Queen (positions in the same row or column or diagonal), and minus signs (−) elsewhere, as shown at the left for the Queen in position (3,4).

(a) Construct a flowchart solution without using either lists or arrays.
(b) Construct a flowchart solution without using arrays, but with lists permitted.
(c) Construct a flowchart solution with an array permitted.

3. Flowchart an algorithm to printout an hourglass figure surrounded by a line border, as shown at the left for the print character, "*", and the dimension, 7. Make the frame fit snugly about the hourglass and read in only two items of information, that is, values for the print character, C, and the dimension, i.

4. At the end of this problem there is a partially completed modification of the flowchart in Problem 5, Exercises 3·6, Set D. This modification uses iteration boxes. When completed, the new flowchart is intended to accomplish the same net effect as the old flowchart, although it may not be identical in the finest detail. The iteration box numbered 1-7-8 is intended to replace boxes 1, 7, and 8 of the original flowchart, and the iteration box numbered 3-5-6 is intended to replace boxes 3, 5, and 6.

Evaluate the truth or falsity of the following six assertions:

(a) Box 3-5-6 can be completed as

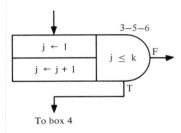

(b) The "F-exit" of box 3-5-6 should be connected to the initialization compartment of box 1-7-8.

(c) When completed, box 1-7-8 should be

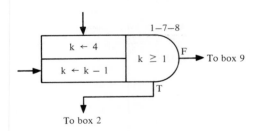

When boxes 1-7-8 and 3-5-6 are properly completed and box 3-5-6 is properly connected to box 1-7-8, are the following assertions true or false?

(d) This flowchart will be more efficient in its execution than the one that did not use iteration boxes.

(e) The efficiency of the two flowchart algorithms will be comparable, but the one that uses iteration boxes may be easier for a programmer to understand.

(f) Only one of the values input at box 2 the first time through is preserved when execution reaches box 10, and this is the value of A_4.

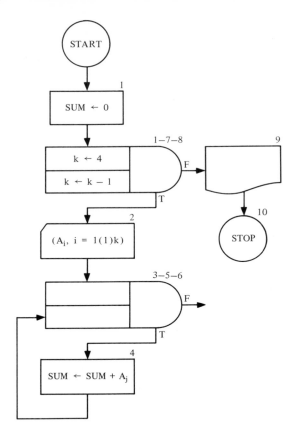

5. The flowchart fragment in Figure 5·5 represents a special summing process on a subset of a matrix A having n rows and n columns. Now assume the following matrix A is already in storage

$$A = \begin{bmatrix} 6 & -2 & 5 & 4 & -3 & 1 \\ 9 & 0 & -8 & 3 & -2 & 6 \\ 1 & 8 & 5 & -4 & 1 & -1 \\ 8 & -3 & 7 & -3 & 6 & 3 \\ 5 & -5 & 4 & -8 & 1 & 2 \\ 3 & 2 & -1 & 6 & -4 & 8 \end{bmatrix}$$

and assume that n has been assigned the value 6.

(a) What is the range of rows from which elements can be taken for the summing process in box 5?

(b) Will any matrix elements actually be retrieved (for summing) from row 2? If not, why not?

(c) Draw a border around that portion of the matrix A that will be accumulated in the sum by the flowchart of Figure 5·5.

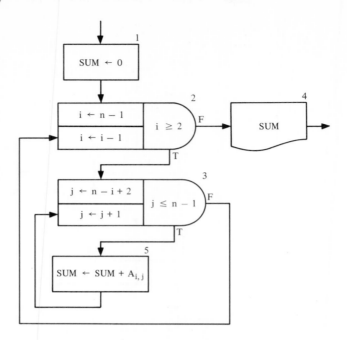

FIGURE 5·5

6. This question concerns an algorithm for producing a coded version of a message. The algorithm uses two lists, IN and OUT, such as those shown below. Each list contains each of the 26 letters of the alphabet, but the ordering of the letters is different in the two lists. The algorithm operates as follows.

(a) Initial values for the IN and OUT lists are input.
(b) M, the number of characters in the message, is input.
(c) The message is read into the list MSGE, one character per list element. (Assume that the message contains only letters—no blanks, numbers, etc.)
(d) Each letter of the message is encoded by locating it in the IN list, then replacing it by the corresponding letter from the OUT list, where the "corresponding element" means the one with the same subscript. (E.g., for IN and OUT shown below, each occurrence of D in MSGE would be replaced by Q, since D is IN_4 and Q is OUT_4.)
(e) The encoded message is output.

IN | A | B | C | D | E | F | G | H | I | J | K | L | M | N | O | P | Q | R | S | T | U | V | W | X | Y | Z |

OUT | I | C | T | Q | Y | J | W | E | V | A | O | K | B | H | P | R | G | L | S | X | D | N | Z | M | U | F |

An incomplete flowchart for this algorithm is shown on the next page. Your job is to complete it.

7. Consider the following problem. Input a number N and a list of length

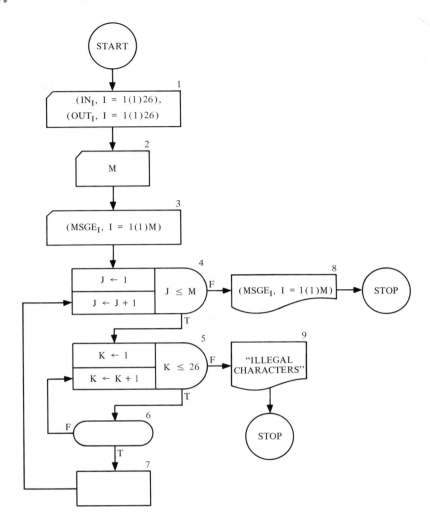

N. The list may contain duplicated values; that is, several of the elements may be equal (see the example below). Find the value that occurs the maximum number of times (i.e., the "most duplicated" value) and output that value and the subscript corresponding to the first position in which the value occurs in the list.

Example

    $N = 7$
    List elements: 7, 8, 4, 8, 9, 8, 7
    Values printed: 8 (most duplicated value)
                     2 (subscript of first occurrence)

An incomplete flowchart for the solution is shown on the next page. Your job is (a) to specify the contents of box 7 and (b) to complete the second assignment statement in box 10.

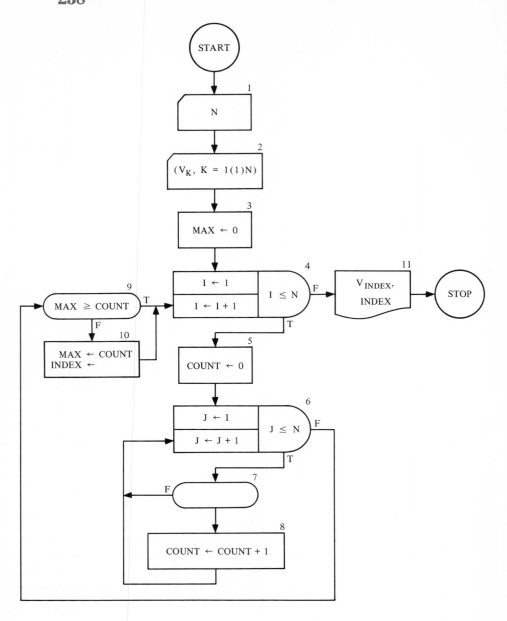

8. Trace the flowchart shown on the next page using the given data. What values will be output when box 10 is executed?

The assumed data set
is: m = 3, n = 4

$$P = \begin{bmatrix} 5 & 7 & 4 & 3 \\ 6 & 3 & -1 & 6 \\ 8 & 5 & 2 & 2 \end{bmatrix}$$

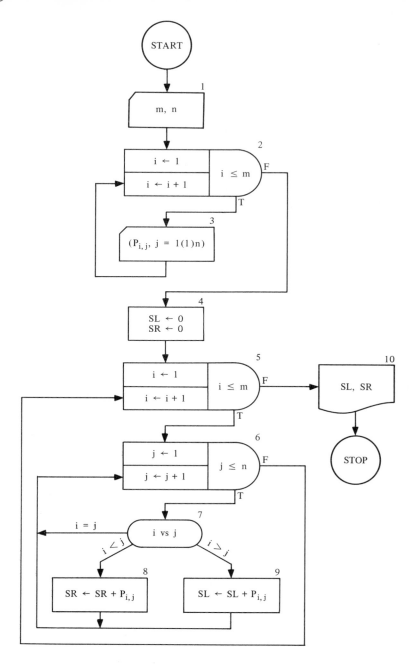

9. This question refers to the flowchart given on the next page.

(a) True or false: The flowchart describes an algorithm that inputs data for an m-row by n-column matrix called A and sums the elements of a particular row.

(b) True or false: The flowchart cannot be correct—no matter what

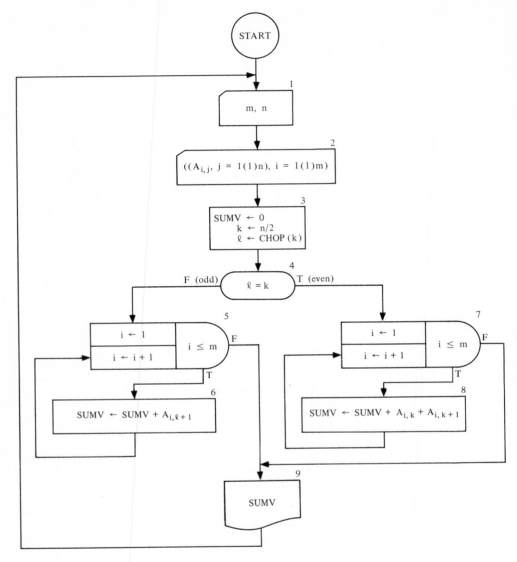

its intended purpose—because the two inner loops share a common flowchart box (i.e., box 9) and hence the flowchart is ambiguous.

(c) What value will be printed if the following input data are used with the *above* flowchart?

$$m = 5$$
$$n = 4$$

$$A = \begin{bmatrix} 1 & 2 & 3 & 4 \\ 5 & 6 & 7 & 8 \\ 9 & 10 & 11 & 12 \\ 13 & 14 & 15 & 16 \\ 17 & 18 & 19 & 20 \end{bmatrix}$$

(d) What value will be printed if the flowchart *below* is executed using the following input data?

$$m = 4$$
$$n = 5$$

$$A = \begin{bmatrix} 1 & 2 & 3 & 4 & 5 \\ 6 & 7 & 8 & 9 & 10 \\ 11 & 12 & 13 & 14 & 15 \\ 16 & 17 & 18 & 19 & 20 \end{bmatrix}$$

(e) Are the two flowcharts used in this problem *equivalent* (i.e., given the same data, do they produce the same result)?

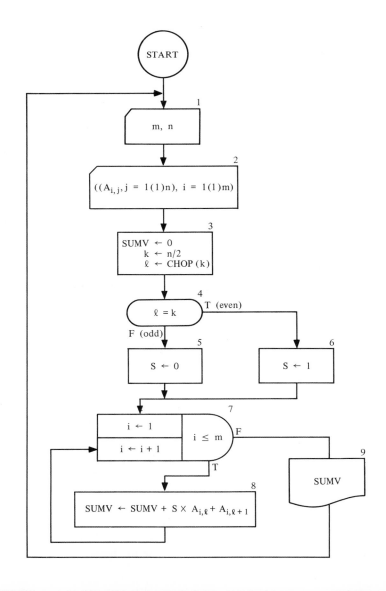

10. Trace through the flowchart fragment shown below assuming that the given data values have previously been assigned. What are the values of the elements in matrix A and in B after execution?

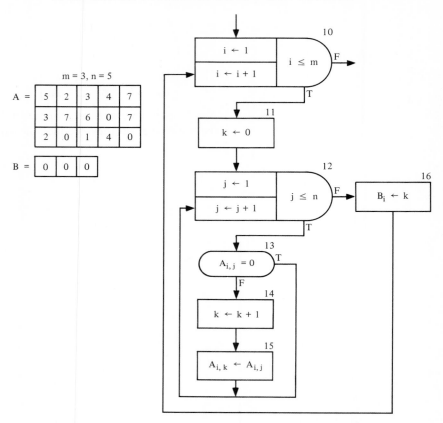

m = 3, n = 5

$$A = \begin{array}{|c|c|c|c|c|} \hline 5 & 2 & 3 & 4 & 7 \\ \hline 3 & 7 & 6 & 0 & 7 \\ \hline 2 & 0 & 1 & 4 & 0 \\ \hline \end{array}$$

$$B = \begin{array}{|c|c|c|} \hline 0 & 0 & 0 \\ \hline \end{array}$$

11. Suppose values for the matrix P have been read from data cards as shown by the following table:

23	−8	13
9	−3	0
−5	1	0

Trace the execution of the flowchart fragment given at the top of the next page assuming that the values of P are as shown in the table, and answer questions (a) through (c).

(a) At the time the *false* exit is taken from box 1, the value of $P_{2,1}$ is (choose one):
  (1) 3.
  (2) 2.
  (3) 8.
  (4) − 8.
  (5) None of these.

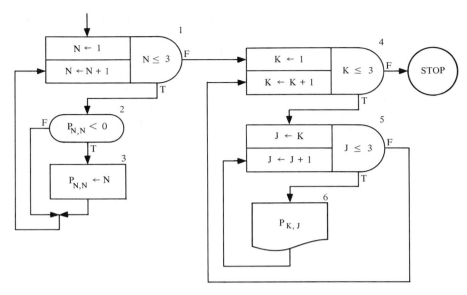

(b) At the time the *false* exit is taken from box 1, the value of $P_{2,2}$ is (choose one):
   (1) 3.
   (2) -3.
   (3) 0.
   (4) 2.
   (5) None of these.

(c) When box 7 is reached, the sequence of values that has been printed is (choose one):
   (1) 23, -8, 13, 2, 0, 0.
   (2) 23, 9, -5, 2, 1, 0.
   (3) 23, -8, 13, 9, -3, 0, -5, 1, 0.
   (4) 23, -8, 2, 13, 0, 0.
   (5) 23, 9, -5, -3, 1, 0.

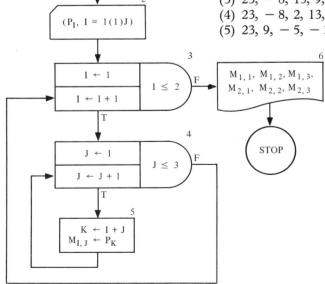

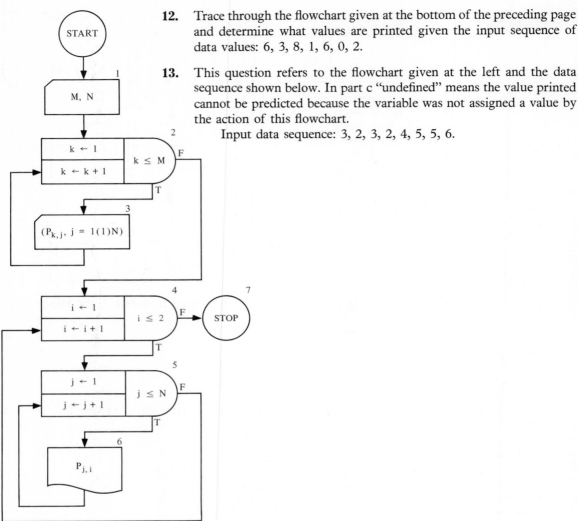

12. Trace through the flowchart given at the bottom of the preceding page and determine what values are printed given the input sequence of data values: 6, 3, 8, 1, 6, 0, 2.

13. This question refers to the flowchart given at the left and the data sequence shown below. In part c "undefined" means the value printed cannot be predicted because the variable was not assigned a value by the action of this flowchart.

Input data sequence: 3, 2, 3, 2, 4, 5, 5, 6.

(a) What value is associated with the variable $P_{3,2}$ at the instant that execution takes the *false* exit from box 2?

(b) At the instant that execution takes the *false* exit from box 2, list the variables to which values already have been assigned together with the assigned values.

(c) The values printed at the time execution reaches box 7 are (choose one):

   (1) No values are printed because of the error made in attempting to print an undefined value.
   (2) 3, 2, 4, 5, 5, 6.
   (3) 3, 2.
   (4) 3, 4, 2, 5.
   (5) 3, undefined, 2, undefined, 5, 6.

14. This question concerns the following flowchart. Suppose that the execution of box 1 resulted in the values

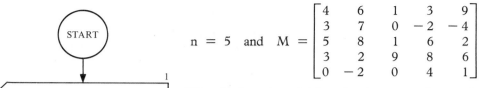

$$n = 5 \quad \text{and} \quad M = \begin{bmatrix} 4 & 6 & 1 & 3 & 9 \\ 3 & 7 & 0 & -2 & -4 \\ 5 & 8 & 1 & 6 & 2 \\ 3 & 2 & 9 & 8 & 6 \\ 0 & -2 & 0 & 4 & 1 \end{bmatrix}$$

What is the value of M at the time execution reaches box 8?

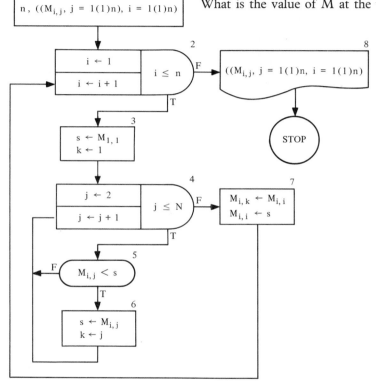

The Prime Factor Algorithm   In Section 4·1 (Figure 4·12) we considered the problem of finding the cofactors of an integer N. Now our problem is to represent N as a product of *prime* factors. These two problems may sound similar to you. To see how they differ, compare the following. The integer factors of 360, in the order they would be printed when executing the algorithm in Figure 4·12, are:

1, 360, 2, 180, 3, 120, 4, 90, 5, 72, 6, 60,
8, 45, 9, 40, 10, 36, 12, 30, 15, 24, 18, 20

On the other hand, the complete factorization of 360 *as a*

product of primes is

$$2 \times 2 \times 2 \times 3 \times 3 \times 5$$

When we output the results from our algorithm, however, the multiplication operators will be omitted.

Before attempting to construct a flowchart let's see how we carry out this process in practice. Look at the decomposition of the number 5280. We exhibit this work in Table 5·1.

TABLE 5·1
Factorization of 5280 into Prime Factors

Line Numbers	Number to be factored (N)	Trial Divisor (K)	Prime Factor Found (and Output)
1	5280	2	2
2	2640	2	2
3	1320	2	2
4	660	2	2
5	330	2	2
6	165	2	—
7	165	3	3
8	55	3	—
9	55	4	—
10	55	5	5
11	11	5	—
12	11	6	11

We need two variables, N, the number to be factored, and K, the trial divisor. We start N off with the given value, 5280, and we start K with the smallest possible nontrivial divisor (i.e., we exclude 1). If N has a factor K, we output K (last column in the table) and replace N by N/K, as this quotient will be the product of all the so far unfound prime factors. We keep repeating this process with the same trial divisor as long as that trial divisor works, as in the case of repeated prime factors. As we can see, this division happens successfully five times with the factor 2.

When the trial divisor fails to divide the current value of N, as it eventually must, the trial divisor is incremented by 1. Lines 7 and 8 of the table show that 3 is a divisor (but only once).

Line 9 of the table contains a surprise—we test for divisibility by 4, which is not a prime. Why should we do this? Well, although we can see by eye that 4 is not a prime, there is no general way to communicate to the computer the information as to whether a given number is prime or not, unless we supply it with a list of primes. Of course, we know that all even numbers greater than 2 are not prime, but testing for *primeness* (or nonprimeness) of each trial divisor may cost more time than is wasted in trying nonprime divisors. We can be sure, however, that no composite number will ever be printed out in our list of factors because by the time any composite trial divisor is reached, all of its prime factors will have been factored out of N.

Finally, we consider the question of how the value 11 came to be printed out on the last line of the table. Each time we use a new trial divisor, K, we make the test

$$K^2 \leq N$$

If this is false, then, as seen in the discussion of the integer factors algorithm (Figure 4·12), N can have no divisors $\leq \sqrt{N}$ other than the trivial divisor, 1. Thus either the current value of N is prime or it is equal to 1.

Now it is easy to see how to flowchart the process described above. The flowchart developed by stepwise decomposition is seen in Figure 5·6.

The top-level view is shown in Figure 5·6a. We copy the given value of M into N and then proceed to compute and display all of N's prime factors (by a process that changes the value of N, but not the original value, M), printing a concluding message (box 4) before terminating the process.

Prime factors are computed and displayed as shown in Figure 5·6b. For each trial divisor K, we divide out and print all factors, if any, of value K. Trial divisors start with K = 2 and are incremented by 1 as long as $K^2 \leq N$, as seen in boxes 5 and 6 of Figure 5·6b. As explained in the preceding discussion, when the F exit from the while box is taken, either N = 1 or N is prime. Thus we want to add N to the printed list of prime factors, unless N = 1. (See boxes 9 and 10.)

The details for removing and printing factors of value K are seen in Figure 5·6c.

Note that we have chosen a while box to control the loop in Figure 5·6b instead of an iteration box because the loop is an indefinite iteration. That is, the number of times box 6 is to be executed cannot be predicted because the value of N may change if and when box 13 is executed. We reserve the iteration box for cases when the number of transits through

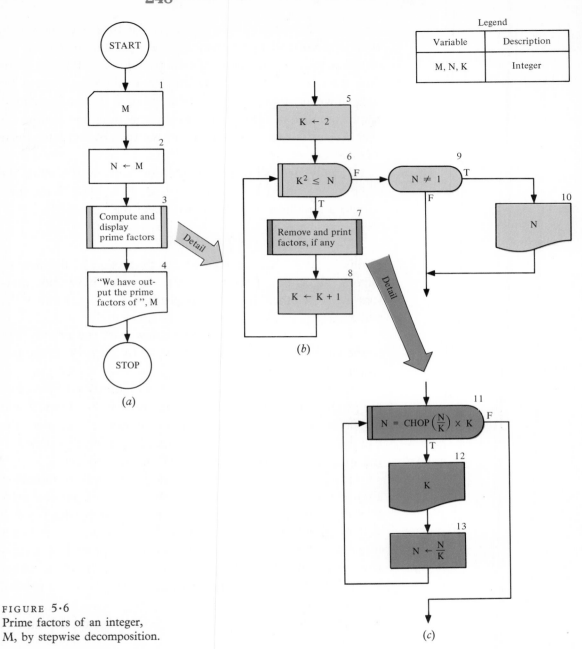

FIGURE 5·6
Prime factors of an integer,
M, by stepwise decomposition.

the loop is predictable before entering the loop. Similarly, in Figure 5·6c, box 11 is a while box because we cannot predict how often boxes 12 and 13 will be executed.

EXERCISES 5·1,
SET D

1. In mathematics an ordered set of numbers is called a *vector*. We recognize that what the mathematician calls a vector is what we call

a *list* of numerical values. We may define the product of two vectors (of the same length M) as follows.

$$A \otimes B = A_1 \times B_1 + A_2 \times B_2 + \ldots + A_M \times B_M$$

The operator $\otimes$ denotes vector multiplication, whereas $\times$ means the ordinary multiplication of two numbers. Note that the result of $\otimes$ is a single number.

This notion may be extended to define multiplication of a matrix and a vector. If C is an $M \times N$ matrix (M rows, N columns), and A is a vector of length N, then $C \boxtimes A$ is defined to be a vector D of length N, calculated as follows.

D_1 is the vector product (i.e., the operation $\otimes$) of row 1 of C, and A

D_2 is the vector product of row 2 of C and A

$\vdots$

D_N is the vector product of row N of C and A

(a) Write the value of

$$\begin{pmatrix} 6 & 2 \\ -4 & 5 \\ 1 & 0 \end{pmatrix} \boxtimes \begin{pmatrix} 2 \\ 3 \end{pmatrix}$$

(b) Draw a flowchart fragment to compute $C \boxtimes A$ and assign the result to D, assuming M, N, the vector A, and the matrix C have already been assigned values. Use the stepwise decomposition method for developing your flowchart.

2. Using the stepwise decomposition method, draw a flowchart for an algorithm that determines whether a given square matrix is a so-called "magic square." A magic square is a matrix for which certain subsets of matrix elements add up to the same value. In particular, a square array is a magic square if the elements of each row, column, and main diagonal sum to the same value. For example,

8	1	6
3	5	7
4	9	2

or

16	3	2	13
5	10	11	8
9	6	7	12
4	15	14	1

or

17	24	1	8	15
23	5	7	14	16
4	6	13	20	22
10	12	19	21	3
11	18	25	2	9

Your algorithm should:

(a) Input n, the "order" (i.e., number of rows and columns) of a candidate magic square.
(b) Input the entire $n \times n$ matrix.
(c) Print out a copy of the matrix.
(d) Determine whether it is a magic square and print "hooray", or

some such message if it is, and "sorry, try again", or an equivalent message if it is not a magic square.

(e) Return to step (a) to try another square.

3. Study the algorithm given at the left.

(a) Your first job is to prepare detailed flowchart steps equivalent to box 2.

(b) Your next job is to prepare detailed flowchart steps equivalent to boxes 3, 4, and 5.

Note that parts a and b are logically independent of one another. That is, the method of search in box 3 is not dependent on whether (or how) the data may have been previously rearranged by sorting. Use iteration boxes wherever possible in your flowcharts.

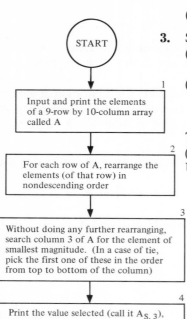

4. Explain how we could have N = 1 in box 9 of Figure 5·6.

5. Study the flowchart of the accompanying figure and answer the following questions.

(a) If execution reaches box 5, is n a real number or an integer? Why?

> In answering parts b to e of this exercise assume the value of n is 25.

(b) List the values that will be assigned to the subscript j in box 6.

(c) List the values that will be assigned to A_j in box 6.

(d) If we exit box 9 having printed "5" as the value of j, for what actual subscript values i will A_i be set to zero in box 11?

(e) List the first 7 values output by the algorithm.

(f) Describe, in your own words, what the algorithm is doing.

(g) Suggest an initialization of k in box 10 that will improve the efficiency of the algorithm by eliminating the possibility of setting the same A_i to zero more than once.

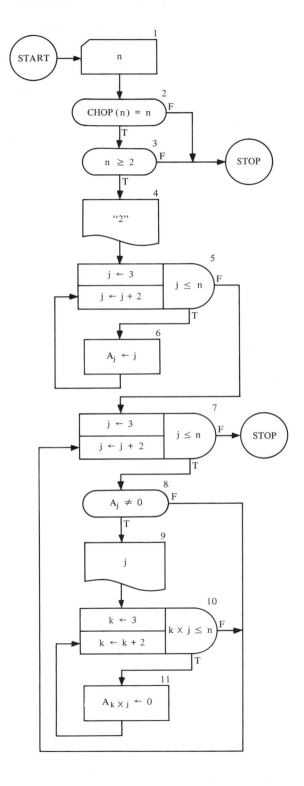

Graphing by Computer

Suppose we want to have a computer print the graph of a function. One very illuminating way to do this uses an array that we will call GRAPH. Because a line printer has approximately 60 lines per page and may have 132 characters per line, let us say GRAPH is to have 60 rows and 132 columns. With this array at our disposal we can assign whatever value we choose to any of the 60×132 elements of GRAPH.

To begin with we want to make sure the array is clear, or "clean." It is good practice to start off by "erasing"; we can do this by the following double loop in which the blank character, "□", is assigned to every position in GRAPH.

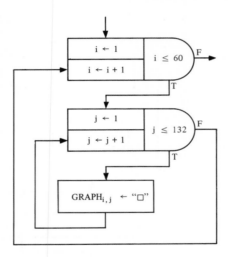

Next, we may want to "draw" axes on our graph. For our first graph let us place the origin essentially at the center of the page, say at the 30th row and 66th column. We can use the hyphen character to draw the x-axis by assigning "$-$" to every element in the 30th row. Similarly, for the y-axis we can assign "$|$" to every element in the 66th column.

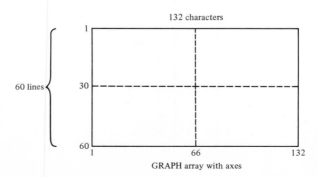

GRAPH array with axes

Suppose the function we are to graph is $y = \sin x$, and we want the domain to be $-\pi \le x \le \pi$. We need to interpret the 132 column indices of the GRAPH matrix so that they correspond to about 2π units on our graph. If we let the unit between two horizontal indices represent $\pi/64$, then 128 of these units will be 2π. This interpretation is called *scaling*; the horizontal scale will be $\pi/64$ per unit. In the vertical direction, we have 60 indices (units), and the range of the sine function is $-1 \le y \le 1$. If we let one vertical unit represent $1/28$, 56 of these units will represent the full range of the sine function; the vertical scale is $1/28$ per unit.

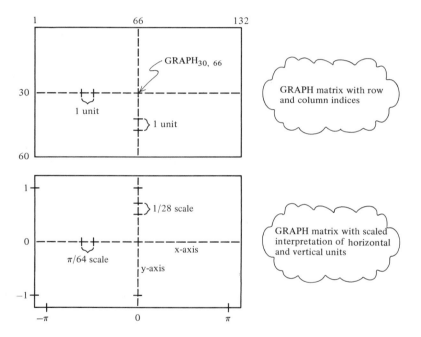

Now let us see how to "plot" a point on the graph. Suppose $x = \pi/4$. The library sine function will compute the value $y = \sin(\pi/4) = .70711$. We want to assign a certain symbol such as an asterisk (*) to some matrix element to represent the data pair $(\pi/4, .70711)$. But which matrix element should get the asterisk? To convert $\pi/4$ into matrix units we divide by $\pi/64$ to obtain 16 units to the right of the origin. Therefore the scaled x-coordinate, $\pi/4$, corresponds to $16 + 66 = 82$ as a column index in matrix notation. (The 66 is added because it is the column index of the origin.)

Now we must find the proper matrix correspondence for the y-value, .70711. First we divide the y-value by $1/28$ to convert it to matrix index units. But, since all matrix indices are integers, we must also round the resulting value to the nearest integer. Thus by adding .5 and then chopping we will have CHOP (.70711 × 28 + .5). We notice at this point that the sine function is positive in the upward direction, while the matrix rows are numbered positively in the downward direction. Therefore, to compute the row index of the matrix element that should be assigned the asterisk, we take the coordinate of the origin, 30, minus the y-value computed above.

The three assignment statements needed to plot the point are then

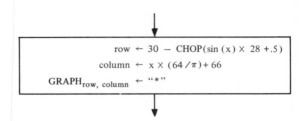

If we let x run through the values from $-\pi$ to π in steps of $\pi/64$ and compute the above assignments for each value of x, we can then print the graph by executing the single flowchart step

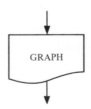

By appropriate changes in the function and, if necessary, in the scaling factors and the origin, many other functions can be plotted for regions of interest. The following exercises will help you get started.

EXERCISES 5·1, SET E

1. Construct a flowchart to "draw" the x- and y-axes on the GRAPH array with origin at the 30th row and 66th column, as described in the text.

2. Incorporating the solution to Exercise 1, construct a flowchart to clear the graphing array, draw axes, and plot the function y = sin x for $-\pi \leq x \leq \pi$. If you have a computer available, have it execute your flowchart.

3. Modify your flowchart for Exercise 2 to plot y = cos x for $-\pi \leq x \leq \pi$. Choose a different plotting symbol than an asterisk.

4. Having completed Exercises 2 and 3, construct a flowchart to plot both y = sin x and y = cos x for $-\pi \leq x \leq \pi$ on the same axes, using a different plotting symbol for each function.

5. Modify your flowchart for Exercise 4 to plot not only y = sin x and y = cos x, but also y = sin x + cos x all on the same axes, using three different plotting symbols. It will be necessary to rescale the y-axis for these graphs because y = sin x + cos x has a range $-2 \leq y \leq 2$. Change the vertical scale from 1 / 28 to 1 / 14. Construct a flowchart to plot the graphs for the domain $-\pi \leq x \leq \pi$ and run the resulting computer program.

5·2 Procedures—an outgrowth of decomposition

Look back at the abominable sorting algorithm of Section 3·6, Figure 3·29. The purpose of the algorithm was to take a given list of numbers and "sort" or "rearrange" it in increasing order. We went through the list from left to right, looking for a consecutive pair out of order. As soon as we found two adjacent numbers out of order, we interchanged them.

$$A_1 \quad A_2 \quad A_3 \quad A_4 \quad A_5 \quad A_6 \quad A_7 \quad A_8 \quad A_9$$

$$2 \quad 7 \quad 9 \quad 11 \quad 3 \quad 8 \quad 7 \quad 12 \quad 5$$

$$2 \quad 7 \quad 9 \quad \boxed{3} \quad \boxed{11} \quad 8 \quad 7 \quad 12 \quad 5$$

Then we started over again, treating this "interchanged" list as a new problem. The algorithm was easy to describe, but wasteful. The reason for this wastefulness is the rechecking of all the pairs preceding the interchanged pair. Those are already known to be in increasing order! We look for an algorithm to eliminate the waste.

Let's start over again from scratch with the original list above. We locate the first pair (11,3) that is out of order, as before. We put one finger on this spot for future reference. Then we put the 3 aside and shove the 11 over in its place.

Vacant place

TEMP.

Now we have a vacant space, and we want to move one place to the right all those numbers already ordered that are larger than the one we put aside. So we compare 9 and 3 and shove 9 over to the right one place, as shown below; compare 7 and 3 and shove 7 over one place. When we compare 2 and 3, we find 3 is larger, and so we insert 3 into the vacant place between 2 and 7.

Then we go back and resume our original comparisons, starting just to the right of where we put our finger before.

The flowchart in Figure 5·7a expresses the overall structure of the algorithm we have just described: check the values of all n-1 successive pairs, (A_j, A_{j+1}) to see if they are already in order. If the jth pair of values is out of order, then the value of A_{j+1} is taken out of the list and inserted where it belongs among its predecessors, as shown in Figure 5·7b.

Box 3b

```
                      3b
    ┌──────────────────┐
    │ ┌──────────────┐ │
    │ │  Determine k │ │
    │ └──────────────┘ │
    └──────────────────┘
              │
              ▼
```

refers to the detailed steps of determining the new position k, at which to make the insertion. Finding the right value of k is achieved by testing and moving each higher-valued predecessor of the saved value copied from A_{j+1}, each time decrementing k from the starting value j. These details are seen in Figure 5·7c. Whenever all n-1 pairs are in order or have been put in order, the sorting process is finished. The whole algorithm is called a *bubble sort*.

Birth of the "Procedure" Concept

There are two ways we can think about the successive levels of detail of our new sort algorithm of Figure 5·7. The first way is familiar: simply regard boxes 3a through 3c as the detail

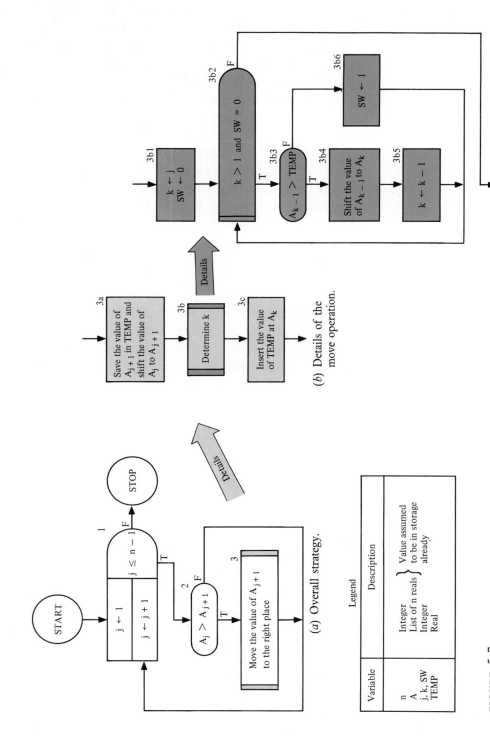

(a) Overall strategy.

(b) Details of the move operation.

(c) Details of the determine k operation.

FIGURE 5·7
A bubble sort algorithm.

Legend

Variable	Description	
n	Integer	Value assumed to be in storage already
A	List of n reals	
j, k, SW	Integer	
TEMP	Real	

for which box 3 acts as a *shorthand*. With this view, we are free at any time, if it suits our convenience, to replace box 3 with the program fragment consisting of boxes 3a through 3c. (The same approach can be taken for boxes 3b1 through 3b6 with respect to box 3b.)

The second way we may view this decomposition is to regard the detailed program fragment as a subordinate component or subalgorithm of the main flowchart. This recasting of roles is reflected in Figure 5·8 by giving the fragment of Figure 5·8b the unique name MOVE and by regarding box 3 of the main flowchart as a *call on* or reference to the subalgorithm whose name is MOVE. By identical reasoning, we may also give the fragment of Figure 5·8c a unique name, Determinekay, and regard box 3b as a reference to the subalgorithm having that name. We refer to such a subordinate component as a *procedure*.

Using this terminology, box 3 may now be regarded as a call or request to execute the procedure named MOVE and, upon completing the steps of this procedure, to resume activity in the main flowchart at the *successor* to the call box. In this example, the successor to the call box is the incrementation of j at box 1. Likewise, box 3b of MOVE may now be regarded as a call or request to execute the procedure Determinekay. Upon completing the steps of this procedure, activity is to resume in MOVE at the successor to call box 3b, which is box 3c.

To make each procedure a complete, self-identified subflowchart, we give it a start box clearly marked with its name, for example

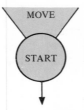

We also mark its terminus with a new form of stop box to

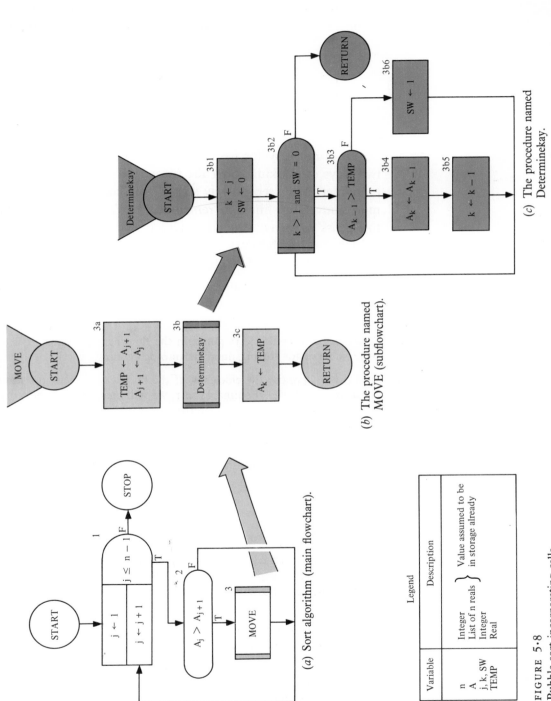

(a) Sort algorithm (main flowchart).

(b) The procedure named MOVE (subflowchart).

(c) The procedure named Determinekay.

Legend

Variable	Description	
n	Integer	Value assumed to be
A	List of n reals	in storage already
j, k, SW	Integer	
TEMP	Real	

FIGURE 5·8
Bubble sort incorporating calls
on MOVE and Determinekay.

indicate that control is to return to the flowchart box that immediately follows the point of reference, in this example

It is not easy for us at this point to judge which of the two ways of thinking about the successive levels of detail has more merit. The second way seems more complicated; that is, more conventions must be remembered. We are not yet ready to discuss its many advantages. One type of advantage will be brought out in the next section, and many more advantages will be explained in Chapter 9.

EXERCISES 5·2

1. To compare properly the abominable sorting algorithm (Figure 3·29) with the one in Figure 5·8, redraw the former using an iteration box for control of the inner loop.

2. What changes would be required in the flowchart of Figure 5·8 to make it serve for sorting numbers into descending order?

3. In order to appraise the efficiency of the bubble sort method and to compare it with the abominable sort, we will again equate the work of sorting to the number of comparisons required. In this case, the sorting work would be proportional to the total number of times boxes 2 and 3b3 (Figure 5·8) are executed. (See Exercises 3.6 Set B.)

    (a) How many times are the tests in boxes 2 and 3b3 executed from

if the values to be sorted are 7, 2, −5, 4?

    (b) How many times are the tests in boxes 2 and 3b3 executed if the values to be sorted are − 9, 5, 9, 12?
    (c) How many times are the tests in boxes 2 and 3b3 executed if the values to be sorted are 12, 9, 5, − 9?

4. Suppose the values of the elements A_1, A_2, A_3, . . . , A_N are in descending numerical order.

    (a) Show that to sort the list A into ascending numerical order using the bubble sort algorithm of Figure 5·8 requires $N^2 - N$ comparisons. (How many comparisons are required if N = 1000?)
    (b) Show that to sort the list A into ascending numerical order using the abominable sort algorithm of Figure 3·29 requires

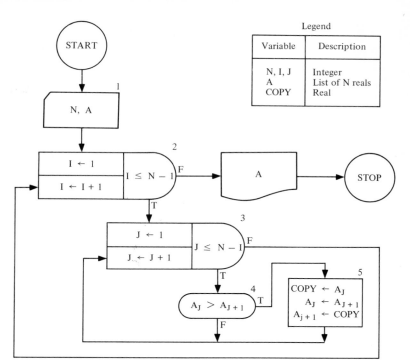

FIGURE 5·9
A sleeper?

$(N^3 - N)/6$ comparisons. (How many comparisons are required if $N = 1000$?)

5. A student brings into class the algorithm shown in Figure 5·9. He makes the following claims. Your job is to verify or refute each claim.

   (a) It is an algorithm for sorting numbers in ascending algebraic order.
   (b) It is more efficient than the algorithm in Figure 5·8.

6. Draw a flowchart to do the following.

   (a) Find the number of distinct (i.e., no two congruent) triangles with sides of integer length and no side greater than 100 in length.
   (b) Find the sum of the perimeters of the triangles in part a.
   (c) In part a replace the condition "no side greater than 100 in length" by "with perimeter $\leq$ 100" and redraw the flowchart.
   (d) Redraw part b with the replacement condition specified in part c.

**5·3
An illustrative
problem**

We are now ready to undertake a fairly substantial problem* to explore further the advantage of stepwise decomposition using loops and procedures. First, we will state the problem

*The problem in this section grew out of a similar problem presented in *The Language of Computers* by B. A. Galler (New York: McGraw-Hill Book Co., Inc., 1962). This section may be skipped on a first reading without loss of continuity.

in general terms. In what follows, the word "coding" will cover both encoding and decoding. *Encoding* is the process of converting (enciphering) an easily interpreted string of characters into one whose interpretation is not at all obvious. *Decoding* or deciphering is the inverse process.

Problem Statement

We are given two alphabets of 39 characters each. The first we call STAND, short for the *stand*ard alphabet. The second is called KEY, for the *key* alphabet. We want to construct a flowchart that will accept messages written in either alphabet and translate each message character by character into the other alphabet. The encoding translation is not to be just a simple substitution. If each character were always encoded into the same key character, it would be too easy to break the code.

The method of encoding that we will use results in code that is considerably more difficult to interpret (break). The method is based on a "shift" operation, and the idea can be grasped from Figure 5·10.

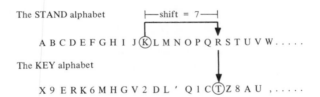

The STAND alphabet

A B C D E F G H I J Ⓚ L M N O P Q R S T U V W . . . . .

The KEY alphabet

X 9 E R K 6 M H G V 2 D L ' Q 1 C Ⓣ Z 8 A U , ...

FIGURE 5·10

As seen in this figure, a shift value of 7 applied to the letter K in the standard alphabet encodes to the letter T in the key alphabet. In our method, the shift value is to be dependent on the position of the character, not in either alphabet, but in the message being encoded.

The algorithm we want to construct first inputs the standard and the key alphabets. Then an unlimited series of messages is input and processed, that is, encoded or decoded according to a switch value or *signal* that precedes each message. The structure of this algorithm is seen in Figure 5·11.

The standard (STAND) alphabet consists of the 26 letters of the English alphabet, in order, followed by the digits 1 through 9 and 0, followed by the apostrophe ('), comma (,), and slash (/). The KEY alphabet is some chosen permutation of these 39 characters.

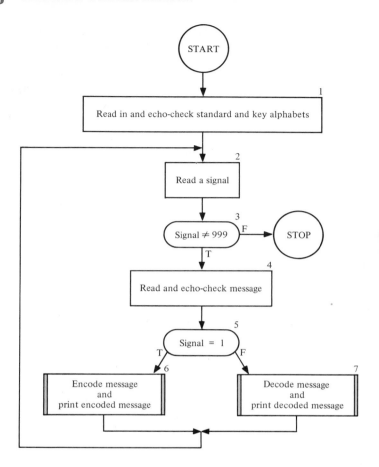

FIGURE 5·11
General coding flowchart.

Here is how the actual encoding of a message character is done. The given character is searched for in the standard alphabet to determine the subscript value of its position. The correct shift value is then added to this index, and that sum determines the subscript value of the encoded character in the key alphabet.

In case the shifting process results in a subscript beyond the range (1–39), *modular* arithmetic may be used to bring the subscript back into range. One interpretation of modular arithmetic for this case is as follows.

One may imagine that each alphabet is repeated over and over in both directions. Having computed the index of the proper character in the coded alphabet, one may simply "slide backward or forward" one whole alphabet at a time, by subtracting or adding 39, to arrive at an index in the range 1 through 39. This value will identify the wanted character in the target alphabet. More on how to determine the correct shift value will be discussed later.

In outputting encoded messages, each five characters should be followed by the space character to break up the printed line into wordlike groups. In messages to be encoded, words should be separated by slashes, since the space symbol (□) is not a character in either alphabet. Figure 5·12 shows a sample of the output that is desired from the coding program.

```
THE STANDARD ALPHABET IS
A B C D E F G H I J K L M N O P Q R S T U V W X Y Z 1 2 3 4 5 6 7 8 9 0
' , /
THE KEY ALPHABET IS
X 9 E R K 6 M H G V 2 D L ' Q 1 C T Z 8 A U , J I Y 7 N F O O S / B 4 W
3 P 5

THE MESSAGE IS
MR/COLLINS/WAS/NOT/A/SENSIBLE/MAN/AND/THE/DEFFICIENCY/OF/NATURE/HAD/
BEEN/BUT/LITTLE/ASSISTED/BY/EDUCATION/OR/SOCIETY//PRIDE/AND/
PREJUDICE/BY/JANE/AUSTEN/

ENCODED, IT READS
TNQ,X EHV80 1K72W 1USC, 7DEC7 U84// DK,'8 P/B8L QQJOW 9VG8A 4FCWC LDO,H
'1HHA Z7N4R G,'A6 VBD'O 4SDOW 8I849 O4WRS DUYG4 P,CNS ,RDP, JCNFV 85KY/
FF449 8Q13K WM,2A 877B, ET'SN NB8,F Z/J

THE MESSAGE IS
TNQ,X EHV80 1K72W 1USC, 7DEC7 U84// DK,'8 P/B8L QQJOW 9VG8A 4FCWC LDO,H
'1HHA Z7N4R G, 'A6 VBD'O 4SDOW 8I849 O4WRS DUYG4 P,CNS ,RDP, JCNFV 85KY/
FF449 8Q13K WM,2A 877B, ET'SN NB8,F Z/J

DECODED, IT READS
MR/COLLINS/WAS/NOT/A/SENSIBLE/MAN/AND/THE/DEFFICIENCY/OF/NATURE/HAD/
BEEN/BUT/LITTLE/ASSISTED/BY/EDUCATION/OR/SOCIETY//PRIDE/AND/
PREJUDICE/BY/JANE/AUSTEN/
```

FIGURE 5·12
Typical output from coding program.

Copies of both alphabets are printed first. Then a copy of each input message is followed by a display of its coded form, encoded or decoded, as the case may be.

The general flowchart in Figure 5·11 is partially detailed in Figure 5·13 in which, as the legend shows, list data structures and their dimensions are specified for the important variables. As one can see, detailed decisions for the encoding and decoding process have been deferred.

It is characteristic of the stepwise decomposition approach

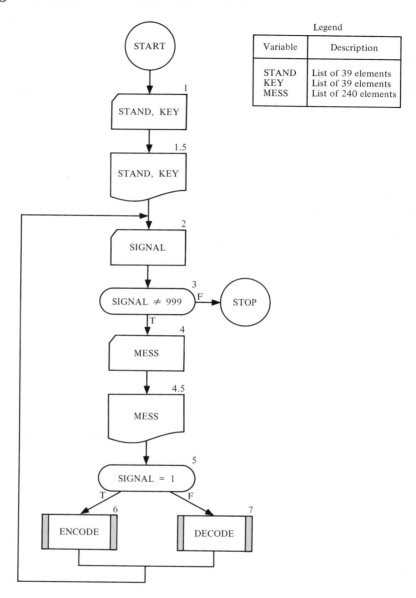

Legend

Variable	Description
STAND	List of 39 elements
KEY	List of 39 elements
MESS	List of 240 elements

FIGURE 5·13
Coding of main flowchart.

to problem solving that the expansion from one level of detail to another may be, and nearly always is, done piecemeal. That is, any one step of an algorithm may normally be selected for further expansion of detail, independently of the other steps.

ENCODE Procedure

We are now ready to think about the procedure ENCODE. This part of the flowchart must scan the message, character by character, identifying each one in the standard alphabet, shifting, and translating to the appropriate character in the key alphabet and assembling a coded message for printout. Figure 5·14 shows the algorithm that is developed through the following discussion. "Scan the message character by character" suggests a loop controlled by an iteration box, provided we know the length of the message.

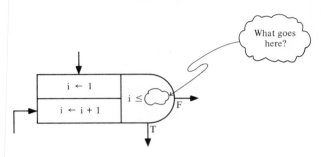

Now we have a choice. We can count the number, N, of characters in our message, and input this value for use as the upper limit on the condition governing the loop. Or we can avoid having to count the characters by using the dimension of the message list, 240, as the upper limit. But then we should also add the condition

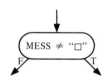

to cause a skip over any blank characters that are found anywhere in the message (boxes 6.1 and 6.2 in Figure 5·14).

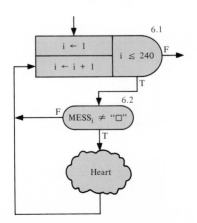

Having found a nonblank character in the message, we must determine the position j of the matching character in the standard alphabet. The idea is shown below.

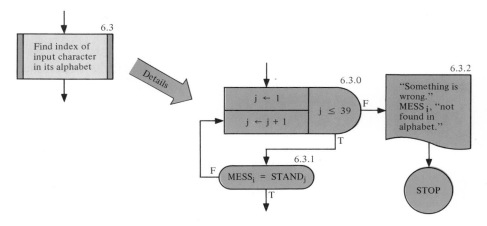

Once we have determined the index of the given character in its own alphabet, we are ready to convert it to the corresponding character in the target alphabet.

The position, newj, in the target alphabet is computed as follows. First, obtain the correct shift; then add this to j, the position in the input alphabet. To be sure that newj lies between 1 and 39, the value of j + shift must be reduced by 39's until it lies within the correct range. One way this can be done is:

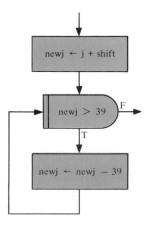

Recalling the carnival wheel exercises in Section 2·4, you should have no trouble convincing yourself that the same value for newj may be obtained by:

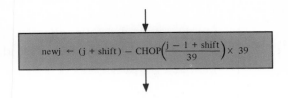

$$newj \leftarrow (j + shift) - CHOP\left(\frac{j - 1 + shift}{39}\right) \times 39$$

You must have noticed that we have not yet decided how the value of shift itself will be determined. This decision has been postponed to this point, but we will end the suspense here.

Let us say that the first character in our message will be shifted 5 places to the right, and that each succeeding character will be shifted 5 more places, that is, the second character will have a shift of 10, and so forth. If the value of shift is initialized to zero at the beginning of the procedure, then the step required to compute newj is better shown as:

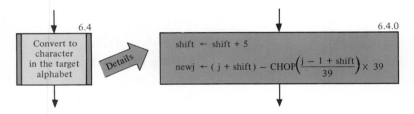

Finally, having calculated a value for newj, we can copy KEY_{newj} and append this character value to the output list, which we call TEXT.

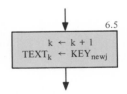

When the algorithm is ready to print the coded message, a subscript pointer, k, should be pointing to the last character assigned to the output list. Thus it is expedient to initialize k to zero at the beginning of the coding step and to increment it (in box 6.5) the instant before each new character is assigned to TEXT. The computation portion of the loop that processes each character is completed by the insertion of a space after each fifth character (box 6.6).

Figure 5·14 summarizes our just-completed design of ENCODE. Box 6.7, not mentioned previously, prints the encoded message.

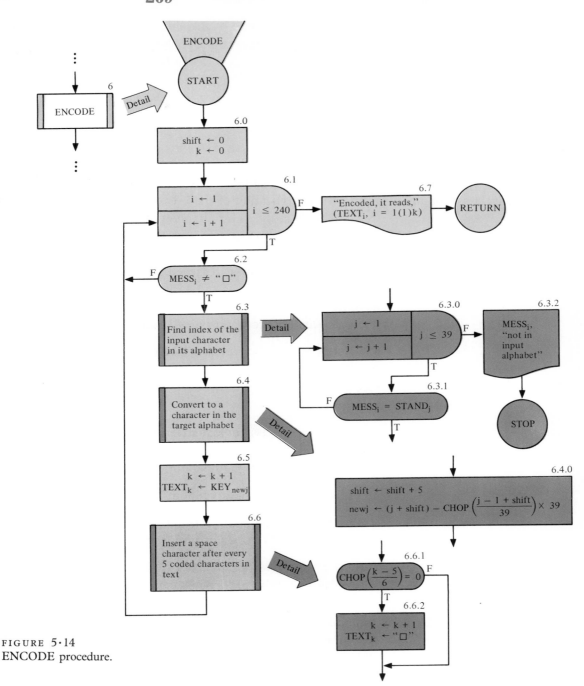

FIGURE 5·14
ENCODE procedure.

DECODE Procedure

The procedure DECODE shown in Figure 5·15 does the analogous and nearly symmetric job of decoding. The input message characters (except for spaces) must be located in the key alphabet. The corresponding index is then *un*shifted, that is, reduced by the value of the shift. Then the corresponding character from the standard alphabet is appended to the output list. Only the colored boxes in DECODE differ from those of Figure 5·14. Even the differences seem trivial. But notice that in decoding no spaces need to be inserted to break up the output because the slash character separates words.

Generalized Procedure for Encoding or Decoding

We are prompted to ask, is there any way one can avoid the almost total duplication of these two procedures? That is, can we somehow get by with only one procedure, call it CODER, say, and let it do the job of either encoding or decoding as required? The answer is definitely yes. There are several ways this condensation can be achieved. We suggest one way here and leave for you the discovery of still better ways after you have studied Chapter 9.

A systematic comparison of the two procedures reveals:

1. References to the alphabet STAND in one procedure correspond to references to the alphabet KEY in the other and vice versa. (Compare, e.g., boxes 6.5 and 7.5 and boxes 6.3.1 and 7.3.1).

2. In the second assignment statement of box 6.4.0 the operator that precedes occurrences of the variable, shift, is "+", whereas in box 7.4.0, the operator is "−".

3. Box 6.6 has no counterpart in Decode.

4. The message in box 6.7 begins with the word "Encode," whereas in box 7.7 it begins with the word "Decode".

Figure 5·16 gives a silhouette of CODER showing details only where there is a change made from the corresponding version of ENCODE or DECODE. The overall structure is unmodified. To call CODER for purposes of encoding or decoding it is only necessary to make preassignments to the alphabets ALPH1 and ALPH2, and to the special multiplier m that is used in box 8.4.0 in Figure 5·16.

For encoding we want the alphabets STAND and KEY to be preassigned to ALPH1 and ALPH2, respectively, and the value 1 preassigned to the multiplier m. For decoding we want, instead, to have the alphabets KEY and STAND preassigned to ALPH1 and ALPH2, respectively, and the value −1 preassigned to the multiplier m. Figure 5·17 now shows the main flowchart partially silhouetted with the discussed changes.

EXERCISES 5·3

1. If you have access to a computer, program the coder algorithm and code the following two messages. (If you don't have a computer, try tracing the algorithm by hand.) Use the alphabets given in the sample output.

Message to encode:

```
TO/BE/SURE/ANY/COMPUTER/BEHAVIOR/CAN/ULTIMATELY/BE/DESCRIBED/IN/TERMS/
OF/THE/UNDERLYING/CIRCUITRY/BUT/THIS/IS/OFTEN/NO/MORE/HELPFUL/THAN/IT/
WOULD/BE/TO/DESCRIBE/MAN'S/BEHAVIOR/IN/TERMS/OF/THE/ATOMS/MAKING/UP/
HIS/BODY/
```

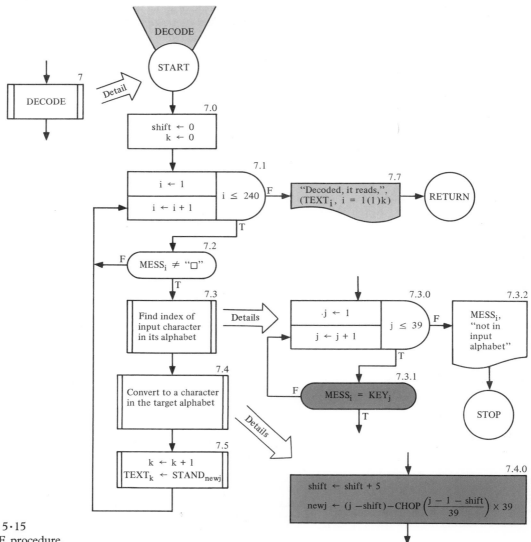

FIGURE 5·15
DECODE procedure.

Message to decode:

```
IIQUO OQUJ1 1UXCW KUI/R H31EV TYJ2E 'UGC8 PF1DI ZNA64 HY6LA AOW1K IAZ7O
SMCH/ ,99LP ZQ'5S BBAZ' 8P31K QL2ZO KBT27 OEUF' TENA7 ENETR J85FR B'8VN
4R44G 2,S7H RWUQL OUWL3 Y,BO7 N4RRF FZNB' E,ZCI IRWQR 01,05 3J174 UWM3,
LOOEN GKRFU JJOQQ TFQ/Y 9KQL2 33Y56 AM'SY LS
```

2. Design your own input alphabet, choosing the particular characters you want to use. Permute them in some fashion to obtain a key alphabet. Use CODER to encode messages in your own secret code. Check your process by also decoding your messages. Then challenge your friends to break your coded messages.

Warning Because a blank is inserted after each 5 encoded characters, encoded messages will be longer than original messages if the average word length of the original message exceeds 5 characters. This means that if the original message fills MESS, the TEXT list should have more than 240 elements.

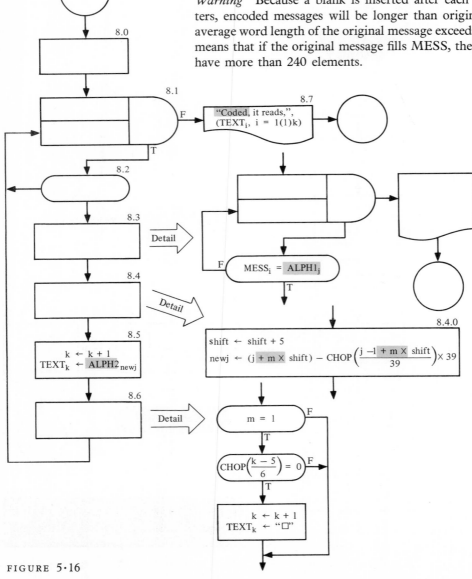

FIGURE 5·16

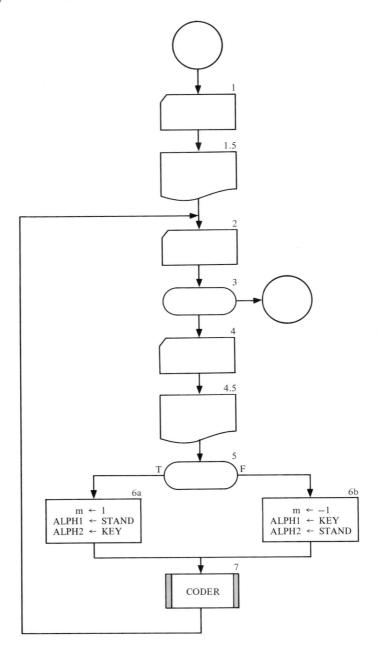

FIGURE 5·17
Main flowchart modified to
use CODER as an Encoder or
as a Decoder. Preassignments
of box 6a prepare for
*En*coding. Preassignments of
box 6b prepare for *De*coding.

5·4
Problem solving,
program quality, and
structured
programming

It is well known that when asked to flowchart the solution to
a problem, students produce a wide variety of flowcharts. Some
of these flowcharts may be incorrect in that they do not satisfy
some requirement of the problem and, even among those that
are essentially correct, some will be recognized as being "better" than others. These observations lead us to wonder whether

there are techniques we can learn that will help us to construct correct and even superior flowcharts.

Years ago the expense and difficulty of building a large, fast computer was such that the overriding criterion for a "good" program was that it use the least possible computer time. Computer storage was much more limited then than now, and the time it took to input (or output) information into (or from) storage during a computation was relatively long. Therefore to consume the least possible computer time implied not only that an algorithm was fast but also that it conserved computer storage and reduced to a minimum the input (or output) of information.

In view of this criterion, the "programmer's art" tended to emphasize the elimination of unnecessary instructions and the creation of tricky shortcuts. Programmers became proud of their ability to fit programs into a limited amount of storage and to find ways to trade storage for additional speed in execution.

Unfortunately, tricky programs (which often involve complicated branching back and forth between remote parts of the program) are extremely difficult to check or test. The programmer who created the "masterpiece" was often the only one who understood how the program worked, and often even he did not understand it well enough. Of course, programs can be tested for correctness under a wide variety of conditions, but such tests also use computer time and they can never guarantee that the program will still give correct results under an untested set of conditions. When a program is to control airline traffic or monitor patients in a hospital, we need more than a hit or miss assurance that it is both dependable and correct.

Although computers are still expensive and the need for program efficiency still cannot be ignored, important changes have taken place. Today the cost of creating programs often far exceeds the cost of using the computer, and so it has become essential to make the process of writing and testing programs more efficient. Today many computers have time-sharing systems that execute several jobs concurrently while the users share the computer storage. In such systems the cost of bringing new information into storage becomes relatively less, since another job uses the computer while the new information is brought in. The computer hardly ever waits idly by. Furthermore executing branches to remote parts of a program has become less efficient since all parts of a large program will probably not be in storage at the same time.

Such changing conditions as we describe must affect the criteria by which good programming is measured. Today we place a stronger emphasis on the need to demonstrate conclusively that programs are correct. It would be nice if methods existed to prove correctness mathematically. Such methods are still in their infancy. But it appears that even as these methods improve, they will only transfer the possibility of human error from the area of program construction to the area of formulating the mathematical criteria for correctness.

In practical applications only programs whose design adheres to a certain discipline can be demonstrated to be correct. Fortunately, that discipline, called *structured programming*, consists essentially in a more conscious and organized use of the techniques that we have already begun to use in this book.

In structured programming we subdivide a given task into a short sequence of subtasks. Decomposition is done in such a way that, at *any stage*, it is absolutely clear that the aggregate of the subtasks, executed in their proper sequence, achieves the desired result. For this to be "absolutely clear," three conditions must hold.

1.   The number of subtasks in any sequence must be small.

2.   Each subtask must be described precisely, so that there can be no confusion as to what the subtask does.

3.   The subtasks must not "overlap." To achieve this condition it is necessary but not sufficient to require that a subtask have only one entry and one exit. (One inference of this condition is that a subtask must not have *side effects*; i.e., it must not do anything that can have an unintentional effect on another subtask. Certain techniques to help avoid unintended side effects will be discussed in Chapter 9.)

Once we have accomplished this first decomposition we in turn decompose the subtasks in the same way. This decomposition continues until the subtasks are representable as simple statements in a language that is intelligible to the machine that will execute the algorithm. That language, in the case of SIMPLOS, is our flowchart language. Decomposition allows focusing of attention on ever smaller fragments of the main task.

If we achieve the nonoverlapping feature (condition 3) we need never worry about the effect that an activity in one subtask has on another subtask. That is, the demonstration of the correctness of each subtask is completely independent of the other subtasks. Thus, after the first decomposition, it is no longer necessary to have a grasp of the entire program. The same observation holds at each level of decomposition.

There are many problems in which the best choice of data representation is not obvious. Each step in the stepwise decomposition may require some decision concerning the data representation. In addition the programmer must exercise his ingenuity in deciding how to devise each decomposition step. Moreover, each decomposition must be regarded as tentative and subject to replacement if further analysis suggests that an earlier choice at another level is not optimal.

The problem of selecting an appropriate set of subdivisions of a given task is an intellectual, not a mechanical one. Inventiveness, insight, analysis, experience, and trial and error are often required. Selecting appropriate subdivisions is a design activity whose importance cannot be minimized. Some subtasks are trivial to decompose, as the first subtask (box 1)

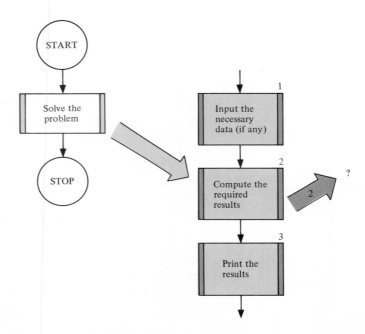

FIGURE 5·18

in Figure 5·18, with which we are all quite familiar. Unfortunately, the second subtask (box 2) in Figure 5·18 may not be so easy to decompose, and this is the more usual situation.

The function of the human programmer is always a vital one in the identification of subtasks and the design of subsequent decomposition. The discipline of structured programming involves the methods for structuring the subtasks *after* the programmer has selected (designed) each decomposition. These methods are actually surprisingly simple, but they are worth far more than a passing remark.

GOOD versus BAD Structure

What constraints, if any, does the discipline of structured programming impose on the way branching and looping are to be expressed in a flowchart? Experience has shown that when poor programming practice occurs, it usually involves bad branching or looping.

Each branch as well as each loop of a task must be thought of as a complete subtask. The branch step consists of a decision box that makes a selection among two or more (usually two) action paths.

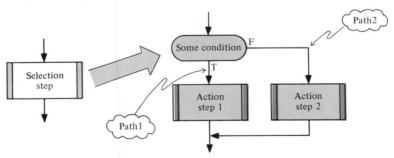

One or the other of the two action paths may in fact have no action; for example,

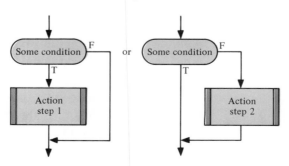

The important point to remember is that only after the two action paths *rejoin* is the branch or *selection* step completed!

Since it is beyond human intellectual capacity to remember too many details at once, it is bad practice to branch to a remote location of an algorithm where the action path may include another branch to still another remote location of the program, and so forth. Such branching requires the programmer to have the whole program in mind right down to the lowest level of detail.

The loop must be thought of as a single step in a decomposition, that is, one entry point and one exit point. In our flowchart language a loop step consists of an iteration box or a while box controlling a computation that itself should be thought of as a single action step; for example,

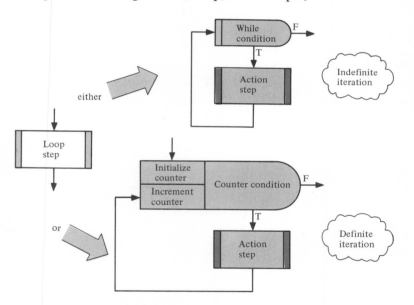

The initialization of the variables associated with the loop operation is best considered part of the loop step's decomposition. This is, of course, always true for the counter-variable that is initialized in an iteration box, but it should also be true for other variables. Two decompositions that illustrate this point are shown on the next page.

In each decomposition of a loop step the single exit point from the loop structure is the *false* exit from the loop control box. The principal programming offense regarding looping occurs when we allow execution to enter or exit from a loop

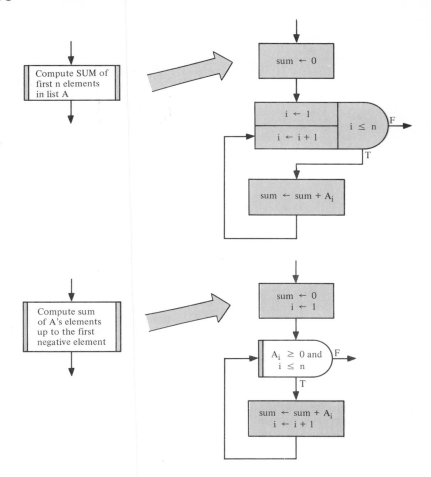

in the middle, that is, to or from places other than the "official" entry point or exit point. When this offense is committed, it becomes almost impossible to be sure what will happen in all possible cases of the program's execution. In short it becomes much more difficult to make sure the program will behave as the programmer intended under all conditions.

In a two-way selection either action step may itself be either an assignment step, a procedure step, another selection step, a loop step, or any sequence of these. The same can be said for the action step within a loop step. Figure 5·19 shows some examples of the nested structures that are possible and perfectly permissible within the constraints of structured programming. Because of the strict nesting of the structures, each substructure can be considered as a step in the decomposition of its "parent" structure. For example, Figure 5·19*d* can be

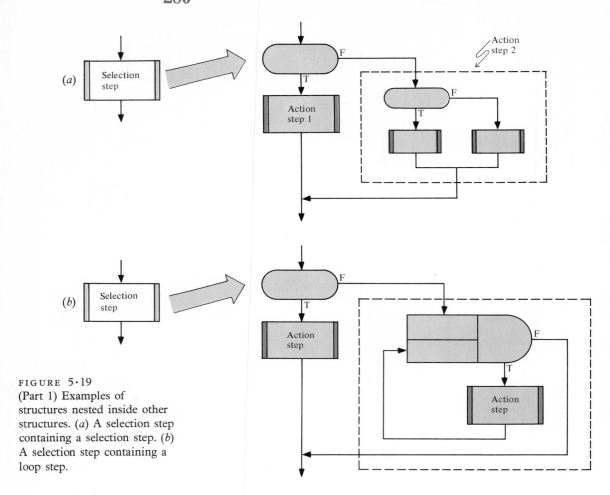

FIGURE 5·19
(Part 1) Examples of
structures nested inside other
structures. (*a*) A selection step
containing a selection step. (*b*)
A selection step containing a
loop step.

viewed more effectively as the decomposition sequence shown
in Figure 5·20.

Now that we have seen the numerous examples of good
loop structure, what are some examples of *bad loop structure?*
How can this bad structure be avoided? Bad loop structure
nearly always comes about as a result of a *premature exit from
a definite iteration.* A good example of this bad structure is
seen in Figure 5·21.

It is assumed that the cloud marked V includes various
steps, some of which may alter the value of B. At some point
in the iteration, before i exceeds n, B may no longer be less
than 0. In this case, exit from the loop is through box 5 in-

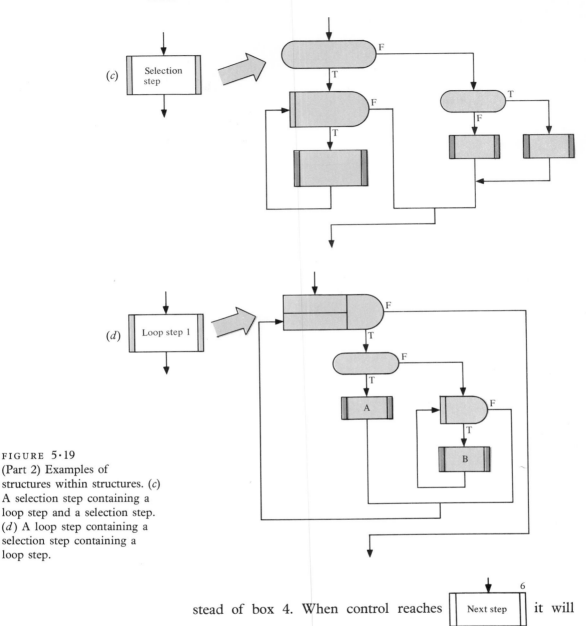

FIGURE 5·19
(Part 2) Examples of structures within structures. (c) A selection step containing a loop step and a selection step. (d) A loop step containing a selection step containing a loop step.

stead of box 4. When control reaches [Next step] it will

not be apparent (without further testing) which path was taken to get to that next step. And it may be a matter of considerable importance! Frequently the programmer fails to include the tests that would indicate which exit was taken from the loop. Often the wrong tests are made, especially if several bad loop

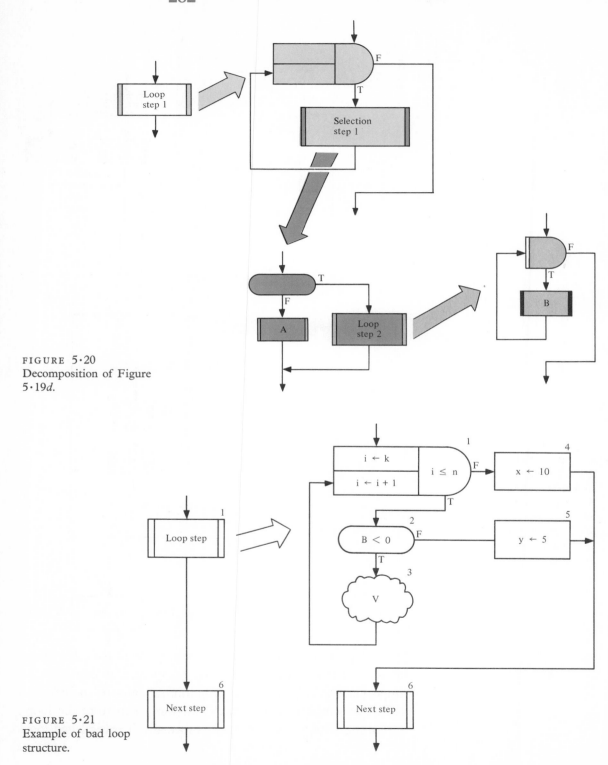

FIGURE 5·20
Decomposition of Figure
5·19d.

FIGURE 5·21
Example of bad loop
structure.

structures come before the point where the tests are inserted or if one bad loop structure contains not one, but several premature exits.

What simple rules can be followed systematically to avoid this premature exit problem? A little thought shows that the difficulty arises when an iteration box is used in the loop structure instead of a while box. The loop step displayed in Figure 5·21 should be thought of as an indefinite iteration. Figure 5·22 shows a three-step logical metamorphosis from the bad structure of Figure 5·21 to the good structure in Figure 5·22c. The key ideas are:

1. First replace the iteration box with the extra steps needed for a while structure (boxes 0, 1, and 6 of Figure 22a).

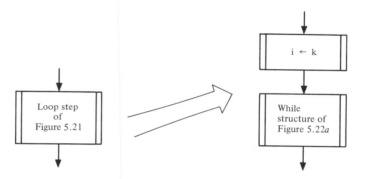

2. Next, break up the while structure into two separate steps.

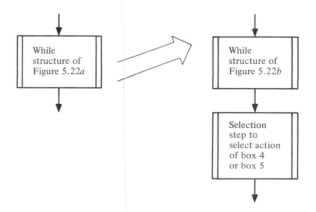

This is done by forcing the two separate exits of the loop to join and then appending to that joined exit a selection step that selects either the action of box 4 or box 5.

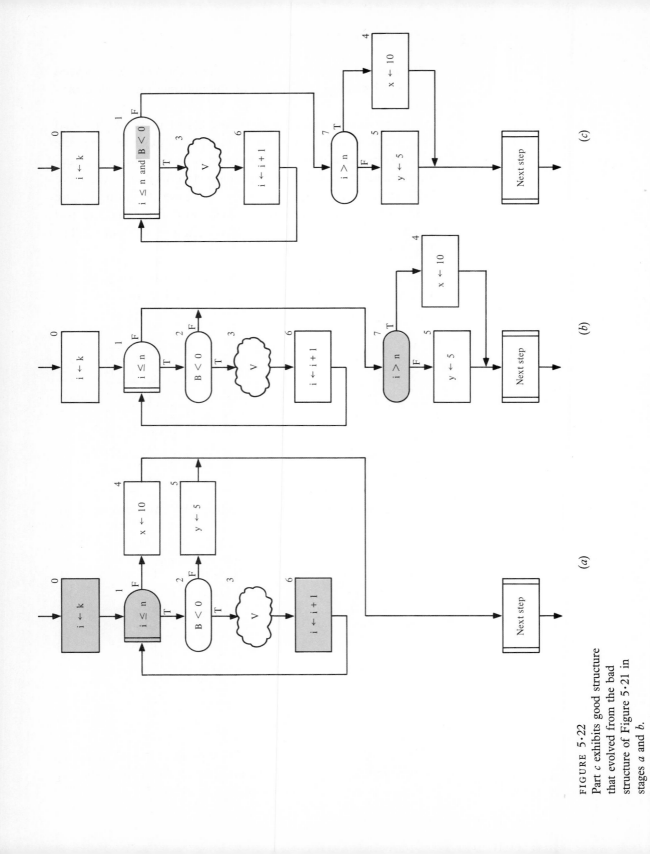

FIGURE 5·22
Part c exhibits good structure
that evolved from the bad
structure of Figure 5·21 in
stages a and b.

3.   Finally, eliminate the extra exit from the new while structure by "absorbing" the test, $B < 0$, into the while box, as
shown in Figure 5·22c. It is possible to eliminate the extra
exit in this way because, as we know from Section 3·3,

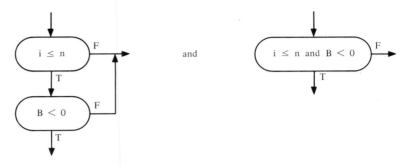

are logically equivalent.

Notice that a price has been paid to achieve the improved
structure. The final version is in two respects less efficient than
the original one. (1) The final one has more boxes at the
detailed level, 8 versus 6, hence more machine instructions,
and (2) one or two extra tests must be made in executing the
final version. We gladly pay this price for the cleaner structure
until it has been clearly demonstrated that greater efficiency is
essential.

   Is it always such a simple matter to go from a structure
such as Figure 5·22b to Figure 5·22c? Unfortunately, not if
the body of the loop contains other steps *between* the while
box and the test in box 2. Figure 5·23a shows such a structure
where the computation U intervenes. Now it is not possible
to absorb the test $B < 0$ into the while box because

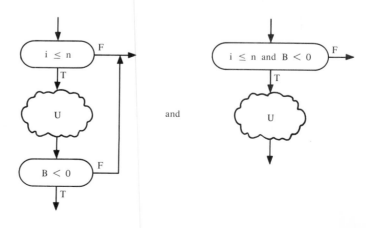

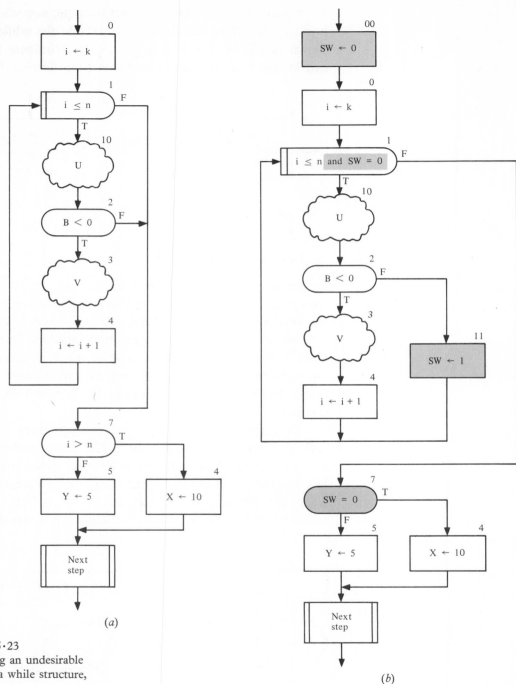

FIGURE 5·23
Eliminating an undesirable
exit from a while structure,
general case.

(a)

(b)

are not logically equivalent. To see this, suppose i is less than n, but B is not less than zero. In the first case the computation U is executed. In the second case it will not be executed.

How then, in this more general case, can the extra exit from the loop structure be avoided, if at all? Figure 5·23*b* provides one answer.

Eliminating the extra exit now comes at a slightly increased cost. We must introduce a new switch variable, reset it (to zero) in a separate step before entering the while box, set it (to one) whenever $B < 0$ is false, and test it as part of a compound condition within the while box. Although the cost of executing the loop structure has not gone up appreciably, we have had to add two more boxes to the structure (box 00 and box 11).

Is it ever too costly to eliminate the extra exits? Eventually, perhaps yes. For each extra exit eliminated within a loop structure there will need to be a more complex (multiway) switch that must be tested inside the while box, as well as later outside the structure, to decide what caused the exit. When the cost of executing all these extra steps becomes prohibitive, a programmer may well choose to stop short of the full cleanup operation, but in doing so, he should be aware of the trade-off he is making and the risks he is taking.

To highlight this trade-off between clean structure and efficiency and to close out this discussion, we illustrate with Figure 5·24 a case where there are three alternate exits from a loop. Figure 5·24*a* shows the bad structure. Figure 5·24*c* shows the cleanly structured form with the extra steps necessary to achieve it. Figure 5·24*b* shows the compromise (for the sake of efficiency), but always beware of such compromises. For example, it is easy to see that Figure 5·24*b* is not equivalent to Figure 5·24*a* or 5·24*c* if the execution of clouds 5 or 7 can alter the value of B or if the execution of cloud 7 can alter the value of C. For, suppose the execution path in Figure 5·24*b* takes the F exit from box 8 after B has been assigned a positive value, say during execution of cloud 7. Then the test at box 16 will be true, causing the assignment in box 12 to be executed instead of the assignment in box 14.

Lest the reader be lulled into the belief that use of the multiway switch variable offers no risk, we remind him that the switch variable does its job effectively only if used for no

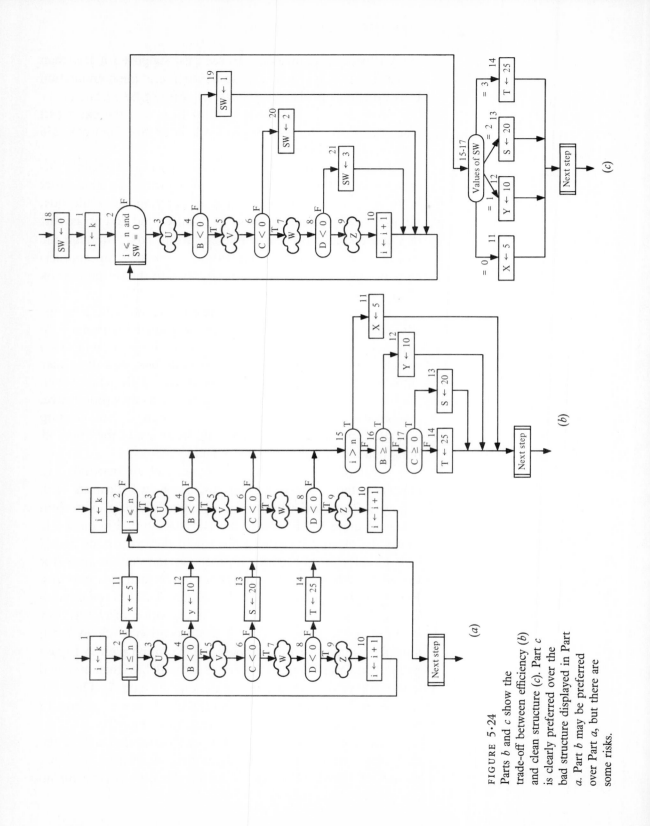

FIGURE 5·24
Parts *b* and *c* show the trade-off between efficiency (*b*) and clean structure (*c*). Part *c* is clearly preferred over the bad structure displayed in Part *a*. Part *b* may be preferred over Part *a*, but there are some risks.

other purpose than the one we have given it. If it is accidentally modified in clouds 3, 5, 7, or 9, then Figure 5·24c is no better a solution to the problem than Figure 5·24b is.

EXERCISES 5·4

In each of the following exercises your job is to convert the flowchart fragment to one that is *well structured*.

1.

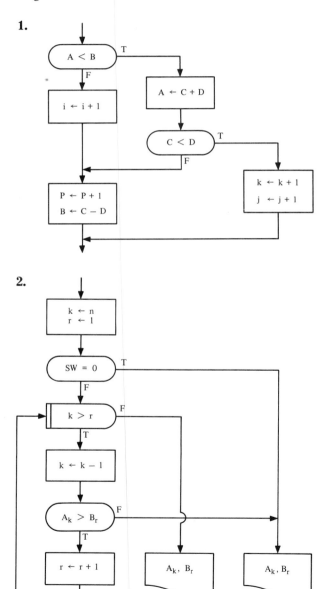

2.

3.

4.

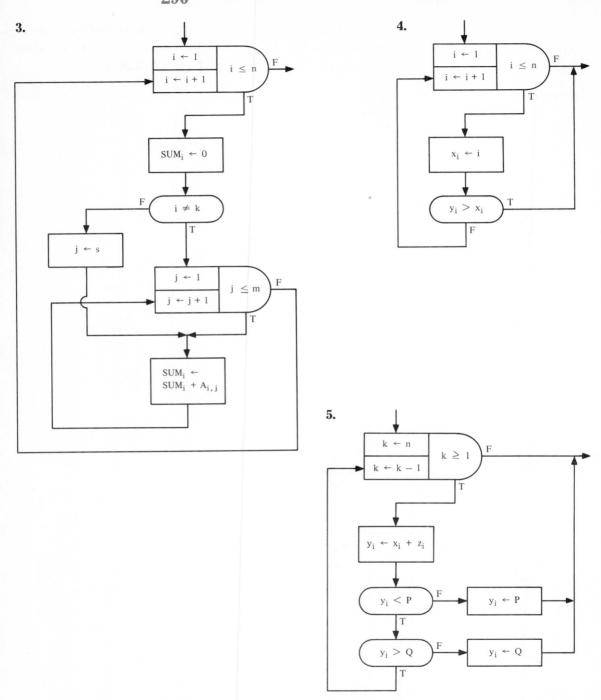

5.

6.   Find at least two flowchart fragments in the exercises for Section 3·4 that exhibit bad structure, and then show how each can be modified to exhibit good structure.

5·5
Restructuring a bad example

In most of the flowcharts in previous chapters we followed the precepts of structured programming even though we did not point this out at the time. However, we saved (at least) one bad example at which we could point the finger of scorn after the principles of structured programming were introduced. This is the flowchart for our first "abominable" sorting algorithm seen in Figure 3·29. We repeat this flowchart here as Figure 5·25.

Boxes 4, 6, and 7 constitute one loop while boxes 3, 4, and 5 constitute another loop. These two loops share flowchart box 4. This is obviously quite horrible from the point of view of structured programming. Consequently we will attempt to redesign this algorithm to meet the requirements of structured programming. It will be easier to start over again instead of repairing the given flowchart.

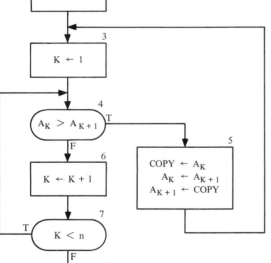

Legend

Variable	Description
n	Integer
A	List of n reals
K	Integer

FIGURE 5·25

Before we begin, a warning is needed. Just improving the structure of the algorithm's flowchart representation will not make a more efficient sorting algorithm. The job we are about to do is a case in point. When our task is completed, the abominable sort algorithm will have good structure, but it will still be abominable in the sense that it is outrageously inefficient even relative to, say, the bubble sort algorithm, which is certainly not the most efficient of all known sorting algorithms. With this warning in mind let us redescribe the algorithm in simple English.

Verbal Description of
Abominable Sort Algorithm

Scan the list, A_1, A_2, ... , A_n, from the beginning for an out-of-order pair of adjacent elements. If such a pair is found, perform an interchange, and then repeat the scan until a complete scan of the list finds no out-of-order pair.

The first step of decomposition brings us to Figure 5·26. We can see that only box 3 requires further decomposition. How should this be done to carry out the verbal description? The clue is the phrasing: "scan the list . . . and then repeat the scan until . . . ." We need a *while* structure because the number of times the scan operation is to be performed is *indefinite;* that is,

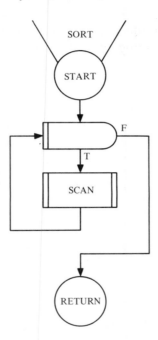

What test can be applied in the while box to tell when it is no longer necessary to scan the list? Enter the switch variable! Suppose we let SW be given an initial value of 1 and then rely on the inner workings of SCAN to set SW to 0 when the list is found to have no out-of-order pair. Although this strategy forces on SCAN, the responsibility to "signal" SORT concerning this event, our decision to use SW in this way allows us to complete the second step of decomposition, as seen in Figure 5·27.

What about the details for SCAN? This step has two basic functions. It must search the list A for a pair of adjacent

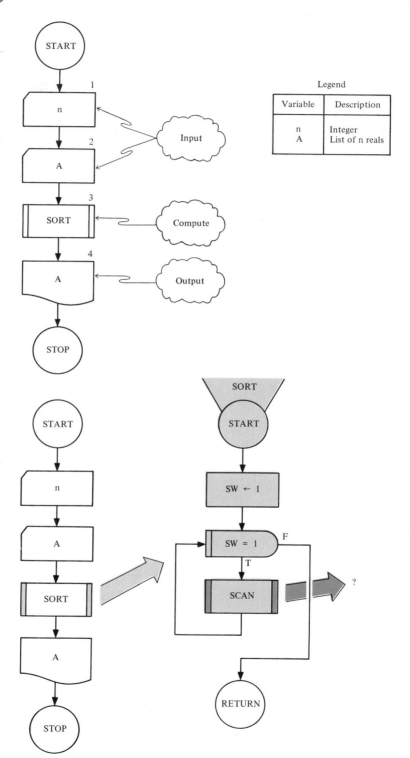

FIGURE 5·26
The first and easy
decomposition step.

FIGURE 5·27

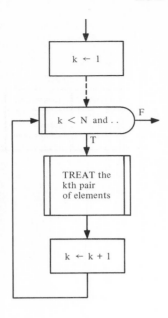

elements out of order (indefinite iteration), and it must guarantee to set SW to 0 should no pair be found out of order. Let k be the index for identifying the elements of A. Then the scan must have a loop structure that is roughly as shown at the left.

Some escape mechanism must still be supplied so that the loop will terminate when an out-of-order pair has been found. How can this be done? Again we can use a switch variable. Another switch can be added. SW2 might originally be set to 0 to signify that we assume the list is in perfect order. SW2 would then be reset to 1 by TREAT whenever an out-of-order pair is found. We would then have the structure something like:

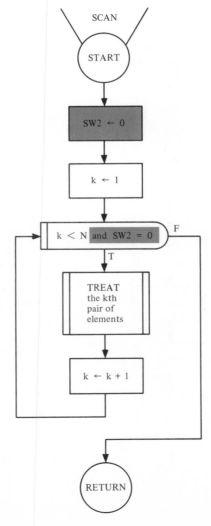

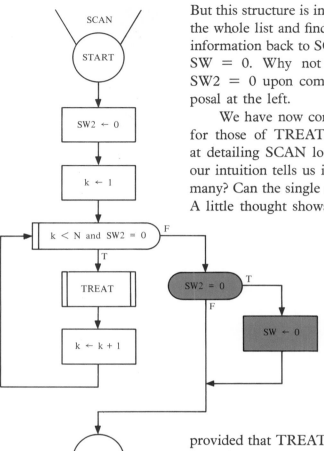

But this structure is incomplete because when SCAN examines the whole list and finds it to be in order, it must transmit this information back to SORT. What SORT wants is a signal that SW = 0. Why not then let SCAN set SW to 0 when SW2 = 0 upon completion of the while loop? See the proposal at the left.

We have now completed all the details for SCAN except for those of TREAT. But wait a minute! The last attempt at detailing SCAN looks suspiciously more complicated than our intuition tells us it should be. Do we have one switch too many? Can the single switch SW be made to do the job alone? A little thought shows that SW can, indeed, do double duty, provided that TREAT is coded to set SW to 1 instead of SW2 to 1 when an out-of-order pair is found. But this is no problem, since the details of TREAT have been conveniently postponed up to this point. Figure 5·28, therefore, shows our third step of decomposition as we would like it, and we are ready to consider the final set of details, those of TREAT.

What are the functions of TREAT? They are to compare the pair A_k, A_{k+1}, and, if out of order, interchange them and then set the switch SW to 1. If SW is set to 1, then on return to SCAN, that procedure will complete its loop and return execution to SORT which, because SW = 1, will *continue* its loop by again calling on SCAN. It's like magic! It all works, and it works in a well-structured manner. That is, each decomposition level is understandable merely by assuming that the details at the next lower level are somehow carried out properly. See the final step of decomposition in Figure 5·29.

And so we have seen that even the unpromising example

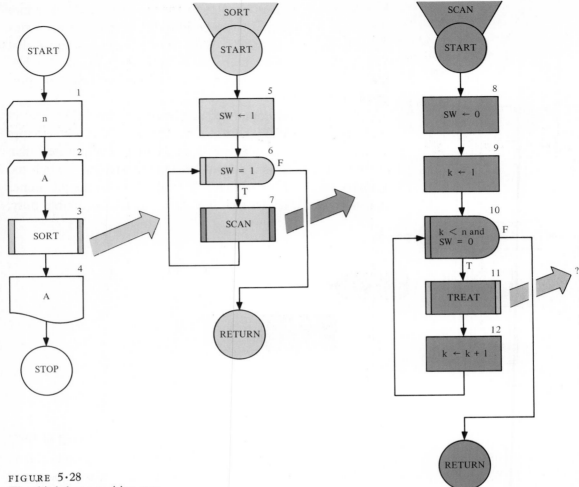

FIGURE 5·28
The third decomposition step.

presented in this section has yielded to the requirements of structured programming. The creation of switch variables as seen in this example is characteristic of structured programming, because each program must know *what* each of its subtasks accomplishes, but not *how* each subtask is accomplished. Thus, to carry any information back to the calling program (such as whether or not a search was successful), there must be variables provided to return this information.

We do not demand that every program be decomposed down to the level of the three primitive forms: assignment steps, selection steps, and loop steps. However, the flowcharts

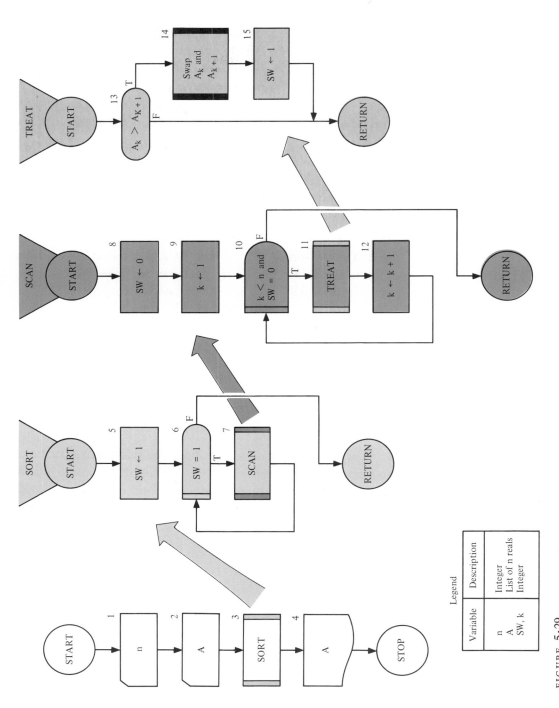

FIGURE 5·29
The fourth and last
decomposition step.

Legend

Variable	Description
n	Integer
A	List of n reals
SW, k	Integer

should be so drawn that this ultimate decomposition is easily possible—almost obvious at sight.

As a test that the task of structuring a program is complete we should be able to supply simple descriptions in words of the activities carried out by each of the subtasks. Only then can a reader verify from the top down that the program actually carries out the desired task. To illustrate we give below such word descriptions for each of the subtasks of Figure 5·29.

MAIN.   Inputs a list A, sorts it, and outputs the sorted list.

SORT.   Rearranges entries in the list A in increasing order by repeatedly executing the subtask SCAN until A is free of out-of-order pairs (i.e., until SW = 0).

SCAN.   Scans successive pairs in the list $A_1, A_2, \ldots, A_n$ for the first out-of-order pair, if any. SCAN calls on TREAT to examine the individual pairs of elements. If an out-of-order pair is found, SW equals 1 when control returns to SORT. If no out-of-order pair is found, SW equals 0 when control returns to SORT.

TREAT.   For a given value of k, tests whether $A_k > A_{k+1}$. If so, the values of A_k and A_{k+1} are interchanged and SW is given the value 1 before control returns to SCAN. If not, then the value of SW is left unchanged, that is, remains equal to 0, and control is then returned to SCAN.

There is actually more that should be said about structured programming, but this is best postponed until Chapter 9, where we discuss ways to insure the isolation and insulation of subtasks one from another so that they do not overlap in unexpected ways. (See the subsection entitled "Structured Programming and Parameters.")

Chapter 6   Trees

6·1
Tree examples

The use of flowcharts to represent algorithms has helped us to recognize their underlying *structure*. Furthermore, attention paid to the structure of an algorithm usually results in a better understanding of the computational process, and often results in our recognizing alternatives and potential improvements to the original design. Similar rewards result from attention paid to the structural relationships among the components of a set of data.

There is, in fact, a close connection between the steps we need to express an algorithm and the way we choose to think about or *represent* the data that are to be transformed by that algorithm. Experience in constructing algorithms fosters an increased appreciation of this interdependence. You will gain some of this experience by studying the next several chapters. Your ability to analyze the structure of a set of data and how alternate representations of it can affect algorithms using such data, undoubtedly will improve. We have already considered two structural forms for data, lists and arrays. Another type of structure is called a *tree* (Figure 6·1). Tree structures are important in representing certain types of data and, oddly enough, the essential steps of a number of algorithms exhibit a treelike structure.

First we will give two simple examples of a process whose strategy of execution (algorithm) can be pictured as a tree and two examples of data that can be pictured as a tree. Later, we will tackle three fascinating problems, the first one at the end of this chapter and the other two in Chapter 7. When we have finished this study, we may claim the title *tree expert*.

Let us agree now, before we get too far along, that trees in this chapter will be drawn upside down (Figure 6·2). We

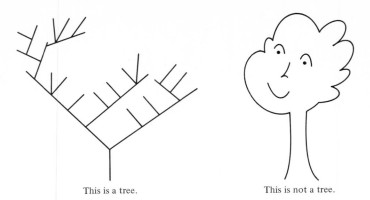

FIGURE 6·1

This is a tree.   This is not a tree.

do this only because it is convenient. You have to be willing to think of a tree growing toward the earth, its trunk "hanging" from the sky.

Example 1.
Treelike Algorithms

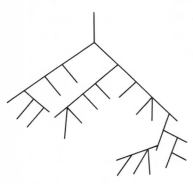

FIGURE 6·2
This is an upside-down tree.

Our first example shows how we can represent the 16 conclusions to the well-known eight-coin problem as a "decision tree." The problem is this. You are given eight coins, a, b, c, d, e, f, g, and h, and are told that they are all of uniform weight except one, which is either heavier or lighter than the others. You are given an equal arm balance, but you may only use it three times for comparing coins or groups of coins. Your job is to determine the maverick coin and whether it is lighter or heavier than the rest.

Here is a strategy to use (see Figure 6·3) for all possible cases.

1. Compare the weights of two subsets of equal numbers of coins and consider the significance of the *three* possible outcomes. If the weights of the two subsets are equal, the coin in which we are interested cannot belong to either of the compared subsets.

2. Once we have isolated a pair containing the "odd" coin and we want to know whether one of them is heavy or light, we weigh one of the two candidates against any other that is known to be "standard."

There are 16 possible cases, each of which may occur, given the eight labeled coins. The algorithm shown in Figure 6·3 has a treelike structure. Conclusions are reached by follow-

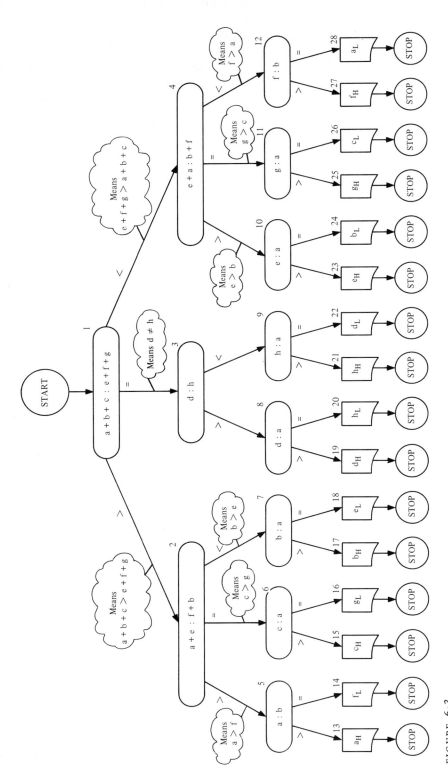

FIGURE 6·3

Tree diagram of a strategy to
identify the odd coin.

Conclusions are subscripted:
subscript H means *heavy*;
subscript L means *light*.

ing a unique path (a sequence of three weighings) from the top or *root* of the tree diagram to one of the terminal boxes or *leaves* at the bottom.

EXERCISES 6·1,
SET A

1. For decision box 2 in Figure 6·3, explain why:

    (a) If the relation $a + e > f + b$ is true, one may conclude that $a > f$.
    (b) If the relation $a + e = f + b$ is true, one may conclude that $c > g$.
    (c) If the relation $a + e < f + b$ is true, one may conclude that $b > e$.

2. Explain why b may be regarded as a "standard" coin at decision box 5 but not at decision box 7.

3. Suppose you are given 12 seemingly identical balls and are told that one ball is *heavier* than the others, which are of the same weight. Draw the tree diagram algorithm to identify the heavy ball in three weighings.

4. Suppose you are given 12 seemingly identical balls and are told that one ball is *different* in weight (either heavier or lighter). Draw a tree diagram algorithm to identify the odd ball and to determine whether it is heavier or lighter in three weighings.

5. Are all decision sequences tree structures? Consider the three flow-charts below.

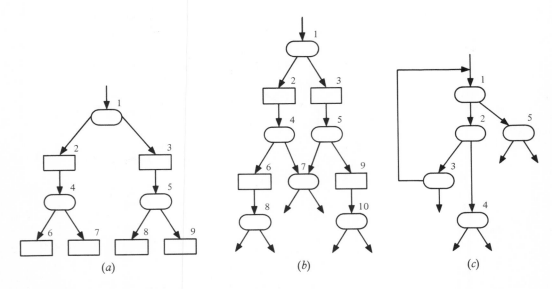

(a)   (b)   (c)

(a) Which of these are tree structures?
(b) Consider the following attempt to define a tree structure.

(1) A node having no segments extending from it is a *terminal* node.

(2) A node having one or more segments extending from it is a *nonterminal* node.

(3) A tree structure is a terminal node *or* a nonterminal node whose segments consist either of terminal nodes or tree structures.

What corrections or additions, if any, are needed in the above definition so that, when applied to flowcharts *a, b,* and *c,* you will reach the same conclusions that you came to in the answer to part a of this problem?

Example 2.
Game Trees

A more interesting type of decision tree, frequently referred to as a *game tree,* shows the moves made by the players. Each time a player makes a move, he selects among the available choices of "legal" moves. Each line segment of the tree represents one choice by one player during the playing of one game. Figure 6·4 is a tree for the game of "Eight." This two-player game is so trivial you may not enjoy playing it very long. Its tree is simple enough, however, that we can study it easily, and it serves as a good illustration of similar but far more complicated games.

The rules of "Eight"

Each player takes a turn at picking a number from one to three, adding this number to a running sum that is initially set at zero. The first player has a free choice of numbers 1, 2, and 3. The choice in each play thereafter is restricted. A player may not choose the opponent's preceding selection. The player who brings the running sum to a total of exactly eight wins the game; a player exceeding eight loses. There is no draw possible.

When we study the game tree, we can observe that a complete game from start to finish is represented by one path (e.g., the colored line) from the beginning or *root* of the tree down to an end or terminal point. Player A always moves first. Thus, on the green line, A chooses 1 from among the three initial choices. Then B chooses 3, then A chooses 1, and so forth, until at the last move for A the running sum is 7, and his choices are 1 and 3. So he chooses 1 to make the sum 8 and wins. Triangular-shaped endpoints denote a win for A. Square-shaped endpoints denote a win for B.

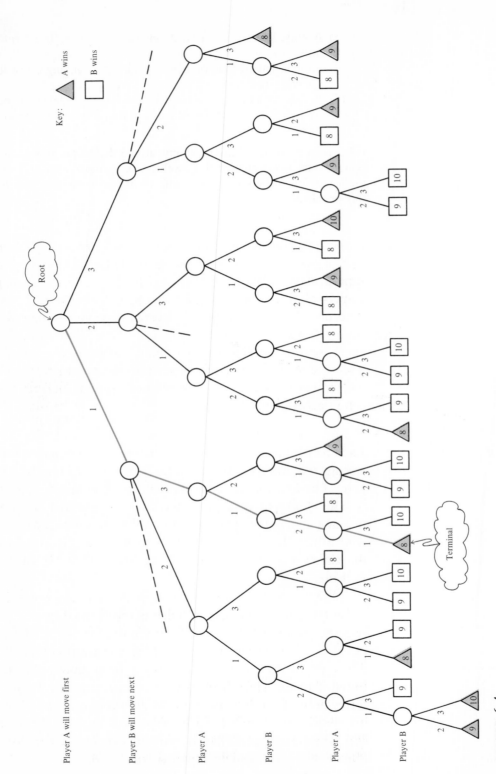

FIGURE 6·4
Tree for the game of Eight.

Each time a player makes a move, you can imagine he looks at three choices 1, 2, and 3. After the very first choice he rules out one of these, as the game rules demand. *Inadmissible* moves would not ordinarily appear in the tree because they tend to clutter the diagram. We have shown them as dashed lines for B's first move only as a reminder.

1. (a) How many distinct games of "Eight" are there?

Imagine the game of Eight is played by children at the local kindergarten in the following way. Player A twirls the arrow of a three-part spinner, to select the initial move. Thereafter, each player flips a coin to decide among the two admissible choices. (heads the smaller, tails the larger.)

   (b) What percentage of games played will follow the color line path in Figure 6·4?
   (c) What are A's chances of winning? Express this result as the number of games won for every 100 games played.
   (d) If each player chooses each move as shrewdly as possible, what do you think are A's chances of winning if A plays first? The answer is 0 times out of 100. See if you can develop a proof of this assertion. In Chapter 7 we will take another look at this problem.

In each of the next two exercises, you are given the rules of a simple, two-player game. Your job in each case is to show part or all of the game tree with at least four complete games displayed.

Column

	1	2	3
1	● 1	● 2	● 3
Row 2	4	5	6
3	● 7	● 8	● 9

2. The game of *Hex* (or Hexapawn) uses a 3 by 3 checkerboard. Each player begins the game with three pieces on his base line, as shown in Figure 6·5. Play alternates between green and gray. The rules of the game are as follows.

   (a) Either green or gray, in his turn, can move forward one space to an unoccupied position.
   (b) Or he can move diagonally one space to capture an opponent. A captured piece is removed from the board.
   (c) The game is won by reaching the opponent's baseline.
   (d) Or by leaving the opponent without a move.
   (e) Or by capturing all opponent pieces.

FIGURE 6·5
Board position at the beginning of the game of Hex.

Hint Each segment of the tree should be labeled to indicate the move it represents. One way would be to show the *before* and *after* row, column values of the piece that is moved. For example, on green's first play he has three choices: $(3,1) \rightarrow (2,1)$, or $(3,2) \rightarrow (2,2)$, or $(3,3) \rightarrow (2,3)$. Each of these moves can be further abbreviated to four-digit numbers without loss of information, that is, 3121, 3222, and 3323, respectively.

Alternatively, if we give the squares of the board the explicit names shown as small digits in the lower right corner of each square in Figure 6·5, then we can use a somewhat more compact representation of a move. Instead of four-digit abbreviations (e.g., 3121, 3222, and 3323), we can use two-digit abbreviations (e.g., 74, 85, and 96, respectively) with no risk of confusion.

3. *The game of "31."* Take a die and roll it. The side that turns up gives the running sum's initial value. Thereafter, each player moves by tilting the die over on its side (one of four possible sides, of course, and remember that opposite faces

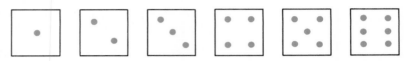

always add to seven). The side that turns up after the tilt-over is then added to the running sum. The game proceeds tilt after tilt. A player whose tilt brings the total to exactly 31 wins the game; a player exceeding 31 loses. There are no draws.

Data Trees

Flowcharts of algorithms often have the characteristic treelike structure, but it is also interesting that *data* can be arranged in a treelike structure. Here are two examples.

Example 3.
Monotone Subsequences

Suppose you are given a sequence (i.e., a list) of N numbers, all guaranteed to be different. What is the longest *monotone subsequence* in the given sequence?

By a *subsequence* we mean the list that remains after "crossing out" some numbers in the original list. If, for example, the given list is

5 0 9 6 1 12 3 7 2,

then one of the 511 ($2^9 - 1$) possible subsequences of this sequence is:

5̷ 0̷ 9 6 1̷ 12 3 7̷ 2

that is, 9 6 12 3 2.

The reason for explaining this idea in terms of "crossing out" is to make it absolutely clear that the order of the *remaining* terms is not altered. By a *monotone* subsequence we mean one in which either the values are increasing from left to right or one in which they are decreasing. Thus the preceding subsequence,

9   6   12   3   2

is not monotone, but the following two are, the first being increasing and the second decreasing.

5̸ 0 9̸ 6̸ 1 1̸2̸ 3 7 2̸
5 0̸ 9̸ 6̸ 1 1̸2̸ 3 7̸ 2

You can check that the increasing subsequence is the longest possible; that is, there is no increasing subsequence with more than four elements. The decreasing one is not the longest possible, since the subsequence

9   6   3   2

is longer.

It is possible to develop an algorithm for determining longest monotone subsequences of a given sequence. Our interest here is a bit different. Suppose you are asked to picture *all* the possible monotone decreasing subsequences of our example sequence,

5   0   9   6   1   12   3   7   2

A hopeless task? Not if we think in terms of trees! See the answer in Figure 6·6.

A most revealing discovery! We have taken a string of numbers, posed a particular problem concerning that string, and discovered that the problem's answer could lie in inspecting a related tree. Notice that every monotone decreasing subsequence in S can be represented as a *path* running from the root S to one of the terminal squares. From now on, we'll call these circles and squares *nodes*.

The longest of such subsequences is easy for the eye to pick out once the tree is drawn. It is the one whose *terminal node* is found at a level of the tree farthest from the root node. In this example, only one path reaches to level 4, so there is only one longest monotone decreasing subsequence.

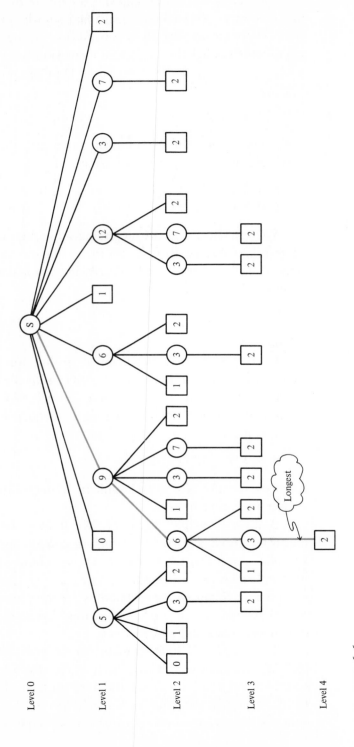

Level 0

Level 1

Level 2

Level 3

Level 4

Longest

FIGURE 6·6
Tree of monotone *decreasing*
subsequences for the list
S = 5, 0, 9, 6, 1, 12, 3, 7, 2.

If a computer is to be used for this approach, we must have an algorithm that, in effect, systematically scans the entire tree. This is the interesting part, which will be taken up starting with the next section.

1. Construct a tree that displays all monotone *increasing* subsequences of the same sequence given in Figure 6·6.

2. Draw the tree that displays all monotone decreasing subsequences for the sequence S defined as

$$S = \{3, 2, 1, 0\}$$

3. Imagine you are a student registering at a university and you have decided to enroll in a particular group of five courses. The five courses, together with the available sections and the times each will be taught, are listed in Figure 6·7. We presume these data are extracted from the official class schedule. Notice that the time periods are letter coded for convenience.

Course	Open Sections		
ENG 132	D (9–10	MWF)
	E (10–11	MWF)
	F (11–12	MWF)
FRE 141	F (11–12	MWF)
	H (1–2	MWF)
	Q (10–11:30	TTH)
HIS 231	F (11–12	MWF)
	H (1–2	MWF)
MTH 172	D (9–10	MWF)
	F (11–12	MWF)
	Q (10–11:30	TTH)
CSC 131	F (11–12	MWF)
	H (1–2	MWF)

Timetable

Course	Letter Codes for Possible Sets				
	No. 1	No. 2	No. 3	No. 4	No. 5
ENG 132					
FRE 141					
HIS 231					
MTH 172					
CSC 131					

FIGURE 6·7
Data taken from the printed class schedule.

Does a possible set of nonconflicting sections for the five courses exist? That is, is it possible to select a set with no time conflicts? If so, how many distinct feasible sets can be selected? To be distinct, a set need differ in no more than one section from other possible sets. Complete a column of the timetable shown in Figure 6·7 for each feasible set.

Hint This problem and others like it can be solved systematically by constructing a tree of labeled nodes. The structure for the tree could be such that the set of nodes along any path emanating from the root represents a set of nonconflicting course sections. For example, labeled nodes at level 1 could represent the various available sections of ENG 132 (Figure 6·8). Nodes at level 2 could correspond to various sections of FRE 141, and so forth. Any path running from the root to level 5 such that every node has a different label would represent a feasible set of courses.

FIGURE 6·8

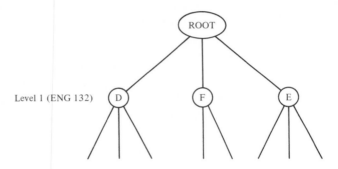

4. Imagine you are a student registering at a university and assume that you have decided to enroll in the following *six* courses:

Communications 267	(COM 267)
English 337	(ENG 337)
French 231	(FRE 231)
Geography 233	(GGY 233)
Mathematics 272	(MTH 272)
Music 120A	(MUS 120A)

Below are data taken from the printed class schedule. Imagine that when you reach the registration desk, you find that certain sections of four of the desired courses are closed (as indicated). Prepare a tree diagram that shows whether there are one or more possible programs open to you at this time, permitting you to enroll in all six of the desired courses with no time conflicts. If one (or more) program(s) is (are) available, prepare a filled-out timetable whose format is similar to that given in Figure 6·7.

5. A student who was planning to work every afternoon (1–5 p.m.) for the Athletics Department was also hoping to enroll in all of the following six courses: COM 267, MUS 120A, GGY 233, MTH 272,

COM 267	TV-FILM SCENE AND LIGHT		
P601	117–KUHT	930–11AM TTH	COLLINS
MUS 120A	MUSICIANSHIP I		
E601	129–E	10–11AM WF	MILLER
H602	129–E	1–2PM WF	MILLER
P603	129–E	9–10AM TTH	HORVIT
Q604	101–E	10–11AM TTH	BENJAMIN
GGY 233	WORLD REALMS		
F601	101–AH	11–12 MWF	HYER
H602	101–AH	1–2PM MWF	PALMER
S603	210–AH	1–2:30PM TTH	SHERIDAN
U604	101–AH	4–5:30PM TTH	COFFMAN
MTH 272	CALCULUS III		
D602	204–AH	9–10AM MWF	RADER
E603	216–AH	10–11AM MWF	
H604	116–T	1–2PM MWF	
P607	7–AH	8:30–10AM TTH	RADER
P608	111–Z	8:30–10AM TTH	
S610	211A–SR	1–2:30PM TTH	
FRE 231	INTERMEDIATE FRENCH		
E601	303–AH	10–11AM MWF	MCLENDON
F602	106–Z	11–12 MWF	JANSSENS
H603	105–Z	1–2PM MWF	
I604	105–Z	2–3PM MWF	
Q605	111–Z	10–11:30AM TTH	MCDERMOTT
S606	112–Z	1–2:30PM TTH	HOWARD
ENG 337	SHAKESPEARE		
D601	105–C	9–10AM MWF	HENDERSON A
E602	110–C	10–11AM MWF	EAKER
P604	110–C	8:30–10AM TTH	EAKER
S605	113–C	1–2:30PM TTH	THOMAS

closed sections

FRE 231, and ENG 337. He received special permission to register early (i.e., no *closed sections* to worry about). How many different feasible programs could he select, given the printed schedule used in Problem 4 (ignoring closed sections), and still take the afternoon job without a time conflict?

Example 4.	Suppose we are given
Tree Representation	
of Expressions	

$$((a \times w + b) \times w){\uparrow}2 / (d \times y)$$

It seems obvious that whoever first wrote this string of characters intended that it have a mathematical meaning. By now, you are quite expert at interpreting such strings. This interpretation, remember, involved the application of a relatively complicated set of rules (Tables 2·1 and 2·3). Figure 6·9

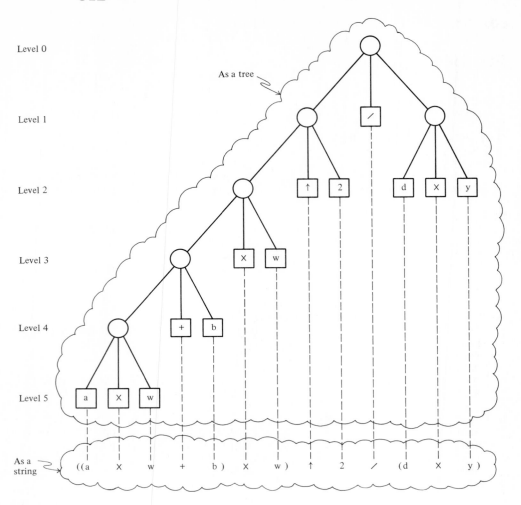

FIGURE 6·9
A tree representation of an
arithmetic expression.

shows how we can represent the same string as a tree and give
it the same interpretation. We will quickly discover that the
rules for evaluating an expression represented as a tree are
much simpler to state because *part of the interpretation is inherent in the structure of the tree.*

Before proceeding with this line of thought, it will be
helpful to summarize and supplement the tree terminology
developed thus far. This is done with the aid of Figure 6·10*a*.

We see that every tree has a *root node* from which extend
segments (one or more) to other nodes, which in turn branch
to others, eventually ending in *terminal* or *leaf nodes*. (Notice
that a root node alone is not a tree.) Every segment leads to
the root of a subtree, which may be a terminal node. Nodes

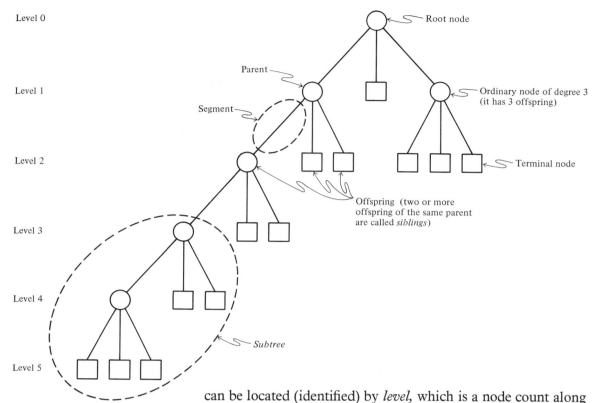

Level 0

Root node

Parent

Level 1

Ordinary node of degree 3
(it has 3 offspring)

Segment

Level 2

Terminal node

Offspring (two or more
offspring of the same parent
are called *siblings*)

Level 3

Level 4

Level 5

Subtree

FIGURE 6·10*a*
Tree terminology.

can be located (identified) by *level,* which is a node count along a *path* from the root node to a terminal. The level we associate with the root node is purely arbitrary, but we will usually take it to be zero. The nodes along a path are often thought of as having an *ancestral* relationship one to another. By analogy with family trees, moving from a root toward a terminal, each node is the *parent* of its immediate successor nodes (*offspring*). Two or more nodes having a common parent are sometimes called *siblings.* Finally, we can say that the *degree* of a node is the number of its immediate offspring.

A node may also be identified in terms of the *path* that leads from the root to that node. How can we represent that path? An answer comes to mind when we realize that representing a tree in two dimensions imposes an ordering on the segments that emanate from each node. And we might as well recognize this fact of life by numbering the segments in some way, say from left to right or right to left. For simplicity and consistency we will generally number segments from left to right, as suggested in Figure 6·10*b*. These ordinal numbers amount, in effect, to *names* for the segments.

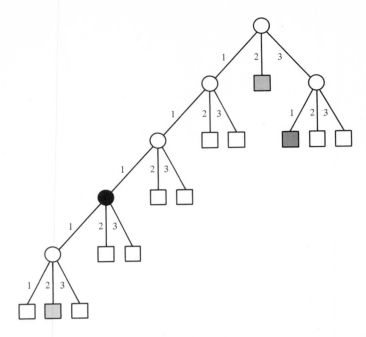

FIGURE 6·10*b*

Now a node can be designated uniquely by listing the *names of all the segments in the path leading to that node*. For example, the light green node in Figure 6·10*b* may be designated by the list (1, 1, 1, 1, 2), the dark green node by the list (3, 1), the gray node by the one-element list (2), and the black node by (1, 1, 1). (How would the root node be designated in this scheme?) Distinct nodes have distinct paths and hence distinct lists.

The *expression tree*, by its very structure, provides the key to evaluating the expression that is represented. For example, suppose values for the variables of our expression are:

a	w	b	d	y
3	2	2	− 1	7

A subtree of the form shown in Figure 6·11, together with the above table, can be understood to mean: Look up the values of a and w, compute $a \times w = 3 \times 2 = 6$, and replace the subtree by the terminal node 6.

Correspondingly, the subtree shown on the left can be interpreted as: Compute $d \times y = -1 \times 7 = -7$ and replace the subtree by the terminal node − 7.

Figure 6·12 represents a sequence of meaningful substi-

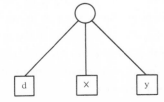

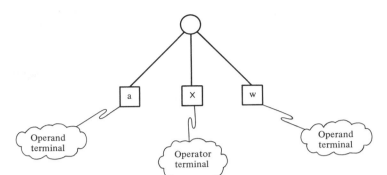

FIGURE 6·11

tutions that, when carried out, will ultimately lead to the replacement of the whole tree, root node and all, by a single terminal, which represents the value of the expression.

Proper evaluation is guaranteed if we follow one simple *replacement rule* that says:

> *Whenever you find a subtree consisting of a root node leading to three terminals (an operator and two operands), replace that subtree by a single terminal value.*

Thus the replacement sequence in Figure 6·13, although different from that of Figure 6·12, leads us irrevocably to the same value, $\boxed{\dfrac{-256}{7}}$. A computer performing either sequence would evaluate the same indicated quotient $\boxed{\dfrac{-256}{7}}$, notwithstanding the fact that computer operations on floating-point numbers are nonassociative, a fact explained in Chapter 11. Another point to note from the figures is that the treelike representation of a complicated arithmetic expression allows us to see all the meaningful subexpressions (all the subtrees) at a glance.

Once an expression is represented as a tree, evaluation depends only on repeatedly searching and finding subtrees that are subject to the replacement rule. At any given time, an expression tree, if not already fully evaluated, will exhibit at least one such subtree.

A question that has no doubt been uppermost in the minds of some readers is: How should tree structures be represented in storage? Linked lists, introduced in Chapter 4, suggest one

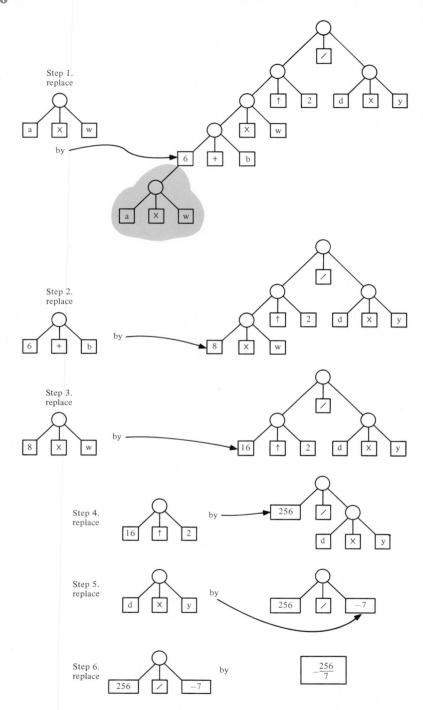

FIGURE 6·12
A stepwise evaluation of a tree
expression.

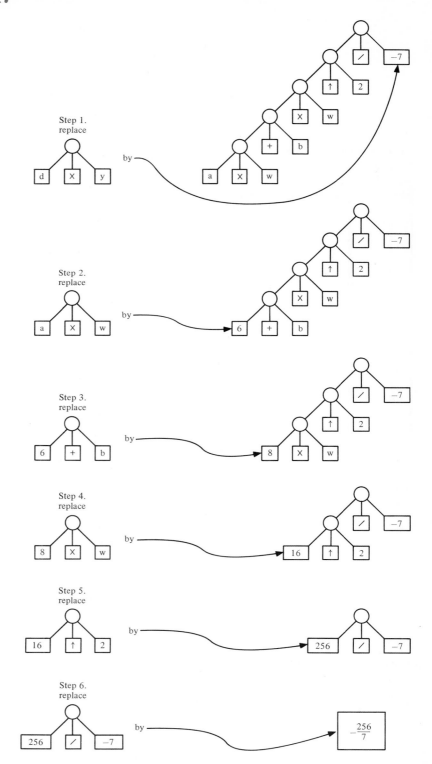

way. With this approach, one storage representation for the expression

$$((a \times w + b) \times w)\uparrow 2 / (d \times y)$$

is shown in Figure 6·14. A four-column table is used. Each row represents a node with row 1 representing the root node.

Tree Table

Node Number	Value (String)	Links		
		Left	Middle	Right
1	□	2	15	16
2	□	3	13	14
3	□	4	11	12
4	□	5	9	10
5	□	6	7	8
6	a	—	—	—
7	×	—	—	—
8	w	—	—	—
9	+	—	—	—
10	b	—	—	—
11	×	—	—	—
12	w	—	—	—
13	↑	—	—	—
14	2	—	—	—
15	/	—	—	—
16	□	17	18	19
17	d	—	—	—
18	×	—	—	—
19	y	—	—	—

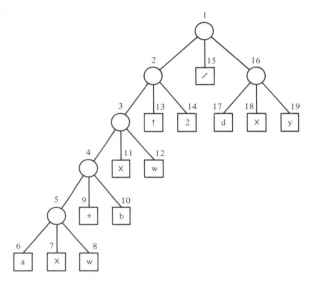

FIGURE 6·14
Tabular representation of an expression tree.

The first column holds the value of the node if it is a terminal or some special mark, for example, □, if the node is nonterminal. The remaining three columns hold node numbers that designate the left, middle, and right offspring. These positions may be left empty (undefined) for terminal nodes. Node numbers in the left, middle, and right columns serve as *links* to other nodes. Other tabular descriptions of tree structure using the linked list approach are discussed in Chapter 7.

A Peek at Some Future Models of SIMPLOS

We noticed in the expression tree of Figure 6·12 that two separate subtrees

and

had only terminal nodes as offspring. At the start of evaluation we could invoke the replacement rule on either of these subtrees. It was immaterial which we picked first. This will always be the case for subtrees whose root nodes are siblings or the offspring of sibling nodes (i.e., cousins once or more *removed*). From the standpoint of expression evaluation, such subtrees are *mutually independent.*

Under what circumstances can a computer work on the evaluation of two or more independent subtrees at the same time? With our present SIMPLOS model the answer is never, because at any one time there is only one team of personnel (Master Computer, Affixer, Reader, and Assigner) available to do work. On the other hand, advanced models of computer systems having several, perhaps many teams of personnel, are quite feasible.

Although it may boggle the mind to think about it, one may anticipate that future computers will evaluate mutually independent subtrees concurrently, that is, *in parallel,* whenever more than one team of personnel is available for the purpose. In cases where speed is essential the capability of concurrent computation offers the opportunity to solve problems that cannot be solved fast enough in any other way. Examples of such problems already abound in our technological society. More can be found on this topic in advanced texts.

EXERCISES 6·1,
SET D

1. Evaluate the expression trees below, using the given values for the variables.

(a)

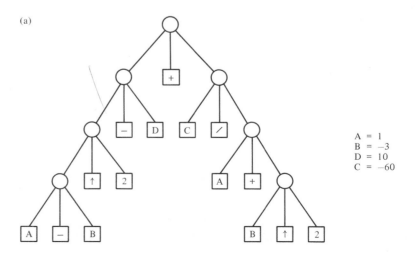

A = 1
B = −3
D = 10
C = −60

(b)

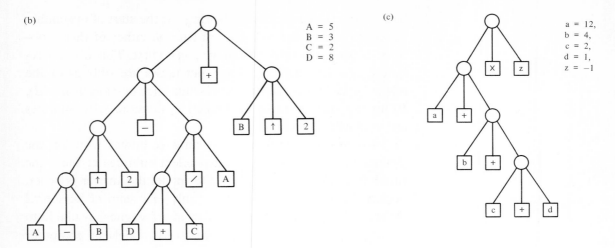

A = 5
B = 3
C = 2
D = 8

(c)

a = 12,
b = 4,
c = 2,
d = 1,
z = −1

(d)

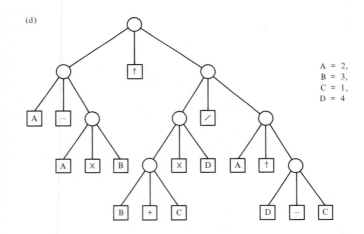

A = 2,
B = 3,
C = 1,
D = 4

2. Draw a tree representation for the expression

$$B{\uparrow}2 - 4 \times A \times C$$

3. The following are two proposed tree representations for the expression

$$I - N \times A{\uparrow}N / D + O \times U - T$$

Which, if either, of these trees, evaluated by the replacement rule, yields a result computationally equivalent to the result we get by following the evaluation rules laid down in Tables 2·1 and 2·3? If the evaluation of either one of the trees is not compatible with these rules, describe the discrepancy.

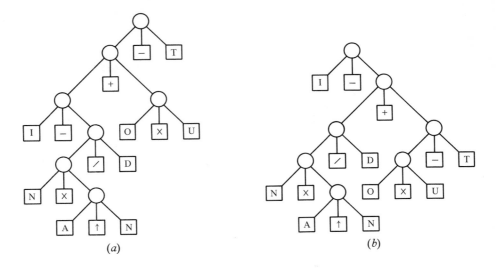

(a)   (b)

4. Draw a tree representation for the expression

$$(a - b) \times (c - d) / (e \times (f + g))$$

5. Find which of the three trees given below correctly represents the given expression and exhibit the expression represented by each of the other trees.

$$y\left(\frac{4 - 2y}{3}\right) + y^2$$

(a)

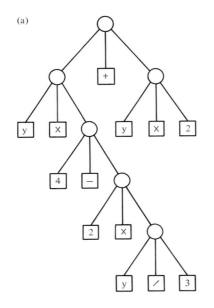

(b)

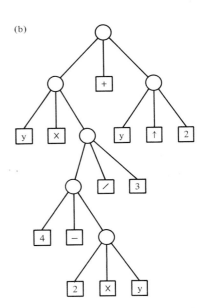

(c)

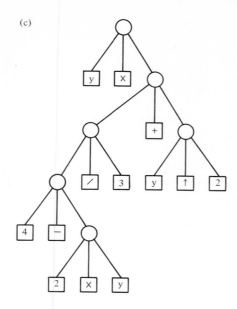

6. Find the tree among the four given below that represents the given expression correctly and exhibit the expressions represented by each of the other trees.

$$a \times b < c + d / (f + g)$$

(a)

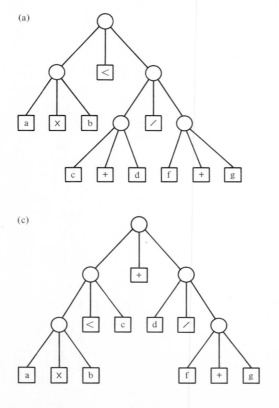

(b)

(d)

(c)

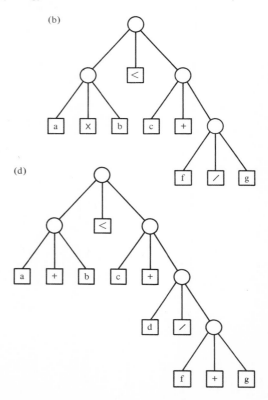

7. Convert the trees below into the corresponding arithmetic expressions.

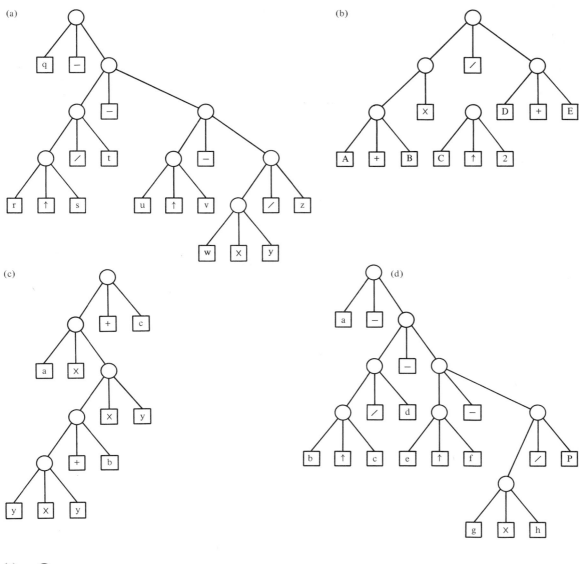

(a)

(b)

(c)

(d)

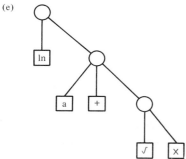

(e)

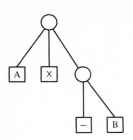

8. How would you draw the expression tree for the expression $A \times (-B)$? The problem here is to decide how one should represent a unary operation. One possibility is shown in the tree on the left.

    Here the subtree expression $-B$ is treated as a root node having a unary operator $\boxed{-}$ and one argument $\boxed{B}$ as offspring nodes. One can deduce that the operator is unary by the fact that the (left-hand) operand node is missing. Functions such as $\sqrt{}$, cos, and so forth, can be thought of as unary operators. Using the above expression scheme, or another of your own choosing, develop expression trees for:

    (a) $A + \sqrt{x}$
    (b) $\cos(x^2 + y^2)$

    (c) $\sqrt{\frac{1}{2} \times (1 + q / \sqrt{p^2 + q^2})}$

9. Which of the following statements is false?

    (a) A terminal node has one ancestor node and no descendant nodes.
    (b) A root node has no ancestor nodes and may have no descendant.
    (c) A nonterminal node has no descendant nodes.
    (d) A nonterminal node may have only one ancestor node.
    (e) A terminal node can be connected to an ancestor.

    Hint If you have any question as to the meaning of "ancestor" and "descendant" just think of a family tree.

10. Any given two-dimensional matrix can be represented as a tree. For example, the matrix

    $$A = \begin{bmatrix} 3 & 4 & 5 & 6 \\ 8 & 3 & 2 & 9 \\ 1 & 17 & 4 & 6 \end{bmatrix}$$

    can be expressed as the tree:

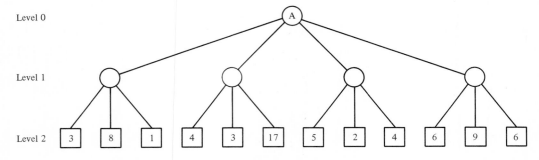

    (a) Given the representation above, the four nodes at Level 1 correspond to (choose one):

        (1) The four elements of the main diagonal of the given matrix.
        (2) The four elements of row 1 of the given matrix.

(3) The four columns of the given matrix.

(4) The sums of the elements in each of the columns of the given matrix.

(5) None of the above.

(b) Show at least one other way to represent the matrix A as a tree structure.

11. Using list notation, give the paths for the nodes labeled $\boxed{D}$, $\boxed{U}$, and $\boxed{\uparrow}$, in the second of the two trees referred to in Problem 3 of this exercise set.

12. Develop a scheme to denote the saving in time that, in principle, is possible in a computer having multiple processing units that can execute concurrently in the same expression. Show how your scheme would work on the following expressions.

(a) $a^2 + b^2 + c^2$

(b) $(a - b) \times (c - d) / (e \times (f + g))$

(c) $(\sqrt{x} + \cos y) / z$

13. In the text we have always shown the operator symbol of an expression tree as a terminal node, so each nonterminal node of the tree has three offspring if the operator has two operands, and two offspring if the operator has one operand. Another way to draw the tree is to place each operator symbol *at* its parent (nonterminal) node. For example, the tree for the expression

$$A + B \times C$$

may be drawn as

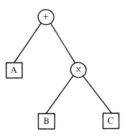

instead of as

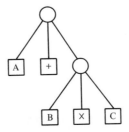

The new form, which we shall call a *binary* expression tree, has fewer nodes but the same amount of information.

Refer to Figure 6·14 and:

(a) Produce the binary expression tree equivalent to the expression tree given in the figure.

(b) Show how the tree table in that figure can be changed in structure and in content to represent the binary tree you developed in part a.

(c) Which tree table would require less storage in a computer representation?

6·2
Tree searches

We have now seen enough of trees to have observed their main structural characteristics; segments of a subtree always connect to new nodes that form a continuation of the same subtree; there is no looping back to nodes closer to the root; and there is no crossing or crisscrossing between subtrees.

There are many ways one can construct and store a tree structure. Depending on what use is to be made of the tree, some representations (we will call these *storage structures*) are better than others. Trees are searched for one reason or another, either to gain specific information, to reach a conclusion, or to modify the tree in a certain way. A tree search lies at the heart of a number of mathematical problems and a great number of games.

Natural-order Tree Search

There is a systematic way to scan all the nodes of a tree that is used frequently in solving problems. We call it *natural-order* searching. Although a squirrel may have better ways of finding nuts in a tree, it will help us to understand natural-order search if we imagine a nutseeking squirrel willing to follow these rules.

1. Start at the trunk (root) and don't stop trying segments until you reach a leaf (terminal node) unless you find a nut and choose to stop at that point.

2. Upon reaching a terminal without finding a nut, back up to the node you just passed, that is, to the *parent* node of this terminal.

3. Now, choose the next untried segment, if any, and move forward along it toward another leaf node.

4. If there are no untried segments, crawl backward to the predecessor (parent) node and repeat the process of trying to reach another leaf node.

5. If you ever find yourself back at the root having already tried all segments from the root without finding a nut, you have finished searching the entire tree in natural order and can report a failure to find a nut.

Figure 6·15 shows a natural-order search of a tree. The numbers beside the nodes indicate the sequence in which they

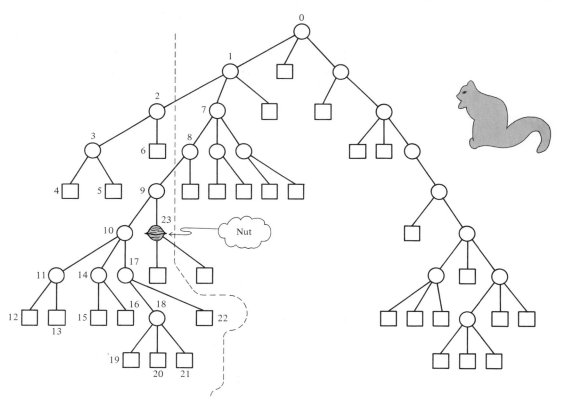

FIGURE 6·15
Systematic (*natural-order*)
search for a nut.

are first encountered (i.e., as the squirrel sees them in its forward progress). We picture one of these nodes as a nut. It is the 23rd node encountered. Notice the systematic, left-to-right selection of segments at each node.

Algorithm for Natural-Order
Tree Search

Now suppose we wish to construct a tree search algorithm that generally follows the stated set of rules. One of our problems is how to interpret rule 3, that is, how to choose among the remaining untried segments. If we recall, however, that the segments emanating from each node are, or always can be, *ordered*, then a simple interpretation comes quickly to mind: choose the segment, if any, whose ordinal number name is one higher than that of the segment previously tried.

To make this choice implies that the algorithm can always identify the ancestor or parent node from which the "previously tried" segment emanated. That is, the algorithm can only identify additional segments in terms of the common parent. This *backup* capability is assured if the algorithm at all times has an up-to-date record of where it is in the tree search and can represent this data in the form of a path list. For example, suppose it has been discovered that the segments from the node whose path designation is (1, 1, 2, 1) need be examined no further (Picture 1).

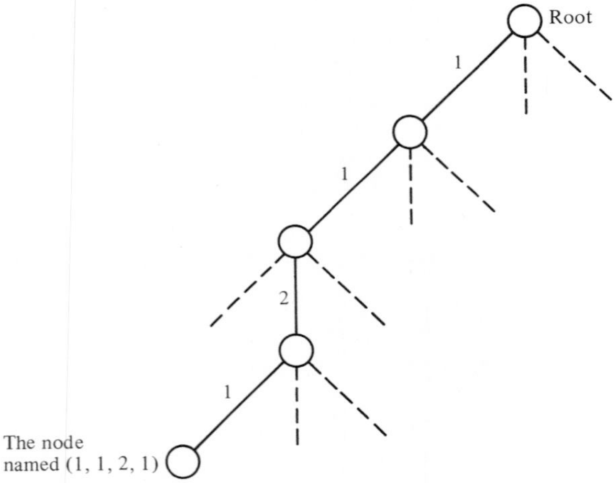

The node named (1, 1, 2, 1)

PICTURE 1

What is the path name for the parent of that node? The answer is (1, 1, 2).

How do we apply rule 3 to this parent (1, 1, 2)? (Rule 3: choose the next untried segment, if any, and move forward along it toward another leaf node.) The answer is, if there *is* a node whose path is (1, 1, 2, 1 + 1), try it (Picture 2).

In general, suppose we have tried the segment leading from node (1, 1, 2) to node (1, 1, 2, i) and the subtree whose root is (1, 1, 2, i) has failed to contain the nut we are looking for. To select the next untried segment, if any, of node (1, 1, 2), we have only to check whether there exists a valid node

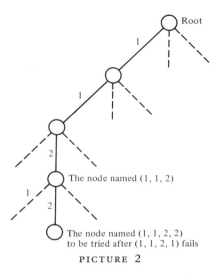

Root

The node named (1, 1, 2)

The node named (1, 1, 2, 2)
to be tried after (1, 1, 2, 1) fails

PICTURE 2

whose path is $(1, 1, 2, i + 1)$. If so, select the segment leading to this node and if not, back up, and check whether there is a valid node $(1, 1, 2 + 1)$. If so, select the segment leading to this node, but if not, back up again and see whether $(1, 1 + 1)$ is valid, and so on.

We now sense that by starting out with a path list that represents the root node (an empty list of segments), and by continuing to update that list as we move through the tree to reflect where we are in the search, then simple adjustments to the path allow us to determine each new direction of search.

Figure 6·16 shows a systematic procedure, that is, an algorithm for conducting natural-order tree search. The algorithm is represented in top-down style, with Figure 6·16a giving the topmost view. Any necessary data are input in box 1 and the tree search begins at box 2. In Tree_Search, whose details are given in Figure 6·16b, there are two key variables: *level* and *path*. The value of level tells us the number of elements in path. Values of these two variables determine the *current node* of the search. In a sense the current node is the one we are standing on while we try to find the next node to move to. These variables are initialized in box 1 of Figure 6·16b. Tree_Search sets some sort of switch to indicate success or failure. (Recall that a root node by itself does not constitute a tree. There must be at least one subtree. For this reason the first time box 2.2 is executed the Yes outlet will be taken.) Upon exit from Tree_Search, the main program, in effect, tests

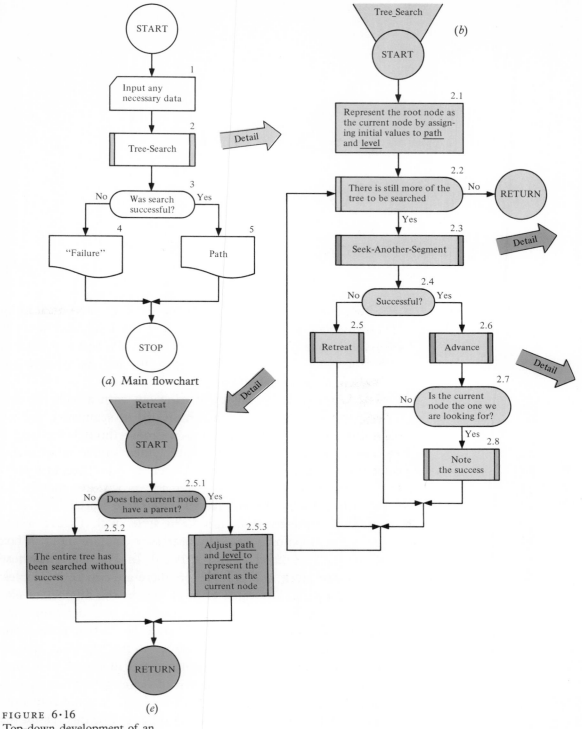

START

1
Input any
necessary data

2
Tree-Search

Detail

3
No   Was search   Yes
      successful?

4
"Failure"

5
Path

STOP

(a) Main flowchart

Detail

Tree_Search

(b)

START

2.1
Represent the root node as
the current node by assigning initial values to path
and level

2.2
There is still more of the   No   RETURN
tree to be searched

Yes

2.3
Seek-Another-Segment

Detail

2.4
No   Successful?   Yes

2.5
Retreat

2.6
Advance

Detail

2.7
No   Is the current
node the one we
are looking for?

Yes   2.8
Note
the success

Retreat

Detail

START

2.5.1
No   Does the current node   Yes
      have a parent?

2.5.2
The entire tree has
been searched without
success

2.5.3
Adjust path
and level to
represent the
parent as the
current node

RETURN

(e)

FIGURE 6·16
Top-down development of an
algorithm for natural-order
tree search.

(c)

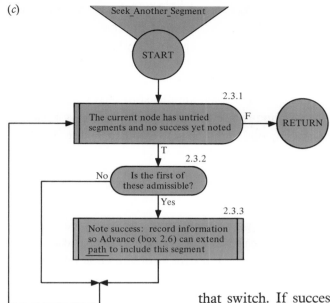

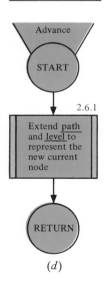

(d)

that switch. If success is indicated, the path list is displayed, identifying the location in the tree where the nut was found; otherwise a failure message is displayed.

To simplify the details of Tree_Search, three of its boxes are given in more detail in Figure 6·16c, 6·16d, and 6·16e. Notice that rule 3 is implemented in box 2.3 as a call to a procedure, "Seek_Another_Segment," whose details (Figure 6·16c) include a test for admissibility of untried segments. Although not shown in the level of detail given in Figure 6·16c, we imagine that some sort of switch is set by Seek_Another_Segment, which can be tested upon return to Tree_Search so that the former's success or failure can be determined at box 2.4. If successful, there is a new node to which the search may *advance* (details in Figure 6·16d). If unsuccessful, it is necessary to *retreat* to the parent node, if any (Figure 6·16e). (Remember that Seek_Another_Segment reports failure only after *all* segments have been tested.)

The bookkeeping of the retreat operation (box 2.5.3) is a two-step process.

1. Detach the last element of *path*, which is a segment number, and save it to use the next time Seek_Another_Segment is called at box 2.3.

2. Decrement *level* by one to reflect the shortened length of *path*.

The segment number saved in step 1 is needed in boxes 2.3.1 and 2.3.3. When a new segment number is selected in box 2.3.3, it in turn is saved for use by Advance, the next time that procedure is called at box 2.6. Advance increments *level* by one and appends the new segment number on to the end of *path*. We leave to the reader the pleasure of reviewing these details and convincing himself of their correctness. As a parting remark, it is worth observing that the nature of the admissibility check hinted at in box 2.3.2 may be crucial to the success of the search. As many inadmissible structures as possible must be ruled out at each stage. For example, the squirrel should recognize each dead limb and not search it. Otherwise, the proportion of useless paths may grow rapidly, meaning that the efficiency of the search method can plummet toward zero. Next we examine several interesting problems that employ this type of search in their algorithmic solution.

EXERCISE 6·2

1. List the nodes of the tree below in the order in which they would be encountered in a natural-order search.

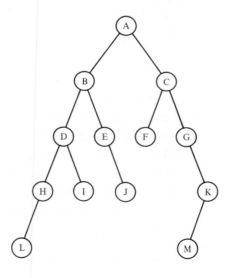

6·3
The four-color problem

Maps are colored to make it easy to see at a glance the extent of each country. It is necessary that neighboring countries (i.e. countries with a common boundary line) be assigned different colors. Does the mapmaker then need more than four colors to do his job? He doesn't care, but we *do*.

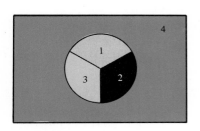

FIGURE 6·17

This problem was one of the most celebrated challenges in mathematics. It is of great intellectual interest and has intrigued many people from all paths of life. Actually, its solution has little or nothing whatsoever to do with making maps. A mapmaker is and always will be able to print maps using as many different colors as he needs.

A checkerboard is an example of a map that can be colored with only *two* colors. The four-country map shown in Figure 6·17 requires *four* colors. Because each pair of countries is adjacent, no two can have the same color.

It didn't take us long to find a map requiring four colors. Yet, in over 100 years of searching, no one has succeeded in finding a map requiring five! It is natural to conjecture that every map can be colored with four colors, and many mathematicians have racked their brains trying to prove this conjecture. The best they have been able to do so far is to show that every map can be colored using no more than five colors.*

We are about to see how computer methods can be applied to the four-color problem. We will not use the computer to show that the four-color conjecture is *true*. Indeed, it is entirely possible that no computer can ever prove this. However, true or false, we can use the computer to determine whether *a particular map* can be colored in only four colors. This is the task for which we want to construct an algorithm.

Before starting on this algorithm, a few remarks concerning the coloring of maps may be helpful.

A *minimal five-color map* is a map requiring five colors, so that every other map requiring five colors has at least as many countries. Of course, no minimal five-color map has ever been found. But mathematicians have shown that if such maps exist at all, then some of them satisfy these two conditions.

1. No point is a boundary point of more than three countries.

2. Each country is a neighbor of at least five others.

Moreover, it can be shown that *every* minimal map, if any exist, must satisfy the second condition.

It is therefore customary to consider as candidates for counterexamples to the four-color conjecture only maps fulfilling these conditions.

*A simple proof of the five-color theorem exists. It may be found, for example, in *What is Mathematics?*, Oxford University Press (1941), by Courant and Robbins.

Four-Coloring as a Tree Search

We can model the problem of four-coloring a given map, say, the one pictured in Figure 6·18, as one of traveling along a path through a tree such as that shown in Figure 6·19. Each segment represents a decision to color a country, with colors 1, 2, 3, or 4. The ith segment in a path from the root corresponds to the coloring of the ith country of the map.

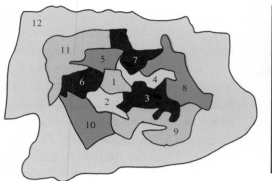

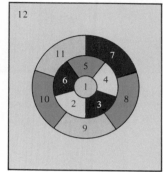

FIGURE 6·18

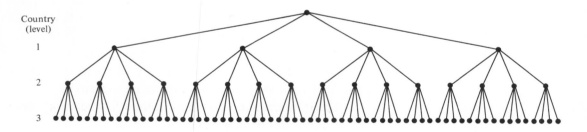

Country (level)

1

2

3

etc.

FIGURE 6·19

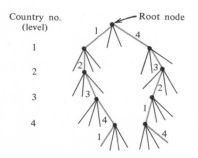

Country no. (level)   Root node

1

2

3

4

FIGURE 6·20

Observe that many paths through the tree turn out to represent identical colorings of the map except for renaming of the colors, and it is desirable to avoid searching through such duplicate patterns. (E.g., the two heavy-line paths in Figure 6·20 represent the same coloring patterns with different names used for the colors.) One way to avoid the unnecessary search is to fix at the outset in a quite arbitrary way the colors for neighboring countries 1, 2, and 3 and to begin the real search with the coloring of country 4.

In coloring all countries, from the fourth country on, as seen in Figure 6·21, we assume that all four choices are possible. Most of the time, however, as can be seen in Figure 6·22, only one, two, or three of these choices will be admissible. Sometimes even all four choices will be inadmissible, as ex-

FIGURE 6·21
Showing coloring tree and one path representing the coloring of the first six countries (colored line).

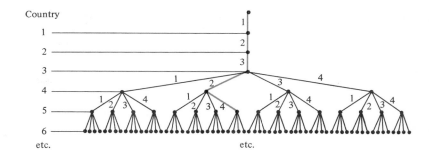

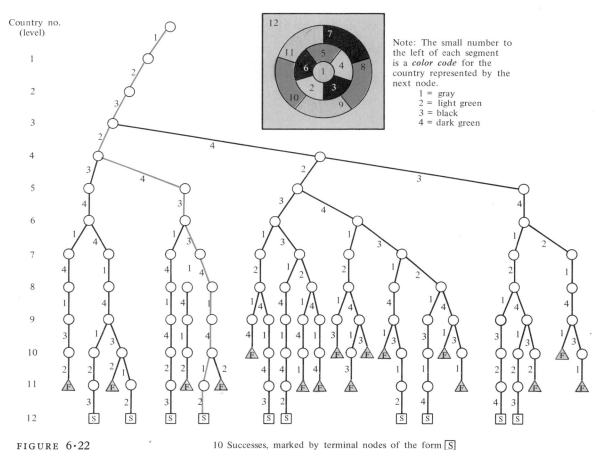

FIGURE 6·22
An entire coloring tree showing how to four-color the map of Figure 6·18.

10 Successes, marked by terminal nodes of the form ⬜S

16 Failures, marked by terminal nodes of the form △F

emplified by terminal nodes marked F in Figure 6·22. Only 10 paths lead to S (success) terminals.

1. Compute the theoretical maximum number of possible terminal nodes for the coloring tree of the 12-country map in Figure 6·18.

   Hint Use Figure 6·21 as a guide.

2. Assume that it takes only 1 microsecond to check another path to a terminal, and that the search of half of these paths is required before the desired terminal is reached. How long would the computer chug away before it found what it was looking for in a 39-country map? Assume all segments to be admissible. Express your answer in units of *years*.

3. By renumbering the countries on the map of Figure 6·18, show that a coloring tree can have nodes with three and even four permissible segments emanating from them.

4. Using a form similar to that of Figure 6·22, draw a "coloring tree" for the map shown below.

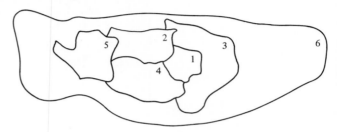

A Four-Coloring Algorithm

Let us see how to apply what we have just learned about tree search to an actual problem. It is one thing to discuss a tree in the abstract and another to start with a problem, define in some detail the tree search that is involved, and then develop a detailed flowchart algorithm. In this case, we will take as our problem statement: Develop a detailed flowchart algorithm for four-coloring any n-country map.

The first step toward this objective might be to devise a method to represent any n-country map. To do this we need a sample map for study as, for example, in Figure 6·23. The

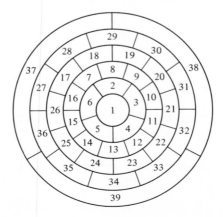

FIGURE 6·23
Example of map to be four-colored by a computer algorithm.

map consists of 39 countries, and the countries have been numbered or indexed in the order that the algorithm will attempt to "color" them.

The efficiency of the algorithm will be greatly improved if each country borders on as many lower-numbered countries as possible. We do not absolutely insist on this but, if you have done Problem 3 of Exercise 6·3, you will appreciate why we recommend this approach. We do, however, require that the first three countries all be neighbors of each other.

How do we represent the map in computer storage? One way is to construct a "connection table," listing after each country all of its neighbors in increasing order. This is shown for our example in Table 6·1.

Our algorithm should consult this table when deciding how to color a particular country. For example, if we were coloring country 15, we could see in row 15 that countries 5, 6, and 14 are neighbors already colored. Our choice of color for 15, then, depends solely on the currently chosen colors for 5, 6, and 14.

Knowing that country 15 also has neighbors numbered 16, 25, and 26 appears to be superfluous. This leads us to the idea of a shaved-down table, which we will call the "*reduced* connec-

TABLE 6·1
The Connection Table for the Map in Figure 6·23

Country	Neighbors						Country	Neighbors					
1.	2	3	4	5	6		21.	10	11	20	22	31	32
2.	1	3	6	7	8	9	22.	11	12	21	23	32	33
3.	1	2	4	9	10	11	23.	12	13	22	24	33	34
4.	1	3	5	11	12	13	24.	13	14	23	25	34	35
5.	1	4	6	13	14	15	25.	14	15	24	26	35	36
6.	1	2	5	7	15	16	26.	15	16	17	25	27	36
7.	2	6	8	16	17	18	27.	17	26	28	36	37	
8.	2	7	9	18	19		28.	17	18	27	29	37	
9.	2	3	8	10	19	20	29.	18	19	28	30	37	38
10.	3	9	11	20	21		30.	19	20	29	31	38	
11.	3	4	10	12	21	22	31.	20	21	30	32	38	
12.	4	11	13	22	23		32.	21	22	31	33	38	39
13.	4	5	12	14	23	24	33.	22	23	32	34	39	
14.	5	13	15	24	25		34.	23	24	33	35	39	
15.	5	6	14	16	25	26	35.	24	25	34	36	39	
16.	6	7	15	17	26		36.	25	26	27	35	37	39
17.	7	16	18	26	27	28	37.	27	28	29	36	38	39
18.	7	8	17	19	28	29	38.	29	30	31	32	37	39
19.	8	9	18	20	29	30	39.	32	33	34	35	36	37	38
20.	9	10	19	21	30	31							

TABLE 6·2
Reduced Connection Table for the Map in Figure 6·23

Country i	Neighbors CONN_{ij}				Width w_i	Country i	Neighbors CONN_{ij}						Width w_i
1					0	21	10	11	20				3
2	1				1	22	11	12	21				3
3	1	2			2	23	12	13	22				3
4	1	3			2	24	13	14	23				3
5	1	4			2	25	14	15	24				3
6	1	2	5		3	26	15	16	17	25			4
7	2	6			2	27	17	26					2
8	2	7			2	28	17	18	27				3
9	2	3	8		3	29	18	19	28				3
10	3	9			2	30	19	20	29				3
11	3	4	10		3	31	20	21	30				3
12	4	11			2	32	21	22	31				3
13	4	5	12		3	33	22	23	32				3
14	5	13			2	34	23	24	33				3
15	5	6	14		3	35	24	25	34				3
16	6	7	15		3	36	25	26	27	35			4
17	7	16			2	37	27	28	29	36			4
18	7	8	17		3	38	29	30	31	32	37		5
19	8	9	18		3	39	32	33	34	35	36	37 38	7
20	9	10	19		3								

tion table." It is constructed by striking out of each row in the table all numbers greater than the number of the row itself. The reduced connection table for our example is seen in Table 6·2 and can be thought of in this case as a 39-row by 7-column array called CONN. The number of nonnull elements in each row is given by elements of an associated list w. Thus the algorithm can search the first w_i elements in the ith row of CONN to determine which neighbors have already been colored.

If we are to apply our generalized tree search algorithm (Figure 6·16) to the map-coloring problem, we must also decide how to represent the *current node* (i.e., how to represent the variables *path* and *level*). The variable *path* is a list of elements, each of which designates a segment choice. Our decision to use color codes 1, 2, 3, and 4 for the four possible color choices leads us directly to the decision that a search from a node may be accomplished by selecting (trying) the segments in the same order, 1, 2, 3, and 4. The decision to make this correspondence between the color codes and the segment order imposes the required ordering on the segments from each node of our coloring tree. Moreover, the ith element of *path* automatically identifies the color chosen for the ith country! This means that whenever we have been able to choose a valid color for the nth country, the current contents of the path is the desired list of colors for the n countries of the map. Nothing could be simpler. For this problem, let us call the path list COLOR, since it is more suggestive of our desired objective.

Figure 6·24 shows a flowchart algorithm incorporating the foregoing concepts and details and following the identical top-down structure given in the generalized search (Figure 6·16). It will be easy to verify the claimed similarity. If you have any difficulty in following Figure 6·24, remember that boxes with corresponding numbers in the generalized flowchart have similar meanings. Only Figure 6·24*f,* the detail of the admissibility test in box 2.3.2, is really new.

Discussion

Box 1 of Figure 6·24 is a counterpart to box 1 of Figure 6·16. In the detailed algorithm we must input the data explicitly to represent the map if we are going to deduce the actual structure of the tree. In Figure 6·24*b,* to keep track of what tree level has been reached, a level or path length counter k is needed. This counter is initially set to 0 in box 2.1 to reflect the start of the search at the root node. [The algorithm could be made more efficient by initializing the level counter to 3 and path to (1, 2, 3) to reflect coloring the first three countries with the first three colors, as suggested in Figure 6·21.]

Success_Switch is a three-valued switch variable that is initially set to "undecided" (at box 2.1), and then is set to either "Yes" if the tree search succeeds or to "No" if the search fails. To see why or where this switch is set to either "Yes" or to "No," you may have to descend to the next levels of detail. Thus, whenever we discover that the search is about to backtrack to level zero, the search has failed (boxes 2.5.1 and 2.5.2 of Retreat). If $k - 1 = 0$ in box 2.5.1, the current node is at level 1. In other words we have backtracked to the first country. The first country was colored with color 1 at the beginning of the search. We have not tested colors 2, 3, or 4 on country 1. Should we? Not really, because we know that any coloring we find will simply be a renaming of a previous coloring (if any) when country 1 had color 1. We won't find

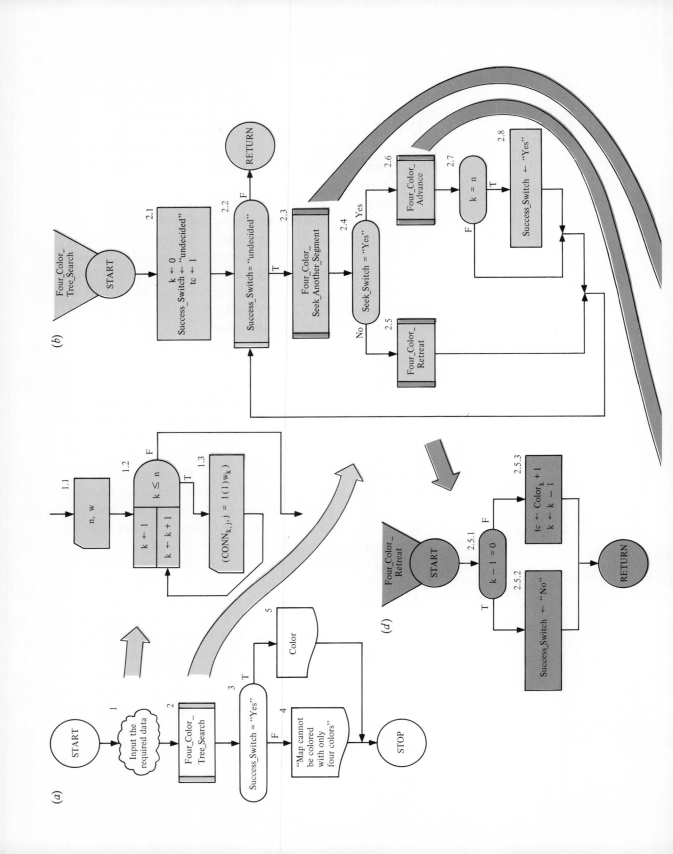

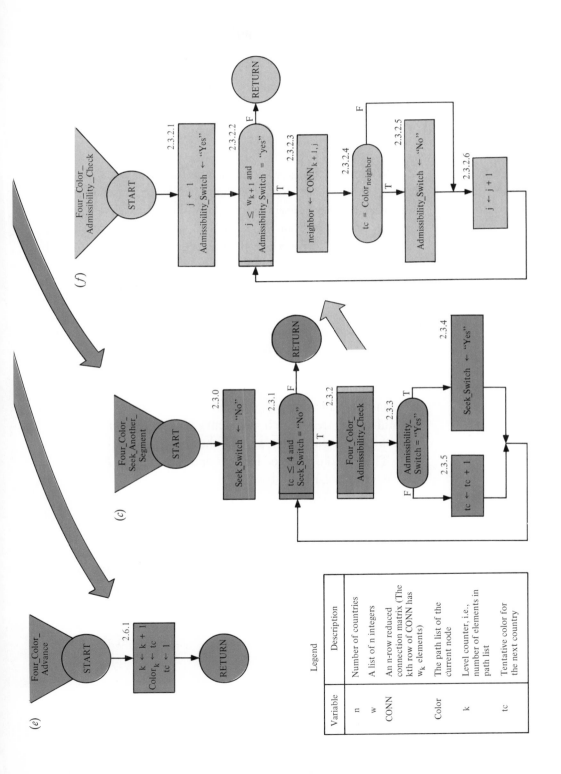

FIGURE 6·24
Four-coloring algorithm.
Top-down approach.

any new patterns. If we want to search the complete tree, however, including the four possible colors for the first country, we have only to change the test in box 2.5.1 to read

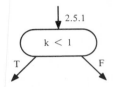

Whenever the level counter k is found to equal n (boxes 2.7 and 2.8 of Tree_Search), Success_Switch is set to "Yes." The variable Seek_Switch tested by Tree_Search in box 2.4 is set to either "Yes" or "No" by Seek_Another_Segment (Figure 6·24c). This procedure in turn reports success if and only if the subprocedure Admissibility_Check reports success. This latter procedure (Figure 6·24f) determines whether any of the previously colored neighbors (there are w_{k+1} of them) have the same color as the *tentative color*, tc, that is being considered for the k + 1 st country. If so, Admissibility_Switch is set to "No" so that, after the RETURN to Seek_Another_Segment, another (the next) color may be tried. Notice that only in Admissibility_Check is there any reference to the map's representation. This suggests that detailed flowcharts for different natural-order tree search problems will differ mainly in the details of this particular part of the search algorithm.

The bookkeeping of Retreat and Advance in Figure 6·24 uses auxiliary variable, tc, tentative color. This variable is also used in Seek_Another_Segment during the search for an admissible segment and, in box 2.3.5, tc is incremented whenever an inadmissible segment is found. In Advance, k is incremented to represent the longer successful coloring path. The successful tentative color is stowed away in $Color_k$, and the auxiliary variable tc is reset to 1. (See box 2.6.1.) During *Retreat* the current color choice for country k must be remembered so that the search for another segment of country k's parent can resume at a value of tc that is one greater than the last one tried. The saving of this information is accomplished by the assignment step,

$$tc \leftarrow Color_k + 1$$

as seen in box 2.5.3. Then the path length k is shortened by 1.

In the problem set that follows, you are introduced to several well-known problems involving tree search. Here is your chance to apply our generalized natural-order tree search method.

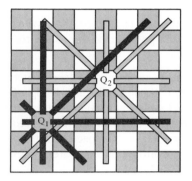

FIGURE 6·25
A chessboard with two Queens on different rows, columns, and diagonals.

1. *The Eight Queens Problem.* A chessboard is an eight-by-eight array of positions. The Queen is the most powerful piece in the game of chess in that it can capture any other piece encountered on the same row, column, or diagonal. The problem is to so place eight Queens on the chessboard so that no Queen can capture another Queen.

If there is a solution to the Eight Queens Problem, it is evident that each Queen must be on a different row, column, and diagonal of the chessboard (Figure 6·25). This suggests the need for a systematic way of placing the eight Queens on the board, one at a time. It is certainly immaterial where the first Queen should go but, to be systematic, we can think of putting it somewhere in column 1 with the object of placing each successive Queen in a succeeding column.

In placing the first Queen in column one, there are eight choices, each of which eliminates some of the choices for placing a Queen in column two. These eight choices may be represented by a tree with eight segments emanating from the root node. As one moves down this tree of choices, there will be fewer and fewer admissible branches. A solution to the Eight Queens Problem is represented by a path through the tree reaching all the way to level eight.

The natural-order tree search is suitable for searching the tree, but it is necessary to be explicit about the test to determine which segments of the tree are admissible. Although it is tempting to represent the chessboard as an eight-by-eight array, it is easy to see that a single eight-element list, say $\{Q_i, i = 1(1)8\}$, will suffice, since in the Q list we can store the row number for each Queen.

Suppose that k Queens have already been placed admissibly in the first k columns of the board. To determine whether the next Queen can be placed in position j, k + 1, at least two tests must be made.

(a) Is there already a Queen in row j? That is, has the value j already been assigned to an element of the Q list? If so, this position (j, k + 1) is inadmissible.

(b) Is there already a Queen on one of the two diagonals that pass through the new position? The first diagonal, which we will call a "major" diagonal, slants from upper left to lower right. The second one, a "minor" diagonal, slants from lower left to upper right.

If the answers to all these tests are negative, the new position is admissible. You should give thought to various ways of representing the needed data and performing the required tests. One way to record the positions of the Queens (least amount of storage) is with a single eight-element list whose ith element is the row number of the ith

Queen. A second way to represent the data uses a total of three lists, the first list being the same as the eight-element list just mentioned. The two additional lists, each of 15 elements, are used to record the presence or absence of Queens on the major and minor diagonals. This second way uses more storage, but requires less computation.

(a) Construct a flowchart and legend for a tree search algorithm following the guidelines of Figure 6·16 and using the tests for admissible segments discussed above to find one solution of the Eight Queens Problem.

(b) Modify the flowchart you developed in part a so that, when executed, the algorithm will find *all* possible solutions of the Eight Queens Problem.

2. *The Instant Insanity Problem.* Four cubes with faces colored light green, gray, white, or dark green are to be stacked one on top of the other so that on each side of the stack only one face of each color is visible. The six faces of a cube can be unwrapped and numbered as shown. Each cube has 24 possible orientations in space, since any one of the six faces can be turned to the bottom and there are always four vertical faces from which to select the face to be placed in front. Thus the stacking of four cubes can be represented by a tree with

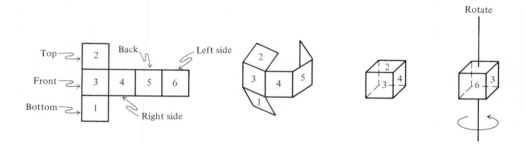

up to 24 segments coming from each node. (Many segments should be classified as inadmissible because they make a color reappear on the same side of the stack.) A successful solution to the Instant Insanity Problem is an admissible path from the root node reaching to the fourth level of the tree.

The four cubes to be stacked have their faces colored as follows: (*Dark Green, White, Gray, Light Green*)

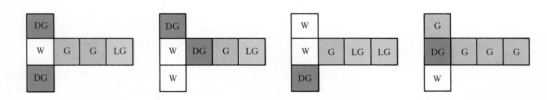

Your task is to develop a tree search algorithm to search for *all* successful solutions to Instant Insanity and to print the path from the root node for each successful solution.

Hint You may find it useful to construct an "orientation table," each row of which describes one of the 24 possible orientations of a cube. You can use the row numbers of the orientation table to number the segments emanating from any node of the tree. Other useful tables are COLOR, with four rows and six columns, to record the given coloring of the four cubes, and STACK, again with four rows and six columns, to represent the coloring of the current stacking of the cubes.

3. A surveyor has laid out a subdivision as shown in Figure 6·26.

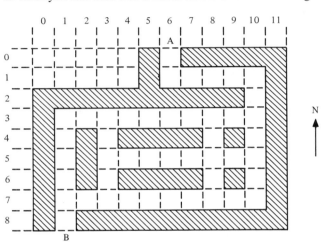

FIGURE 6·26
Plan of the subdivision.

Possible vehicular traffic flow through the subdivision is to be studied. One member of the planning team has proposed a series of traffic rules as follows.

(a) There is only one entrance (the place marked A).
(b) There is only one exit (the place marked B).
(c) North-south roads (called streets) are to be *one-way* from North to South.
(d) East-west roads (called avenues) are *two-way*.
(e) No U turns are allowed.

The first step of the traffic study is to determine all possible traffic paths from A to B through the subdivision. (Later, a study of these paths can decide what are good locations for a school, a park, a library, etc.) The set of all possible traffic paths can be represented as a tree, with the root node representing flow beginning at the entrance, A, and with terminal nodes representing "flow" past the exit, B.

(a) Construct the tree of all possible paths, mentioned above, for the subdivision, that "obeys" the stated traffic rules. To make your tree meaningful to another person, you will have to label the nodes, or the segments, or the levels of the tree (or some combination of these) and indicate the meaning of these labels.

(b) If one were interested in constructing a computer algorithm that displays all the paths of the tree, one would need first to decide on a representation for the structure (layout) of the subdivision, much as it was necessary to decide on a representation for an n-country map in order to construct a four-coloring algorithm. Show and explain a representation of the subdivision for storage in a digital computer.

(c) Develop a flowchart that follows the generalized top-down structure for natural-order tree search given in Figure 6·16 that, if executed, would search out every terminal node of the tree, printing out for each terminal node, its "path list."

4. *The Jumping Game.* Fifteen spots are arranged in a triangle. All but one of the spots are covered by checkers. A checker may be moved only by "jumping" one other checker along a straight line in any direction, in which case the jumped checker is removed from the triangle. The object of the game is to find a sequence of jumps resulting in only one checker remaining in the triangle.

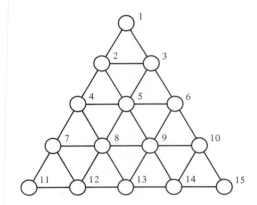

Begin by numbering the spots of the triangle. It will be helpful to have a table showing permissible jumps, for example, the Jump Table (Table 6·3). We will also build a list, called the "empty list," of the spots that are not covered at each stage. Suppose we begin the game with spot 5 not covered. The jump table shows that two jumps are possible; either 12 jumping 8 or 14 jumping 9. Then the game tree would start with two segments, one labeled (12,5) and the second (14,5). If the first segment is chosen, 5 would be removed from the empty list and both 8 and 12 added to the empty list. Next look at the jump table for 8 empty and for 12 empty. There are a total of four possibilities, each requiring two spots (the jumper and the jumped) to be covered. One of the possibilities, 5 jumping 8 with 12 empty, is inadmissible because 8 is now in the empty list. Thus,

TABLE 6·3
Jump Table for the Game Described in Problem 4

Empty Spot	Jumper Spot	Jumped Spot	Empty Spot	Jumper Spot	Jumped Spot
1	4	2	12	5	8
	6	3		14	13
2	7	4	13	4	8
	9	5		6	9
3	8	5		11	12
	10	6		15	14
4	1	2	14	5	9
	6	5		12	13
	11	7	15	6	10
	13	8		13	14
5	12	8			
	14	9			
6	1	3			
	4	5			
	13	9			
	15	10			
7	2	4			
	9	8			
8	3	5			
	10	9			
9	2	5			
	7	8			
10	3	6			
	8	9			
11	4	7			
	13	12			

from the (12,5) segment, there are just three admissible segments (3,8), (10,8), and (14,12). The path through the game tree is a sequence of jumps, each jump identified by a pair of integers.

Your task is to develop a flowchart and legend for a tree search algorithm to search out (and display) one sequence of jumps that leaves just one checker on the triangle.

Chapter 7

More on tree search and storage concepts

7·1
Level-by-level tree search

Having studied Chapter 6, you are well on the way to becoming a tree expert. Tackling the problems in this chapter will substantially increase your ability to produce algorithmic solutions to difficult problems. With the first problem, we will consider alternate ways of performing a tree search and see how each approach suits the needs of the problem. We will also introduce several new concepts in the storing of arrays and data trees and in the retrieval of information from these structures.

Is *natural*-order tree searching, as described in Chapter 6, the *only* systematic way to search a tree? Figure 7·1 suggests what we will call the *level-by-level* tree search, which can be thought of as a companion piece to Figure 6·15.

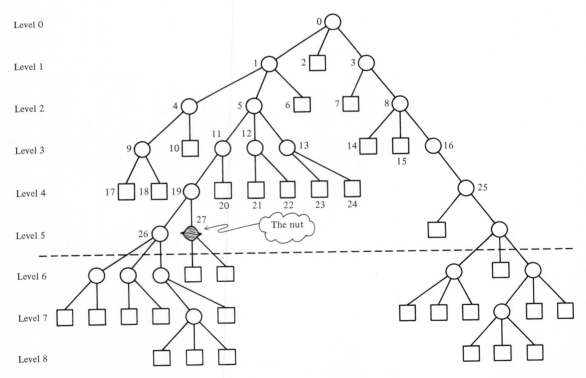

FIGURE 7·1
Search in level-by-level order.

It may be difficult to imagine a nut-hunting squirrel using this search strategy, but we will explain the search in "squirrel context" anyway. In this approach the squirrel searches for a nut *nearest*-the-root-node. He begins the search at the root, then at level 1, and so forth. The squirrel moves from one node to the next at the same level. If he fails to find a nut at level 1, he jumps to the next level (level 2), looks at all the nodes there, and so on, until he does find a nut or searches the entire tree without success.

Algorithms for level-by-level search, depending on the particular application, may halt after the first *desired* node is located, or they may continue to search the current level for more such nodes, if any, stopping at the end of the level. Or they may continue the search, level by level, until the entire tree has been scanned, collecting all the nuts in the tree. In the next section we will see that there are penalties involved in making a level-by-level search as compared with a natural-order search. However, the ensuing rewards can often far overbalance these penalties.

7·2
The border-crossing
problem

To set the stage for this problem, we offer the following bit of computer science fiction. It is entitled "Traveling Overland in the United States of Europe."

In 1984 the 26 countries shown on the map (Figure 7·2) agreed to form a federal union. For the first 10 years of the union, they further agreed to continue the practice of maintaining customs at the various borders between their states.

The first few years of the union proved to be somewhat unstable. Individual states were suspicious of one another. Borders between neighboring states were sometimes closed for several hours (days, or even months) while the legislatures of the disputing states fought tariff and other problems having political overtones.

By 1988 the frequency of these state versus state discords became so high that the federal government's Bureau of Public Roads began offering a computer service to assist in the solution of the routing problems of interstate trucking firms.

If a client phoned in giving his source (state) and destination (state), the computer would reply (almost instantly) giving:

1.   The route with the minimum number of OK border crossings (custom inspections), avoiding all border crossings currently closed.

2.   Any other routes (if more than one) that involve this minimum number of border crossings.

The trucker could then select among the choices reported by the computer, if any. In some (unfortunate) cases, the computer would phone a message such as, "You can't get there from here. Suggest you ship by air freight."

It will be interesting to see if we can develop an algorithm that provides essentially the same service as the one given by the USOE's Bureau of Public Roads. Any algorithm we develop should be general enough to be applicable to any federation of contiguous states.

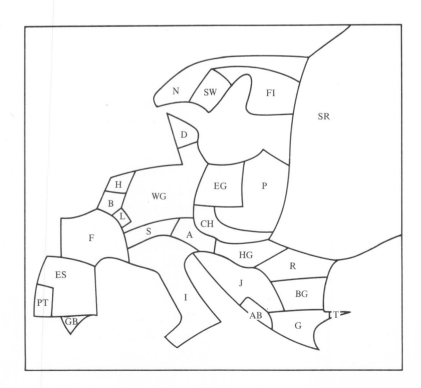

FIGURE 7·2
Map of Europe in 1984.

The Tree Search Strategy   Even if we know nothing about computers, we can sense that some kind of tree search is involved here. For example, suppose we want to travel from Spain (ES for España) to Holland (H) using a best path (minimum number of borders crossed).

First, we consider Spain's neighbors (at level 1), which are Portugal (PT), Gibraltar (GB), and France (F). Then we ask where we can go from each of these countries (level 2), moving on in this way from level to level (of the tree) until we reach a level that contains among its countries the one we call our destination. This tree is sketched in Figure 7·3.

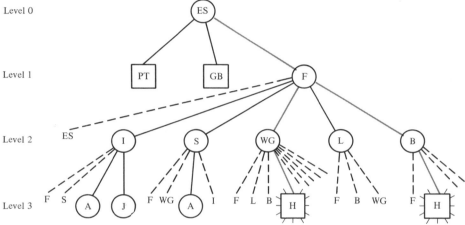

FIGURE 7·3
Traveling from Spain to Holland along best paths (colored lines).

There are two conclusions we can deduce from the tree.

1. A minimum of three border crossings is required to get from Spain to Holland.

2. The two colored paths that reach terminals marked H show that there are, in this case, two best paths.

There are also several things to keep in mind about the actual *construction* of the tree.

1. This tree is built from the root node *one level at a time* in some order, such as left-to-right order.

2. Certain uninteresting terminals can be encountered at any level. Thus, at level 1, GB has only one neighbor, ES. The same is true for PT. Hence the path from ES through GB cannot continue (except, of course, to return to ES, which we do not allow).

3.   A segment emanating from the node for country P at level n is *inadmissible* if it leads to another country Q, and Q has already appeared *anywhere* in the tree at a level equal to or lower than n. For example, at level 2 the node for Italy has four possible segments emanating from it, but only two are admissible. Segments to F and S are both inadmissible because each appears as a node at level 2 or less.

4.   When considering the segments emanating from a node, if any one is discovered leading to the destination node, there is no need to consider any more segments *from that node*. This is suggested by the way we have drawn the segments emanating from WG (Figure 7·4).

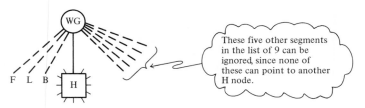

FIGURE 7·4

5.   After reaching our destination by a segment from one node at a certain level, it is still necessary to look for other possible occurrences of the destination by "expanding" the remaining nodes at this level (in left-to-right order). Thus, expanding at level 2, even though we have found that H can be reached from WG, we complete the expansion of nodes L and B, the other nodes on this level. In this way we find the second occurrence of H at level 3.

6.   Finally, there is absolutely no point in looking for an H node at a level higher than level 3. Any such nodes will represent tree paths *exceeding* the minimum "length."

To summarize, the level-by-level search goes hand in hand with the construction of the tree, drawing on whatever data is needed. Figure 7·5 displays a generalized algorithm for such a search. It is given in top-down style. Figure 7·5a assumes there is available a procedure called One_Level_Searcher. This procedure, whose flowchart is given in Figure 7·5b, in turn assumes the availability of the procedure called Node_Expander. Finally, the details for Node_Expander are given in Figure 7·5c. See pages 354 and 355.

1. If the nodes of the tree given below were numbered in the order in which they would be examined in a level-by-level search, what number would be given to the square node? (Assume the root node is numbered one.)

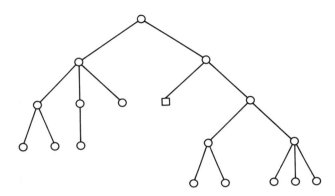

2. True or false: If node X is at level 2 of a tree and node Y is at level 3 of the same tree, then node X will *always* be examined *before* node Y in a level-by-level search and *after* node Y in a natural-order search.

3. True or false: If a certain node is the ith node encountered in a level-by-level search of a tree and if that same node is the jth node encountered in a natural-order search of the same tree, then it is always the case that $i \leq j$.

4. True or false: Natural-order tree search can be characterized as being "depth first," whereas level-by-level tree search can be characterized as being "breadth first."

5. True or false: Any tree search algorithm must retain in computer storage all parts of the tree that have already been searched, since it is not certain where the desired node will be found.

Data Structures Required for Level-by-Level Tree Search

We are now ready to consider what input data are required in the computer algorithm of the border-crossing problem and what storage arrangement will be appropriate. We must also think about the tree data that will be *generated* by the algorithm and its appropriate storage structure.

It may be well to digress momentarily to compare storage requirements of this problem with those of the four-color problem of Chapter 6. In the latter case, only one path of the coloring tree was of interest to us at any one time. This was the path from the root to the node currently under consideration (in the natural-order search). We suggested that a record

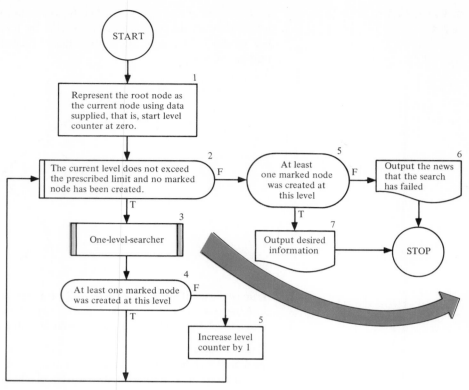

FIGURE 7·5a
Generalized algorithm for
level-by-level tree search (with
concurrent tree construction).
See also Figure 7·5b and
7·5c.

of this path be kept in the form of the COLOR list. If the
current node ever turned out to be a terminal node, then
COLOR's contents could be output, and that was that. But
in this problem we must somehow keep a record of the *entire
tree so far traversed* (e.g., the solid lines of Figure 7·3). The
reason is that any one (or several) of these paths may prove
to be the one(s) containing the destination terminal. In the
example of Figure 7·3, for instance, when the scan of level
3 is completed, the algorithm must be able to recover and print
out the nodes along the two (or, in general, several) best paths
that were found. The easiest way to do this is to keep a record
of the tree itself.

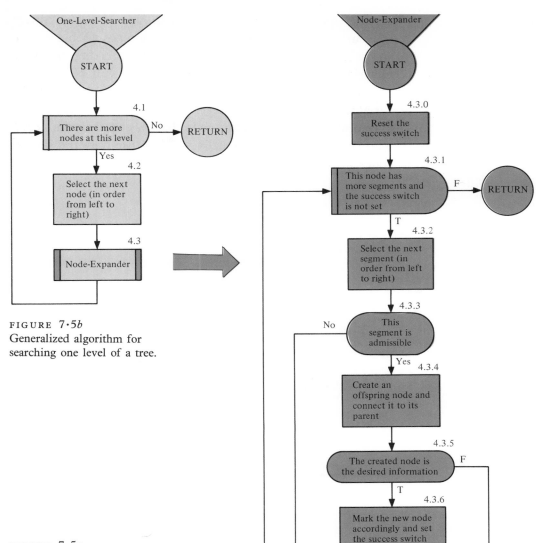

FIGURE 7·5*b*
Generalized algorithm for searching one level of a tree.

FIGURE 7·5*c*
Generalized algorithm for expanding a node, that is, to see if any of its offspring is a desired node.

Representing the
Map of Europe

Having studied the four-color problem, you would be correct in assuming that the connection table approach (Table 6·1) is an eminently suitable method for the digital coding of maps. However, as you can see in Table 7·1, we will be adding a new twist. Table 7·1 shows the connection table having 26 variable-length rows. An integer code for each country is displayed along with the letter code that was used in the actual map (Figure 7·2). Occasionally, we will use only the integer codes in our discussion of the computer algorithm.

TABLE 7·1
Map of Europe

Country		Access List,	Neighbors								
Number	Name	AL	1	2	3	4	5	6	7	8	9
1	GB	1	3 ES								
2	PT	2	3 ES								
3	ES	3	2 PT	1 GB	5 F						
4	L	6	5 F	6 B	8 WG						
5	F	9	3 ES	10 I	9 S	8 WG	4 L	6 B			
6	B	15	5 F	7 H	8 WG	4 L					
7	H	19	8 WG	6 B							
8	WG	21	5 F	4 L	6 B	7 H	11 D	25 EG	18 CH	19 A	9 S
9	S	30	5 F	8 WG	19 A	10 I					

TABLE 7·1 (Continued)

Country		Access List,	Neighbors								
Number	Name	AL	1	2	3	4	5	6	7	8	9
10	I	34	5 F	9 S	19 A	20 J					
11	D	38	8 WG								
12	N	39	13 SW	14 FI	15 SR						
13	SW	42	12 N	14 FI							
14	FI	44	13 SW	12 N	15 SR						
15	SR	47	26 R	17 HG	18 CH	16 P	14 FI	12 N			
16	P	53	25 EG	15 SR	18 CH						
17	HG	56	15 SR	26 R	20 J	19 A	18 CH				
18	CH	61	15 SR	17 HG	19 A	8 WG	25 EG	16 P			
19	A	67	10 I	9 S	8 WG	18 CH	17 HG	20 J			
20	J	73	10 I	19 A	17 HG	26 R	23 BG	22 G	21 AB		
21	AB	80	20 J	22 G							
22	G	82	21 AB	20 J	23 BG	24 T					
23	BG	86	22 G	20 J	26 R						
24	T	89	22 G								
25	EG	90	16 P	18 CH	8 WG						
26	R	93	15 SR	23 BG	20 J	17 HG					
		97									

Closed borders

The table entries encircled by clouds refer to closed borders. If, for example, we are told that the border between France and West Germany is closed, we have to remove it or specially mark it (e.g., with a cloud). See the WG entry on row F and the F entry on row WG. Also shown is another closed border between Norway and Finland. We sense that the closing of these borders will not greatly complicate the problem of finding best paths, so we will temporarily forget about this part of the problem.

Access lists

The column headed "Access List, AL" in Table 7·1 is something new. It is especially useful in case one wants to conserve storage for "jagged" arrays like this map of Europe. That is, if you consider the map as a 26-row array, it would require nine columns to contain the row with the most elements, while other rows would be longer than necessary and thus space is wasted. Because storage space may be at a premium, we consider another way to store such a table.

A space-saving method we suggest here is to represent the whole table as a single list, which we will call MAP. For n countries this list would have n subdivisions (Figure 7·6). The ith subdivision would hold codes for the countries that border country i. To reference a particular row of the table, say row i, one would only need to know the index in the MAP list that corresponds to the first element (word) of the ith subdivision. The purpose of the access list, AL, is to hold n + 1 index values such that the ith element of AL holds the index of the ith subdivision within MAP. Moreover, the difference, $AL_{i+1} - AL_i$ gives the number of elements in the ith subdivision. This pointer scheme is illustrated in Figure 7·6 for the first five rows of the connection table.

To reference the jth element in the ith row of the table, that is, table$_{i,j}$, we would now use the expression

$$MAP_{AL_i+j-1}$$

As a quick check on the validity of this expression, let's compare the two ways of getting at the second element in the fourth row of the connection table.

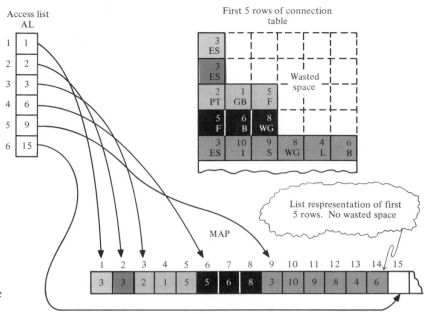

FIGURE 7·6
Use of an access list to reference elements of the connection table stored in the MAP list.

Table$_{4,2}$ is seen to have the value $\boxed{\begin{smallmatrix}6\\B\end{smallmatrix}}$. Correspondingly, for the access list approach,

$$AL_4 = 6$$
$$AL_4 + 2 - 1 = 7$$

Hence,

$$MAP_7 = \boxed{6}$$

We get the same code value either way.

Representing the Tree in Storage

We must keep a record of the tree in storage at all times, you will recall, because when we have completed the tree through some level, k, on which one or more destination terminals have been found, we must print out all paths from the root node to the destination nodes at level k. The storage representation that we design for the tree should make these data retrieval operations easy.

In Figure 7·7 (top half) we illustrate an acceptable type of storage representation. This is based on our earlier example of a path from Spain to Holland. The tree in this figure shows only the solid lines from the earlier illustration (Figure 7·3)

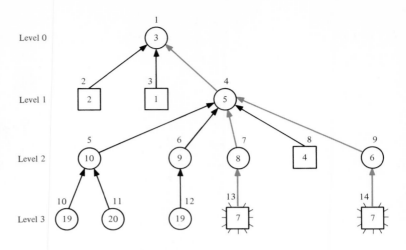

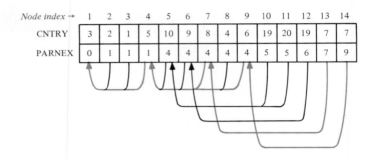

FIGURE 7·7
Sample tree and its storage
representation.

and, moreover, uses integer codes in place of letter codes for the countries.

In trying to think how a "two-dimensional" tree can be stored, one should try for a representation in which the tree's essential information can somehow be strung out in a line or sequence of storage containers such as a row or column of a table. What comes to mind is the picture of the tree as a set of nodes, arranged as the elements of a list. In this case each list element (node) should have some kind of link relationship to the list element that represents its parent node. For example, we could store two pieces of information for each node.

1. The country number ($CNTRY_i$) to identify the node.

2. A link or pointer to (i.e., index of) the list element that represents the parent of this node.

It seems reasonable that we should store the information

for each node of the tree in the order that we search the tree, that is, level by level. Since each node is to hold a pair of values (identification number and pointer), we could well use two lists with the pairs consisting of the corresponding elements. The lower part of Figure 7·7 offers this simple approach, showing the use of two lists, called CNTRY (each element of which is a country code), and PARNEX (each element of which is the index in CNTRY of the parent node).

For example, node 9 is represented by the pair (6,4), meaning that the parent of the country numbered 6 at node 9 may be found be consulting $CNTRY_4$, which is country 5. The ith node encountered in the level-by-level search will be stored as the pair of values

$$CNTRY_i \quad \text{and} \quad PARNEX_i$$

Notice that since node number 1 (the root node) has no parent, $PARNEX_1$ has the value zero.

Once the elements of CNTRY and PARNEX have been assigned values, as shown in Figure 7·7, the problem is essentially solved. We have only to output the codes for the list of countries encountered along each of the tree paths backward from the discovered destination nodes, that is, the green 7's, to the root node. Starting from one of the easily recognized terminal elements in the CNTRY list, we can *"climb"* back up the tree to the root rather easily. Figure 7·8 shows how. A terminal can, of course, be recognized by the fact that the value in $CNTRY_i$ is the known destination code.

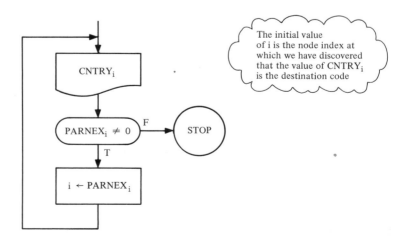

FIGURE 7·8
Printing out a best path by "climbing" to the root node from the destination node and printing the country numbers that are encountered along the way.

A Computer Algorithm

We will leave it to you to develop a detailed flowchart algorithm for the border-crossing problem. If you have studied the foregoing material, you should be well prepared to proceed. Be sure to consult the generalized level-by-level search algorithm in Figure 7·5 as a guide.

We suggest the following plan. First, develop your algorithm on the assumption that the closing of a border will never occur. In this case the overall flowchart will resemble Figure 7·9.

If you are successful in producing the foregoing algorithm, it should be easy for you to add the necessary boxes to recognize the possibility of closed borders.

EXERCISES 7·2,
SET B

1. It was stated in the text that the storage structure we design for a tree should relate closely to the way we intend to *use* the tree. Consider the effect on box 6 of the border-crossing algorithm (Figure 7·9) if we change the storage representation of the tree (Figure 7·7) as

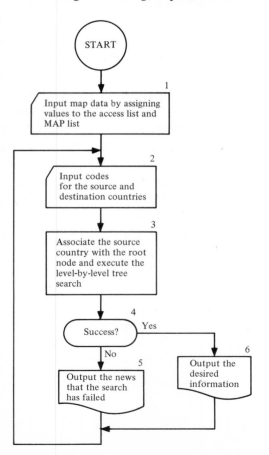

FIGURE 7·9
Top-level border-crossing
algorithm.

follows. Instead of assigning to the list elements $PARNEX_i$, the *index* to the parent node, we assign to $PARNOD_i$ the actual country code for the parent of node i. (Note the new name for this list.)

(a) Redraw the lower half of Figure 7·7 under this change.
(b) Construct a new flowchart for box 6 of Figure 7·9 and compare it critically with the one you have already developed.

2. Shown here is an algorithm that processes the tree described in Figure 7·7.

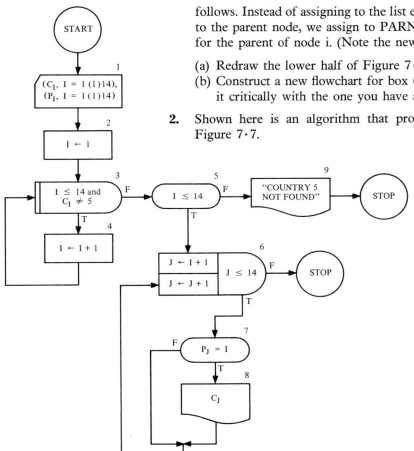

The lists CNTRY and PARNEX of Figure 7·7 are renamed here as C and P, respectively.

Node index →	1	2	3	4	5	6	7	8	9	10	11	12	13	14
C	3	2	1	5	10	9	8	4	6	19	20	19	7	7
P	0	1	1	1	4	4	4	4	4	5	5	6	7	9

(a) Assuming that the values input at box 1 are those shown in the above table, what values are printed by this algorithm?
(b) What process is carried out by this algorithm? (Choose one.)

   (1) The algorithm prints the code numbers of all the countries bordering on the root node.
   (2) The algorithm prints the code numbers of the terminal nodes of the tree.

(3) The algorithm prints all paths from the root node to terminals going through country number 5.

(4) The algorithm prints the code numbers of those neighbors of the country coded 5 that appear below it in the diagram of the tree.

(5) The algorithm prints the code numbers of the countries that are immediate descendants of the fifth node in the tree.

3. Consider Figure 7·7, which shows one way to represent a tree in storage. That tree representation identifies the *parent* node for each node of the tree, and thus that representation was convenient for tracing paths from terminal nodes to the root. That tree was constructed while a level-by-level search was being carried out.

In this problem, we will consider another way to represent a tree in storage. The new representation will contrast with the one above in the following ways. First, the representation will deal with trees in general; we will not tie ourselves to some particular context, such as a map. Second, the representation will be one in which it is convenient to search or trace paths in a *downward* direction, that is, from nodes to their "daughter" nodes (i.e., immediate descendants). Third, we will consider search algorithms that are useful in the situation where the tree already exists in memory before the search begins.

Let us begin by considering the following sample tree.

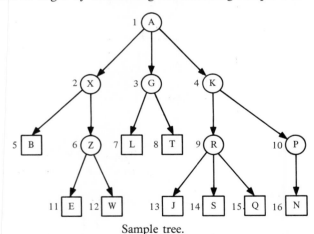

Sample tree.

Notice that each node contains an item of information; here we have used a letter of the alphabet. We will not specifiy any *meaning* for these node contents, but simply realize that it is often desirable to store (associate) information at (with) the nodes of a tree, and that we should include this capability in our representation.

In the diagram, the terminal nodes can readily be distinguished from nonterminal nodes. This should also be possible in our tree representation.

We now display the representation of the sample tree as it will appear in storage. The nodes have been numbered in the sample tree, and information for node i in the tree is found in the tree representation as follows.

$CONT_i$ holds the *contents* of node i,

row_i of DAUGH holds the node numbers (indices) of the *daughters* of node i,

W_i holds the "width" of row i of DAUGH, that is, the number of daughters of node i.

	CONT		W		DAUGH		
1	A	1	3	1	2	3	4
2	X	2	2	2	5	6	
3	G	3	2	3	7	8	
4	K	4	2	4	9	10	
5	B	5	0	5			
6	Z	6	2	6	11	12	
7	L	7	0	7			
8	T	8	0	8			
9	R	9	3	9	13	14	15
10	P	10	1	10	16		
11	E	11	0	11			
12	W	12	0	12			
13	J	13	0	13			
14	S	14	0	14			
15	Q	15	0	15			
16	N	16	0	16			

For example, we see that the sixth node contains the letter "Z" and has 2 daughters, nodes 11 and 12. The nodes in this example have been numbered and placed in the tables in level-by-level order, but this is not a requirement of the representational scheme. All that we do require is that $CONT_i$, W_i, and ($DAUGH_{i,j}$, $j = 1(1)W_i$) all contain information about the *same* node. Let us also agree that node 1 will be the root.

A logical extension of this representation is to use the access list technique to store the rather "sparse" matrix DAUGH.

(a) Draw a flowchart for an algorithm to carry out a *natural-order search* to find a node whose contents is "S" and to print the contents of all nodes in the path from the root to the first "S" found (if any). The flowchart should assume that the tree has already been stored in CONT, W, and DAUGH, and that node 1 is the root. The list, PATH, should be used to store the node numbers (indices) of the nodes in the path from the root down to the node currently being searched. Paired with the PATH list should be a list called ALT for use when the search has to "backtrack." ALT_i tells how many ALTernatives have already been tried immediately under the node in $PATH_i$, that is, how many of the daughters of the node in $PATH_i$ have been examined.

(b) Draw a flowchart for an algorithm to print the contents of all terminal nodes of a tree represented as above.

7·3 Analysis of tree games

In this section we leave behind the idea of level-by-level tree search. Here, after some preliminary definitions and orientation, we will again resort to natural-order tree search to solve a very interesting problem.

As suggested in Chapter 6, many two-player games can be modeled by trees. We have called these "tree games." Among these are chess, checkers, go, nim, and tic-tac-toe, and each has a characteristic tree. In any of these trees, if we follow a path from the root node to a terminal, the segments we traverse represent a set of legal moves constituting one completed game. The move made *from* the next-to-last node in the path represents a win for A, a win for B, or a draw (if a draw is allowed).

These games are finite in the sense that every path from the root node ends in a finite number of steps, and there can be only a finite number of paths.

There is a fascinating problem associated with every such finite tree game. It is known by the utterly drab and unrevealing name "analysis." For example, what we would mean by *analysis of checkers,* if it were possible to do it in practice, is a study that would lead us to the following conclusion.

> Given that A is the first player and B the second player, and assuming that each player makes each move in the best way possible, the game of checkers will inevitably end in a foreordained way as a ⬚.

Unfortunately, we don't know how to end the last sentence because checkers has never been *analyzed*. But, because checkers is a finite game, we do know that one of the following three phrases completes the sentence.

> Win for A

> Win for B

> Draw

Our first challenge is to appreciate fully what we have just said, that is, to understand that finite tree games are indeed *predetermined* in this way. Our second challenge is to learn how to go about developing an algorithm to analyze *any* such finite tree game.

Analyzing a Simple Game

The approach to game analysis can be best illustrated by a very simple game. We will pick for study the game of Eight. Figure 7·10 is a reproduction of the game tree in Figure 6·4. To streamline its appearance, we've stripped off the segment labels and modified the appearance of the terminals.

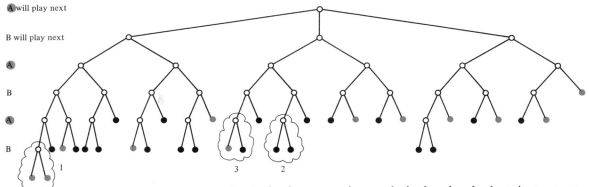

A will play next

B will play next

A

B

A

B

● Means A wins
● Means B wins

FIGURE 7·10

Control of a game is a relatively simple but important concept in the analysis of any game. When, for example, during a game of bridge, each player holds three cards, and you hold the Ace, King, and Queen of the trump suit, it is possible to lay down your cards face up and say, "I take the last three tricks." It is not necessary to *play out the hand* because you *control* the remainder of the tricks, that is, you will win each remaining trick no matter what cards each of your opponents chooses to play on each of the last three tricks.

Subtrees of a game tree can be inspected for similar situations of control. Look, for example, at subtree 1 in Figure 7·10.

The unmarked node leading to the green terminals represents a point in a game of Eight where it is B's play and, no matter which of the two possible moves he makes, A wins. What can we infer about this unmarked node? If the play ever reaches this node, we know the game is won for A, so we can just as well color the node green, as suggested in Figure 7·11.

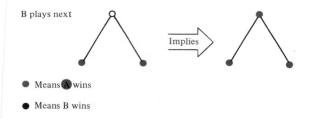

FIGURE 7·11

By similar reasoning, if we have the situation that is shown in subtree 2

where it is clear that the unmarked node can now be considered a black node because, no matter what play A makes from this point, the game for A is lost.

We take one more example before drawing an interesting generalization. Suppose we have this situation, as in subtree 3 (of Figure 7·10);

It's A's turn. He examines his alternatives and, if he's playing "heads up" Eight, he can be counted on always to select the move that leads to the green terminal. In other words, in this situation, the unmarked node might as well be green.

If you study Figure 7·12, which shows all possible control situations for the game, you cannot help but arrive at the following *node-marking rule.*

> A node representing a player's turn to move can be marked as a *win* for that player, if at least one segment emanating from the node leads to a win for that player; otherwise, the node should be marked as a win for the other player.

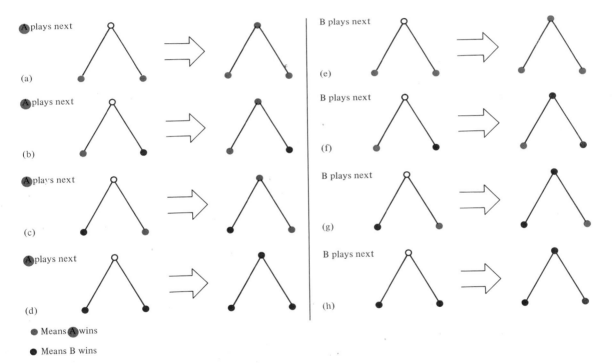

(a) A plays next
(b) A plays next
(c) A plays next
(d) A plays next
(e) B plays next
(f) B plays next
(g) B plays next
(h) B plays next

● Means A wins
● Means B wins

FIGURE 7·12
The eight possible control situations.

It's possible by now that you already see how one can analyze a game tree such as the one in Figure 7·10. In principle, it's an astonishingly simple process. Given a picture of the tree, all you do is repeatedly apply the node-marking rule until you are able to mark the root node by the same rule. *Remember:* marking a node green, for example, is equivalent to recognizing that A *controls* the game *from this node* down. That is, no matter what B chooses to do henceforth, A will win. Since the root node *controls* all the rest of the tree, marking it green is equivalent to concluding that A controls the entire tree; marking it black is equivalent to concluding that B controls the entire tree.

EXERCISES 7·3,
SET A

1. Suppose A plays with the situation

How should the root node of this subtree be colored?

2. Suppose we wish to analyze a game whose game tree has branching of *degree* more than two as in the case suggested in Problem 1. (See Figure 6·10a for the meaning of degree.) How should the fact that the degree of a tree or subtree may exceed 2 affect the way we express our *node-marking rule?*

In a game tree as small as Eight's, it is only a five-minute exercise to determine the root node's color *if you are already given the full tree with all terminals properly colored.* Moreover, it makes very little difference how you go about it. One approach is to color nodes at each level, beginning with the level immediately above the terminals, then to color nodes at the next level, and so on, until you reach the root. This is certainly a systematic approach, and we couldn't quarrel with it. But keep in mind that in a typical game that is hard to analyze, *you are not given the tree at all.* For one thing, the tree is probably too big to be drawn without the aid of a computer.

Figure 7·13 suggests one very efficient method. In this method we follow what is basically a *natural-order tree search* algorithm (recall Figure 6·16) in the hunt for terminal nodes. After we find one, we retrace our steps to the preceding node and, at this point, attempt to color that node, *if sufficient information is available.* If not, we continue with the search for terminals. Eventually, we'll return to the same node with enough information to color it. Thus, in Figure 7·13, node 1 is colored green after the two terminals emanating from it are determined. Retracing to node 2, there is sufficient information to color it immediately, on the basis of node 1's color alone, *by applying*

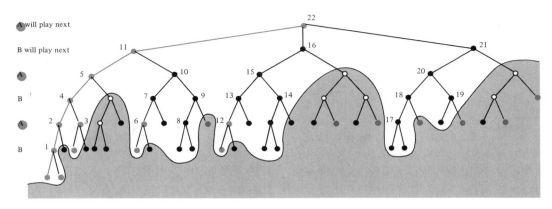

FIGURE 7·13

the node-marking rule. Backing up to node 4 where it is B's play next, we have this situation:

We can't decide whether B controls this node until we determine the color of the nodes below node 3. After determining that the leftmost of these is a terminal and green, and retracing to node 3, we can then color 3 green, and then 4 green, and so on, during the execution of the natural-order search.

We see that as we proceed through the tree in this fashion, it is possible to reach a color decision on the root node even though we ignore several branches of the tree (the shaded areas). You can now see why we suspect that this method of modified natural-order searching will prove to be very efficient for game tree analysis.

EXERCISES 7·3,
SET B

1. This question is related to the tree for a game named "X" shown at the top of page 372. A plays first. The terminal nodes are marked "A" or "B" to indicate a win for A or a win for B. (There are no draws in this game.)

   (a) Who controls the game at node 3?
   (b) Who controls the game at the root node (node 1)?

2. This question relates to the game tree shown on the bottom of page 372. The tree represents some finite two-person game in which player A moves first. The terminal nodes are labeled A or B, indicating a win for player A or B, respectively.

A will play first

B will play next

A will play next   3

B

A

B

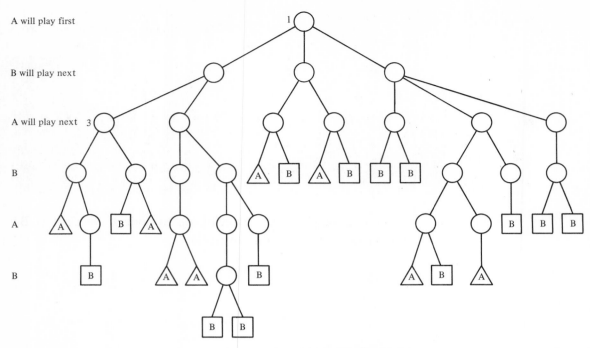

(a) Analysis of this game reveals that if both players always use the best possible strategy, then (choose one):

(1) Player A will always win.
(2) Player B will always win.
(3) A draw will always occur.
(4) The outcome cannot be determined.
(5) Each player will win an average of 50% of the time.

A will play next

B will play next

A

B

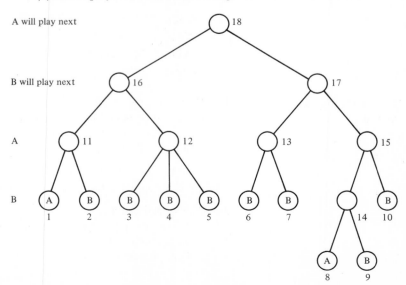

(b) If the game tree is analyzed using the modified natural-order search plan described in the text, the nodes which will *not* need to be examined are (choose one):

(1) 2, 4, 5, 7, 9, 10.
(2) 2, 3, 4, 5, 6, 7, 8, 9, 10, 12, 13, 14, 15, 17.
(3) 2, 8, 9, 10, 14, 15.
(4) All nodes must be examined.
(5) All nodes but node 2 must be examined.

3. Shown below is the game tree for some finite, two-person game in which there are no draws. The players are referred to as A and B, with A moving first. The terminals are labeled △A (A wins), ⬛B (B wins), or ⊙? (someone wins, but you are not told who). If both players use the best possible strategy, which of the following is a *true* statement?

(a) Player A can always win, regardless of the winner at the ⊙? terminals.

(b) Player B can always win, regardless of the winner at the ⊙? terminals.

(c) The winner cannot be determined from the information given in the tree.

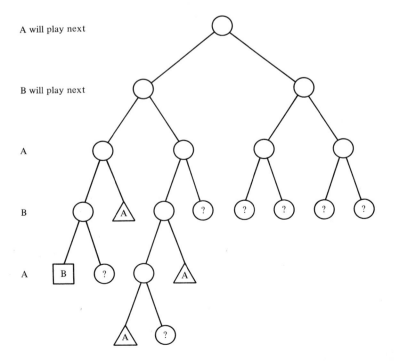

4. Shown below is the game tree for some finite, two-person game in which player A moves first. The terminal nodes of the tree are labeled Ⓐ (win for player A), ⃞B (win for player B), or "?" (outcome unknown). Your job is to determine whether the "?" nodes prevent analysis of the game and, if not, who will win (assuming best play by both players).

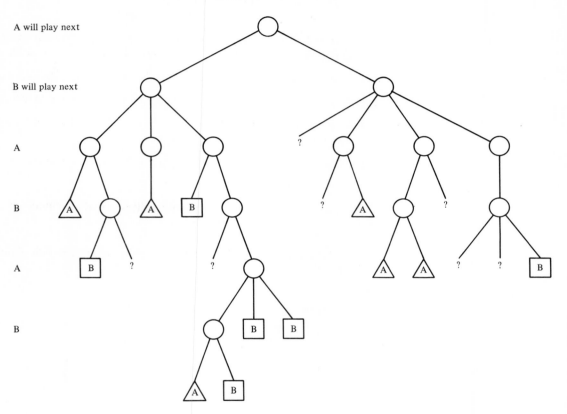

A will play next

B will play next

A

B

A

B

Analysis of the game tree above shows that (choose one):

(a) Player A will always win.
(b) Player B will always win.
(c) The winner cannot be determined unless the value of at least one of the "?" nodes is known.

5. Suppose that the analysis of a game tree indicates that player A will always win over player B if both use the best possible strategy.

(a) What will happen if B makes one or more moves according to some other strategy? Is it still true that A will always win?
(b) Can the outcome be predicted if neither player uses the "best possible" strategy?

6. Shown below is the game tree for a finite, two-person game in which draws are possible. The terminal nodes have been labeled A (win for player A), B (win for player B), or D (draw). Player A moves first.

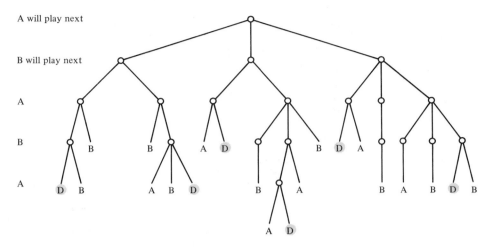

A will play next

B will play next

A

B

A

(a) Even though draws are possible, this game can be analyzed using the technique described in this chapter. Assuming that each player uses the best possible strategy (and that a win is better than a draw), carry out the analysis. Show on the tree which player controls the game at each node. The player controlling the root node is, of course, the winner.

(b) Player A claims that he can always force a draw if he so desires. Analyze the tree to determine whether this claim is correct. Remember that for this analysis the "desired" nodes for A are draws and the desired nodes for B are anything else (i.e., a win for A or B). Draw the tree showing your analysis. Use the label " + " on the nodes from which A can force a draw, and the label " − " on the other nodes.

Analysis of "31"

Because we are now expert tree game analysts, we will appreciate a look at a detailed algorithm that when executed, analyzes a game such as "31" using the tree search method just described. That method can be regarded as a slightly modified natural-order tree search and our generalized search algorithm (Figure 6·16) should, therefore, be our *point of departure*. One algorithm that can analyze "31" is given in Figure 7·14, which we will discuss after restating the rules of the game. The rules of "31" are:

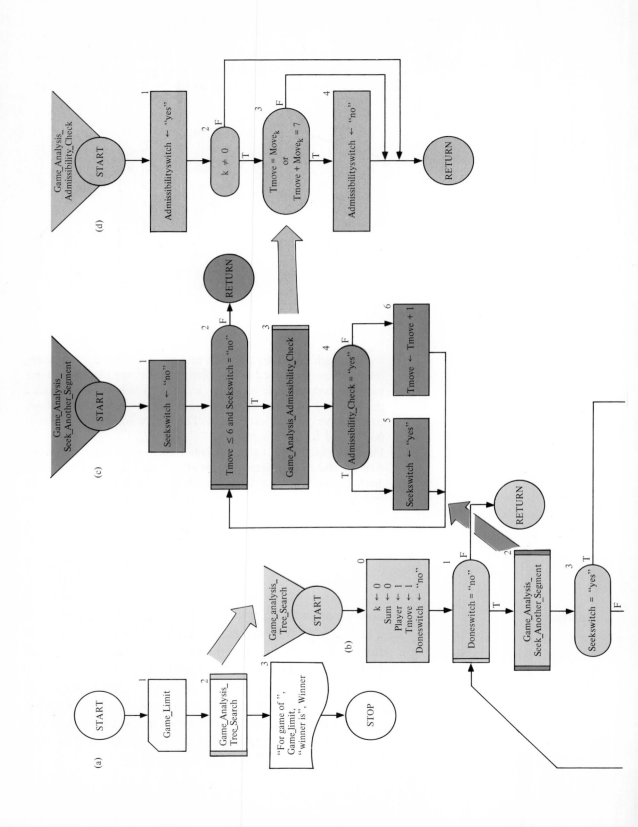

(a)

START → Game_Limit [1] → Game_Analysis_Tree_Search [2] → "For game of ", Game_limit, "winner is", Winner [3] → STOP

(b)

Game_analysis_Tree_Search START →

k ← 0
Sum ← 0
Player ← 1
Tmove ← 1
Doneswitch ← "no" [0]

→ Doneswitch = "no" [1] — T → Game_Analysis_Seek_Another_Segment [2] → Seekswitch = "yes" [3] — T

F (from Doneswitch) → RETURN

F (from Seekswitch)

(c)

Game_Analysis_Seek_Another_Segment START →

Seekswitch ← "no" [1] → Tmove ≤ 6 and Seekswitch = "no" [2] — T → Game_Analysis_Admissibility_Check [3] → Admissibility_Check = "yes" [4]

F (from Tmove ≤ 6) → RETURN

Admissibility_Check = "yes":
  T → Seekswitch ← "yes" [5]
  F → Tmove ← Tmove + 1 [6]

(d)

Game_Analysis_Admissibility_Check START →

Admissibilityswitch ← "yes" [1] → $k \neq 0$ [2]

$k \neq 0$:
  T → Tmove = Move_k or Tmove + Move_k = 7 [3]
  F → RETURN

Tmove = Move_k or Tmove + Move_k = 7:
  T → Admissibilityswitch ← "no" [4]
  F → RETURN

Admissibilityswitch ← "no" [4] → RETURN

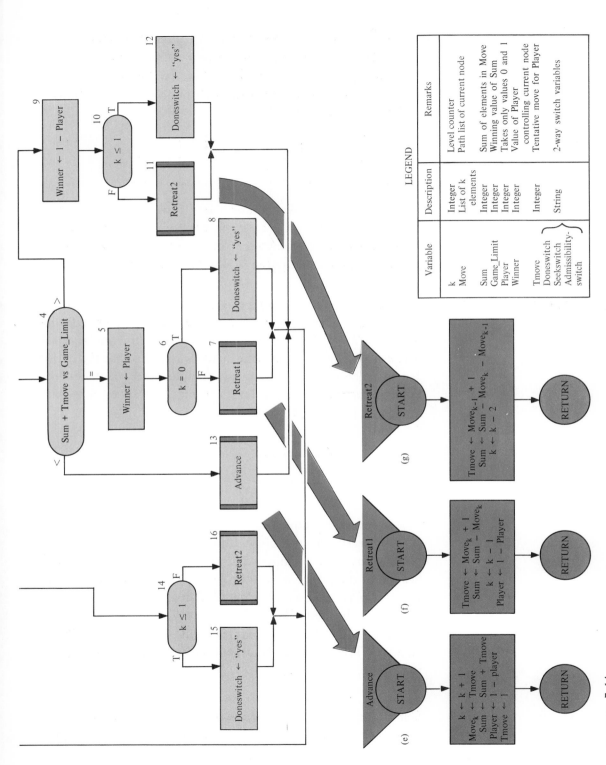

FIGURE 7·14
Algorithm for game analysis.

The first player chooses an initial orientation for a die. The side face up gives a running sum's initial value. Thereafter, each player moves by tilting the die over on its side (one of four possible sides, of course. And remember that opposite faces always add to seven).

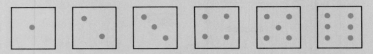

The side that turns up after the tilt-over is then added to the running sum. The game proceeds tilt after tilt. A player whose tilt brings the total to exactly 31 wins the game; a player exceeding 31 loses. No draws.

Main Flowchart

One distinction between game analysis and tree search for a nut should be clear in your mind before you examine the details of Figure 7·14. Although a squirrel can stop his tree traversal whenever he finds a nut, game analysis requires that the entire game tree be traversed before any "results" can be announced. For this reason the test in box 3 of the generalized flowchart for tree search (Figure 6·16a)

is not relevant here; the game analysis is *always* successful. That is, a squirrel may not always find a nut, but this kind of a game always has a winner. The result produced is the identification of the player who is the predetermined winner, assuming best play and assuming player A makes the first move.

Thus the main flowchart (Figure 7·14a) contains a box to read the value of Game_Limit, a call on Game_Analysis_Tree_Search, and an output box to print the value of the variable, Winner.

Tree_Search

Game_Analysis_Tree_Search starts by initializing the level counter, k, to zero, the level of the root node. Since the path list for the root node is null, the variable Sum is initialized to zero. Player A, coded as Player 1, will make the first move so the variable Player is initialized to 1. Player B is coded as Player 0 and moves second. Each time the players change, this fact is recorded by switching the value of the variable Player from 1 to 0 or 0 to 1. Such switching actually takes place in either Advance (Figure 7·14e) or Retreat1 (Figure 7·14f). Player always has the value of the player *about to move,* that is, the player for whom an admissible move (segment) is sought. The current node is always identified with the node reached in the most recently *executed* play or action. Thus, as in the natural-order tree search (Figure 6·16), the current node is the node on which we stand while we seek the next move for Player.

The list, Move, indexed by the level counter, k, at any time holds a record of the individual decisions in one partial or full play-through of the game. This list corresponds to the game *path* and serves precisely the same role as the list Color in the four-color algorithm. That is, Move represents a path from the root node to the current node. The variable Sum keeps a running total of the values of the path or move choices. Tmove holds the segment number of the move under consideration for Player.

The variable Doneswitch has sole charge of controlling the while loop that carries out the search in Figure 7·14b. Doneswitch is initially set to "no" and is reset to "yes" only when the marking for the root node has been determined, as will be seen presently. When Doneswitch is interpreted as "yes", the search ends and control returns to box 3 of Figure 7·14a, where the result is displayed.

The logic for determining whether advance or retreat is in order begins in box 3 of Figure 7·14b and is necessarily more complex here than in, say, the *four-color* algorithm. This is because we now have more than one condition justifying retreat and, moreover, depending on who controls the game at the current node, the choice is made to retreat one level or two levels. We will return to the detail for this decision shortly.

Seek_Another_Segment and Admissibility_Check

Each player has six possible choices per move. After the first move, two of these are inadmissible by the rules of the game (box 3 of Figure 7·14d). The variable Tmove (*tentative move*), serves the same role as tc (*tentative color*) in the four-coloring algorithm; it is a tentative choice for the next move, $Move_{k+1}$. Seek_Another_Segment sets Seek_Switch to "yes" in box 5 of Figure 7·14c if an admissible move has been found. The situation is further analyzed in boxes 3 and 4 of Figure 7·14b. If Seekswitch is "yes" then a legal move *is possible*. If the new sum would be less than the value of Game_Limit (< 31, for instance) then an advance is executed in box 13. But if the new sum would *equal* the value of Game_Limit, then Player (i.e., the player who would actually make that move) should be recognized now at the current node as in control of that node. This is done by the assignment, Winner ← Player, in box 5. There is no point in checking out other *higher-valued* segments as tentative moves for Player, since he already controls the current node. Now a retreat of one level should be executed so we can proceed with the marking of the parent of the current node.

Moving back one level involves changing players so that the *other* player can replay his last move (i.e., try the next segment) searching for a win instead of a loss for him. Figure 7·15 shows the reasoning in terms of tree nodes. (See also Figure 7·12.)

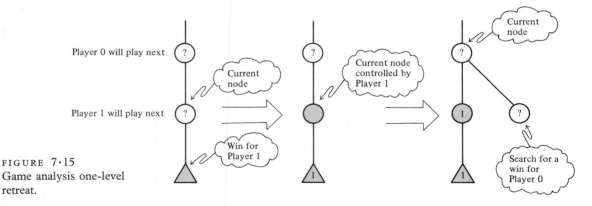

FIGURE 7·15
Game analysis one-level retreat.

On the other hand, if the new value of Sum + Tmove in box 4 of Figure 7·14b exceeds Game_Limit, then Player would lose the game if he made this play. This means that the *other player* should be recognized as in control of the game at the current node, as is done in box 9 by the assignment:

Winner ← 1 − Player

When a tentative move would carry the total beyond Game_Limit, there is no point in checking higher-numbered segments. They would only increase the total, which is already too large. Thus retreat is in order. How far should we retreat? Well, the other player made the move leading to the current node that has been marked as controlled by him. Therefore the node *preceding* the current node can also be marked as controlled by the other player. Thus we should retreat *two* levels (box 11) to the point at which Player made *his* previous move, and let him try the next segment to see if he can find a play leading to a win for him. The details are taken care of in Retreat2 (Figure 7·14*g*). Figure 7·16 illustrates this reasoning in terms of tree nodes.

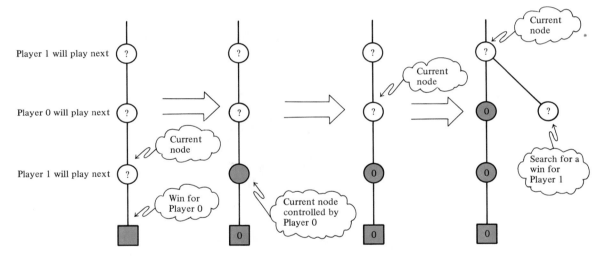

Player 1 will play next

Player 0 will play next

Player 1 will play next

Current node

Win for Player 0

Current node controlled by Player 0

Current node

Current node

Search for a win for Player 1

FIGURE 7·16
Game analysis two-level retreat.

Now let us investigate the situation in the case that the test in box 3 of Figure 7·14*b* fails. In this case the Seekswitch is "no", that is, no admissible value for Tmove was found by Seek_Another_Segment. Thus the current node is a win for the *other* player. The situation is analogous to that in Figure 7·16 and, in general, a retreat of two levels is in order. If, however, the value of the level counter is already less than or equal to 1 *before* the two level retreat is to be executed, then Game_Analysis is complete because we know how to mark the root node. The value of Winner denotes the correct marking for the root node.

As can be seen from Figures 7·15 and 7·16, each *node-marking* chain from a terminal node backward toward the root marks each node successively with the same value (0 or 1) unless there is a branch off to the right which causes the node marking value to change. But the chain that finally succeeds in marking the root node progresses all the way from a terminal node where Winner was assigned a value right up to the root node without any change in node marking value. Thus Winner has the correct value to mark the root node.

We leave to the student the exercise of understanding the remaining details of Figure 7·14.

Computer Results for Analysis of "31"

Table 7·2 gives actual computer results showing that the first player, Player A, is the fore-ordained winner of "31," assuming best play. The first line of the table was obtained by programming the algorithm of Figure 7·14 exactly, except that a tally was added to count the number of times Seek_Another_Segment was called. A spectacular 135 to 1 improvement in the execution time for the game analysis was effected by the

TABLE 7·2
Computer Results for Analysis of "31"

	Winner	Tally	Execution Time in Seconds[a]
Method of Figure 7·14	Player A	640,224	67.72
Modified Figure 7·14	Player A	4,276	.5

[a]As run on an IBM System 360/67 at Stanford University with the program coded in the Algol-W language.

simple expedient of examining the potential moves in the order 6, 5, 4, 3, 2, 1 instead of in the natural order 1, 2, 3, 4, 5, 6. These results are shown in the second line of Table 7·2.

If you have not already done so, get together with a friend and play a game such as "31," keeping careful statistics on Move, Winner, and Tally. Then you will understand the miraculous improvement in the execution time of Figure 7·14, brought, about by testing segments for admissibility in the order 6, 5, 4, 3, 2, 1 instead of in natural order. To incorporate this reversal in the order of segment selection into Figure 7·14, it is obvious that some change is required in Figure 7·14c, Seek_Another_Segment. But some alteration is also required in Figure 7·14b, Tree_Search, and trivial changes must be made to Figure 7·14e, 7·14f, and 7·14g. (See exercise 4 below.)

1. Explain why the first step in Figure 7·14f assigns to TMOVE the value Move$_k$ + 1 instead of 1.

2. Should the value of Move$_k$ be reset to zero in Retreat1 and should the value of Move$_k$ and Move$_{k-1}$ be reset to zero in Retreat2 of Figure 7·14?

3. The details in box 0 of Figure 7·14b do not initialize the MOVE list. Is this an omission that can cause an error when control reaches Figure 7·14f and 7·14g? Could the algorithm in retreating call for evaluation of a Move$_k$ to which a value had not been assigned?

4. Revise Figure 7·14b, 7·14c, 7·14e, 7·14f, and 7·14g, making all changes required so that values of Tmove are initialized and tested in the order 6 to 1, as described above. Run both versions on a computer, if possible, to check that the winner outputs are the same. *Hint.* In Revising Figure 7·14b check out carefully the "$>$" branch from box 4. If one segment number is too large, what about the next one?

5. Is the *same* player *always* the predetermined winner of the game in Figure 7·14? Run the program for various values of Game_Limit, or trace the algorithm for these values and make a table of Game_Limit versus Winner.

6. This is a project. After studying the algorithm for the analysis of "31," you should try your hand at writing an algorithm to analyze the game of HEX, whose rules are given in Problem 2, Exercises 6·1, Set B.

    You should not need much help with this project but, just in case, here are a few suggestions to consider after you've had a go at it yourself.

    Although the analysis of HEX is, in principle, similar to that of "31," there is more bookkeeping involved in the former. In "31" we saved, in the list element MOVE$_k$, an integer that could later be used to tell what segments had not yet been tried from the node at level $k - 1$. Saving this information amounts to saving the state of the game at every point in its history. In HEX we will also need to save the game's state at each move.

    When we backtrack, we also have a problem in *reversing* the play to recover the earlier state of the HEX board. In "31" recovering the earlier state simply amounted, by careful design, to subtracting values of MOVE$_k$ or values of both MOVE$_k$ and MOVE$_{k-1}$ from SUM. (See Figure 7·14f and 7·14g.) In HEX, however, it may prove more convenient simply to save the full description of the HEX board, say, as a 3 by 3 array, or as a nine-element list, for each state of the game. Then, to return to the condition of the board at an earlier level in the tree, it would merely be necessary to adjust the level index so that it corresponds to the desired array or list. To be more specific, the condition of the HEX board could be coded thus.

Value Assigned to Array Element	Interpretation
1	Presence of a black pawn
9	Presence of a green pawn
0	An empty square

Now, for example, the HEX board can be pictured by the grid shown in Figure 7·17. Information in this grid could, in turn, be saved as a "row" of nine elements.

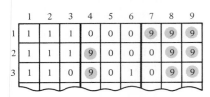

Imagine that this row belongs to an array of nine columns. We could then store the state of the game in each succeeding row after each move. We dub such an array the HEXH (for HEX History) and picture it below after green makes his first move, say, by moving his leftmost piece forward, followed by a similar move by *black*.

	1	2	3	4	5	6	7	8	9
1	1	1	1	0	0	0	9	9	9
2	1	1	1	9	0	0	0	9	9
3	1	1	0	9	0	1	0	9	9

You might also consider ways to think about (and to code) the up-to-nine choices each player may have when he takes his turn. One way to picture these choices is as a 3 by 3 array, say, with rows corresponding to each of the three *pawns* a player has to play with, and with columns corresponding to each of the three different *directions* each pawn might be allowed to move forward (diagonal left, straight, and diagonal right). Row and column indexes could be updated appropriately as each new choice for a move is considered. Once a move is selected and we prepare to move along a chosen segment to the next node, we can save the associated row and column index values for later use whenever we have to backtrack to this node and scan the remaining choices.

Strictly speaking, we need to save only one number, call it the choice index. (An integer from one to nine will do.) This value could then be converted into the row and column indexes by these simple rules.

$$\text{row} \leftarrow \text{CHOP}\left(\frac{\text{choice} - 1}{3}\right) + 1$$

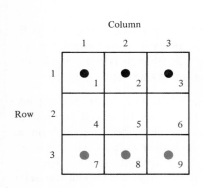

FIGURE 7·17

and

$$\text{column} \leftarrow \text{choice} - 3 \times (\text{row} - 1)$$

There is clearly a trade-off here between storage space and computer time. If you allocate space for pairs of indexes (row and column) in place of space for one index (choice), you avoid having to compute repeatedly the row, column pairs.

Interpreting and compiling

8·1
Interpreting and compiling

A program written in a procedural language such as FOR-TRAN or ALGOL may be executed by a conventional computer in one of two ways. (1) Statements of the program may be *interpreted* and executed one at a time, in the fashion of our Master Computer and his assistants. That is, each time a statement (flowchart box) comes up for execution, the meaning or intent of the statement is determined (or redetermined) and then carried out. No matter how many times the same statement comes up for execution, say when it appears in a loop, the same work is performed to interpret what action is wanted. (2) The statements of the program may be converted into an equivalent list of machine language (e.g., SAMOS) instructions to form a new representation of the algorithm. In this approach, it is the new program that is actually executed by the machine instead of the original program. The process of converting a procedural language program into a program expressed in a language directly executable by a machine is called *compiling*.

The main advantage of the first, or *interpreter,* approach is ease of debugging. From the perspective of the programmer, the program behaves as if it is being executed on a *higher*-level language machine. The fact that this machine is, in effect, simulated by a *lower*-level language machine is transparent to the programmer (i.e., he cannot *see* the lower level of mapping). The result is that if the program malfunctions *while executing,* the malfunction can be understood in terms of the higher-level machine and in terms of the program statement being executed. A compiled program has seldom preserved any direct connection to higher-level statements.

The main advantage of the second, or *compiler,* approach is efficiency. The instructions of a machine language program can be decoded directly by the computer hardware, whereas normally the instructions in the higher-level languages must be decoded by procedures (software) that are themselves expressed in machine language.

Currently there is a trend in computer design to build

machines so that the hardware (possibly with the aid of micro-code) decodes statements of a higher-level language. Little software is needed for this purpose. Machines of this type combine the flexibility of the interpreter with the efficiency of the compiler. Many such computers have already been built, some experimental, some commercial. They execute the higher-level instructions of Algol, APL, COBOL, RPG, and so forth.

Whichever approach is taken, compiling, interpreting, or some combination of the two, essentially similar algorithms must be executed to deduce the meaning of the program statements. This chapter emphasizes these common points of analysis and algorithmic structure. Moreover, if the trend in computer design that was just mentioned changes from a ripple to a wave, more people may want to understand how these newer computer models work. A study of this chapter will provide *some* of the necessary concepts.

8·2
Polish strings

When compiling or interpreting a program on a machine such as SAMOS, each statement is scanned character by character to determine the meaning. In the case of the compiler, the purpose of this analysis is to generate a list of machine language instructions for the scanned statements.

For example, on SAMOS, the procedural language statement

$$A \leftarrow A + B \times C$$

would be converted into machine language instructions somewhat as follows. (We assume that A, B, and C have been given the storage locations 1001, 1002, and 1003.)

±	OPER				ADDRESS			REMARKS
1	2 3 4	5	6	7	8 9	10	11	
	L, D, A		,	,	1, 0,	0,	2	Put B in accumulator
	M, P, Y		,	,	1, 0,	0,	3	Multiply accumulator by C
	A, D, D		,	,	1, 0,	0,	1	Add A to accumulator
	S, T, O		,	,	1, 0,	0,	1	Assign value in accumulator to A

Even with the notational improvements made in Section 2·3, it is awkward to analyze and convert our customary notation for arithmetic expressions into machine language instructions. We will show you why this is so.

Consider the arithmetic expression

$$\frac{B + \sqrt{B^2 - 4 \times A \times C}}{2 \times A}$$

which represents the *negative* of one of the roots of the equation

$$A \times X^2 + B \times X + C = 0$$

(We have omitted the minus sign in front of the first B above to avoid the complication of a *unary* minus at this point.)

Adopting the modifications of Section 2·3, the above expression takes the form

$$(B + (B\uparrow2 - 4 \times A \times C)\uparrow.5) / (2 \times A)$$

Let's number the operations in this expression in the order in which the operations are performed in the evaluation process. This is the order in which they will appear in our list of machine language instructions.

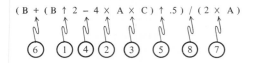

Now we see the difficulty. The machine must engage in a great deal of back-and-forth scanning of the expression to find the next operation to be performed. The difficulty would remain even if we were to drop the precedence relations among the operators and rely exclusively on parentheses to force special orderings. Thus, in a *right-to-left* scan with no operator precedence, as used in the language APL, we would have

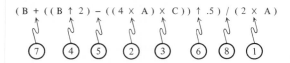

To eliminate this difficulty, the machine makes a preliminary translation of arithmetic expressions into *Polish string notation* (so called after the Polish mathematician, Lukasiewicz, who originated this kind of notation). This notation has the

advantage that operations appear in the order in which they are actually performed in the evaluation.

The basic idea behind Polish string notation is that operators are written at the end of the expression instead of in the middle. Thus A + B would be written as AB+. In this new form, the operator + is viewed as a command to add the values of the two variables immediately preceding it.

In computing we have permitted a variable to be a string of characters, and this permissiveness introduces the risk of a certain confusion in the use of Polish notation unless we are alert to the problem. For example, the expression

AA / AAA

if converted into Polish notation, would be

AAAAA /

Unfortunately, the same form will result when AAA / AA, A / AAAA, AAAA / A, and so forth, are expressed in Polish notation. Thus, unless we take special precautions, an expression in the form of Polish string notation can be unclear in that we may not be able to identify it uniquely with an expression in the *usual* notation.

To avoid this ambiguity, we insist that every variable be delimited, that is, its beginning and end must be identified. In the usual notation we partially depend on the operators to delimit the variables, but in Polish notation this no longer works. There are a number of ways of delimiting variables; one is to insist that a variable consist of only one character, another is to insert some distinguishing mark, say, the blank (□) after (or before) each variable when the expression is being converted into Polish notation. Then the expression

AA / AAA

can be converted, without ambiguity, into

AA AAA /

Nearly all modern compilers and interpreters *preedit* input expressions using an equivalent to the above technique. Typically each multicharacter variable, constant, or operator is replaced by a uniquely coded symbol usually of fixed length. (Sometimes a special delimiting code is used to indicate the end of the symbol.) In Chapter 13 we will return to this subject.

In the comparatively simple examples that follow, it will be convenient to use expressions having only single-character variables. This will save us the trouble of inserting marks between elements of an expression when it is displayed in Polish notation.

Here is an example of how this *postfix* (or operators-at-the-end) notation replaces the customary *infix* (or operators-in-the-middle) notation in a more complicated expression.

Infix   Postfix

$(A + B) \times (C - D)$ $(AB+)(CD-) \times$

In the postfix form, the operator $\times$ is viewed as a command to multiply the values of the two expressions $(AB+)$ and $(CD-)$ immediately preceding it.

How can we devise general rules for translating from infix to postfix? Well, if we represent our infix expression as a tree, then, to make this translation, we merely go through the tree and bend the branches at each node, so that the operator branch is brought to the right. See, for example, Figure 8·1.

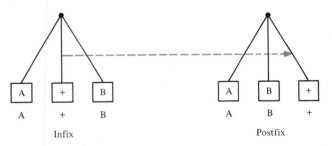

FIGURE 8·1

As another example, consider the infix expressions $A + (B \times C)$ and $(A + B) \times C$ in Figure 8·2. Here, the original infix expressions

$$A + (B \times C) \quad \text{and} \quad (A + B) \times C$$

are different in appearance only in the way in which the parentheses were inserted. But this is not the case with their postfix translations

$$A(BC\times) + \quad \text{and} \quad (AB+)C\times$$

Here we see that the operators occur in different positions in the two expressions. The locations of these operators alone are

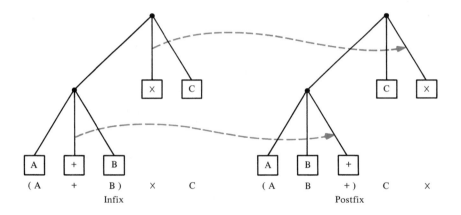

FIGURE 8·2

sufficient to indicate the intended operations. No parentheses are necessary. Thus we may write

$$ABC \times + \quad \text{and} \quad AB + C \times$$

in place of the above expressions and no confusion can arise. No "precedence rules" are necessary for the operations.

Another way of saying this is that in any Polish string expression, there is only one way in which to insert parentheses to obtain a meaningful result. That is, there is only one way to insert parentheses so that the entire expression and each subexpression will have the form

*expression*1 *expression*2 *operator*

You should satisfy yourself that this is the case in the above examples.

To understand the meaning of a Polish string, one must be able to identify the subexpressions on which each operator is operating. We will show how this is done for the quadratic formula expression discussed at the beginning of the section. In the initial editing, we replace 2 by the symbol T, 4 by F, and .5 by H, and the expression then has the infix form

$$(B + (B{\uparrow}T - F \times A \times C){\uparrow}H) / (T \times A)$$

The translation of this expression to a Polish string (which you will soon be asked to make, using tree manipulation) has the form

$$BBT{\uparrow}FA \times C \times {-}H{\uparrow}{+}\ TA \times /$$

Using brackets, we will identify the subexpressions and the operators acting on them according to the following rules.

1. Variables are subexpressions; put a bracket under each variable.

2. Each time we come to an operator, place a bracket under that operator together with the two immediately preceding subexpressions, thus forming a new subexpression.

The work starts out like this:

$$\underline{B}\ \underline{B}\ \underline{T}{\uparrow}F\ \ A\ \times\ C\ \times\ -\ H{\uparrow}\ +\ T\ \ A\ \times\ /$$

and the finished job appears as

$$\underline{B}\ \underline{B}\ \underline{T}{\uparrow}\ \underline{F}\ \underline{A}\ \times\ \underline{C}\ \times\ -\ \underline{H}{\uparrow}\ +\ \underline{T}\ \underline{A}\ \times\ /$$

The secret of the success of Polish string notation is that each operator is the terminal symbol in exactly one subexpression.

We can see that the order in which the *variables* occur is the same for the infix and postfix expressions, but the order in which the *operators* occur is radically different. In Figure 8·3 we compare the order in which the operations are performed in the infix and postfix expressions.

The fact that operations are performed in exactly the order in which they occur in postfix notation shows the importance of this notation in computing. No back-and-forth scanning is necessary.

Order in Which Operations are Performed	
Infix	Postfix
$(B+(B{\uparrow}T-F{\times}A{\times}C){\uparrow}H)/(T{\times}A)$	$BB T{\uparrow}FA{\times}C{\times}-H{\uparrow}+TA{\times}/$

FIGURE 8·3
The sequence of evaluation of the quadratic expression.

EXERCISES 8·2

1. Translate the expression for one solution of the quadratic equation, that is,

   $$(B + (B{\uparrow}T - F \times A \times C){\uparrow}H) / (T \times A)$$

   to Polish form by first developing an expression tree for the given infix expression, bending the operator branches, and "reading off" the postfix equivalent, that is, by listing the terminal nodes found during natural-order traverse of the tree.

2. Translate the expression

   $$A / B / C \times D \times C / B \times A$$

   to Polish form. In the translated expression, identify all subexpressions and verify that each is terminated by an operator.

3. The sum of the first n terms of an arithmetic progression is given by

   $$(n / 2) \times (2 \times a + (n - 1) \times d)$$

   where a is the first term and d is the common difference between successive terms of the progression. Rewrite the expression in Polish notation.

4. The sum of the first n terms of a geometric progression is given by

   $$a \times (1 - r{\uparrow}n) / (1 - r)$$

   where a is the first term and r is the common ratio of successive terms of the progression. Rewrite the expression in Polish notation.

5. You are given the following expression.

   $$a / b \times c / (a - b) \times (a - c)$$

   (a) Convert it to an expression tree using the usual rules of precedence.
   (b) Next, by bending the branches, as suggested in Problem 1, arrive at the postfix form for the given expression.

6. Which of the following is a correct postfix equivalent of the following expression tree?

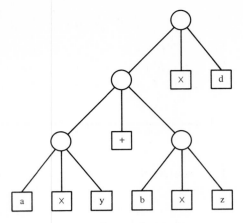

(a) $(a \times y + b \times z) \times d.$
(b) $a\ y\ \times\ +\ b\ z\ \times\ d.$
(c) $a\ y\ \times\ b\ z\ \times\ +\ d\ \times.$
(d) $a\ y\ \times\ +\ b\ z\ \times\ d\ \times.$
(e) None of the above.

7.   Below we give an expression tree equivalent to the following logical (infix) expression.

$$a > b \times c \quad or \quad f = b^2 - 4 \times a \times c$$

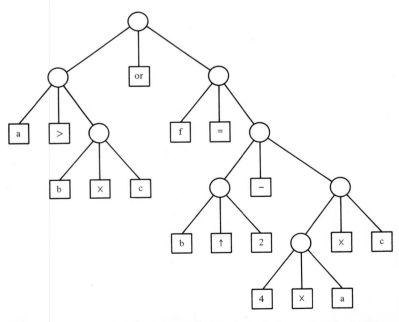

What is the postfix equivalent of the given infix expression? (Note that Table 3·4 precedence levels are assumed and the logical operator *or* has a precedence level *below* that of the relations, i.e., less precedence than the relations.)

8. Given an expression tree such as the one in the preceding problem, describe how you would scan this tree to produce as output an *infix* expression that is equivalent to this tree with parentheses placed around each subexpression.

9. Modify the description developed in Problem 8 so that the output is not the infix equivalent of the given tree but the *postfix* equivalent. In short, the modifications called for represent an algorithmic instead of a graphical procedure for bending the branches.

10. This question relates to the binary expression tree on the left. In a binary expression tree the operator is placed *at* its parent node. (See Problem 13, Exercises 6·1, Set D.)

During natural-order search of a tree, each terminal node is encountered only once, but each nonterminal node is encountered *three* times (i.e., just prior to descent to the left subtree, just prior to descent to the right subtree, and just prior to ascent to the parent node).

Let us define a natural-order tree scan as one in which the terminal node values are copied onto a list (from left to right), as they are encountered, and the nonterminal node values are consistently copied onto the same list at a selected one of the three points of encounter as described above. Show the list of values obtained for the given tree using each of the three scanning methods. Explain the significance of each result. As an example: If we are given the tree

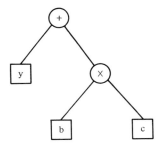

the three scanning methods respectively yield these lists.

(a) + y × b c
(b) y + b × c
(c) y b c × +

8·3
Evaluating polish strings

In order to understand Polish string expressions and appreciate their efficiency, we will inspect the simple single-scan method of evaluating them.

The method works like this. As we scan the expression, character by character (from left to right), we construct a special form of list called a "stack." This list is constructed so that whenever we come to an operator, the values on which that operator is to act are the most recent two that have been entered in the stack.

The rules for constructing this list (stack) are as follows.

1.   When a *variable* is scanned, its value is entered at the open end or "top" of the stack.

2.   When an *operator* is scanned:
  (a) The most recent two entries are removed from the stack.
  (b) The indicated operation is performed on these values.
  (c) The result computed in part b is entered at the open end of the stack.

We show how this works with our old standby, the quadratic formula expression in Polish notation,

$$\text{BBT}{\uparrow}\text{FA} \times \text{C} \times\, - \,\text{H}{\uparrow}\, + \,\text{TA} \times /$$

with the values of the variables being

A	B	C	F	H	T
3	7	−20	4	.5	2

(Remember that the value of this expression will be the *negative* of a root of the equation $3x^2 + 7x - 20 = 0$.)

To show the construction of the stack, we have written in Figure 8·4 the expression vertically at the left. On the right, we show the condition of the stack after the character in the left column has been scanned.

The purpose of Figure 8·4 is to show the condition of the stack at all stages of the process. In applying the method, you would not make all these copies of the stack; your final work would look like Figure 8·5.

At the end (for a correctly written postfix expression), everything should be crossed out except the value appearing under the last operator. This is the value of the expression.

The reason for the use of the word "stack" is now apparent, since the stack works very much like a stack of plates in a cafeteria. During the lunch hour, customers are lifting plates off and employees are adding plates on to the stack. Removals and additions are made at the same end of the stack so that

Single Scan Evaluation of BBT↑FA × C × −H↑ + TA × / with Values Given		
Character Scanned	Computation (If Any)	Condition of Stack (Open End at the Right)
B		7
B		7 7
T		7 7 2
↑	7↑2 = 49	7 7 2 49
F		7 7 2 49 4
A		7 7 2 49 4 3
×	4 × 3 = 12	7 7 2 49 4 3 12
C		7 7 2 49 4 3 12 −20
×	12 × (−20) = −240	7 7 2 49 4 3 12 −20 −240
−	49 − (−240) = 289	7 7 2 49 4 3 12 −20 −240 289
H		7 7 2 49 4 3 12 −20 −240 289 .5
↑	289↑.5 = 17	7 7 2 49 4 3 12 −20 −240 289 .5 17
+	7 + 17 = 24	7 7 2 49 4 3 12 −20 −240 289 .5 17 24
T		7 7 2 49 4 3 12 −20 −240 289 .5 17 24 2
A		7 7 2 49 4 3 12 −20 −240 289 .5 17 24 2 3
×	2 × 3 = 6	7 7 2 49 4 3 12 −20 −240 289 .5 17 24 2 3 6
/	24 / 6 = 4	7 7 2 49 4 3 12 −20 −240 289 .5 17 24 2 3 6 4

FIGURE 8·4
Detailed scan of a quadratic expression.

B	B	T	↑	F	A	×	C	×	−	H	↑	+	T	A	×	/
7	7	2	49	4	3	12	−20	−240	289	.5	17	24	2	3	6	4

FIGURE 8·5
A shorthand way of following the condition of the stack.

the most recent plate added is the first to be removed (*last in, first out*). And so it is with the stacks used in evaluating arithmetic expressions.

EXERCISES 8·3,
SET A

1. In parts a and b below, you are given a postfix expression and values for the variables involved. Your job is to find the value of the expression.

(a) A B C − × D +

$$A = 1$$
$$B = 4$$
$$C = 2$$
$$D = 3$$

(b) R Y Z × W Q↑ − X

$$R = 2$$
$$Y = -1$$
$$Z = -4$$
$$W = 3$$
$$Q = 2$$

2. Evaluate the postfix expression

$$K \ I \ J \uparrow + \ L /$$

using the values $K = 5, I = 4, J = 2, L = 3$.

3. In Problem 3, Exercises 8·2, you converted the formula for summing an arithmetic progression to Polish notation. Apply the converted formula to evaluate the first eight terms of the progression

$$3, \ 7, \ 11, \ 15 \ , \ . \ . \ .$$

by using an evaluation scheme similar to the one shown in Figure 8·5.

4. In Problem 4, Exercises 8·2, you converted to Polish notation the formula for summing a geometric progression. Apply the converted formula to evaluate the first eight terms of the progression

$$2, \ 4, \ 8, \ 16, \ . \ . \ .$$

using an evaluation scheme similar to Figure 8·5.

5. Suppose we use a list P to represent a *stack* and let the value of the variable PTR designate the position (subscript) in P corresponding to the last (most recently) stacked item.

(a) Are the following steps sufficient to represent the stacking of two more items L and M? If not, what changes are needed?

$$
\begin{aligned}
P_{PTR+1} &\leftarrow L \\
P_{PTR+2} &\leftarrow M \\
PTR &\leftarrow PTR + 2
\end{aligned}
$$

(b) Do the following steps represent the removal of the last three items from the stack P, assigning these in last-in, first-out order to I, J, and K, respectively? If not, what changes are needed?

$$
\begin{aligned}
I &\leftarrow P_{PTR} \\
J &\leftarrow P_{PTR-1} \\
K &\leftarrow P_{PTR-2} \\
PTR &\leftarrow PTR - 3
\end{aligned}
$$

Postfix Machines (POSTOS)

We have just seen that evaluation of postfix expressions offers the advantage of a simple single scan method. *Postfix machines* are computers that are organized so that postfix representation is, in effect, the language of the machine. Some of the most familiar *actual* postfix machines are the hand-held calculators and computers such as the model illustrated in Figure 1·36. It may be instructive to see how a computer of this type, which we will call POSTOS (*Post*fix-Oriented *SAMOS*), works.

Consider the infix expression

$$(A + B) \times (C - D)$$

and its postfix equivalent

$$A \quad B + C \quad D - \times$$

In the language of the postfix machine, the list of instructions necessary to produce the value of the postfix expression would be something like what is shown below on the left.

Stack A		Stack 1001
Stack B		Stack 1002
ADD		ADD
Stack C	$\Longrightarrow$	Stack 1003
Stack D		Stack 1004
SUB		SUB
MPY		MPY

Strictly speaking, if we assume that A, B, C, and D have been allocated storage locations 1001, 1002, 1003, and 1004, this list of instructions would actually look more like what is shown above on the right of the open arrow.

This machine language is easily understood in terms of stack operations. The stack of the machine can be thought of as a list of storage registers that take the place of an Accumulator register in a conventional machine such as SAMOS. The computer circuitry "knows" at all times the location of the register in the list that was last filled with a value, that is, it "knows" the location of the "top of the stack."

Suppose that before the execution of the above list of instructions, the stack is empty. An empty stack is pictured to the left by showing a *top-of-stack* indicator pointing to a special cell or register that is not used.

We are now ready to see what the above instructions mean, although you have probably already figured it out. For purposes of illustration, let us assume that locations and current values for A, B, C, and D, are:

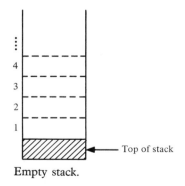

Empty stack.

Variable	Location	Value
A	1001	2
B	1002	4
C	1003	3
D	1004	7

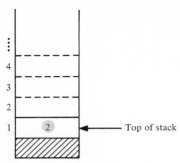

After execution of Stack 1001.

The instruction,

Stack 1001

means, fetch a copy of the value at location 1001 and "push" it on to the top of the stack. This action is shown pictorially at the left.

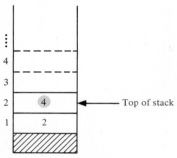

After execution of Stack 1002.

By the same reasoning, execution of

Stack 1002

causes the value 4 to be assigned to the next cell in the stack, as shown on the left.

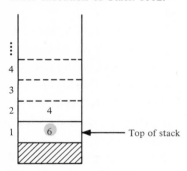

After execution of ADD.

The next instruction,

ADD

has a very interesting interpretation. No operands (addresses) are required in this instruction. The action is to (1) form the sum of the values found in the top *two* registers of the stack and assign that sum to the "lower" of these two registers, that is, to the next-to-top position—as shown, and (2) adjust the top-of-stack indicator so it points to the new result. (The old value at the old top-of-stack position remains where it was, but it will never be used again, as you will see.)

The succeeding steps,

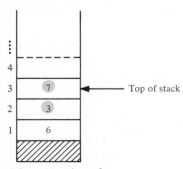

After execution of
Stack 1003
Stack 1004.

Stack 1003
Stack 1004

cause the stack to appear as shown. (Notice that execution of the first of these two instructions replaces the residual value, 4, with the new value, 3.)

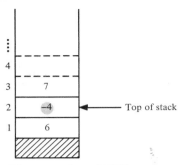

After execution of SUB.

By analogy with ADD, executing the next instruction

SUB

causes the computer to form the difference between the next-to-top and top values of the stack, place this difference in the lower of the two registers, and adjust the indicator so it points to this result.

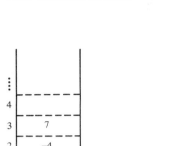

After execution of MPY.

Finally, execution of

MPY

causes the computer to form the product of values in the top-most two positions, assign that product (-4×6 in this case) to the lower of these two positions, and adjust the top-of-stack indicator.

To recapitulate, the postfix machine employs the topmost position or positions of the stack in some sense like the SAMOS machine uses an Accumulator. Because the postfix machine always adjusts the top-of-stack indicator in an appropriate manner after each instruction, it is always true that at the very end of an expression evaluation, the top-of-stack indicator points to the computed result.

A statement of the form

$$A \leftarrow (A + B) \times (C - D)$$

will have the postfix representation

$$A \ A \ B + C \ D - \times \ \leftarrow$$

Here we treat the assignment symbol "$\leftarrow$" as another operator of even lower precedence than that of "$+$" or "$-$". With this extension, one more postfix machine instruction completes the job of assigning the value of the expression to A. It is

Unstack 1001

This instruction not only stores the value found at the top of the stack in the location assigned to A, but it also adjusts the top-of-stack indicator to signify an empty stack.

For a postfix machine, once we associate storage locations with the variables, for example, establish that "Stack A" means "Stack 1001," and so forth, the postfix representation *is*, in effect, the machine language. When we get to the end of this chapter, it will be interesting to compare the lists of instructions for postfix machines such as the one just described, with the lists of generated instructions for SAMOS-like machines— for various types of expressions.

The hand-held calculator illustrated in Figure 1·36 is a postfix machine that has a small number of storage cells—nine, to be exact. These are designated by addresses 1 through 9. There is also a stack that has only four registers. Such a calculator is nevertheless powerful enough to evaluate most "everyday" mathematical expressions.

Since the illustrated Brand X calculator is not able to store a postfix program, you must enter the instructions as a sequence of key strokes each time you wish to evaluate an expression. (More advanced hand-held models have space to store instructions, so in those models postfix expressions can be stored as part of a larger program.)

On the Brand X calculator the *stack* instruction is accomplished by striking the recall key $\boxed{\text{RCL}}$, followed by the name of the storage cell whose copied value is to be *pushed* onto the stack. Thus $\boxed{\text{RCL}}$ $\boxed{3}$ pushes a copy of register 3's contents onto the stack. The Brand X calculator has no instruction key corresponding exactly to the *Unstack* instruction of POSTOS, but there is a store instruction that copies the value at the top of the stack into a designated register. For example, the key sequence $\boxed{\text{STO}}$ $\boxed{4}$ assigns a copy of the value at the top of the stack to storage register 4.

Now let us see how we can evaluate

$$(A + B) \times (C - D)$$

on the Brand X calculator. Suppose that variables A, B, C,

and D correspond to storage registers, 1, 2, 3, and 4, respectively, and that these registers already hold the proper values. Recall that the postfix expression we wish to evaluate is

$$A\ B + C\ D - \times$$

We see below the flowchart box equivalent, the corresponding POSTOS instructions and, finally, the required key stroke sequence for the Brand X calculator.

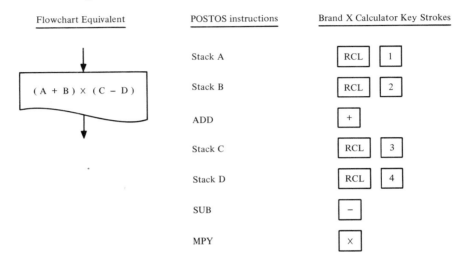

Flowchart Equivalent	POSTOS instructions	Brand X Calculator Key Strokes
	Stack A	RCL 1
$(A + B) \times (C - D)$	Stack B	RCL 2
	ADD	+
	Stack C	RCL 3
	Stack D	RCL 4
	SUB	−
	MPY	×

A total of 11 key strokes are required. When this sequence has been keyed in, the resulting value of the expression appears in the calculator display register. Note the similarity to our earlier POSTOS notation.

The value of the expression just calculated can be saved by executing a *store* instruction designating which storage cell is to receive this value. For example, if the original expression had been part of the assignment statement

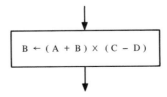

then the assignment action is achieved by the key sequence

STO 2

following the original 11 key sequence that evaluated the expression.

1. For each of the four cases below develop a list of instructions for the postfix machine that would execute the given assignment step. Assume that cells located at 1001 through 1006 are associated with variables A through F, respectively and, in each case, identify the index of the topmost register of the stack that was actually required for evaluation. For cases c and d assume the operator DIV forms the quotient of the values in the top two registers and, by analogy with SAMOS, leaves the integral part of the quotient in the next-to-top register of the stack.

    (a) F ← A + B + C + D + E
    (b) F ← A + (B + (C + (D + E)))
    (c) F ← A / (C + D)
    (d) F ← A / (C / (D + E))

2. Obtain a copy of an "Owner's Handbook" for a postfix calculator similar to Brand X and study it until you know how to instruct that machine to evaluate a variety of expressions such as those given in Problems 4, 5, 6, and 8 of Exercises 6·1, Set D. Be sure to study how unary operations such as $\sqrt[n]{}$, cos, and absolute value are keyed in on such a machine. Now outline an explanation of how to use this calculator to evaluate expressions. Your explanation is for someone who has not studied this text and is unfamiliar with postfix machines.

8·4
Translating from infix to postfix

We have examined one method of translating from infix to postfix: manipulating the branches of a tree. (Exercise 9 of Section 8·2 suggests that systematically manipulating the branches amounts, in effect, to a special tree search.) However, this method is complicated and time consuming. We are motivated to find a method based on a single scan of the infix expression.

Let's look at an infix expression and its postfix translation.

INFIX: A × B + C × D ↑ E / F − G × H

POSTFIX: A B × C D E ↑ × F / + G H × −

As we have seen before, the variables occur in the same order in the two expressions, but the operators are radically rearranged. How do we know where to put the operators? How do we know, for example, when we are ready to write the + in the above postfix expression? In this example, the left and

A × B + C × D ↑ E / F − G × H

Left-hand Sub-expr

Right-hand Sub-expr

right expressions operated on by the + in the infix expression are as indicated on the left. But how did we know where the end of the right-hand expression was? Is there anything special about the letter "F" that gives us this information? No! The answer lies in the symbol "−". The reason that the minus is not included in the bracket is that it is an operator whose precedence level is not higher than that of "+". That is the reason that the "−" signals the end of the right-hand subexpression acted on by the "+".

This principle can be implemented in the translation process by using the notion of a stack that was introduced in the preceding section. However, instead of stacking scanned *operands*—as was done in the scheme for evaluating an expression—we will use the stack to save scanned *operators*. Here is how the translation to postfix works.

1. When the element scanned is a variable, it is immediately placed at the right end of the postfix expression being created.

2. When the element scanned is an operator, it is placed at the open end of a stack.

3. *But,* before the operator is placed at the end of the stack, the operator presently at the end of the stack is inspected. It is transferred to the right end of the postfix expression if its precedence level is *equal to or higher than* that of the new operator to be added to the stack. The next operator so uncovered in the stack is likewise inspected *until* the stack is empty or the operator at the end of the stack has a lower precedence level than that of the operator being added to the stack.

4. When there are *no more characters* to be scanned, the elements of the stack are popped off the end of the stack one by one and transferred to the end of the postfix expression.

In Figure 8·6 we show how all this works in the case of the foregoing expression. Trace the operations by studying this figure line by line.

Character Scanned	Stack	Postfix Expression
A		A
×	×	A
B	×	AB
+	× +	AB ×
C	+	AB × C
×	+ ×	AB × C
D	+ ×	AB × CD
↑	+ × ↑	AB × CD
E	+ × ↑	AB × CDE
/	+ × ↑ /	AB × CDE↑ ×
F	+ /	AB × CDE↑ × F
−	+ / −	AB × CDE↑ × F / +
G	−	AB × CDE↑ × F / + G
×	− ×	AB × CDE↑ × F / + G
H	− ×	AB × CDE↑ × F / + GH
□	− ×	AB × CDE↑ × F / + GH × −

FIGURE 8·6
Translating from infix to
postfix.

The handling of parentheses is still to be discussed. The rules are simple and should be self-explanatory.

1. When a left parenthesis is scanned, it is placed directly in the stack. Nothing is removed from the stack.

2. When a right parenthesis is scanned, operators are transferred one at a time from the end of the stack to the postfix expression until a left parenthesis is reached.

3. Now this parenthesis pair is discarded and no longer appears anywhere in the stack or in the postfix expression.

Figure 8·7 demonstrates this process, using our favorite (quadratic formula) expression.

$$(B + (B{\uparrow}T - F \times A \times C){\uparrow}H)/(T \times A)$$

The reader must satisfy himself that the rules given above do, in fact, accomplish the desired translation. And, also, he must be sure he sees why operators are removed from the stack in the first-in, last-out order. Figure 8·7 should be studied carefully, as well as the exercises that follow.

The stack has been displayed somewhat differently here than in the preceding section. The crossed-out entries, instead of remaining in the list, have disappeared entirely. In working

Character Scanned	Stack	Postfix Expression
(	(	
B	(	B
+	(+	B
(	(+ (	B
B	(+ (	B B
↑	(+ (↑	B B
T	(+ (↑	B B T
−	(+ (↑ −	B B T ↑
F	(+ (−	B B T ↑ F
×	(+ (− ×	B B T ↑ F
A	(+ (− ×	B B T ↑ F A
×	(+ (− × ×	B B T ↑ F A ×
C	(+ (− ×	B B T ↑ F A × C
)	(+ (− ×	B B T ↑ F A × C × −
↑	(+ ↑	B B T ↑ F A × C × −
H	(+ ↑	B B T ↑ F A × C × − H
)	(+ ↑	B B T ↑ F A × C × − H ↑ +
/	/	B B T ↑ F A × C × − H ↑ +
(	/ (	B B T ↑ F A × C × − H ↑ +
T	/ (	B B T ↑ F A × C × − H ↑ + T
×	/ (×	B B T ↑ F A × C × − H ↑ + T
A	/ (×	B B T ↑ F A × C × − H ↑ + T A
)	/ (×	B B T ↑ F A × C × − H ↑ + T A ×
□	/	B B T ↑ F A × C × − H ↑ + T A × /

FIGURE 8·7
Translation of an expression
with parentheses.

examples, the student may prefer to continue crossing out the
deleted entries.

EXERCISES 8·4

Use the stack technique described in this section to translate the
following five infix expressions to postfix form.
Hint Use the format of Figure 8·7 as a guide until you feel safe
in using a shorthand form.

1. $(n / 2) \times (2 \times a + (n − 1) \times d)$

2. $a \times (1 − r{\uparrow}n) / (1 − r)$

3. $2 \times \pi \times ((a{\uparrow}2 + b{\uparrow}2) / 2){\uparrow}.5$
   (approximate circumference of an ellipse with semiaxes a and b)

4. $((u − x){\uparrow}2 + (v − y){\uparrow}2){\uparrow}.5$
   (distance between points (x,y) and (u,v)

5. $p \times (1 + i / q){\uparrow}(n \times q)$
   (value of principal p at interest i compounded q times per year
   after n years)

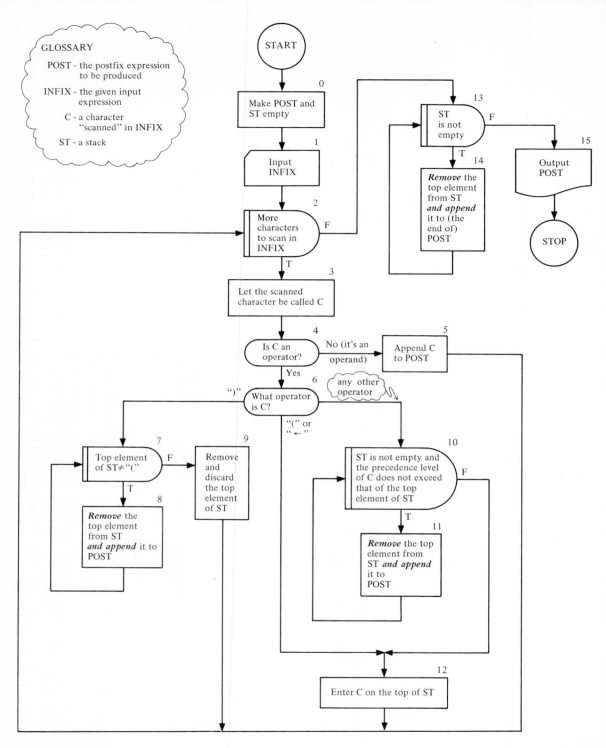

FIGURE 8·8
Generalized flowchart for
single-scan infix-to-postfix
translation.

6. In what way will the stack technique have to be modified to handle the expression

$$a + (b - c) \times d < f \quad \text{or} \quad q + r \geq t$$

8·5
Flowcharting the translation process

The translation process described in the preceding section can be flowcharted easily. A brief examination of the flowchart in Figure 8·8 should reveal that it is almost self-explanatory and faithfully reflects the verbal description given in the preceding section. The reader should satisfy himself that the various while loops will all terminate if the infix expression being processed is a correct one. For example, if the character value of C is determined to be a right parenthesis, the loop of boxes 7 and 8 must terminate, since a matching left parenthesis must have been placed on the stack at an earlier point in the scan.

Of course, a flowchart can be constructed showing the operations on POST, INFIX, and the stack, ST, in greater detail. Before going to greater detail one needs to decide how POST, INFIX, and ST are to be represented, for example as lists or as strings. We will first assume they are lists *whose elements are single characters,* that is, each list element is a string of length one. (The detail may be developed with even greater ease using strings, once certain string manipulation techniques are developed. See Chapter 13.) In the list approach, three indices, or pointers, are needed, one for each list:

1. n, the position of the latest entry in the stack, ST.

2. i, the position being scanned in the infix expression, INFIX.

3. k, the position of the most recent entry in the postfix expression, POST.

Here are some possible mappings to lower levels of detail.

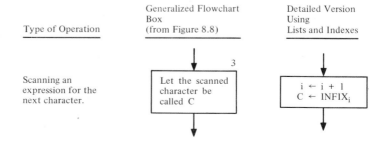

Type of Operation	Generalized Flowchart Box (from Figure 8.8)	Detailed Version Using Lists and Indexes
Scanning an expression for the next character.	Let the scanned character be called C	$i \leftarrow i + 1$ $C \leftarrow INFIX_i$

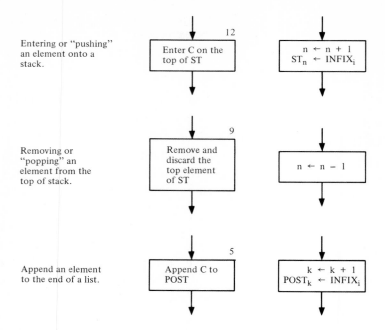

Entering or "pushing" an element onto a stack.

Removing or "popping" an element from the top of stack.

Append an element to the end of a list.

We may wonder how box 10 of Figure 8·8

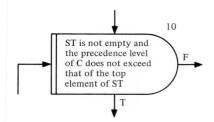

is to be expressed in more detailed notation. We might define a function called LEV, that, when applied to a character, returns an integer value representing the precedence level of the given character. The complete tabulation of LEV is given in Table 8·1. With such a function at hand, box 10 could be mapped to

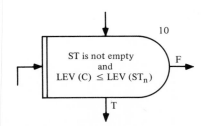

and boxes 4 and 6 could be replaced by

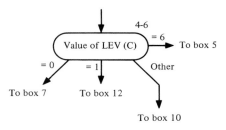

CHAR	LEV(CHAR)
Any variable	6
↑	5
×, /	4
+, −	3
<, >, ≤, ≥, =, ≠	2
(, ←	1
)	0

Taking stock, we have seen in Figure 8·8 an algorithm for converting expressions and statements from infix form, an external representation of our program, to postfix form, which may be regarded as an internal form especially suitable for further processing on a computer. This additional processing is the conversion of the postfix form to a generated list of SAMOS-like instructions. The next section shows how the algorithm of Figure 8·8 can be modified to perform this additional processing step. Of course, for postfix machines, that is, machines that can interpret postfix form directly, this last processing step is unnecessary.

EXERCISES 8·5

In Problems 1, 2, and 3, you are asked to provide details for some of the boxes in the Figure 8·8 flowchart—continuing to assume that INFIX, POST, and ST are represented as lists of single characters—with indexes i, k, and n used for the respective lists.

1. Give a detailed representation for box 2. Explain any assumptions you choose to make.

2. Give a detailed representation for box 0.

3. Using the results of the preceding exercises and the additional suggestions given in the text, construct the detailed representation for the entire Figure 8·8 flowchart.

4. Assume preediting has placed a blank between each two characters of INFIX. Show the changes that would be required to the flowchart of Problem 3 to accommodate this new infix form.

5. Assume a blank character is to be inserted *after* each character of the postfix form. Show the changes that would be required for the flowchart of Problem 3.

6. Suppose preediting has placed a blank between each two elements of the infix expression, but assume these elements are *not of fixed length*. Show the changes that would be necessary for the flowchart of Problem 3.

8·6
Interpreters and compilers

The algorithm (Figure 8·8) for converting from infix to postfix is only a heartbeat away from being either an interpreter algorithm or a compiler algorithm. We will first discuss the conversion of this flowchart into an interpreter.

Interpreter

The essential modification is that each time we are about to place an *operator* at the end of POST (boxes 8, 11, and 14 of Figure 8·8), we do something else instead, such as:

> 1. Remove from the end of POST the two operands that go with this operator.
>
> 2. Calculate the value of the infix expression using this operator and these operands.
>
> 3. Place the calculated value at the end of POST.

To clarify this process we present in Figure 8·9 a trace comparing the execution of the INFIX-to-POSTFIX algorithm with that of the INTERPRETER algorithm. These algorithms differ only when an operator is about to be appended to POST (boxes 8, 11, and 14 of Figure 8·8). In this trace we will use the expression

$$A \leftarrow B \times C - D / E$$

where B, C, D, and E are assumed to have the values 4, 2, 6, and 3, respectively. Characters printed in dark green have just been appended to the lists they appear in; those printed in light green have just been removed. When you study the trace in Figure 8·9, remember that the condition of the stack

CHAR Being Scanned	Flowchart Box of Figure 8·8	ST	INFIX-TO-POSTFIX Algorithm (Figure 8·8)	INTERPRETER Algorithm Figure 8·8 with Figure 8·10 version of boxes 8, 11, and 14	
			POST	POST	Calculation Performed
A	5		A	A	
←	12	←	A	A	
B	5	←	AB	AB	
×	12	← ×	AB	AB	
C	5	← ×	ABC	ABC	
−	11	← ×	ABC ×	A BC	$B \times C = 4 \times 2 = 8$
				A8 ◄－－－－－－－－－－／	
	12	← −			
D	5	← −	ABC × D	A8D	
/	12	← − /	ABC × D	A8D	
E	5	← − /	ABC × D E	A8DE	
No more characters	14	← −́ /	ABC × DE /	A8DE	$D / E = 6 / 3 = 2$
				A82 ◄－－－－－－－－－／	
	14	← −	ABC × DE / −	A 82	$8 - 2 = 6$
				A6 ◄－－－－－－－－／	
		←	ABC × DE / − ←	A6	A ← 6
Final State			ABC × DE / − ←	(empty)	A ← 6

FIGURE 8·9
Trace comparing effect of INFIX-TO-POSTFIX algorithm with that of INTERPRETER algorithm. Each algorithm is executed using the following data set:

INFIX = "A←B×C−D/E"

and

B = 4, C = 2,
D = 6, E = 3

will be the same no matter which of the two algorithms is being executed.

We see that the net effect of the interpreter algorithm is to perform the assignment

$$A \leftarrow 6$$

which is the assignment called for by the (initial) infix expression in

$$A \leftarrow B \times C - D / E$$

and by the (final) postfix expression

$$A \ B \ C \times D \ E \ / \ - \ \leftarrow$$

when B, C, D, and E have the specified values.

There is a difficulty with our approach to interpreting that we have purposely glossed over. This difficulty arises from our assumption that POST is a list of characters, which implies that each item appended to or removed from POST must be a single character. Fortunately, in the trace just considered, the calculated values (8, 2, and 6) appended to the end of POST met this requirement—they were single characters. But we can't expect calculated values to always be so cooperative. Thus we must resort to some other means of storing calculated values. For example, we could relax our assumption about the structure of POST and allow its elements to have values of any type, for example, strings of any length, or integers, or reals, as may be required. Another way, which is more useful when programming the algorithm in a language such as FORTRAN or ALGOL, is to create a second stack for saving the numeric "temporaries." Then each time we make a calculation, as in the last column of Figure 8·9, we place the calculated value on the top of TEMP. We also put an asterisk (*) on the end of POST to indicate that the numeric value of the desired operand can be found at the top of TEMP. Thus, if the character we remove from POST (as in the trace in Figure 8·9) turns out to be an asterisk, we know that the numeric value of the desired operand represented by this asterisk will be found on the top of TEMP.

The flowchart of Figure 8·10 incorporates this latter feature. The interpreter algorithm is seen in silhouette form in Figure 8·11, where every box is identical with its match in Figure 8·8 except for boxes 8, 11, and 14, which are now calls on the procedure in Figure 8·10, which is entitled Interpreter_version_of_Remove_and_Append. It should be noted in Figure 8·10 that the assignment operator must be handled a little differently from the other operators.

A trace of this interpreter algorithm will be found in Figure 8·12. This trace is exactly the same as that in Figure 8·9 except that it includes the TEMP feature. Detailed programming of this algorithm will be considered at the end of Chapter 13.

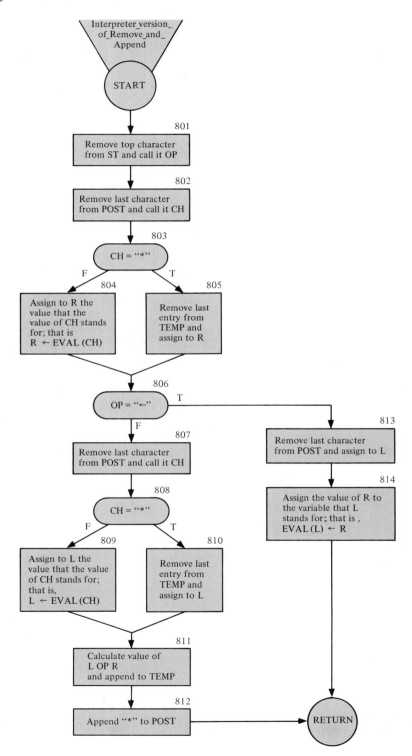

FIGURE 8·10

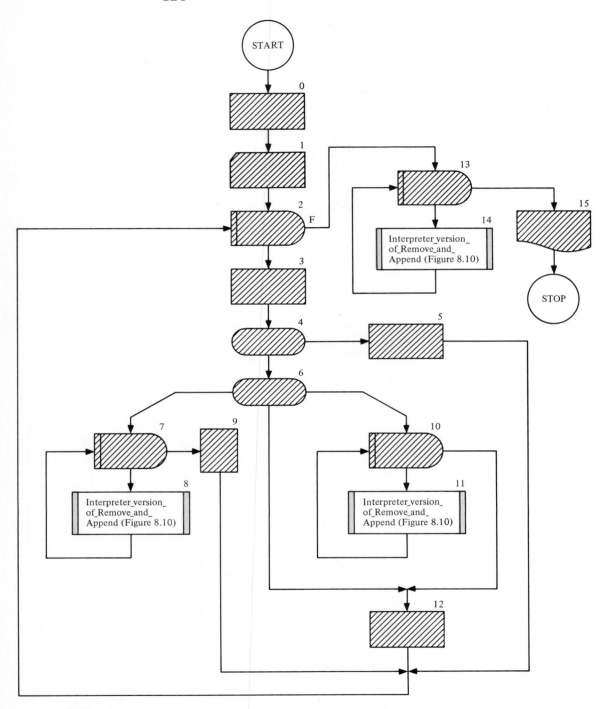

FIGURE 8·11
Interpreter algorithm.

CHAR Being Scanned	ST	POST	Calculation Performed	TEMP Stack
A		A		
←	←	A		
B	←	AB		
×	← ×	AB		
C	← ×	ABC		
—	← ×	ABC	$B \times C = 4 \times 2 = 8$	8
	←	A*		
	← —	A*		
D	← —	A*D		
/	← — /	A*D		
E	← — /	A*DE		
No more characters	← — /	A*DE	$D/E = 6/3 = 2$	8,2
	← —	A**		8,2
	← —	A**	$8 - 2 = 6$	8,2
	←	A*		6
	←	A*	$A \leftarrow 6$	6
Final state			$A \leftarrow 6$	

FIGURE 8·12
Repetition of the trace of Figure 8·9 with TEMP feature included. Here we INTERPRET the assignment statement
$A \leftarrow B \times C - D/E$ where $B = 4, C = 2, D = 6, E = 3$

Compiler

Converting the INFIX-to-POSTFIX algorithm to a *compiler* algorithm is virtually the same task as converting it to an interpreter. The only difference is that, instead of actually executing the operations, we generate the machine language (for us, SAMOS) instructions to accomplish this execution.

This requires a modification of boxes 811 and 814 of Figure 8·10. Modifications relating to the handling of temporaries are also necessary. In the *interpreter* algorithm we actually made the calculations and placed the calculated values on the top of the stack of temporaries. In the *compiler* algorithm we will instead generate instructions for making these calculations and for placing the calculated values on top of the stack of temporaries. To do this will require a variable, j, the index of the next temporary to be used. (The variable, j, must be initialized to 1 in box 0 of the flowchart of Figure 8·8.) Figure 8·13 shows the details of the Remove_and_Append step for use in compiling. Figure 8·14 is a silhouette of the compiler algorithm showing only the required changes in boxes 0, 8, 11, and 14.

Two remarks are needed to explain some of the details of Figure 8·13. We must realize that the compiler represented by Figure 8·14 is not complete. For example, it does not treat the allocation of storage addresses (cells) for the variables. For this reason *symbolic* SAMOS instead of actual SAMOS is compiled. The difference is this: in actual SAMOS a statement to add the value of B to the accumulator would have a form such as

    +ADD□□□1004

where 1004 is the address associated with the variable, B. But, when the compiler executes (i.e., at "compile time"), it does not have available the addresses of the variables, so it can generate only the "symbolic SAMOS" statement

    +ADD□□□B

When the addresses of the variables finally become known, this statement can be modified, replacing "B" by the address associated with B. Also, in symbolic SAMOS, statements involving temporaries will look like

    +STO□□□2

This statement is an instruction to assign the value of the accumulator to the *second* temporary (because the second temporary is currently the *top* temporary).

The compiler algorithm of Figure 8·14 differs from the interpreter of Figure 8·11 only in those flowchart boxes in which calculations are performed and in which values are appended or removed from TEMP. A trace of the compiler algorithm is shown in Figure 8·15. In this trace we use the same assignment statement

$$A \leftarrow B \times C - D/E$$

used in the trace (Figure 8·11) of the interpreter algorithm. It will be highly instructive to compare these traces.

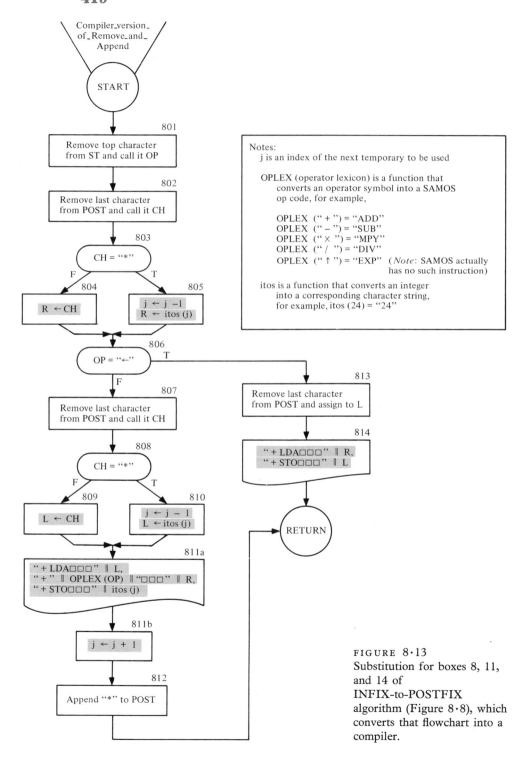

Notes:
  j is an index of the next temporary to be used

  OPLEX (operator lexicon) is a function that
    converts an operator symbol into a SAMOS
    op code, for example,

  OPLEX (" + ") = "ADD"
  OPLEX (" − ") = "SUB"
  OPLEX (" × ") = "MPY"
  OPLEX (" / ") = "DIV"
  OPLEX (" ↑ ") = "EXP"   (*Note*: SAMOS actually
                                has no such instruction)

  itos is a function that converts an integer
    into a corresponding character string,
    for example, itos (24) = "24"

FIGURE 8·13
Substitution for boxes 8, 11,
and 14 of
INFIX-to-POSTFIX
algorithm (Figure 8·8), which
converts that flowchart into a
compiler.

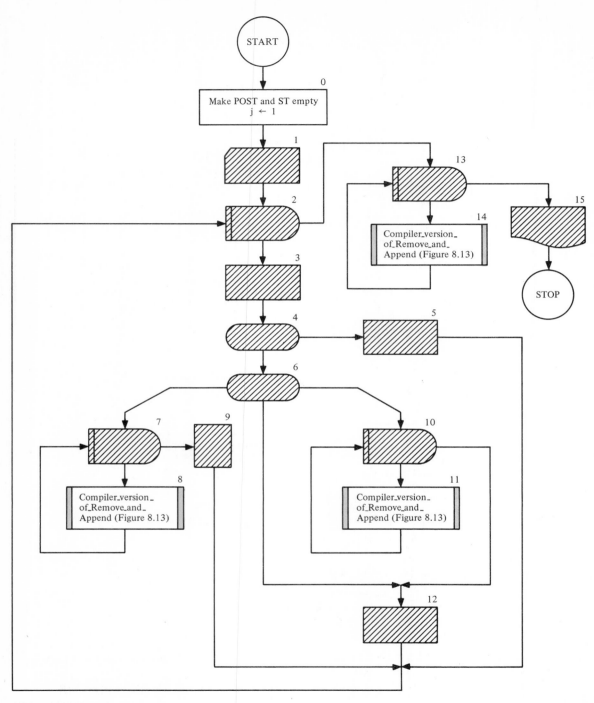

FIGURE 8·14
Compiler algorithm.

CHAR Being Scanned	Flowchart Box of Figure 8·14	ST	POST	Value of j	Symbolic SAMOS Statements Output
	0			1	
A	5		A	1	
←	12	←	A		
B	5	←	AB		
×	12	← ×	AB		
C	5	← ×	ABC		
−	11	← ×	ABC		+LDA□□□B
		←	A		+MPY□□□C
					+STO□□□1
		←	A*	2	
	12	← −	A*		
D	5	← −	A*D		
/	12	← − /	A*D		
E	5	← − /	A*DE		
No more characters	14	← − /	A*DE		+LDA□□□D
		← −	A*		+DIV□□□E
					+STO□□□2
			A**	3	
	14	← ─	A**	2	+LDA□□□1
		←	A	1	+SUB□□□2
					+STO□□□1
			A*	2	
	14	←	A*	1	+LDA□□□1
					+STO□□□A
Final state				1	

FIGURE 8·15
Trace of the compiler algorithm (Figure 8·14). The assignment statement A ← B × C − D / E is compiled into symbolic SAMOS.

1. Trace the interpreter algorithm given in Figure 8·11 for the statement

$$D \leftarrow (B + (B\uparrow2 - 4 \times A \times C)\uparrow.5)/(2 \times A)$$

where the values of A, B, and C are 1, − 2, and − 15, respectively. Use the variables T, F, H to stand for the constants 2, 4, and .5, respectively. Tracing should be done with a table structure similar to the one in Figure 8·12. Check your final value of D by a hand calculation.

2. Trace the compiler algorithm given in Figure 8·14 for the statement

$$D \leftarrow (B + (B\uparrow2 - 4 \times A \times C)\uparrow.5)/(2 \times A)$$

First replace the constants 2, 4, and .5 by T, F, and H, respectively. Tracing should be done with a table structure similar to the one in Figure 8·15.

3. In the symbolic SAMOS program produced in the trace of Figure 8·15, there is a pair of consecutive statements that are superfluous (i.e., eliminating both statements would leave the SAMOS program effectively the same).

    (a) Identify these superfluous statements.
    (b) Discuss the modifications of the flowchart of Figure 8·14 that would be necessary in order to eliminate such superfluous statements.

4. Map the interpreter flowchart of Figure 8·10 to a lower level of detail using such mappings as described in the table on pages 409–410. (I.e., replace word statements by statements in our (more) formal flowchart language.)

5. Repeat Problem 4 for the compiler flowchart of Figure 8·14.

Chapter

Procedures and functions

In this chapter we will greatly expand the capabilities and usefulness of procedures. Before doing so we should reconfirm our initial understanding of the procedure concept that was developed in Chapter 5. Our frame of reference is again the SIMPLOS model. Recall from Chapter 1 that each time an algorithm is executed, the first step is to create a data storage environment consisting of a set of storage boxes, one for each variable present in the flowchart.

The Master Computer establishes this environment with the help of the Sticker Affixer. When execution is complete, the collection of storage boxes is no longer needed, and the Affixer is ordered to disestablish the environment. He does this by returning all storage box resources to the warehouse for recycling, so they are available for reuse when another algorithm is to be executed. The meanings of (START) and (STOP) are simply: *establish* and *disestablish the requisite environment*.

Translated into terms of an actual computer, execution of a program cannot begin until a set of storage cells has been allocated, that is, made addressable, accessible, and related one to one, to the variables of the program. The close-out operation of halting a computation on an actual computer that operates to serve many users, involves a deallocation of the program's data storage resources. There is clearly a close analogy between SIMPLOS and an actual computer system.

When an algorithm consists of a main flowchart and one or more procedures that call one another, we should pay special attention to the matter of data storage environments and how they may be altered as the scene of action in the computation shifts from one flowchart to another. Although we have not treated this matter in the past, we will do so now. In fact, much of what we will do in this chapter to expand our understanding of the application and power of procedures will be a direct result of focusing carefully on data storage environments. In particular we will be concerned with how these environments are created and/or shared among the several subflowcharts of an algorithm, and how they may be made inaccessible upon close out of certain parts of the computation.

Why is it that we have been able so far to build extensive flowchart structures including numerous subflowcharts without having to worry about environments? The reason is simple. Each subflowchart was initially viewed as a set of detailed steps of the main flowchart. As such, it was reasonable to assume that *all* variables of the computation, wherever they appeared, referred to and determined one data storage environment. Execution of (START) therefore meant establishing properly stickered boxes, not only for the variables that appeared in the main flowchart, but also for any other variables that were mentioned only in the subflowcharts. Likewise, (STOP) meant recycling *all* stickered boxes of the algorithm, not just the ones for the variables that appeared in the main flowchart. This may have implied a little more work for the Master Computer and the Affixer at the start and stop points, but that hardly matters.

The benefit of viewing the situation in this way is the peace of mind of knowing that for each computation, no matter how large or complex, no matter how many procedure flowcharts, no matter at how many levels of detail, there will be one and only one set of distinctly stickered boxes made immediately accessible to the Reader and Assigner from the start to the stop of the program. But wait a minute! Is this really the very best arrangement? Possibly it is for some programs we write, but can there be a fly or two as yet undiscovered in this ointment?

These flies will be seen and heard from shortly, but for now, we will continue with the assumption that variables appearing in procedures belong to the same set as those that appear in the main flowchart. Moreover, we will refer to this *arrangement* (the only one that we have really considered so far) as the case where all variables are *global,* meaning that there is one and only one environment and the storage boxes within it are accessible from all parts of the algorithm. Since this is the case, it behooves us to be a bit more careful in documenting our flowcharts. From now on, each main flowchart should be accompanied by a legend that lists and describes *all* the global variables of the algorithm—including those that may not actually appear in the main flowchart itself. (In any actual computer program, this legend is always supplied, explicitly or implicitly, usually in the form of *declarations.*)

Soon we will feel the need to revise our all-variables-are-global arrangement and, when we do, it will not only be desirable to have a legend for the main flowchart, but it will also be important to have legends for each of the procedures.

To recapitulate, all the variables we have considered thus far in this book have the characteristic of *globality*. They are accessible when referred to from any part of an algorithm. Perhaps you have already guessed that under other arrangements, soon to be discussed, we may want certain variables to have the contrasting characteristic of *locality,* that is, accessible only when referred to from certain limited parts of an algorithm. We invite the reader to pursue this subject further, beginning with the next section.

9·1 Parameters and arguments, local and global variables

The following illustration shows the limitations of the procedures we have used so far.

Example Members of teams B and C are to be paired in alphabetical order for a bowling match. A preliminary flowchart to print a list of pairings is seen in Figure 9·1.

Two things are worth noting about the legend that accompanies this main flowchart. (1) It is not necessarily complete. Although all variables appearing in the flowchart are listed, there may be other variables that appear in the sorting procedure that do not appear in Main. If this proves to be the case, we will have to add these to the legend. (2) We have changed a heading in the legend. Beginning with this one, we replace "variable" with a more general heading, "identifier." Later it will be desirable to list other types of "flowchart entities" besides variables in this column of the legend.

We have already developed a sorting procedure that we would like to use in this example (Figure 9·2). You will recognize it as one adapted from Figure 5·8. Notice that this flow-

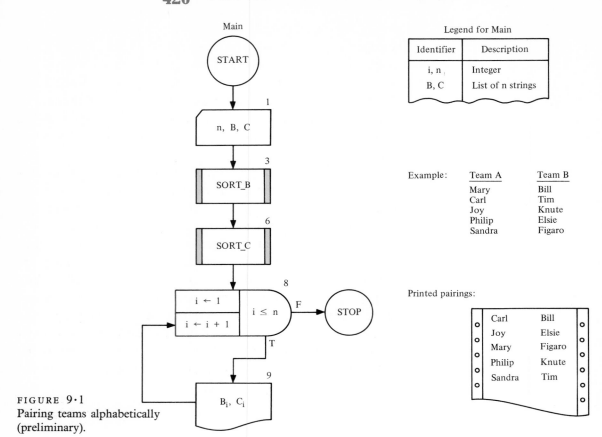

FIGURE 9·1
Pairing teams alphabetically
(preliminary).

chart sorts a list called A and to use it as a procedure in our pairing algorithm, both lists to be sorted will have to be designated as A. This necessitates the modification of Main shown in Figure 9·3. (Note that the new legend is complete.) With the pre- and postassignments of lists seen in boxes 2, 4, 5, and 7 we can force the SORT procedure to sort the lists B and C.

Now let us review the meaning of the calls on SORT in boxes 3 and 6. Thinking back to Chapter 5, there are two possible interpretations. These boxes can be regarded as shorthand for the SORT flowchart, that is, the SORT flowchart could have appeared in place of flowchart box 3 and again in place of flowchart box 6. In this text-substitution interpretation, the use of the procedure merely saves us the effort of writing out over and over again the details of this flowchart block. In the second interpretation we regard flowchart boxes 3 and 6 as *execute* or *call* boxes. Thus box 3 calls for the execution of the SORT procedure, which is a separate but subordinate

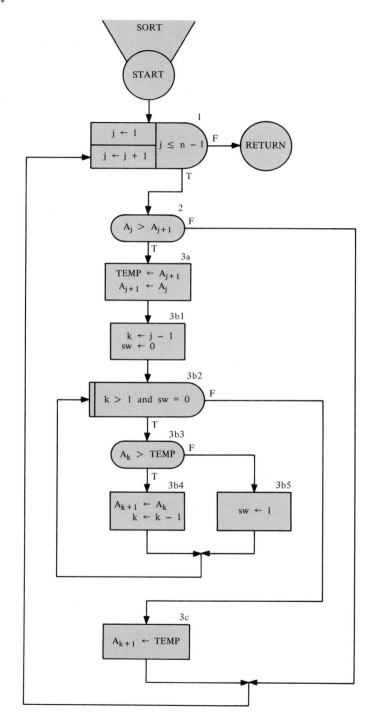

FIGURE 9·2
Bubble sort.

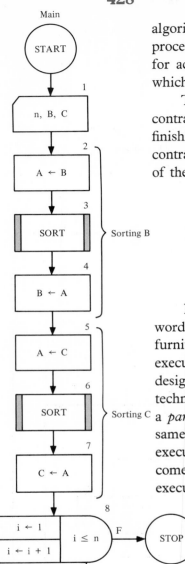

Main

FIGURE 9·3
Final pairing algorithm.

algorithm. Likewise, box 6 calls for the execution of the same procedure. Here we view the main flowchart as the program for action of a contractor who prepares to do a job, part of which he plans to farm out to subcontractors (i.e., procedures).

To pursue this analogy, let us suppose that a decorator contracts to redecorate a house and farms out the job of refinishing the dining room table and a study desk to a subcontractor—a furniture refinishing firm. We represent the plans of the contractors by flowcharts in Figure 9·4.

Legend for Main

Identifier	Description
i, n, j, k	Integer
A, B, C	List of n strings
TEMP	String

Looking at the subcontractor's flowchart, we see that the word FURNITURE does not refer to any particular piece of furniture. When the subcontractor is given a job (as in the execution of *call* boxes 3 and 4), the word FURNITURE designates the particular item he is given to work on. In the technical terminology the word FURNITURE is regarded as a *parameter*. It is not a variable in the strictest sense. In the same way D.R.TABLE and DESK are called *arguments*. When execution of the procedure is called for, the parameter becomes a name for the argument mentioned in the call for execution.

This new point of view can be used to modify the treatment of the bowling team pairing algorithm, as we see in the flowcharts of Figure 9·5. The flowchart in Figure 9·5b is exactly the same as that in Figure 9·2 except for the *parameter list* in the hopper, and the legend for the procedure. Corresponding to the parameter list there is an "argument list" in each procedure call (boxes 2 and 3) of the main flowchart.

The legend for the procedure is now a necessary part of the documentation because the identifiers of SORT are no longer global variables. Instead, n and A are parameters and

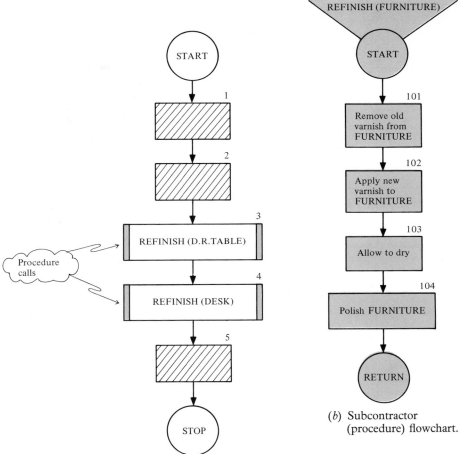

FIGURE 9·4
Contractor and subcontractor.

(*a*) Decorator flowchart.

(*b*) Subcontractor (procedure) flowchart.

j, k, sw, and TEMP are *local* variables. These characteristics are spelled out in a column headed Treatment. The fact that j, k, sw, and TEMP are locals and hence are accessible only while SORT is being executed is a matter of great significance. We will come back to this point soon.

When the execution of SORT is called for in box 2 of Main, the parameter list and argument list are matched up one to one

$$(n, A) \qquad \text{parameter list}$$
$$(m, B) \qquad \text{argument list}$$

and the SORT procedure is executed with m playing the role of n and B playing the role of A.

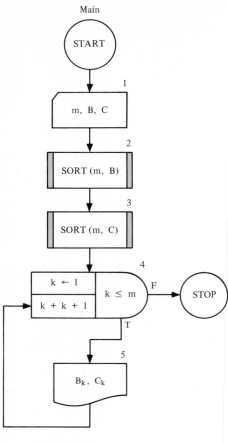

Legend for Main

Identifier	Description
k, m	Integer
B, C	List of m strings

(a)

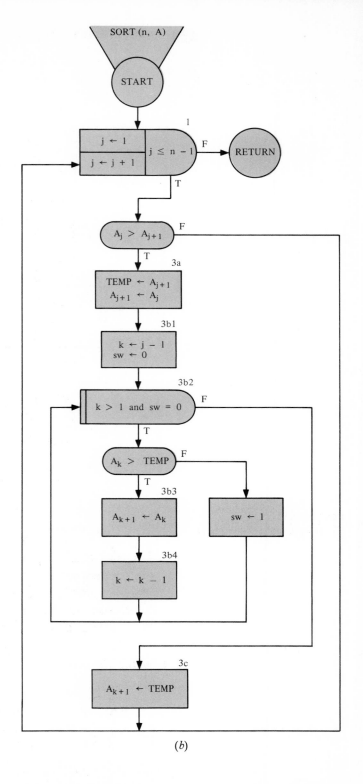

Legend for SORT

Identifier	Treatment	Description
n	Parameter	Integer
A	Parameter	List
j, k, sw	Local	Integer
TEMP	Local	String

(b)

FIGURE 9·5
Introducing parameters and arguments.

Remember now that one way to interpret the call box is as a "text" substitution step. That is, the detail or *body* of the procedure flowchart is substituted for the call box, and this body is executed. If the call box contains a list of arguments, editing of the text (of the procedure) is required before execution. The editing could be done by starting with a fresh copy of the procedure flowchart and replacing every occurrence of a parameter by the matching argument.

Alternatively, execution of a procedure with parameters may be viewed as executing the procedure flowchart but temporarily using n as the name for m's storage box and temporarily using A as the name for B's storage box. This second view resembles more closely the actual computer operation and is the view we will emphasize here.

Let's take a detailed look at how execution of a procedure might be accomplished in the SIMPLOS model. When the Master Computer comes to box 2 of the main program

he writes down the argument list

on a piece of paper, walks across the room to the desk of *another Master Computer,* the SORT Master Computer. The Master Computer for the main flowchart hands the argument list and a baton (signifying control) to his colleague and then goes out for a short coffee break (Figure 9·6).

The SORT Master Computer lines up the argument list with the parameter list from his SORT flowchart.

(n, A)   parameter list from SORT
(m, B)   argument list from Main

Now the SORT Master Computer reaches up on the shelf, takes down a packet of SORT stickers and asks the Affixer to put

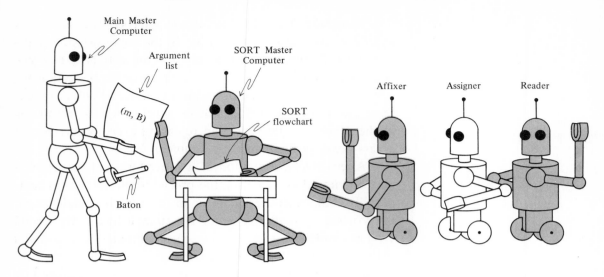

FIGURE 9·6
Control passing to the SORT
Master Computer.

n and A stickers on the window boxes of the main flowchart
variables m and B (respectively).

When the Affixer returns from this job, the SORT Master
Computer looks again at the SORT legend and finds that he
needs local variables j, k, sw, and TEMP. He therefore directs
the Affixer to get four *un*labeled boxes from the storeroom and
place the appropriate SORT stickers on them. The resulting
configuration of storage is shown in Figure 9·7.

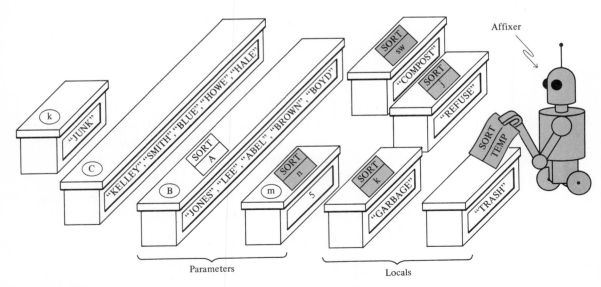

FIGURE 9·7
Storage configuration for first
execution of SORT.

Now the SORT procedure is executed. During the execution the Assigner and Reader are instructed to use only storage boxes with SORT stickers on them. For example, references to k in the procedure apply only to the storage box with the sticker. The procedure will neither use nor alter the value in the box labeled Ⓚ used for Main.

When the RETURN instruction is reached, the Affixer removes the SORT stickers and hands them as a packet back to the SORT Master Computer, who returns them to the shelf. The baton is now passed back to the main program Master Computer.

We see then that calling on SORT causes an addition to and rearrangement of the accessible data storage environment. Figure 9·8 summarizes this change schematically. Figure 9·8*a* depicts the environment accessible to Main's Master Computer before and after execution of SORT, and Figure 9·8*b* shows the environment after it has been augmented and restructured for use by the SORT Master Computer.

The variable C of the main program is a global variable,

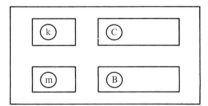

(*a*) Environment of the Master Computer for Main.

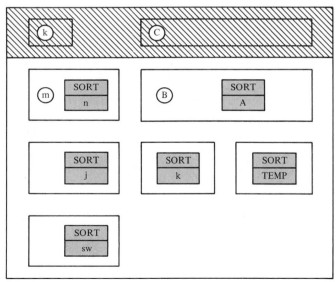

(*b*) Environment of the Master Computer for SORT while executing the first call (box 2). Cells shaded over are inaccessible.

FIGURE 9·8
Schematic summary of changes to the accessible environment before and after the first call on SORT.

so strictly speaking, it should be accessible to the Master Computer of SORT. However, since C is not referred to at all in SORT, and is not listed in the legend for SORT, we show C as inaccessible to the SORT Master Computer.

What would have been the situation, had the SORT variables j, k, sw, and TEMP been designated as *global* variables instead of local variables? That is, what is the situation if the flowchart legends are as follows?

Legend for Main

Identifier	Description
j, k, m, sw	Integer
B, C	List of m strings
TEMP	String

Legend for SORT

Identifier	Treatment	Description
n	Parameter	Integer
A	Parameter	List
j, k, sw	Global	Integer
TEMP	Global	String

In that event a reference within SORT to any of the variables j, k, sw, or TEMP would use the same storage box as was allocated at the start of Main. More specifically, Figure 9·9 summarizes the accessible environments before and after the first call on SORT.

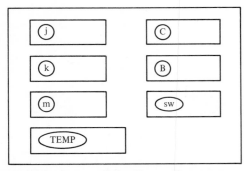

(*a*) Environment of the Master Computer for Main.

FIGURE 9·9
Schematic of the accessible environments assuming j, k, sw, and TEMP were listed in the legends as global variables.

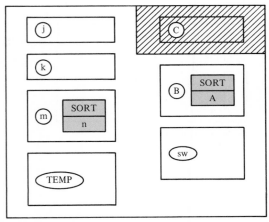

(*b*) Environment of the Master Computer for SORT.

Using local variables in preference to globals allows us truly to achieve the effect of "subcontracting" a part of our program. To see why this is so, let us think again about the analogy of the decorator and the refinisher. More detailed flowcharts of their activities might show that they both use a

BRUSH. If the BRUSH referred to in the refinisher's program is a local variable, then it refers to a BRUSH in the refinisher's shop so that the decorator can be confident that *his* paint BRUSH will not be all stuck up with varnish after the table has been refinished. If, however, BRUSH were a global variable, then the decorator and refinisher would be using the same BRUSH.

The analogy with computer programs is very close. Often we wish to use procedures written by some other programmer. A quick look at the funnel and legend of the procedure will make clear what the parameters are and how they are used. However, for each global variable listed in the legend, one must examine both the body of the procedure and the main program very carefully to see whether execution of the procedure can cause any change in the value of this global variable, which can have an undesired effect when execution resumes in the main program and the value of this global variable is used. If, on the other hand, all the procedure variables are either parameters or locals, then the main programmer can remain indifferent to what names are used for the procedure locals because changes in the values of local variables can have no effect on main program variables of the same name. Thus using locals in preference to globals has the effect of setting up a separate "environment" for variables used in the execution of the procedure, rather like the furniture refinisher's shop. In this case the only communication between the main program and the procedure is through the identifiers in the argument and parameter lists.

In some programming languages, for instance, some versions of BASIC, we have to get by entirely on global variables because in these languages parameters and local variables are not available for procedures. Fortunately, restriction to global variables is acceptable when procedures are used only to cut the program up into bite-size chunks. It may also be acceptable when we write the main program and the procedure at the same time, since we can then naturally be careful not to mix up our own variables. However, when one plans to store away a procedure for future use (by himself or others) and when the procedure is to be called by various main programs, then one must be especially careful in the selection of variables.

A safe approach to use in a language such as BASIC is

to choose different variables in the main program and in the procedure unless the variable serves the same purpose in both environments. We have already seen how to achieve the effect of parameters by the use of pre- and postassignments.

A few words of caution may help to avoid a programming catastrophe arising out of confusion as to which of several storage boxes a variable has reference to.

1. If we are careful to use only parameters and locals, there can be no confusion as to which storage boxes they refer to, since the Master Computer in any program (main or procedure) insures that the Assigner and Reader will always refer to storage boxes in his immediate environs, that is, to boxes with his own characteristic stickers on them.

2. If only globals are used, then again, no confusion can arise as to which storage boxes our variables have reference to. There is only one environment—only one kind of sticker.

3. If, however, a procedure executes with globals as well as locals or parameters, then there is some opportunity for confusion although not in our flowchart language with the SIMPLOS machine. Here the rules for finding the right global variable are very simple:

> A variable of the currently executing procedure that is not local or a parameter has total globality. Thus no matter how many procedures may list that variable as global, there will be only one storage box in the total environment of the computation that has a sticker with that global's name on it. Hence, the Reader and Assigner will have no trouble finding it.

However, in many programming languages, the globality of a variable need not be total. To see what this implies, picture the following variant of our SIMPLOS model. In quest of a global variable, the Reader and Assigner must move out of the immediate environment to find the storage boxes for the global variables. To which environment do they go to find the globals, to the main program's environment or to that of the procedure that called on the currently executing procedure? As we have implied, different programming languages (FORTRAN, ALGOL, and APL, e.g.) use different accessing (search) rules. For this reason mixing globals with parameters and locals will have meaning and be a sensible thing to do only within the framework of a particular programming language or machine whose fixed rules clearly spell out the way to find the correct storage boxes outside the immediate environment of the executing procedure. Such rules can be found in reference manuals for each language.

EXERCISES 9·1

1. Here is a procedure call and the funnel of the corresponding procedure.

Which is the parameter list and which is the argument list?

2. If no treatment is prescribed for an identifier listed in the legend of a procedure then the identifier S is a: local variable, global variable, parameter, "can't tell-something is wrong." Choose one.

3. The process of integer division consists of starting with two positive integers N and D (called the dividend and divisor respectively) and finding two other nonnegative integers Q and R (the quotient and remainder) so that

$$N = Q \times D + R \quad \text{and} \quad R \geq 0 \quad \text{and} \quad R < D$$

Taken together, the main flowchart and a tentative procedure flowchart on the next page input the dividend and divisor and calculate and output the quotient and remainder.

(a) Are the variables in INTDIV treated as parameters, locals, or globals?
(b) If the input values of N and D are 43 and 12, give the complete output.
(c) Modify the procedure INTDIV so as to eliminate the use of globals so that the procedure can be called by other main programs using other names for the dividend and divisor. This modification will consist of a parameter list and a legend.

4. If the main flowchart in Problem 3 is modified as shown on the lower left panel of the next page, but INTDIV is left in its original form, there will be a change in the output.

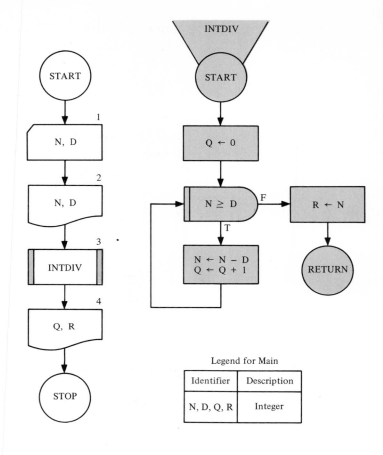

Legend for Main

Identifier	Description
N, D, Q, R	Integer

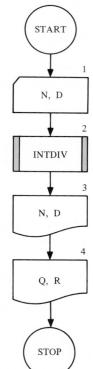

(a) Give the complete output when the input values of N and D are 43 and 12, as in Problem 3(b).

(b) Which statement, if any, in INTDIV is responsible for the change in the output?

(c) Suggest a modification to INTDIV that will correct this situation.

5. Construct a main flowchart and its legend for a computation that:
(a) Inputs a list B of p real elements.
(b) Locates the largest element in B.
(c) Interchanges that element with B_1.
(d) Displays the modified list.
In constructing Main, you are to minimize its complexity by employing the procedures MAX and INTERCHANGE, whose flowcharts and legends are given on the next page.

9·2
Protection and
call by value

When we call for the execution of one of those subcontracted procedures (i.e., with parameters and locals) we give the procedure Master Computer access to a number of main flowchart

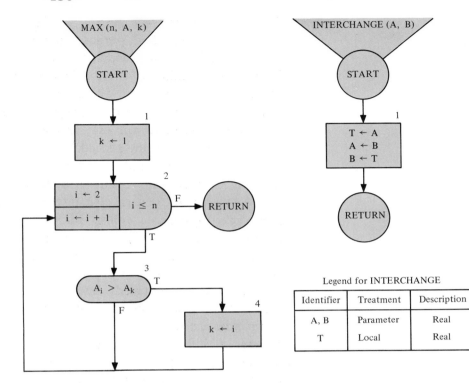

Legend for MAX

Identifier	Treatment	Description
n, k	Parameter	Integer
A	Parameter	List of reals
i	Local	Integer

Legend for INTERCHANGE

Identifier	Treatment	Description
A, B	Parameter	Real
T	Local	Real

variables (the arguments). We do this with one of two purposes in mind.

1. To allow the procedure Master Computer to gain access to the values of these variables for use in calculations.

2. To allow the procedure Master Computer to cause values to be assigned to these variables for use when execution resumes in the main flowchart environment.

We can appreciate the distinction between these two purposes very clearly in the procedure call

SORT (m, B)

from the flowchart of Figure 9·5a. Here the argument B is communicated with both purposes in mind. We expect the list B to be examined and modified. That is, it will be returned in an altered condition (sorted). On the other hand, when the procedure is executed, we expect the value of m, the length of the list B, to be returned unchanged. Thus m is communicated to the procedure with only purpose 1 in mind. We would be most distressed if the procedure were to change the value of m. Since we are familiar with what the SORT procedure does, we know that no such change in the value of m will occur.

And yet, in the general case, if we are using someone else's procedure, we cannot, without studying the flowchart of the procedure, know for sure which variables will have their values changed and which will not. It may happen that some variables, when turned over to the tender mercies of a procedure, return with their values "mangled" despite our intentions to the contrary. This disaster is usually caused by either carelessness or a misunderstanding of the effect of another programmer's procedure. In either event the situation can be remedied by "protecting," in one of several ways, the variables whose values are supposed to remain unchanged.

The Catastrophe

We next give an example in which the above-mentioned catastrophe occurs and then discuss ways to provide the "protection." But first we develop a mathematical formula needed for the flowcharting.

In this example the procedure is GCD, greatest common divisor. The main flowchart calls on GCD in the course of computing the least common multiple, LCM, of two given integers A and B. Use is made of the well-known equality that the least common multiple, LCM, of A and B is equal to the product of A and B divided by the greatest common divisor, GCD, of A and B, that is,

$$LCM(A,B) \equiv \frac{A \times B}{GCD(A,B)}$$

For example,

$$LCM(15,10) = \frac{15 \times 10}{GCD(15,10)} = \frac{15 \times 10}{5} = 30$$

A possible procedure for GCD is given in Figure 9·10c, and a main flowchart for calculating the LCM of two integers is given in Figure 9·10a. You will recognize that the flowchart in Figure 9·10c is simply a "procedurized" version of our most primitive GCD algorithm from Chapter 3.

In box 3 of Figure 9·10a we call for the execution of a procedure that calculates the value of the GCD of A and B; the variable D is included in the argument list as a *receptacle* to carry the value of the GCD back to the main flowchart environment.

If the flowcharts of Figure 9·10a and 9·10c were supplied to the Master Computer and the values 15 and 10 were input for A and B we would expect the value 30 to be output when flowchart box 4 is finally reached. But the actual output value would be 0. What went wrong?

The solution to this mystery is easily found upon further inspection of the flowcharts of Figure 9·10a and 9·10c. Although the user of the LCM flowchart expected that only the value of D would be changed by execution of GCD, this turned out not to be the case. We can see that the storage boxes of A and B were made accessible to the GCD personnel under the names of M and N. Inspection of the GCD flowchart shows that in boxes 104 and 106 assignments were made to M and N, which changed the values of the main program variables A and B. See Figure 9·11.

We see that the value of the GCD returned to the main flowchart in the D storage box is the correct one, 5; but, as a "side effect," the values of A and B were changed as well. Thus when the output value is calculated in box 4 we get

$$(5 \times 0)/5 = 0 \qquad \text{instead of} \qquad (15 \times 10)/5 = 30$$

This example demonstrates the need for "protecting" the main flowchart variables whose values we don't want changed by the procedure.

Protection may be supplied either in the main flowchart or in the procedure flowchart. The first type of protection is seen in Figure 9·10b where we modified the LCM flowchart by assigning the values of A and B to R and S and, in our argument list, replaced A and B by R and S. Now R and S (not A and B) will be altered by the execution of the procedure, but this doesn't matter to us as we won't use R and S again.

The alternative method of protection is seen in Figure

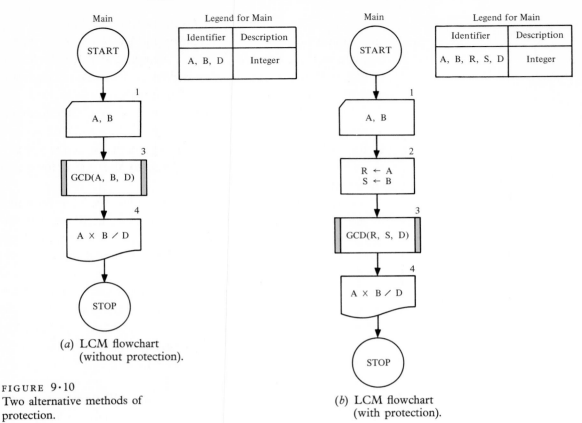

(a) LCM flowchart
(without protection).

FIGURE 9·10
Two alternative methods of
protection.

(b) LCM flowchart
(with protection).

9·10d. Here we modified the GCD procedure by replacing M
and N in the parameter list by P and Q. In box 101 we assigned
P and Q to *local* variables M and N (see the legend). The
parameters P and Q were never again referred to; the modification of the values of the local variables M and N will not

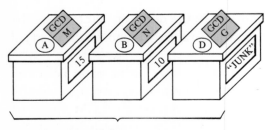

(a) Before the call for
execution of GCD.

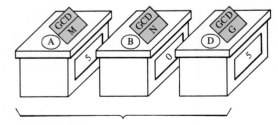

(b) After the call for execution
of GCD.

FIGURE 9·11
Change in the state of data
storage.

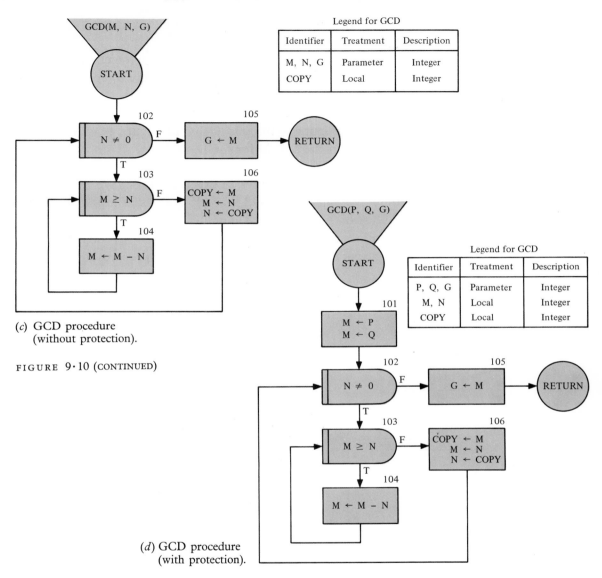

(c) GCD procedure
(without protection).

FIGURE 9·10 (CONTINUED)

(d) GCD procedure
(with protection).

alter the values of any main flowchart variables. Protection is guaranteed by the use of the protected version of either LCM or GCD (or, of course, both) from Figure 9·10.

Automatic Protection

The means of protection described above are not entirely satisfactory because we are forced to resort again to the awkward preassignments that were employed in Section 9·1. The treatment of parameters as discussed up to now is known as *call by reference*. SIMPLOS offers another way of treating parameters, *call-by-value,* and it leads to another method of protection.

With this treatment we can achieve protection using the flowcharts of Figure 9·10*a* and 9·10*c* merely by specifying that the parameters M and N are to be called "by value." To explain the meaning of call-by-value, we reproduce the flowcharts of Figure 9·10*a* and 9·10*c* in Figure 9·12 with only a change in the legend for GCD.

Let's see what happens when the Master Computer for the main flowchart comes to execute box 3. (We assume that the input values of A and B are 15 and 10, as in the preceding discussion.) The Master Computer for the main flowchart first examines the legend of the GCD procedure. Noting that some of the parameters are called-by-value, he prepares for the Mas-

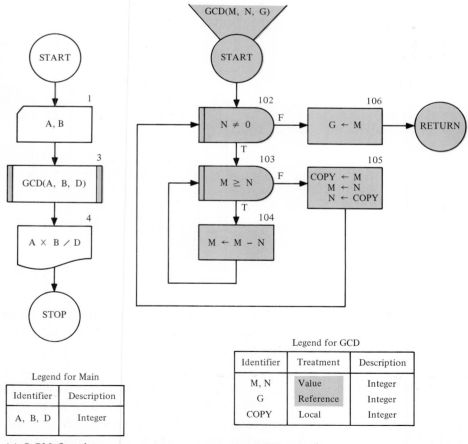

Legend for Main

Identifier	Description
A, B, D	Integer

Legend for GCD

Identifier	Treatment	Description
M, N	Value	Integer
G	Reference	Integer
COPY	Local	Integer

FIGURE 9·12
Call by value.

(*a*) LCM flowchart
(without protection).

(*b*) GCD procedure.

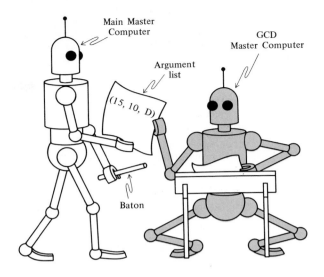

FIGURE 9·13

ter Computer of the GCD procedure a different argument list than before. For those parameters treated by value, the argument list contains not the variables but *copies of their values* (as seen in Figure 9·13).

The GCD Master Computer, in lining up the argument list with the parameter list

(M, N, G)   parameter list

(15, 10, D)   argument list

carries out the following activities.

1. Instructs the Affixer to create new variables M and N to be treated as locals.

2. Instructs the Assigner to assign the values 15 and 10 to M and N (respectively).

3. Treats the remaining variables by reference as described in the preceding section.

4. Instructs the Affixer to create a local variable COPY.

The resulting configuration of storage is shown in Figure 9·14. In this way we see that the procedure staff gets hold of the *values* of A and B but not their storage boxes. Hence the variables A and B are protected and no preassignments are necessary. By examining the legend of the procedure, the

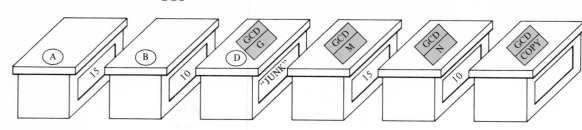

FIGURE 9·14
Resulting storage
configuration.

programmer can quickly check that his variables are protected
without studying the flowcharts.

Observe that since only the values of arguments are used
and not their storage boxes, it is quite permissible to have
expressions in the argument list for arguments that correspond
to call-by-value parameters. Thus

$$GCD (B^2 - 4 \times A^2, \ 27, \ D)$$

is a perfectly valid procedure call when the parameters M and
N in the procedure GCD(M, N, D) are called by value.

Two Pertinent Observations

1. It is somewhat unusual for all the parameters in a
procedure to be called by value, since no computed values
can be carried back to the main program.

2. In a legend for a procedure we will always indicate
whether parameters are called by value or by reference.

More on Protection

One might also wonder if it is valid to let an expression
argument match a call-by-reference parameter. Perhaps so, but
why bother? After all, the main purpose of a call-by-reference
parameter is to let a called procedure "communicate" with its
caller through a shared storage box that can serve as a receptacle for a value generated by the procedure. Since the argument
in this case is an expression *and not a variable*, the purpose
of the communication can only be to transmit a value from
the caller to the called procedure, and not the reverse.

It is still of interest to ask how the expression argument
is handled in this case and a surprise is in store for the reader
who chooses to read on. Here is how it is done in the SIM-
PLOS model. Consider a call on a procedure P(X, Y), where

X and Y are both reference parameters and the call has at least one expression argument, for example,

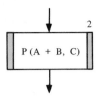

The first step taken by the Master Computer is to evaluate each expression in the argument list. In this case there is only one. Let us say the expression A + B has the value 7. The Master Computer then hands over to the Master Computer of the procedure P a revised argument list, (7,C). Then the matching of parameters to arguments gives

(7, C)　　revised argument list

(X, Y)　　parameter list for procedure P

Now, when the Master Computer for P sees that a value instead of a variable is matched to the reference parameter X, he asks the Affixer for a *stickerless* storage box. The sticker $\frac{P}{X}$ is then placed on this box and the value 7 is assigned to it.

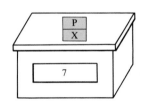

When the execution of P is about to terminate, there can be only the one sticker on the storage box. Therefore, during the return to P's caller, when all stickers of P are peeled off, the box that had the sticker $\frac{P}{X}$ will no longer have any sticker on it, so that box will be eligible for recycling. Certainly P's caller will not know how to make a reference to it. The box is effectively inaccessible.

In short, when an expression argument is matched to a reference parameter, the parameter behaves precisely like call-by-value! A special storage box is created and used as a local variable. Its "lifetime" is just the period during which the called procedure is executed. Therefore, there can be no way that the calling algorithm can be affected by a change in the value assigned to the matching parameter.

Argument expressions matched to reference parameters turns out to be just another way to achieve protection! (In many popular programming languages, such as FORTRAN, there is no such thing as a call-by-value parameter. All parameters are handled by reference. That is why the simple "trick" of using expression arguments is often resorted to in FORTRAN when protection is needed. For example, the call

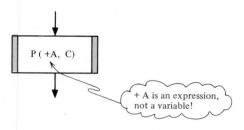

may be used to protect A from being assigned a new value by the procedure P.)

EXERCISES 9·2

1. Below we see one modification of the flowcharts and legends of Problem 3, Exercises 9·1.

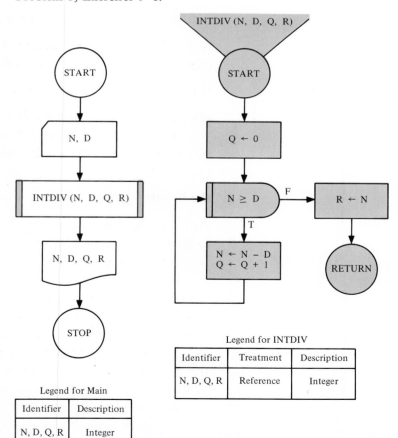

Legend for Main

Identifier	Description
N, D, Q, R	Integer

Legend for INTDIV

Identifier	Treatment	Description
N, D, Q, R	Reference	Integer

(a) Which variables (if any) in the argument list are apt to have been made available to the procedure for the purpose of (i) only transmitting their values *to* the procedure without any intention of having their values changed by the procedure? (ii) only receiving information *from* the procedure (i.e., the procedure makes no use of values that these variables may have had in the main program)? (iii) for both of the above purposes?

(b) According to your replies to part a, which variables should be protected?

(c) Show three methods of effecting this protection.
   (i) By a modification in the main flowchart.
   (ii) By a modification in the procedure flowchart and legend.
   (iii) By a modification in the procedure legend only.

(d) In the flowcharts above without protection, what actual error occurs? (See Problem 4, Exercises 9·1.) Explain.

2. Below we see a flowchart for a GCD (greatest common divisor) algorithm that makes use of the procedure INTDIV as a subprogram.

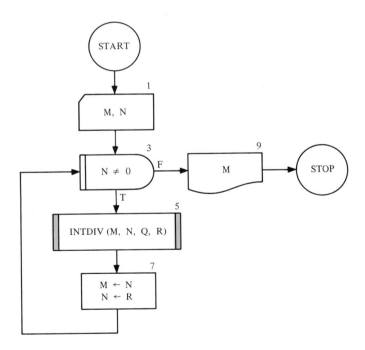

(a) The variable, Q, is not used in this algorithm. Why must it be included in the argument list?

(b) If we wanted to output the input values of M and N in box 9 as well as the value of the GCD we would be frustrated by the fact that the values of M and N have been "clobbered" by the assignments in box 7. Make a modification that will correct this situation.

3. The greatest common factor (GCF) of several numbers can be found by successive use of the GCD of two numbers. Thus

$$GCF(A, B, C) = GCD(GCD(A, B), C)$$

and

$$GCF(A, B, C, D) = GCD(GCF(A, B, C), D)$$
$$= GCD(GCD(GCD(A, B), C), D)$$

Accordingly, we can construct a flowchart for finding the GCF of the components of a list

$$A_1, A_2, \ldots, A_k$$

We present below such a flowchart that makes use of the GCD procedure of Figure 9·10*d*.

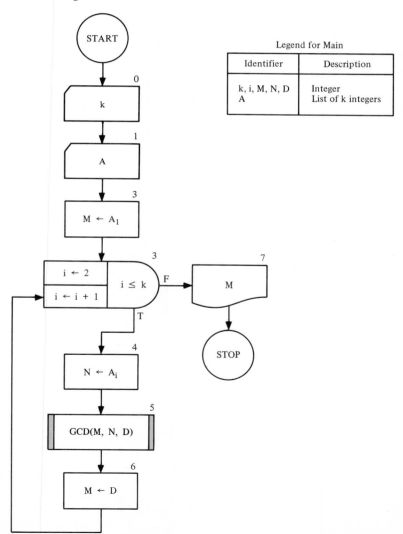

Legend for Main	
Identifier	Description
k, i, M, N, D	Integer
A	List of k integers

(a) Your task is to convert this flowchart into a procedure, GCF. Here the input and output will disappear and be replaced by items in the parameter list. The legend should include only reference parameters, value parameters, and locals, using value parameters only when they are necessary.

(b) In studying roots of a polynomial equation with integer coefficients of the form

$$a_n \times x^n + a_{n-1} \times x^{n-1} + \ldots + a_2 \times x^2 + a_1 \times x + a_0 = 0$$

it is convenient to simplify by dividing all the coefficients by their greatest common factor.

Accordingly, construct a flowchart that, when executed, inputs the coefficients, finds their greatest common factor using the procedure of part a, divides the coefficients by the GCF, and outputs the coefficients of the simplified equation.

4. Having studied the distinction between call-by-reference and call-by-value parameters, it should now be meaningful to revisit Problem 5, Exercises 9·1 to decide which type of parameters each of the two procedures MAX and INTERCHANGE should have.

(a) Can parameters A and B of INTERCHANGE be call-by-value? Justify your answer.

(b) What would be the disadvantage, if any, of letting the parameter k be call-by-value?

(c) Can parameter A of MAX be call-by-value? Justify your answer.

5. EQUILAT is a procedure that determines whether a triangle whose sides are A, B, and C is equilateral and, if so, prints "EQUILAT-ERAL". In any case, the procedure sets k to 0 or 1 to denote failure or success respectively.

(a) Construct a flowchart and legend for EQUILAT such that the procedure has no locals and no globals.

(b) Choose and justify call-by-value or call-by-reference treatment for each parameter.

(c) Illustrate the use of EQUILAT by showing a simple main flowchart that calls on EQUILAT, then tests to see whether success or failure resulted and, depending on the outcome, chooses between two different action paths. Be sure to provide a legend for the main flowchart.

6. ISOSC is a procedure that determines whether a triangle whose sides are A, B, C is isosceles (two and only two sides are equal). If so it prints "ISOSCELES". In any case ISOSC sets the global variable k to 0 or to 1 to denote failure or success, respectively.

(a) Construct a flowchart and legend for ISOSC, letting k be the only global variable.

(b) Illustrate the use of ISOSC by constructing a main flowchart and legend. Main should call ISOSC and then choose between two action paths, depending on the success/fail outcome "reported" by the procedure.

7. Construct and illustrate the use of a procedure called LARGE that displays the largest value found in the first n elements of the list called A. Use no globals. Show the legend for LARGE and justify the treatment that you select for the parameters.

8. Draw a flowchart and legend for a procedure named printisosc that, when called, will print the pattern of a right isosceles triangle whose dimension and display character are given as arguments (See Problem 3, Exercises 2·3, Set B).

9. Modify the procedure printisosc that you developed in Problem 8 so that, when called, it will print n complete triangles (space permitting) from left to right across the page having a width of 120 spaces. Each triangle should be separated horizontally by h characters, with values of n and h given as arguments. For example, for n = 3

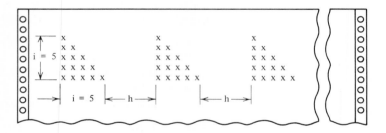

10. Draw a flowchart and legend for a procedure named printdiamond that, when invoked, will print a diamond whose dimensions and display character are given as arguments (See Problem 4, Exercises 2·3, Set B).

11. Modify the procedure printdiamond developed in Problem 10 so that a string of n diamonds are printed left to right across the page with h spaces between the edges of each diamond. For example, for n = 4, the diamonds would line up as

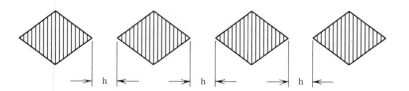

The values for n and h should be supplied as arguments for the modified procedure. The number of diamonds printed should either be n or the maximum number that can be printed across a page having 120 spaces, whichever is the smaller.

9·3
Functions

We have already used functions in our flowcharts in such situations as

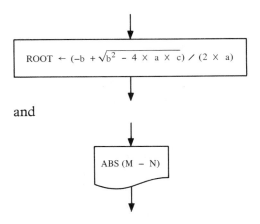

$$\text{ROOT} \leftarrow (-b + \sqrt{b^2 - 4 \times a \times c}) / (2 \times a)$$

and

$$\text{ABS}(M - N)$$

where we see the square root and the absolute value functions. Often such functions are called *library functions,* meaning that programs to evaluate them are stored as part of the computer software available to any user on demand. In this section we will see how to construct a flowchart for any function we choose.

In computer parlance a *function* is nothing more nor less than a slightly modified procedure. The distinguishing features of a function are enumerated below.

1. The call to execute a function comes not from encountering an execute box but from encountering the name of the function in any expression.

2. The computed value of a function (functional value) is not returned to the main program in a receptacle provided for the purpose (i.e., as the value of a variable.) Instead, the "bare" value is returned directly to the Master Computer of the calling algorithm for use in the course of his computations.

3. The execution of a function normally does not change the value of any main program variable (except for possible and usually unfortunate "side effects"). In a function reference we usually employ call-by-value parameters in order to avoid such effects.

Some of the actions we accomplished by use of procedures could have been carried out more simply by functions. We illustrate this by comparing the procedure version of the calcu-

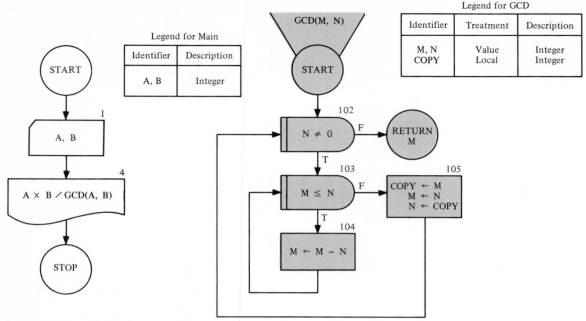

(a) Main (LCM) flowchart.   (b) GCD function.

FIGURE 9·15
Finding the LCM with the
GCD function.

lation of the LCM from the preceding section (Figure 9·12) with the same calculation using a function, as seen in Figure 9·15.

Suppose in Figure 9·15 the input values of A and B are 15 and 10, as before. After these values are put away in their appropriate storage locations (box 1), the main flowchart Master Computer begins to evaluate the expression in box 4. He multiplies A by B, obtaining 150, and then observes that he requires the *functional value* GCD(A, B). [Note all of the simplications that we have achieved as compared with the method of Figure 9·12. We do not require an execute box in order to call for the calculation of this functional value (i.e., no box 3). Furthermore, note that the "receiving" argument D is omitted from the argument list since, as we will soon see, there is no need of a receptacle to carry the functional value back to the main flowchart environment.] At this point the main program Master Computer transmits the values of his arguments to the Master Computer of GCD just as described in the previous section. (Note the absence of the call-by-reference parameter G in the GCD parameter list; it will not be needed.)

Now the GCD function goes into operation, all the calculations being the same as in the procedure of Figure 9·12 until we emerge from the F exit of box 102. At this point the variable M has as its value the GCD of A and B. But we see that this value is not assigned to a call-by-reference parameter. Instead, a slightly modified RETURN box is employed. It contains the variable M. When the GCD Master Computer comes to this flowchart box, he sends his Reader out to read the value of the variable M (which is 5). On receiving this value, the GCD Master Computer gets up from his desk and takes this value to the Master Computer of the main flowchart along with the baton. The main flowchart Master Computer now resumes his evaluation of the expression in box 4 using the value 5 just received as the value of GCD(A, B). Thus he obtains $150/5 = 30$, which is immediately output.

It should be clear that this computer interpretation of function is entirely equivalent to the mathematical concept of a function. However, the situation is different if the arguments are matched to call-by-reference parameters, as illustrated in Figure 9·16.

Here all parameters are called by reference and, from the discussion in the previous section, we know that in the body of the GCD procedure the values of A and B will have been changed from 15 and 10 to 5 and 0, respectively. This is a potentially dangerous "side effect"; a function that changes its arguments in the course of calculating functional values! (Alas, many programming languages offer the programmer only limited help against side effects. For example, the parameters of a function defined in FORTRAN must be called by reference. It is therefore incumbent on the FORTRAN programmer to

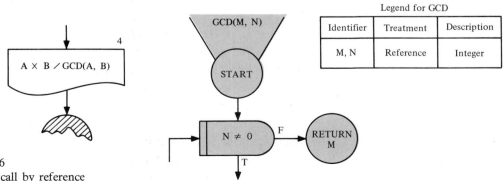

FIGURE 9·16
Switching to call by reference

guard against side effects by using protection mechanisms such as those described in the preceding section.)

To illustrate the delicate protection problems arising from use of call by reference, let us see what happens to the value output in box 4 in the calculation under discussion. When the value 5 is returned to the Master Computer for use as the value of GCD(A, B), it is true that the values of A and B are changed. However, this has no effect on our program, since the value of A × B has already been computed as 150 before the interruption. Thus the output value is 30, as with call by value. However, if box 4 had been written as shown in Figure 9·17, which is mathematically equivalent to box 4 in Figure 9·16, then the value of A × B is calculated *after* the function call. Accordingly, the expression is evaluated with the values A = 5 and B = 0, so that the output value is 0. It is hoped that this illustration will reinforce the message of the need for protecting the arguments by one means or another to properly achieve the effect of a mathematical function.

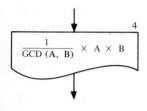

FIGURE 9·17

One slight disadvantage of functions compared with procedures is that the functional values are not permanently stored in our main flowchart environment for possible reuse later in the flowchart. This can, however, always be achieved by assigning the returned value to a variable of the main flowchart, such as

Approximating Functional Values

We have been operating on the assumption that our SIMPLOS computer (as most actual computers) is endowed with a "library" square root function. We tend to regard all such library functions as if they were *primitives* like addition and multiplication. We depend on the computer to give us the correct answer, but we usually have no need of knowing how it is done. (A primitive operation is one that is not itself defined in terms of any other operations.)

If the machine were not endowed with such library functions we would have to construct them ourselves. How would one go about doing this for the square root function? To this end we reproduce in Figure 9·18 the square root flowchart

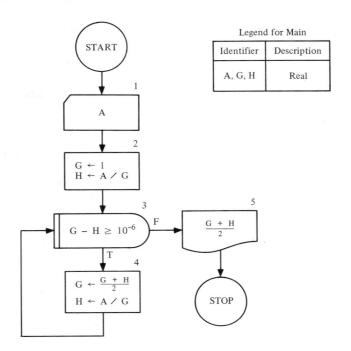

FIGURE 9·18
The square root algorithm
revisited.

from Chapter 3. Recall that this flowchart approximates the square root of A with accuracy $\varepsilon = 10^{-6}$.

The value to be returned is the value of the expression $(G + H)/2$. The "functionized" flowchart is seen in Figure 9·19. Of course, this function flowchart does not produce the

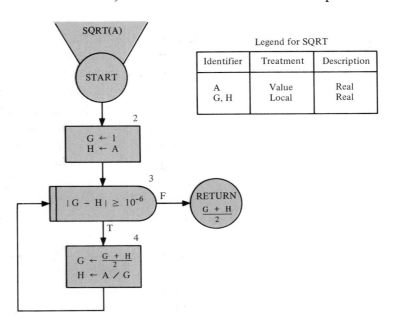

FIGURE 9·19
Square root function.

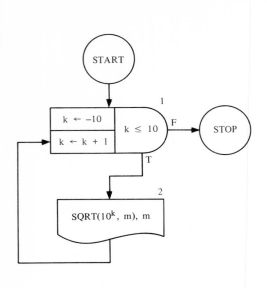

Legend for Main

Identifier	Description
k, m	Integer

(a) Selecting values to be tested.

Legend for SQRT

Identifier	Treatment	Description
A	Value	Real
n	Reference	Integer
G, H	Local	Real

(b) Modified SQRT function.

FIGURE 9·20
Test of efficiency of SQRT function.

exact values of the mathematical square root function but only a suitably accurate approximation.

Suppose that, as a test of the efficiency of our function, we want to count the number of times the loop of boxes 3 and 4 is executed for each value of A. This can be done by deliberately allowing our function to have a *useful* side effect. Such a test is illustrated in Figure 9·20, where our SQRT function has been modified to provide for this test capability.

Here we are testing the SQRT function with powers of 10 from 10^{-10} to 10^{10}. The functional value returned is the same as for the flowchart in Figure 9·19 but, in this case, the argument m receives as its value a count of the number of times that the loop inside SQRT was executed. This particular side effect was desirable, but the effect of such a function flowchart is different from that of a mathematical function that only produces a functional value. (Incidentally, the use of a fixed error estimate, 10^{-6}, over such a wide range of values of A is unrealistic.)

1. Draw a flowchart for the function f(x, y) where

$$f(x, y) = \frac{(x^3 + y)^2 + 5}{|x| + 2}$$

2. (a) Prepare a flowchart to evaluate the function

$$\text{RIGHT}(a, b, c) = \begin{cases} 1, \text{ if a, b, c are lengths of the sides of a right} \\ \quad \text{triangle} \\ 0, \text{ otherwise} \end{cases}$$

   (b) Prepare a main flowchart to print out all triples of integers (i, j, k) with $i \le j < k \le 100$ such that i, j, k are the sides of a right triangle. Use the function RIGHT in part a.

3. Construct a flowchart and legend for the function QUAD, defined as follows: given the values of x and y, the function QUAD (x, y) is to return the value 1, 2, 3, or 4 according to which quadrant of the plane the given point (x, y) lies in. In cases where x and/or y equals zero, QUAD (x, y) = 0.

4. The Cheerful Finance Company loans money at $1\frac{1}{2}\%$ per month compound interest. That is, each month $1\frac{1}{2}\%$ of the balance due is added to the balance.

   (a) Prepare a flowchart and legend for the function BAL(L, n) that returns the balance due at the end of n months on a loan of L dollars.
   (b) Prepare a main flowchart using BAL(L, n) to find the number of months when the balance first exceeds twice the amount of the loan when the principal is $100.

5. In general, any procedure whose net effect is to modify one variable in the environment of the main flowchart can be converted into a function. Here the procedure GCF from Problem 3, Exercises 9·2 is tentatively revised in Figure 9·21 as a function. (The value returned is the GCF of the components of the list A.) The function GCD called in box 5 is taken from Figure 9·15*b*.

   The main flowchart in Figure 9·21 (which calls on the GCF function in box 107) attempts to divide the components of B by the GCF of the components of the original list, B. (See Problem 3b, Exercises 9·2.) However, this flowchart is very bad on two counts. First, it is highly inefficient; second, it doesn't work.

   For example, if the input value of B is (18, 24, 30), then the GCF of the components is 6, so that dividing through by 6, the expected output is (3, 4, 5). However, the actual output would be (3, 8, 30).
   (a) Explain the discrepancy between the expected and actual outputs.

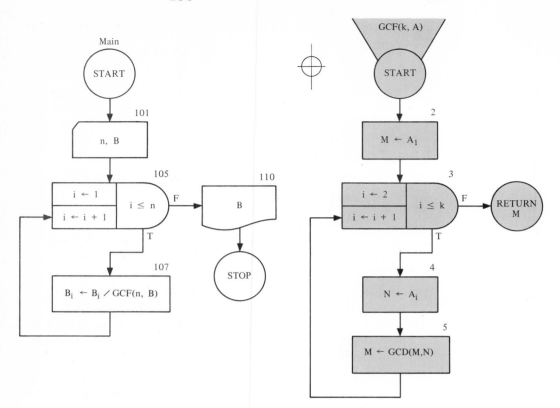

Legend for Main

Identifier	Description
i, n	Integer
B	List of n integers

Legend for GCF

Identifier	Treatment	Description
k	Value	Integer
A	Value	List
i, M, N	Local	Integer

FIGURE 9·21
The GCF procedure revised
as a function.

(b) Explain why the program would be very inefficient even if it were to work.

(c) Make a small modification in the main flowchart above that disposes of both objections.

6. In the preceding exercise you modified GCF, given in Figure 9·21. Use this new GCF to modify the output of Problem 2b so as to eliminate similar triangles. Thus, for example, (6, 8, 10) will not be output, since this triangle is similar to (3, 4, 5). In general any right triangle in which the sides have a GCF different from 1 is not to be output.

7. Construct a flowchart and legend for the function WHICH as follows. Given a list A of n real elements, WHICH returns a value, 0, 1, or 2 according to the following rule. Let S1 be the sum of the elements

in the first "half" of the list, and let S2 be the sum of the elements in the last half of the list. Then

$$\text{WHICH } (n,A) = \begin{cases} 0 & \text{if} \quad S1 < S2 \\ 1 & \text{if} \quad S1 = S2 \\ 2 & \text{if} \quad S1 > S2 \end{cases}$$

Use no globals.

8. Construct a flowchart and legend for the function RMS (root mean square). Given two real values, A and B,

$$\text{RMS } (A,B) = \sqrt{\frac{A^2 + B^2}{2}}$$

Use no globals and no locals.

9. Using no globals, construct a flowchart and legend for the function EXTREM. This function has three parameters, n, A, and CODE. Given a list A of n real elements, EXTREM returns values as follows.

$$\text{EXTREM } (n,A,CODE) = \begin{cases} \text{smallest value in the list A, if} \\ \text{CODE} = 0 \\ \text{largest value in the list A, if} \\ \text{CODE} = 1 \\ \text{value of CODE, if CODE} \neq 0 \\ \text{and CODE} \neq 1 \end{cases}$$

10. Construct a main flowchart and legend and select data sets that can be used to test the *correctness* of the function EXTREM that is defined in the preceding exercise. For each data set that you select explain what aspect of the "behavior" of EXTREM you expect to test. A function is considered to be *correct* if it does what it is supposed to do and never does what it is not supposed to do.

9.4
Chains of procedure and function calls

Procedures may call on procedures to form what amounts to *chains of procedure calls.* Rules for executing any procedure in such a chain, in particular the rules for accessing variables, are independent of the length of the chain. (Even the work involved in locating the referenced storage boxes need not increase with the length of the chain, so long as no globals are involved.) One may also observe that renaming the local variables or parameters within a procedure in a consistent way introduces no confusion for the Master Computer and his staff, even though such renaming may increase (or decrease) the difficulty for a human reader to trace the same chain of procedure calls. The example of this section is designed to illustrate the above observations with the aid of our SIMPLOS model.

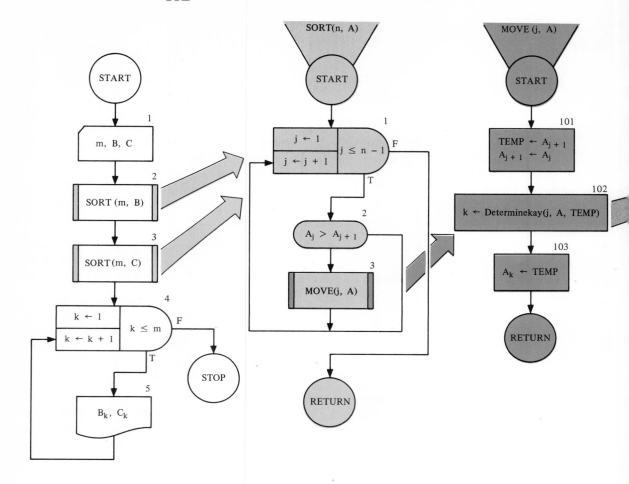

FIGURE 9·22
Bubble sort structure revised
to include parameters.

Legend for Main	
Identifier	Description
k, m	Integer
B, C	List of m strings

Legend for SORT		
Identifier	Treatment	Description
n	Value	Integer
A	Reference	List
j	Local	Integer

Legend for MOVE		
Identifier	Treatment	Description
j	Value	Integer
A	Reference	List
k	Local	Integer
TEMP	Local	String

Chains of procedure calls are not unfamiliar to us. The sorting procedure as originally shown in Figure 5·8 involved a chain of three calls: SORT → MOVE → Determinekay. Figure 9·22 reproduces that structure for SORT but now provides each procedure component in the chain with an appropriate set of parameters and clarifying legend.

As a refresher, recall that the procedure MOVE puts the

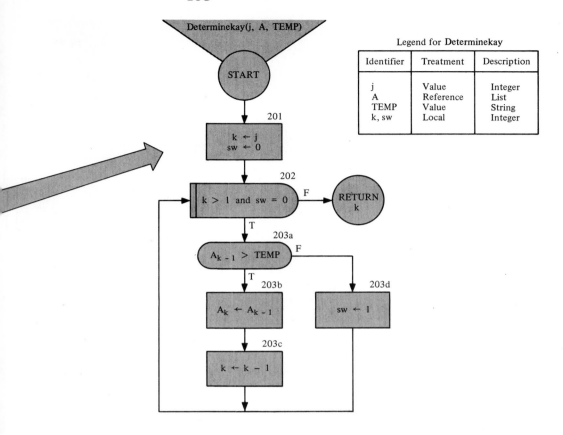

Legend for **Determinekay**

Identifier	Treatment	Description
j	Value	Integer
A	Reference	List
TEMP	Value	String
k, sw	Local	Integer

value of TEMP in the correct position in an already sorted list $(A_1, A_2, \ldots, A_{j-1}, A_j)$. The correct position is found by appealing to the procedure Determinekay, which in Figure $9 \cdot 22$ has been revised as a function that returns the value k, that is, the correct position.

Moving from legend to legend beginning with the one for SORT, we note the following.

1. The parameter n which is of interest only to SORT is called by value, since there is no need to give it a new value.

2. The parameter A is passed from SORT to MOVE to Determinekay, and at all levels must be called by reference, since new values may be assigned to elements of A by both MOVE and Determinekay.

3. MOVE and Determinekay both need to know the value of j as determined by SORT, but neither MOVE nor Deter-

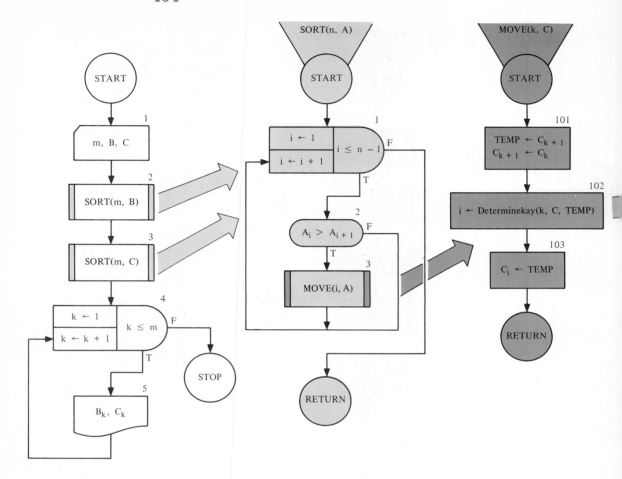

FIGURE 9·23
Same as Figure 9·22 except
for renaming of some
parameters and locals.

Legend for Main	
Identifier	Description
k, m	Integer
B, C	List of m strings

Legend for SORT		
Identifier	Treatment	Description
n	Value	Integer
A	Reference	List
i	Local	Integer

Legend for MOVE		
Identifier	Treatment	Description
k	Value	Integer
C	Reference	List
i	Local	Integer
TEMP	Local	String

minekay need to alter j, so it is treated as a call-by-value parameter in both instances.

4. Determinekay also needs TEMP as a value parameter. The value of TEMP is defined by MOVE and passed along by it to Determinekay.

One purpose in bringing up this complex example is to emphasize the degree of independence that can be achieved

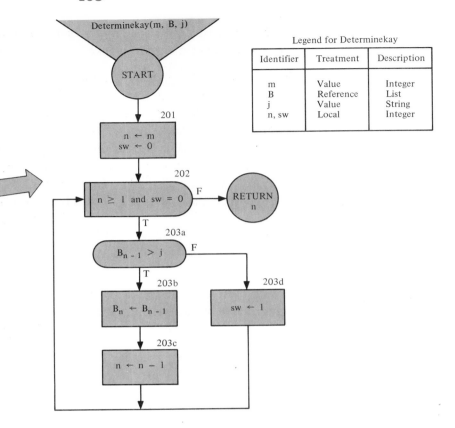

Legend for Determinekay

Identifier	Treatment	Description
m	Value	Integer
B	Reference	List
j	Value	String
n, sw	Local	Integer

once all globals have been removed. Names of parameters and locals of any component flowchart may now be changed consistently within that flowchart without affecting the interrelationship among all the flowcharts. Breaking up an algorithm in this way gives *modularity* to its construction. That is, any one module can, with relative ease, be replaced by a revised version of itself without adversely affecting the existing interrelationships among the component modules. To illustrate, Figure 9·23 shows the algorithm in Figure 9·22 with some parameters and local variables of SORT, MOVE, and Determinekay renamed.

The confusion of the variables in MOVE with those of the other flowcharts is now potentially about as bad as possible. In spite of these changes there is no problem in tracing the execution if the rules for affixing stickers to storage boxes and if the other working rules of the SIMPLOS model are adhered to, namely:

1. For a call-by-value parameter or for a *local* variable the Affixer must place the sticker on an unlabeled box.

2. For a *call-by-reference* parameter the Affixer must place the sticker on a previously labeled box bearing a sticker with either the name of the invoking procedure or the main flowchart shape. (For example, the reference parameter, C, of MOVE can only be matched to an argument in the environment of SORT, which has invoked MOVE. When, in particular, C is matched to the argument A, then the sticker for C can only be placed on a

box that already carries the sticker $\boxed{\begin{array}{c} \text{SORT} \\ \hline A \end{array}}$.)

With these ideas in mind we look (in Figure 9·24) at the configuration of storage when, for the flowchart in Figure 9·23, SORT has been invoked in box 2 of the main program and

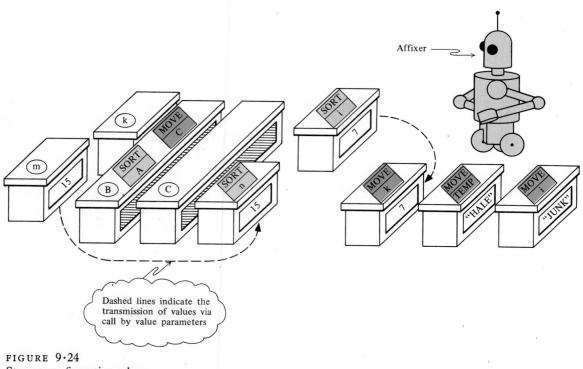

Dashed lines indicate the transmission of values via call by value parameters

FIGURE 9·24
Storage configuration when MOVE is called.

then MOVE has just begun executing after having in turn been invoked in box 3 of SORT.

MOVE goes into execution using only the storage boxes with the MOVE stickers, that is, its own parameters and locals. The fact that i, k, and C are used as variables for other purposes in the other environments is completely irrelevant and immaterial. Thus MOVE stickers cannot be placed on storage boxes created in a previously constructed environment unless these boxes have SORT stickers on them. That is, since SORT has no globals either, parameters of MOVE can match only locals or parameters of SORT. Of course, a parameter of SORT can itself match a variable of the main program, so a storage box can have more than two stickers pasted on it.

Moreover, during execution of SORT, the Reader has been instructed that he may not copy values from any box except one that is either a local in SORT or a parameter of SORT. To illustrate this point, suppose the variable m of the main flowchart is changed to i. Now both Main and SORT have a variable i.

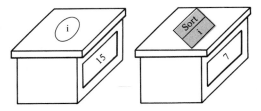

Even so, there can be no confusion as to which variable i has its value passed to MOVE when SORT calls MOVE in Figure 9·23.

The storage box with the oval sticker $\left(i\right)$ is invisible to SORT's Master Computer because that box does not also carry a SORT sticker, but SORT's Master Computer can of course see

the box with the sticker
SORT
i
and it is from this box that the

value of the argument is copied and passed to MOVE.

Structured Programming and Parameters

Any reader who has been studying this chapter will recognize that "procedures" are the "subtasks" that result from stepwise decomposition. Our discussion of the treatment of identifiers for procedures has a direct application to achieving nonoverlapping subtasks. We review this interesting possibility here.

As we have observed, each task must know what its subtasks accomplish but not how the subtasks carry out their work. From the point of view of the calling program, the result of a subtask will usually be the modification of the values of certain variables of the calling program. Such variables must correspond to call-by-reference parameters of the subtask. It may also be necessary to communicate to the subtask values of certain variables of the calling program, values, incidentally, that are not to be changed by the subtask. These transfers should be done by call-by-value parameters. *All other variables of the subtask should be locals.* Adopting these conventions will greatly clarify the nature of the communication between the various subtasks or procedures.

We redraw in Figure 9·25 the flowcharts of Figure 5·29 with full legends to illustrate this principle.

EXERCISES 9·4
SET A

1. For the schematic main program and procedures in Figure 9·26 draw a sketch showing the configuration of storage (labeling of storage boxes) when RUTH goes into operation. Use arrows to show passage of values of variables matched to call-by-value parameters.

2. In this problem you are asked to pursue further the example illustrated in Figure 9·24. Update the storage configuration that is diagrammed to show the situation just after Determinekay of Figure 9·23 begins executing after having been invoked by MOVE for the first time.

3. A set of flowcharts, incomplete legends, and values for one data set for a computation are given on page 471.

(a) Complete the legends with as much detail as you can.
(b) Assume that the flowcharts are executed using the given data set. Draw the storage configuration for the computation at the instant just after box 12 has been executed for the *third* time. The storage configuration should show all the labeled storage cells (storage boxes) and their values if they are defined. Storage cells may be depicted in two dimensions to make the diagram simpler. For example, the box on the left might be represented as

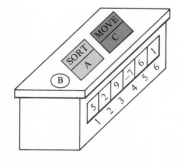

B, A(SORT), C(MOVE)	5	2	9	−7	6	1

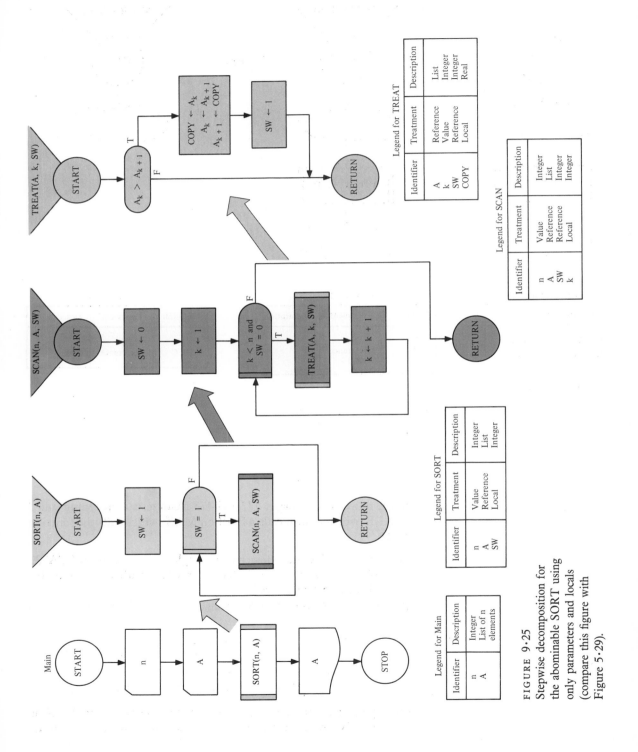

FIGURE 9·25
Stepwise decomposition for the abominable SORT using only parameters and locals (compare this figure with Figure 5·29).

Main

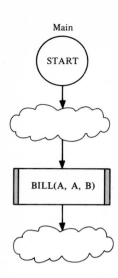

BILL(B, C, D)

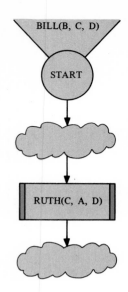

RUTH(D, B, C)

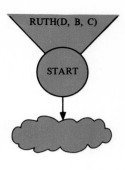

Legend for Main	
Identifier	Description
A, B	Integer

Legend for Bill		
Identifier	Treatment	Description
D B, C A	Value Reference Local	

Legend for Ruth		
Identifier	Treatment	Description
D B, C	Value Reference	

FIGURE 9·26

4. In the flowcharts on pages 472 and 473 Main tests a procedure called SCALE, which in turn calls a function MAX, which calls the function NEG.

   (a) After studying these flowcharts, complete the legends for SCALE, MAX, and NEG in a fashion consistent with the rest of the information that is provided.

   (b) Show the output produced using each of the following two data sets.

Data Set 1	Data Set 2
$k = 4$	$k = 5$
$p = -3$	$p = 2.2$
$A = (6., 3., 0.0, 12.)$	$A = (8.2, -7.5, 0.0, 12., 15.)$

   (c) Using data set 1, assume the Master Computer for MAX is currently executing box 3 for the first time. At this point, some

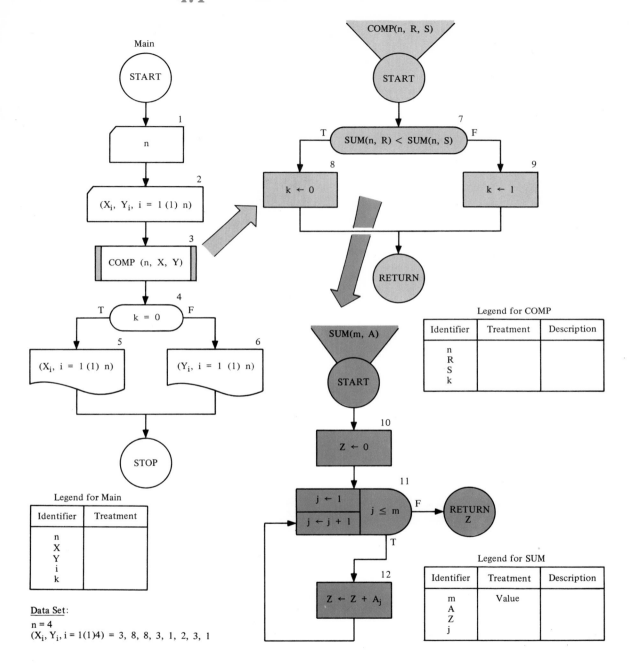

Main

START

1

n

2

$(X_i, Y_i, i = 1 (1) n)$

3

COMP (n, X, Y)

4

T   k = 0   F

5

$(X_i, i = 1 (1) n)$

6

$(Y_i, i = 1 (1) n)$

STOP

COMP(n, R, S)

START

7

T   SUM(n, R) < SUM(n, S)   F

8

k ← 0

9

k ← 1

RETURN

SUM(m, A)

START

10

Z ← 0

11

j ← 1
j ← j + 1   j ≤ m   F   RETURN Z

T

12

$Z ← Z + A_j$

Legend for COMP

Identifier	Treatment	Description
n		
R		
S		
k		

Legend for Main

Identifier	Treatment
n	
X	
Y	
i	
k	

Data Set:
n = 4
$(X_i, Y_i, i = 1(1)4)$ = 3, 8, 8, 3, 1, 2, 3, 1

Legend for SUM

Identifier	Treatment	Description
m	Value	
A		
Z		
j		

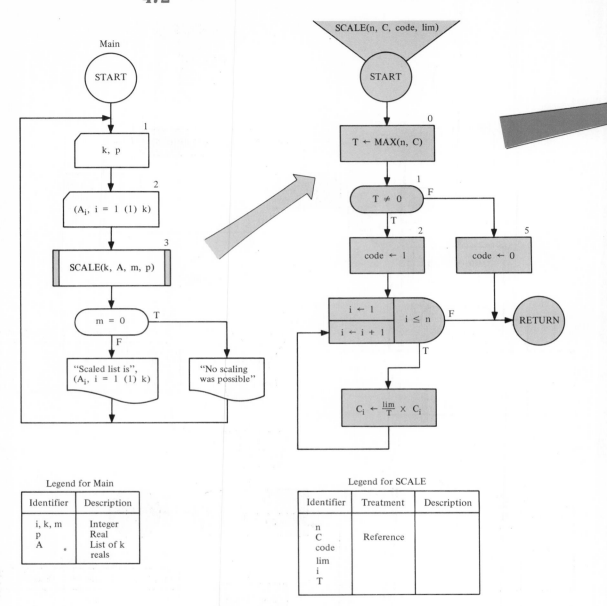

Main

START

1 k, p

2 $(A_i, i = 1 (1) k)$

3 SCALE(k, A, m, p)

m = 0   →T

F

"Scaled list is",
$(A_i, i = 1 (1) k)$

"No scaling
was possible"

SCALE(n, C, code, lim)

START

0 $T \leftarrow MAX(n, C)$

1 $T \neq 0$ F

T

2 code ← 1   5 code ← 0

i ← 1
i ← i + 1 $i \leq n$ F   RETURN

T

$C_i \leftarrow \dfrac{lim}{T} \times C_i$

Legend for Main

Identifier	Description
i, k, m	Integer
p	Real
A	List of k reals

Legend for SCALE

Identifier	Treatment	Description
n C code lim i T	Reference	

but not all, of the storage cells of the computation are accessible
to that Master Computer. List each accessible cell and show,
according to our SIMPLOS model, what stickers appear on each
accessible cell.

5.   This exercise is an extension of Problems 9 and 11, Exercises 9·2.
Construct a procedure named printpattern that, when invoked, will
call on printisosc or printdiamond to print m rows of right isosceles
triangles or m rows of diamonds.

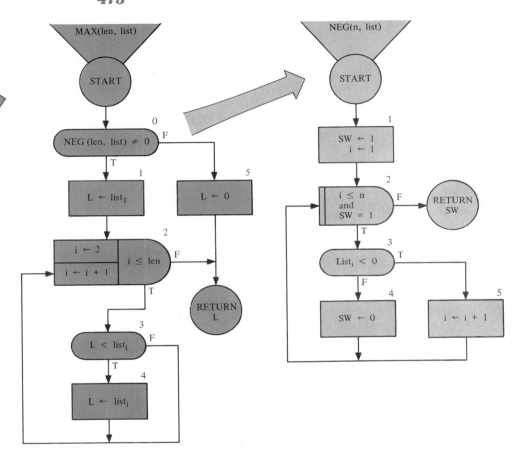

\-	Legend for MAX	\-
Identifier	Treatment	Description
len list L i	Reference	

\-	Legend for NEG	\-
Identifier	Treatment	Description
n List SW i		

Some of the information supplied to printpattern is used directly, while other information supplied to printpattern is passed along to either printisosc or printdiamond, that is,

m = number of rows of "figures" (triangles or diamonds) to be printed

k = $\begin{cases} 1 \text{ if triangles} \\ 2 \text{ if diamonds} \end{cases}$

n = number of figures on a row

h = number of horizontal spaces separating two figures

i = height / width of the figure

c = display character

In Figure 5·6 a flowchart to find the prime factorization of an integer was presented. We repeat that flowchart in Figure 9·27 with a slight modification: the factors are stored in a list, FACS, and printed out all at once at the end instead of being printed as they are found.

From the discussion in Section 5·1 we see that each prime factor of N found in box 201 is divided out of the current value of N and stored in the list FACS in box 202. Upon taking the F exit from box 102, N has no factors $\leq \sqrt{N}$ and, therefore, no factors at all. If, in box 104, the current value of N is not equal to 1, then N is prime and is therefore a prime factor, so N is appended to the list of factors (box 105).

Your task is to convert Figure 9·27*b* and 9·27*c* into procedures (and boxes 3 and 103 into procedure calls). You are to

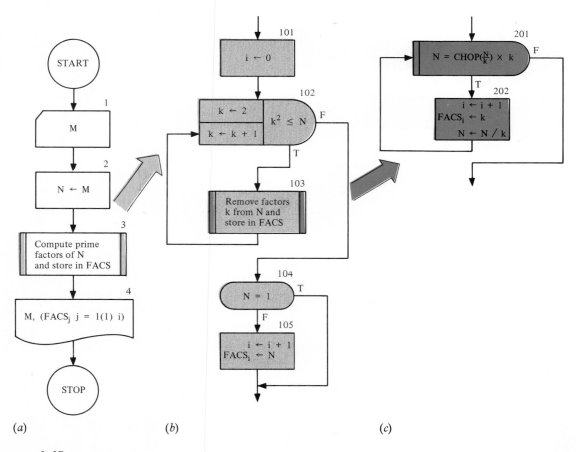

(*a*)   (*b*)   (*c*)

FIGURE 9·27

do this conversion in three different ways, as described in the exercises below. (Be sure to include legends in all cases.)

1. In this problem the converted flowcharts for Figure 9·27b and 9·27c should be called FACTORIZE1 and REMOVE1, respectively. Use no parameters. All variables are global. Has all the necessary protection been provided?

2. In this problem the converted flowcharts for Figure 9·27b and 9·27c should be called FACTORIZE2 and REMOVE2, respectively. Use no globals. Use only locals and call-by-reference parameters. Also, draw a sketch showing the storage boxes with their stickers at the point at which REMOVE2 is ready for execution (after REMOVE2 stickers have been affixed.) Show storage boxes for all variables: M, N, i, j, FACS, k.

    (a) Which variables appearing in Figure 9·27a will *not* be found in the argument list in the procedure call replacing box 3?
    (b) What are the locals (if any) in FACTORIZE2?
    (c) What is the significance of the fact that the variables FACS and i that appear in Figure 9·27a have never been given values by assignment or input in that flowchart?
    (d) What are the locals of REMOVE2 (if any)?

3. In this problem the converted flowcharts for Figure 9·27b and 9·27c should be called FACTORIZE3 and REMOVE3, respectively. Use locals and call-by-value parameters. Use call-by-reference parameters only when necessary.

    Explain why the variable M may be deleted in this approach so that boxes 1 and 2 may be replaced by $\boxed{\begin{smallmatrix}1\text{-}2\\ N\end{smallmatrix}}$. (This illustrates that the purpose of box 2 is protection. If protection is always used then there is no need for call-by-value.)

9·5 Procedure and function name parameters

Sometimes we are asked to design a procedure P that, when invoked, calls on still another procedure (or function), f, and yet, as designers of P, we do not know and cannot know which particular procedure (or function) P is to call. Only the (main) program that calls P can supply this information. As an example, in Chapter 12 we will develop a procedure to find the area under the graph of a function f between two lines, $x = a$ and $x = b$, as illustrated in Figure 9·28a. The process of finding this area is independent of the particular function f being referred to and is also independent of the particular interval [a,b]. Moreover, anyone using this process at all is likely to use it frequently.

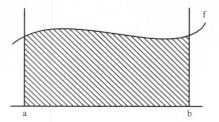

FIGURE 9·28a

Accordingly, it will be useful to program this area calculation as a procedure in which [a,b] and f do not refer to a
particular interval and a particular function, but instead to an
interval and a function supplied by the main or "calling"
program. In other words we would like the end points of the
interval and the function name to be parameters of the procedure.

This approach implies an interaction among three programs as indicated in Figure 9·28b. Thus, when the procedure,
AREA, is invoked, the parameter f will be treated as a name
for the function indicated in the corresponding position in the

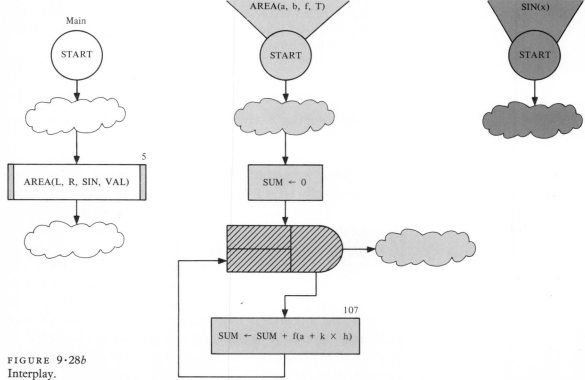

FIGURE 9·28b
Interplay.

argument list in box 5 of the main program. Accordingly, when the value of f(a + k × h) is called for in box 107 of AREA, the value of SIN(L + k × h) will be calculated by reference to the flowchart for the SIN function. (Here k and h are local variables of the AREA procedure. The argument VAL matched to parameter T provides a receptacle for returning the computed area to the main program.)

The foregoing observations clearly demand a new kind of treatment for parameters, called "procedure name" (we make no distinction between procedures and functions in this context), which must be indicated in the legend. Appropriate legends for the flowcharts of Figure 9·28b are shown in Figure 9·29.

Legend for Main

Identifier	Description
L	Real
R	Real
VAL	Real
SIN	Real function
—	—
—	—

FIGURE 9·29
The missing legends for Figure 9·28(b).

Legend for AREA

Identifier	Treatment	Description
a,b	Value	Real
T	Reference	Real
f	Procedure name	Returns real value
k	Local	Integer
h	Local	Real
SUM	Local	Real
—	—	—

Legend for SIN

Identifier	Treatment	Description
x	Value	Real
—	Local	—
—	—	—
—	—	—

There is probably no need for further exploration of the handling of procedure parameters by the SIMPLOS model. In case anyone wishes to pursue the model he can take the point of view that an empty storage box is labeled f and filled with the value "SIN", as illustrated in Figure 9·30. When evaluation of the "dummy" function f is called for in the AREA procedure, the box labeled f is consulted to find the actual function to be evaluated.

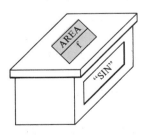

FIGURE 9·30

EXERCISES 9·5

1. In Problem 3, Exercises 5·1, Set E a flowchart was constructed to plot the graph of a function. At that time we had no knowledge of procedures, so that the explicit calculation of required function values,

that is, cos (x) in that case, had to be included in the program. Your task now is to redesign that program as a procedure Plotter that will plot the graph of *any* function supplied by the main or "calling" program. Other parameters of Plotter should be the coordinates of the origin, the horizontal and vertical scale factors, and the endpoints of the domain. The graph array (60 × 132) can be local to the procedure. (The next step in the graphing development is to have the procedure figure out the scaling factors and the proper location, if any, for the origin. We leave that as a challenge to students.)

2. Trace the program given in the flowcharts and legends on page 479 for the data set

$$r = 7 \quad A = (4, -5, 7, 9, -4, 8, 6)$$

and show that the printed results should be:

```
25
11
19
```

3. This problem is an extension of Problem 5, Exercises 9·4, in which you developed a procedure named *printpattern*. We want to modify printpattern so the type of figure to be printed in the pattern is not specified by an integer parameter, k, but by a procedure parameter, *figure*. This parameter is to be matched by the name of the procedure to be used for printing the figure, for example, printisosc, or print-diamond, but certainly not limited to these two.

   (a) Show what changes are needed in the flowchart and legend of printpattern to accomplish the required modification.
   (b) What limitations are there, if any, on the nature of the procedure arguments that match the procedure parameter in your modified flowchart? (*Hint.* Must all the matching procedure arguments have the same number and types of parameters?)

9·6
Recursion

We have just seen how one procedure can call on another. Now we ask the question, "Can a procedure call on itself?" At first one wonders if this can work. Is it like defining a word in terms of itself? If so, then executing such a procedure will put the Master Computer in an endless loop. To answer this question consider the following "recursive" definition.

> hu'-man be'-ing (n) — a creature whose mother is a human being

In order to determine whether a creature is a human being you have to find out whether its mother was a human being,

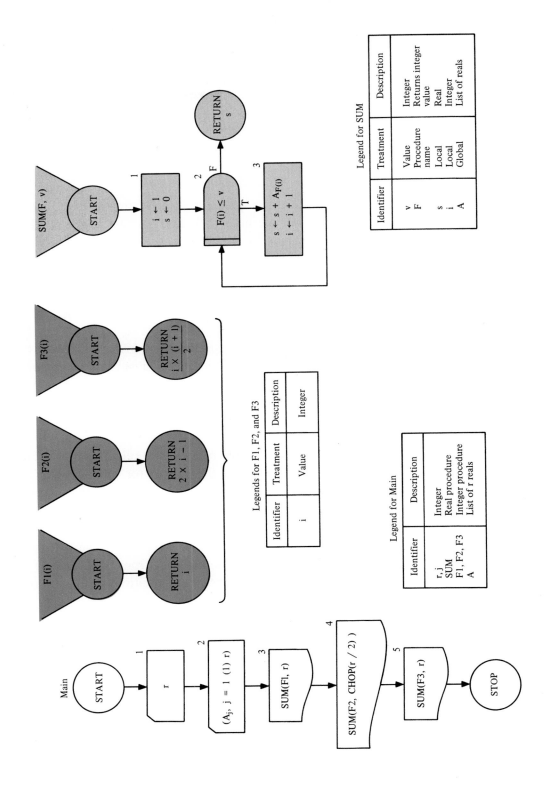

SUM(F, v)

START

1
i ← 1
s ← 0

2
F(i) ≤ v

3
s ← s + A_{F(i)}
i ← i + 1

RETURN
s

Legend for SUM

Identifier	Treatment	Description
v	Value	Integer
F	Procedure name	Returns integer value
s	Local	Real
i	Local	Integer
A	Global	List of reals

F1(i)

START

RETURN
i

F2(i)

START

RETURN
2 × i − 1

F3(i)

START

RETURN
$\dfrac{i \times (i+1)}{2}$

Legends for F1, F2, and F3

Identifier	Treatment	Description
i	Value	Integer

Legend for Main

Identifier	Description
r, j	Integer
SUM	Real procedure
F1, F2, F3	Integer procedure
A	List of r reals

Main

START

1
r

2
(A_j, j = 1 (1) r)

3
SUM(F1, r)

4
SUM(F2, CHOP(r / 2))

5
SUM(F3, r)

STOP

which requires finding out whether *her* mother was a human being, and so on, ad infinitum. Or does it go on forever? Not according to the Biblical view of creation! Let's modify the above definition.

hu'-man be'ing (n)—a creature that is either (a) Adam or Eve, or, (b) whose mother is a human being.

With this "escape hatch" (of Adam and Eve) included in the definition one finds that the recursive test applied to any person (such as you) will always terminate. The chain of mothers terminates eventually with Eve. Working back down the chain again one finds that each mother is a human being because her mother is a human being. Finally, when the base of the chain is reached, one finds that, among others, even you are a human being.

The situation is entirely analogous when recursive procedure calls are made. There must always be an escape hatch that is guaranteed to get us out of the recursive loop. A recursive process is like eating an onion by first boring down to the innermost layer and then eating the onion, layer by layer, from the inside out.

Here is an example of recursive calculation of n factorial (n!), but first we review the normal (or iterative) way of calculating n factorial. Figure 9·31 presents two functionalized flowcharts for the iterative calculation.

Observe that in either case, FACT1 or FACT2, the multiplication instruction in box 3 is repeated (iterated) over and over again until execution emerges from the F exit of box 2. What is important is that each multiplication is completed before the next one is begun.

Now consider an entirely different approach to the calculation of n!. Start with the "recursive definition" of n!.

$$\text{FACT}(n) = \begin{cases} 1, \text{ if } n = 0 \\ n \times \text{FACT}(n-1), \text{ if } n \neq 0 \end{cases}$$

How can this definition be used to find the value of FACT(6)? First look at the expression, FACT(6) and check

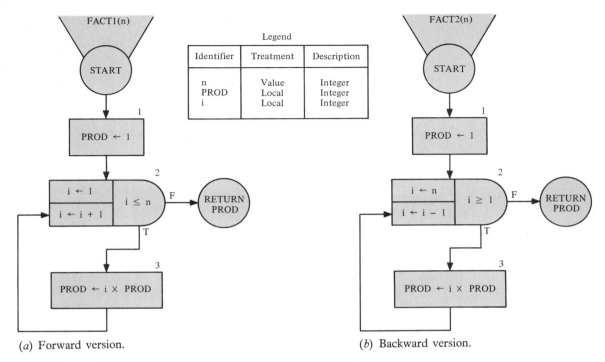

(a) Forward version.

(b) Backward version.

FIGURE 9·31
Iterative calculation of n
factorial.

whether $6 = 0$ is *true;* it isn't, so according to the recursive definition

$$FACT(6) = 6 \times FACT(5).$$

But you can't carry out the indicated multiplication until you know what the value of FACT(5) is. Therefore, you must interrupt the indicated calculation to find the value of FACT(5). Check whether $5 = 0$ is *true;* it isn't, so

$$FACT(5) = 5 \times FACT(4).$$

Now you can use the definition to write down the whole process, as in Figure 9·32. First write the first half of each of the equations in the order shown from top to bottom, checking at each step whether any function argument is equal to 0. No product can be completely evaluated until you come to the bottom, where the function argument of FACT is zero. This time you use the "escape hatch" clause of the recursive definition, writing FACT(0) = 1.

Now for the climb back up the ladder. First, substitute 1 for FACT(0) in the next to last line, allowing the calculation

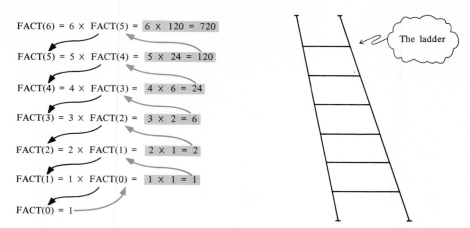

FIGURE 9·32
Recursive calculation of
FACT(6).

of FACT(1) to be completed. This in turn allows the calculation of FACT(2) to be completed, and so forth. The path back
up the ladder is represented by the upward arrows in Figure
9·32. The path terminates when the calculation of FACT(6)
is completed.

   Obviously this example does little to illustrate the need
for recursion, since it can be handled more easily by iteration.
And unfortunately, most examples of recursion, simple enough
to understand as a first illustration, are also trivial in the sense
that they can be solved more easily by other means.

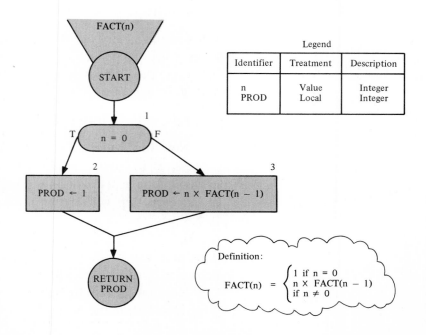

FIGURE 9·33
Recursive evaluation of
factorial.

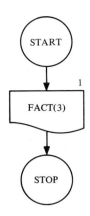

FIGURE 9·34
Main flowchart.

Can we draw a flowchart for this computation? It is easier than you might imagine! The flowchart of FACT, as seen in Figure 9·33, is a straightforward rendition of its mathematical definition.

Although the flowchart has a deceptively simple structure, convincing oneself that its execution gives a correct result is not so easy. Once again, we may appeal to our SIMPLOS model. For this purpose we use an extremely simple main program (Figure 9·34).

When the Master Computer for the main program gives the argument, 3, to the Master Computer for FACT, the latter has the Affixer set up the storage configuration shown in Figure 9·35. Note that when the FACT Master Computer comes to

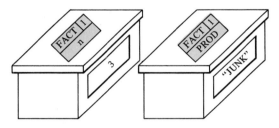

FIGURE 9·35
Storage configuration for first call on FACT.

box 3 in his flowchart (Figure 9·33), he gives the value of $n - 1$ (which is now 2) to a new Master Computer, who will execute FACT with 2 as the given value of n. When this Master Computer goes to the sticker bin to get FACT stickers for the Affixer, the stickers he finds are marked | FACT | 2 | because those marked | FACT | 1 | are currently in use. He hands this second set of stickers to the Affixer, who modifies the storage configuration, as seen in Figure 9·36. While exe-

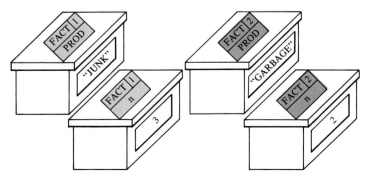

FIGURE 9·36
Storage configuration established by second call on FACT.

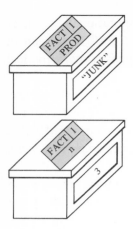
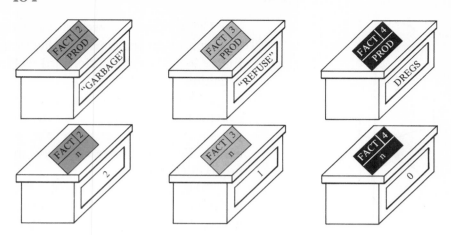

FIGURE 9·37
Storage completed.

cuting in this second run through FACT, the Assigner and

Reader will be able to see only the [FACT 2] stickers.

This process is repeated through the four "activations" of FACT, thus creating four environments in storage, as depicted in Figure 9·37.

Just before each successive return step, a value is assigned to the local variable PROD, which is used to identify the value to be returned. The values of PROD assigned at successive

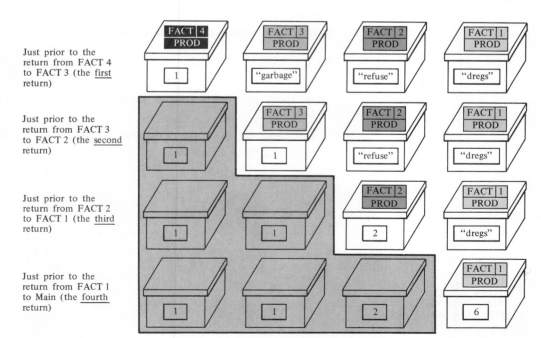

Just prior to the return from FACT 4 to FACT 3 (the first return)

Just prior to the return from FACT 3 to FACT 2 (the second return)

Just prior to the return from FACT 2 to FACT 1 (the third return)

Just prior to the return from FACT 1 to Main (the fourth return)

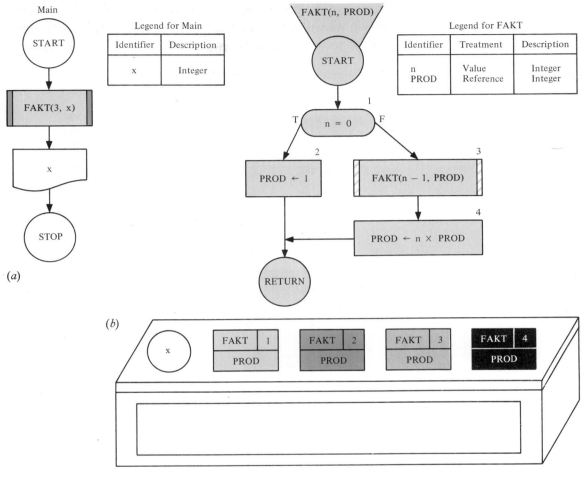

FIGURE 9·38
A factorial procedure.

returns form the sequence 1, 1, 2, 6. As the baton is passed back from the FACT4 Master Computer to the FACT3 Master Computer the sticker is peeled off that box. Each successive return of the baton is accompanied by the removal of another such sticker. All this business has been diagrammed in the lower part of page 484. The shaded boxes represent those whose stickers have already been removed.

Procedures may be defined recursively whether or not they return a functional value. For example, we may reexpress FACT as a procedure using a call-by-reference parameter as a means of transmitting a result to the calling "site," as seen in Figure 9·38a. During the fourth invocation of FACT, *five* stickers may be seen (Figure 9·38b) on the same storage box because of the call-by-reference parameter PROD. In the next section we will introduce a sequence of increasingly interesting uses of recursive procedures.

EXERCISES 9·6

1. The greatest common divisor, algorithm, GCDR, can be represented very easily as a recursive function, as seen in the flowchart below.

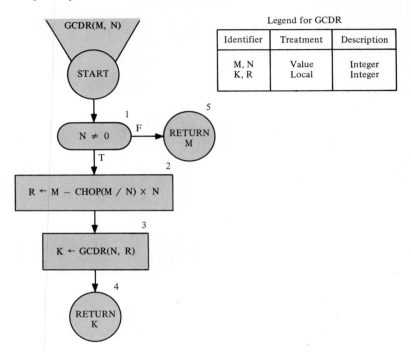

Legend for GCDR

Identifier	Treatment	Description
M, N	Value	Integer
K, R	Local	Integer

(a) Which is the escape hatch of GCDR?
(b) Which of the two return statements will be the first to be executed and why?
(c) Describe the activities that take place after the first RETURN is executed.
(d) A student has claimed that the return box

is equivalent to the sequence of boxes 3 and 4 in the above algorithm. Explain why you agree or disagree with this claim.
(e) Assume that the main flowchart at the left is executed using as data a = 65 and b = 35.

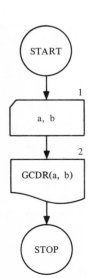

Trace the execution of the call on GCDR at box 2 by filling out the table below.

Call Number Is	M	N	K	R	Value Returned
1					
2					
3					
4					
5					
. . .					

Note As the answer to part c shows, although these procedures are recursive in structure, the activities after the first RETURN are trivial in nature. In fact, the value returned in box 5 gets returned all the way up the ladder to the calling program.

2. The algorithm for the prime factorization of an integer N can be expressed as a recursive procedure very simply if we are not too concerned with efficiency. For instance, consider the flowchart for FACTOR1 on the next page. It is fairly obvious that this process works by the following reasoning: once a factor is found and printed (box 3), and then divided out of N (box 4), the whole process starts over (box 5). On emerging from the F exit of box 1, we are sure that the current value of N has no prime factors $\leq \sqrt{N}$ and hence is either a prime or is equal to 1. Boxes 7 through 9 deal appropriately with this situation.

   The flowchart for FACTOR1 is open to two fundamental objections.
   (a) The process is extremely wasteful in that when box 5 is invoked, the factorization process again tests 2 as a factor, whereas we know that N has no factors less than the most recent value of k.
   (b) The main program may not be satisfied with having the prime factors output by the procedure but may wish to use these prime factors for other purposes. Accordingly, it might be better to store these prime factors in a list FACS instead of outputting them. (See Problem 2, Exercises 9·4, Set B for clarification.)

   Objection a can be eliminated by modifying the procedure to one that removes all factors starting with i, as suggested at the left.

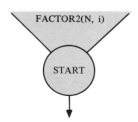

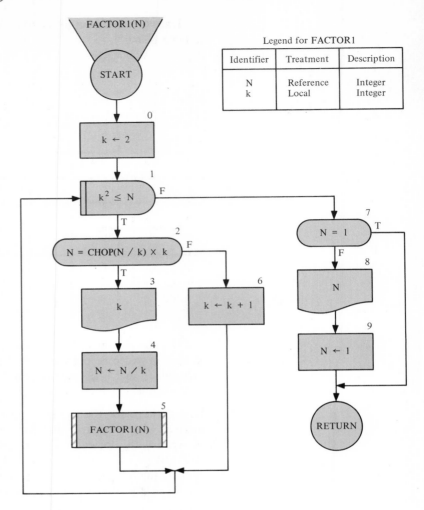

Legend for **FACTOR1**

Identifier	Treatment	Description
N	Reference	Integer
k	Local	Integer

The procedure call in box 5 will then be changed to

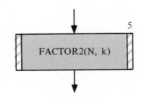

Now do the following exercises.

(a) How must box 0 be modified to deal with the change? Explain.
(b) To actually obtain the prime factorization, the main program procedure call must have the form shown at the left. Explain the M and the 2 in the argument list.

(c) Since N is to be a reference parameter, after the first RETURN all further tests in box 7 will result in emerging from the T exit. Explain. (*Hint.* The key is found in box 9.)

(d) All of the above discussion is geared to the removal of objection a. If objection b is to be dealt with as well, then the parameter list must also be changed, suggesting further modification, for example,

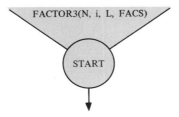

where L is the length (or dimension) of FACS. Must L and FACS be called by reference or may they be call-by-value parameters?

(e) The main program procedure call must now have the form

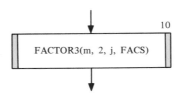

What should be the value of the argument j just before box 10 is executed? Explain.

(f) How must boxes 3 and 8 be modified to accommodate storage of factors rather than output?

(g) What is the escape hatch in this program? How can we be sure that it will eventually be reached?

(h) Show a flowchart and legend for FACTOR3 that satisfactorily eliminates objections a and b.

4. Study the flowcharts and legends given on the next page.
   (a) Trace execution of the computation for the given data set and show what is displayed as a result of executing box 4 of Main.
   (b) Revise the flowcharts and legends to remove all globals from the procedures without changing the purpose of procedures Pattern or Filltheline.

   The given data set:
   $n = 4, A = (\text{"S"}, \text{"T"}, \text{"O"}, \text{"P"})$

5. Use the flowcharts of the preceding exercise as a guide for constructing flowcharts (and legends) that, when executed, will accomplish the following. If the input values are $n = k, A = (a_1, a_2, a_3, \ldots, a_n)$, where the a_i's are single characters, the algorithm will produce as output k "concentric" squares. The outermost square is

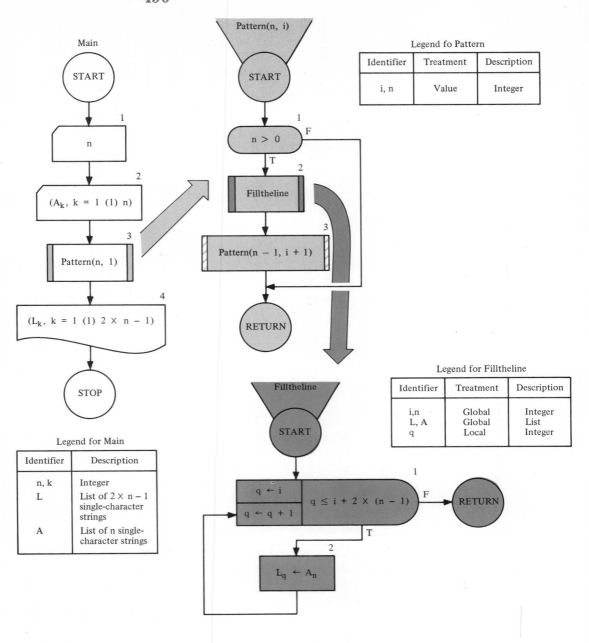

Main

Legend fo Pattern

Identifier	Treatment	Description
i, n	Value	Integer

Legend for Fishtheline

Legend for Filltheline

Identifier	Treatment	Description
i,n	Global	Integer
L, A	Global	List
q	Local	Integer

Legend for Main

Identifier	Description
n, k	Integer
L	List of 2 × n − 1 single-character strings
A	List of n single-character strings

made up of the letter a_k. The square inside of that is made up of the letter a_{k-1}, and so forth, with the innermost square consisting simply of the letter a_1. For example, if the data were:

$$n = 5, A = (\text{"Q"}, \text{"U"}, \text{"E"}, \text{"E"}, \text{"N"})$$

then the executed program should display the following:

```
N  N  N  N  N  N  N  N  N
N  E  E  E  E  E  E  E  N
N  E  E  E  E  E  E  E  N
N  E  E  U  U  U  E  E  N
N  E  E  U  Q  U  E  E  N
N  E  E  U  U  U  E  E  N
N  E  E  E  E  E  E  E  N
N  E  E  E  E  E  E  E  N
N  N  N  N  N  N  N  N  N
```

6. Design and construct a flowchart and legend for the recursive procedure Evaluate which converts numbers in base 4 representation to numbers in base 10 representation. For example, if the parameter list of Evaluate were (n, B, R), then the procedure might assign to R the base 10 equivalent of the list B of n + 1 elements, each element being a digit in base 4. Thus the value assigned to R might be

$$B_0 \times 4^0 + B_1 \times 4^1 + B_2 \times 4^2 + \ldots + B_n \times 4^n$$

Evaluate should recognize error conditions and return a value of 0 for R and print an appropriate error message as well. Error conditions include:

(a) Some element of B is negative.
(b) Some element of B exceeds 3.
(c) The parameter n is negative.

7. For the preceding exercise show a collection of data sets that might be used by a main flowchart for testing the correctness of Evaluate. Explain what each data set is designed to accomplish and why you feel the collection of such data sets is complete for the purpose intended.

8. Show what changes would be needed in the flowchart and legend of Evaluate (as constructed in Problem 6) so that this procedure can convert numbers from any base, b < 10, to representation in base 10.

9·7
Tree traversal and recursion

So far each example of a recursive procedure or function can be characterized by the fact that execution leads to an unbranched chain of recursive calls and returns. Figure 9·39a gives this view for the case of Main calling FACT with the argument 3. The downward chain links are labeled with the arguments for the successive calls on FACT, and upward links are labeled with the values provided in the successive returns.

One can also view such a chain as a tree that has at each nonterminal node only one offspring. Each node is connected to its single successor by a double link or "double segment." In the figure the black segments represent *calls* and the green ones represent returns.

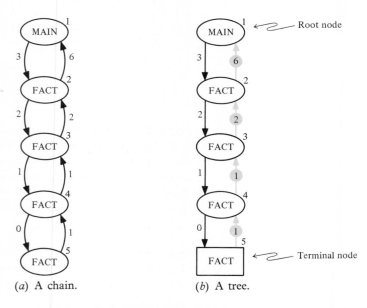

(a) A chain.   (b) A tree.

FIGURE 9·39

What aspect of recursive procedures or recursive functions leads to single chains? Alternatively, what property of a recursive procedure can lead to chains of calls that in turn split into two or more chains like ordinary trees? For example, can we have a recursive procedure P that, when called, leads to a call chain such as the following?

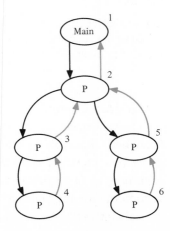

A little thought will lead us to the answer. A recursive procedure whose flowchart contains only one self-reference (call on itself), can develop only a single chain of calls when it is executed. In order for branching of the call chain to occur, the procedure must contain at least two distinct references to itself within the body of its flowchart.

For our first illustration of "recursive branching" we take a problem familiar to every college algebra student, the calculation of the "binomial coefficient," BC. We recall that the binomial coefficient refers to the kth coefficient of the polynomial resulting from the expansion of a binomial of the form a + b raised to the nth power.

$$(a + b)^n = a^n + n \times a^{n-1} \times b + \frac{n \times (n-1)}{2!} \times a^{n-2} \times b^2$$

0th term　　1st term　　2nd term

$$+ \frac{n \times (n-1) \times (n-2)}{3!} \times a^{n-3} \times b^3 + \ldots$$

3rd term

An explicit formula for the kth term of the nth degree polynomial is

$$BC(n,k) = \frac{n \times (n-1) \times (n-2) \times \ldots \times (n-k+1)}{k!}$$

which can also be expressed as

$$BC(n,k) = \frac{n!}{k! \times (n-k)!}$$

Using this formula one could, of course, compute BC(n,k) by making three separate calls on the factorial function. There is a second way to compute binomial coefficients, of greater interest for our particular discussion. That way suggests itself through an examination of Pascal's triangle, which is formed by writing down the coefficients for each polynomial beginning with degree 0 (Figure 9·40).

Pick any number "inside" the triangle, for example, BC(6,4) which is 15, and you will find it to be the sum of its two neighbors, the one immediately above it, 5, and that neigh-

Degree	Term number, k							
n	0	1	2	3	4	5	6	7
0	1							
1	1	1						
2	1	2	1					
3	1	3	3	1				
4	1	4	6	4	1			
5	1	5	10	10	5	1		
6	1	6	15	20	15	6	1	
7	1	7	21	35	35	21	7	1

FIGURE 9·40
Pascal's triangle provides the binomial coefficients for the kth term of the nth degree polynomial.

bor's left-hand neighbor, 10. By "inside the triangle" we mean any coefficient that is neither on the left edge of the triangle ($k = 0$) nor on the diagonal ($n = k$). Of course, these coefficients are always one.

With these observations in mind we can now write down a recursive definition of BC in mathematical form and its direct analog in flowchart form (Figure 9·41). The mathematical form is

$$BC\ (n,k) = \begin{cases} 1, \text{ if } k = 0 \text{ or if } n = k \\ \text{else} \\ BC\ (n - 1, k) + BC\ (n - 1, k - 1) \end{cases}$$

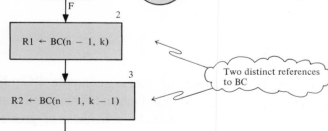

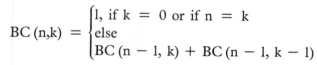

Legend for BC		
Identifier	Treatment	Description
n, k	Value	Integer
R1, R2	Local	Integer

FIGURE 9·41
A recursive definition for the BC procedure.

Note Here, for the first time, we see a recursive procedure exhibiting more than one recursive call within its definition. In this case these calls appear in boxes 2 and 3 of Figure 9·41. Tracing the execution of BC, when called to compute BC (4,2), we find branching in the chain of calls (Figure 9·42).

FIGURE 9·42
Executing BC(4,2) results in execution of a tree of calls in the order shown by the small numbers beside each node. Each downward-directed segment represents a call on BC, and the number pair that labels the line is the argument list. Upward-directed segments represent returns, and the green-shaded numbers shown beside these segments are the returned values.

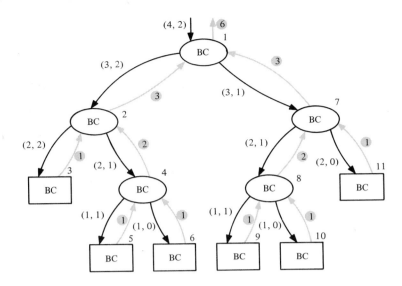

One important thing to notice in Figure 9·42 is that the nodes of this tree are numbered in the order that the calls are actually made, which you will recognize is the same as in *natural-order tree search.*

In Figure 9·41 the order in which box 2 and box 3 are executed is immaterial. If the order were reversed, the same tree of calls would still be executed, but the order in which the nodes were encountered would be different. (To verify your understanding of this assertion, trace the execution of, say, BC(3,2) two ways: (1) with boxes 2 and 3 in their present order, and (2) with boxes 2 and 3 reversed.)

A second observation worth making is that the tree of calls that is "traversed" during execution of BC is a *binary* tree, that is, every nonterminal node has two and only two offspring nodes. We suspect, therefore, that the structure of the BC algorithm suggests the structure for any recursive traversal of a binary tree. Indeed, a little thought produces an analogous algorithmic structure, as seen in Figure 9·43.

The key idea to keep in mind when verifying your understanding of this algorithm is that each time control takes the No exit of box 1, that is, each time a nonterminal node is being examined, there are two and only two steps that must be taken before returning to the caller; first, the left subtree must be traversed and, second, the right subtree must be traversed. It's as simple as that!

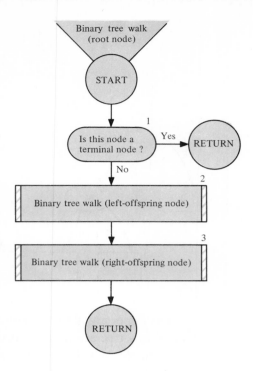

FIGURE 9·43
Recursive structure for a
binary tree traversal algorithm.

Some readers have probably begun to race ahead with
thoughts about how this algorithm can be generalized to trees
whose nonterminal nodes have three, four, . . . , or n subtrees.
An *n-ary* tree is one whose every nonterminal node has exactly
n offspring. One way to modify Figure 9·43 to handle the
search of an n-ary tree is to replace boxes 2 and 3 with n such
boxes. For example, if n = 4, as in the map-coloring problem
of Chapter 6, we might consider the scheme in Figure 9·44.

This approach is basically an unsatisfying solution, but
it does inspire us to see how to go about structuring an algorithm to traverse any tree, even a tree whose nonterminals do
not have a fixed number of offspring nodes. Of course, an
algorithm that will search a general tree structure will also be
capable of traversing any special, n-ary tree as well. The approach to be taken is sketched in Figure 9·45. Here we see
a while loop controlling a sequence of recursive calls on the
tree walk procedure, one call for each offspring of the node
currently being considered. The structure sketched here is
sufficiently general to merit attempts to apply it to some specific
problems.

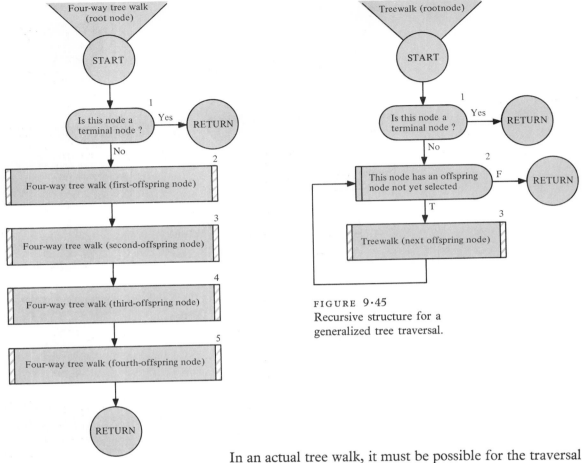

FIGURE 9·44
A recursive approach to the
4-ary tree traversal problem.

FIGURE 9·45
Recursive structure for a
generalized tree traversal.

In an actual tree walk, it must be possible for the traversal algorithm to determine certain vital information associated with each node of the tree. In particular the traversal algorithm must at least be able to determine for each node how many offspring it has. How is this information obtained in actual practice? As we have seen from the applications in the chapters on data structures, sometimes the information is found in a table or other data structure that serves as an explicit representation of the tree and its associated properties. In other cases the tree data is represented implicitly in the form of a set of rules or functions. We will not concern ourselves too much with these details here.

Even so, the additional detail presented in Figure 9·46 will shed considerable light on how an actual recursive tree-traversal procedure could be flowcharted. The pair of arguments matching the call-by-value parameters, *path* and *length*,

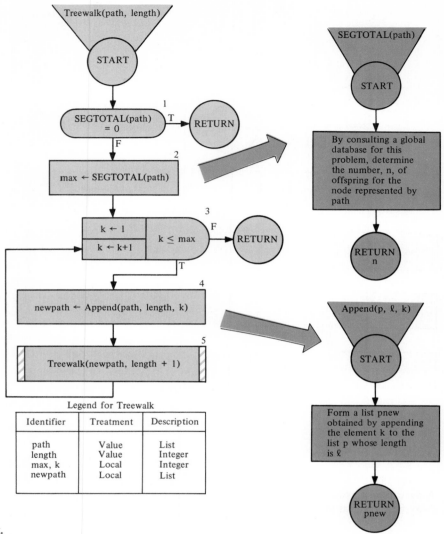

FIGURE 9·46
Partial detail for Treewalk.

furnished by the main program will always represent the root node. Remember that the root node's path list is empty and its level is 0, and the level is the same as the *length* of the path list. To determine whether a node is a terminal node, the algorithm appeals to a function SEGTOTAL which, in turn, somehow has access to the representation of the tree. SEGTOTAL returns the number of offspring of the node represented by *path*. If zero, the node is a terminal node; otherwise, the value returned by SEGTOTAL is used as the upper bound in the iteration box used to control the number of recursive calls on Treewalk from the given node. Forming the argument list for each such call requires the construction of new values for path and length (box 4). The function Append (whose details are purposely suppressed) is employed to form a new list called newpath, which represents the offspring node to serve as the root of the subtree earmarked for the next traversal (box 5).

Additional sophistication can, of course, be added to the traversal strategy. For example, we might add an admissibility check to avoid searching subtrees that are not feasible. The addition of these details is left for the exercises.

Our final concern is to consider how to convert our traversal algorithm into a *search* algorithm. While a traversal must "visit" *every* node in the tree, a search should be allowed to halt when a node with some desired attribute is encountered.

Figure 9·47 suggests how a search algorithm can develop

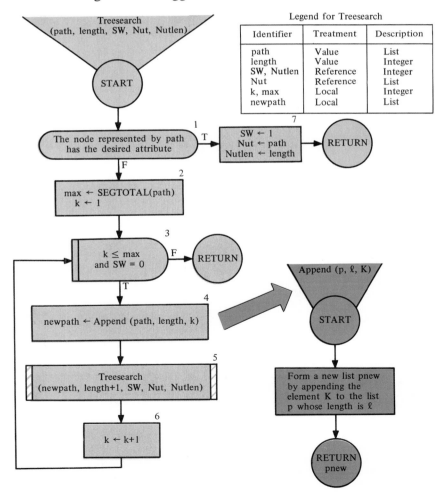

FIGURE 9·47
Partial detail for recursive treesearch.

from the structure of the traversal algorithm. The important new features are as follows.

1.   At least one more parameter is needed, in this case a call-by-reference switch, called SW, to force return from each call in the current chain of recursive calls. For clarity we also introduce two other reference parameters. Nut is used to return the designation of the (first) node found to have the desired attribute, and Nutlen, is used to return the *len*gth of Nut. By setting SW to 1 as soon as the desired node has been found, any remaining returns that are still "pending" will be executed without further search of the tree. At the same time that SW is set to 1, the current value of path and its length are *captured* by assignment to Nut and Nutlen. Notice that if no node is found with the appropriate attribute, the full tree will be traversed without at any time setting SW to 1. Thus the main program may invoke the search procedure with a call sequence of the form

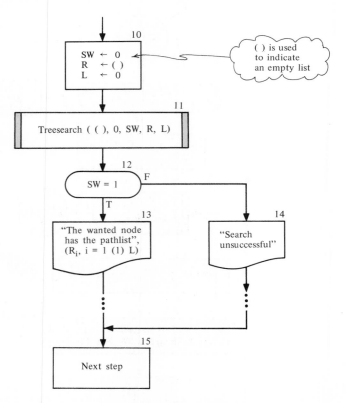

and thereby learn whether the search has been successful.

2. The details of box 1 of Treesearch, were they provided, must include an appeal to the representation of the tree, for example, a global data base or function that can retrieve a recorded property associated with each node. Such details, as those of the function SEGTOTAL, depend on the data representation chosen for the particular problem.

The tree search strategy, like that of the tree walk, can also be improved by introducing steps to determine whether or not a node is admissible. Again we leave such improvements for the exercises.

EXERCISES 9·7
SET A

1. It is not always practical to compute a function value using a recursive definition for the function, even when that definition seems simple and natural. For example, the value of the Fibonacci sequence can be computed using a function on the nonnegative integers expressed as follows.

$$\text{FIBR (n)} = \begin{cases} \text{if n } = \text{ 0, then 0} \\ \text{if n } = \text{ 1, then 1} \\ \text{else FIBR (n } - \text{ 1) + FIBR (n } - \text{ 2)} \end{cases}$$

(a) Construct a flowchart for the function FIBR based on the above definition.
(b) Draw the tree of calls on FIBR that will be executed when evaluating FIBR (4). As a guide for drawing this tree you might consult Figure 9·42. Be sure to indicate arguments and returned values for all calls.
(c) Estimate the number of calls on FIBR required to compute FIBR(10).
(d) Construct a flowchart and legend for the function FIBRWORK that, when executed, will return the number of calls required to compute FIBR(n) for a given value, n.

2. Construct a flowchart and legend for a function, FIBI that, when executed will compute *iteratively* (and return) the value of the nth term of the Fibonacci sequence for a given value of n. Compare your function FIBI with FIBR produced in the preceding problem.
(a) For what values of n will the computation of FIBI(n) be more efficient than that of FIBR(n)? Explain, stating any assumptions you may have made in arriving at your answer.
(b) For what values of n, if any, might the computation of FIBI(n) be less efficient than that of FIBR(n)? Explain, stating any assumptions you may have made in arriving at your answer.

EXERCISES 9·7
SET B

1. Complete a trace table that *audits* the execution of Treewalk (Figure 9·46) for traversal of the accompanying tree. Assume that in the call that invokes Treewalk the arguments for path and list are ( ) and 0, respec-

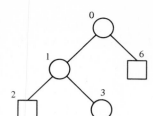

tively, where ( ) represents the empty list. What is the maximum length of the chain of calls on Treewalk during traversal of this tree?

2.   Modify the Treewalk algorithm of Figure 9·46 to include provision for "pruning" as the traversal proceeds. That is, before the subtree defined by each node is "walked," the algorithm executes steps that test for admissibility. For guidance, you may wish to review how this strategy was achieved in the nonrecursive treesearch algorithm given in Chapter 6 (Figure 6·16).

3.   Complete a trace table that *audits* the execution of Treesearch (Figure 9·47) in the search for the first nut found in the following tree. Assume

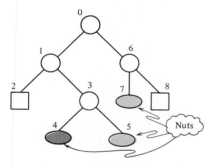

that in the call from the main program that invokes Treesearch, values for the arguments are as follows.

    path = ( )
    length = 0
    SW = 0
    R = ( )
    L = 0

where ( ) represents the empty list.
Pay special attention during this trace to the steps taken that insure returns from the chain of calls when the nut at node 4 is discovered. The value of nut upon return to the main program should be (1, 2, 1). Be sure you understand why this is so before you begin your trace efforts.

4. Show what modifications are needed to the Treesearch algorithm (Fig. 9·47) to eliminate the need for reference parameters Nut and Nutlen.

5. Prepare modifications to the Treesearch algorithm (Figure 9·47) similar to those described in Problem 2.

6. Review the four-coloring algorithm given in Figure 6·24. Adapt the Treesearch algorithm that you prepared in Problem 4 and substitute it for the nonrecursive version used in Figure 6·24. Comment on the simplifications, if any, that result from this substitution.

7. The Towers of Hanoi puzzle is probably familiar to most readers. We are given a board from which three posts project. On the left post is a stack of graduated disks such that the bottom one has the largest diame-

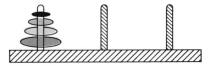

ter and no larger disk rests on a smaller one. The problem is to devise an algorithm for moving n disks from the left post to the right post observing the two following rules.

(a) Only one disk can be moved at a time.
(b) No disk is ever to rest on a smaller one.

The algorithm should print out some kind of directions that a person can follow to carry out the actions required to move the disks.

A simple recursive solution to this problem is suggested. First, notice that the problem is easily solved if we have only two disks (n = 2) to be moved from the left post to the right post. We use the following three-step action.

(n = 2) (a) Move the *top disk* from the left post to the middle post.
        (b) Move the remaining disk from the left post to the right post.
        (c) Move the *disk* from the middle post to the right post.

The strategy for n = 3 can be expressed in nearly the same terms as for n = 2. We need alter only the italicized words in steps a and c.

(n = 3) (a) Move the *top two disks* from the left post to the middle post.
        (b) Move the remaining disk from the left post to the right post.
        (c) Move the *two disks* from the middle post to the right post.

Notice that the procedure for moving two disks between two designated posts in steps a and c is exactly the same as in the corresponding steps for n = 2. But in applying the rules for the n = 3 case we will also have to apply the rules for the n = 2 case, changing the names of the posts.

To solve the general problem, that is, for n ≥ 2, we need only give general names for the posts involved in the operation and re-express our strategy for n = 3 as follows:

n ≥ 2 (general case)
- (a) Move the *top n − 1 disks* from the *from-post* to the *intermediate post.*
- (b) Move the remaining disk from the *from-post* to the *to-post.*
- (c) Move the *n − 1 disks* from the *intermediate post* to the *to-post.*

Notice that this recursive approach guarantees that at each level the largest ("remaining") disk is always moved by itself to an empty post so it is clearly on the bottom. Also notice that steps a and c amount to recursive calls to reemploy the same method, so the algorithmic solution will give rise, during its execution, to a binary tree of procedure calls.

For n = 2 the task requires 3 instructions and for n = 3, $3 + 1 + 3 = 7$ instructions are required. In general it takes $2^n - 1$, which can be a very large number of instructions! Devise a recursive algorithm (flowchart and legend) to solve this puzzle for an arbitrary number of disks but, when you actually try out your algorithm, use $n \leq 7$. Call your procedure Hanoi with parameters FP, IP, TP, and n, where FP, IP, and TP are the post names, standing for *from-post, inter-mediate-post,* and *to-post,* and n is the number of disks in the Tower.

Chapter 10

Introduction to data processing

10·1
Computer systems for record keeping*

The 20-year period from 1955 to 1975 has produced a steady stream of technological advances in computer systems and, as a result, the use of computers for record keeping has become more and more attractive to business and government. A *record* is a set of facts or attributes about a particular person or item. A record can be retrieved by the name of the individual or by some other identifying label, for example, the social security number for a person or the license plate number for an automobile record. Each fact or attribute in a record is usually contained in a separate *field;* the collection of fields makes up the record. A *file* is a set of records about individuals or items in a particular class, such as an employee personnel file, a customer account file, an automobile dealer parts-inventory file, or a file of persons claiming insurance payments or income tax refunds.

Manual record systems use hand-operated files based on written or printed records. In a *computer* record system the files are stored in computer-readable form, and the records can be searched, rearranged, or updated by electronic processing methods. Whether the system is operated manually or by computer, usually only a few different types of operations are performed on the data files of a record system. Hereafter our discussion will concentrate primarily on computer record systems.

Information too voluminous to hold in the central store of a computer can be kept in computer-readable form in auxiliary storage, typically on a magnetic tape or disk, or on a drum whose surface is similar to that of tape. A central or satellite computer can then be programmed to control such auxiliary storage devices, to search for and transfer records or groups of records to or from the files, or to or from the central storage. Major advances in computer system technology have resulted

*This section was drawn by permission from "Fundamentals of Computer Technology," in *Databanks in a Free Society* by Alan F. Weston and Michael A. Baker, Quadrangle New York Times Book Company, © 1972.

in increased speed, capacity, and reliability of auxiliary storage media.

Two types of computer processing for record keeping have evolved, each strongly influenced by this improved technology of auxiliary storage devices. These are known as *batch processing* and *on-line processing*. Batch processing gathers together a number of transactions that need to be executed, say, a day's worth of laboratory reports to be entered into medical patient records, or a day's worth of sales slips to be used in updating customer account records in a department store. Then batch processing sorts these records into proper sequence, such as alphabetically, by name, and the computer system "performs" the transactions in a single pass through the entire file. The next three sections of this chapter develop illustrative computer algorithms for some typical batch processing operations. A department store customer accounting system serves as the principal example in the development of these algorithms.

Batch processing is often associated with systems in which information is stored on magnetic tape, historically the first auxiliary storage medium brought under computer control with sufficient speed and capacity to do large-scale record keeping. Reading a tape file from beginning to end requires minutes, but reading a single transaction, for example, one laboratory test result, after the tape has been positioned to read that information, may take as little as a few millionths of a second. For the sake of efficiency all transactions must be handled in a single pass through each tape.

Batch processing systems are not designed to update records at the time the transaction information becomes available. This is because updating one record of a file may require locating the appropriate file tape, mounting it on the equipment, searching possibly the entire length of the tape for the right record, updating it, rewinding, and restoring the tape. If this series of steps were carried out for each transaction, the efficiency goals for the computer system would surely be defeated.

On-line processing usually involves transactions whose information can be keyed directly into the computer, as in the case of a flight reservation inquiry in an airlines reservation system. On-line systems work best when the bulk of the records are stored on *random-access* devices, such as disks or drums, in which it is possible to reach every record (every flight passenger list), with essentially the same speed, in a matter of milliseconds. As the technology for large-capacity, highly reliable disk storage devices has been perfected in the last 10 years, on-line systems have become more and more feasibile. On-line systems are especially useful where continuous access to a file or files is required, for example, to make and check airline reservations as requests come in 24 hours a day, or to check on the status of orders for automobile parts from the factory, or to maintain or use a directory of guests registered at a large hotel or room reservations for a chain of hotels.

On-line processing works well when a file has a comparatively small number of records, for example, 490 records for a file representing seats on a jumbo jet flight, but it becomes more and more expensive as the number of records in the file grows. Thus on-line processing is just becoming economical in cases where a file has several million records, as in government census data or large electric-utility customer data. Moreover, an on-line system is probably not justified when only periodic access to a file is required, such as to process a payroll once a week or to audit income taxes once a year. Some of the algorithmic techniques developed in the last half of this chapter are applicable to on-line processing.

In this chapter we will explore a few important data processing concepts, operations, and applications. We can by no means exhaust the subject. However, the ideas presented in this chapter are all relevant and applicable to the data processing of the business and financial world, the world of government, education, and so forth, in fact, to any area of activity where it is necessary to work with a large volume of information.

10·2 Sequential files

Before considering the batch processing approach to record keeping, we will review how data are organized in sequential files and discuss how data are stored on tapes and retrieved from them. Any collection of similar groupings of data is called a *file*. The white pages of a telephone directory may be thought of as a file. Each individual line within the directory constitutes a *record* as, for example,

BARTON, ROBERT	CATALINA ISLAND	327–1730
Name	Address	Phone number

This record subdivides naturally into three parts—the name, address, and phone number—each of which is a *field*. We could have considered the first and last names to be separate fields, but that may not turn out to be as useful. The design of a record as a collection of data fields is done by the system analyst or programmer and deserves careful thought.

When a file is ordered according to the values of a certain field within it, that field is called the *key* field. The same file at different times can be ordered according to different key fields. For example,

EARL DOUGLAS	1259 LAIRDAV	582–6350
EARL GEORGE	1620 LAIRDAV	359–9692
EARL GLENN	1209 LAIRDAV	467–6903

Key field

and

EARL GLENN	1209 LAIRDAV	467–6903
EARL DOUGLAS	1259 LAIRDAV	582–6350
EARL GEORGE	1620 LAIRDAV	359–9692

Key field

illustrate the same records ordered according to different key fields.

As another example, consider the file that a department store keeps of the monthly activity of its charge account customers for use in preparing bills at the end of the month. A typical record from such a file might be the one shown at the top of the next page. All this information comprises one record. The number of fields in such a record may vary from customer to customer and from day to day. Here, however, the first five fields (the top line in the illustration) will appear in every record, while the number of succeeding fields may vary, since the recording of each purchase adds four additional fields.

The programmer can also subdivide his files into groups of records called *blocks* or subdivide his records into groups of fields by use of special separator symbols. He can place a special mark at the end of a group of fields, at the end of a

Charge account number	Name	Address	City code (Minneapolis)	Balance due from last month
506172	JOSEPH CONRAD	3357 OLSON BLVD	MPLS	37.65

Branch D = Downtown S = Suburban	Department	Date	Amount of purchase
D	BOYS SHOES	6 MAR 75	19.95

D	CAMERA	17 MAR 75	48.50

S	STYLE SHOPPE	22 MAR 75	99.95

record, at the end of a block, or at the end of a file. *End-of-record* marks and *end-of-file* marks are almost always useful or necessary for efficient processing of a sequential file.

Now that we have a little idea of how data are organized, we are ready to examine how data are stored. Until now, in discussing such algorithms as sorting, we assumed that all the relevant data was located in the computer's primary (e.g., core) storage. But with the large quantity of data we wish to consider in this chapter, this is no longer practical. The primary storage in a typical computer facility cannot hold such a mass of data all at one time, and to increase the size of the primary storage to accommodate the data would be prohibitively expensive.

If the data are stored as a sequential file, say, on magnetic tape, the records may be read into the primary storage one at a time or a few at a time. The magnetic tape storage can be thought of as an adjunct to the primary computer storage. Ordinarily, however, this auxiliary tape storage differs from primary storage in that it is not directly addressable. Our algorithms must take account of this limitation.

To distinguish the terms "addressable" and "nonaddressable," suppose for the moment that the information for a telephone directory is located in primary storage as a table, T. Then, if the first subscript denotes the index of the record and the second subscript denotes the index of the field, $T_{i,j}$ refers to a certain field in a certain record. The exact field denoted depends, of course, on the values of i and j. In this case we say that all the fields are "addressable"; in order to retrieve the contents of any field all that is required is to supply the values of the subscripts i and j. The field is located directly without control having to pass through or examine any other fields or records. On the other hand, if the telephone directory is stored as a sequential tape file, then the task of retrieving the contents of any field normally requires that the records be read into the primary storage one at a time, until the required record is found. Only when a record has been located whose key field value matches the one sought, can the desired field value be retrieved. Thus the fields are said to be nonaddressable in the sense of not being directly addressable.

The nonaddressability of individual tape files is an interesting fact of life in the search and retrieval algorithm shown in Figure 10·1. TAPESEARCH (Figure 10·1) begins by rewinding tape A. The REWIND instruction in box 1 is included to make sure the reading of the tape in box 2 starts at the beginning of the tape. If the tape is already rewound, the REWIND instruction will cause no action.

In box 2 the instruction to read a record advances the tape past a read-write head (Figure 10·2) where the pattern of magnetic pulses constituting the record is read from the tape and stored in an area S of core storage, large enough to accommodate an entire record. When a certain pattern of pulses denoting the end-of-record mark is reached, the tape automatically stops. We regard the variable S as a "record" variable that is subdivided into fields whose values may be of any type, for instance, string, integer, or real.

In box 3 of Figure 10·1 there is a compound condition. The first half of the condition compares the value of the name

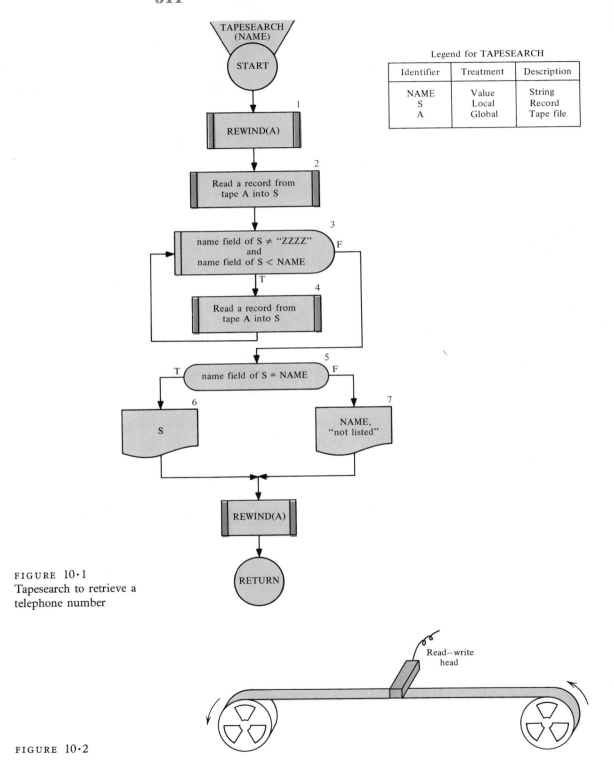

Legend for TAPESEARCH

Identifier	Treatment	Description
NAME	Value	String
S	Local	Record
A	Global	Tape file

FIGURE 10·1
Tapesearch to retrieve a
telephone number

FIGURE 10·2

field of the record variable S with "ZZZZ". When S ≠ "ZZZZ" is false, the last real record has already been processed and a dummy or sentinel record has been read in. The second half of the compound condition compares the value of the parameter NAME with the value of the name field in the record variable S. This comparison is done alphabetically, as in a dictionary. If the value of the name field of S is less than the value of NAME (and the last record has not been read in), then another record should be read in to S because the current name field value is too low.

When control reaches box 5, a test must be made to determine which of the two conditions in box 3 caused the exit from the loop. If it was the end-of-file sentinel, the name searched for was not contained in the file. Otherwise a copy of record S containing the correct name field value is output in box 6, and the tape is rewound.

10·3
Merging and updating files

The department store example in the preceding section, with its files of monthly activity, is continued here. Suppose that at the end of every day each of the two branches, the downtown store and the suburban store, sends to the store's main data processing center a file of all the sales transactions in that branch for that day. A record from either of these files will have the form

Account number	Name	Address	City code
506172	JOSEPH CONRAD	3357 OLSON BLVD	MPLS

Branch (D or S)	Department	Date	Amount of purchase
D	CAMERA	17 MAR 75	48.50

Assume that the files received from each branch have already been sorted in order of increasing account numbers and are now to be merged into one single sorted file.

An algorithm to carry out this process is seen in the MERGE flowchart of Figure 10·3. The rewind instructions of boxes 1 and 7 have already been explained in Section 10·2. Rewinding tapes before and/or after processing them is a re-

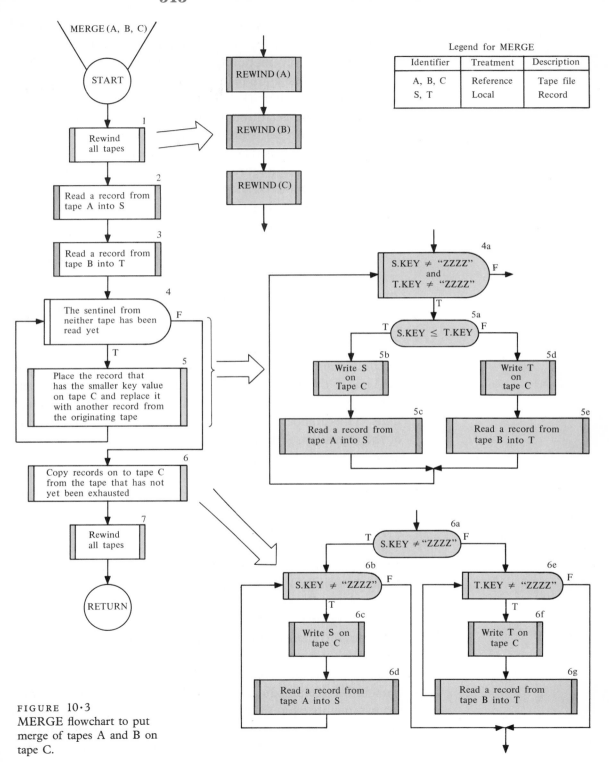

FIGURE 10·3
MERGE flowchart to put merge of tapes A and B on tape C.

quirement for any tape handling. Thus rewinding is also a necessity with tapes for any audio or video tape recorder or with films for any motion picture projector. Here the first records on each tape are read into primary storage where their key fields can be compared.

On each transit through the loop of boxes 4 and 5 the keys of the two records are compared and the record having the smaller key is copied on to tape C and replaced with another record from the same source tape. To understand these details, we employ a notational shorthand in boxes 4a and 5a; instead of writing "key field of S" and "key field of T", we write "S.KEY" and "T.KEY". We will use this type of shorthand wherever it is convenient, as in boxes 6a, 6b, and 6c. Box 6 determines which tape, if any, is not exhausted and copies the remaining records of that tape on to tape C. Boxes 6b to 6d are used if tape A is not exhausted and boxes 6e to 6g if tape B is not exhausted.

In order to get some cost estimate for executing the algorithm, note that each record on each of the files A and B is read once into primary storage and is written once onto tape C. Thus if there are L records on tape A, and M records on tape B, we will have, in all, L + M of these read-write operations. This number, L + M, serves as a measure of the cost of the algorithm. A little later in this section we will use this measure to decide whether or not the merging process is an economically viable operation.

There is a slight variant of the merge algorithm that occurs in practice frequently: merging-with-elimination-of-duplicates. Let us consider a scenario illustrating this variant.

Two computer societies, the ACM (Association for Computing Machinery) and the DPMA (Data Processing Management Association) have collaborated in preparing a special publication, "Contemporary Data Management," to be sent to everyone on the combined membership lists. Of course, the publication could be sent to all the ACM members and to all the DPMA members, but there is a great overlap in the memberships of the two societies, and it will accordingly be very economical to eliminate the duplicates. Thus we want to merge the two membership files, eliminating the duplicates to obtain a mailing list for the special publication. This process will not require a brand new flowchart; in fact it is just a minor modification of the flowchart in Figure 10·3, as seen in Figure 10·4.

Notice that box 5a has been changed from a two-way branch in Figure 10·4*a* to a three-way branch in Figure 10·4*b* because any duplicates (= exit from box 5a in Figure 10·4*b*) must be given special treatment. We see in boxes 5f, 5g, and 5h that one of the duplicate records has been entered on tape C (box 5f), while both of the duplicate records in storage have been discarded (i.e., replaced by the next records.) This guarantees that duplicate records will not appear on file C if there were no duplicates on files A and B.

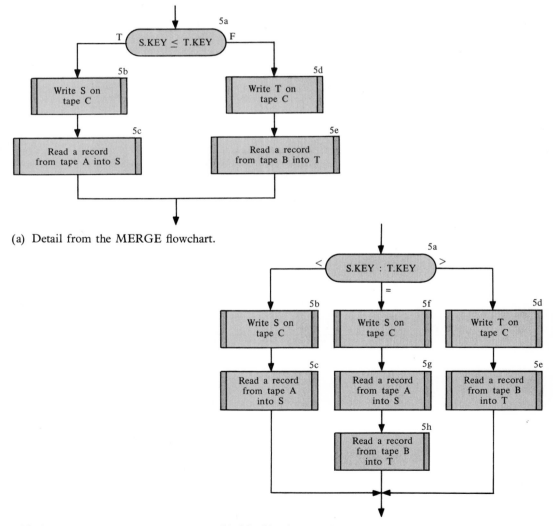

(a) Detail from the MERGE flowchart.

(b) Modification to eliminate duplicates.

FIGURE 10·4

Now let's take one more trip back to that department store. Recall that the data processor had just finished merging the daily transactions from the two stores to form a single sorted file of daily transactions. What will happen to this sorted file now? It will be used to update the records in the monthly activity file, and the mechanics of the updating process are remarkably similar to the merging process. Again we have two files, the file D of *d*aily transactions and the file M of *m*onthly activity. The records in both files are ordered (keyed) by account numbers; in other words, the files have been sorted according to increasing account numbers. The main operation in the updating process occurs when matching account numbers have been found in two records, one from each file, as illustrated in Figure 10·5.

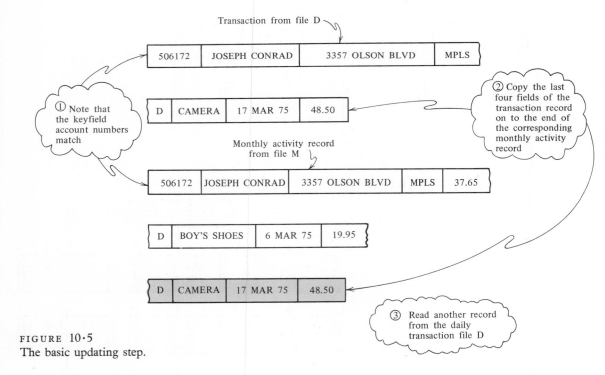

FIGURE 10·5
The basic updating step.

Next, we want to develop a flowchart fragment to carry out the updating step. We assume that when the key fields exactly match, the daily transaction record is located in S in primary storage, while the monthly activity record is located in T, also in primary storage. The flowchart fragment for carrying out the process in Figure 10·5 is seen in Figure 10·6.

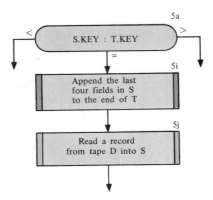

FIGURE 10·6
Flowchart fragment for the
basic updating step.

Next we wonder what to do when control emerges from the other two exits of box 5a in Figure 10·6. In the case of ">" (i.e., S.KEY > T.KEY, or key of daily record > key of monthly account) we see that there are no more transactions to be entered in the monthly activity record under examination, so we want to move this monthly activity record onto a tape of *updated* monthly activity records (tape U) and read a new record into T. Control is not expected to emerge from the < exit of box 7. Such an exit would indicate that a purchase had been made under a nonexistent account number. A message to this effect should be printed out so that this anomaly can be investigated by the credit department.

Once these features have been added to Figure 10·6, the rest of the updating flowchart (except for the names of the tapes) is essentially identical with the MERGE flowchart in Figure 10·3. In Figure 10·7 we see the UPDATE flowchart with the boxes in green where they differ from the corresponding boxes of MERGE.

The amount of processing required is the same as if the files were merged. Each record in each of the files D and M must be read into primary storage and then written onto another tape as another record. (We expect that boxes 5b and 6c will not ever be executed, but even if they are, the amount of work involved is equivalent to that in writing a record on a tape.) Thus, if d is the number of records on tape D and m is the number on tape M, then there will be d + m reading operations and d + m writing operations, so that 2(d + m) serves as a measure of the cost of the algorithm.

Now let us try to measure the advantage of having sorted data. Suppose that both files D and M were *unsorted*. In that

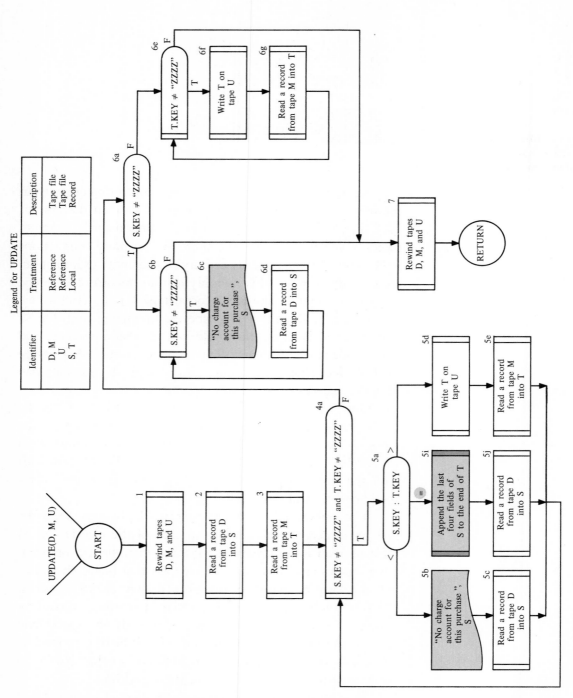

FIGURE 10·7
The UPDATE procedure.

case we would have to make an exhaustive search of file D for each record in file M, updating the monthly activity record each time a matching account number was found, and finally writing the updated monthly account record when file D was exhausted. Since d transactions are read for each monthly activity record, the number of transaction records read in all would be $d \times m$. The number of monthly activity records read would be m for a total of $(d + 1) \times m$ reading operations. The number of writing operations would be the same as in the sorted case, $d + m$, as discussed earlier in this section, so that the total number of operations, reading and writing, would be $d \times m + 2m + d$ as compared with $2 \times (d + m)$ in the sorted case.

We can best appreciate the magnitude of the difference by supplying some actual numbers. Let us suppose that the department store has 100,000 charge account customers, that about one customer in 25, that is, 4000 customers, will be shopping in the store on a given day, and that each shopper will buy 3 items on the average. Then we have $m = 100,000$ and $d = 4000 \times 3 = 12,000$ so that

$$2 \times (d + m) = 224,000$$

On the other hand,

$$d \times m + 2m + d = 1,200,212,000$$

so that the unsorted version will be more than 5000 times as expensive as the sorted version. The case that one of the files is sorted and the other unsorted is just about as bad as the completely unsorted version. Now we can appreciate the value of having sorted data.

There is one other economic question that we wish to consider before closing the book on updating. You will recall that the department store data processing center received *sorted* transaction lists from each of the two branches of the store, which were then merged before updating. The question is whether the decision to merge before updating was economically viable compared with updating the account file using the files from each of the stores separately. The comparative calculations follow.

1. *Updating without first Merging transaction tapes A and B*

    Update file M with file A $2 \times (a + m)$ operations
    Update file M with file B $2 \times (b + m)$ operations
    Total $2 \times (a + b + 2m)$ operations

2. *Updating after first Merging the transaction tapes A and B*

    Merge file A and file B into file C
    $$2 \times (a + b) \text{ operations}$$
    Update file M with file C
    $$2 \times (a + b + m) \text{ operations}$$
    Total $2 \times (2a + 2b + m)$ operations

Here we see that the comparison is rather close. In fact, if $m > a + b$, we should merge, while if $m < a + b$, we should not merge. In the case of the department store where the number of accounts is considerably greater than the number of daily purchases, merging the daily purchase tapes first does, in fact, pay off.

10·4
Ordering the records of a sequential file

Suppose the department store chooses to order the daily transactions file so that the updating of the monthly account file can be done by merging. How should the ordering of the transaction file be done? Suppose there are 10,000 transaction records on the file that is to be ordered. We had better assume that there is not enough space in primary storage to hold all these records. If there were, we could employ a procedure like our bubble sort (or possibly an even more efficient one) to rearrange the records and then write out the records on a new tape, ordered by account number. Even if the 10,000 records could fit in the primary storage of *some* computer, sooner or later we are sure to encounter a file that is too large to be sorted "internally." What methods for ordering a file of tape records are then feasible? A practical sorting method independent of the number of records to be sorted is what is needed.

We observe that the tape merging operation of the preceding section exhibited just such a property. No matter how long the files are that are to be merged, it is never necessary to hold in primary storage more than one record for each input tape. Let us take a hint from this observation and see how the repeated use of a tape merge operation can order a tape file.

We will begin by considering two unordered tape files, A and B, each containing a sequence of blocks of m records (see Figure 10·8). Furthermore, let us assume that the m records written in each block are already in order according to the value in the key field to be used for the sort.

FIGURE 10·8
Unordered tape files A and B
with records grouped in
blocks of m records each. The
records of each block are
assumed to be ordered.

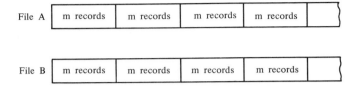

If a merge algorithm is applied to the first block in file A and the first block in file B, an ordered block of length 2m records will be produced on a file named C. (Here we assume that any duplicates that might occur are retained.) Suppose we then apply the merge algorithm to the next two blocks of file A and file B. This step yields a second ordered block of length 2m, which can also be placed on the new file named C. Applied repeatedly to successive pairs of blocks in file A and file B, the merge algorithm will produce an output tape file that contains $N/(2m)$ ordered blocks, each of length 2m, where N is the total number of records in files A and B combined.

Now we have only one half the original number of blocks, but each is twice as long, and each is *ordered*. Can the merge operation be applied again? Yes, indeed! Suppose we split off the last half of tape C as a new tape. Call it tape D. The two new tapes (C and D) will contain an equal number of ordered blocks, each of length 2m. The merge process can then be repeated on these two tapes to produce yet another new tape, this time containing ordered blocks of length 4m. Clearly, if this process is pursued to its logical conclusion, we should be able to produce a tape consisting of one ordered block that contains all the N records.

To recap our discussion to this point, suppose there are N records to be sorted with half the records on tape file A and half on tape file B. Tape A will then contain $N/(2m)$ ordered blocks of length m, as will tape B. We assume here that m and $N/(2m)$ are both integers and that N can be expressed as an integral power of two:

$$N = 2^P$$

These assumptions introduce no restriction on the method being proposed, since we can always "pad out" the tape to be sorted with "dummy" records, each having a sort key whose value is larger than any of the original records, so that the number of records (N) is exactly a power of two.

Notice that if at the outset m = 1, each block will be of length 1 and naturally the records of each block are ordered! If we then perform the merge of the tape files A and B, the successive values of m at the start of each application of the tape merge will be m = 2^0, m = 2^1, m = 2^2, m = 2^3, ..., m = 2^{P-1}, where P = $\log_2 N$. The result of the last merge operation will be one ordered tape of 2^P or N elements. It can be shown that this process, called *merge-sorting,* is, relatively speaking, a highly efficient way to order the records of a tape file.

To get an idea how the repeated merge-sorting would work in a specific example, Figure 10·9 displays the various tapes for repeated merges. For simplicity, records are represented only by numerical keys. For this illustration we use very small files (N = 8), and start with the block length m = 1.

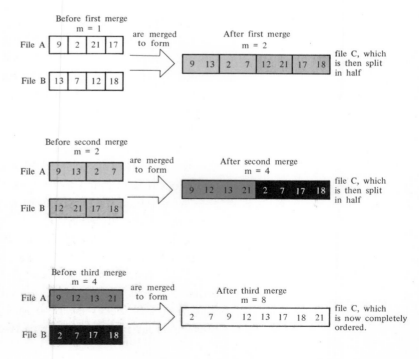

FIGURE 10·9
Showing how repeated merges double the length of the ordered blocks until a final merge yields a completely ordered file as one ordered block. Note that the individual integers shown in the files stand for complete records having the integers as their sorting keys.

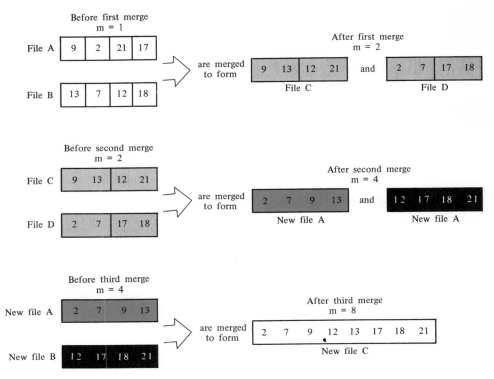

FIGURE 10·10
Showing how repeated merges may be used to order files A and B. During each tape merge, blocks of ordered records are written out alternately, first on one tape then on the next, until there are no more blocks left to write out.

Notice the apparent inefficiency introduced by first forming one output tape file C and then splitting it in half into two new ones again called file A and file B. Wouldn't it be better if each merge of two tape files yielded *two* output tapes that are all ready to be remerged? This improvement, which is illustrated in Figure 10·10 for the same pair of files, should be studied until you become convinced that the new method yields the same end result as the one originally described. Notice that in the Figure 10·10 method, records are written in blocks on the output tapes in an alternating fashion, first on one tape, then on the other. We will now follow the method of Figure 10·10 to develop a merge-sorting algorithm.

A stepwise decomposition of the tape-sorting process suggests that procedures are needed at three levels of (increasing) detail. These levels are described at the top of page 526. Figure 10·11 displays the Mergesort procedure as a sequence of decompositions. We will explain these steps in the order of their decomposition.

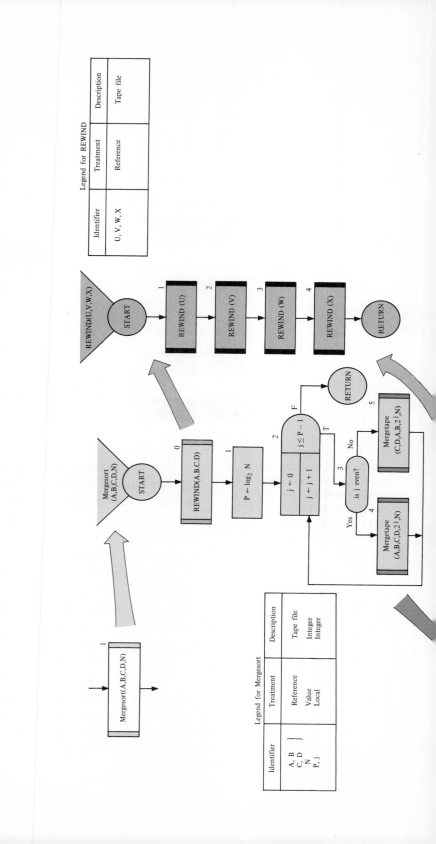

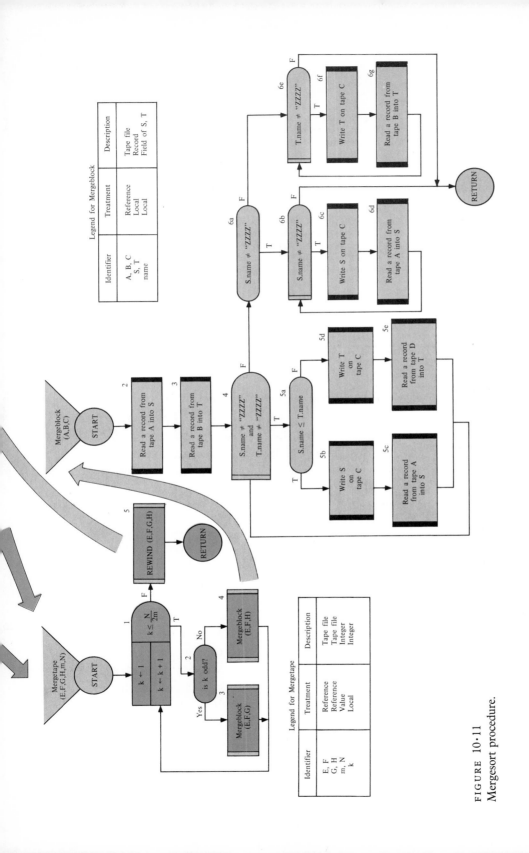

FIGURE 10·11
Mergesort procedure.

Level	Name of Procedure	Purpose	Number of Times Called
1.	Mergesort	Produce a single ordered tape file of one block by repeatedly calling Mergetape	Once from the main program
2.	Mergetape	Merge *all the pairs of ordered blocks* from a pair of tape files and output the merged blocks onto two output tapes, alternating between the two output tapes	P times for each invocation of Mergesort, where $N = 2^P$ = total number of records to be sorted
3.	Mergeblock	Merge *one pair of ordered blocks* of m records each and output the merged block of 2m records on an output tape	$\frac{N}{2m}$ times for each invocation of Mergetape

Call on Mergesort

Box 1 shows that the overall objective is to sort tape files A and B using auxiliary tapes C and D. There are a total of N records to be sorted (half on file A and half on file B). Note that A, B, C, and D, the reference parameters of Mergesort, are of type *tape file*, while N is a value parameter of type integer. The first step of Mergesort rewinds all tapes by a call to a procedure REWIND.

Call on Mergetape

The main structure of Mergesort is an iterative loop taken P times (where $P = \log_2 N$). Mergetape is called alternately first at box 4, then at box 5 during this iteration, the purpose being to alternate the names for the input and output files. To begin with (box 4 of Mergesort), A and B are named as the input files and C and D are named as the output files. The next call on Mergetape will take place when j is odd at box 5 of Mergesort. Here C and D are designated as the input files, while A and B are specified as the output files. The next call on Mergetape will again be at box 4 of Mergesort, and so forth.

Note that to minimize the confusion with the parameters of Mergesort, the parameters of Mergetape are E and F for the input file names and G and H for the output file names. The call-by-value parameter m is the length of the blocks on the input file, and the call-by-value parameter N is the total number of records. Just before returning to its caller, Mergetape calls REWIND to rewind all tapes.

Call on Mergeblock

The structure of Mergetape is an iterative loop taken N / 2m times (which is the number of blocks on each input tape file). In the body of the loop, calls on Mergeblock are made alternately, first at box 3, then at box 4, the purpose being to alternate the names of the output file, G then H, on which the merged block of records is to be written. The names of the input files, of course, do not change during the alternate calls on Mergeblock. Notice, too, that we already have from the preceding section (Figure 10·3) a perfectly satisfactory algorithm for merging record blocks, provided we eliminate the steps of rewinding tapes.

EXERCISES 10·4

1. The Mergesort algorithm of Figure 10·11 will produce a single-ordered output file on one of the tapes A, B, C, or D. On which tape will the output file be found and under what circumstance?

2. If the work done by the Mergesort algorithm of Figure 10·11 is measured by the total number of records read from tape files during its execution, what is that number, if the total number of records to be sorted by Mergesort is N?

3. *Project.* The merge-sort algorithm is well adapted to the situation in which the lists to be sorted are too long to be held in the main storage of a computer. Since, at any stage, only one element from each list need be available for comparison in the main storage, the rest of the list elements can be kept on some other storage medium (most commonly, magnetic tape).

   In this exercise you are to *simulate* the behavior of magnetic tape units (whether or not your computer has such storage) so that the merge-sort algorithm can operate as though tape units were available.

   Magnetic tape is a linear storage medium. File elements are recorded sequentially. Reading from the tape transfers an element from the tape to storage and advances the tape so that the next element in sequence is positioned to be read. Writing on the tape transfers an element from storage to the tape and advances the tape so that it is positioned to receive the next element. A special end-of-tape mark (we suggest you use an asterisk) is written after the last element on a tape and, when read, identifies the end of the used part of the tape. Most magnetic tape units can be read from and written on only while moving in the "forward" direction. Therefore, when a tape is completely used (either read or written), an instruction is given to rewind the tape to its starting position.

To simulate this behavior, represent each tape by a list (which can be kept in storage). Prepare procedures RTAPE and WTAPE to simulate reading and writing of an element from and to a tape. Prepare other procedures WEOT and REWIND to write an end-of-tape mark and to reposition a tape at its start. The RTAPE procedure should include a test for an end-of-tape mark, using one of its parameters as a switch to signal the calling procedure when this mark has been sensed.

After you have defined the necessary tape procedures, modify the Mergesort algorithm (Figure 10·11) to call on these procedures and, if feasible, test the new program on an actual computer.

10·5 Representation of variable-length records for internal sorting

Files with a moderate number of records can be kept in addressable storage and, while there, such files may be processed in various ways. In this section we consider some ways that such "small" files may be structured in storage for internal sorting. One of the characteristics of real-life files is that records typically vary in length. To handle this problem, *access list* methods are quite useful. These will be explained shortly. Even if the records do not vary in length, they usually have at least one field other than the key field.

The best internal sort method studied so far was the bubble sort (Figure 5·8). Another sort of some interest, known as the *radix* sort, is examined in the exercises (Set A of this section). Both the bubble sort and the radix sort can be adapted to deal with records having more than one (the key) field.

One way to represent multifield records is to store the fields of each record as corresponding elements in separate but associated lists. For example, the list A could contain only the key field and lists B, C, and so forth could contain the other fields. Thus the ith record would consist of the values of A_i, B_i, C_i, and so forth. Then, when the jth pair of keys is found to be out of order, it is necessary not only to interchange A_j and A_{j+1} but also B_j and B_{j+1}, C_j and C_{j+1}, and so forth. A study of this approach is also left as an exercise.

In many practical applications the key field is fairly long, for example, the name field in a telephone directory. Hence, when sorting alphabetic information like names, in a word-organized machine such as SAMOS, the key field may span several words. Coding comparisons of multiword fields in such machines can be a nuisance at the machine language level and even at higher language levels. Probably the most obvious technique for dealing with multiword key fields is to detail the comparison step of the sorting algorithm so that if comparison of the most significant part of the key field produces an equality, then a comparison of the next most significant portion of the key field will be made, and so forth. We leave as another exercise the details of specifying such a scheme. Note, however, that with a bit-organized machine such as BITOS, a key field of any length can be defined and treated as a unit. Thus a BITOS-like machine is well adapted to sorting or merging records on alphabetic key fields.

EXERCISES 10·5, SET A

1. *Radix sorting* is a way of dealing with multiword key fields. The idea is to first apply a sorting algorithm to the entire file using the least significant word (or character) of the key field as the search key. This guarantees that records that differ only in the least significant word will not only become ordered but will also remain ordered. Next, reapply the sorting algorithm to sort the entire file on the next most significant word (or character) of the key field and continue until the file has been sorted on all words of the key field. Try out this scheme by a purely manual process using, say, a small group of three-digit numbers, each written on a separate slip of paper.

For example, the following table shows one group of 16 three-digit integers in four states: (a) original ordering; (b) after sorting on the units position; (c) after sorting on the "10's" position; and (d) after sorting on the "hundreds" position.

a	b	c	d
224	341	801	129
325	801	313	224
243	422	416	243
873	452	617	313
341	792	917	325
801	243	817	341
416	873	422	416
617	313	224	422
129	224	325	429
917	325	129	452
429	416	429	617
422	617	341	792
452	917	243	801
792	817	452	817
313	129	873	873
817	429	792	917

Your job is to prepare flowcharts for a modified bubble sort procedure and its activating program to carry out a radix sort on a list of 6-character strings.

2. Modify the flowchart for the bubble sort (Figure 9·22) so that three lists A, B, and C are input, each having n elements. These lists are to be considered as though collectively they represent an n-record file, where fields of the kth record are A_k, B_k, and C_k. Your new algorithm should sort the file using elements of list A as the key field.

3. Modify the flowchart for the bubble sort (Figure 9·22) so as to be able to sort a file for a telephone directory on the name field. Assume that on a SAMOS-like machine the kth name field requires four words of storage and hence is divided into four subfields, for example, $Name_{k,1}$, $Name_{k,2}$, $Name_{k,3}$, and $Name_{k,4}$.

Access Lists

Figure 10·12 shows a collection of records stored as a table, each row being one record and each column entry of a row

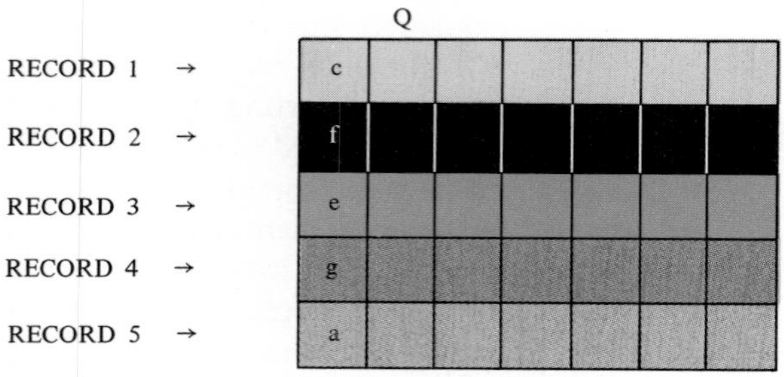

Q

RECORD 1 →
RECORD 2 →
RECORD 3 →
RECORD 4 →
RECORD 5 →

FIGURE 10·12

being a field. Suppose we wish to rearrange the rows of this table so that they are in order according to a key field, which happens to be the first entry in this case. Is it necessary to relocate whole rows? That could amount to a lot of (computer) work. One approach might be to rearrange only the key field, as in Figure 10·13. But then each sorted item loses its connection with the rest of the record of which it is a part.

FIGURE 10·13

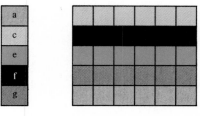

Alternatively we could start with an ordered set of pointers that are in one-one correspondence with the records, including their keys (Figure 10·14). Then we could reorder the pointers

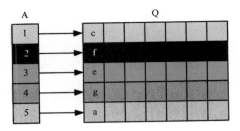

FIGURE 10·14

based on the contents of the respective keys (Figure 10·15). Note that records remain in fixed locations. The pointers are moved, but the connection between each pointer and its corresponding record is preserved. So merely by rearranging pointers, we can access records of a file in any desired order.

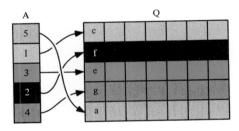

FIGURE 10·15

In Figures 10·14 and 10·15 the pointers belong to a list A called an *access list*. Each pointer is nothing more than an index to the corresponding row of the Q array that holds the corresponding record. Figure 10·15 shows the access list whose elements have been "sorted" based on the contents of the keys. The basic comparison step for such a sorting algorithm (for ascending order) is

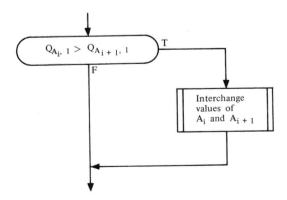

If, after completing the sort depicted in Figure 10·15, we now

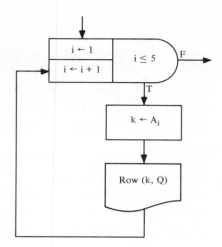

wish to print the five records in sorted order, the strategy shown in Figure 10·16 can be used.

For simplicity we have been assuming that all the records have the same length, whereas in actual applications that is rarely the case. A file whose records vary in size can be thought of as a *jagged array,* for example, R in Figure 10·17. For-

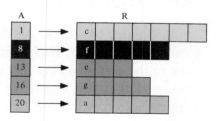

tunately, even when the records differ in length, we can still use the idea of an access list provided the records of such a jagged array are stored one following the other as a single list so that individual record elements can be accessed using a single subscript instead of a pair of subscripts. (Recall that this approach was used to represent the connection table for the map of Europe in Figure 7·6.) If this linear form is used then, as suggested in Figure 10·17, each pointer of the access list will be a linear index of a list instead of a row index of an array. Thus the value of the ith element in the access list is an index into the list to identify the first element of the ith record. For example, since the first two records of R (in Figure 10·17) have 7 and 5 elements, respectively, the third record must begin at index position 13. Hence $A_3 = 13$.

Notice that the length of each record (except the last) is easily calculated as the difference between adjacent access list values. However, if the access list is rearranged as was done in Figure 10·15, the ability to calculate this useful information is lost. So it is helpful to include the length of the record in each entry of the access list, as shown in Figure 10·18. (Note that now the access list amounts to a two-column array.)

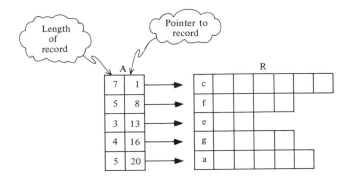

FIGURE 10·18
Access list including record-length values.

If the access list is rearranged, the length of each record must now be carried along with the pointer (see Figure 10·19).

To print the five records in sorted order, we can now use the strategy of Figure 10·20.

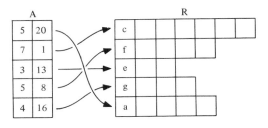

FIGURE 10·19
A sorted jagged array.

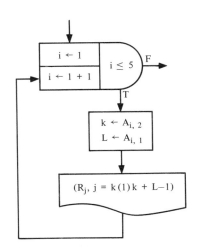

FIGURE 10·20
Printing a jagged array.

If each record of the file is thought of as a character string, then an attractive way to think of the file in directly addressable storage is as a single (very long) string, formed by concatenating the individual records (strings). This view is shown in

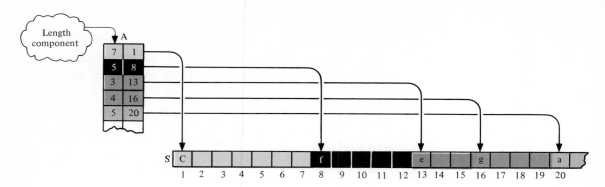

FIGURE 10·21
Picturing a file of records as a
string.

Figure 10·21. Here the length component of each access list element now refers to the number of *characters* in the record and not to the number of *words*.

We now have the basic ideas for using an access list to sort records of variable length. One top-level view of the problem is shown in Figure 10·22.

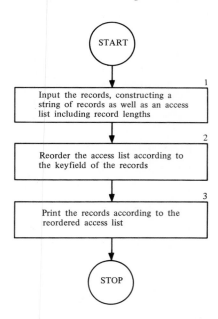

FIGURE 10·22
A first stage analysis.

The basic strategy for completing box 3 has already been shown in Figure 10·20. Box 2 can be detailed by straight forward modifications of one of the sorting algorithms (see Exercises 10·5, Set B).

A strategy for box 1 of Figure 10·22 is shown in Figure 10·23. We treat each record as a string and utilize the string operations for length and concatenation that were introduced

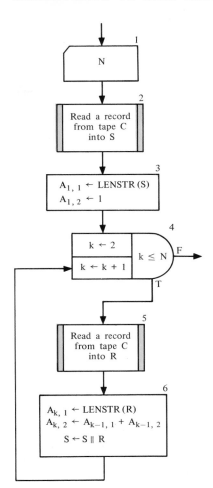

Legend

Identifier	Description
C	Tape file
S, R	String record
N, k	Integer

FIGURE 10·23
Input of a file of
variable-length records.

in Chapter 2. Recall that, given the name of the string, the length function LENSTR counts the elements in the string and returns that value. We have assumed that the number of records, N, which is at least one, is known beforehand, so the records can be counted as they are read into directly addressable storage. Alternatively, the reading can be controlled by a sentinel at the end of the file. Magnetic tape input devices are designed to recognize special marks such as the end-of-file mark. An input step that reads a tape record can be programmed to branch (conditionally) to a designated instruction when an end-of-file mark is recognized by the tape reading device.

To this point we have assumed that the records of a file are held in directly addressable storage if they are to be sorted without moving them. Now suppose, instead, this file is held on random-access disk storage. Is it possible to sort such a file and print out the records in sorted order by keeping in main storage only the access list itself? The answer is *yes,* if each pointer of the access list now refers to the *disk address* of the corresponding record. It would appear, however, that each reference to the key field of a record requires input of the whole record so, even though it is not necessary to interchange the records on the disk, it seems necessary to input a record whenever it is necessary to examine its key field. A compromise approach might be feasible, however, in which the keys are duplicated and made part of the access list. Thus each element of the access list could hold an address of a record on disk, the length of that record, and a copy of the key field for that record. We leave to the reader the challenge of exploring the details of a scheme to sort records stored on disk, applying the ideas developed in this section.

EXERCISES 10·5,
SET B

1. Develop a complete flowchart for sorting variable-length records using the bubble sort algorithm and an access list.

2. Shown below is an array B partially filled with alphabetic information, one character per element. Array elements with no character shown are to be considered "empty." We have described a technique by which the information in the array B could be stored rowwise in a list, say LIST, using an auxiliary access list AL to "point" to the beginning of each name in LIST. The following questions relate to this alternate method of sorting the information. (It may be helpful to fill in the value of LIST and AL in the diagram.)

W	I	L	L		
J	I	M	□	L	E	E
A	L	F	R	E	D	
R	O	Y			
M	A	C	K		

LIST

AL

(a) If the access list method of storage is used, the value of AL_3 is (choose one):

   (1) 18
   (2) 5
   (3) 15
   (4) 12
   (5) None of the above

Suppose the first character of each record (consider each row of the original array to be a record) is used as a key field and that the records are to be sorted into alphabetical order on the basis of this field.

(b) Show the contents of AL after the sort is completed.

(c) Show the final contents of LIST after the sort is completed.

(d) Of what use would a sixth element of AL be?

3. This question relates to the table of stock market data shown below. The table contains the code names and quarterly prices of four stocks. The code names, which are "XYZ", "AB", "S", and "CDQ", are stored one character per table element, but prices are stored as one complete price per table element. After each price is a special "end marker", the character "*".

X	Y	Z	72	75	74	80	*	
A	B	50	55	60	70	*		
S	95	80	85	63	*			
C	D	Q	25	28	30	30	*	

(a) Suppose that this table is to be stored as a single list, LIST, using an access list to identify the beginning of each stock record within LIST. (Code names will be stored one character per list element.) Note that the presence of an end marker in each record (the last one, in particular) may eliminate the need for a fifth access list element. What would be the contents of the access list? (Choose one.)

1. | 1 | 9 | 17 | 24 |

2. | 1 | 2 | 3 | 4 |

3. | 1 | 9 | 16 | 22 |

4. | X | A | S | C |

5. | 3 | 11 | 17 | 25 |

(b) Suppose that the access list is called AL, and that the list LN holds the lengths of the names of the stocks, that is, LN is

| 3 | 2 | 1 | 3 |

Which of the following is a correct expression for the *first* price of the fourth stock (CDQ)?

(1) $LIST_{AL_4}$

(2) $LIST_{AL_4 + LN_4}$

(3) $LIST_{AL_{LN_4}}$

(4) $LIST_{AL_4 + LN_4 - 1}$

(5) $AL_{22 + LN_4}$

(c) Suppose the stocks are sorted into increasing order based on the *first* price given for each stock, and suppose further that this sort is accomplished by rearranging the access list instead of by moving information in LIST. Construct the resulting access list.

4. Shown below is an incomplete flowchart that is designed to input character strings from N data cards, store them in a list called L, and construct an access list AL such that AL_K is a pointer to the leftmost nonblank character from the Kth card. Note the following

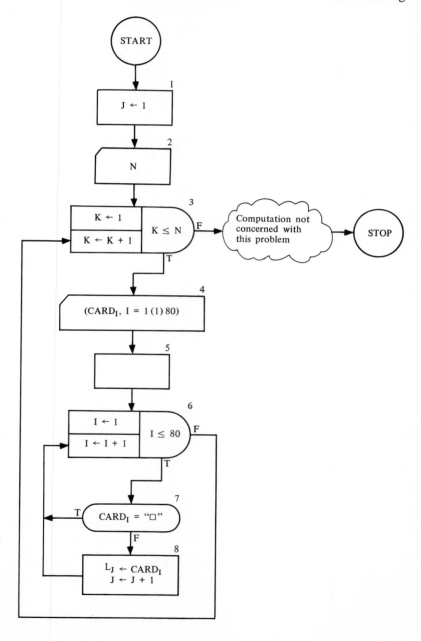

details: the second and all succeeding data cards are read so that the 80 characters of a card are temporarily assigned to corresponding elements of a list called CARD. Nonblank characters from the list CARD are then copied into the list L.

(a) Box 5 should be completed to read (choose one):

(1) $AL_K \leftarrow AL_{K-1} + 1$
(2) $AL_K \leftarrow K$
(3) $AL_K \leftarrow J$
(4) $AL_K \leftarrow K + 1$
(5) $AL_J \leftarrow J + 1$

(b) Suppose the available data cards contain the information shown on the following lines, respectively,

```
4
MIGHTY□□ .................................□□
COU□G□AR□S ...............................□□
BEA□□□T□□ ................................□□
S□T□ATE□□ ................................□□
```

(where "......." stands for blank columns). Then, after the *false* exit from box 3 has been taken, the contents of AL would be (choose one):

(1) 1, 7, 17, 23, 31
(2) 1, 81, 161, 241
(3) 1, 7, 14, 18
(4) 1, 2, 3, 4
(5) 1, 6, 13, 17

10·6 Table management with hashing

In our earlier approach to the table lookup problem there was the tacit assumption that the contents of the table are not altered very often, and that between changes the table is searched for information rather frequently. The alphabetically ordered telephone directory is a good example. The high cost of putting such a large table in order is justified because it will be used many times in its ordered form. However, it is easy to think of a counterexample where the "tables are turned" (pun intended), that is, where there is a high frequency of change in the contents of a table relative to the number of times the table is needed between table changes.

Consider the problem of maintaining an up-to-date directory of guests in a fairly large metropolitan hotel. During some rush hours, hundreds of people may check in or out every hour. For each check-in a record must be inserted in the directory and for each check-out the corresponding record must be found and removed. Many guests may never receive a single telephone call during their stay, but a few guests may receive several calls, especially during the period immediately before and after check-in or check-out. Requests such as "Has John Bennett of Seattle registered yet?", "What is John Bennett's room number?", "Please connect me with John Bennett.", or "Is John Bennett still registered with you?" are typical.

In the face of the high rate of registration and check-out, the problem of keeping a directory of the registered guests up to date, say in alphabetical order, so that the hotel operator can quickly and accurately respond to such requests, seems formidable.

No matter how the solution to this problem is achieved, whether by manual means alone or partly with computer assistance, a careful algorithm design is needed. You might like to think out a solution and then compare it with actual manual or computer practice in a hotel in your vicinity. Since our interest in the hotel problem is primarily to devise a computer approach to problems of this type, we will deal only with computer issues.

A simple-minded "brute force" (computer table lookup) search solution, always maintaining the hotel directory in alphabetical order, will probably prove unsatisfactory. It may take too much computer time to fix up the directory to reflect every new check-in and check-out. One reason why insertion can be so time consuming is that the steps required include not only finding the right spot for the insertion (in the alphabetically ordered list) but also making room for the new record by "shifting down" all subsequent records by the space of one record. (On the average the records of half the registered guests will be pushed down for each new registration). Deletion requires a similar number of operations to locate and remove an entry and to "push up" the rest of the records to close the gap. Even if good use is made of access lists, as discussed in the preceding section, and perhaps with the actual records kept on disk storage, it is still necessary to shift the access list elements up or down. So there may still be a lot of shifting to be done.

Taking stock, in a hand-operated card file it is easy to insert or remove a card, but within a computer these operations may not be so simple. Moreover, if the computer is being time-shared with other hotel data processing operations, it could well take many seconds, perhaps a full minute, to insert a new entry in the already ordered list, preserving alphabetical order in the process. If, during one of these insertion operations, the hotel operator attempts to enter a request for John Bennett's phone number on his computer console and if he finds the computer is busy, he may be forced to say to the caller, "Just a minute, please" and put the caller "on hold" for up to one full minute. With guests checking in or out at more than one a minute (in a hotel that has several desk clerks on duty), it would be out of the question to carry out the time-consuming insertion and deletion operations after each transaction (registration or check-out) or even after each group of 5 or 10 transactions. There would still be occasions in the day when anyone "asking the computer" for a guest's phone number would have to be told to wait what might be an intolerable length of time for a reply.

What is needed is a maintenance system for the directory such that the computer time used to insert or delete an entry in the stored directory is short, and such that the time required to search for it is also short. If the cost of maintaining the list in *alphabetical* order is prohibitive, do there exist other feasible ways of handling the list?

If no order is maintained in the stored directory, it seems as though every search would have to be *exhaustive!* If so, the *search* time may then become prohibitive. For example, suppose it takes quite a few seconds to perform one search of the directory, but only one or two seconds to insert or delete an entry. Then a bottleneck may develop at the telephone switchboard during hours when incoming calls are at their peak rate.

There are two reasons why this bottleneck is not always solved by simply saying "just get a faster computer."

1. Higher-speed computers cost more money and the additional cost may not be justified economically. It may be cheaper to revert to a manual method.

2. Even if speed is not a limiting factor in the hotel example, there must exist some case in which speed (and hence cost) *will* be a limiting factor if a much larger table must be maintained with similar relative frequencies for making entries, deleting them, and searching for them.

Fortunately, solutions to this type of problem *do* exist. The *hashing technique,* described below, is one of several known table management methods that are applicable to this problem. These solutions have the nice property that they are workable and economical over a wide range of computer speeds and table sizes. A basic idea of the hashing technique is that the location or *index* of a table entry is *computed* instead of searched for. The computation is based on the value of the *search key* of the entry. Thus the key for John Bennett's entry in the hotel example is "John Bennett." In the *search method* of locating this entry we kept looking through the directory until we found an entry whose name field contained "John Bennett," but in the *hashing method,* we take the value "John Bennett" and *hash it,* or map it, with the aid of a special hashing function, into a table index. The same hashing computation is always performed to locate the position of John Bennett's entry, whether in a procedure to create the table entry, to delete it, or to "look" for it in the table.

A hash function maps a string of characters (a value), such as a guest's name, into a relatively narrow range of the integers. For example, if the hotel directory can take 1000 entries, then a hash function should map from the domain of all possible guest names into the integer range 0 to 999. The ideal hashing function would map each guest name into a different integer from 0 to 999. As we will see, this ideal rarely, if ever, is achieved.

In the ideal case, the cost of finding the correct place to insert an entry, to delete it, or to read its contents reduces to executing a call on the hashing function, for example,

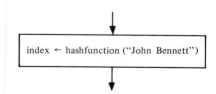

Most hashing functions are simple and require only a moderate amount of computation. It is easy to invent hashing functions. One, for example, named hash, is sketched in Figure 10·24. This function does the following:

1. Selects the even-indexed characters of a given name and

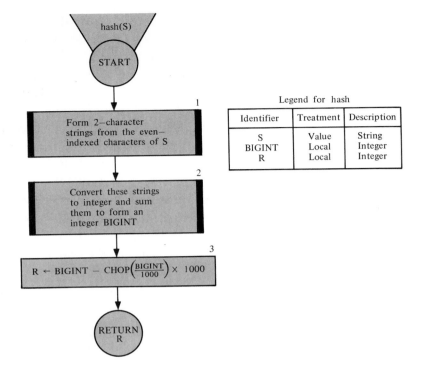

FIGURE 10·24
A possible hashing function for the hotel directory problem.

groups them two by two. For example the even-indexed characters of "John□Bennett" are "O", "N", "B", "N", "E", "T". Paired off, we get "ON", "BN", and "ET". (In case there are an odd number of selected characters the last one would be paired with "□".)

2.   Converts the bit string used to code each of these character pairs into a binary integer and sums these integers. (In SAMOS, e.g., each pair of characters converts to a 12-bit binary integer.)

3.   The remainder produced by dividing the integer computed in step 2 by 1000 is the result returned by this hashing function. It is an integer in the desired range from 0 to 999 inclusive.

Functions such as hash often map from a *huge* domain to a very *small* range. Thus, if names may be up to 32 characters in length and if each character in the name is drawn from a 26-character alphabet, then the domain of hash is 26^{32}. Wow! With a range of only 1000, the function maps many names to each index. This means that it will be frequent instead of rare for several guest names to map to the same directory index.

Such many-to-one occurrences are called "collisions." Collisions can be expected to occur even if there are more positions or *slots* in the table than actual entries, for example, even if there are many fewer than 1000 registered guests.

Only one entry can occupy one slot of the directory at any given time, so only one of the entries involved in a collision can be placed exactly at its *home position,* that is, in the slot computed by the hash function. Fortunately, appropriate positions for the other colliding entries can be computed easily, so that the hash method works well even though a table may be composed of many groups of colliding entries. We will now develop the details to show how all this works.

A hashed table or directory that is not completely filled will have its entries scattered, as you can see in Figure 10·25.

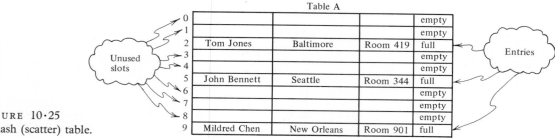

FIGURE 10·25
A hash (scatter) table.

Any algorithm that accesses a hash table entry must be able to determine (1) whether or not the accessed slot of the table contains an entry, and (2) if so, what is the identifier that goes with that entry. Thus each hash table slot should contain a *use* field to denote whether the slot is in use as an entry or not in use. For our examples we will use the indicator "empty" to denote *not in use* and "full" to denote *in use.*

If a new entry is to be made for Mary Heath and this entry collides with, say, that of John Bennett, then one approach for handling this collision is to select the first empty slot below that of John Bennett for the Mary Heath entry. Later, when looking for Mary Heath's entry, application of the hash function will lead us to examine slot 5 first. Then, if a match on the name leads to a discovery that this slot does not contain Mary Heath's entry, we would continue searching successive slots until Mary Heath's entry is found. In the example shown, a test of the very next slot (6) would turn up the desired entry. However, as a hash table becomes more full, empty slots for Mary Heath's entry become more rare and might be far away (in terms of sequential search) from the slot indicated by the hash function.

Other methods may be used for the management of hash table slots. We will use the technique (useful in many other data processing situations) of *linked lists* or *chains*. A chain, as mentioned in Chapter 4, is a sequence of entries each containing a link or pointer to the next entry of the chain.

If we want to use linked lists, a link field must be added to each entry in the directory, as suggested in Figure 10·26, which shows how a new entry for Mary Heath is linked to a colliding entry for John Bennett. The directory table, to be

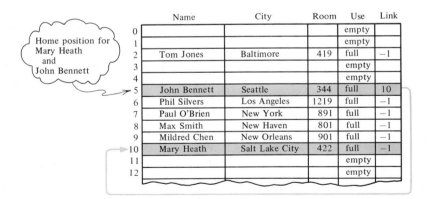

FIGURE 10·26a
The table prior to making an entry for Mary Heath, whose home position is slot 5.

	Name	City	Room	Use	Link
0				empty	
1				empty	
2	Tom Jones	Baltimore	419	full	−1
3				empty	
4				empty	
5	John Bennett	Seattle	344	full	−1
6	Phil Silvers	Los Angeles	1219	full	−1
7	Paul O'Brien	New York	891	full	−1
8	Max Smith	New Haven	801	full	−1
9	Mildred Chen	New Orleans	901	full	−1
10				empty	
11				empty	
12					

Home position for John Bennett

FIGURE 10·26b
The table after creating the entry for Mary Heath at slot 10 and linking that entry to the one for John Bennett.

	Name	City	Room	Use	Link
0				empty	
1				empty	
2	Tom Jones	Baltimore	419	full	−1
3				empty	
4				empty	
5	John Bennett	Seattle	344	full	10
6	Phil Silvers	Los Angeles	1219	full	−1
7	Paul O'Brien	New York	891	full	−1
8	Max Smith	New Haven	801	full	−1
9	Mildred Chen	New Orleans	901	full	−1
10	Mary Heath	Salt Lake City	422	full	−1
11				empty	
12				empty	

Home position for Mary Heath and John Bennett

called A, becomes an array of n rows. Each row is an entry having five columns, one for each of five parts or *fields:*

1. Name   (name of the hotel guest)   (string)

2. City   (home town of the guest)   (string)

3. Room   (room number of the guest)   (string)

4. Use   (use indicator for this slot   (string)
             "full" or "empty")

5. Link   (index of the next slot in the chain. A   (integer)
             negative link value, e.g., -1,
             denotes the tail element of the
             chain)

To manage and use this table, three procedures must be developed, *Insert, Lookup,* and *Delete.* In simple terms the job of *Insert* is to place an entry in the table, given a name, hometown, and room number for a guest. The job of *Lookup* is to find and report the contents of the entry, given the name of the guest, and the job of *Delete* is to delete the table entry for a guest, given his name. In the absence of collisions, the entry involved in all three cases will be located at the home position for the given guest name.

But let us take a second look at each of these operations, bearing in mind that chains of entries may exist in the table at the time an insertion, lookup, or deletion operation is to be performed.

If, when we attempt to insert an entry at its home position, that slot is found to be empty by a check of the use indicator (column 4), there is, of course, no problem. But what if there is already an entry positioned in this slot? In fact, there are two possible classifications for an entry already placed in the home position. We must know to which classification this particular entry belongs before we can take the appropriate action to complete the insertion operation.

Classification 1. Does the entry at the home position belong to the same "collision family" as the entry we wish to insert? We can answer this question affirmatively simply by hashing the value in the name field of this home position and finding that the result of this hashing is identical with the index of the home position.

Classification 2. Is the entry at the home position a *foreigner,* that is, does it belong to *another* collision family? If so, it is already chained on a list to all the elements representing that family, and the head of that list is located elsewhere in the table (at *its* home position). We can always recognize a foreigner because its name field hashes to some other slot of the table.

After Insert determines to which classification the entry at the home position belongs, what action should be taken then? If the home position entry belongs to classification 1, the new entry is colliding with a member of its own collision family and, in particular, is colliding with the "head" of that family. It is only necessary to find an empty slot, fill it with the information for the new entry, and attach or link that entry to the chain. Figure 10·27 shows how this insertion can be done for Mary Thompson, whose home position we will assume is slot 5. The chain starting at slot 5 is searched to its tail, and the new entry for Mary Thompson is linked to the end of this chain. The entry for Mary Thompson becomes the new tail element of the chain (all of whose members are assumed to hash to slot 5).

If the home position entry belongs to classification 2, then the foreigner entry must be moved to some unused slot so a new chain can be started at this home position. The new slot found for the foreigner must be linked into its chain as before. Let us look at an actual example. Suppose the table's condition is as found in Figure 10·27, at which point we wish to insert

	Name	City	Room	Use	Link
0				empty	
1				empty	
2	Tom Jones	Baltimore	419	full	−1
3				empty	
4				empty	
5	John Bennett	Seattle	344	full	10
6	Phil Silvers	Los Angeles	1219	full	−1
7	Paul O'Brien	New York	891	full	−1
8	Max Smith	New Haven	801	full	−1
9	Mildred Chen	New Orleans	901	full	−1
10	Mary Heath	Salt Lake City	422	full	11
11	Mary Thompson	Denver	1801	full	−1
12				empty	

FIGURE 10·27

an entry for Tom James, whose computed home position is slot 10. This slot is occupied by the entry for Mary Heath, a member of the "slot 5 family" and hence a foreigner at slot 10. Figure 10·28 shows that the entry for Mary Heath has been moved to slot 12, the first empty slot that follows slot 10. Moreover, slot 10 has been reused for Tom James. Notice that the chain beginning with John Bennett's entry is preserved by adjusting the link to the new Mary Heath entry in the link

	Name	City	Room	Use	Link
0					
1					
2	Tom Jones	Baltimore	419	full	−1
3				empty	
4				empty	
5	John Bennett	Seattle	344	full	12
6	Phil Silvers	Los Angeles	1219	full	−1
7	Paul O'Brien	New York	891	full	−1
8	Max Smith	New Haven	801	full	−1
9	Mildred Chen	New Orleans	901	full	−1
10	Tom James	Bell Isle	1722	full	−1
11	Mary Thompson	Denver	1801	full	−1
12	Mary Heath	Salt Lake City	422	full	11

FIGURE 10·28

field of Mary Heath's predecessor. In this case that means adjusting the link field of the John Bennett entry.

Although we now have a working understanding of how to handle each type of collision when making an insertion, some readers will have noticed that the search for an empty slot can become quite long if full slots bunch up "below" the head of a collision chain as they have in our examples. Later we will see that there is an easy way to guarantee that the job of locating an empty slot is always a trivial one (no searching required). For now, we will simply ignore this problem in the interest of completing the picture of what the three procedures Insert, Lookup, and Delete must do and how they may be flowcharted.

Lookup has the job of deciding whether the wanted entry is in the table and either reporting on the contents of that entry, if found, or reporting failure. This procedure must examine the home position of its argument and, on the basis of the contents of this home position, decide among three possibilities (just as in the case of Insert). If the home position is empty, the wanted entry cannot possibly be present in the table, so failure must be reported. If the home position is full, but has a foreigner entry, again the wanted entry cannot possibly be present. Only if the home position contains the head element of a collision chain for the Lookup argument is the matter worth pursuing. At this point the chain beginning at the home position is searched for an entry whose name field matches the Lookup argument. If a match is found, the Lookup procedure then can assign the contents of the matching entry to reference parameters and return successfully; otherwise, if the entire chain is searched without success, the Lookup operation ends in failure.

The several failure cases of Lookup can be illustrated by referring to Figure 10·28 and considering several possible home positions for Bill Smith while looking up his room number.

1.   If the home position is slot 3, we have a failure because the slot is empty.

2.   If the home position is slot 11, we have a failure because the entry at slot 11 is a foreigner. (The name field, by previous assumption, hashes to slot 5 and not to slot 11.)

3.   If the home position is slot 2, we again have a failure because the chain that begins (and also ends) at slot 2 does not have a single entry whose name field matches "Bill Smith."

To delete an entry, the *Delete* procedure must first locate that entry, so this operation must be very similar to Lookup. Once the wanted entry is found, it can be deleted from the chain on which it is found by, for example, moving its successor to the slot occupied by the one to be deleted and freeing the slot of the successor element. The delete procedure need return only a report of success or failure. It is either able to find the entry and then delete it, or it fails to find it and hence fails to accomplish its purpose.

Figure 10·29 illustrates the successful action of Delete for two of the entries pictured in Figure 10·28. The new figure shows the effect of deleting the entry for Max Smith and then deleting the entry for John Bennett. Notice that the entry for

FIGURE 10·29
The table after deleting entries for Max Smith (slot 8) and John Bennett (slot 5). The slot 5 entry has been overwritten with a copy of the entry at slot 12, which was the successor element of the John Bennett entry.

Table A

	Name	City	Room	Use	Link
0				empty	
1				empty	
2	Tom Jones	Baltimore	419	full	−1
3				empty	
4				empty	
5	Mary Heath	Salt Lake City	422	full	11
6	Phil Silvers	Los Angeles	1219	full	−1
7	Paul O'Brien	New York	891	full	−1
8	Max Smith	New Haven	801	empty	−1
9	Mildred Chen	New Orleans	901	full	−1
10	Tom James	Bell Isle	1722	full	−1
11	Mary Thompson	Denver	1801	full	−1
12	Mary Heath	Salt Lake City	422	empty	11

Max Smith, whose home position is slot 8, has no successor. Deletion of this entry simply amounts to marking that entry *empty*. On the other hand, deletion of the John Bennett entry, which *has* a successor, is accomplished by copying the successor element (the entry for Mary Heath) into the John Bennett slot and marking the old Mary Heath slot 12 as *empty*. Finally, consider what action would be needed to remove the entry for Mary Thompson at slot 11 under the conditions shown in Figure 10·29. This entry has no successor, but *does* have a predecessor entry (that of Mary Heath at slot 5). To delete the Mary Thompson entry, what type of change in the table is needed that was not needed in deleting the Max Smith entry?

We are now ready to specify the implementation of our table management system by presenting and discussing a set of flowcharts that represent all the operations just explained. Figure 10·30 shows the skeleton structure common to all

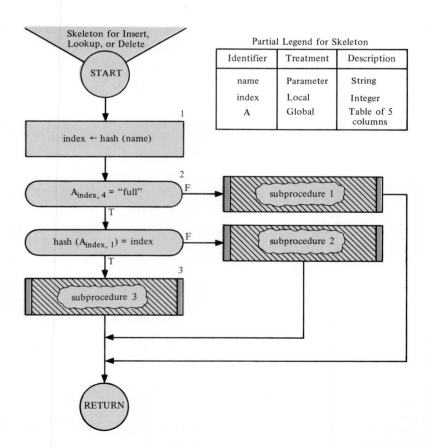

FIGURE 10·30

of the three principal procedures Insert, Lookup, and Delete. The skeleton has a simple structure. Box 1 computes the index value of the home position. The next two tests determine which of the three possible cases is under consideration, each case being handled by a subprocedure.

Subprocedure 1 covers the case where the home position is empty, subprocedure 2 covers the case where the home position contains a foreigner, and subprocedure 3 covers the case where the home position contains the head of the collision family that hashes to index, the value computed in box 1. The flowcharts for Insert, Lookup, and Delete will be explained in terms of the skeleton.

Figure 10·31 shows a complete breakdown for Insert and all its subprocedures with the exception of hash, which has already been discussed. The three parameters, name, city, and room, match the values that are to be inserted in the new entry. The fourth parameter, scode, (for *success code*) is used to return a message to the hotel operator to indicate success or the nature of the failure, as the case may be.

When you look at the flowchart for Insert, you see immediately the first level of detail for its three subprocedures (marked sub1, sub2, and sub3). Sub1 calls on the Makeentry procedure (lower left), which generates a new entry at the home position, given the appropriate values for its parameters. An scode of "yes" is then assigned to indicate success. Sub2 calls on the Moveforeigner subprocedure to find an empty slot and move the foreigner to that slot. If Moveforeigner is successful, recognized by the test in box 12, the Makeentry is called to generate the new entry. If Moveforeigner is not successful, an scode message such as "storage is full" is returned (box 14). Sub3 first calls on the Searchchain procedure to see if an entry already exists under the given name of the guest. If Searchchain is successful (F exit of box 5) then Insert reports a failure with a message such as "already registered." If Searchchain fails (T exit of box 5) then Findemptyslot is called to locate a slot to house the new entry (box 6). The new entry is linked into the end of the chain by the operation in box 8.

We now mention some of the highlights of the subprocedures, but leave detailed understanding of these as an exercise for the interested reader.

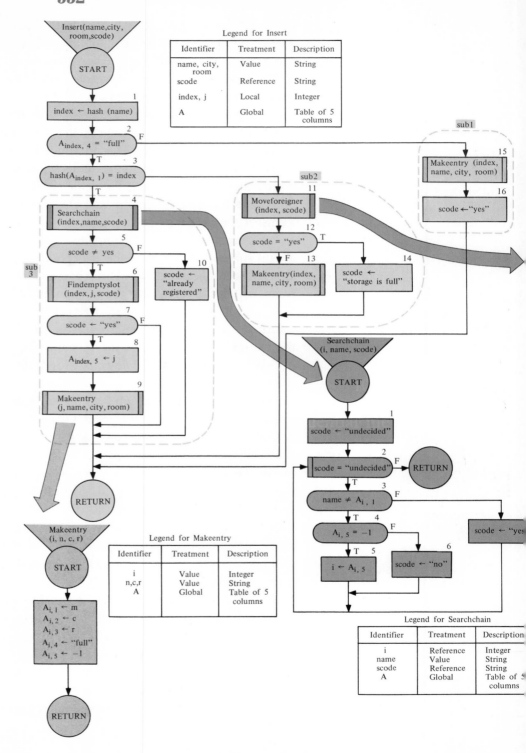

FIGURE 10·31

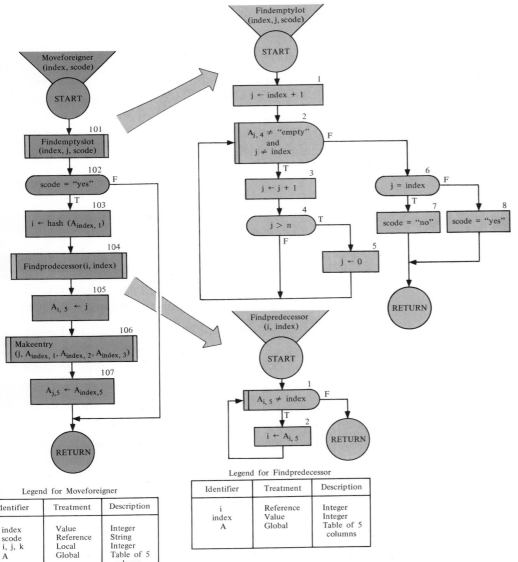

Legend for Findemptyslot

Identifier	Treatment	Description
index	Value	Integer
j	Reference	Integer
scode	Reference	String
n	Global	Integer
A	Global	Table of 5 columns

Findemptylot (index, j, scode)

START

1 $j \leftarrow index + 1$

2 $A_{j,4} \neq$ "empty" and $j \neq index$

3 $j \leftarrow j + 1$

4 $j > n$

5 $j \leftarrow 0$

6 $j = index$

7 scode = "no"

8 scode = "yes"

RETURN

Moveforeigner (index, scode)

START

101 Findemptyslot (index, j, scode)

102 scode = "yes"

103 $i \leftarrow hash (A_{index, 1})$

104 Findprodecessor (i, index)

105 $A_{i, 5} \leftarrow j$

106 Makeentry $(j, A_{index, 1}, A_{index, 2}, A_{index, 3})$

107 $A_{j,5} \leftarrow A_{index,5}$

RETURN

Findpredecessor (i, index)

START

1 $A_{i, 5} \neq index$

2 $i \leftarrow A_{i, 5}$

RETURN

Legend for Findpredecessor

Identifier	Treatment	Description
i	Reference	Integer
index	Value	Integer
A	Global	Table of 5 columns

Legend for Moveforeigner

Identifier	Treatment	Description
index	Value	Integer
scode	Reference	String
i, j, k	Local	Integer
A	Global	Table of 5 column

Moveforeigner

To move a foreigner it is necessary to adjust the link field of its predecessor to point to the new slot for the foreigner (box 105). Finding the predecessor is accomplished by first finding the index i of the head element on the chain to which the foreigner is attached (box 103). Once the index i is found, the Findpredecessor procedure, a simple search loop, is called (box 104) to get the index of the predecessor. Moving the foreigner to its new slot, j (boxes 106 and 107) is accomplished in part by a call on the Makeentry procedure.

Searchchain

This procedure is a search loop that ends on one of two conditions: a matching entry is found or the entire chain is searched without success. To control the search loop, the reference parameter scode is used as a three-way switch initialized to "undecided" and later reset to either "yes" or "no" to end the loop.

Findemptyslot

This procedure is coded here as an exhaustive search for an empty slot beginning at index $+1$ and continuing, if necessary, around the end of the table (slot n) and to its beginning (slot 0). As indicated in the exercises, this costly procedure can be replaced by a trivial operation if the empty slots are all prelinked into a chain of empty slots and maintained as such.

The *Lookup* procedure, which is flowcharted in Figure 10·32, is very easy to follow. Again, we need examine only the subprocedures sub1, sub2, and sub3. The actions of sub1 and sub2 are simply the assignment of failure messages to scode. Sub 3 starts with a call to Searchchain, whose detail has already been mentioned in connection with Insert. If Searchchain is successful, the returned value of index points to the slot of the wanted entry, so box 6 shows the steps necessary to retrieve and return the desired information. If the search fails, a failure message is returned.

The *Delete* procedure, which is flowcharted in Figure 10·33, appears almost as simple as the Lookup procedure. As before, the actions of sub1 and sub2 are simply the construction of failure messages. Sub3 begins with a call to the procedure Searchtodelete, whose detail is left for the exercises. This procedure is similar to Searchchain except that when the wanted

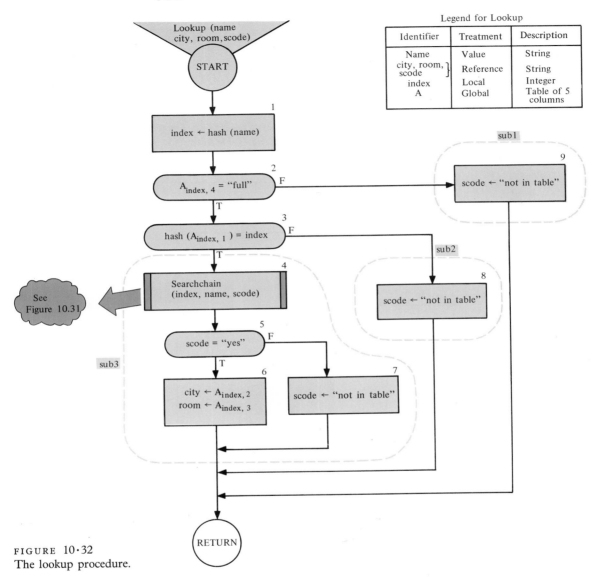

Legend for Lookup

Identifier	Treatment	Description
Name	Value	String
city, room, scode }	Reference	String
index	Local	Integer
A	Global	Table of 5 columns

FIGURE 10·32
The lookup procedure.

entry is found, it is deleted by making an appropriate adjustment to the chain, as was illustrated in our earlier discussion of the delete operation.

This concludes a very brief illustration of table management using hashing. The collection of procedures that were displayed were closely interrelated. By attempting to develop the structure of Lookup, Insert, and Delete first, it was possible to discover as we went along several necessary or useful subprocedures. Notice that some of these have been called by two

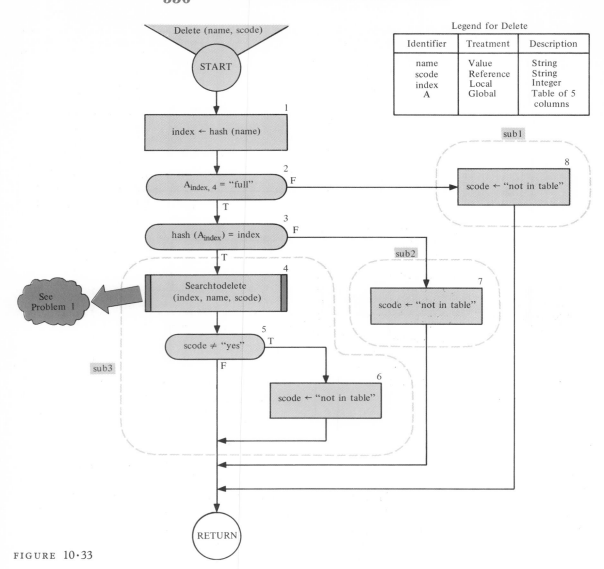

FIGURE 10·33

or more of the other procedures, as seen in the summary graph of the program organization in Figure 10·34.

The efficiency of the operations so far described strongly depends on the fraction of the table that is empty. As this fraction shrinks to zero (i.e., as the table fills up), so does the efficiency shrink. The chains that must be searched tend to grow longer, which means added work when such procedures as Searchchain or Searchtodelete are invoked. The work of Findemptyslot shoots up even more rapidly. For, when the table has only one empty slot left, Findemptyslot, which uses

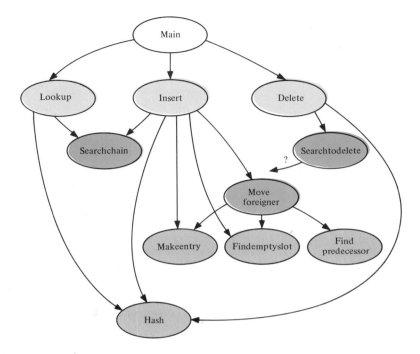

FIGURE 10·34
Summary graph for table management showing procedure call chains from Main to various subprocedures. (Calls from Searchtodelete, if any, are left for the exercises.)

an exhaustive search method, must examine, on the average, half the slots in the table to find the empty one. The following exercises consider several possible improvements to eliminate or drastically reduce some of these shortcomings.

EXERCISES 10·6

1. Construct a flowchart and legend for the procedure Searchtodelete that is called by Delete in the flowchart of Figure 10·33. Recall that there are three types of delete actions, depending on where the entry to be deleted is found on its chain.
   (a) It has a successor.
   (b) It has no successor and no predecessor.
   (c) It has no successor, but it does have a predecessor.

2. Develop one procedure, Search, that can be used in place of either Searchchain or Findpredecessor.

3. Develop a procedure Removeentry that cuts an entry from the chain by changing pointers instead of by moving entries. Assume that

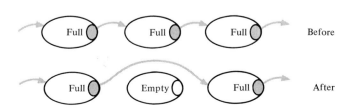

Removeentry is given value parameters that specify the index of the entry to be deleted and the index of the predecessor.

4. A technique often used in programming with linked lists is to organize storage from the start as a chain. Begin with *all* storage connected as a *chain of available entries* (CAE). The head of CAE is in a fixed storage location and is itself never available for use as an entry. Insert will always take the first entry after the head of CAE for insertion into a chain. Delete will return the entry removed from a chain to CAE as the first entry after the head. Revise the procedures of this section to use the chain of available entries idea. One of the advantages of this is that the full/empty indicator is no longer needed since, by definition, entries on CAE are vacant and all other entries are used. State one other advantage of the chain of available entries method for table management.

5. A refinement of the linked list idea is that of *doubly linked lists*. **In** such a list each entry has *two* links. One link points to the successor entry, while the other points to the predecessor entry, as illustrated below where the gray links point to successors and the light green ones point to predecessors.

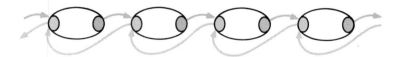

(a) Which procedures shown in Figure 10·34 could be eliminated by use of doubly linked lists?

(b) Imagine that storage is organized as a doubly linked chain of *available* entries (see Problem 4). Flowchart the procedures for "Attachentry" and "Detachentry" that are to produce the results shown in the diagram below. Draw modified flowcharts for Lookup, Insert, and Delete in terms of the primitives Searchchain, Attachentry, and Detachentry.

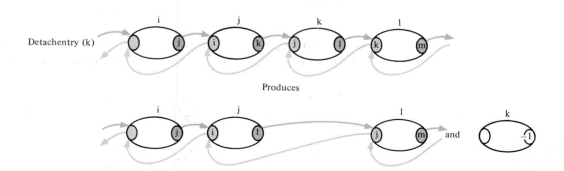

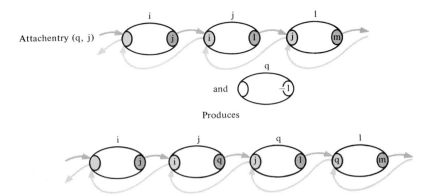

Attachentry (q, j)

and

Produces

10·7
Available
storage lists

One of the improvements to our hotel directory "system" that was studied in the exercises above is discussed and extended here to help us see how the same directory may be given multiple use. It has been assumed all along that the initial state of the directory is empty. Thus every slot is marked "E" for *empty,* but other fields in each slot are neither defined nor made zero. That is why finding an empty slot implies exhaustive search. Suppose instead that the directory is initially arranged as one long linked list of available slots. We can picture, for example, that beginning with slot 0 the link field of each entry is initialized to point to the next slot. That is, we assume that the link of slot i has been assigned the initial value $i + 1$, for i ranging from 0 to 998, and that the link in slot 999 is assigned a negative value to denote the tail of the list. Furthermore, we assume that a variable, HEAD, has been initialized to point to the head element of the available list, as seen in Figure 10·35.

Each time Findemptyslot is invoked it can now select the slot pointed to by the value of HEAD. Then the value of

FIGURE 10·35
Initial condition of the
directory as a linked list.

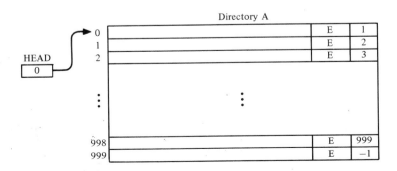

HEAD can be adjusted by assigning to it the link value copied from the selected slot

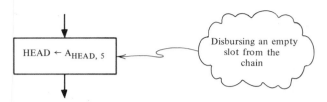

so that the next available slot is the new head of the chain.

Any time a slot is removed from a chain as a result of a deletion (check-out), that slot can easily be linked into the list of available slots to become the head of the list. Thus, if the deleted entry is at slot j and if slot k is the current head of the available list, then slot j may be returned to this list by the action

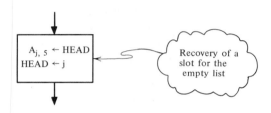

Figure 10·36 pictures storage after "recovery" of slot j.

We have just learned how to manage and to preserve an *inventory* of empty storage slots by disbursing slots and recovering these slots to and from a linked list. By letting slots in the directory match the actual rooms of the hotel one for one, the available storage list immediately becomes the list of empty

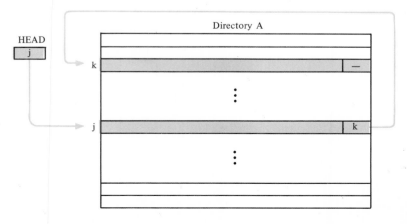

FIGURE 10·36
Showing the head of the "available" list after recovery of slot j.

hotel rooms, so the desk clerks can now use the same table for assigning rooms to guests as part of the registration process. To add this second use, it is only necessary to initialize each slot with a room number, as in Figure 10·37.

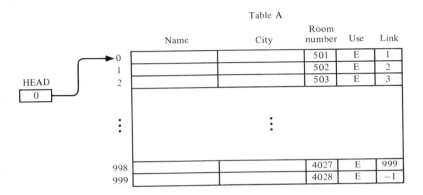

FIGURE 10·37
Initial state of the hotel directory modified so its list of available slots also serves as an inventory of rooms (assumes the hotel has 1000 rooms on floors 5 through 40).

Ordinarily, guests wish to choose among several types of rooms, for example, single, double bed, or twin bed, but for our first view of this method, we will assume that the guest has no choice, imagining that the hotel has only single rooms. We will leave for the exercises consideration of the more realistic case where the desk clerk must choose an empty room of a desired type.

After altering the design and purpose of the table, it is fairly easy to see how, using their computer terminals, the desk clerks might execute a procedure such as Registerguest, which can pick a room from the head of the empty-room list and then insert an entry for the registering guest into the directory, showing his name, hometown, and the selected room number.

The procedure Registerguest would replace Insert in our table management system. The steps taken by Registerguest are very similar to those of Insert, but a few extra steps are

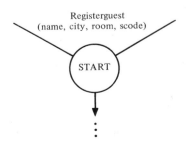

required. To see what these are, suppose the clerk is trying to register Tom Jones.

Registerguest would first select the first entry on the list of available rooms. We will suppose this entry is found at slot 12. After hashing Tom Jones and getting, say, the index 21, the usual test is made to see if slot 21 is empty or full. If full, the logic follows identically that of Insert, except that it is not necessary to call Findemptyslot at box 6, since slot 12 has already been found and may be used to create the desired entry. Hence box 6 is simply replaced by steps to detach slot 12 from the empty room list. If the home position at slot 21 is empty, however, that means that this entry also belongs to the emptyroom list, so to use this slot for the entry of Tom Jones, it is necessary to:

1.   Detach slot 21 (instead of 12) from the empty room list.

2.   Interchange values in the room-number fields of slots 12 and 21.

3.   Fill in the entry at slot 21 with Tom Jones' name, city, and so forth. This case is illustrated in Figure 10·38.

The exercises that follow provide opportunities for the reader to consider alternate ways to treat table management operations and to design systems that are useful in other familiar business applications.

All our discussion of table management in the preceding section and all our discussion of available storage lists in this section have assumed that the tables are kept in main (directly addressable) storage to achieve *on-line processing*. But this assumption is not essential. If the actual table, possibly accessed through a hashing function, is too large to be held in main storage, the bulk of the table can be kept on disk. In this case, an *access list* must be kept in main store. Each element in the access list must then contain, as a pointer, the disk address of the corresponding slot of the table. More efficient access to the table may be achieved if, space permitting in main store, each access list entry can also include the *use* field and the key field. (In our hotel directory example, the key field is the name field.)

The space on the disk reserved for the table may also be managed using available storage (linked list) strategies similar

(a) *Before* registering Tom Jones (after discovering that slot 12 shows that room 509 is available and after determining that the home position for Tom Jones at position 21 is empty).

(b) *After* registering Tom Jones (slot 21 is detached from the empty rooms list. Its room number, 2014, has been interchanged with the corresponding value in slot 12, that is, 509, and the remainder of the entry at slot 21 is completed as shown).

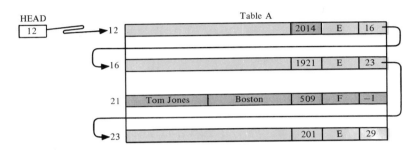

FIGURE 10·38
Showing the condition of the directory before and after registering Tom Jones using the Registerguest procedure.

to those described in this section. If table entries are disbursed from an available storage list and then always linked to other lists, only the heads of all such lists need be kept in main store. However, if the table is to be searched by hashing techniques, then an access list will also have to be kept in main store. Each access list entry, space permitting, might then contain not only a disk address to the actual slot and a key field, but also a link field to hold the disk address of the successor slot, if any. Techniques for using and managing space on disks by methods suggested here are subjects of study that can be pursued either in courses on data structures and data management or by independent study. (Consult the reading list on this topic at the end of this book.)

EXERCISES 10·7

1. Revise the hotel management system summarized in Figure 10·34 by modifying the directory structure to include a list of available rooms such as shown in Figure 10·37. In particular, draw flowcharts and legends for the following procedures.

   (a) *Initialize* puts the hotel directory into its initial form, for example, as in Figure 10·37.
   (b) *Registerguest* as described in the text.
   (c) Auxiliary procedures that you determine to be useful.

2. Show what changes are required in the system you developed in the preceding exercise to handle the case where the hotel offers three types

of rooms, for example, single (s), double (d), and twin bedrooms (t). In particular, show what changes, if any, are needed in the data structure of the system and what changes are needed in the procedures of the system. Note that adding a new field to each entry in the directory as a code for the type of room may not be the best approach if the available rooms are kept on only one list. This is because the Registerguest procedure would then have to search this available list until an entry is found of the desired type. One can imagine that such a search may take too long if a large number of entries of the "wrong" type are bunched up at the head of the empty room list.

3. *Project.* Design a table management system that can be used by the recently reorganized Repair Division of the State Highway Dept. The Repair Division is to operate as follows. On the first day of its operation (day 1), a work force of 1000 men will report for duty. Requests for repairs will be received daily and each request will specify a project name and the number of repair crewmen needed. Each repair will take at least one day, counting travel time for the crew, but it is not known in advance how many (whole) days each repair job will require. At the beginning of each new work day those men who have finished their jobs on the previous day will report in and be available for a new assignment (along with any crewmen who have not yet been assigned to any job).

A table is to be designed and maintained whose contents should enable the managerial group of the division to keep track, day by day, of each crewman's status and to what job, if any, he is assigned. A crew-assignment rule is to be followed: the man who has waited the longest is always given the first opportunity for work on the next project that requests manpower assistance from the Repair Division. This division, which wants to do its bookkeeping by computer, will keep three lists:

(a) A list of all men currently idle and available for work assignment.
(b) A list of all jobs currently in progress.
(c) For each job, a list of the men assigned.

The main procedures of this system are:

Getmenforjob   This procedure requests n men for assignment to a project, PROJ. If not enough men are available, an appropriate message is to be returned. No request is to be honored if it would draw off more than 30% of the available manpower.

Jobcomplete   This procedure adjusts the "books" of the system to reflect the fact that a given project, PROJ, is now completed. The crew assigned to it are released and join the list of those available for new job assignments.

Reportonjob	This procedure displays the names of the men currently working on a given project PROJ.
Fullreport	This procedure gives a display of the data on every project in progress within the system and for each one gives the list of names of the crew assigned to it. The report also gives names of those on the available list.

Solution of this problem will be easier if you first focus on selecting and then designing the table or tables appropriate for this problem. Will one table be sufficient? What should each filled slot in the table represent, a crewman or a project? Can both types of entries be accommodated in the same table? How many different list head variables will be required and how should they be represented? How should the tables and list heads be initialized? Is the use of a hashing function appropriate in this system?

4. In this problem your task is to modify the manpower allocation record-keeping system designed in the preceding problem. At the end of each 250 working days (one year), cash bonuses are to be awarded to repair crewmen on the basis of days actually worked during that period. The bookkeeping system is then started afresh, that is, all the tables are reinitialized.

   The system is to be revised to keep track of days worked and to report for each crewman his total days worked at the end of the bonus period based on the following method: a fourth list is to be maintained, which is a list of men currently on sick leave or on leave of absence. The total days worked for each crewman is to be kept current by incrementing this figure with the number of days worked upon completion of each project to which the crewman has been assigned. (To keep things simple, assume that all projects currently in progress on the 250th work day of the bonus period will be automatically "completed" on that day.)

   Two new procedures should be designed (with accompanying modifications to the table structures) as follows.

Takeoffavailable	Given a crewman's name, this procedure transfers the entry for him from the available list to the sick/leave-of-absence list.
Putonavailable	Given a crewman's name, this procedure transfers the entry for this crewman to the end of the available list. Crewmen are always assigned to jobs in the order of their entries on the available list, beginning with the head entry.

Chapter 11

Numerical approximation

So far in this book we have assumed that our algorithms are executed on an *ideal* machine like SIMPLOS. A SIMPLOS storage box is assumed to have an unlimited capacity to store information, and therefore we have also been able to assume that every indicated computation in a flowchart can be carried out exactly. So far then, the SIMPLOS model has been extremely helpful. It has made sense to emphasize the similarities and to minimize the differences between SIMPLOS and actual computers. Nevertheless, the behavior of an actual machine departs in important ways from the behavior of SIMPLOS when certain numerical computations are executed.

Storage cells of *actual* computers are finite and most often fixed in size like SAMOS words. This is in contrast to the limitless storage boxes of SIMPLOS, which we assume can store numerical values over an infinite range with infinite precision. Fortunately, this difference is unimportant for non-numerical values such as letters or other symbols on which logical processes such as matching or substitution are carried out. However, when we consider executing numerical computations with storage cells of finite (and fixed) capacity, many new considerations and problems come into play. These considerations arise partly from the fact that the number system represented in a computer is not, and cannot be, a perfect simulation of the real-number system of mathematics.

Our main task in this chapter is to understand what numbers are available in an actual computer such as SAMOS, how arithmetic operations are carried out on them, and how the results differ from the ideal mathematical results.

The number systems of mathematics are beautiful intellectual creations. There are an *infinite* number of integers equally spaced along the number line. There are an *infinite* number of real numbers and, between any two of them, there are infinitely many more. But a computer is a real-life device designed to do practical real-life computation, and any such computer can represent only a *finite* number of numbers.

It is clear that there must be discrepancies and difficulties when the integers or the real numbers are simulated by any finite set. Furthermore, certain numbers, for instance, π and $\sqrt{2}$, require an infinite number of digits in their digital representation; hence, fitting them into any finite storage will require approximation.

In the two sections that follow we will restrict our attention to fixed word length machines, and we will frequently use the SAMOS computer with its 11 character word for illustrations.

11·1 Floating-point numbers

The real numbers are represented in SAMOS, as in most computers, by so-called *floating-point numbers*. SAMOS floating-point representation was discussed in Section 1·8, but let us review how it works.

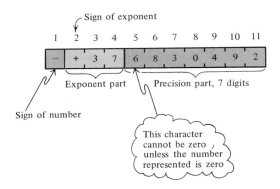

The above display represents the number $-.6830492 \times 10^{37}$. The exponent part can range from -99 to $+99$, including zero. The precision part, which in SAMOS always has 7 digits, can range from .1000000 to .9999999, which means that there are $9999999 - 999999$ or 9000000 different precision parts. Thus the total number of floating-point numbers in SAMOS is

$$\underset{\substack{\text{Number} \\ \text{of signs}}}{2} \times \underset{\substack{\text{Number of} \\ \text{exponent} \\ \text{parts}}}{199} \times \underset{\substack{\text{Number of} \\ \text{precision} \\ \text{parts}}}{\underbrace{9 \times 10^6}} + \underset{\substack{\text{The number} \\ \text{zero}}}{1} = 3582000001$$

By contrast, $2 \times 10^{10} - 1$ integers can be represented in a SAMOS storage word, i.e., all integers, N, in the range.

$$- 9999999999 \leq N \leq + 9999999999$$

This is seen schematically in Figure 11·1.

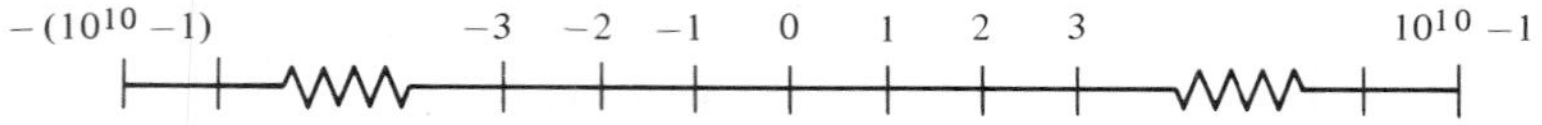

FIGURE 11·1
Integers representable in SAMOS.

Some computers also provide what are called *double precision floating-point numbers*. For the SAMOS design this would mean numbers to which two words of storage are allocated. The first word would contain the sign, the exponent and 7 digits of precision, while the second word would contain 10 more digits of precision. Any machine works more slowly when double precision numbers are used, but the number of representable numbers is significantly increased. In SAMOS with double precision

$$2 \times 199 \times 9 \times 10^{16} + 1$$

numbers would be representable.

The floating-point numbers in SAMOS, or in any computer, are not all evenly spaced on the number line as are the SAMOS integers. The following observations show why. There is, in fact, a closest-to-zero positive floating-point number, $.1 \times 10^{-99}$, that is,

and a closest-to-zero negative floating-point number, $-.1 \times 10^{-99}$, that is,

Between many other pairs of numbers, for example, between $.1 \times 10^{-99}$ and $.1 \times 10^{-98}$, there is a block of evenly spaced floating-point numbers, that is, all the 9 million possible precision parts following $\boxed{+ \quad - \ 9 \ 9}$ in the SAMOS word. The distance between any successive two of these particular numbers is only $.0000001 \times 10^{-99} = 10^{-106}$, a very close spacing. On the other hand, consider the spacing between, for instance, $.1 \times 10^{10}$ and $.1 \times 10^{11}$. Here, too, there are 9 million evenly spaced floating-point numbers, but these numbers are spaced at $.0000001 \times 10^{10} = 10^3$, a fairly wide spacing. In fact, all the SAMOS floating-point numbers lie in contiguous blocks of evenly spaced numbers with the numbers 10^a ($-100 \leq a \leq 99$) marking the boundaries between blocks.

As with the SAMOS integers, there is a largest and a smallest SAMOS single precision floating-point number. The largest is $.9999999 \times 10^{99}$ and the smallest $-.9999999 \times 10^{99}$. No numbers larger or smaller than these can be represented in SAMOS floating-point form.

In general each floating-point number has to represent or serve as an approximation for a whole interval of real numbers, that is, those real numbers for which it is the "best" floating-point number in SAMOS. This means, for example, that

+	+	0	1	3	1	4	1	5	9	7

represents π in SAMOS and also every other real number x such that $3.1415965 \leq x < 3.1415975$ if the machine rounds, or $3.141597 \leq x < 3.141598$ if the machine chops. This idea will be discussed further below.

Floating-Point Operations

The floating-point numbers are only an imperfect model of the real-number system. In particular, if two SAMOS floating-point numbers are *mathematically* added, subtracted, multiplied, or divided, the result can fail to be a SAMOS floating-point number. But, for useful computation, each result of an arithmetic operation on floating-point numbers must be a floating-point number, that is, must be computer representable. Therefore the usual arithmetic processes are slightly modified to insure floating-point results.

Addition

Let's see first how to perform a simple floating-point addition in SAMOS. All arithmetic operations use the accumulator register. This register must be longer than an ordinary SAMOS storage word to allow numbers of unlike magnitudes to be added. For floating-point addition the SAMOS accumulator has a precision part of 14 digits, twice that of an ordinary word. (Actually only two or three of the extra digits are really required).

Suppose we want to add $+.6493287 \times 10^7$ and

$+.5372642 \times 10^4$. First, the summand with the greater absolute value is entered into the accumulator just as it appears in a SAMOS word, with the sign and exponent and precision digits packed into the left half of the precision part of the accumulator. The precision part of the second summand is now "positioned" (as it were) under the first summand but shifted a number of spaces to the right equal to the difference of the exponents, in this case $7 - 4 = 3$ spaces.

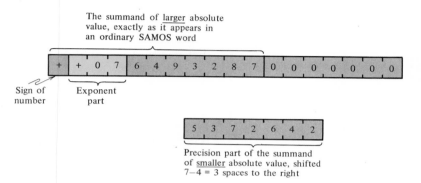

Addition setup.

Now the computer adds or subtracts, respectively, according to whether the summands have the same or different signs, respectively. In this case we add with the resulting configuration as shown below.

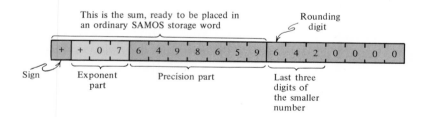

Addition complete.

But this particular result is not a SAMOS floating-point number. That is, before the answer can be stored, the precision part must be trimmed to seven digits to fit into an ordinary SAMOS word. If the machine accomplishes this trimming by "chopping," then everything after the seventh precision digit is lopped off and the SAMOS representation of the sum is as follows.

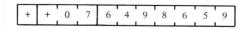

However, if the machine accomplishes its trimming by "rounding," then the following method is typical. The eighth digit is examined and if this digit is 5 or greater (as it was in this case) the seventh digit is increased by 1. Then the stored floating point sum is

But suppose, instead of the above addition, we want to add $+.6493287 \times 10^7$ and $+.5372642 \times 10^7$, the same precision parts as above, but multiplied by the *same* power of 10. Then the addition must proceed in two stages, of which the first is similar to the above.

First stage of addition.

When the computer adds together the precision parts of the two summands, it will sense an overflow in the addition of the most significant digits $6 + 5$. This overflow will trigger a second stage in which:

1. All the precision digits of the sum are shifted one place to the right.

2. The overflow digit (1) is assigned to the leftmost position of the precision part.

3. The exponent is increased by 1.

Thus the sum in the accumulator becomes

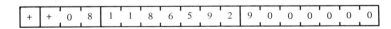

But again this is not a SAMOS floating-point number. If the computer chops we will instead store the result as

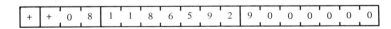

while, if the computer rounds, we will store it as

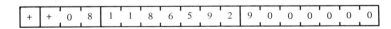

The difference between the floating-point sum and the mathematical sum of two floating-point numbers is called the *roundoff error* of addition. In the above example the roundoff error of addition, if the computer *rounds* (to the nearest number), is $.00000001 \times 10^8 = 1$, while if the computer *chops,* it is 9.

A different kind of overflow occurs when we add the floating-point numbers $.6000000 \times 10^{99}$ and $.4000000 \times 10^{99}$. The first stage of the addition is

| + | + | 9 | 9 | 6 | 0 | 0 | 0 | 0 | 0 | 0 | 0 | 0 | 0 | 0 | 0 | 0 | 0 |

| 4 | 0 | 0 | 0 | 0 | 0 | 0 |

When the second stage in the addition is triggered by the overflow of $6 + 4$, the precision part of the sum becomes 1000000 but, when the exponent is increased by 1, there is an overflow in the exponent part of the sum. *Exponent overflow* will usually cause a computer to terminate the computation because the result is beyond the floating-point range and cannot be expressed.

There is still another addition configuration that has interesting implications. Suppose the summands we want to add have exponent parts that differ by more than 7, the number of digits of precision in a SAMOS floating point number; that is, suppose we want to add $.6493287 \times 10^{17}$ and $.5372642 \times 10^8$. The first stage of the addition process places the larger summand in the accumulator

Addition setup, first stage.

with the precision part of the smaller summand shifted to the right by the difference of the exponent parts, in this case $17 - 8 = 9$. But if the addition were actually to be performed, we can see ahead of time that all the digits from the precision part of the second summand would be lost in the roundoff error of addition, since the sum would be stored as $.6493287 \times 10^{17}$. In general, if two floating-point numbers have exponents whose difference is more than the number of digits of precision of either number, the summand with the smaller exponent can contribute nothing to the sum and therefore the second stage of the addition process is simply omitted.

Multiplication

While some mathematical sums of floating-point numbers are themselves floating-point numbers, that is, there is no roundoff error of addition, this is almost never the case in multiplication. To understand this, let us look at how multiplication is done in SAMOS, using the example of multiplying

$$.1111111 \times 10^7 \text{ by } .1020201 \times 10^{-2}$$

A SAMOS product is always developed in the accumulator and proceeds in two stages. For the above product the first stage is as follows.

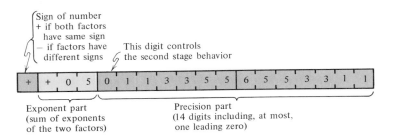

Multiplication: first stage.

In the first stage the exponent part is computed as the sum of the exponents of the two factors. In the precision part appears just what you would get in multiplying:

$$.1111111 \quad \text{by} \quad .1020201$$

by hand, which turns out to be

$$.01133556553311$$

Now the leading digit of the precision part is examined and found to be zero. This fact causes the second stage of multiplication to be performed. The second stage, sometimes referred to as *normalizing*, consists of shifting each of the remaining 13 digits in the precision part one place to the left and reducing the exponent by 1. If the leading digit had not been zero the second stage would have been omitted, as the product would already have been represented in the correct form.

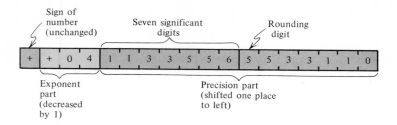

Multiplication: second stage.

But the result is not a SAMOS floating-point number, and some floating-point number must be selected to represent it. If the computer chops, the SAMOS number

will be chosen as the sum with a roundoff error of multiplication equal to $.0000000553311 \times 10^4 = .000553311$. If the computer rounds, the SAMOS floating-point number

will be used with a roundoff error of $.000446689$.

Exponent overflow is more likely to occur in a product than in a sum, and there is yet another phenomenon called *exponent underflow*, which is also more likely to occur in a product than in a sum. Suppose SAMOS computes the product of $.5 \times 10^{-40}$ and $.6 \times 10^{-60}$, both floating-point numbers. The precision part of the product will be $.3000000$. But the exponent part of the product is $-40 + (-60) = -100$. The mathematical product is not a SAMOS floating-point number. Its value lies between zero and the smallest positive floating-point number, $.1 \times 10^{-99}$.

How do actual computer systems cope with exponent underflow? One of the following three design approaches is usually taken.

1. The result in the accumulator that has been sensed as underflow is replaced by zero, and the computation continues with the next instruction in sequence, as if the previous result were equal to zero. This way of proceeding is unsatisfactory if the "pseudo zero" result is later used as the denominator in a division operation. It is also rather unsatisfying to observe

that with this approach, a sequence of multiplications such as

$$\underbrace{10^{-50} \times 10^{-50}} \times 10^{60} \times 10^{40}$$
exponent underflow

would yield a result of zero, whereas the mathematically equivalent sequence

$$10^{-50} \times 10^{60} \times 10^{-50} \times 10^{40}$$

would yield the correct result, 1.

2. The sensing of the underflow causes an unconditional branch to an instruction sequence that, when executed, attends to the problem, usually by printing out an error message indicating where and when the underflow occurred, and then terminates the computation. To have one's computation stopped in midstream, however, is often very unsatisfying, especially if the number that underflowed was really negligible.

3. Another approach is to have the computer replace the underflowed result with the closest to zero floating-point number with the same sign, and proceed with the computation.

Still other ways to resolve the underflow problem are of potential interest. If you are interested consult the subject "Unnormalized Mode" in the book by Sterbenz or the paper by Kahan in the selected reading list for this chapter.

We terminate this discussion of floating-point addition and multiplication with the following two observations.

1. The mechanisms described for implementing floating-point addition and multiplication guarantee the property of commutativity, that is, that $a + b = b + a$ and that $a \times b = b \times a$, if a and b are floating-point numbers.

2. Texts on computer arithmetic can be consulted for further details on the floating-point operations of subtraction and division. A study of division will reveal few surprises, but there is more to subtraction than one might guess.

To be sure, subtracting two floating-point numbers of *like* sign is, in essence, the same problem as adding two floating-point numbers of *unlike* sign. But on actual computers this operation can lead to significantly different results because the methods vary. Let us see why. First we explain how SAMOS does subtraction to provide a basis for comparison.

When two floating-point numbers, a and b, of like sign, are nearly equal in magnitude, the first stage of subtraction results in a precision part that has one or more leading zeros because of cancellation. These leading zeros are taken care of in the second stage, which is called a *normalization* step. Here the precision part is shifted left until there are no more leading zeros and, at the same time, the exponent part is appropriately adjusted (i.e., decremented by one for each shift of one position). Any digits remaining in the lower-order half of the accumulator, usually called the *guard digits,* are then chopped off. So the three substeps in SAMOS are: *subtract* with full 14 digits of precision (i.e., subtract with 7 guard digits), then *normalize* and then *chop*. The SAMOS approach (type 1) is used by many computer manufacturers, who may incidentally use fewer than 7 guard digits. Alternatively, other manufacturers do subtraction (with guard digits) and then chop and then normalize. Still others (type 3), often makers of "shirt-pocket" calculators, first chop, then subtract, and then normalize, using no guard digits.

To give some idea of how different the results can be, consider the floating-point subtraction of 0.9999999 from 1 on actual computers that do 7-digit precision arithmetic.

On type 1 computers with one guard digit, the result is $.1 \times 10^{-6}$.

On type 2 computers with one guard digit, the result is zero.

On type 3 computers with no guard digits, the result is $.1 \times 10^{-5}$.

EXERCISES 11·1

1. Approximate the following fractions as SAMOS floating-point numbers: $1/3$, $1/7$, and $1/21$.

   Let p, q, and r represent the three approximations just obtained. Show that the SAMOS floating-point product $p \times q$ is less than r. Now show that for *any* positive integers a, b $< 10^8$, such that p and q are the respective SAMOS approximations for $1/a$ and $1/b$ and r is the approximation for $1/(a \times b)$, that $p \times q \leq r$.

2. For floating-point addition it was stated that the summand of greater absolute value is packed into the accumulator and the smaller sum-

mand is added to it. State a simpler but equally effective test for deciding which summand is to be packed into the accumulator.

3. (a) Show that 199 is the largest integral power of π that can be expressed as a SAMOS floating-point number.
   (b) Show that -230 is the smallest integral power of e that can be expressed as a SAMOS floating-point number, where e is the base of the natural logarithms.

4. 186,000 miles per second is a frequently cited approximation of the speed of light. It is certainly not exact. The three trailing zeros are included merely as placeholders to locate the decimal point. The floating-point notation $.186 \times 10^6$ would be more suggestive. Assuming that these three digits of precision are correct in the sense of "the best possible 3-digit approximation" (but using no additional information):

   (a) What is the maximum possible absolute error?

   $$\text{absolute error} = \text{true value} - \text{computed value}$$

   (b) What is the maximum possible relative error?

   $$\text{relative error} = \frac{\text{true value} - \text{computed value}}{\text{true value}}$$

5. Repeat Problem 4 using each of the following familiar approximations.

   (a) The distance from the earth to the sun is 93 million miles.
   (b) There are 365 days in a year.
   (c) The acceleration of gravity at the earth's surface is 32 feet per second squared.

11·2
Some implications of finite word length

The representation of rational numbers (ratios of integers) in various number bases has surprisingly important implications for computer computations. Consider the ratio of the number one to the number two. Expressed decimally in the base 10, this ratio is .5. In base 2 the ratio is .1. Expressed similarly in base 3, however, this ratio is .1111 . . . , as may be derived by long division.

$$\begin{array}{r} .1 \\ 2\overline{\smash{\big)}\,1.0} \\ \underline{2} \\ 10 \end{array}$$
base 3 long division

This infinite repeating expression can not be stored exactly in a finite word of any length. Or, look at the ratio of 1 to

10. In base 10 decimal notation this ratio is .1, but in base 2 it becomes $1 / 1010 = .0001100\dot{1}\dot{1}$, as may be derived by long division.

$$
\begin{array}{r}
.0001100 \\
1010\overline{)1.0000000} \\
1010 \\
\overline{1100} \\
1010 \\
\overline{1000}
\end{array}
$$

The result is a repeating binary expression whose storage requires approximation.

Is the base in which numbers should be expressed determined by the nature of computer storage? No. There is nothing implicit in the storage occupied by a computer word that requires a number stored there to be represented in a particular base. However, to carry out arithmetic computations correctly, the overflow *carry* from one accumulator position to the next left position occurs differently according to the base in which the numbers are expressed. The carry occurs at 2 for base 2 numbers, at 10 for decimal numbers, and so forth. Thus the base in which the stored numbers are expressed is tied to the computer arithmetic and vice versa.

As long as integer overflow does not occur, one really need not know in what base *integers* are represented in a computer. But because of roundoff in floating-point arithmetic, the base in which *floating-point numbers* are represented becomes important to understanding the results. For instance, suppose we evaluate the expression $1 + 1/8$ in 3-precision digit base 2 arithmetic. The computation would have roundoff error as follows.

$$
\left.\begin{array}{r}
1.00 \\
+ \ .001 \\
\hline
1.00\dot{1}
\end{array}\right\}
\begin{array}{l}
\text{one plus one eighth} \\
\text{in base 2 arithmetic}
\end{array}
$$

The final result is 1.00. But in 3-precision digit base 4 arithmetic the sum has no roundoff error. It is exact!

$$
\left.\begin{array}{r}
1.00 \\
+ \ .02 \\
\hline
1.02
\end{array}\right\}
\begin{array}{l}
\text{one plus one eighth} \\
\text{in base 4 arithmetic}
\end{array}
$$

The result is $1 + 2 \times 4^{-2} = 9/8$.

In base 8 arithmetic the sum is also exact, but in base 10 there is again roundoff error for 3-precision digit arithmetic.

Computers presumably can be designed to operate with floating-point numbers expressed in any reasonable base, but only 2, 8, 10, and 16 are generally used. And, even though a computer accepts numbers in decimal notation as input data, the numbers may still be stored and the arithmetic done in one of the other bases followed by a reconversion back to decimal form for output.

In order to understand which floating-point numbers your computer makes available to you (i.e., which numbers you can use without any approximation), you need to know the precision length of the floating-point numbers and the base in which they are expressed. With this information you can determine whether a certain rational number can be expressed exactly in your computer or not (if indeed it can be expressed at all). It may, of course, be too large or too small. To get a handle on the range, you need information on the limits of the exponent e in the expression for floating-point numbers.

$$x = \pm . d_1 d_2 \ldots . d_n \times b^e$$

Here x is any floating-point number and b is the base in which the number is represented, d_1 is any integer from 1 to $b - 1$, that is, $1 \le d_1 \le b - 1$ and the other d_i, $1 \le i \le n$, satisfy the relation $0 \le d_i \le b - 1$. The value of n is the number of digits of precision in the computer word.

Increased insight into the limitations of floating-point numbers can be gained through a deeper study of one system, preferably a "toy" or model system in which only a few numbers can be represented exactly. We make such a study in the remainder of this section. However, readers who are satisfied that they already have sufficient familiarity with the subject may skip to Section 11·3.

The toy system we will study can represent only 33 real numbers exactly. For this system, $b = 2$, $n = 3$, and $-1 \le e \le 2$. The possible nonzero precision parts of the numbers, disregarding sign, are

$$.100_2 = 1/2$$
$$.101_2 = 1/2 + 1/8 = 5/8$$
$$.110_2 = 1/2 + 1/4 = 3/4$$
$$.111_2 = 1/2 + 1/4 + 1/8 = 7/8$$

The possible values of the exponent e are -1, 0, 1 and 2, and thus b^e can have the values $1/2$, 1, 2, and 4. Combining the possible precision parts with all the exponent values we get the 32 values $\pm 1/4$, $\pm 5/16$, $\pm 3/8$, $\pm 7/16$, $\pm 1/2$, $\pm 5/8$, $\pm 3/4$, $\pm 7/8$, ± 1, $\pm 5/4$, $\pm 3/2$, $\pm 7/4$, ± 2, $\pm 5/2$, ± 3, and $\pm 7/2$. These numbers together with zero make up the floating point system graphed in Figure 11·2.

FIGURE 11·2
33-valued floating-point number system.

We can get a feeling for the limitations of a floating-point system by doing some simple exercises. For example, suppose in our toy system we want to add $7/8$ to itself repeatedly to arrive at $10 \times 7/8$.
First,

$$\frac{7}{8} + \frac{7}{8} = \frac{7}{4}$$

The result, $7/4$, is a floating-point number, as can be seen by glancing at Figure 11·2, so the sum is exact. Now,

$$\left(\frac{7}{8} + \frac{7}{8}\right) + \frac{7}{8} = \frac{7}{4} + \frac{7}{8} = \frac{21}{8}$$

which is *not* a floating-point number in our system. The "closest" such number, using rounding as opposed to chopping, is $5/2$, so in this system

$$\left(\frac{7}{8} + \frac{7}{8}\right) + \frac{7}{8} = \frac{5}{2}$$

Likewise,

$$\left(\left(\frac{7}{8} + \frac{7}{8}\right) + \frac{7}{8}\right) + \frac{7}{8} = \frac{5}{2} + \frac{7}{8} = \frac{27}{8}$$

which again is not a floating-point number. The closest such number is $7/2$, so

$$\frac{5}{2} + \frac{7}{8} = \frac{7}{2}$$

continuing,

$$\left(\left(\left(\frac{7}{8} + \frac{7}{8}\right) + \frac{7}{8}\right) + \frac{7}{8}\right) + \frac{7}{8} = \frac{7}{2} + \frac{7}{8} = \frac{35}{8}$$

which is outside the range of the number system (exponent overflow). A computer executing in this number system could handle the result in several ways. One way is to approximate the result $35/8$ by the largest value in the system. Then

$$\frac{7}{2} + \frac{7}{8} = \frac{7}{2}$$

Observe that no matter how many more times $7/8$ is then added to $7/2$, the result would remain $7/2$. Another possible handling of the situation is to stop the computation and print a message to the effect that the sum has overflowed.

Before we leave the 33-number floating-point system, let's take one more look at this problem of adding $7/8$ to itself 10 times. Expressed in binary decimal form, $7/8$ is .111. As a binary floating-point number, we would write it as $.111 \times 2^0$. Table 11·1 shows a consolidated display of the solution to this problem as discussed above, based on roundoff to the nearest floating-point number. Table 11·2 shows a comparable display of the solution based on chopping excess digits as the roundoff rule. Notice that whichever roundoff rule is used, the same effect is observed: before ten $7/8$'s are accumulated, exponent overflow occurs.

Suppose we were to deal with the 65-number floating-point system where the base b is again 2 and n is again 3, but where the exponent e ranges from -1 to 3 instead of from -1 to 2. Now an entirely different effect can be observed when we add $7/8$ to itself repeatedly. When we add $7/2 + 7/8$ as on line 6 of Table 11·2, the result, $.100 \times 2^3$, that is, 4, is now a valid floating-point number, so the next addition gives:

Fractional Notation	Base 2 Decimal Notation	Scratch Pad	Chopped Result in Base 2 Decimal Notation	Remarks
$4 + \frac{7}{8}$	$.100 \times 2^3 + .111 \times 2^0$	$\begin{array}{r} .100 \times 2^3 \\ +.000111 \times 2^3 \\ \hline .100111 \times 2^3 \end{array}$	$= .100 \times 2^3$	No change!

Adding two numbers whose exponents differ by the number of precision digits and chopping means that the summand of smaller magnitude *has no effect on the sum*. Hence all subse-

TABLE 11·1

Adding $\frac{7}{8}$ to itself repeatedly in the 33-number toy floating-point system. *Roundoff is to the nearest number in the system.*

Number of $\frac{7}{8}$'s Accumulated	Fractional Notation	Base 2 Decimal Notation	Scratch Pad	Rounded Result in Base 2 Decimal Notation	Remarks
2	$\frac{7}{8} + \frac{7}{8}$	$.111 \times 2^0 + .111 \times 2^0$	$.111 \times 2^0$ $+.111 \times 2^0$ $\overline{1.110 \times 2^0}$ round down	$= .111 \times 2^1$	
3	$\frac{7}{4} + \frac{7}{8}$	$.111 \times 2^1 + .111 \times 2^0$	$.111 \times 2^1$ $+.0111 \times 2^1$ $\overline{1.0101 \times 2^1}$ round down	$= .101 \times 2^2$	
4	$\frac{5}{2} + \frac{7}{8}$	$.101 \times 2^2 + .111 \times 2^0$	$.101 \times 2^2$ $+.00111 \times 2^2$ $\overline{.11011 \times 2^2}$ round up	$= .111 \times 2^2$	
5	$\frac{7}{2} + \frac{7}{8}$	$.111 \times 2^2 + .111 \times 2^0$	$.111 \times 2^2$ $+.00111 \times 2^2$ $\overline{1.00011 \times 2^2}$ round down	$= .100 \times 2^3$ $\Downarrow$ $.111 \times 2^2$	Exponent overflow Replace with the largest number in this system
6	$\frac{7}{2} + \frac{7}{8}$	$.111 \times 2^2 + .111 \times 2^0$	$.111 \times 2^2$ $+.00111 \times 2^2$ $\overline{1.00011 \times 2^2}$ round down	$.111 \times 2^2$	
7					

quent additions of 7/8 to 4 will yield 4. The same type of effect can be observed, when rounding to the nearest number is used, if the exponent range for the floating-point number system becomes -1 to 4. In this system, after the sum reaches 8, successive additions of 7/8 will have no further effect. Try it and see for yourself.

TABLE 11·2

Adding $\frac{7}{8}$ to itself repeatedly in the 33-number toy floating-point system. *Roundoff is by chopping excess digits.*

Number of $\frac{7}{8}$'s Accumulated	Fractional Notation	Base 2 Decimal Notation	Scratch Pad	Chopped Result in Base 2 Decimal Notation	Remarks
2	$\frac{7}{8} + \frac{7}{8}$	$.111 \times 2^0 + .111 \times 2^0$	$.111 \times 2^0$ $+.111 \times 2^0$ $\overline{1.110 \times 2^0}$	$= .111 \times 2^1$	
3	$\frac{7}{4} + \frac{7}{8}$	$.111 \times 2^1 + .111 \times 2^0$	$.111 \times 2^1$ $+.0111 \times 2^1$ $\overline{1.0101 \times 2^1}$	$= .101 \times 2^2$	
4	$\frac{5}{2} + \frac{7}{8}$	$.101 \times 2^2 + .111 \times 2^0$	$.101 \times 2^2$ $+.00111 \times 2^2$ $\overline{.11011 \times 2^2}$	$= .110 \times 2^2$	
5	$3 + \frac{7}{8}$	$.110 \times 2^2 + .111 \times 2^0$	$.110 \times 2^2$ $+.00111 \times 2^2$ $\overline{.11111 \times 2^2}$	$= .111 \times 2^2$	
6	$\frac{7}{2} + \frac{7}{8}$	$.111 \times 2^2 + .111 \times 2^0$	$.111 \times 2^2$ $+.00111 \times 2^2$ $\overline{1.00011 \times 2^2}$	$= .100 \times 2^3$	Exponent overflow
				$.111 \times 2^2$	Replace with the largest number in this system
7	$\frac{7}{2} + \frac{7}{8}$	$.111 \times 2^2 + .111 \times 2^0$	$.111 \times 2^2$ $+.00111 \times 2^2$ $\overline{1.00011 \times 2^2}$	$.111 \times 2^2$	
$\vdots$					

EXERCISES 11·2

1. Construct a diagram similar to that of Figure 11·2 for a floating-point number system whose characteristics are:

$$b = 2$$
$$n = 2$$
$$-1 \leq e \leq 2$$

where b = base

n = number of precision digits

e = exponent

2. For the system described in Problem 1 and using a chopping rule for rounding, express:

(a) the sum

$$-\frac{3}{2} + 1$$

(b) the products

$$\frac{3}{4} \times \frac{3}{8}$$

and

$$-\frac{3}{8} \times \frac{3}{8}$$

(c) $3 / 4$ added to itself five times.

3. Repeat the computations of Problem 2 using rounding to the nearest floating-point number.

4. Consider a floating-point system where b = 2, n = 6, and the range of e is from very large negative to very large positive.

(a) Express $1 / 10$ as a floating-point number in this system.
(b) Using chopping as the rounding rule, form the product $10 \times 1 / 10$ and show that the value obtained is $63 / 64$ in this system.
(c) Using chopping as the rounding rule, add $1 / 10$ ten times and show that the value obtained is $61 / 64$ in this system.
(d) If the computer outputs the result of parts b and c in the decimal system chopped to three decimal precision digits, show the printed results in each case.

5. For the floating-point number system defined in Problem 4, express as floating-point numbers the values of $3 / 10$, $7 / 10$, and $9 / 10$ obtained by dividing and chopping.

6. How can the values $2 / 10$, $4 / 10$, $6 / 10$, and $8 / 10$, expressed in the floating-point number system defined in Problem 4, be obtained from previous results without using division? Find these values.

**11·3
Floating-point
numbers in
decision steps and
loop control**

Floating-point roundoff can have effects that are difficult to predict, especially when the value of some variable represented as a floating-point number is used to control path selection in a flowchart. For example, we will now show how the execution of an iteration box can be affected by floating-point numbers. For this little "case study" we will assume that our floating-point number system has base $b = 10$ and $n = 3$ (i.e., 3 decimal precision digits). Also, we will use chopping for roundoff and will ignore for the moment any limitation on the range of the exponent. In such a system, for example, $.333 \times 10^0$ is the best approximation for $1/3$. Now consider executing the loop

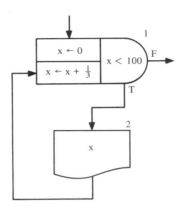

where values are represented and all arithmetic operations are carried out in floating point. The variable x is initially set to zero. When the increment $1/3$, that is, $.333 \times 10^0$ is successively added to x, we obtain new values for x, as shown in Table 11·3.

After 10 additions of the increment, x has the value $.331 \times 10^1$, or 3.31. The roundoff error of addition has caused an error of .02, since we would expect $10 \times .333$ to equal $.333 \times 10^1$.

If we study the trace in Table 11·3, can we see a pattern in the addition? Yes, we can. In the first three additions the summands have their precision digits aligned directly under each other, because the exponents in their floating-point representations are equal, for example,

$$
\begin{array}{r}
.333 \times 10^0 \\
+ \ .333 \times 10^0 \\
\hline
.666 \times 10^0
\end{array}
\quad \text{and} \quad
\begin{array}{r}
.666 \times 10^0 \\
+ \ .333 \times 10^0 \\
\hline
.999 \times 10^0
\end{array}
$$

But in the following additions the exponents of the summands differ by 1, and thus the precision digits of the increment are shifted right by one, for example,

$$.133 \ \times 10^1$$
$$+ \ .0333 \times 10^1$$
$$\overline{.1663 \times 10^1}$$

In the rounding process that completes each of these next additions, the final digit is always rounded off. Only the first two digits contribute anything, so the effect is the same as if $.330 \times 10^0$ had been added instead of $.333 \times 10^0$. This will continue to be the case until the sum "spills" or overflows into another digit position to the left, that is, until the sum reaches 10, after which the effective increment will be .300 instead of .330.

From Table 11·3 we see that the sum spills over 10 after 31 increments, and it reaches 100 after 331 increments.

TABLE 11·3
Values for x Upon Successive Execution of $\boxed{x \leftarrow x + \dfrac{1}{3}}$ Using 3-Decimal Digit Arithmetic

Number of Times the Increment $\frac{1}{3}$ Has Been Added	Old x	$+\frac{1}{3} \ \Rightarrow$	New x	Effective Increment
1	0	$.333 \times 10^0$	$.333 \times 10^0$	
2	$.333 \times 10^0$		$.666 \times 10^0$	.333
3	$.666 \times 10^0$		$.999 \times 10^0$	
4	$.999 \times 10^0$		$1.332 \times 10^0 \Rightarrow .133 \times 10^1$	
5	$.133 \times 10^1$		$.1663 \times 10^1 \Rightarrow .166 \times 10^1$	
6	$.166 \times 10^1$		$.1993 \times 10^1 \Rightarrow .199 \times 10^1$	
7	$.199 \times 10^1$		$.2323 \times 10^1 \Rightarrow .232 \times 10^1$	.330
8	$.232 \times 10^1$		$.2653 \times 10^1 \Rightarrow .265 \times 10^1$	
9	$.265 \times 10^1$		$.2983 \times 10^1 \Rightarrow .298 \times 10^1$	
10	$.298 \times 10^1$		$.3313 \times 10^1 \Rightarrow .331 \times 10^1$	

Values of x at Various Other Stages of Incrementation

20	$.628 \times 10^1$	$.333 \times 10^0$	$.6613 \times 10^1 \Rightarrow .661 \times 10^1$	
30	$.958 \times 10^1$		$.9913 \times 10^1 \Rightarrow .991 \times 10^1$	
31	$.991 \times 10^1$		$1.0243 \times 10^1 \Rightarrow .102 \times 10^2$	
131	$.399 \times 10^2$		$.40233 \times 10^2 \Rightarrow .402 \times 10^2$	
231	$.699 \times 10^2$		$.70233 \times 10^2 \Rightarrow .702 \times 10^2$	
300	$.906 \times 10^2$		$.90933 \times 10^2 \Rightarrow .909 \times 10^2$	.300
330	$.996 \times 10^2$		$.99933 \times 10^2 \Rightarrow .999 \times 10^2$	
331	$.999 \times 10^2$		$1.00233 \times 10^2 \Rightarrow .100 \times 10^3$	
332	$.100 \times 10^3$		$.100333 \times 10^3 \Rightarrow .100 \times 10^3$	.000
⋮				

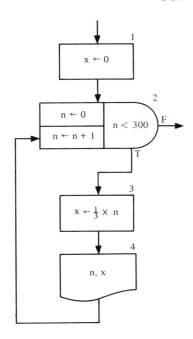

From the iteration box we might have expected 300 increments of $1/3$ to bring x to 100, but Table $11 \cdot 3$ shows that x is only 90.9 at that point. Part of the 9.1 difference is caused by the roundoff error of addition. The rest of the difference is caused by the error of representing $1/3$ by .333. The roundoff error of addition is the difference between the floating-point sum 90.9 and the mathematical sum, $300 \times .333 = 99.9$. Thus the roundoff error of addition is 9.0, and this leaves only .1 as the error caused by representing $1/3$ by .333.

Before we leave this problem consider what would happen if the limit test in the iteration box on page 585 were

$$ x < 200 \quad \text{instead of} \quad x < 100 $$

Once the sum reaches 100, as Table $11 \cdot 3$ shows, the effective increment becomes zero, and x will increase no further. This is because the exponent parts of x and of the increment differ by 3, the number of precision digits; i.e.,

$$
\begin{array}{r}
.100 \quad \times 10^3 \\
+ \ .000333 \times 10^3 \\
\hline
.100\cancel{333} \times 10^3
\end{array}
$$

Such an iteration becomes an endless loop!

From the above discussion it should be evident that a floating-point number is *not* a satisfactory translation for the *increment* in an iteration box. *Loop counter values should always be integers* so that there will be no roundoff error. Thus a better flowchart fragment to output the values of x is shown at the upper left. Now the printed table *will* have 300 lines and the last value of x will be 99.5.

Suppose we are still executing in the 3 precision digit floating-point decimal number system, and we have before us the flowchart fragment shown at the lower left.
Is the loop satisfactory?

We have all the information we need to decide this question. First, $1/3$ is chopped to .333 as before, to fit the 3-digit precision word length. From the data in Table $11 \cdot 3$ we know that 30 additions of .333 give x the value $.991 \times 10^1$, and the 31st addition makes it $.102 \times 10^2$. In other words, x goes from a value of 9.91 to 10.2 and *never* has the value 10. Therefore

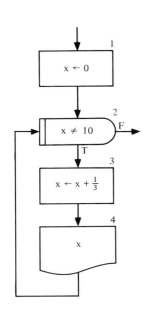

the T-path out of box 2 will always be followed, and this loop will never terminate! Although x increases from a value less than 10 to a value greater than 10, we failed to capitalize on this fact. What we want is a test that recognizes when the expression x − 10 changes sign. Thus, if the control box 2 is replaced by

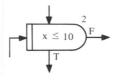

the value of the assertion will change from *true* to *false* when the expression x − 10 has a change in sign. Since the sign must change eventually, we know this loop will terminate.

EXERCISES 11·3

1. (a) In a floating-point system where b = 10 and n = 3, that is, in a 3 precision digit decimal system, what would be the effect of the stopping condition, x = 4, in the following iteration box?

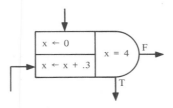

(b) What is your answer to part a if the stopping condition were altered to x = 4.2?

11·4 Nonassociativity of floating-point arithmetic

Because it is cumbersome always to write floating-point numbers as they appear in SAMOS storage, we will illustrate our points in this section using 3-digit precision decimal numbers and rounding results by chopping. Suppose we wish to evaluate the following sum.

$$.143 \times 10^3 - .164 \times 10^3 + .209 \times 10^2 - .100 \times 10^0$$

If we proceed from the left we compute

$$\underbrace{.143 \times 10^3 - .164 \times 10^3}$$
$$\underbrace{- .210 \times 10^2 + .209 \times 10^2}$$
$$\underbrace{- .100 \times 10^0 - .100 \times 10^0}$$
$$- .200 \times 10^0$$

On the other hand, if we rearrange the terms in the above sum slightly without changing its mathematical value, that is,

$$(.143 \times 10^3 + .209 \times 10^2) - (.164 \times 10^3 + .100 \times 10^0)$$

then the computed sum becomes

$$.163 \times 10^3 - .164 \times 10^3 = -.100 \times 10^1$$

We obtained a very different result simply by changing the order of computation. From study of the above computations it is evident that several of the intermediate additions involved roundoff. When the order of summing terms was changed, the intermediate summations were subject to different roundoffs in each case, and thus the final results were different.

A more formal way of stating the above fact is: *floating-point addition is not associative.*

The same phenomenon of nonassociativity occurs with multiplication. Consider the product $(a \times b) \times c$ versus the product $a \times (b \times c)$. Different roundoffs may be involved in obtaining the partial products, $a \times b$ in the first instance, and $b \times c$ in the second instance, so floating-point multiplication is also not associative.

In the case of multiplication and division, the nonassociativity usually does not matter very much. It may lead to a result that is wrong by a few units in the last place. For instance, if one computes a binomial coefficient, $n! / [r! (n - r)!]$, the result may not come out to be exactly an integer, although we know it should. But the answer will be close to the correct one.

With floating-point numbers, the order of operations is likely to affect the results. Let us explore this point further. Suppose we wish to compute

$$\text{sum} = \sum_{i=1}^{10} \frac{1}{2^i}$$

that is,

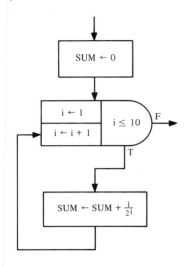

In Table 11·4 we have computed the exact decimal equivalents of the 10 terms to be added, as well as their 3-digit precision decimal equivalents. We have also summed the exact values.

TABLE 11·4

i	$1/2^i$	Exact Decimal Equivalent	3-Digit Precision Decimal Equivalent
1	$\frac{1}{2}$	.5	.500
2	$\frac{1}{4}$	.25	.250
3	$\frac{1}{8}$	.125	.125
4	$\frac{1}{16}$	.0625	.0625
5	$\frac{1}{32}$	.03125	.0312
6	$\frac{1}{64}$	.015625	.0156
7	$\frac{1}{128}$	.0078125	.00781
8	$\frac{1}{256}$	.00390625	.00390
9	$\frac{1}{512}$	.001953125	.00195
10	$\frac{1}{1024}$	.0009765625	.000976
		.9990234375 ◄	

(Exact sum)

Now let us add in the "normal" way, from top to bottom, using 3-digit precision decimal floating-point addition with chopping.

$$.500 + .250 \quad = .750$$
$$.750 + .125 \quad = .875$$
$$.875 + .0625 \quad = .937$$
$$.937 + .0312 \quad = .968$$

$$.968 + .0156 \quad = .983$$
$$.983 + .00781 \quad = .990$$
$$.990 + .00390 \quad = .993$$
$$.993 + .00195 \quad = .994$$
$$.994 + .000976 = .994$$

This result differs from the exact value by .005, which is not very good. Now let us try adding the same values in the reverse order.

$$.000976 + .00195 = .00292$$
$$.00292 + .00390 = .00682$$
$$.00682 + .00781 = .0146$$
$$.0146 \quad + .0156 \quad = .0302$$
$$.0302 \quad + .0312 \quad = .0614$$
$$.0614 \quad + .0625 \quad = .123$$
$$.123 \quad + .125 \quad = .248$$
$$.248 \quad + .250 \quad = .498$$
$$.498 \quad + .500 \quad = .998$$

Here the error from the exact result is only .001, or one-fifth of the previous error.

The given examples use only 3-digit precision arithmetic in order that the step-by-step execution of the process can be followed with greater ease. However, similar effects occur in floating-point operations on actual computers, where much longer series of calculations are performed. As an example, we have computed the sum of the first 10,000 terms of the series $\Sigma \ 1/i^2$ by two algorithms. The "forward" one is displayed in Figure 11·3. The result of executing this algorithm with 8-digit arithmetic is 1.6444743. Now, using the "backward" algorithm shown in Figure 11·4, we get 1.6448339, a difference of .0003596. Since the true sum, rounded to 8 decimal digits of precision, is 1.6448341, we see that the "backward" summing yields a result that is in error by only 2 in the 8th digit, versus 3598 in the 8th digit for the forward summing method.

Note from the above examples that adding terms in order of *increasing absolute value* is generally preferable to the reverse order. This is because the cumulative effect of a large number of small terms has a better chance to make itself felt.

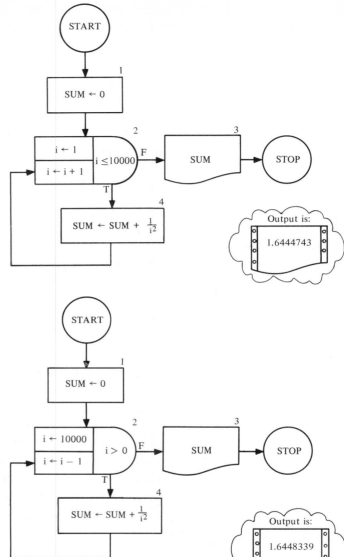

FIGURE 11·3
Summing the series $\sum \frac{1}{i^2}$ forward.

FIGURE 11·4
Summing the series $\sum \frac{1}{i^2}$ backward.

As with all general rules, there are exceptions, and the following summation is one of these exceptions. The sum

$$102 + (-91.2) + (-9.66) = 1.14$$

with no roundoff, whereas the mathematically equivalent sum

$$-9.66 + (-91.2) + 102 = 2.00$$

because of roundoff on the first partial sum.

Computing with Extended Precision

Roundoff errors are the fundamental cause of the lack of associativity in floating-point arithmetic. If the roundoff error could be reduced to zero, then the order of operations would not matter and the computed results would be accurate. Thus it makes sense to search for ways to reduce roundoff error. Roundoff error usually occurs if at all in the least significant or rightmost digits of a computed result. Roundoff potentially affects every intermediate result and there is a chance that the roundoff "contamination" will grow to affect more and more of the precision digits of the final result. This, of course, is the reason for providing *double precision arithmetic.*

If double the normal storage, for example, two computer words, are used to hold each value and each intermediate result, then more digits of the final result should be uncontaminated by roundoff errors. If a computer has the capability to do double precision floating-point arithmetic, that is, if it is "built in" to the system, it is probably reasonably efficient and should be used where needed to combat roundoff error. The cost to the user is (1) somewhat slower execution, which only matters in large problems, and (2) twice as much storage is required for the variables that are to be represented in double precision, which may or may not matter.

You may wonder what organizational changes are required to enable a computer to perform floating-point arithmetic operations on double precision as well as single precision operands. For example, how might SAMOS be modified to do this? The last section of the SAMOS Appendix answers this question.

The analysis of roundoff errors in arithmetic and algebraic computations is not an easy subject and should be approached with caution. However, it is possible to get a rough measure of the roundoff in a single precision computation by running it in single and again in double precision and then comparing the results. The digits in the single precision result that are in agreement with the double precision result are probably correct and, of course, even more digits of the double precision result are probably also correct.

Are there any ways other than double precision to combat roundoff error? Yes there are, although if improvement in a computation is possible, the method required may go well beyond the scope of this book. However, let us consider evaluating a polynomial. If we calculate the value of the polynomial $x^3 - 6x^2 + 4x - .1$ in its given form, about six intermediate results seem to be necessary, as will be seen shortly. If we rearrange the polynomial into $((x - 6)x + 4)x - .1$ before computing the value, only four intermediate results are required, as shown in Table 11·5.

TABLE 11·5
Two Methods for Evaluating a Polynomial

Algorithm 1: $y \leftarrow x^3 - 6x^2 + 4x - .1$	Algorithm 2: $z \leftarrow ((x - 6) \cdot x + 4) \cdot x - .1$
Compute $i1 = x^2$	Compute $i1 = x - 6$
Compute $i2 = x^3$	Compute $i2 = i1 \times x = (x - 6) \times x$
Compute $i3 = 6x^2$	Compute $i3 = i2 + 4 = (x - 6) \times x + 4$
Compute $i4 = i2 - i3 = x^3 - 6x^2$	Compute $i4 = i3 \times x = ((x - 6) \times x + 4) \times x$
Compute $i5 = 4x$	Compute $z = i4 - .1 = ((x - 6) \times x + 4) \times x - .1$
Compute $i6 = i4 - i5 = x^3 - 6x^2 - 4x$	
Compute $y = i6 - .1 = x^3 - 6x^2 - 4x - .1$	

We would expect the second algorithm to probably give better results. For $x = 5.24$ the exact value of the polynomial is $-.007776$. Using 3 precision digit arithmetic and chopping the intermediate results, the first algorithm gives $-.200 \times 10^0$ and the second evaluates to $.004$. Thus the first algorithm gives a result 30 times as large as it should be. On the other hand, the second algorithm gives a result that is about the right size but has the wrong sign!

How could we get an acceptable answer? The error in the second or nested form evaluation of the polynomial comes when the four intermediate results are stored. But notice the sequence of computations in the nested form evaluation; each succeeding computation uses the result of the previous one. Our floating-point arithmetic has had us compute each intermediate result in a double length accumulator, apply a rounding function (chop) to store it in a single length word, only to immediately return the chopped value to the accumulator in the next operation of the computation.

Suppose our computer could skip that intermediate rounding and storing if the value in question is to be used in the very next computation. As a matter of fact, this is done in a computer having a good compiler or interpreter, and it improves the arithmetic result dramatically. In the polynomial evaluation above (Algorithm 2) *all* intermediate rounding can thus be eliminated, in which case, the final value in the accumulator is −.007776, agreeing perfectly with the exact value. Of course, when this result is stored it will be chopped to −.00777, but the three significant digits are correct.

If one happens to know the roots of a polynomial, the best way to evaluate it usually is to use the *factored form*. Thus, for a third-degree polynomial whose three roots are a, b, and c, the factored form is:

$$(x - a) \times (x - b) \times (x - c)$$

We turn now to the problem of repeated addition, and we will see that the above discussion is relevant. Suppose we have a large number of terms to add up, as suggested in Figure 11·5.

In the normal addition process every intermediate result occurring in the double length accumulator is rounded off to the word length of the computer when it is stored. In this problem each value of SUM + x is rounded off as it is assigned to SUM. This happens 10,000 times. But here, as in

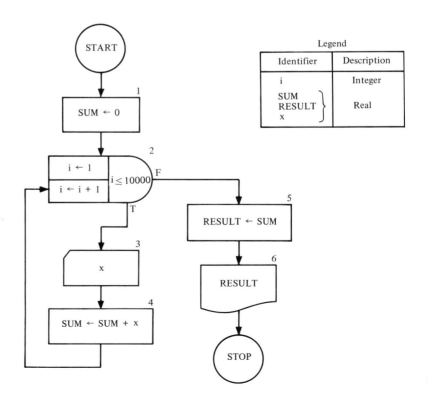

FIGURE 11·5

the nested polynomial evaluation, every computation uses the result of the last one. If the storing of the intermediate results (the partial sums) can be bypassed by the computer, 10,000 roundoff errors can potentially be eliminated. If you program this algorithm, say in standard FORTRAN, it is a simple matter to declare SUM as a double precision real variable. Then, in the actual FORTRAN computation, each assignment of a value to SUM will be the double precision value in the accumulator, and each time the value of SUM is brought to the accumulator, it will cause a "reinstatement" of that double precision value for the next addition of x to SUM.

Another way of looking at the situation is to say that the sum should accumulate in double precision, since the accumulator is a double length word. Only when the loop is ended should the variable RESULT receive the rounded (chopped) value of the double precision result built up in SUM.

EXERCISES 11·4, SET A

1. One way to appreciate the usefulness of double precision floating-point arithmetic is to sum up many numbers both with and without this feature. You will probably (because of cost) have to restrict yourself to well under a million terms, but somewhere in the range of 100,000 to 250,000 terms should be feasible. For numbers of terms in this range the error when *not* using double precision could appear in the fourth from the last precision digit of the single precision result. If your machine has some hidden guard digits (i.e., actually does its computation with higher precision than it prints out its answers for single precision), then the comparison will be less dramatic.

The only question is how to select the terms to be summed. Here are a few suggestions.

(a) Let TERM = $1/3$. Then you can compare the results your computer gives with those in the Table 11·3.

(b) Let TERM = $1/[i \times (i + 1)]$ (where i is the loop variable.) Here the correct value of the sum of N terms is easy to calculate since

$$\frac{1}{i(i + 1)} = \frac{1}{i} - \frac{1}{i + 1} \text{ so that}$$

$$\frac{1}{1 \cdot 2} + \frac{1}{2 \cdot 3} + \frac{1}{3 \cdot 4} + \cdots + \frac{1}{N(N + 1)}$$

$$= \left(1 - \frac{1}{2}\right) + \left(\frac{1}{2} - \frac{1}{3}\right) + \left(\frac{1}{3} - \frac{1}{4}\right) + \cdots + \left(\frac{1}{N} - \frac{1}{N + 1}\right)$$

which is equal to $1 - \dfrac{1}{N + 1}$ because all the other terms cancel out.

(c) Let TERM = $1/i$ (where i is the loop variable). Here the correct sum of N terms cannot be given exactly but, for large N, the sum can be shown to be close to $.57 \ldots + \log_e N$. (Here $\log_e N$ denotes the natural log of N and $.57 \ldots$ denotes Euler's constant.)

2. This exercise is an extension of Problem 1b.

Let the term summed be $1/i - 1/(i+1)$ (where i is the loop variable). Here, as in Problem 1b, the sum of N terms is $1 - 1/(N+1)$. At first glance, one expects that the cancellation error resulting from the subtraction step in the computation of each "difference" term will lead to much poorer results for the sum of this series as compared with results obtained upon summing the "product" term, $1/[i \times (i+1)]$.

(a) Compute the difference term and the product term sums for $N = 10$, using a computer that chops or using an available calculator. If a calculator is used, compute both sums using 6-decimal precision arithmetic, chopping each intermediate result. The exact sum, correct to 6 places, is .909091.

(b) Repeat the above experiment taking 10 terms in the sum beginning at $i = 100$. The exact sum correct to 6 places is .000909091.

Comment on the results obtained. Note that product terms are computed accurately to 6 places, whereas cancellation in the computation of difference terms results in a loss of two significant digits in each value computed for these terms. Can you explain why results summing the product terms are not *much* better than results using difference terms? On the computer available to you, which method (product sum or difference sum) will be faster when summing a very large number of terms?

3. *Backward Adding.* Suppose we want to sum up a large number of terms whose absolute values are steadily decreasing toward zero. For example,

(a) $1 + \dfrac{1}{2} + \dfrac{1}{3} + \dfrac{1}{4} + \dfrac{1}{5} + \dfrac{1}{6} + \cdots + \dfrac{1}{N}$

(b) $\dfrac{1}{1 \cdot 2} + \dfrac{1}{2 \cdot 3} + \dfrac{1}{3 \cdot 4} + \dfrac{1}{4 \cdot 5} + \dfrac{1}{N(N+1)}$

(c) $1 + \dfrac{1}{2} + \dfrac{1}{4} + \dfrac{1}{8} + \dfrac{1}{6} + \cdots + \dfrac{1}{2^N} = 1 - \dfrac{1}{2^N}$

(Examples a and b) were used in parts c and b, respectively, of Problem 1.

In such cases, if we are using single precision arithmetic, it helps to add from right to left instead of from left to right. The reason is that as the partial sum gets larger so does the next term to be added, so that the two summands are more nearly equal in size if we use backward adding rather than forward adding. Backward adding gives the aggregate of the smaller terms a better chance to have some impact on the sum. Example c illustrates this idea quite well because the next TERM to be added (summing right to left) will always be nearly identical to the SUM of those added so far. However, in this example, the high-order terms go to zero so rapidly that their sum doesn't amount to anything anyhow.

(a) Compute the sums by both forward adding and backward adding for Examples a and b above and compare the results with the double precision results determined in parts b and c of Problem 1. (Use a value of N on the order of 100,000.)

(b) Apply a combination of double precision adding and backward adding to the same examples as in part a and compare the results of all three methods.

Batch Adding and Magic Adding

In some computers extended precision arithmetic cannot be used because the length of the accumulator is only equal to or slightly greater than a single computer storage word. Even so, there are ways to sum a very large number of terms of reasonably equal size and have less roundoff error than occurs when small terms are added to large partial sums. Two such methods are considered in the following problem set. The first method is called "batch adding." We call the second method "magic adding" because it *works like magic.*

The basic idea of batch adding is very simple. We add up the summands in small *batches,* say 10 terms to a batch. Once the sum of one batch of 10 has been computed, it is summed with the totals of other such batches to form the sum, say, for a batch of 100. This process is continued to produce sums for batches of 1000 terms, 10,000 terms, 100,000 terms, and so forth. In this way the effect of each new term or each new batch is significant because it is always added to a group of terms or to groups of batches that are of approximately the same magnitude.

We can develop an algorithm for the above process by first noting that batch adding is closely modeled on our *method of counting* in the decimal system. The algorithm shown in Figure 11·6 counts from 1 to N where $N \leq 999,999,999$. It works very much like an automobile odometer. The variables $R_9, R_8, \ldots, R_1$ play the roles of the wheels on the odometer. Each time the value on one of these registers (wheels) goes over 9, as noted in box 8, this register (wheel) is set back to zero and the value in the next register (wheel) is incremented by 1, as seen in box 9. At any stage in the process, the variables $R_1, R_2, R_3, \ldots$ record, respectively, the units digit, tens digit,

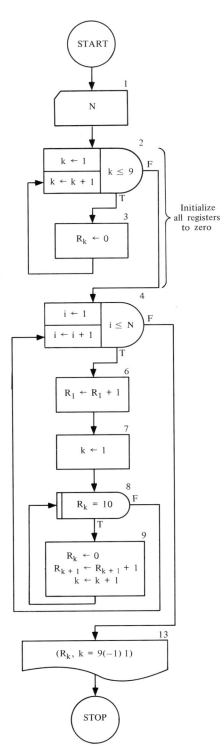

Legend

Identifier	Description
N	Integer $< 10^{11}$
i, k	Integer
R	List of 9 integers

FIGURE 11·6
Odometer algorithm (counting in base 10).

hundreds digit, and so on, of the number to which we have counted.

For batch adding, we can use the same basic flowchart, but introduce *sum* registers, SUM_1, SUM_2, . . . SUM_9. Each time we increment R_1 by 1, we get a new term and add it to SUM_1. Each time we "reset" R_k to zero and increment R_{k+1} by 1 we also increment SUM_{k+1} by SUM_k and then reset SUM_k to zero.

In this way, terms are added in SUM_1 until 10 terms have been added to form a batch. These batches are, in turn, added up in SUM_2 until 10 additions have been performed, thus obtaining a batch of 100, and so on. If the terms being added do not differ much in magnitude, roundoff error will not grow too rapidly. For example, to see how this method works when *most* applicable, we can imagine adding up many floating-point

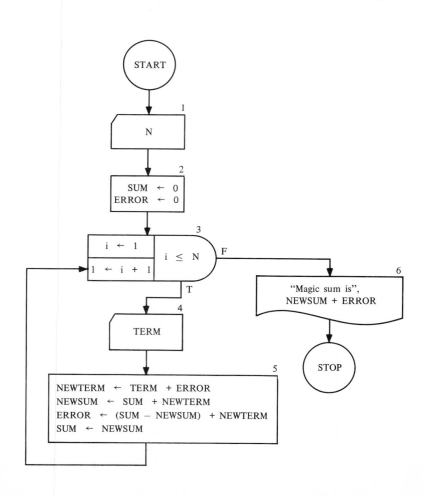

FIGURE 11·7
Summing by the Magic Adding method.

numbers each having the same exponent part. Then, adding 10 terms will yield a sum whose exponent is at most one greater than the individual terms. Adding 10 batches of 10 will yield a sum of 100 terms whose exponent is no more than one greater than that of a batch of 10, and so on.

Prediction of the expected roundoff error for batch adding is a difficult mathematical task. Nevertheless, it is easy to show cases where the results using this method are spectacular. See Problem 2 in the following exercise set.

In the magic adding method, the roundoff error caused by adding each new term is subtracted out when the next term is accumulated. Figure 11·7 shows a flowchart for this algorithm. The negative of the roundoff error introduced in the second (assignment) step is computed and saved in the third assignment step of box 5 and then it is added back into the sum in the first assignment step of box 5 on the next transit through the loop, thus cancelling out its effect. In the third assignment step of box 5 it is essential that the difference, (SUM — NEWSUM), be computed first, as indicated by the parentheses. It is also essential that the whole computation be executed on a processing unit equipped with at least one accumulator guard digit.

EXERCISES 11·4
SET B

1. Convert the odometer algorithm in Figure 11 · 6 into a batch adding algorithm as explained in the above discussion.
2. Verify the results reported in Table 11 · 6 using any pocket or desk-type calculator that has floating-point arithmetic with a precision of at least 8 digits. That is, calculate what the sum would be if 1 million

TABLE 11·6
Batch Adding Results

Adding 1 Million Terms Each Equal to $\frac{1}{3}$	Result
8 precision digit floating-point addition	330909.91
8 precision digit batch adding (floating-point) addition	333333.30
Mathematical sum	333333.33

terms, each equal to 1/3, were summed using 8-precision digit floating-point addition (with chopping), first assuming straight addition, and then assuming you followed the batch adding technique described above.
3. Verify that the magic adding method (Figure 11·7) yields good results by adding ten equal terms of 1/3 in 3-precision digit floating-point

arithmetic (with chopping). The expected result is 3.33, as compared with the result shown in Table 11·3, which was 3.31.

4. Modify the flowchart algorithm in Figure 11·7 to simulate 3-precision digit floating-point arithmetic. Now write an equivalent computer program and run it on any available computer or programmable calculator. Show that using magic adding, the sum of 300 terms, each equal to 1/3, gives 99.9 as the result, i.e., as good an answer as can be obtained using 3 precision digits.

5. Execute a computer program equivalent to the flowchart for magic adding in Figure 11·7 to obtain the sum

$$\sum_{i=1}^{10,000} \frac{1}{i^2}.$$

Compare your answer with the true sum which, as reported in the text, is 1.6448341, rounded to 8 decimal digits of precision.

6. Use the batch adding algorithm and the magic adding algorithm to recompute the sums you developed for Problem 1, Set A of this section. Compare the results obtained for batch adding, magic adding, double precision method, and single precision method. If possible also compare the time required on your computer using each of the four methods. What conclusions can be drawn?

11·5
Pitfalls

As we have shown so far in this chapter the floating-point numbers are only an approximation to the real-number system of mathematics. While the approximation is quite good enough for many purposes, the user must be aware of and have a healthy respect for the possible effects of roundoff errors because rounding is inherent in floating-point computation. In this section we will explore some disquieting rounding possibilities that can occur by blindly applying such a simple algorithm as the familiar quadratic formula.

In high school algebra we learned that if a, b, and c are any real numbers and if a $\neq$ 0, then the quadratic equation

$$ax^2 + bx + c = 0$$

has exactly two solutions given by

$$(1) \quad x1 = \frac{-b + \sqrt{b^2 - 4 \times a \times c}}{2 \times a}$$

and

$$(2) \quad x2 = \frac{-b - \sqrt{b^2 - 4 \times a \times c}}{2 \times a}$$

Assume for this discussion that the discriminant $b^2 - 4 \times a \times c$ is not negative, i.e., the mathematical solutions are real, not imaginary.

The first example we want to solve is

(3) $x^2 - 10^5 x + 1 = 0$

If we substitute in the above formulas using 8-precision digit arithmetic, we have:

$$x1 = \frac{10^5 + \sqrt{10^{10} - 4}}{2} \qquad x2 = \frac{10^5 - \sqrt{10^{10} - 4}}{2}$$

$$x1 = \frac{10^5 + \sqrt{10^{10}}}{2} \qquad x2 = \frac{10^5 - \sqrt{10^{10}}}{2}$$

$$x1 = 10^5 \qquad\qquad x2 = 0$$

> To 10 significant decimal digits the "true" answers are
>
> $x1 = 99999.99999,$
>
> $x2 = .1000000000 \times 10^{-4} \cong .00001$

The value we computed for x1, 100000, is not very wrong, but x2 is computed as zero although its true value has a 1 in the 5th decimal place! The quadratic formula has led us to an answer that is plausible, i.e., it has the right order of magnitude, but the zero answer is absolutely wrong! (For an algorithm to give incorrect plausible answers is "unforgiveable." We will return later in this section to the question of when a computer algorithm is adequate.)

What happened and why? In the computation of the discriminant $b^2 - 4ac$, the value of b^2 was so much larger than $4ac$ that the $4ac$ was rounded off completely. In computing x1, this fact did not matter too much because, in the next step, there was an addition of two large terms of like sign. But in computing x2, the roundoff in the $b^2 - 4ac$ was followed by a subtraction. The roundoff led to computing the difference between two equal terms, and thus a result of zero. The rounded-off value became crucial in this case. As a matter of fact, cancellation is often a signal that one should seek another method of computation.

Although the difference between zero and 10^{-5} may not be great in some contexts, the *relative error* in x2 is

$(.00001 - 0)/.00001 = 1$ or 100%. A small relative error is generally accepted as a good measure of accuracy in the evaluation of the solution of a quadratic. The straightforward evaluation of the quadratic formula has not led us to an adequate computer algorithm but, before we discard it completely, we should see if we can do better.

At the beginning of this section we showed the solutions to the quadratic equation as

(1) $$x1 = \frac{-b + \sqrt{b^2 - 4 \times a \times c}}{2 \times a}$$

and

(2) $$x2 = \frac{-b - \sqrt{b^2 - 4 \times a \times c}}{2 \times a}$$

By a little algebra we can fortuitously transform these equations into two others. Multiply the numerator and denominator of Equation 1 by $-b - \sqrt{b^2 - 4 \times a \times c}$ and of Equation 2 by $-b + \sqrt{b^2 - 4 \times a \times c}$. Then we have

$$x1 = \frac{b^2 - (b^2 - 4 \times a \times c)}{2 \times a(-b - \sqrt{b^2 - 4 \times a \times c})}$$

$$x2 = \frac{b^2 - (b^2 - 4 \times a \times c)}{2 \times a(-b + \sqrt{b^2 - 4 \times a \times c})}$$

or

(4) $$x1 = \frac{2 \times c}{-b - \sqrt{b^2 - 4 \times a \times c}}$$

(5) $$x2 = \frac{2 \times c}{-b + \sqrt{b^2 - 4 \times a \times c}}$$

Now, if $a \neq 0$ and $c \neq 0$, we have found an alternate expression for both solutions x1 and x2. The important point to notice is that if $b > 0$, there is cancellation in Equations 1 and 5 but not in either Equation 2 or Equation 4. Thus, if $b > 0$, we should use (2) to compute x2 and (4) to compute x1. On the contrary, if $b < 0$, there is no cancellation in (1) or (5), so we should use (1) to compute x1 and (5) for x2.

Figure 11·8 expresses the computation of this alternate solution to the quadratic equation as an algorithm. Check for

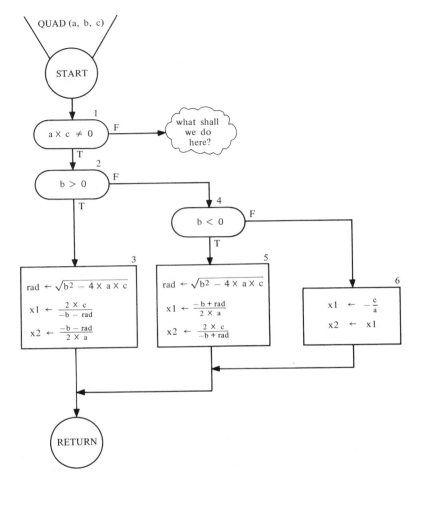

FIGURE 11·8
Improved quadratic equation
solver.

yourself that this algorithm will compute the solutions to the
first quadratic (3) correctly.

Since Figure 11·8 essentially requires no more computation than the original equations (1 and 2), we will henceforth
follow this improved approach.

Next we want to solve another quadratic.

(6) $1.667x^2 - 7.0007x + 7.35 = 0$

Using the improved algorithm in Figure 11·8, we compute
the discriminant with 8 precision digits and have:

$$b^2 = (7.0007)^2 = 49.009800$$
$$4 \times a \times c = 49.009800$$
$$b^2 - 4 \times a \times c = 0$$

Since $b < 0$, we arrive at the solutions:

$$(7) \quad \begin{cases} x1 = -\dfrac{b}{2a} = \dfrac{7.0007}{2 \times 1.667} = 2.0997900 \\[2ex] x2 = \dfrac{2 \times 7.35}{7.0007} = 2.0997900 \end{cases}$$

The algorithm gives us two *equal* roots for this quadratic, but that is really *not* the case at all, as you will see.

The true value of b^2 was 49.00980049, but the final two digits were lost to roundoff. The true value of $b^2 - 4 \times a \times c$ was .00000049 and not zero. The roots should have been computed as

$$(8) \quad x1 = \frac{(7.0007 + .0007)}{3.334} = 2.1000.$$

$$x2 = \frac{2 \times 7.35}{7.0007 + .0007} = 2.0995800$$

The equal roots shown in Equation 7 are actually the roots of the quadratic equation

$$(9) \quad 1.667x^2 - 7.000699860x + 7.349999779 = 0$$

whose coefficients differ by at most 3 units in the 8th significant digit from the coefficients in Equation 6. But the roots of Equation 9 differ already in the 5th significant digit from the roots of Equation 6. Thus a small change in the coefficients has produced a relatively large change in the roots. This is an example of *hypersensitivity* or *instability*. The algorithm in Figure 11·8 has not solved exactly the problem we gave it, but has instead solved a *nearby problem*.

Should we therefore discard the algorithm of Figure 11·8? That depends on whether we have a better one to use instead. As it is, we have been able to interpret the errors in terms of small perturbations in the given coefficients. This type of study is called a "backward" error analysis. It is newer and considerably less difficult than the traditional "forward" error analysis, which must analyze the roundoff error in every floating-point operation in the computation.

Can we improve the algorithm of Figure 11·8 so it will solve Equation 6 correctly? Yes! If we use double precision for the calculations of b^2, $4 \times a \times c$, and the difference

$b^2 - 4 \times a \times c$ in computing the discriminant, the solutions will be computed correctly. But the phenomenon of hypersensitivity will not therefore go away. Hypersensitive problems appear in many areas and are characterized by the fact that an algorithm produces the solution to a nearby problem instead of the given one.

Effects of Data Errors.

Coefficients in real-life computations are often taken from measured data and are themselves subject to error. Consider the system of equations

$$x + .98y = 1.98$$
$$.99x + .98y = 1.97$$

Using exact arithmetic, we get the solution $x = 1$, $y = 1$. Check it! Now suppose we change just one of the numbers involved in the problem slightly, say 1.97 to 1.96, and solve the system

$$x + .98y = 1.98$$
$$.99x + .98y = 1.96$$

We get the solution $x = 2$, $y = -2/98 = -.0204$ to three significant digits. Thus a very minor change in just one coefficient causes an extreme change in the solution.

There is a fairly simple geometrical explanation for this change that becomes evident when one draws the graphs of the three equations involved in the two systems. It would be very difficult to distinguish the three lines with the naked eye. They are almost parallel but, since they are not exactly parallel, the two pairs of lines have two distinct and separate points of intersection. Changing the slope of one line slightly, or shifting it slightly parallel to itself, can move those points of intersection a long way. In a real-life problem, the coefficients of a system of equations are usually determined by earlier computations, which themselves are subject to error.

The hypersensitivity situation described above, where a small change in the coefficients of the equation causes an extreme change in a solution to the system, is not the result of a bad choice of equations but rather is inherent in the problem itself, i.e., with the natural phenomenon modeled by the equations.

To return to a question raised earlier in this section: When can a numerical computer algorithm be regarded as adequate? Professor W. Kahan of the University of California at Berkeley says an algorithm can be regarded as adequate if for any input it gives one of the following answers.

(1) It returns an answer and says, "Here is your answer. It is correct." And the accompanying answer *is* correct.

(2) It says "Your problem doesn't have a decent answer and here is why." And the explanation that follows is correct.

(3) It says "I don't know the answer." But this reply does not occur very often.

From the above description and from our own experience thus far it is clear that most computer algorithms are not adequate! Even though an algorithm is not adequate, we should not discard it unless we can substitute a better one. We should also not condemn algorithms even though imperfect if they try to do something no other program has managed to do.

The object of this section has been to make the reader aware of the discrepancy between real arithmetic and floating-point arithmetic. However, in an ordinary small problem this difference is not apt to be significant.

EXERCISES 11·5

1. The quadratic equation

$$ax^2 + bx + c = 0$$

can be transformed into an equivalent one,

$$Ax^2 + 2Bx + C = 0$$

whose roots are

$$x = \frac{B \pm \sqrt{B^2 - A \times C}}{A}$$

which is a simpler formula because it requires fewer multiplications. Show the changes required in the algorithm of Figure 11·8 to take advantage of this simplification.

2. Find the roots of

(a) $x^2 - 9000x + 2 = 0$

and of

(b) $x^2 - 756 + 2 = 0$

to seven digits of precision, assuming in each case that the coefficients are precise. Use the algorithm given in Figure 11·8.

3. Draw a flowchart for the best algorithm you can devise for a QUADSOL procedure whose "masthead" and legend are given below. QUADSOL should find all the real roots if any of a quadratic equation and either output a message or return a warning through an additional switch variable if the roots are imaginary. Treat separately the special cases when any of the coefficients A, B, or C is zero as well as the cases that two or more of the coefficients are zero.

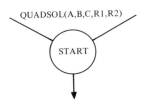

QUADSOL(A,B,C,R1,R2)

START

Legend for QUADSOL

Identifier	Treatment	Description
A, B, C	Value	Real
R1, R2	Reference	Real

4. Consider the equation system

$$.0001x + y = 1$$
$$x + y = 2$$

The true solution, rounded correctly to the number of decimals shown is

$$x = 1.00010$$
$$y = 0.99990$$

(a) With 3-precision digit decimal arithmetic solve this system by using the first equation to eliminate x from the second equation, that is, by multiplying the first equation by 10000 and then subtracting the resulting equation from the second equation.

(b) Next interchange the two equations, that is, start with

$$x + y = 2$$
$$.0001x + y = 1$$

and again solve the system using the same approach and the same precision arithmetic.

(c) If you computed the results for parts a and b correctly your answers should have been:

For part a: $y = 1.00$
$\qquad\qquad\quad x = 0.00$
For part b: $y = 1.00$
$\qquad\qquad\quad x = 1.00$

Explain the large discrepancy in these results and consider how you might construct an algorithm that would prevent the accuracy loss encountered in part a.

11·6
Truncation error

There are many *infinite processes* one might want to simulate on a computer; one of them is adding up the terms of an infinite series. Quite a number of functions can be written as the sum of an infinite series, for instance,

$$\sin x = x - \frac{x^3}{3!} + \frac{x^5}{5!} - \frac{x^7}{7!} + \frac{x^9}{9!} - \dots$$

$$\cos x = 1 - \frac{x^2}{2!} + \frac{x^4}{4!} - \frac{x^6}{6!} + \dots$$

$$e^x = 1 + x + \frac{x^2}{2!} + \frac{x^3}{3!} + \dots$$

The "...." at the end of each series indicates that it continues on and on in the same pattern. Let S be the true sum of the infinite series. Let S_n be the sum of the first n terms of the series. The difference $|S - S_n|$ is called the *truncation error*.

There is a mathematical theorem (given here without proof) to the effect that if the terms of a series *alternate* in sign and if the value of the terms become closer and closer to zero as the series continues, then the sum, S_n, gets closer to the sum S and the truncation error, $|S - S_n|$, *is less than the value of the first term omitted.*

For example, if x = 1 radian and if only three terms of the above series for sin x are included in the summation, we have

is "approximately equal to"

$$\sin 1 \approx 1 - \frac{1}{3!} + \frac{1}{5!} = 1 - \frac{1}{6} + \frac{1}{120} = .841666667$$

The truncation error $|S - S_n|$ is less than the value of the first term omitted, thus the truncation error

$$E = |\sin 1 - .841666667|$$

$$< \frac{1}{7!} = \frac{1}{5040} < .000198413$$

But to 9 digits of precision, the actual value is

$$\sin 1 = .841470985$$

and we see that our approximation differs from this by .000195682. Thus the calculated truncation error was indeed an upper estimate for the error in this case.

Suppose we want to calculate sin x for some other value of x, and we guess that 4 terms of the series will be sufficient. Then we can write

$$\sin x \sim x - \frac{x^3}{3!} + \frac{x^5}{5!} - \frac{x^7}{7!}$$

with a truncation error

$$E < \frac{|x^9|}{9!}$$

Since $9! = 362880$, the error will be small if $|x|$ is small. Can we make x small? That is, can we force x to be small in all cases where we want to compute sin x by this series? Fortunately, $y = \sin x$ is periodic (Figure 11·9). The functional

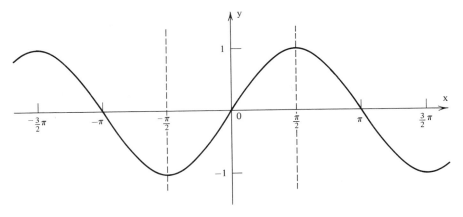

FIGURE 11·9
y = sin x.

values simply repeat after 2π radians; that is, for any integer n,

$$\sin x = \sin (x \pm 2 \pi n)$$

Thus, if we are given an angle A in radians, we can always find another angle A′ such that $\sin A = \sin A'$ and $|A'| \leq \pi$. The domain, $-\pi < A' \leq \pi$, contains one complete period or cycle of the function.

We have shown so far that we can reduce any angle to one no larger in absolute value than π radians. But can we do better? Remember that the sine graph is symmetric about the line $x = \pi/2$, and this symmetry means that

$$\sin\left(\frac{\pi}{2} + x\right) = \sin\left(\frac{\pi}{2} - x\right)$$

So, if our angle A' lies between $\pi/2$ and π radians, there is another angle A'', symmetrically located with respect to $x = \pi/2$, such that $\sin A' = \sin A''$ and $0 \leq A'' \leq \pi/2$. In the same way the symmetry of the sine function about $x = -\pi/2$ enables us to replace an angle A' in the domain, $-\pi \leq A' \leq -\pi/2$, with an angle A'' in the domain, $-\pi/2 \leq A'' \leq 0$, and the two angles have the same sine. In short, if we need to compute the sine of any angle y, we can always do it by computing the sine of some angle x, such that $|x| \leq \pi/2$.

Therefore, for any $|x| \leq \pi/2$, the 4-term approximation to $\sin x$ above will have a truncation error

$$E < \frac{(\pi/2)^9}{9!} < .00017$$

An even more interesting challenge now presents itself. Suppose we are given not only an angle x, but also the size of the allowable truncation error. How do we proceed to compute $\sin x$ to that accuracy? In that case we observe that the nth term for the sine series can be written in the following way.

$$(-1)^{n-1}\frac{x^{2n-1}}{(2n-1)!}$$

If we are given the value, for example, 10^{-5}, for the allowable truncation error, we can find k, the number of terms that must be included in the calculation of $\sin x$ to insure that the truncation error will be less than 10^{-5}. Since the first omitted term will be the $k + 1$st term, then the inequality

$$\left|\frac{(-1)^k x^{2k+1}}{(2k+1)!}\right| < .00001$$

must be satisfied. For ease of computation, let us again assume $x = 1$ radian. Then the above inequality becomes

$$\frac{1}{(2k+1)!} < .00001$$

A glance at Table 11·7 shows that $1/N!$ is less than .00001 for $N \geq 9$. (I.e., it can be seen that $1/9!$ is the first entry less than .00001.) Thus $2k + 1 = 9$, or $k = 4$. So four terms are sufficient to evaluate $\sin 1$ to a precision of .00001. To

TABLE 11·7
Factorials and Their Inverses

N	N!	1 / N!
1	1	1
2	2	.5
3	6	.166666667
4	24	.041666667
5	120	.008333333
6	720	.001388889
7	5040	.000198413
8	40320	.000024802
9	362880	.000002756
10	3628800	.000000276

verify this conclusion, we note that in actually carrying out the 4-term summation we compute

$$\sin 1 = .84147$$

to 5 decimal places. As mentioned earlier, the true value is

$$\sin 1 = .841470985$$

to 9 digits of precision. Thus the actual truncation error is indeed less than .00001, the given limit.

If we utilize the further trigonometric identity that

$$\sin x = \cos\left(\frac{\pi}{2} - x\right)$$

then we can go one step further in reducing the size of the angle for which we need to compute a sine or cosine function. If any angle lies between $\pi/4$ and $\pi/2$, its complement, $\pi/2 - x$, will lie between 0 and $\pi/4$. In this way it should be clear that if we have the capability to compute both sines *and* cosines, we can compute the sine (or cosine) of any angle by computing a function of an angle no larger than $\pi/4$.

Now let us develop a flowchart to compute sin x, given a value of x (in radians) and a value for the allowable truncation error, trunc. Notice that for any term in the series

$$\frac{(-1)^{n-1}x^{2n-1}}{(2n - 1)!}$$

the next term may be obtained by multiplying this one by the

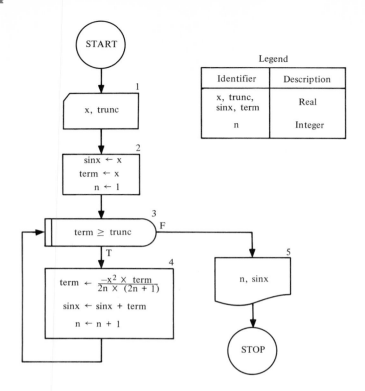

FIGURE 11·10
Algorithm for computing sin x
for an allowable truncation
error.

factor

$$- \frac{x^2}{2n \times (2n + 1)}$$

For example, for n $=$ 7, the seventh term is

$$(-1)^6 \frac{x^{13}}{(13)!} \quad \text{or} \quad \frac{x^{13}}{13!}$$

and the next term is

$$\left(- \frac{x^2}{14 \times 15}\right) \times \left((-1)^6 \frac{x^{13}}{13!}\right) = - \frac{x^{15}}{15!}$$

These relationships are applied in a straightforward manner
in the flowchart of Figure 11·10.

Roundoff Error versus
Truncation Error

Truncation error can be expressed as the difference between
the sum of an infinite number of terms and the sum of a finite
number of terms approximating the infinite sum. We intuitively
sense that the truncation error must, in some sense, decrease

as the number of terms gets larger and larger. Exactly how the error decreases depends on how the approximating sum converges to the infinite sum. This is a subject area belonging to numerical analysis. Some approximating sums converge very rapidly and some rather slowly. Sometimes a series of slowly converging sums can be converted into a rapidly converging one.

On the other hand, if we add up a sum of n floating-point numbers, the potential *roundoff error grows with the number of terms added*, the more terms, the more roundoff error possible. Thus there is a kind of tradeoff between truncation error and roundoff error in the computation of approximating sums. When too few terms are used, the truncation error is too large but, when too many terms are taken, the roundoff error may swamp the result. A happy medium must be struck to obtain best results and, unfortunately, there is no formula for accomplishing this. On the sine series used as an example in this chapter, the truncation error declined very rapidly before the roundoff error had built up. In Chapter 12, especially in Section 12·2, you will find situations in which there is a tradeoff of truncation error and roundoff error. For example, Figure 11·11 shows how the calculation of π, by a method discussed in Chapter 12, converges to the true value as more and more terms are added, but only up to a point. Beyond this point,

FIGURE 11·11
Calculation of π by a series of approximations. In 8-digit precision floating-point arithmetic, accumulated roundoff error overtakes the truncation error after about 4000 terms have been summed. The algorithm used for this approximation is discussed in Chapter 12.

Number of Terms	8-Digit Precision Sum	First 8 Digits of 16-Digit Precision Sum	
1	2.0000000	2.0000000	
2	2.7320508	2.7320508	True value
4	2.9957091	2.9957091	of π rounded
8	3.0898191	3.0898191	to 8 decimal
16	3.1232530	3.1232530	digits is:
32	3.1351023	3.1351024	3.1415927
64	3.1392967	3.1392969	
128	3.1407803	3.1407808	
256	3.1413048	3.1413056	
512	3.1414894	3.1414912	
1024	3.1415534	3.1415568	Closest
2048	3.1415732	3.1415800	approach to
4096	3.1415746	3.1415882	the true
8192	3.1415638	3.1415911	value of π
16384	3.1415385	3.1415921	

adding more terms results in a divergence from the true value because of the accumulated roundoff error.

The calculated results are shown using both 8 precision decimal and 16 precision decimal floating-point arithmetic. The double precision computation continues to converge on π when the single precision computation begins to diverge, confirming that in summing series, the accumulated roundoff error can exceed the truncation error.

The buildup of roundoff error as truncation error diminishes is a characteristic phenomenon in infinite series approximation, but it is by no means characteristic of all types of functional approximation computed by iterative processes. For example, the square root algorithm developed in Section 3·3 employs a repetitive process similar to the summing of terms of a convergent series. However, in that algorithm (Figure 3·14), the *new* approximates G and H, which incidentally always lie on opposite sides of $\sqrt{A}$, are obtained from the old approximates as follows.

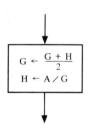

The new G is always the arithmetic average of the old G and the old H. The arithmetic average of two numbers always lies halfway between them. Thus each new G is a much better approximation to $\sqrt{A}$ than the old G. But equally important is the fact that the new H is obtained by dividing G into A. Thus, at the end of each stage, the product of G and H is A or, in other words, each is an approximation to $\sqrt{A}$, one greater than the true value and the other smaller than the true value. But there is no buildup of error from one stage to the next; moreover, the convergence to $\sqrt{A}$ is exceedingly rapid.

EXERCISES 11·6

1. Construct a flowchart analogous to that in Figure 11·10 for approximating values of cos(x).

2. Develop a flowchart that inputs a value x in the interval $0 \leq |x| \leq \pi/4$ and outputs both sin(x) and cos(x) to within a

prescribed error bound, trunc. Use a variable, TERM, that, after being updated, is alternately added to cos(x) and sin(x). The meaning is seen in the partially structured flowchart fragment given here.

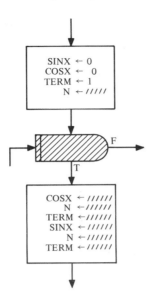

3. (a) Develop a flowchart feature for inputting any positive number x and finding a value y, where $0 \le y \le \pi/4$, so that sin(x) is equal to one of the four values: sin(y), cos(y), $-$ sin(y), or $-$cos(y). Which of these four values is appropriate will depend on the remainder obtained when CHOP(x / (π / 4)) is divided by 8, i.e., on the value of SEC defined by

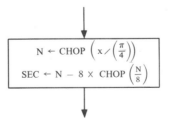

   (b) Augment the feature in part a so as to handle negative values of x as well.
   (c) Develop features in parts a and b for the cosine function.

4. Incorporate the features in Problem 3 into the flowchart of Figure 11·10 so as to have a flowchart that will calculate sin(x) and cos(x) for any x.

5. As with the sine and cosine functions, the arctangent function also has a series expansion.

$$\arctan(x) = x - \frac{x^3}{3} + \frac{x^5}{5} - \frac{x^7}{7} + \frac{x^9}{9} - \cdots$$

valid only for $-1 \leq x \leq 1$. [This series looks much like the sine series except that the factorials (!) are missing in the denominators.] As with the sine and cosine series so with this one, $\arctan(x)$ lies between any two consecutive partial sums, so that the same kind of calculation of error bounds as for the sine and cosine functions is valid here. This series enables us to approximate π from the fact that $\pi/4 = \arctan(1)$. However, the series converges very slowly for $x = 1$.

(a) How many terms would we have to use in order to calculate $\pi/4$ with truncation error $< 10^{-7}$ by using $x = 1$ in the arctan series? Is such a calculation practical?

(b) It is easy to see that $\pi/4 = \arctan(1/2) + \arctan(1/3)$ as follows. Let $A = \arctan(1/2)$, $B = \arctan(1/3)$, so that $\tan(A) = 1/2$, $\tan(B) = 1/3$. Now the *sum formula* for tangents tells us that

$$\tan(A + B) = \frac{\tan(A) + \tan(B)}{1 - \tan(A) \times \tan(B)} = \frac{\frac{1}{2} + \frac{1}{3}}{1 - \frac{1}{2} \times \frac{1}{3}} = 1$$

Thus $A + B = \arctan(1)$. That is,

$$\arctan(\tfrac{1}{2}) + \arctan(\tfrac{1}{3}) = \frac{\pi}{4}$$

Thus we can find the value of $\pi/4$ by approximating $\arctan(1/2)$ and $\arctan(1/3)$, using the series and adding the results. How many terms would be required to find $\arctan(1/2)$ with truncation error less than 2×10^{-7} and to find $\arctan(1/3)$ with the same accuracy?

(c) Draw a flowchart and write a program for calculating $\arctan(x)$ with a given truncation error bound, ERR.

(d) Run the program in part c using the results in part b so as to find an approximation to the value of $\pi/4$ and then find an approximation to π itself. Get the truncation error as small as you can on your machine. [As additional output, print out the number of terms used in computing $\arctan(1/2)$ and arctan $(1/3)$.]

(e) Make an estimate of the maximum possible roundoff error that could occur in part d. (Some students have developed their own multiple-precision procedures and have used the methods in this exercise to compute the value of π to thousands of digits.)

Numerical applications

In this chapter we attack four fundamental computational problems that arise frequently in many areas of scientific and technological endeavor. The flowcharted solutions for these four problems can be applied in many practical situations, even though no more advanced mathematics than college algebra is required to obtain these solutions. Since we only scratch the surface of this subject (numerical methods), it should not be surprising that the methods selected are not necessarily the most powerful.

The four problems solved are:

1. Finding the roots of nonlinear algebraic equations by the method of *bisection* (Section 12·1).

2. Computing the area "under a curve" by methods usually referred to as *numerical integration* (Sections 12·2 and 12·3).

3. Solving systems of linear algebraic equations using the *Gauss method of elimination* (Section 12·4).

4. Predicting the dependence of Y on X, given observed X, Y data pairs, by use of a statistical analysis often called *linear regression.* (Sections 12·5, 12·6, and 12·7.)

12·1
Roots of equations

In algebra courses considerable energy is devoted to solving equations such as

$$7x + 5 = 4x + 3$$

or

$$x^2 = 3x + 5$$

The only solution to the first equation above is $-\frac{2}{3}$, while the second equation has two solutions, given by the quadratic formula

$$\frac{3 + \sqrt{29}}{2}$$

and

$$\frac{3 - \sqrt{29}}{2}$$

When we consider more complicated equations such as

$$5 \sin x = x + 2$$

or

$$x^5 = x^4 - 3x^2 + 1$$

it develops that explicit formulas for the exact solutions are either exceedingly complicated or else such formulas do not exist at all. When numerical answers to such problems are required, only approximate solutions can be supplied. In practical applications we are usually satisfied if a method is available that approximates the solution to whatever degree of accuracy we desire. There are many methods for making such approximations but the bisection method presented in this chapter is probably the simplest and, in an actual computer implementation, generally gives good results.

Any equation such as

$$3x^3 = 7x + 2$$

can always be rewritten as

$$3x^3 - 7x - 2 = 0$$

Thus we can consider the function defined by

$$f(x) = 3x^3 - 7x - 2$$

and find the values of x for which

$$f(x) = 0$$

The solutions of the equation

$$3x^3 = 7x + 2$$

are then the roots of the function f defined by

$$f(x) = 3x^3 - 7x - 2$$

Locating a Root
by Graphing

Graphical methods are perhaps the easiest of the many methods for finding roots of equations. If the equation is written in the form $f(x) = 0$, then you have only to calculate $f(x)$ for a suitable set of values of x and plot the graph of $y = f(x)$. Wherever this graph crosses the x-axis, there will be a root of the equation. Of course, you can get only an approximate result by such a graphical procedure because there is a limit to the accuracy with which you can draw the graph. You may also have difficulty in finding the right domain for the values of x to use in plotting the graph.

Suppose you want to approximate the roots of the equation

$$3x^3 - 7x - 2 = 0$$

First calculate a small table of values and then draw the graph.

x	− 3	− 2	− 1	0	1	2	3
y	− 62	− 12	2	− 2	− 6	8	58

As shown in Figure 12·1, there are three roots: between − 2 and − 1, between − 1 and 0, and between 1 and 2, respectively.

Alternatively, one could write the equation to be solved in the form $f_1(x) = f_2(x)$ and plot the graphs of $y = f_1(x)$ and $y = f_2(x)$. The x-coordinates of the points where these graphs intersect are the roots of the equation.

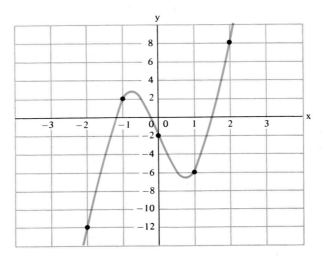

FIGURE 12·1
Graph of $y = 3x^3 - 7x - 2$.

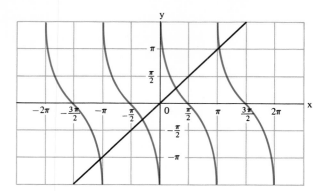

FIGURE 12·2
Graphs of y = x and
y = cot x.

For example, to obtain approximations for the roots of the equation $x = \cot x$, draw the graph of $y = x$ and $y = \cot x$ (Figure 12·2). You can see that there are infinitely many roots, the smallest ones being near $\pm \pi/4$. The other roots lie near to $\pm k\pi$, $k = 1, 2, 3, \ldots$.

EXERCISES 12·1,
SET A

1. For each of the following two equations, plot the graph of $y = f(x)$, where $f(x)$ denotes the left-hand side. Obtain approximate roots for each equation.

    (a) $x^3 - 2x - 5 = 0$
    (b) $x^2 - 3x - 4 \sin^2 x = 0$

2. By plotting the graphs of $y = f_1(x)$ and $y = f_2(x)$ for suitably chosen $f_1(x)$ and $f_2(x)$, obtain approximations for the roots of the following equations.

    (a) $x = \tan x$
    (b) $5 - x = 5 \sin x$

3. By plotting the graph of

    $$y = x^4 - 13.2x^3 - 60.96x^2 + 804.67x - 2655.42$$

    find an approximate root.

The Method of
Successive Bisection

Either of the graphical methods just described will give an approximation to a root of the equation. Once we have an idea of where the root lies, we can improve the accuracy of the root.

Many of the methods used to solve such problems on a computer are essentially methods of search. Because a computer calculates rapidly, we do not hesitate to have it evaluate a function often. At the same time, of course, the methods should be systematic and efficient, and every function evaluation should be absolutely necessary.

The general strategy in methods of search is to establish that the target (in this case, a root of an equation) is to be found in some interval of values and then use some test or criterion to reduce the size of this interval. The method of successive bisection applies a rather simple technique to repeatedly reduce the size of the interval in which one root of an equation is found. The method is designed to be used when the function is known in advance to be continuous (i.e., no breaks in the graph) and to have just one root in the given interval. Incidentally, the method will produce one of the roots in the case that the function has an odd number of roots in the interval. If the number of roots in the interval is even, the method is inapplicable.

Suppose we seek a root of the equation $f(x) = 0$, and suppose further that $f(x_1) < 0$ and $f(x_2) > 0$ are true. The graph of $y = f(x)$ is below the x-axis at $x = x_1$ and above the x-axis at $x = x_2$. This situation is illustrated in Figure 12·3a. If the graph of $y = f(x)$ has no gaps or jumps between $x = x_1$ and $x = x_2$, then it must cross the x-axis between x_1 and x_2 and, hence, there must be a root of $f(x) = 0$ between x_1 and x_2.

Now bisect the interval (x_1, x_2) and denote the midpoint by x_M so that

$$x_M = \frac{x_1 + x_2}{2}$$

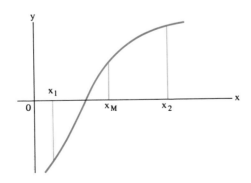

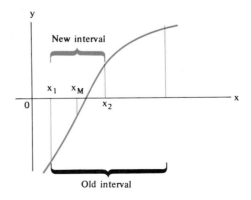

FIGURE 12·3a
Graph of some f(x) with a
root between x_1 and x_2.

FIGURE 12·3b
New interval after one
bisection.

If $f(x_M) = 0$ is true, then we have found a root. However, if $f(x_M) > 0$ is true, as in Figure 12·3a, then the root must be between x_1 and x_M. If we assign the value of x_M to the variable x_2, then once again we can denote the interval in which the root lies by (x_1, x_2), but the length of the new interval is only one half of the original interval, as shown in Figure 12·3b.

Again, we calculate the value of the function at the midpoint x_M of the (new) interval. This time in this example $f(x_M) < 0$ is true, as shown in Figure 12·3b, and therefore the root lies between x_M and x_2. Again the root has been isolated in an interval half the length of the previous interval. If we now assign the value of x_M to the variable x_1, we can still denote by (x_1, x_2) the current interval containing the root.

By repeating this bisection process, we can theoretically come as close to the root as we please because at each step we halve the length of the interval in which the root lies. Thus 10 steps will reduce the length of the interval by a factor of 2^{10} or roughly 1000, while 20 steps will reduce it roughly by a factor of 1 million.

Example   We again consider the equation

$$3x^3 - 7x - 2 = 0$$

The corresponding graph is drawn in Figure 12·1. If we write $f(x) = 3x^3 - 7x - 2$, we see that $f(1) < 0$ and $f(2) > 0$ are true and so we know there is a root of the equation between 1 and 2. Bisecting this interval, the midpoint is $x_M = 3/2$. By substitution

$$f\left(\frac{3}{2}\right) = -\frac{19}{8} \qquad \text{so} \qquad f\left(\frac{3}{2}\right) < 0$$

is true. Thus the root lies in the interval $(3/2, 2)$. The midpoint of this interval is $x_M = 7/4$. But

$$f\left(\frac{7}{4}\right) = \frac{117}{64} \qquad \text{so} \qquad f\left(\frac{7}{4}\right) > 0$$

is true. Hence, the root lies in the interval $(3/2, 7/4)$.

We can continue this process, halving the interval as many times as we wish, each time finding in which half interval the root lies.

1. Use the method of bisection to find approximate values for the indicated roots of the following equations. In each case, start with the indicated interval, which is known to contain a root, and use the indicated number of bisection steps.

(a) $x^3 - 2x - 5 = 0$ (2, 3)   4 steps
(b) $x = \tan x$ (3, 5)   4 steps

Compare your results with the results found graphically in Exercises 12·1, Set A.

In flowcharting the bisection process we will use X1, X2, and XM instead of x_1, x_2, and x_M because only simple variables are required. The basic operation to be accomplished is the replacement of the interval (X1,X2), in which a root of F is known to lie, by a subinterval of half its length in which the root is known to lie. If we assume that the initial values of X1 and X2 are such that F(X1) and F(X2) have opposite signs, then the partial flowchart of Figure 12·4 describes the steps of this operation. In box 5 the midpoint XM is calculated. In box 6 we see an easy way to decide whether F(X1) and F(XM) have the same or opposite signs. They have the same or opposite signs according to whether their product is positive or negative. If their product is zero, then F(XM) must be zero [since we are assuming that F(X1) is known to be different from zero]. In this case, we set a switch SW to 1 to signal that we have found the root, XM.

At each stage, before we replace the interval (X1, X2) by an interval half as long, we need to check two conditions. First, is the switch variable SW still equal to zero? If not, then the

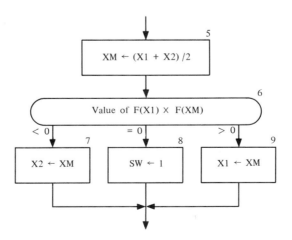

FIGURE 12·4
Partial flowchart of bisection process.

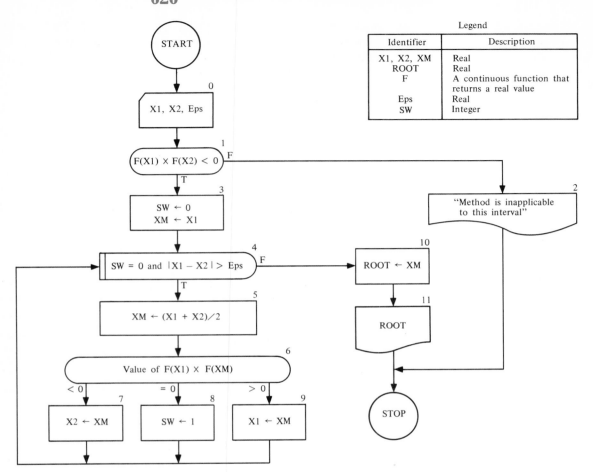

FIGURE 12·5
Flowchart and legend for the
method of bisection.

unlikely event has occurred that an endpoint XM of an interval
exactly coincided with a root. We don't need any more bisection. We can assign to the variable ROOT the value XM. The
other condition we need to check is the length of the interval,
the absolute value of the difference, X1 − X2. If it is sufficiently
small (say, smaller than a given value, Eps), we can accept the
value XM at the midpoint of the interval as the root of the
equation. Otherwise, we repeat the operations of the flowchart
of Figure 12·4.

Figure 12·5 is a complete flowchart and legend to find
a root by the bisection method. The end points of the interval,
X1 and X2, as well as the error tolerance, Eps, are input in
box 0. The function F, for which the root is sought, must return
a real value. We seek to calculate the root with an error less

than Eps. More precisely, the true root is to lie within an interval of length Eps centered on the calculated root. In an actual calculation with floating-point numbers there is a very real limit to the number of times bisection can be repeated profitably. This limit is set by the number of digits of precision in the computation. For instance, with 3 decimal digits of precision an error tolerance less than .001 makes no sense at all. (See Chapter 11.)

One last comment should be made concerning Figure 12·5. Just before box 1 we could have assigned the value of F(X1) to an auxiliary variable Y1. This would have saved reevaluating F(X1) when control reached box 6. Moreover, since control reaches box 9 only when F(X1) and F(XM) have the *same* sign, the assignment X1 ← XM will not ever result in F(X1) changing sign. Thus, in box 6, we could just as well always make the test on the product Y1 × F(XM) instead of on F(X1) × F(XM).

EXERCISES 12·1,
SET C

1. Step through the flowchart of Figure 12·5 with the indicated functions, the indicated intervals, and the indicated values of Eps. Determine whether there are an odd number of roots in the interval and, if there are, determine the value of ROOT. Slide-rule accuracy is adequate.

(a) $x^3 - x - 1 = 0$ [0,2] Eps = 0.1
(b) $x + \ln x = 0$ [.1,1] Eps = 0.15
(c) $5 - x = 5 \sin x$ [0,2] Eps = 0.4
(d) $x^3 - 3x - 2 = 0$ [0,2] Eps = 0.1
(e) $x^3 - 2x^2 - 13x - 10 = 0$ [0,4] Eps = 0.1

The following example can be used as a guide.

Problem. $3x^4 - 2x^3 + 7x - 4 = 0$ [0,1] Eps = 0.4

Solution.   An odd number of roots. For Eps = 0.4 the root is 0.625:

$$f(x) = 3x^4 - 2x^3 + 7x - 4 = 0$$

Step	X1	Sign of F(X1)	X2	Sign of F(X2)	XM	Sign of F(XM)	|X1 − X2|
	0	−	1	+	0.5	−	1
1	0.5	−	1	+	0.75	+	0.5
2	0.5	−	0.75	+	0.625	+	0.25

2. Convert the flowchart of Figure 12·5 to a procedure called ZERO. The effect of calling this procedure should be:

(a) To set the value of some switch variable to indicate success or failure in finding a root.

(b) In the event of success, to set the value of some result variable to the computed root.

3. If you have studied Chapter 9, then your design of ZERO (in Problem 2 above) should reflect the principles of protection explained there. Thus ZERO might be designed with local variables and parameters but no globals. In this case, you should indicate in the legend for ZERO which parameters are called by value and which are called by reference.

4. Show what further modifications are needed for the procedure ZERO and its legend, which you developed in the preceding exercise, so that it can compute the roots of *any* given function. (*Hint.* Review Section 9·5.)

12·2
Computing areas

An important part of theoretical and applied mathematics deals with problems involving areas of regions with curved boundaries. These problems, especially that of finding the area of a circle, have been of interest to mathematicians since the dawn of history. About 2300 years ago, the Greek mathematician, Archimedes, severely handicapped by the poor notation available in those days to represent numbers, was still able to prove mathematically that the area of a circle of radius 1 (the number known as π) is less than $3\frac{1}{7}$ and more than $3\frac{10}{71}$. This has always been considered an outstanding mathematical achievement.

Expressing Archimedes' estimates in decimal form, we find that

$$3.140845 < \pi < 3.142857$$

Taking the average of these two estimates yields

$$3.141851$$

as an approximation for π with a maximum error of .001006 (Figure 12·6). Today, routine methods are available for calculating such areas to any desired degree of accuracy. We know that the value of π correct to eight decimal digits is 3.1415926. Some people have made a hobby of calculating π to a great many decimal places. In fact, the value of π is known to hundreds of thousands of decimal places. It would be quite easy for you to program a computer to make such a computation

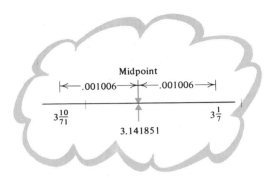

FIGURE 12·6

if anyone were willing to supply the computer time for such a frivolous activity.

To study *area* we need to make a few basic assumptions—all very simple and, we hope, intuitively obvious. These are as follows.

5 Properties of Area

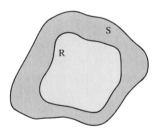

FIGURE 12·7

1. For every region that can be outlined in a plane, there is an associated nonnegative number called the area of the region.

2. If a region R is contained in a region S, then the area of R is less than or equal to the area of S. This is exemplified in Figure 12·7, where R is the region enclosed by the inner curve and S is the entire region enclosed by the outer curve.

3. If a region is subdivided into a number of nonoverlapping parts, then the area of the entire region is the sum of the areas of the parts. Thus the area of the entire region R in Figure 12·8 is the sum of the areas of the regions labeled 1, 2, and 3.

FIGURE 12·8

FIGURE 12·9

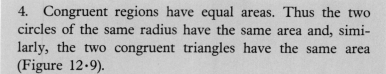

4.   Congruent regions have equal areas. Thus the two circles of the same radius have the same area and, similarly, the two congruent triangles have the same area (Figure 12·9).

5.   The area of a rectangle is the product of the length and the width (Figure 12·10).

FIGURE 12·10

On the basis of these five properties, we are prepared theoretically to approximate areas of regions with curved boundaries to any desired degree of accuracy.

The established mathematical approach to area is to consider the areas of regions bounded on the bottom by the x-axis, on the sides by vertical lines, and on the top by a curve—the graph of a function. This is seen in Figure 12·11.

FIGURE 12·11
Graph of f(x) showing the region under the function in the interval from a to b.

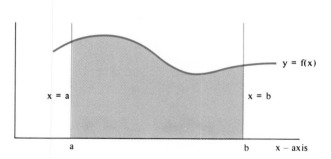

This is not the specialization that it might appear, since we can find the areas of regions, such as those in Figure 12·12, as differences of areas of regions of the standard type. We see how in Figure 12·13. (Notice how area property 3 is called into use here.)

FIGURE 12·12

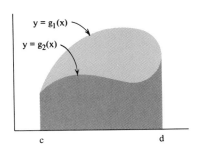

FIGURE 12·13
Suggesting how to compute
the area of a region by taking
differences of areas.

Let us consider for the moment a rather crude attack on the problem of finding the area under the graph of

$$f(x) = \frac{1}{x} \quad \text{between} \quad x = 1 \quad \text{and} \quad x = 2$$

Figure 12·14 shows three reproductions of this graph as it would appear on a sheet of graph paper with five squares between $x = 1$ and $x = 2$.

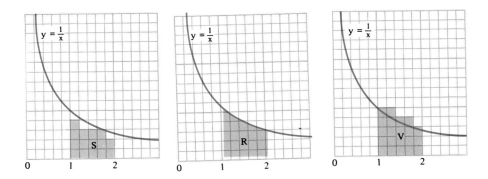

FIGURE 12·14
Regions S, R, and V.

Since the region S is contained in the region R, which is in turn contained in V, we have, by area property 2, the inequalities

$$\text{area (S)} \leq \text{area (R)} \leq \text{area (V)}$$

Since S is composed of 15 little squares, each having (by property 5) the area $1/5 \times 1/5 = 1/25$, we see by property 3 that the area of S is $15 \times 1/25$ and, similarly, the area of V is $21 \times 1/25$. Thus we have firm upper and lower estimates for the area of R.

$$.60 = 15 \times \frac{1}{25} \leq \text{area (R)} \leq 21 \times \frac{1}{25} = .84$$

This method can be refined by drawing a larger picture, say, 10 divisions between 1 and 2 or 100 divisions. But we could hardly manage to estimate the area with accuracy to more than three decimal places (which would require counting almost a million little squares). In addition to being tedious, this method is not very instructive, relying as it does on accurate drawing, and so forth. Still, it serves as an introduction to the fundamental method we present next.

Using the same example, the area under the graph of $f(x) = 1/x$ between $x = 1$ and $x = 2$, we see in Figure $12 \cdot 15$ three pictures of the region under discussion.

In Figure $12 \cdot 15a$ we see that a staircase-shaped region S has been inscribed in R, while in Figure $12 \cdot 15c$ we see R inscribed in another such staircase-shaped region. As before, application of property 2 shows that

$$\text{area}(S) \leq \text{area}(R) \leq \text{area}(V)$$

and application of properties 3 and 5 shows that the areas of S and V are each the sum of the areas of four rectangles given respectively by:

$$
\begin{aligned}
\text{area}(S) &= \frac{1}{4} \times f\left(\frac{5}{4}\right) + \frac{1}{4} \times f\left(\frac{3}{2}\right) + \frac{1}{4} \times f\left(\frac{7}{4}\right) + \frac{1}{4} \times f(2) \\
&= \frac{1}{4} \times \left(f\left(\frac{5}{4}\right) + f\left(\frac{3}{2}\right) + f\left(\frac{7}{4}\right) + f(2) \right) \\
&= \frac{1}{4} \times \left(\frac{4}{5} + \frac{2}{3} + \frac{4}{7} + \frac{1}{2} \right) \cong .634523 \\
\text{area}(V) &= \frac{1}{4} \times f(1) + \frac{1}{4} \times f\left(\frac{5}{4}\right) + \frac{1}{4} \times f\left(\frac{3}{2}\right) + \frac{1}{4} \times f\left(\frac{7}{4}\right) \\
&= \frac{1}{4} \times \left(f(1) + f\left(\frac{5}{4}\right) + f\left(\frac{3}{2}\right) + f\left(\frac{7}{4}\right) \right) \\
&= \frac{1}{4} \times \left(1 + \frac{4}{5} + \frac{2}{3} + \frac{4}{7} \right) \cong .759523
\end{aligned}
$$

Thus we have

$$.634523 \leq \text{area}(R) \leq .759523$$

Using the average of these upper and lower estimates as an approximation for the area (Figure $12 \cdot 16$), we have

$$|\text{area}(R) - .697023| \leq .0625$$

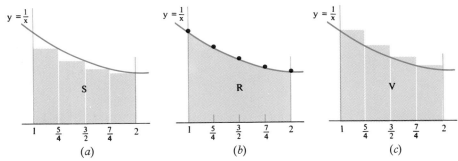

FIGURE 12·15
Regions S, R, and V revisited.

That is, when we use .697023 as an approximation for the area of R, the error cannot exceed .0625 = 1 / 16. (Actually, the error turns out to be about .0042. We will have something to say later on about why the error is so small.) If we divide the interval [1,2] into a large number of parts instead of just four, the error becomes much smaller.

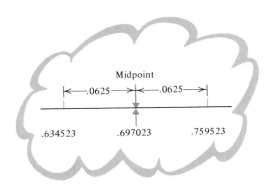

FIGURE 12·16

The only property of the function f(x) = 1 / x that has been used in this presentation is the property that the functional values change monotonically as x increases. Our analysis then applies as well to any decreasing function with any interval [a,b] replacing [1,2].

In Figure 12·17 we see a decreasing function f over an interval [a,b], which is partitioned into four subintervals. The width of the subintervals, denoted by w, is (b − a)/4. The shaded areas in Figure 12·17a and 12·17b represent upper and lower sums, U and L, which may be calculated as:

$$U = w \times f(a) + w \times f(a + w) + w \times f(a + 2w) + w \times f(a + 3w)$$
$$L = w \times f(a + w) + w \times f(a + 2w) + w \times f(a + 3w) + w \times f(b)$$

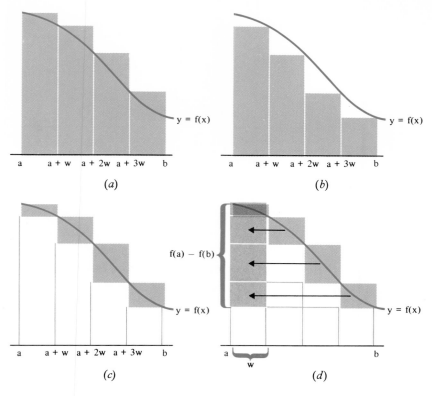

FIGURE 12·17
Four views of a decreasing
function f(x) on the interval
[a,b].

And now, letting R as before denote the true area under the curve,

$$L \leq area(R) \leq U$$

The shaded area in Figure 12·17c represents the difference between U and L. It is because the function is monotonic that the rectangles in this figure can be "slid" horizontally without overlapping so as to just fit in a rectangle of width w and height f(a) − f(b). That is,

$$U - L = w \times (f(a) - f(b))$$

If the average, T, of U and L,

$$T = \frac{U + L}{2}$$

is used as an approximation to the area under f between a and b (Figure 12·18), then

$$|T - area(R)| \leq \frac{U - L}{2}$$

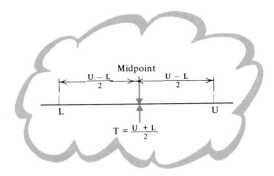

FIGURE 12·18

That is, the error in using $(U + L)/2$ as an approximation for the area under the curve cannot exceed

$$\frac{U - L}{2} = w \times \frac{f(a) - f(b)}{2}$$

Expressing the average $T = (U + L)/2$ in the form:

$$T = \frac{U + L}{2} = w \times \frac{f(a) + f(a + w)}{2}$$
$$+ w \times \frac{f(a + w) + f(a + 2w)}{2}$$
$$+ w \times \frac{f(a + 2w) + f(a + 3w)}{2}$$
$$+ w \times \frac{f(a + 3w) + f(b)}{2}$$

we see that $(U + L)/2$ can be represented as the sum of the areas of trapezoids, as shown in Figure 12·19. For this reason, the method just developed for estimating areas is called the *trapezoid rule*.

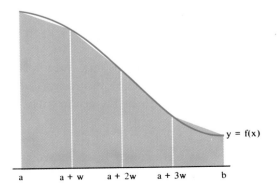

FIGURE 12·19
Estimating areas by the
trapezoid rule.

We can see now that the error in using the area of the trapezoidal region is very small, much smaller than half the difference of U and L, the bound for the error calculated above and depicted in the Figure 12·18. A "tighter" bound for the error will be established in the next section.

In actually computing with four trapezoids, the calculation of the average $T = (U + L)/2$ can also be expressed in the following way:

$$U = w \times [f(a) + f(a + w) + f(a + 2w) + f(a + 3w)]$$
$$L = w \times [\qquad\quad f(a + w) + f(a + 2w) + f(a + 3w) + f(b)]$$
$$\overline{U + L = w \times [f(a) + 2f(a + w) + 2f(a + 2w) + 2f(a + 3w) + f(b)]}$$

$$T = \frac{U + L}{2}$$

$$= w \times \left[\frac{f(a) + f(b)}{2} + f(a + w) + f(a + 2w) + f(a + 3w) \right]$$

$$= w \times \left[\frac{f(a) + f(b)}{2} + \sum_{k=1}^{3} f(a + k \times w) \right]$$

All this was done for four partitions of the interval [a,b]. If, say, n partitions of the interval are used, then the calculations must be modified as follows.

$$T = \frac{U + L}{2} = w \times \left[\frac{f(a) + f(b)}{2} + \sum_{k=1}^{n-1} f(a + k \times w) \right]$$

where

$$w = \frac{b - a}{n}$$

and the bound for the error is

$$|T - \text{area}(R)| \leq \frac{U - L}{2} = w \times \frac{|f(a) - f(b)|}{2}$$

Taking the absolute value of $f(a) - f(b)$ makes the error estimate valid for increasing functions as well as for decreasing functions, as the reader may easily verify.

Flowcharting the Algorithm

We are given f, an increasing or a decreasing function (i.e., monotone), two "endpoints," a and b, and an error tolerance,

Eps. We are to construct a flowchart to compute an approximation to the area under the curve from a to b with error theoretically guaranteed to be less than Eps. The necessary formulas have all been developed in the preceding discussion. Recalling the basic formula for the area calculation,

$$T = w \times \left[\frac{f(a) + f(b)}{2} + \sum_{k=1}^{n-1} f(a + k \times w) \right]$$

we can easily single out the iterative computation that forms the heart of the calculation, namely:

$$\sum_{k=1}^{n-1} f(a + k \times w)$$

A flowchart fragment for this computation is seen in Figure 12·20. The complete computation of this area approximation, which we call TRAP (trapezoid rule), will essentially require only one more box (Figure 12·21). Then the preliminary assignment of values to the variables n and w will complete our task. Recalling the formulas for interval width and error bound

$$w = \frac{b - a}{n} \quad \text{and} \quad w \times \frac{|f(b) - f(a)|}{2} < \text{Eps}$$

we combine them thus:

$$\frac{b - a}{n} \times \frac{|f(b) - f(a)|}{2} < \text{Eps}$$

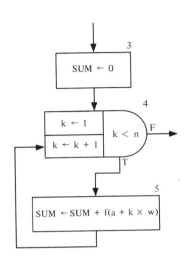

FIGURE 12·20

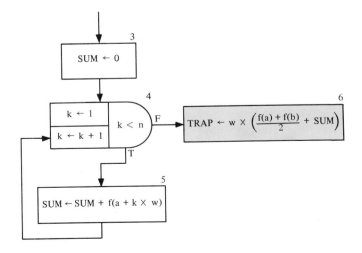

FIGURE 12·21

or

$$n > \frac{(b - a) \times |f(b) - f(a)|}{2 \times \text{Eps}}$$

Since n must be an integer, we use the CHOP function in making the assignment in Figure 12·22. Only input and output

FIGURE 12·22

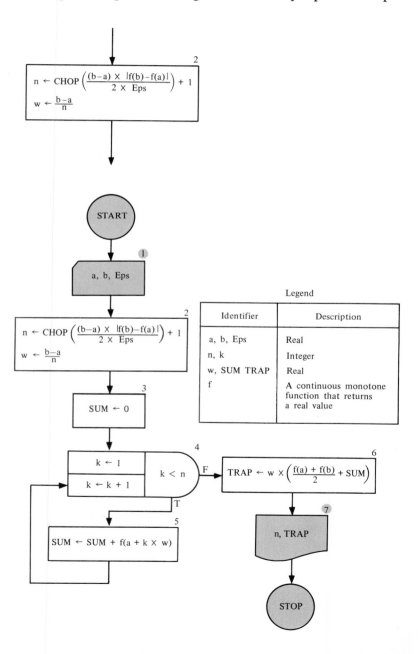

FIGURE 12·23
Approximating area under a monotone function on the interval [a,b] by the trapezoid rule.

need to be added to obtain the complete flowchart shown in Figure 12·23.

An alternative approach is sometimes used for computing areas by the trapezoid rule. Following this second plan, the trapezoidal area approximations are computed with 1, 2, 4, 8, 16, . . . subintervals, stopping only when the calculated error bound is less than an input value Eps. A flowchart using this approach is shown in Figure 12·24. It contains a number of subtleties. You should study it and see how it works. Boxes 2a, 3b, and 3c are the main points of difference from Figure 12·23. Try to understand them all. Which of the two algorithms do *you* think is better? Why?

The algorithm in Figure 12·24 is reminiscent of the process of summing terms of an infinite series as studied in Section 11·6. Estimating an area with 1, 2, 4, 8, 16, and so forth, subintervals is somewhat like estimating a function value, like say, e^x by summing 1, 2, 4, 8, 16, and so forth, terms in the infinite series that defines e^x. The more terms included in the sum, the closer one should get to the true value (in our case the area under the curve). The truncation error decreases as n, the number of subintervals increases, but at the same time the cumulative roundoff error keeps growing. Ordinarily only a small number of subintervals is used in the trapezoid rule computation, for example, less than 100, so that the effect of roundoff is rarely noticed. However if the truncation error decreases too slowly, an excessively large number of subintervals may be required to bring it within the prescribed bound and then the accumulated roundoff error may ruin the accuracy of the result. Consider, for example, the problem of computing the area under the circle curve $x^2 + y^2 = 4$ in the first quadrant.

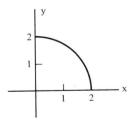

The true area under the curve $f(x) = \sqrt{4 - x^2}$ (i.e., the quarter circle of radius 2) is $\pi \times 2^2 / 4 = \pi$.

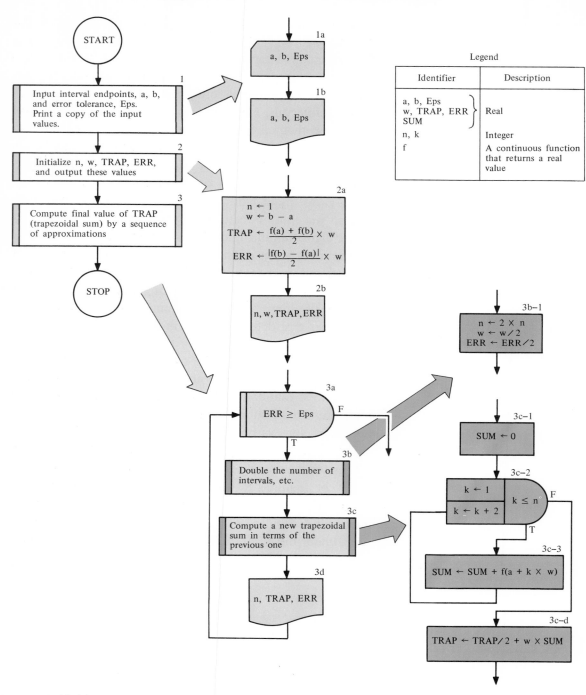

FIGURE 12·24
A sequence of trapezoidal
approximations to the area
under a curve.

The results in Figure 11·11 showed that for 8-precision digit arithmetic the closest approach to the true value of π was achieved when n (the number of terms summed) was somewhere between 2048 and 8192. (In Problem 5 below you will be asked to locate this point more precisely.) Taking any more terms in the sum apparently increases the discrepency between the true and the calculated result. Since, for the quarter circle, the truncation error can be seen to decrease with increasing n, although very very slowly, the growing roundoff error must account for the phenomenon in Figure 11·11. The same difficulty would eventually arise using double precision arithmetic if one tried to compute π accurate to say 15 or 16 significant digits.

EXERCISES 12·2

1. For the areas described below, obtain with the aid of a computer approximations that follow the steps of the flowchart of Figure 12·23.

    (a) Below $y = x^2$, above the x-axis, between $x = 2$ and $x = 4$. Use Eps $= 1.0$. (True area is $56/3$.)
    (b) Below $y = x^3$, above $y = x^2$, between $x = 1$ and $x = 4$. Use Eps $= 0.5$. (True area is $171/4$.)

2. Specialize Figure 12·23 to approximate the value of π to four decimal places.

3. The number x, for which $\ln x = 1$, is a very important mathematical constant designated by the letter e. We now have at our disposal a method (although not the best one) for computing the value of e. This method is based on the fact that e is the root of

    $$\ln x - 1 = 0$$

    Thus, if we can prepare a flowchart to compute the values of $\ln x - 1$ to, say, 6 decimal places, we can then apply the procedure ZERO, discussed in Problems 2 and 3, Exercises 12·1, Set C, to find this root. Remember that the area under the curve $y = 1/x$ for the interval $[1,x]$ is $\ln x$. Use this fact in making the necessary revisions in the flowchart of Figure 12·23 to convert it into a procedure flowchart that returns values of $\ln x - 1$. You will have to decide what to do about a, b, and Eps occurring in Figure 12·23. The main flowchart, which calls on ZERO, will require some preliminary estimates of the interval in which the root lies.

4. One shortcoming of the algorithm in Figure 12·23 should be observed. If Eps is made very small for the purpose of gaining a very accurate result, there is a corresponding increase in the number of terms that must be added to the sum (in box 5). If the number of terms to be

added is very large, the resulting roundoff error of the kind described in Section 11·3 may reduce instead of increase the accuracy of the result.

If you have the computer facilities available, execute the algorithm of Figure 12·23 for $f(x) = \sqrt{4 - x^2}$ in the interval $a = 0$ to $b = 2$, both in single precision and double precision. Run the single precision case, first for an input value of Eps $= .0001$ and again for Eps $= .000001$. Now repeat these calculations in double precision. For each of the four computations, calculate the difference between π and the computed value of π and compare this difference with the corresponding input value of Eps. Explain the discrepencies, if any.

5. The 8-digit precision results in Figure 11·11 (area under $f(x) = \sqrt{4 - x^2}$ from $x = 0$ to $x = 2$) reflect a combination of both truncation error and cumulative roundoff for each value of n. As a first approximation, we may assume that the first 8 digits of the 16-digit result also shown in Figure 11·11 reflect only the truncation error.

    (a) Why is this a good assumption?
    (b) Based on this assumption the difference in reported results in Figure 11·11 for any n is a close approximation to the cumulative roundoff error for 8-precision digit arithmetic. For example, for $n = 4096$, we can assume that the cumulative roundoff error in the reported result, 3.1415746, is approximately $3.1415882 - 3.1415746 = .0000136$. Prepare a graph showing truncation error [or log (truncation error)] plotted versus $\log_2 n$ and also cumulative roundoff error [or log (cumulative roundoff error)] plotted versus $\log_2 n$ in the range $n = 512$ through 16384.
    (c) Based on the graph you prepared in part c, what is the approximate value of n at which, for 8-precision digit floating-point arithmetic, the cumulative roundoff error "overtakes" the truncation error?
    (d) Is the crossover point (i.e., the value of n) you obtained in part c the same for all functions approximated in 8-digit precision floating-point arithmetic using the same summing algorithm? Explain your answer.
    (e) Based on the graph you prepared in part c, what conclusions can you draw about the rate of change in cumulative roundoff error versus n in this calculation? At what rate does truncation error decrease with increase in n in this calculation?

12·3
Better ways to compute areas and to estimate error bounds

A function is said to be convex provided that whenever we choose two points on its graph and draw the chord joining them, then, between these two points the graph of the function lies below the chord. The function is said to be concave if the graph always lies above the chord. These ideas are illustrated in Figure 12·25.

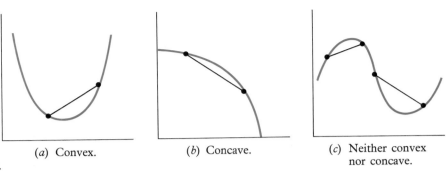

FIGURE 12·25
Three types of functions.

(a) Convex.   (b) Concave.   (c) Neither convex nor concave.

We will deal here with convex functions, although our final conclusions will hold for concave functions as well.

For functions whose graphs are unbroken curves, it is adequate for convexity to prove that for every chord, at the midpoint of the chord, the graph lies below the chord (Figure 12·26). In other words, for every choice of a and b we have

$$f\left(\frac{a + b}{2}\right) \leq \frac{f(a) + f(b)}{2}$$

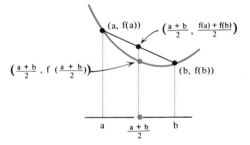

FIGURE 12·26
The function lies below the chord at the midpoint.

To put it still another way, we can say that the function is convex if the process of first averaging a and b and then applying the function produces smaller results than first applying the function to a and b and then averaging.

We need the concept of convexity to discuss another method of approximating area under a curve, called the "midpoint rule." In this method we subdivide the interval as before, and construct for each subinterval a rectangle whose height is the functional value at the *midpoint* of the subinterval. As shown in Figure 12·27, the sum of the areas of the rectan-

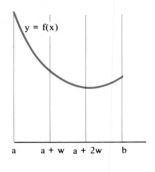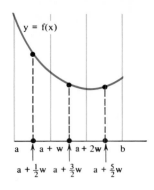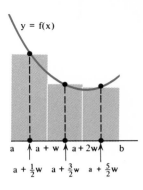

gles can be expressed as

$$M = w \times f\left(a + \frac{1}{2}w\right) + w \times f\left(a + \frac{3}{2}w\right) + w \times f\left(a + \frac{5}{2}w\right)$$

$$= w \times \sum_{k=1}^{3} f\left(a + \left(k - \frac{1}{2}\right) \times w\right)$$

In general, this formula will take the form

$$M = w \times \sum_{k=1}^{n} f\left(a + \left(k - \frac{1}{2}\right) \times w\right)$$

where n is the number of subintervals and

$$w = \frac{b - a}{n}$$

is the common width of the subintervals.

Let us now focus our attention on one of these midpoint rectangles. We can see that if we pivot the top edge of the rectangle about its center, the rectangle is replaced by a trapezoid having the same area as the rectangle. (We can see in Figure 12·28b, using congruent triangles, that the area "lost" on the left is exactly balanced by the area "gained" on the

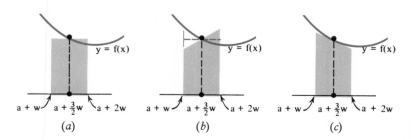

FIGURE 12·28
Showing that the area of the
rectangle is less than the area
under the curve.

right.) And in Figure 12·28c we see the top edge pivoted so as to lie entirely below the graph of the function. (This is always possible for convex functions, although we will not attempt to prove it here.)

Now we can see, as illustrated in Figure 12·29, that for a convex function, f, the midpoint rule gives approximations

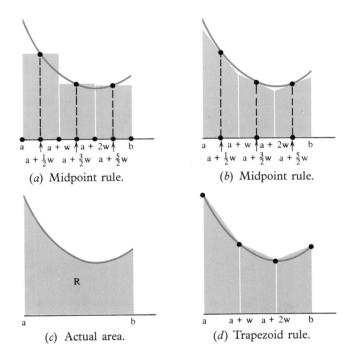

(a) Midpoint rule.

(b) Midpoint rule.

FIGURE 12·29
Comparing the approximations of the midpoint rule with that of the trapezoid rule.

(c) Actual area.

(d) Trapezoid rule.

that are *less* than the actual area under the curve, while the trapezoid rule gives approximations *greater* than the area under the curve. Thus we find that in the case of *convex* functions

$$M \leq \text{area}(R) \leq T$$

where M and T represent the midpoint and trapezoidal areas, respectively. In the case of *concave* functions, we would have

$$T \leq \text{area}(R) \leq M$$

In either case, using $(M + T)/2$ as an approximation for the area of R, the error will be less than $|T - M|/2$. As we saw in Section 12·2,

$$\left| \text{area}(R) - \frac{M + T}{2} \right| \leq \frac{|T - M|}{2}$$

None of this analysis requires that the function f be strictly increasing or decreasing over the interval [a,b].

To see how much better the $|T - M|/2$ estimates of error are than the $|U - L|/2$ estimates of Section 12·2, we may compare them graphically for the example $f(x) = 1/x$ on the interval (1,2) with 4 subintervals. (Figure 12·30).

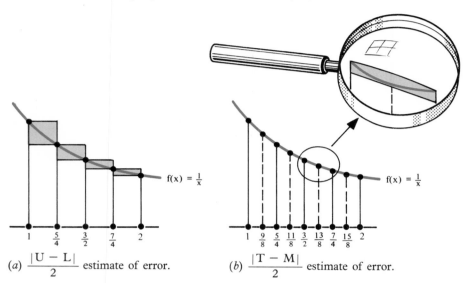

(a) $\dfrac{|U - L|}{2}$ estimate of error.   (b) $\dfrac{|T - M|}{2}$ estimate of error.

FIGURE 12·30
Comparing methods for estimating error in computed area.

The error bound for the trapezoid formula calculated in the proceding section was half the shaded area in Figure 12·30a. The error bound as calculated in this section is represented by half the shaded area in Figure 12·30b, which lies so close to the curve as to be hardly discernible by eye.

Calculating these approximations and estimates by hand, we find that:

$$T = \frac{1}{4} \times \left(\frac{f(1) + f(2)}{2} + f\left(\frac{5}{4}\right) + f\left(\frac{3}{2}\right) + f\left(\frac{7}{4}\right) \right)$$

$$= \frac{1}{4} \times \left(\frac{1 + \frac{1}{2}}{2} + \frac{4}{5} + \frac{2}{3} + \frac{4}{7} \right) \cong .697024$$

$$M = \frac{1}{4} \times \left(f\left(\frac{9}{8}\right) + f\left(\frac{11}{8}\right) + f\left(\frac{13}{8}\right) + f\left(\frac{15}{8}\right) \right)$$

$$= \frac{1}{4} \times \left(\frac{8}{9} + \frac{8}{11} + \frac{8}{13} + \frac{8}{15} \right) \cong .691220$$

$$\frac{M + T}{2} \cong .694122$$

Now we calculate and compare two error bounds: the error bound from the preceding section,

$$|\text{area}(R) - \left(\frac{U+L}{2}\right)| \leq \frac{w}{2} \times |f(a) - f(b)| = \frac{1}{16} = .0625$$

and the error bound from this section,

$$|\text{area}(R) - \left(\frac{T+M}{2}\right)| < \frac{|T-M|}{2} \cong \frac{.697024 - .691220}{2}$$
$$= .002902$$

The comparison becomes even more striking when very fine schemes of subdivision of the intervals are used.

We remark but will not attempt to justify that the weighted average of M and T

$$\frac{2}{3}M + \frac{1}{3}T$$

gives remarkably better results than the ordinary average

$$\frac{1}{2}M + \frac{1}{2}T$$

that we have used here. The two-third, one-third rule for approximating areas is called "Simpson's rule." In the above example, Simpson's rule gives .693155 as the approximate area, as compared with the actual value .693147 . . . , and so gives an error $< .000008$.

The reader can verify that the average $(M + T)/2$ is exactly the result of the trapezoid formula with twice as many partition points. Thus the error estimate $|T - M|/2$ becomes an error estimate for the trapezoid rule with twice as many partition points. These observations are reflected in the flowchart of Figure 12·31.

This flowchart computes approximations for the area under the graph by TRAPezoid, MIDpoint, and SIMPson rules and calculates the ERRor bound established above for the trapezoid rule. The computation is performed for n = 1,2,4,8, ... The process stops when the value of ERR is less than the input value of Eps. No further explanation is given, except for the following. The value assigned to ERR in box 2a is arbitrarily chosen to allow execution to pass through box 3a the first time. The subsequent assignments to ERR in box 3b-1 are genuine error bounds calculated accord-

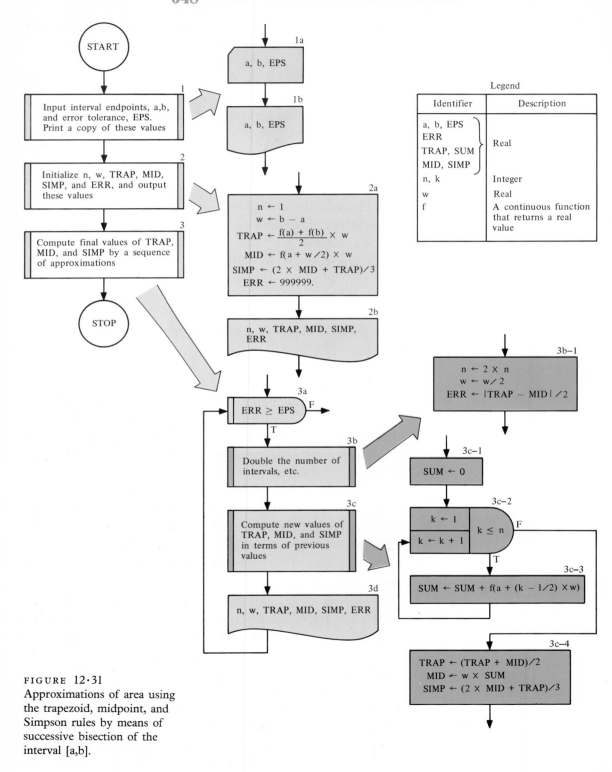

FIGURE 12·31
Approximations of area using
the trapezoid, midpoint, and
Simpson rules by means of
successive bisection of the
interval [a,b].

ing to the preceding analysis. Now study and try to understand the flowchart on the basis of the discussion in this section.

The Figure 12·31 algorithm can be used to emphasize the striking superiority of Simpson's rule. For example, consider the problem of computing the area under the curve

$$f(x) = \frac{1}{1 + x^2}$$

in the interval $[0, 1/\sqrt{3}]$. It can be shown from the calculus that in this interval the area under the curve is exactly $\pi/6$, and that this curve is convex. The fact that the area is $\pi/6$ suggests one way to compute π precisely, namely, to compute the area under the curve

$$f(x) = 6 \times \frac{1}{1 + x^2}$$

in the same interval as above. Table 12·1 shows the results for this computation using a computer with 8-precision digit arithmetic.

TABLE 12·1
Comparison of Trapezoid, Midpoint, and Simpson's Rule Results on the Estimation of π by the Algorithm in Figure 12·31

Area under the curve

$$f(x) = \frac{6}{1 + x^2} \text{ in the interval } \left[0, \frac{1}{\sqrt{3}}\right]$$

n	Trapezoid	Midpoint	Simpson
1	3.0310889	3.1976322	3.1421178
2	3.1143605	3.1552719	3.1416348
4	3.1348162	3.1449848	3.1415952
8	3.1399005	3.1424389	3.1415927
16	3.1411697	3.1418040	3.1415925
32	3.1414868	3.1416452	3.1415924
64	3.1415660	3.1416052	3.1415921
128	3.1415856	3.1415947	3.1415917
256	3.1415901	3.1415911	3.1415908
512	3.1415906	3.1415880	3.1415889
1024	3.1415893	3.1415829	3.1415851
2048	3.1415861	3.1415737	3.1415778

result correct to 8 digits

The results show that to compute π correct to 8 digits by this method, Simpson's rule requires *only 8 subintervals*. The trapezoid rule, on the other hand, requires about 500 subintervals. However, due to roundoff error (chopping) overtaking the truncation error, π can only be computed to 6 digits of precision by the trapezoid rule. The midpoint rule leads to only slightly better results than the trapezoid rule.

Although this example shows how effective Simpson's rule can be, the reader must be aware that even Simpson's rule is not satisfactory for a convex function which has a vertical tangent (infinite slope) anywhere in the interval in which the area is to be computed. This fact can be shown rather vividly if we again compute π, this time as the area under the quarter circle of radius 2 with center at the origin of the x-y coordinates.

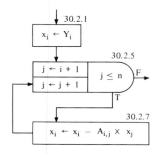

TABLE 12·2
Comparison of Trapezoid, Midpoint, and Simpson's Rule Results on the Estimation of π by the Algorithm in Figure 12·31

Area under the curve
$f(x) = \sqrt{4 - x^2}$ in the interval [0,2]

True value of π rounded to 10 sig. digits = 3.141592654

n	Trapezoid	Midpoint	Simpson	
Part A: 8-precision digit results				
512	3.1414894	3.1416174	3.1415747	
1024	3.1415534	3.1415930	3.1415798	result correct to 5 digits
2048	3.1415732	3.1415761	3.1415751	
4096	3.1415746	3.1415530	3.1415603	
8192	3.1415638	3.1415132	3.1415300	
16384	3.1415385	3.1414334	3.1414685	
Part B: 16-precision digit results rounded to 10 digits				
512	3.141491153	3.141622380	3.141578638	
1024	3.141556767	3.141603164	3.141587698	
2048	3.141579965	3.141596370	3.141590902	
4096	3.141588168	3.141593967	3.141592034	
8192	3.141591068	3.141593118	3.141592434	
16384	3.141592093	3.141592818	3.141592576	result essentially correct to 8 digits

Note: Best results computed by each method up to n = 16384 are shown in clouds.

The function in this case is

$$f(x) = \sqrt{4 - x^2}$$

It is clearly convex over the interval [0,2], but has a vertical tangent at $x = 2$. Table 12·2 shows the results obtained by applying the Figure 12·31 algorithm to this case.

Part A shows that for 8-precision digit arithmetic, Simpson's rule requires about 1000 subintervals, and even so π is computed correct to only 5 digits. Moreover Simpson's rule is not much better in this case than the trapezoid or midpoint rules. Part B shows that even with double precision (16 digit) arithmetic, π can be computed correct to 8 digits only when some 16 thousand subintervals are used. This would be a prohibitive amount of computation when compared with other ways of obtaining equivalent results.

In case a function is not either convex or concave over the entire interval, the error analysis given above will not apply. However, the interval can, in general, be divided into subintervals of convexity and concavity (Figure 12·32) and the approx-

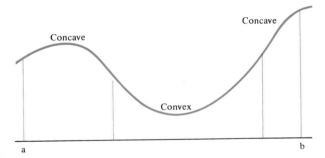

FIGURE 12·32
Showing how to subdivide an interval into concave and convex subintervals.

imations computed by these methods will almost always be very good, even though we are not able (without the aid of calculus) to give bonafide bounds for the error.

EXERCISES 12·3

1. Let T_n and M_n represent the trapezoidal and midpoint approximations for the area under a curve where the interval [a,b] is partitioned into n subintervals:

(a) Give an illustrative example of the relation

$$T_{2n} = \frac{T_n + M_n}{2}$$

for a specific function, f, and a particular interval [a,b] of your choosing.

(b) Verify this relation for the specific example chosen.

2.   In the flowchart of Figure 12·31:

(a) Explain the role of the variable SUM occurring in boxes 3c-1, 3c-3, and 3c-4.

(b) Explain the assignments in box 3b-1 and 3c-4.

3.   Write a computer program for the flowchart of Figure 12·31 and run it with $f(x) = 1/x$ and:

(a) [a,b] = [1,2]
(b) [a,b] = [2,4]
(c) [a,b] = [5,10]

Compare the output from these calculations. Does this motivate you to guess or conjecture some mathematical fact? Can you explain the phenomenon that occurs? In all cases, use an Eps in the range .0001 to .0000001 depending on the word length of your computer.

4.   The function $f(x) = 4/(1 + x^2)$ is neither convex nor concave over the entire interval [0,1]. Thus our error estimates don't apply. Nevertheless, the errors are very small. Use your program for the flowchart of Figure 12·31 to compute the area under this curve between 0 and 1. Compare your output with the results displayed in Table 12·1.

5.   After examining Table 12·2, give an argument justifying the conclusion that the first 8 digits of each 10-digit Simpson's rule result in Part B are free of roundoff error. Based on this conclusion, compute the truncation error and cumulative roundoff error in each Simpson's rule result reported in Part B of Table 12·2. (See Problem 5, Exercises 12·2.) Now plot the truncation error, the cumulative roundoff error, and the sum of these errors as a function of n. (Logarithmic coordinates may prove convenient for this plot.) What is the significance of the value of n at which the sum of the errors is a minimum?

12·4
Simultaneous linear equations

All of our readers have solved systems of two linear equations. Many have solved systems of three or even four equations. In numerous problems of science, engineering, business, economics, and so forth, it is necessary to solve large systems of linear equations involving a great many variables, perhaps as many as 10,000 equations in 10,000 variables. Problems involving this much calculation are virtually impossible without the aid of a computer. And, in fact, such problems constitute one of the principal uses of computers. The algorithms to be developed in this section are, in theory, independent of the number of equations. In practice, however, some modifications are necessary to control the accumulation of roundoff error.

The name of our method is the "Gauss Elimination Algorithm." It is more than 150 years old, but it is nevertheless immediately implementable on the computer. The idea of the method is successive reduction to simpler and simpler problems. Thus the problem of solving 5 equations in 5 variables (or "unknowns") is reduced to that of solving 4 equations in 4 variables, and so forth. We illustrate the method with the specific system of 4 equations in 4 variables shown in Figure 12·33a. The unknowns in this system are x_1, x_2, x_3, and x_4.

$$
\begin{aligned}
{}^2\!\!\!\!-1 \times x_1 + 3 \times x_2 + 2 \times x_3 + 5 \times x_4 &= 9 \\
+\!\!\!\!\Big[\!\!\!\!\longrightarrow -2 \times x_1 - 5 \times x_2 + 0 \times x_3 - 9 \times x_4 &= -21 \\
3 \times x_1 + 7 \times x_2 + 1 \times x_3 + 7 \times x_4 &= 18 \\
-1 \times x_1 - 2 \times x_2 + 4 \times x_3 - 7 \times x_4 &= -20
\end{aligned}
$$

(a) Original system.

$\Longrightarrow$

$$
\begin{aligned}
1 \times x_1 + 3 \times x_2 + 2 \times x_3 + 5 \times x_4 &= 9 \\
0 \times x_1 + 1 \times x_2 + 4 \times x_3 + 1 \times x_4 &= -3 \\
3 \times x_2 + 7 \times x_2 + 1 \times x_3 + 7 \times x_4 &= 18 \\
-1 \times x_1 - 2 \times x_2 + 4 \times x_3 - 7 \times x_4 &= -20
\end{aligned}
$$

(b) After the first step.

FIGURE 12·33
Starting the Gauss algorithm.

We see that the system in Figure 12·33b is obtained from that in Figure 12·33a by multiplying the first equation through by 2 and adding it to the second equation (as indicated by the arrow on the left). The other equations are left alone. What we have to see is that these two systems of equations are equivalent. This means that any values of x_1, x_2, x_3, x_4 satisfying one of these systems satisfies the other as well—which is to say that the two systems have the same solutions.

We know, of course, that if

$$A = B \quad \text{and} \quad C = D$$

then

$$2 \times A + C = 2 \times B + D$$

This continues to hold true when we replace A, B, C, D by more complicated expressions, such as replacing

A by $\quad 1 \times x_1 + 3 \times x_2 + 2 \times x_3 + 5 \times x_4$
B by $\quad 9$
C by $-2 \times x_1 + 5 \times x_2 + 0 \times x_3 - 9 \times x_4$

and

D by -21.

Thus the second equation in the new system follows as a consequence of the first two equations in the original system. Accordingly, any values of x_1, x_2, x_3, x_4 satisfying the original system in Figure 12·33a must also satisfy the modified system in Figure 12·33b.

Moreover, our reasoning is reversible. It is easily checked that if the first equation in Figure 12·33b is multiplied through by -2 and added to the second, then our work is "undone" and we are back to the original system again. Thus any values of x_1, x_2, x_3, x_4 satisfying the modified system must satisfy the original system as well. Therefore the two systems are equivalent.

The Gauss algorithm consists in repeating this process of Figure 12·33 over and over again. In Figure 12·34 we see

$$1 \times x_1 + 3 \times x_2 + 2 \times x_3 + 5 \times x_4 = 9$$
$$-2 \times x_1 - 5 \times x_2 + 0 \times x_3 - 9 \times x_4 = -21$$
$$3 \times x_1 + 7 \times x_2 + 1 \times x_3 + 7 \times x_4 = 18$$
$$-1 \times x_1 - 2 \times x_2 + 4 \times x_3 - 7 \times x_4 = -20$$

(a) Given system.

$$\Rightarrow$$

$$1 \times x_1 + 3 \times x_2 + 2 \times x_3 + 5 \times x_4 = 9$$
$$0 \times x_1 + 1 \times x_2 + 4 \times x_3 + 1 \times x_4 = -3$$
$$0 \times x_1 - 2 \times x_2 - 5 \times x_3 - 8 \times x_4 = -9$$
$$0 \times x_1 + 1 \times x_2 + 6 \times x_3 - 2 \times x_4 = -11$$

(b) After eliminating x_1.

FIGURE 12·34
Eliminating x_1.

three such steps performed at one time to obtain a system that is simpler than the original one, for reasons that we will explain.

In Figure 12·34b we see that the variable x_1 has been eliminated from the second, third, and fourth equations. Thus, in the blocked-off portion, we have three equations in the three variables x_2, x_3, x_4. If we can succeed in solving this (blocked-off) system for x_2, x_3, x_4 then these values can be substituted back into the first equation to solve for x_1.

And how do we solve equations 2, 3, and 4 for x_2, x_3, x_4? By repeating the method above to eliminate x_2 from the third and fourth equations. The work is shown in Figure 12·35.

Now we are ready to repeat the process once more. But this time a new wrinkle appears; the coefficient in the upper left corner of the blocked-off section (called the "pivot element") is not equal to 1 as fortuitously occurred in the previous steps. Accordingly, we first multiply the third equation through by $1/3$ to produce this desirable state of affairs. This process,

$1 \times x_1 + 3 \times x_2 + 2 \times x_3 + 5 \times x_4 = 9$

$-\frac{1}{2}0 \times x_1 + 1 \times x_2 + 4 \times x_3 + 1 \times x_4 = -3$

$+\quad 0 \times x_1 - 2 \times x_2 - 5 \times x_3 - 8 \times x_4 = -9$

$\quad 0 \times x_1 + 1 \times x_2 + 6 \times x_3 - 2 \times x_4 = -11$

(a) System from Figure 12·34b.

$1 \times x_1 + 3 \times x_2 + 2 \times x_3 + 5 \times x_4 = 9$

$0 \times x_1 + 1 \times x_2 + 4 \times x_3 + 1 \times x_4 = -3$

$0 \times x_1 + 0 \times x_2 + 3 \times x_3 - 6 \times x_4 = -15$

$0 \times x_1 + 0 \times x_2 + 2 \times x_3 - 3 \times x_4 = -8$

(b) After eliminating x_2.

FIGURE 12·35
Eliminating x_2.

called "normalizing," is displayed in Figure 12·36. It clearly does not alter the solution of the system of equations.

$1 \times x_1 + 3 \times x_2 + 2 \times x_3 + 5 \times x_4 = 9$

$0 \times x_1 + 1 \times x_2 + 4 \times x_3 + 1 \times x_4 = -3$

$\frac{1}{3} \times [0 \times x_1 + 0 \times x_2 + 3 \times x_3 - 6 \times x_4 = -15$

$0 \times x_1 + 0 \times x_2 + 2 \times x_3 - 3 \times x_4 = -8$

(a) System from Figure 12·35b.

$1 \times x_1 + 3 \times x_2 + 2 \times x_3 + 5 \times x_4 = 9$

$0 \times x_1 + 1 \times x_2 + 4 \times x_3 + 1 \times x_4 = -3$

$0 \times x_1 + 0 \times x_2 + 1 \times x_3 - 2 \times x_4 = -5$

$0 \times x_1 + 0 \times x_2 + 2 \times x_3 - 3 \times x_4 = -8$

(b) After normalizing.

FIGURE 12·36
Normalizing.

Ordinarily we must expect to normalize before each of the elimination steps. We were just lucky that it only had to be done once in this example. Now we perform the final elimination, as seen in Figure 12·37.

$1 \times x_1 + 3 \times x_2 + 2 \times x_3 + 5 \times x_4 = 9$

$0 \times x_1 + 1 \times x_2 + 4 \times x_3 + 1 \times x_4 = -3$

$-\frac{2}{1}0 \times x_1 + 0 \times x_2 + 1 \times x_3 - 2 \times x_4 = -5$

$+\quad 0 \times x_1 + 0 \times x_2 + 2 \times x_3 - 3 \times x_4 = -8$

(a) System from Figure 12·36b.

$1 \times x_1 + 3 \times x_2 + 2 \times x_3 + 5 \times x_4 = 9$

$0 \times x_1 + 1 \times x_2 + 4 \times x_3 + 1 \times x_4 = -3$

$0 \times x_1 + 0 \times x_2 + 1 \times x_3 - 2 \times x_4 = -5$

$0 \times x_1 + 0 \times x_2 + 0 \times x_3 + 1 \times x_4 = 2$

(b) Triangular form.

FIGURE 12·37
Achieving triangular form.

The system in Figure 12·37b is said—for obvious reasons—to be in "triangular form." The characteristic properties of this triangular form are:

1. The coefficients on the "main diagonal" (from upper left to lower right) are all equal to 1.

2. All coefficients below the main diagonal are equal to zero.

Now all that's left is the completely trivial "back solution" process. To accomplish this we write the equations in Figure 12·37b in the opposite order with some terms transposed. See Figure 12·38.

$$x_4 = 2$$
$$x_3 = -5 + 2 \times x_4$$
$$x_2 = -3 - 4 \times x_3 - 1 \times x_4$$
$$x_1 = 9 - 3 \times x_2 - 2 \times x_3 - 5 \times x_4$$

FIGURE 12·38
The back solution.

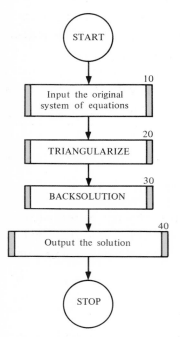

FIGURE 12·39
The Gauss algorithm, first stage.

$$x_4 = 2$$
$$x_3 = -5 + 2 \times 2 = -1$$
$$x_2 = -3 - 4 \times (-1) - 1 \times 2 = -1$$
$$x_1 = 9 - 3 \times (-1) - 2 \times (-1) - 5 \times 2 = 4$$

Substituting the value of x_4 into the expression for x_3, and so forth, we find that the solution of our system is $x_4 = 2$, $x_3 = -1$, $x_2 = -1$, $x_1 = 4$.

Now that we understand the idea behind Gauss elimination, it only remains to devise an algorithm for the process. The first stage or highest level flowchart is seen in Figure 12·39.

Let us first look at the handling of the input data in flowchart box 10. It is unnecessary to write out the system in full for the benefit of the computer. It will suffice to supply the computer with the matrix A of the coefficients of the system, and the list or vector, Y, of constant terms. Thus, in the foregoing worked-out example, the data supplied to the computer would be represented as:

$$\textbf{(1)} \quad A = \begin{pmatrix} 1 & 3 & 2 & 5 \\ -2 & -5 & 0 & -9 \\ 3 & 7 & 1 & 7 \\ -1 & -2 & 4 & -7 \end{pmatrix} \quad Y = \begin{pmatrix} 9 \\ -21 \\ 18 \\ -20 \end{pmatrix}$$

Therefore the input box 10 of Figure 12·39 is expressed in more detail, as in Figure 12·40.

In the example worked out earlier in this section the matrix A had dimension 4 by 4 and the list Y had dimension 4, as seen in (1). However, it is only necessary to replace 4 by n, as in the legend in Figure 12·40, to have the algorithm work for any system of n equations in n variables.

FIGURE 12·40
Detail of flowchart box 1 of Figure 12·39.

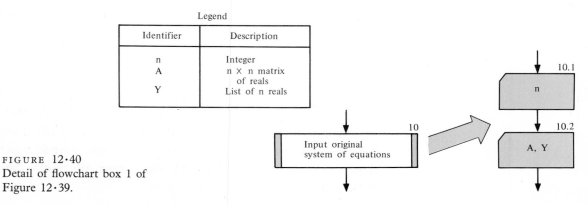

Legend

Identifier	Description
n	Integer
A	n × n matrix of reals
Y	List of n reals

We note that in the coefficient matrix:

$$A = \begin{pmatrix} A_{11} & A_{12} & A_{13} & A_{14} \\ A_{21} & A_{22} & A_{23} & A_{24} \\ A_{31} & A_{32} & A_{33} & A_{34} \\ A_{41} & A_{42} & A_{43} & A_{44} \end{pmatrix}$$

the first subscript on each coefficient denotes the equation in which this coefficient appears, while the second subscript denotes the variable it is multiplied by.

Next we turn our attention to the decomposition of the procedure TRIANGULARIZE. The following word description of this procedure should be checked against the steps in the worked-out example.

> For each value of i from 1 to n we let $a_{i,i}$ be the *pivot* element, that is, the element we are working on, and:
>
> 1. Normalize (i.e., multiply the ith equation through by such a number as to convert the value of the pivot element $a_{i,i}$ to 1).
>
> 2. Eliminate (i.e., add suitable multiples of the ith equation to each equation below it so as to convert the coefficients directly below $a_{i,i}$ to zero).

Accordingly, we have the decomposition of TRIANGULARIZE seen in Figure 12·41.

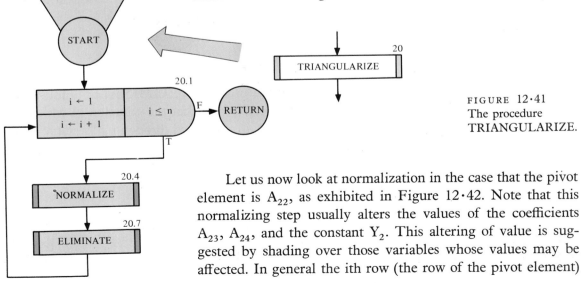

FIGURE 12·41
The procedure
TRIANGULARIZE.

Let us now look at normalization in the case that the pivot element is A_{22}, as exhibited in Figure 12·42. Note that this normalizing step usually alters the values of the coefficients A_{23}, A_{24}, and the constant Y_2. This altering of value is suggested by shading over those variables whose values may be affected. In general the ith row (the row of the pivot element)

$$\frac{1}{A_{22}} \times \begin{pmatrix} 1 & A_{12} & A_{13} & A_{14} \\ 0 & A_{22} & A_{23} & A_{24} \\ 0 & A_{32} & A_{33} & A_{34} \\ 0 & A_{42} & A_{43} & A_{44} \end{pmatrix} \begin{pmatrix} Y_1 \\ Y_2 \\ Y_3 \\ Y_4 \end{pmatrix} \Rightarrow \begin{pmatrix} 1 & A_{12} & A_{13} & A_{14} \\ 0 & 1 & A_{23} & A_{24} \\ 0 & A_{32} & A_{33} & A_{34} \\ 0 & A_{42} & A_{43} & A_{44} \end{pmatrix} \begin{pmatrix} Y_1 \\ Y_2 \\ Y_3 \\ Y_4 \end{pmatrix}$$

Shaded variables may have altered values

FIGURE 12·42
Normalizing the second
equation.

is multiplied by $1/A_{i,i}$ and also Y_i is multiplied by $1/A_{i,i}$. The decomposition of NORMALIZE exhibiting these features is seen in Figure 12·43.

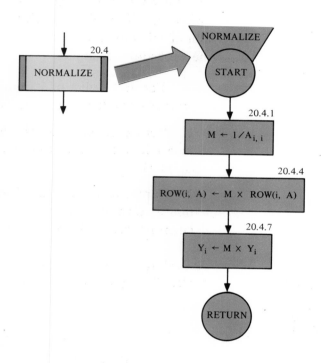

FIGURE 12·43
The procedure
NORMALIZE.

The effect of the procedure, ELIMINATE, is illustrated in Figure 12·44. Here we see that the equation in which the pivot element appears is multiplied through by "suitable numbers" and added to the following equations so as to convert the coefficients directly below the unit pivot element to zeros.

FIGURE 12·44
Elimination.

$$\begin{array}{c} {-A_{42}} \ {-A_{32}} \\ + \end{array} \begin{pmatrix} 1 & A_{12} & A_{13} & A_{14} \\ 0 & 1 & A_{23} & A_{24} \\ 0 & A_{32} & A_{33} & A_{34} \\ 0 & A_{42} & A_{43} & A_{44} \end{pmatrix} \begin{pmatrix} Y_1 \\ Y_2 \\ Y_3 \\ Y_4 \end{pmatrix} \Rightarrow \begin{pmatrix} 1 & A_{12} & A_{13} & A_{14} \\ 0 & 1 & A_{23} & A_{24} \\ 0 & 0 & A_{33} & A_{34} \\ 0 & 0 & A_{43} & A_{44} \end{pmatrix} \begin{pmatrix} Y_1 \\ Y_2 \\ Y_3 \\ Y_4 \end{pmatrix}$$

These "suitable numbers" are the negatives of the coefficients *directly below* the pivot element in the same column. The coefficients directly below the pivot element A_{22} in our example are A_{32} and A_{42}. In general, if the pivot element is $A_{i,i}$, then these coefficients directly below it are $A_{i+1,i}$, $A_{i+2,i}$, . . . , $A_{n,i}$. The decomposition of ELIMINATE is now seen in Figure 12·45.

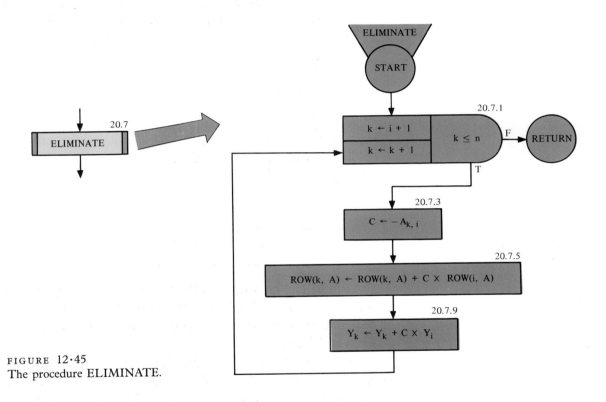

FIGURE 12·45
The procedure ELIMINATE.

It only remains now to break down BACKSOLUTION to a level of greater detail. Using the example of a 4 by 4 system we see that after triangularization has been effected our system has the form

$$1 \times x_1 + A_{12} \times x_2 + A_{13} \times x_3 + A_{14} \times x_4 = Y_1$$
$$0 \times x_1 + 1 \times x_2 + A_{23} \times x_3 + A_{24} \times x_4 = Y_2$$
$$0 \times x_1 + 0 \times x_2 + 1 \times x_3 + A_{34} \times x_4 = Y_3$$
$$0 \times x_1 + 0 \times x_2 + 0 \times x_3 + 1 \times x_4 = Y_4$$

Thus the steps of the back solution are:

$$x_4 \leftarrow Y_4$$
$$x_3 \leftarrow Y_3 - A_{34} \times x_4$$
$$x_2 \leftarrow Y_2 - A_{23} \times x_3 - A_{24} \times x_4$$
$$x_1 \leftarrow Y_1 - A_{12} \times x_2 - A_{13} \times x_3 - A_{14} \times x_4$$

Here, when we calculate the value of x_i, the values of all the x_j with $j > i$ are already known. It is left to the reader to check that the detail of Figure 12·46 calculates x_i once x_{i+1},

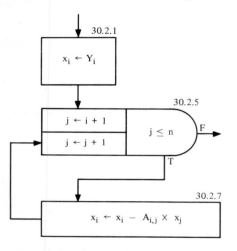

FIGURE 12·46
Calculating x_i.

$x_{i+2}, \ldots, x_n$ are known. To calculate x_i for all integers i, it is only necessary to let i run backwards from n down to 1. The resulting breakdown of the BACKSOLUTION procedure is seen in Figure 12·47.

Now we will put all the bits and pieces together on one page so that the hierarchy of decomposition can be seen as a whole. This is done in Figure 12·48. Note that the solution to be output is now contained in the vector x (as a result of BACKSOLUTION.) The reader should see that there is one further decomposition possible in that the row operations in boxes 20.4.4 and 20.7.5 can be broken down into loops in which the operations are carried out element by element. This will usually be necessary as a preliminary to preparing a computer program. But this activity will be left to the reader.

Partial Pivoting

One contingency that might occur in the Gauss algorithm process was intentionally glossed over in the original discussion. This contingency is that the value of the pivot element

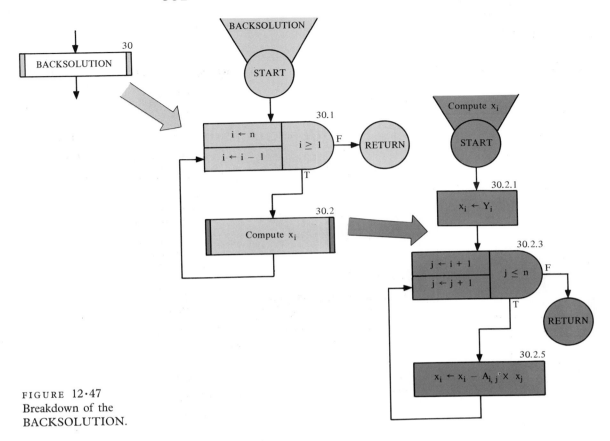

FIGURE 12·47
Breakdown of the
BACKSOLUTION.

might turn out to be zero. That would be an obvious catastrophe. Our NORMALIZE procedure, in which we divide by the pivot element, would then clearly be invalid and the ELIMINATE procedure would also break down.

What is to be done about this? The answer is quite simple; we interchange two equations so as to bring a nonzero entry into the pivot position. This will be represented by the flowchart fragment

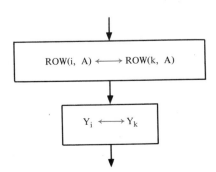

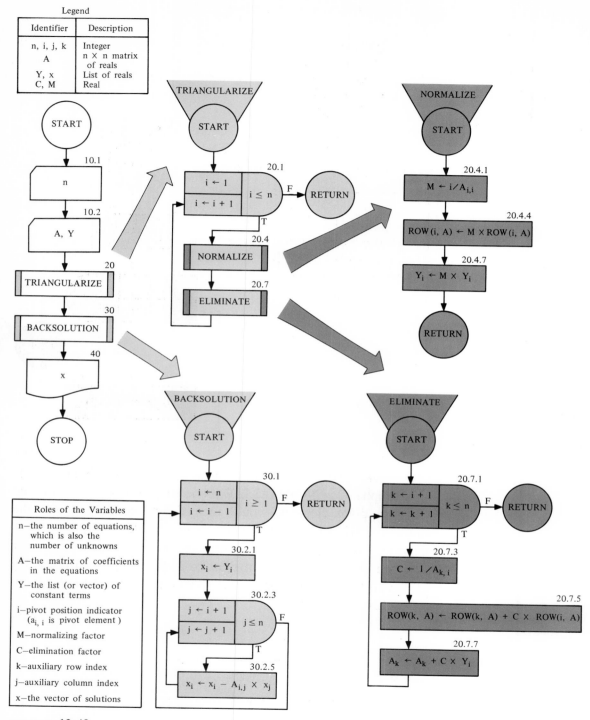

START

10.1 n

10.2 A, Y

20 TRIANGULARIZE

30 BACKSOLUTION

40 x

STOP

TRIANGULARIZE
START

20.1
$i \leftarrow 1$
$i \leftarrow i + 1$ $i \leq n$ F RETURN
T

20.4 NORMALIZE

20.7 ELIMINATE

NORMALIZE
START

20.4.1 $M \leftarrow i / A_{i,i}$

20.4.4 $ROW(i, A) \leftarrow M \times ROW(i, A)$

20.4.7 $Y_i \leftarrow M \times Y_i$

RETURN

Roles of the Variables

n—the number of equations, which is also the number of unknowns

A—the matrix of coefficients in the equations

Y—the list (or vector) of constant terms

i—pivot position indicator ($a_{i,i}$ is pivot element)

M—normalizing factor

C—elimination factor

k—auxiliary row index

j—auxiliary column index

x—the vector of solutions

BACKSOLUTION
START

30.1
$i \leftarrow n$
$i \leftarrow i - 1$ $i \geq 1$ F RETURN
T

30.2.1 $x_i \leftarrow Y_i$

30.2.3
$j \leftarrow i + 1$
$j \leftarrow j + 1$ $j \leq n$ F
T

30.2.5 $x_i \leftarrow x_i - A_{i,j} \times x_j$

ELIMINATE
START

20.7.1
$k \leftarrow i + 1$
$k \leftarrow k + 1$ $k \leq n$ F RETURN
T

20.7.3 $C \leftarrow 1 / A_{k,i}$

20.7.5 $ROW(k, A) \leftarrow ROW(k, A) + C \times ROW(i, A)$

20.7.7 $A_k \leftarrow A_k + C \times Y_i$

FIGURE 12·48
Penultimate version of the
Gauss elimination algorithm
for solving n equations in n
unknowns.

where the symbol "↔" indicates the interchange operation. Now the question is: how do we choose the value of k, the row to be exchanged with the pivot row? This involves searching the column of the pivot position, from the pivot position downward for a nonzero entry.

In theory, any nonzero entry will do. But in practice on an actual computer we must recognize that the entries are not calculated exactly but are, in fact, slightly in error owing to roundoff. Now we recall that in the NORMALIZE procedure we divide the ith equation through by the value of the pivot element. If this pivot element, although not equal to zero, is very small, then dividing by this small number will tend to magnify errors. On the other hand, dividing by a large number tends to reduce errors. Consequently, as a concession to the approximate arithmetic of actual computers, we will search the column of the pivot element not just for *any* nonzero entry, but for the entry of *largest absolute value*. This process is known as *partial pivoting*.

If it should turn out that we find no nonzero entry in our search then we again face an impasse. In this case the system of equations may or may not have solutions. But even if solutions do exist, the nature of the problem changes considerably. We consider it inappropriate to involve ourselves in this book with the mathematics involved in this case and will therefore, if such a misfortune occurs, merely indicate that our Gauss elimination algorithm is inapplicable in this case.

The necessary modification of the TRIANGULARIZE flowchart is seen in Figure 12·49. No further modifications in Figures 12·41, 12·43, or 12·45 are necessary.

Actually, the decomposition indicated in Figures 12·48 and 12·49 has not been entirely reduced to the most primitive level. Boxes 20.2.6, 20.4.4, and 20.7.5 involve row operations that will have to be realized as loops in most languages. Also, boxes 20.2.6 and 20.2.7 involve interchanges that will involve the introduction of COPY variables.

In one of the following exercises you will be asked to incorporate all the procedures in Figures 12·48 and 12·49 into a single flowchart. In Figure 12·50 we give a silhouette of the flowchart that will be useful for comparison in case you have omitted something. This flowchart will be particularly useful in the event that you should want to program the algorithm without the use of procedures.

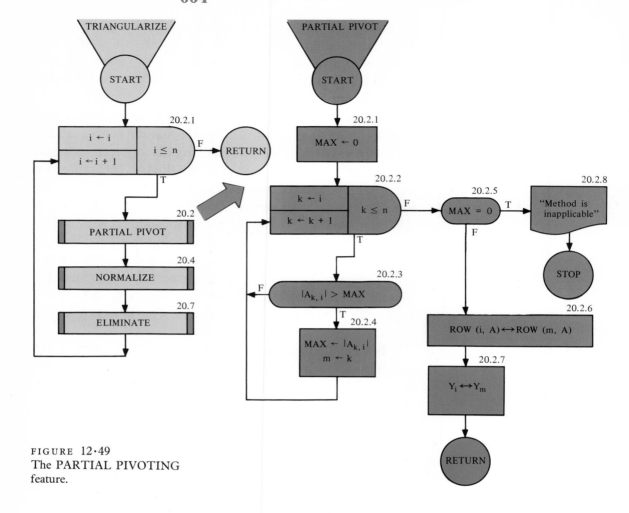

FIGURE 12·49
The PARTIAL PIVOTING
feature.

The methods developed in this section are characterized by cumulative roundoff error that grows rapidly with n, the number of equations in the system being solved. In fact, since the number of arithmetic steps of addition and multiplication in an algorithm such as Figure 12·48 is very large for large n, the effect of roundoff on the quality of the results when n is large can be devastating. Yet every day in the real world very large systems, such as $n > 100$ or even $n > 1000$, are solved many times. Besides extended precision arithmetic a number of other variations and improvements are used to combat roundoff. Getting good numerical solutions to systems of equations is a large subject. We have only scratched the surface.

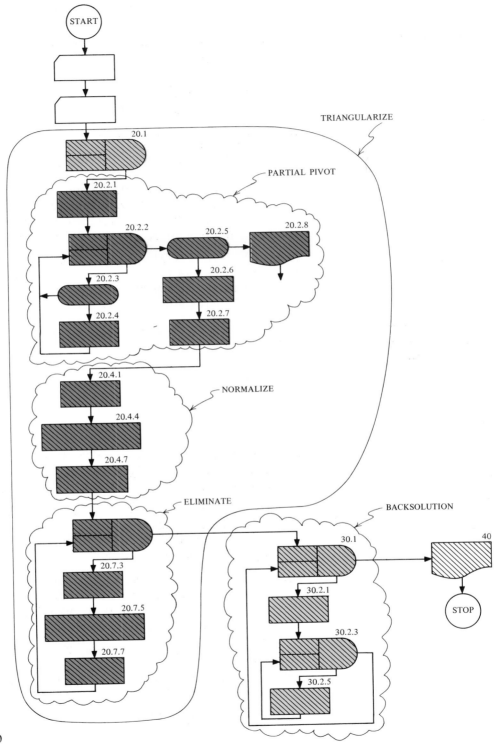

START

20.1

TRIANGULARIZE

PARTIAL PIVOT

20.2.1

20.2.2   20.2.5   20.2.8

20.2.3   20.2.6

20.2.4   20.2.7

NORMALIZE

20.4.1

20.4.4

20.4.7

ELIMINATE   BACKSOLUTION

30.1   40

20.7.3   30.2.1   STOP

20.7.5   30.2.3

20.7.7   30.2.5

FIGURE 12·50
Silhouette of entire algorithm
compressed into a single
flowchart without procedures.

EXERCISES 12·4

1. Trace by hand the flowcharts of Figures 12·48 and 12·49 with the following examples.

(a) $1 \times x_1 - 2 \times x_2 + 2 \times x_3 = 4$
$2 \times x_1 + 1 \times x_2 + 8 \times x_3 = 7$
$-3 \times x_1 + 4 \times x_2 - 8 \times x_3 = -10$

(b) $0 \times x_1 + 3 \times x_2 + 4 \times x_3 = 8$
$2 \times x_1 - 3 \times x_2 + 1 \times x_3 = -5$
$4 \times x_1 - 6 \times x_2 - 7 \times x_3 = -9$

2. (a) For 4 equations in 4 variables find the number of multiplications and the number of additions required (i) in NORMALIZE, (ii) in ELIMINATE, (iii) in BACKSOLUTION, and (iv) in all.
    (b) Repeat this process for n equations in n variables.

3. In the PARTIAL PIVOT procedure, it may turn out that although the true value of MAX is zero, it comes out slightly different from zero on an actual computer owing to roundoff. Describe a modification that could be made in the flowchart box

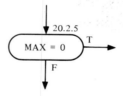

to cope with this possibility.

4. Make the following decompositions of the flowcharts of Figures 12·49 and 12·50 in preparation for actually running a program written in a language such as FORTRAN, BASIC, or ALGOL.

    (a) Decompose the row operations in these figures into loops in which the assignments are made element by element.
    (b) Decompose the interchange ($\longleftrightarrow$) statements in Figure 12·49 into simple assignment statements by using copy variables.

5. (For those interested in efficiency.) We know beforehand that in the final matrix the coefficients below the main diagonal will be zero while those on the main diagonal will be 1. Accordingly, in Problem 2a there is no need to calculate these values.

    (a) Revise the counts made in Problem 2 to eliminate these superfluous calculations.
    (b) For n equations in n variables, estimate the fractional saving of time made in the TRIANGULARIZE procedure by incorporating these features. (Use the number of multiplications as a measure of the time required.)

6. Run the solution algorithm for the following system both with and without the partial pivoting feature.

$$2 \times x_1 + 3 \times x_2 - 1 \times x_3 + 4 \times x_4 = 9$$
$$4 \times x_1 + 6 \times x_2 - 1 \times x_3 + 5 \times x_4 = 9$$
$$6 \times x_1 + 7 \times x_2 + 2 \times x_3 + 7 \times x_4 = 0$$
$$3 \times x_1 - 1 \times x_2 + 3 \times x_3 + 9 \times x_4 = 8$$

Explain the discrepancy in the results.

7. Even when a zero pivot element does not occur, the partial pivoting procedure can greatly improve the accuracy of your results. The following system is especially prepared to exemplify this. If your computer does its arithmetic to 5 or 6 decimal places you will get spectacularly different results with and without partial pivoting. If your computer does its arithmetic to 12 or 13 decimal places no discrepencies will occur. Run both ways and compare results.

$$1.2345\,x_1 + 2.3456\,x_2 + 3.4567\,x_3 + 4.5678\,x_4 + 5.6789\,x_5 = 17.2835$$
$$3.2168\,x_1 - 4.1234\,x_2 - 1.9876\,x_3 + 2.3456\,x_4 + 1.8321\,x_5 = 1.2835$$
$$4.4513\,x_1 - 1.7778\,x_2 + 1.4691\,x_3 + 6.1298\,x_4 - 2.6110\,x_5 = 7.6614$$
$$3.1286\,x_1 + 4.3124\,x_2 - 5.2899\,x_3 + 6.2189\,x_4 + 2.1610\,x_5 = 10.5310$$
$$-1.0101\,x_1 + 3.9886\,x_2 + 2.4141\,x_3 - 6.1298\,x_4 + 4.0001\,x_5 = 3.2629$$

Note It is easily checked that the actual solution is $(x_1, x_2, x_3, x_4, x_5) = (1, 1, 1, 1, 1)$.

12·5
Averages and deviation from the average

One of the principal activities in statistics is that of calculating averages and measuring deviations from the average. We can easily illustrate this method with a set of examination scores. For the purpose of avoiding tedious calculations, we will choose a small class of eight students. The grades on an examination (with 25 points possible) were

$$25, 23, 22, 21, 17, 9, 6, 5$$

If you were asked to calculate the average grade, you would probably add up all the grades and divide by the number of students taking the exam, thus obtaining

$$\frac{25 + 23 + 22 + 21 + 17 + 9 + 6 + 5}{8} = 16$$

This is called the *arithmetic mean* of the test scores.

To measure the deviation (or dispersal or scattering) of the test scores from the mean, it is natural to calculate how much each score differs from the mean and then average these differences. (Here we mean the absolute differences—without regard to sign.) The calculations are tabulated below. Here, then, the average amount by which the test scores deviate from the mean is seven points.

									Total	Arithmetic Mean
Test Score	25	23	22	21	17	9	6	5	128	16
Deviation from mean	9	7	6	5	1	7	10	11	56	7

It is interesting to note that the arithmetic mean is not necessarily the grade from which the test scores deviate the least. In this case, for example, the deviation from the grade of 18 is calculated below. Here, then, we see that on the average the test scores deviate from the grade of 18 by less than they deviate from the arithmetic mean of 16.

									Total	Arithmetic Mean
Test Score	25	23	22	21	17	9	6	5	128	16
Deviation from 18	7	5	4	3	1	9	12	13	54	6.75

It is interesting to consider taking as our "average" score, instead of the arithmetic mean, that score yielding the smallest average deviation (or, what is the same thing, that score yielding the smallest total deviation). We then want to find the number x so that the sum of the deviations from x is a minimum.

That is, we want

$$|25 - x| + |23 - x| + |22 - x| + |21 - x|$$
$$+ |17 - x| + |9 - x| + |6 - x| + |5 - x|$$

to be a minimum.

The problem is much easier to solve than one might think. The method of solution involves considering the deviations in pairs. First, consider the sum of the deviations of the highest and lowest scores.

$$|25 - x| + |5 - x|$$

We can see geometrically that when x is taken between 5 and

25, then $|5 - x| + |25 - x|$ is the length of the interval from 5 to 25 or $25 - 5 = 20$ (Figure 12·51).

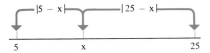

FIGURE 12·51

However, when x is outside the interval [5,25], then the sum $|5 - x| + |25 - x|$ will exceed the length of the interval [5,25] (Figure 12·52). If we pair in the same way, the second highest

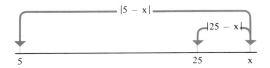

FIGURE 12·52

and second lowest test scores, and so forth, we find that:

$$|25 - x| + |5 - x| \geq 20$$
$$|23 - x| + |6 - x| \geq 17$$
$$|22 - x| + |9 - x| \geq 13$$
$$|21 - x| + |17 - x| \geq 4$$

Each of these inequalities becomes an equality if the number x lies between the innermost pair, 17 and 21 (Figure 12·53).

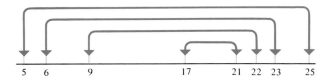

FIGURE 12·53

Hence we find the total deviation from x.

$$|25 - x| + |23 - x| + |22 - x| + |21 - x| + |17 - x|$$
$$|9 - x| + |6 - x| + |5 - x| \geq 20 + 17 + 13 + 4$$
$$= 54$$

The minimum value of 54 is actually achieved if

$$17 \leq x \leq 21$$

Any such value of x is called a *median* grade.

This method of averaging does not always give a unique answer, but it is clear that there will be as many scores above the median as there are below. (In case several papers share the median score, this last sentence will have to be slightly reworded.)

The method of finding the median can be described as follows. Arrange the tests in order of descending scores and count down the list half way. If the number of tests is odd, the middle paper has the median score. If the number of papers is even, then medians are numbers between the lowest score in the top half and the highest score in the bottom half.

EXERCISES 12·5

1. Show that the average deviation from the median is given by

$$\frac{\text{(sum of top half scores)} - \text{(sum of bottom half scores)}}{\text{number of tests}}$$

2. A large number of students (20,000 to 30,000) are taking a college entrance test. The number is sufficiently large that computer sorting of the test scores would use considerable time and a lot of storage. Devise a flowchart for computing the arithmetic mean, the median, and the average deviation from each, without doing any sorting. Test scores are whole numbers between 0 and 100.

3. A large school district has 4000 teachers with salaries ranging between $5000 and $18,000 per year. Compare the methods of finding the median salary with and without sorting.

   (a) In the case that the answer must be exact to the nearest penny.
   (b) In the case that an error of no more than $5 will be tolerated.

12·6 Root-mean-square deviation

The general practice in statistics is to calculate average deviation in a way quite different from that used in the preceding section. To see how it is done, let us return to the test scores in the sample in Section 12·5. We will show how the average deviation from some test score, 18 for example, would be calculated. The method consists of four steps.

Test score	25	23	22	21	17	9	6	5

Step 1 Calculate the deviation from 18 for each score as before.

Test score	25	23	22	21	17	9	6	5
Deviation from 18	7	5	4	3	1	9	12	13

Step 2 Calculate the squares of the deviations.

Test scores	25	23	22	21	17	9	6	5
Deviation from 18	7	5	4	3	1	9	12	13
Squares of deviations	49	25	16	9	1	81	144	169

Step 3 Find the arithmetic mean of these squares.

$$\frac{49 + 25 + 16 + 9 + 1 + 81 + 144 + 169}{8} = \frac{494}{8}$$
$$= 61.75$$

Step 4 Take the square root of the arithmetic mean.

$$\sqrt{61.75} \simeq 7.858$$

This is the number used in statistics as the average deviation from the test score of 18. We can see that it is not the same as the average deviation computed by the method of Section 12·5, which was 6.75. From the above steps we can see that this new method of computing average deviation can be described as "the square *root* of the arithmetic *mean* of the *squares* of the *deviations*." The italicized words reveal the rationale for the name "root-mean-square deviation" that furnishes the title for this section.

Note that virtually all methods of "averaging" used in mathematics are of this general type: we first subject the numbers to be averaged to some treatment (squaring, in this case), take the arithmetic mean of the treated numbers, and finally reverse the treatment (square root) on this arithmetic mean.

As in the preceding section, we would like to find the test score, $\bar{x}$, from which our data deviates the least. That is, so that

$$\frac{\sum_{i=1}^{8} (x_i - \bar{x})^2}{8}$$

is as small as possible. It is clear that the value of $\bar{x}$ making this deviation the smallest will be the value of $\bar{x}$ making

$$\sum_{i=1}^{8} (x_i - \bar{x})^2$$

the smallest.

For the test data in our example, this means finding $\bar{x}$ so that

$$(5 - \bar{x})^2 + (6 - \bar{x})^2 + (9 - \bar{x})^2 + (17 - \bar{x})^2$$
$$+ (21 - \bar{x})^2 + (22 - \bar{x})^2$$
$$+ (23 - \bar{x})^2 + (25 - \bar{x})^2$$

is as small as possible. To solve this problem we expand each of the above squares and add them, as shown below.

$$
\begin{array}{rrr}
\bar{x}^2 - & 10\bar{x} + & 25 \\
\bar{x}^2 - & 12\bar{x} + & 36 \\
\bar{x}^2 - & 18\bar{x} + & 81 \\
\bar{x}^2 - & 34\bar{x} + & 289 \\
\bar{x}^2 - & 42\bar{x} + & 441 \\
\bar{x}^2 - & 44\bar{x} + & 484 \\
\bar{x}^2 - & 46\bar{x} + & 529 \\
\bar{x}^2 - & 50\bar{x} + & 625 \\
\hline
8\bar{x}^2 - & 256\bar{x} + & 2510
\end{array}
$$

Next, we complete the square.

$$
\begin{aligned}
8\bar{x}^2 - 256\bar{x} + 2510 &= 8(\bar{x}^2 - 32\bar{x}) + 2510 \\
&= 8(\bar{x}^2 - 32\bar{x} + (16)^2) - 8(16)^2 + 2510 \\
&= 8(\bar{x} - 16)^2 - 2048 + 2510 \\
&= 8(\bar{x} - 16)^2 + 462
\end{aligned}
$$

Since $8(\bar{x} - 16)^2$ is always ≥ 0, we see that whatever value is taken for $\bar{x}$,

$$8(\bar{x} - 16)^2 + 462 \geq 462$$

is always true with equality only when $\bar{x}$ has the value 16. Thus the minimum value of

$$\sum_{i=1}^{8} (x_i - \bar{x})^2$$

is 462, so the minimum value of the root-mean-square

deviation

$$\sqrt{\frac{\sum\limits_{i=1}^{8} (x_i - \bar{x})^2}{8}}$$

is

$$\sqrt{\frac{462}{8}} = \sqrt{57.75} \cong 7.60$$

In this case we see that the number, 16, from which the test scores had the least root-mean-square deviation, turns out to be the arithmetic mean of the test scores. It is natural to wonder whether this is the case in general. It is, and it is not difficult to prove. In fact, it is largely a repetition of the above calculations in general form. It can be shown (see Problem 2) that

$$\sum_{k=1}^{N} (x_k - \bar{x})^2 = N(\bar{x} - A)^2 - NA^2 + S$$

where

$$A = \frac{\sum\limits_{k=1}^{N} x_k}{N}$$

is the arithmetic mean of the data values and where

$$S = \sum_{k=1}^{N} x_k^2$$

is the sum of the squares of the data values. As before, the expression on the right above has its minimum value when $\bar{x} = A$, and this minimum value is $-NA^2 + S$.

And the root-mean-square deviation can now be calculated as

$$\sqrt{\frac{\sum\limits_{k=1}^{N} (x_k - A)^2}{N}} = \sqrt{\frac{S - NA^2}{N}} = \sqrt{\frac{S}{N} - A^2}$$

Since S/N is the average of the squares of the data values, we see that the expression $S/N - A^2$ inside the square root can be described as the average of the squares minus the square of the average.

The root-mean-square deviation computed in this way is called the *standard deviation*.

In the next section we will meet this problem again. We will have a lot of numbers

$$z_1, z_2, z_3, \ldots, z_n$$

and will want to find the value of B so that

$$\sum_{k=1}^{N} (z_k - B)^2$$

will be as small as possible. This is the same problem as the one discussed above with only the letters changed. The desired value of B is given by

$$B = \bar{z} = \frac{\displaystyle\sum_{k=1}^{N} z_k}{N}$$

EXERCISES 12·6

1. Draw a flowchart for reading a set of data values and calculating the arithmetic mean and standard deviation.

2. By expanding the left side and completing a square in $\bar{x}$, derive the relationship

$$\sum_{k=1}^{N} (x_k - \bar{x})^2 = N(\bar{x} - A)^2 - NA^2 + S$$

given above in the text. Relevant facts are that

$$A = \frac{1}{N} \sum_{k=1}^{N} x_k \quad \text{and} \quad S = \sum_{k=1}^{N} x_k^2$$

3. (a) With the aid of a calculator or computer if you have one handy, or by pencil and paper if you don't, apply the formula for the standard error,

$$d = \sqrt{\frac{S}{N} - A^2}$$

derived in the text, to a set of four values of x, each equal to 55.55.

(i) What value do you get for d when you use 4 decimal digit arithmetic, and round up each intermediate result when its fifth significant digit is 5 or greater?

(ii) Now repeat part i, using chopping as the roundoff rule. What value do you get for d? What conclusion can you draw about using the above formula to compute d?

(b) It is possible to compute the standard error in a different way using recurrence relations. This method avoids the difficulty illustrated in part a where the value under the radical became negative due to roundoff error. We start with two familiar relations

$$\bar{x}_k = \frac{1}{k} \sum_{j=1}^{k} x_j$$

and

$$a_k = \sum_{j=1}^{k} (x_j - \bar{x}_k)^2$$

For $k = 1$, $\bar{x}_1 = x_1$, and $a_1 = 0$. Next we use the recurrence relations

$$\bar{x}_{k+1} = \bar{x}_k + \left(\frac{x_{k+1} - \bar{x}_k}{k + 1} \right)$$

and

$$a_{k+1} = a_k + k \times (k + 1) \times \left(\frac{x_{k+1} - \bar{x}_k}{k + 1} \right)^2$$

to bootstrap our way up to a_n.

And now the standard error of n data values is defined as

$$d_n = \sqrt{\sum_{j=1}^{n} \frac{(x_j - \bar{x}_n)^2}{n}} = \sqrt{\frac{a_n}{n}}$$

Notice that every a_i, for $i > 0$, has been computed as the sum of two terms both of which are definitely nonnegative. Therefore the numerator a_n is nonnegative.

Your job is to construct a flowchart that computes the values $\bar{x}_2, \bar{x}_3, \bar{x}_4, \ldots, \bar{x}_N$ and the values $a_2, a_3, a_4, \ldots, a_N$, and finally computes and displays d_N, given a set of N data values, $x_1, x_2, \ldots, x_N$. Notice that the value $[(x_{k+1} - \bar{x}_k)/(k + 1)]$ need be computed only once in each cycle, if an auxiliary variable is used. Notice also that subscripted variables are not really necessary. Be sure to include a legend with your flowchart.

(c) Derive the two recurrence relations used in part b.

12·7
The mathematics of
prediction

One of the basic problems in statistics is that of prediction or, more specifically, predicting the value of one variable on the basis of the value of another variable.

In order to illustrate our meaning, suppose that we have a spring and a set of weights and that we perform an experiment to see how much weight is necessary to stretch the spring 1 inch, 2 inches, 3 inches, 4 inches, and 5 inches. The results

Amount of stretch (S) in inches	1	2	3	4	5
Weight (W) in pounds	1.4	2.8	4.1	5.5	6.9

of this experiment for a particular spring are tabulated above and graphed in Figure 12·54.

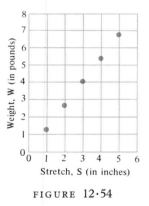

FIGURE 12·54

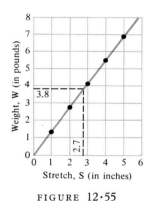

FIGURE 12·55

We can see that all the points on this graph seem to lie on a straight line. In Figure 12·55 we see the line drawn through these five data points.

Suppose an object of unknown weight is hung on the spring, giving a stretch of 2.7 inches. We can use our graph to "predict" that the object will prove to weigh 3.8 pounds. Such an experiment was first performed about 300 years ago by the physicist, Robert Hooke. On the basis of his experiments, he announced "Hooke's Law" for the stretching of springs: the amount of stretch is proportional to the weight causing the stretch.

$$W = K \times S$$

Here, the "spring constant," K, depends on the dimensions of the spring and the metal used in its construction. Hooke's Law of stretching provides the basis for meat scales in use today.

In the above example we have seen how we can predict the value of the variable W from the value of the variable S. In this case it turned out to be particularly simple because the variables were related by the formula

$$W = K \times S$$

However, the same method can be used even when the variables are not "functionally related" in this way, as we will see in our next example.

Scenario

Recently, data were collected to study the relationship between heights of fathers and the heights of their sons. One hundred men with grown sons were selected, and their heights were recorded together with those of their oldest sons at maturity. The results are shown on the graph of Figure 12·56.

Here, for each point plotted, the abscissa represents the height of a father while the ordinate represents the height of his eldest son (at maturity).

A glance at the graph will suffice to establish that the situation here is quite different from that of the stretched spring. On the basis of knowing the height of the father, we are not going to be able to make a reliable prediction of the height of the son. Evidently, some factors other than the heights of the fathers are involved.

And yet there is a definite tendency for taller fathers to produce taller sons. The task we are setting for ourselves is the quantitative measurement of this tendency. As in the case of the stretched spring, we will try to place on this graph the line that best fits these data, the line that will best predict heights of sons from heights of fathers "on the average."

In this case, we cannot locate this line by eye, as in the previous example. In fact, we require a definition of what we mean by the best fitting line. The line we want is the one that shows an average deviation of sons' actual heights from the heights predicted by the line that is as small as possible.

This definition will not be complete until we specify the method to be used in averaging the deviations. The two methods for averaging deviations in the preceding sections were as follows.

1. The arithmetic mean of the absolute values of the deviations.

2. The root-mean-square of the deviations.

In this case, the first method is very cumbersome to work with. Furthermore, advanced study of statistics yields strong theoretical support for the second method. For these reasons, we will adopt the root-mean-square method of averaging our deviations. The best fitting line in this sense is called the "line of regression" of sons' heights on fathers' heights. It is defined as follows.

> The line of regression of sons' heights on fathers' heights is the line producing the smallest possible root-mean-square deviation of the sons' actual heights from those predicted by the line.

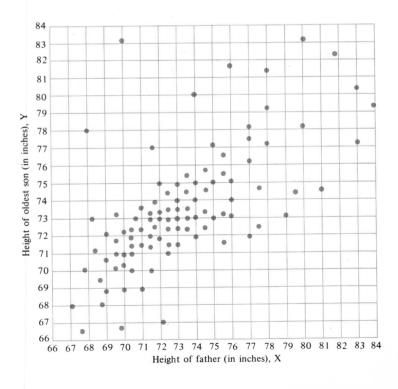

FIGURE 12·56

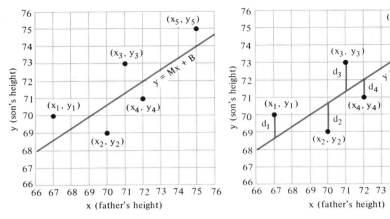

FIGURE 12·57   FIGURE 12·58

First we must investigate how these root-mean-square deviations are calculated. It will be convenient to use an example having fewer data pairs than in Figure 12·56. In Figure 12·57 we see five data points and a line

$$y = Mx + B$$

In Figure 12·58 we see depicted the deviations, d_1, d_2, d_3, d_4, d_5 of the actual values of y from those predicted by the line. The root-mean-square deviation of the sons' actual heights from the predicted values is

$$(1) \qquad \bar{d} = \sqrt{\frac{d_1{}^2 + d_2{}^2 + d_3{}^3 + d_4{}^2 + d_5{}^2}{5}} = \sqrt{\frac{\sum_{i=1}^{5} d_i{}^2}{5}}$$

Noting that when the father's height is x_1, the son's height predicted from $y = Mx + B$ is

$$Mx_1 + B$$

we see that

$$d_1 = y_1 - (Mx_1 + B)$$

and so forth, so that the root-mean-square deviation in Equation 1 can be expressed in the form

$$\bar{d} = \sqrt{\frac{\sum_{i=1}^{5} (y_i - Mx_i - B)^2}{5}}$$

In the general case, with N data points, this, of course, takes the form

$$\bar{d} = \sqrt{\frac{\sum\limits_{i=1}^{N} (y_i - Mx_i - B)^2}{N}}$$

The problem now is to find values of M and B that make this deviation as small as possible. As in the similar situation in the preceding section, these will be the values of M and B that make

$$N\bar{d}^2 = \sum\limits_{i=1}^{N} (y_i - Mx_i - B)^2$$

as small as possible.

Your understanding of the method to be used will be helped by the following analogy. If we want to find the youngest college freshman in the United States, we can first find the youngest college freshman in each state and then pick the youngest from among these statewide winners.

Similarly, if we want to find the line among all lines for which the expression

$$\sum\limits_{i=1}^{N} (y_i - Mx_i - B)^2$$

is smallest, we can regard the problem as a sort of contest in two stages. First, for each value of the slope, M, we find the line with that slope for which

$$\sum\limits_{i=1}^{N} (y_i - Mx_i - B)^2$$

is a minimum. Then, only the winners of each of these contests will compete in the grand finale, the determination of the line, among all the lines, for which

$$\sum\limits_{i=1}^{N} (y_i - Mx_i - B)^2$$

is smallest.

The next step is to show that the following statement is true.

> Among all lines with a given fixed slope M, the one for which
>
> $$N\bar{d}^2 = \sum_{i=1}^{N} (y_i - Mx_i - B)^2$$
>
> is a minimum is the line passing through the point $(\bar{x}, \bar{y})$.

(Here, $\bar{x}$ denotes $\dfrac{1}{N} \times \sum_{i=1}^{N} x_i$ and $\bar{y} = \dfrac{1}{N} \times \sum_{i=1}^{N} y_i$.)

Since lines having the same slope are parallel, and parallel lines have the same slope, the above statement tells us (as

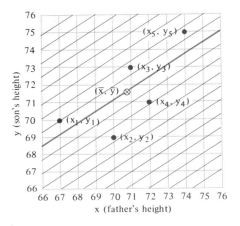

FIGURE 12·59
All lines have same slope M.

illustrated in Figure 12·59) that among a family of parallel lines, the line for which

$$\sum_{i=1}^{N} (y_i - Mx_i - B)^2$$

is a minimum is the one passing through the point $(\bar{x}, \bar{y})$. This point is called the *centroid* of the data points (x_i, y_i). Surprisingly the centroid does not depend in any way on the value of M.

We introduce the notation

(2) $z_i = y_i - Mx_i$

so that

$$\sum_{i=1}^{N} (y_i - Mx_i - B)^2$$

becomes

$$\sum_{i=1}^{N} (z_i - B)^2$$

Since M is given and fixed, each of the z_i's can be calculated as a numerical constant. The minimization problem becomes that of finding the value of B for which

$$\sum_{i=1}^{N} (z_i - B)^2$$

takes on a minimum value. But this problem was solved in the preceding section where we found the value of B to be given by the arithmetic mean of the z_i's.

$$B = \bar{z} = \frac{\sum_{i=1}^{N} z_i}{N}$$

Using Equation 2, we may write

$$B = \bar{z} = \frac{\sum_{i=1}^{N} z_i}{N} = \frac{1}{N} \sum_{i=1}^{N} (y_i - Mx_i)$$

$$B = \frac{1}{N} \sum_{i=1}^{N} y_i - M \cdot \frac{1}{N} \sum_{i=1}^{N} x_i$$

(2a) $B = \bar{y} - M\bar{x}$

Substituting this value of B in the equation $y = Mx + B$ yields us the equation of the minimizing line of that family,

$$y = Mx + \bar{y} - M\bar{x}$$

which can be rewritten as

(3) $y = \bar{y} + M(x - \bar{x})$ or $y - \bar{y} = M(x - \bar{x})$

which is the equation of the line with slope M passing through the point $(\bar{x}, \bar{y})$.

Thus we see that in the search for that line that makes the expression

$$\sum_{i=1}^{N} (y_i - Mx_i - B)^2$$

the smallest, only those lines through the centroid need be considered. As we saw in Equation 2a, the value of B for these

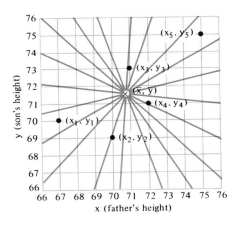

FIGURE 12·60

lines through the centroid is given by $B = \bar{y} - M\bar{x}$ (Figure 12·60) whence, by substitution, we obtain

$$N\bar{d}^2 = \sum_{i=1}^{N} (y_i - Mx_i - B)^2$$

$$= \sum_{i=1}^{N} [y_i - \bar{y} - M(x_i - \bar{x})]^2$$

Hence we seek the value of M that makes this latter expression a minimum. A summary of the steps in the solution is as follows.

Step 1   Expand the square in the expression

$$\sum_{i=1}^{N} [y_i - \bar{y} - M(x_i - \bar{x})]^2$$

Step 2 Change the order of adding to add first "vertically" and then "horizontally."

Step 3 Obtain a quadratic expression in M.

Step 4 Minimize by "completing the square."

We show what this means with $N = 5$:

$$5 \times (\bar{d})^2 = \sum_{i=1}^{5} [(y_i - \bar{y}) - M(x_i - \bar{x})]^2$$

$$= \sum_{i=1}^{5} [M^2(x_i - \bar{x})^2 - 2M(x_i - \bar{x})(y_i - \bar{y}) + (y_i - \bar{y})^2]$$

$$\begin{aligned}
= \quad & M^2(x_1 - \bar{x})^2 - 2M(x_1 - \bar{x})(y_1 - \bar{y}) + (y_1 - \bar{y})^2 \\
+ & M^2(x_2 - \bar{x})^2 - 2M(x_2 - \bar{x})(y_2 - \bar{y}) + (y_2 - \bar{y})^2 \\
+ & M^2(x_3 - \bar{x})^2 - 2M(x_3 - \bar{x})(y_3 - \bar{y}) + (y_3 - \bar{y})^2 \\
+ & M^2(x_4 - \bar{x})^2 - 2M(x_4 - \bar{x})(y_4 - \bar{y}) + (y_4 - \bar{y})^2 \\
+ & M^2(x_5 - \bar{x}) \quad - 2M(x_5 - \bar{x})(y_5 - \bar{y}) + (y_5 - \bar{y})^2
\end{aligned}$$

$$= M^2 \sum_{i=1}^{5} (x_i - \bar{x})^2 - 2M \sum_{i=1}^{5} (x_i - \bar{x})(y_i - \bar{y}) + \sum_{i=1}^{5} (y_i - \bar{y})^2$$

This carries us through Step 3. We now simplify the expression by introducing the notation

$$a = \sum_{i=1}^{5} (x_i - \bar{x})^2, \quad b = \sum_{i=1}^{5} (x_i - \bar{x})(y_i - \bar{y}),$$

$$c = \sum_{i=1}^{5} (y_i - \bar{y})^2$$

Now, the familiar square-completing process takes the form:

$$5 \times (\bar{d})^2 = \sum_{i=1}^{5} [(y_i - \bar{y}) - M(x_i - \bar{x})]^2$$

$$= aM^2 - 2bM + c$$

$$= a\left(M^2 - \frac{2b}{a} M\right) + c$$

$$= a\left(M^2 - \frac{2b}{a}M + \left(\frac{b}{a}\right)^2\right) - \frac{b^2}{a} + c$$

$$= a\left(M - \frac{b}{a}\right)^2 + \frac{ac - b^2}{a}$$

Since the first term in this expression cannot be less than zero, the whole expression takes on its minimum value when the first term is zero, that is, when

$$(4) \quad M = \frac{b}{a} = \frac{\displaystyle\sum_{i=1}^{5}(x_i - \bar{x})(y_i - \bar{y})}{\displaystyle\sum_{i=1}^{5}(x_i - \bar{x})^2}$$

and the minimum value is

$$5 \times \bar{d}^2 = \frac{ac - b^2}{a}$$

$$(5) \quad = \frac{\left(\displaystyle\sum_{i=1}^{5}(x_i - \bar{x})^2\right) \cdot \left(\displaystyle\sum_{i=1}^{5}(y_i - \bar{y})^2\right) - \left(\displaystyle\sum_{i=1}^{5}(x_i - \bar{x})(y_i - \bar{y})\right)^2}{\displaystyle\sum_{i=1}^{N}(x_i - \bar{x})^2}$$

The value obtained by solving for $\bar{d}$ is called the *standard error*.

In the general case with N data points, these formulas are only modified by replacing "5" by "N."

Example Some preliminary computations for the data graphed in Figure 12·57 are shown in Table 12·3.

TABLE 12·3

i	x_i	y_i	$x_i - \bar{x}$	$y_i - \bar{y}$	$(x_i - \bar{x})^2$	$(y_i - \bar{y})^2$	$(x_i - \bar{x})(y_i - \bar{y})$
					a	*c*	*b*
1	67	70	− 3.8	− 1.6	14.44	2.56	6.08
2	70	69	− 0.8	− 2.6	0.64	6.76	2.08
3	71	73	0.2	1.4	0.04	1.96	0.28
4	72	71	1.2	− 0.6	1.44	0.36	− 0.72
5	74	75	3.2	3.4	10.24	11.56	10.88
SUM	354	358	0	0	26.80	23.20	18.60
Arithmetic mean of data	70.8 $\bar{x}$	71.6 $\bar{y}$					

The slope of the line of regression from equation 4 is

$$M = \frac{b}{a} = \frac{18.6}{26.8} \cong .6940$$

The intercept from equation 2a is:

$$B = \bar{y} - M\bar{x} \cong 71.6 - .6940 \times 70.8$$
$$\cong 22.46$$

so the equation of the line of regression from equation 3 is:

$$y = Mx + (\bar{y} - M\bar{x}) = M(x - \bar{x}) + \bar{y}$$
$$y = .6940(x - 70.8) + 71.6$$

and for the standard error

$$\bar{d} = \sqrt{\frac{ac - b^2}{Na}}$$

$$\bar{d} = \sqrt{\frac{26.8 \times 23.2 - (18.6)^2}{5 \times 26.8}} \cong 1.436$$

When N is very large, this is clearly the sort of calculation we would like a computer to do for us. One method of flow-charting these calculations is seen in Figure 12·61.

The calculations in this flowchart divide into four parts that should be self-explanatory.

1. Reading in the data (box 1).

2. Calculating $\bar{x}$ and $\bar{y}$, the means of the list variables X and Y (box 2).

3. Calculating $\sum_{i=1}^{N} (x_i - \bar{x})^2$, $\sum_{i=1}^{N} (y_i - \bar{y})^2$, $\sum_{i=1}^{N} (x_i - \bar{x})(y_i - \bar{y})$, the slope of the regression line, and the standard error (box 3).

4. Outputting the results (box 4).

Figure 12·61 contains a gross inefficiency. In box 1 we have stored the data over which we make two "passes," in boxes 2 and 3. This is wasteful of both time and space, but

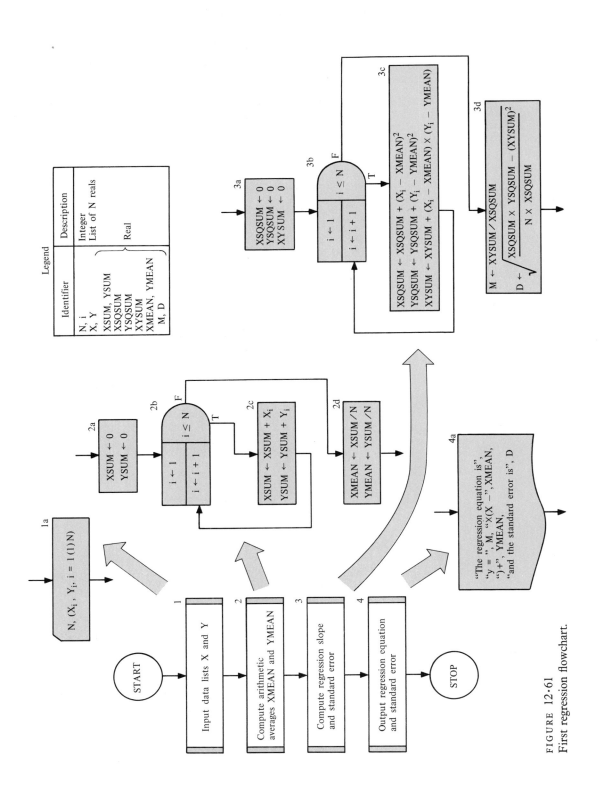

FIGURE 12·61
First regression flowchart.

it seems to be required by the necessity of knowing the values of XMEAN and YMEAN before beginning the next loop of computations, which requires the variables X_i and Y_i to be "adjusted to their means," XMEAN and YMEAN. Surprisingly, this difficulty can be overcome by use of the formulas derived below in which we remember that

$$\bar{x} = \frac{1}{N} \sum_{i=1}^{N} x_i \ \text{ or } \ \sum_{i=1}^{N} x_i = N\bar{x}$$

and

$$\bar{y} = \frac{1}{N} \sum_{i=1}^{N} y_i \ \text{ or } \ \sum_{i=1}^{N} y_i = N\bar{y}$$

And now:

$$\sum_{i=1}^{N} (x_i - \bar{x})^2 = \sum_{i=1}^{N} (x_i{}^2 - 2\bar{x}x_i + \bar{x}^2)$$

$$= \sum_{i=1}^{N} x_i{}^2 - 2\bar{x} \sum_{i=1}^{N} x_i + N\bar{x}^2$$

$$= \sum_{i=1}^{N} x_i{}^2 - 2\bar{x}N\bar{x} + N\bar{x}^2$$

$$= \sum_{i=1}^{N} x_i{}^2 - N\bar{x}^2$$

Similarly,

$$\sum_{i=1}^{N} (x_i - \bar{x})(y_i - \bar{y}) = \sum_{i=1}^{N} (x_iy_i - \bar{x}y_i - \bar{y}x_i + \overline{xy})$$

$$= \sum_{i=1}^{N} x_iy_i - \bar{x} \sum_{i=1}^{N} y_i - \bar{y} \sum_{i=1}^{N} x_i + N\overline{xy}$$

$$= \sum_{i=1}^{N} x_iy_i - \bar{x}N\bar{y} - \bar{y}N\bar{x} + N\overline{xy}$$

$$= \sum_{i=1}^{N} x_iy_i - N\overline{xy}$$

These formulas suggest how we may build up the sums

$$\sum_{i=1}^{N} x_i^2, \quad \sum_{i=1}^{N} y_i^2, \quad \text{and} \quad \sum_{i=1}^{N} x_i y_i$$

as the data are read and then make a single correction (subtracting $N\bar{x}^2$, $N\bar{y}^2$, $N\overline{xy}$, respectively) after $\bar{x}$ and $\bar{y}$ have been computed. This modification also eliminates the necessity for subscripted variables. We provide, instead, for a sentinel value to signal the end of the data. The flowchart is seen in Figure 12·62.

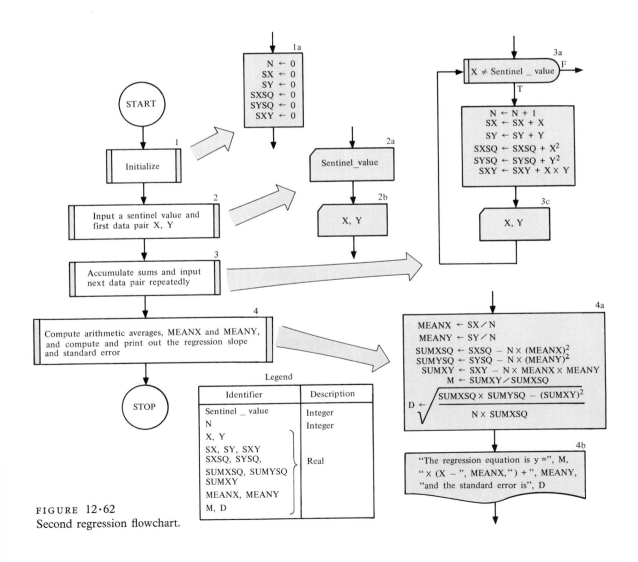

FIGURE 12·62
Second regression flowchart.

EXERCISES 12·7

*1. Forty undergraduates were tested in a verbal discrimination task. X is the number of errors committed during nine learning trials: Y is the number of words recalled in a subsequent free recall test.

S (student)	1	2	3	4	5	6	7	8	9	10	11	12	13	14	15	16	17	18
X	5	5	6	6	6	7	7	7	8	8	8	9	9	9	9	10	10	10
Y	8	10	11	10	8	10	8	7	10	9	5	10	9	7	5	9	8	7

S	19	20	21	22	23	24	25	26	27	28	29	30	31	32	33	34	35	36	37	38	39	40
X	10	10	11	11	11	12	12	12	12	13	13	13	13	14	14	15	15	15	16	16	17	17
Y	5	3	9	6	4	8	7	5	3	8	6	3	2	5	2	6	4	1	2	1	2	1

(a) Make a "scatter diagram" for these data (i.e., a graph such as in Figure 12·56.) Do the data seem to have a straight-line tendency? Does the slope of the line seem to be positive or negative? Sketch in by eye what seems to be the best fitting straight line.

(b) Determine the regression equation for predicting Y from X by running the program of the flowchart in Figure 12·62 with the above data. Draw this line on your scatter diagram and compare it with your eyeball line in part a.

(c) Also, calculate the line of regression for predicting X from Y, by the same method as in part b and sketch this line on your scatter diagram. Be sure to label the two regression lines clearly.

(d) What do we know about the point where these two lines cross?

(e) Comment in a few sentences on the consequences of the two lines of regression not being the same.

2. There are plenty of sources of data close at hand to which you can apply the regression flowchart. Here is one suggestion. Get every student in your class (or in some larger group) to write his height and weight on a slip of paper and find the lines of regression of height and weight and of weight and height, following the outline of Problem 1. (Actually, it would be more sensible to separate the data into male and female categories.)

3. For students who would like to try out the regression algorithms on large masses of data here are some suggestions of where to find such data.

(a) (Easiest since you won't have to punch the cards.) Try to obtain a data deck for an actual statistical sampling. Many Ph.D. Students

*Part of this exercise is borrowed from Edward L. Wike, *Data Analysis*, Aldine Atherton, Chicago & New York, 1971, p. 162.

(in economics, education, biology, etc.) have prepared such decks for use in writing their dissertations and might loan them to you or allow you to copy them.

(b) Almanacs (such as the *World Almanac* or the *Information Please, Almanac* are rich sources of data, ripe for regression analysis. For example, based on data in the education section of the *World Almanac*, one might run a regression of the number of faculty in a college and the number of students in the college. By perusal of an almanac, you can invent a project of your own.

4. Recall Problem 3, Exercises 12·6, which called attention to a pitfall in computing the standard error by the formula

$$d = \sqrt{\frac{S}{N} - A^2}$$

Will the same pitfall show up in the computation of D in box 3d of the Figure 12·61 algorithm and in box 4a of the Figure 12·62? *Hint* Try computing D using the algorithm in Figure 12·62 with the following data set, say with 4 decimal precision arithmetic (use rounding up for the roundoff rule):

N = 5, and

X	Y
2.111	14.55
4.111	24.55
6.111	34.55
8.111	44.55
10.11	54.55

These data fall very near a straight line whose equation is

Y = 3X + 4

5. Develop an alternative regression flowchart to Figure 12·62 so that D is now computed by applying recurrence relations similar to those discussed in Problem 3, Exercises 12·6. Include a legend. Are subscripts necessary?

String processing

A wide variety of everyday problems involves the processing of character string data. It becomes surprisingly simple to express algorithmic solutions for these problems in our flowchart language if we add a very small number of additional primitive operations designed to process character string data. One use of string processing is the editing of text. Typically, text editing is now done manually but, in a rapidly increasing number of situations, computers are being employed. A number of special editing languages have been designed to facilitate the computer programming of editing functions.

One use of computers in editing is to create right-justified margins (squared off on the right) in the typeset columns of books, magazines, or newspapers. Computers are also often used to prepare and periodically revise racing schedules, airline guides, telephone directories, and other such large-formatted tables and lists.

In the field of literature, computers are used to analyze literary works for style and authorship. Some of this is done by carrying out statistical studies, counting the frequency with which certain words, phrases, or ideas are used. A *concordance* of a book, for instance, is a massive ordered list including every nontrivial word occurring in the book and, along with each word, a complete set of citations, chapter, line number, and verse, where that word occurred. The concordance of the Bible, for instance, is a necessary research document for the biblical scholar. In the past the preparation of a concordance required a major manual effort—perhaps lasting many years. Today, concordances and other similar references for scholars are prepared routinely by computers.

Another type of application for text editing is the editing of legal texts. For example, congressional bills are usually voluminous and, as a result of committee deliberations, require many revisions from their original drafts. Computer editing and automatic typesetting speed up the printing of new drafts of such bills. As one further example of string processing, students who are fortunate enough to have access to time sharing systems are able to type and edit their term papers with the aid of the computer.

13·2 Editing

One good way to start investigating the technical aspects of computer editing is to consider an illustrative although hypothetical problem. Let us do this by using the following scenario.

You are taking a laboratory course from Professor S. Kistiakowsky, who insists that each lab report be neatly typed and at least 20 pages in length. Professor K. once thought of himself as a journalist and dislikes seeing such errors as misspelled words, split infinitives, and the like. Moreover, he has strong feelings about certain matters such as the arrangement of mathematical expressions, the proper use of technical abbreviations, and the detailed description of the experimental situation.

You find that your first draft of a lab report is rarely acceptable to Professor K, and usually you are required to revise a report one or more times. For example, Figure 13·1 shows the kinds of changes and corrections to be made on a draft of one of the lab reports. Some of the changes are to be made several times. Thus one word has been misspelled 6 times and one phrase is to be replaced 17 times. Your problem is to find a way to make these changes, produce a neatly typed version and, as part of the process, never have to retype the report completely.

It is reasonable to think that a computer could be helpful. While you may not have a computer at your disposal to help prepare your lab reports, a number of research laboratories, printing and publishing houses, and a few model secretarial offices already use a computer in the solution to this common editing problem. It may not be long before you, too, will routinely use a computer for text editing.

How the Computer Plays Its Role

A text to be edited can be read into a computer from paper tape, punched cards, or magnetic tape or, in many cases, it can be entered through a keyboard, such as a typewriter, attached directly to the computer. The computer, of course, can store

A. Spelling and typographical errors

As it appears now	Approximate number of occurrences	As it should appear
a. litle	6	little
b. stastistics	3	statistics
c. occurrance	4	occurrence
d. *()	1	890

caused by use of wrong case shift

B. Phrase changes

From		To
a. to safely run the experiment	2	to run the experiment safely
b. a terribly costly experiment	1	a costly experiment
c. in order to	17	to
d. cc/s	12	cc/sec
e. normal room temperature	4	normal room temperature, average humidity range and average barometric pressure
f. 4ac	6	$4 \times a \times c$
g. the sum $a \times b + a \times c$	4	the product $a \times (b + c)$
h. LESS * MINUTES	3	LESS ⊛ SECONDS

*number represented by * is to be multiplied by 60 to get a number represented by ⊛.*

the text in memory, print or type it out, or display it a line at a time or a page at a time on a TV screen. The editor can study the typed, printed, or displayed copy and prepare instructions expressed in a special *editing language* to show the changes he wants made. These instructions are then input to the computer and converted into a program that operates on the text as data.

After executing the editor's instructions, the new version of the text is normally printed or displayed so the human editor can decide whether to make still more changes by repeating the process. This editing cycle can be repeated as often as necessary until the human editor is satisfied with the text. Never once is it necessary for the text to be manually retyped.

This chapter does not have as its purpose to study any particular one of the available editing languages. Special editing language primers or manuals are available and may be useful and easy to follow, especially after you have studied this chapter. The programming language SNOBOL, for example, which is a general purpose string processing language, will be especially easy to learn after this chapter. Our initial purpose here is the more basic one of studying the algorithmic processes required to make editorial changes of the type suggested in Figure 13·1. New ways to represent and manipulate text data will be developed, and these will be useful later in this chapter, where we will apply them to the editing, compiling, and interpreting of computer programs.

13·3 Searching a string for a particular string pattern— a review

Computer editing implies the ability to search and *find* particular words or phrases in a text line. If we can't find them, we certainly can't replace them with anything else. In Section 2·2 we introduced the *concatenation operator* and the *inclusion relation* and showed how they could be used to determine by a search whether a given substring occurred in a given list of names. Here we will review briefly what was said there before going on.

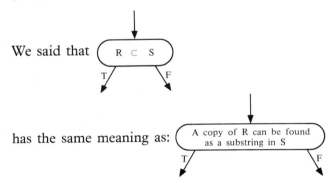

We said that (R ⊂ S) has the same meaning as: (A copy of R can be found as a substring in S)

Here R is any string expression involving string variables, string constants, and the concatenation operator, and S is any string variable. For instance, suppose the value of A is the character string, "UNWILLINGLY", and suppose the value of B is the string, "REPRESENT". The assertion given in box 1 below

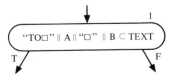

"TO□" ‖ A ‖ "□" ‖ B ⊂ TEXT

is then tantamount to the assertion: a copy of the string of characters "TO□UNWILLINGLY□REPRESENT" can be found as a substring of TEXT. In more general terms, we understand box 1 in the following way. Let the string of characters that represents the value of the string expression (on the left of the inclusion symbol) be called the *pattern*. The assertion in box 1 can then be read as: a substring of characters can be found in TEXT to exactly match the pattern represented by "TO□" ‖ A ‖ "□" ‖ B.

The right-hand operand of the inclusion relation ⊂ is a string variable. The left-hand operand may be any string expression, which we will refer to as the *string pattern*.

We can call a decision box containing an inclusion relation a *string search* decision box. It takes the following general form.

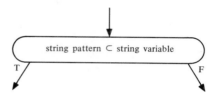

Alternatively, we can refer to this box as a *pattern match*. You should especially remember that if the T exit is taken, there is *at least one occurrence* of the string pattern value in the string variable. We don't know how many occurrences.

To summarize our study of string operations up to this point, we offer the algorithm in Figure 13·2. Here we illustrate a use of the pattern match (box 6), of string assignments (boxes 3, 5, and 10), and of output of the value of a string variable (boxes 7 and 8). The purpose of the algorithm is to determine whether either of the following two phrases occurs in TEXT.

1. "to unwillingly represent".

2. "to represent unwillingly".

Note that the flowchart for the algorithm is essentially independent of the *length* of TEXT.

13·4
Substring operations

The discovery that a string S does or does not contain a pattern P is fundamental to our ability to manipulate strings. However, we will often need to go one step further when the pattern match P ⊂ S is *true*. A replacement operation suggests itself:

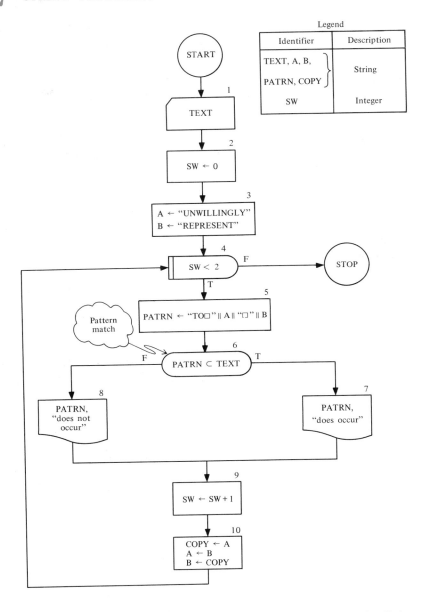

Legend	
Identifier	Description
TEXT, A, B, PATRN, COPY	String
SW	Integer

FIGURE 13·2

when $P \subset S$ is true, replace the matched substring in S by a string R (possibly null).

This operation is a natural concomitant of the pattern-matching process. For an example, let us go back to Figure 13·1. If we find the phrase "a terribly costly experiment" in TEXT, we would like to replace it with the phrase "a costly experiment." This substring replacement is so closely related to the pattern match that in our flowchart notation we want

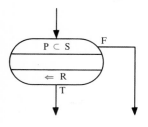

FIGURE 13·3
Pattern match with substring replacement. The *false* exit emerges from the *top* compartment. The *true* branch emerges from the *bottom* compartment.

to include its specification as a second compartment within the pattern match box, as suggested in Figure 13·3. We interpret its meaning as follows.

If $P \subset S$ is *true*, then the first occurrence of the substring in S that matches the pattern P is replaced by the string R and the *true* exit is taken. If $P \subset S$ is *false*, then no replacement takes place and the *false* exit is taken. We use a new operator symbol, $\Leftarrow$, for *substring replacement* to distinguish it clearly from string assignment. When we use this form, the pattern match will always be expressed in the *top* compartment of the box and the *false* exit will always emanate from this part of the oval. The *true* exit will always emerge from the *bottom* compartment. This notation will make it evident that:

1. The pattern match is attempted first.

2. If the pattern match is not successful, the *false* exit is taken.

3. If the pattern match is successful, the substring replacement is performed and then the *true* exit is taken.

Example   If S is the string

"THE RED RED ROSE IS A RED ROSE."

then

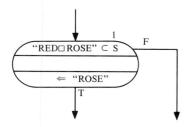

will find the first substring in S that matches "RED□ROSE" (string elements 9 to 16, inclusive) and replace that substring by "ROSE". In effect, the word "RED□" will be eliminated and the string S will read

"THE RED ROSE IS A RED ROSE".

We will know that a replacement has taken place, when we leave the pattern match box via the *true* exit.

Now, suppose we want to replace *each* occurrence of "RED ROSE" in S by "ROSE". This can be accomplished very simply by looping back as shown in Figure 13·4. We see that S will be scanned repeatedly for an occurrence of "RED□ROSE". Each time this phrase is found, it will be replaced by "ROSE" until the phrase no longer occurs and the *false* exit is taken.

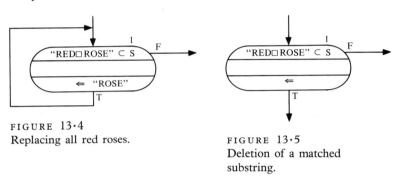

FIGURE 13·4
Replacing all red roses.

FIGURE 13·5
Deletion of a matched
substring.

We will consider *deletion* of a matched substring to be a special case of string replacement. We can express deletion easily in our new notation, as shown in Figure 13·5. This simply means replace the first occurrence of "RED ROSE" in S by the empty or *null string*. An empty string is one that has no characters.

Insertion of a string can also be treated in the framework of replacement. Suppose we wish to insert "□OF□ SHARON" immediately after the first occurrence of "RED□ ROSE" in S. Then the pattern match box will be as shown in Figure 13·6.

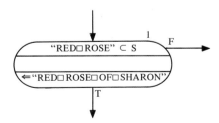

FIGURE 13·6

We remark in passing that the amount of writing can be considerably reduced by a deliberate use of string assignments, as shown in Figure 13·7.

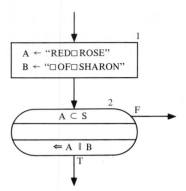

FIGURE 13·7

1. What would happen to TEXT as a result of executing box 1, below, assuming the *true* exit is taken the first time the loop is executed? Is there a lesson to be learned here? If so, what is it?

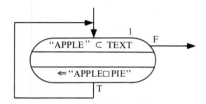

2. You are given below the initial value of the variable TEXT and are to assume that the associated flowchart boxes are executed. Select the string value that correctly represents the printed output.

    The initial value of TEXT is: "Jane and Dick lived in the city. One day Jane met Dick on the street."

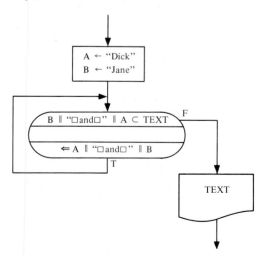

(a) Jane and Dick lived in the city. One day Jane met Dick on the street.

(b) One day Jane met Dick on the street. Jane and Dick lived in the city.

(c) Dick and Jane or Jane and Dick. It makes no difference.

(d) Dick and Jane lived in the city. One day Dick met Jane on the street.

(e) Dick and Jane lived in the city. One day Jane met Dick on the street.

3. Suppose

$$S = \text{"N\$W}\square\text{*S}\square\text{TH} + \square\text{T*M} + \square\text{T\$}\square - \text{*D}\square\text{Y\$/R}\square\text{P} - \text{RTY."}$$

after executing box 2 of the flowchart in Figure 13·8.

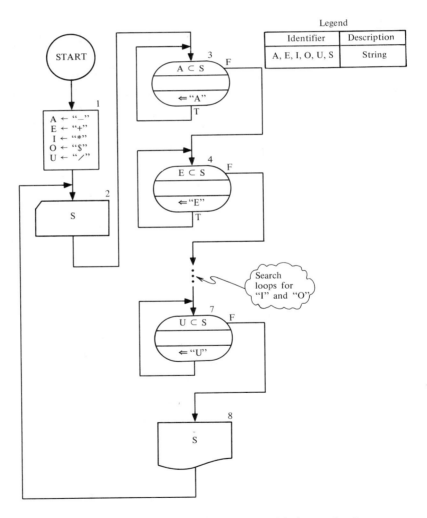

FIGURE 13·8

(a) What will be the output at box 8 with this input data?

Answer   "NOW□IS□THE□TIME□TO□AID□YOUR□PARTY."

(b) Note the five basically similar search loops. Problem 5, Set A at the end of the next subsection reexamines this situation.

13·5
Simple unknowns in pattern match operations

Imagine you have a text for which you need to develop a list of the words immediately preceding a given word. For example, if the given word were "TREE", you might expect to find:

MAPLE TREE,   or SHADE TREE,
or BIRCH TREE,   or FAMILY TREE,
or ORANGE TREE,   or SHOE TREE, etc.

but you wouldn't know in advance what the preceding word was.

To express a search for such a pattern in the flowchart language, we need a special notation for a pattern component that represents an *unknown*, that is, a string of unknown content and length. We choose the double asterisk (**) for this purpose. Then the pattern match

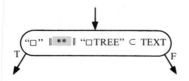

will succeed with all the examples listed above.

Since ** refers to an unknown of *arbitrary* length (including null length), the above pattern match will, in fact, match the substring in TEXT that begins with the *first* blank character and ends with the first occurrence of "□TREE" following the first blank. To illustrate, if TEXT begins with

"□ONLY□GOD□CAN□MAKE□A□GREEN□
TREE.□MORE . . ."

the underbracketed portion will be the substring that is matched by **, and not just "GREEN".

We can have more control over what is matched if we are able to be more specific about the nature of the unknown string. For instance, we can specify the length by writing the number of characters in the string between the two asterisks.

To designate the length of an unknown, we will use such forms as:

   4   meaning any string of four characters

and

   n   meaning any string of n characters

In the sample list of trees at the beginning of this example,

"□" ‖ *3* ‖ "□TREE"   finds no match, but

"□" ‖ *4* ‖ "□TREE"   matches "SHOE TREE",

and

"□" ‖ *5* ‖ "□TREE"   matches "MAPLE TREE", "BIRCH TREE", and "SHADE TREE".

(Note that a blank space must be counted as a character.)

To develop a list of words in TEXT immediately preceding occurrences of the word "TREE", we might try the following pattern match.

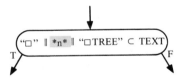

Depending on the exit from this pattern match, we would know that a blank space has or has not been found n spaces before "□TREE" (the blanks are assumed to delimit a word). However, we do not yet have a way to find out what the n intervening characters are. One solution is to assign the value of the unknown string to a designated string variable after the unknown string has been determined in a successful pattern match. Our notation to denote this special kind of assignment is shown in Figure 13·9. Notice that the special assignment will always be represented in the *middle* compartment of the oval. The operation and the notation used are somewhat similar (but in a reverse sense) to that of the pattern match with substring replacement displayed in Figure 13·3. We will sometimes refer to the middle compartment as the *capture* box and refer to the assignment that takes place in this compartment

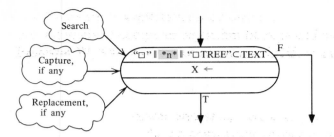

FIGURE 13·9
Determining an unknown
string and capturing it by
assignment to X.

as the *capture of an unknown*. Thus, in Figure 13·9, the unknown is captured by assignment to X.

Now that we are armed with suitable notation, let's draw a flowchart to produce a list of all words containing 3 to 10 characters and occurring immediately before "□TREE". This flowchart is shown in Figure 13·10.

The first box of Figure 13·10 reads in the text to be searched, and the second one assigns the null string as the initial value of the output string. We recall that an empty string is one that has no characters. It is convenient to adopt the convention that we can assign to any variable the value of the empty string simply by showing nothing to the right of the assignment arrow. Thus $\boxed{S \leftarrow}$ means assign to S the empty string.

Box 3 controls repeated searches of TEXT for substrings of length n where n ranges from 3 to 10 characters inclusive. In box 4, TEXT is scanned for the first occurrence of "□TREE" preceded by a blank followed by n characters. If this pattern is found, a copy of the string of n intervening characters is *captured* in, that is, assigned to, X and we go on to box 5. Having found the pattern once and, knowing that we intend to continue searching TEXT for this pattern, we realize we must alter the string already found in TEXT so as not to rediscover the same pattern. Box 5 does this by deleting the word "TREE" where it has been found in the text. This is achieved by refinding the pattern "□" ‖ X ‖ "□TREE" and replacing it with the shorter substring "□" ‖ X ‖ "□".

Box 6 of Figure 13·10 is included to make sure that the output list will not include any string made up of two words preceding "TREE". Because the search is conducted beginning

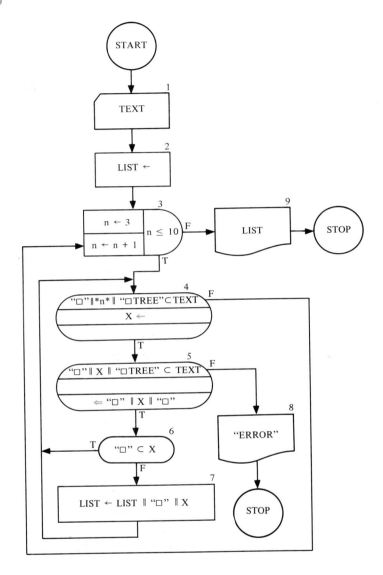

FIGURE 13·10
Making a list of the words
preceding TREE.

with unknowns of short length and going on to longer unknown
strings, the only phrase we think can be excluded by box 6
is "I A TREE". (It will also eliminate one- and two-letter
words that might be included if more than one blank occurred
in succession.) Box 7 appends X, the word found, to the output
string for later printing (box 9).

When a pattern match no longer succeeds in box 4, it
means that there are no more substrings of the desired length
in the text, so we loop back to repeat the search with a larger
value of n.

The text replacement operations accomplished by boxes 4 and 5 are quite common in string searches, but the approach used in Figure 13·10 is not efficient because it implies that *two* scans of TEXT are to be made to find a substring and alter it. In such cases it makes sense to use the single, but more

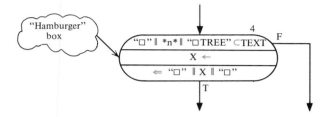

FIGURE 13·11
A fully grown pattern match, capture, and replacement. This box can be used to replace boxes 4 and 5 of the preceding figure.

complex, pattern match box shown in Figure 13·11. Figure 13·11 indicates that:

1. TEXT is scanned for the given pattern.

2. If a substring matching the pattern is found, a copy of the contents of the *unknown* substring is captured by assignment to X.

3. The substring matching the entire pattern is then replaced in TEXT by the new substring given on the right of the replacement symbol ⇐.

By now it has probably occurred to you that the repeated search of TEXT in our improved algorithm (i.e., using the new box 4 to replace the original boxes 4 and 5) is still very inefficient. Once we search a text and find a particular n-character word, we should not have to repeat the scan of the left end of TEXT. Instead, it makes sense to *resume* the search at the point immediately following the last discovered pattern. Unfortunately, a repeated execution of the same pattern match flowchart box will force a new search over "old territory," that is, over a portion of TEXT that cannot possibly contain what we seek. We illustrate a way to avoid this inefficiency by considering the following related problem.

Illustrative Problem

Draw a flowchart to count the number of occurrences of the letter "T" in the string called TEXT. Figure 13·12 contrasts

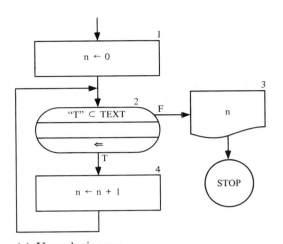

(a) Unaesthetic way to count occurrences.

(b) A good way when TEXT is long and "T" may occur often.

FIGURE 13·12
One unaesthetic and one good way to make successive searches of the same string.

two approaches, one *good* and one *unaesthetic*. The good way may look more complicated (more assignment steps), but the scanning effort is greatly reduced when TEXT is a long string and has numerous occurrences of "T". In the "good" way, box 1 makes a copy of TEXT. After each section of COPY is searched in the pattern match (box 2), the substring beginning with the left end of COPY and ending with the *next* occurrence of a "T" is deleted from COPY. Each reexecution of box 2 searches a shorter copy of COPY. There is never any rescanning of what has been previously searched.

EXERCISES 13·5, SET A

1. You are given below the initial value of the variable TEXT and are to assume that the associated flowchart boxes are executed. Select the string value that correctly represents the printed output.
   The input value of TEXT is:
   "The converted form of (A × T + C) is:"

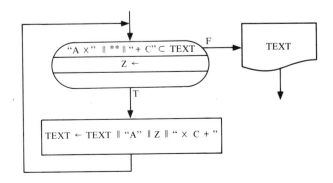

(Choose one)

(a) "The initial input value of TEXT is:".

(b) "The converted form of (A $\times$ T + C) is:".

(c) "The converted form of (A $\times$ T + C) is: A Z $\times$ C + ".

(d) "The converted form of (A $\times$ T + C) is: A T $\times$ C + ".

(e) "The converted form of (A $\times$ T + C) is: A $\times$ T C + ".

2. What will the value of TEXT be after executing the F exit from box 2 in the flowchart fragment shown below?

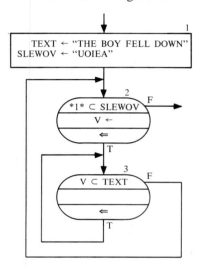

3. Construct a flowchart to scan a given text and output a table showing the number of words that occur for each word length in the range 3 to 20 letters per word (inclusive). For this exercise, you must assume that the text will contain punctuation and that several blanks may occur in sequence.

4. When executed, the flowchart in Figure 13·13 will decipher messages that have been written in a very simple replacement code. The coded messages are input at box 1. Suppose the string input at box 1 is

   "BATJNQMFADPEF"

   (a) What will be the value of X immediately before the first execution of box 8?

   (b) What will be the value of X immediately after the first execution of box 8?

   (c) What will be the value of TEXT that is printed when box 6 is executed?

5. Review Problem 3, Section 13·4. By applying the various ideas and techniques for identifying unknowns, and using the unknown in conjunction with substring replacement and/or deletion, modify the flowchart given in the problem so that the pattern match of S appears in only *one* instead of in *five* flowchart boxes. *Hint* A study of the flowchart in Problem 4 of this set should prove helpful.

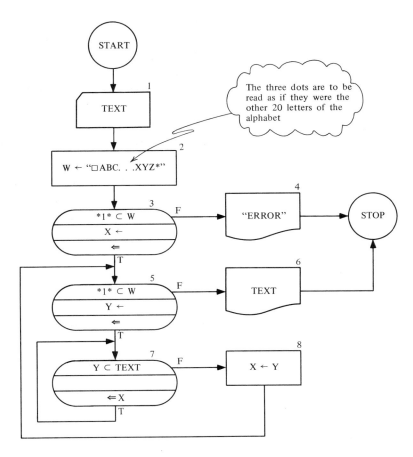

FIGURE 13·13

6. Many procedural programming languages (e.g., FORTRAN and ALGOL) permit the user to intersperse blanks freely anywhere within the body of the statement. The first step in compiling a statement in such a language is usually to remove all blanks within the statement body and to insert a special character not contained within the alphabet of that programming language (say, ";") immediately after the last nonblank character. Usually there is a label field of fixed width (or the equivalent) for each statement that must be handled differently. In the case of FORTRAN, for example, the first six characters in a statement have special significance. Moreover, the statement body is commonly required to lie within a fixed field (e.g., characters 7–72, inclusive, in FORTRAN).

Draw a flowchart for a string manipulation algorithm that will:

(a) Read in a text of 80 characters.
(b) Delete the last eight of them.

(c) Preserve unchanged the first six characters of the input statement.
(d) Remove all blanks from the next 66 characters (statement body).
(e) Append the special character ";" to the statement body.
(f) Print out the modified text.

Multiple Capture of Unknowns

If there is more than one unknown in the search pattern, then we may want to capture the value of more than one unknown. For example, suppose we want to search a text for occurrences of phrases of the form: "The _____ man and his _____ dog" where the underscores are intended to represent (single-word) adjectives, such as:

"The *old* man and his *sleepy* dog"
"The *friendly* man and his *barking* dog", etc.

Having found such phrases, suppose we want to edit the text, (for the fun of it) by interchanging elements of such adjective pairs. Thus our edited text will contain such phrases as:

"The sleepy man and his old dog."
"The barking man and his friendly dog," etc.

The following flowchart fragment suggests a satisfactory notation for multiple capture.

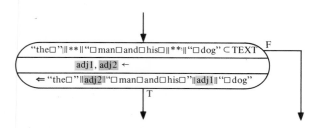

That is, if we have two unknowns in a string pattern, we can capture each of their matching values, assigning them, respectively, to the variables we list in the capture compartment.

It is easy to see how we can extend this idea to the capture of three or more unknowns of a single string pattern. The correspondence between the unknowns in the string pattern of the pattern match compartment and the variables in the capture compartment is maintained purely by the left-to-right ordering within the "hamburger" box.

The trouble with our initial example of multiple capture is that even if we repeat the execution of the hamburger box, only the first occurrence of the search pattern in TEXT will ever be found.

To remedy this defect we will resort to an earlier trick, that is, successively delete the matched patterns from the text being examined. (See Figure 13·12b.)

In our completed version (Figure 13·14) TEXT is assigned to COPY. Each time the wanted phrase is found in

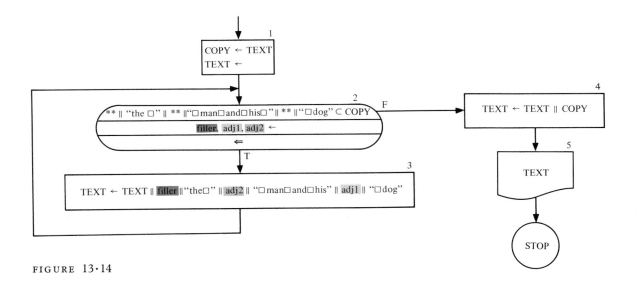

FIGURE 13·14

COPY the phrase and the *filler* to its left are deleted. However, because we now capture the filler as well as the adjective, it is possible in box 3 to rearrange the matched pattern and append it to TEXT. The *empty* string was assigned to TEXT after it was copied in box 1. After we complete the pattern matching loop, anything remaining in COPY is appended to TEXT (box 4). In box 5 the fully edited TEXT is printed out.

EXERCISE 13·5
SET B

1. This question is concerned with the flowchart shown on the next page. Suppose that the execution of box 1 results in the following values for L and Z:

    L = "((A□B) (C□D) (A□E) (D□F) (C□X))"
    Z = "C"

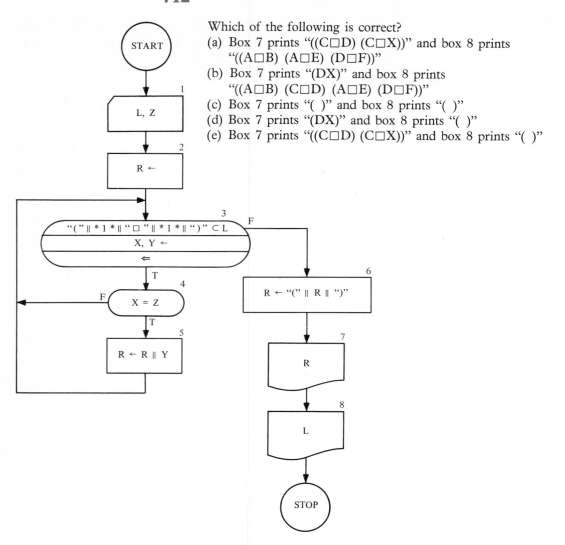

Which of the following is correct?
(a) Box 7 prints "((C□D) (C□X))" and box 8 prints
    "((A□B) (A□E) (D□F))"
(b) Box 7 prints "(DX)" and box 8 prints
    "((A□B) (C□D) (A□E) (D□F))"
(c) Box 7 prints "( )" and box 8 prints "( )"
(d) Box 7 prints "(DX)" and box 8 prints "( )"
(e) Box 7 prints "((C□D) (C□X))" and box 8 prints "( )"

13·6
Other pattern
match operations

String processing is made still easier by the introduction of several additional concepts and operations. This section might be renamed "advanced pattern match operations," except that the ideas presented here are, for the most part, merely refinements or simple extensions of the pattern matching operations discussed in the preceding section. Nevertheless these improvements increase our ability to construct and/or comprehend complex algorithmic processes, as will be seen in the final section of this chapter.

List-Element Unknowns

Are there any other useful ways to qualify unknown string patterns besides specifying their length? Indeed, there are many more! For example, we can have a string that is unknown except that it contains no double letters such as ss, gg, oo, and so forth, or we may have a string that is unknown except that it contains no vowels, or only vowels, and so on. Unfortunately, each new type of qualified unknown we choose to introduce requires a new notational convention for us all to remember. If we are not careful, the flowchart language will become overly difficult to remember and use.

A better question to ask is: are there still one or two other useful ways to qualify unknown string pattern elements that we should know about now? The answer is still *yes*. We offer just one and call it the *list element unknown*. The idea is that the unknown is any substring matching an element of a pre-specified list of strings.

For example, if V is a list of the vowels; that is, if V_1 = "A", V_2 = "E", V_3 = "I", and so forth, we say that *{V}* means "any substring that matches an element of V." Hence, the search

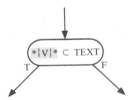

will succeed when the first (if any) vowel in TEXT is discovered. Similarly, executing the loop

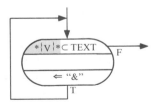

replaces *every* vowel in TEXT with the ampersand symbol. As an exercise, you should satisfy yourself that the following fragment is a more efficient way to accomplish the same task.

Note that although the variable COPY is employed as an auxiliary variable to build up part of the desired string, the

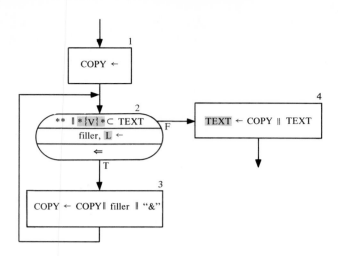

final result is assigned to TEXT, in box 4 above, and *not* to COPY.

Example 1

Suppose we have a text and are interested in counting up all three-letter words whose second letter is a vowel. Moreover, suppose we wish to accomplish this without destroying the "original" text. A flowchart fragment to do this job is seen in Figure 13·15.

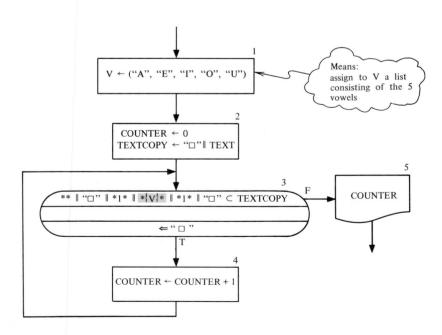

FIGURE 13·15

Note We place a blank character at the beginning of the copied text (box 2) to insure that if TEXT happens to begin with a three-letter word, there will be at least one blank character on its left. Other improvements are needed if the method is to handle cases where three-letter words are followed by punctuation characters, such as the comma or period.

Example 2

Suppose we are interested in knowing how many times each of the following three words appears in a given text: "APPLE", "ORANGE", and "PEAR". A flowchart fragment to do this job is seen in Figure 13·16.

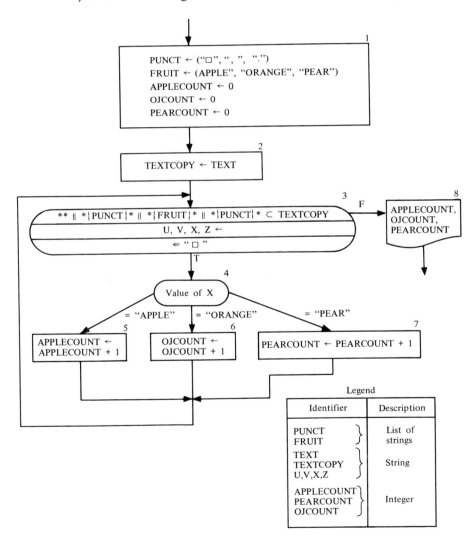

FIGURE 13·16

Example 3
(from Chapter 7 recall the
postfix representation
of an expression)

Suppose the string value of POST is an expression in a *special* postfix form that has each operand or operator separated from the next by a special marker like a comma. For instance:

ordinary infix: $(A + B) \times (C - D)$
standard postfix: A B + C D − ×

and, for this example,

special postfix: A,B,+,C,D,−,×

The flowchart fragment in Figure 13·17 will, when executed, convert any special postfix string assigned to POST to a fully parenthesized infix equivalent, for example,

fully parenthesized
infix equivalent: $((A + B) \times (C - D))$

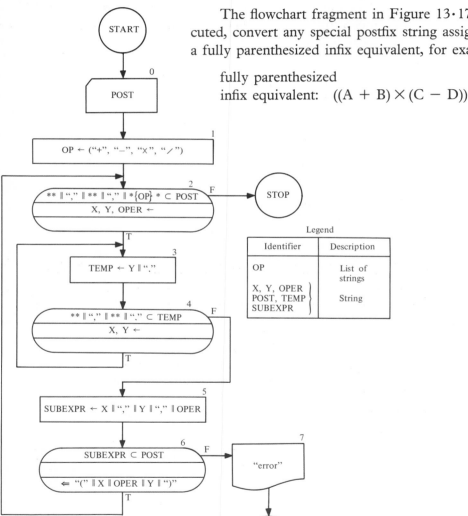

FIGURE 13·17
Transformation of special
postfix to fully parenthesized
infix notation.

TABLE 13·1
Trace of Special Postfix-to-Infix Converter, Figure 13·17. Initial value of POST is "A,B,+,C,D,−,×"

Box Number	Values Assigned to Variables						True or False	Next Box Number
	X	Y	OPER	TEMP	SUBEXPR	POST		
2	"A"						T	3
3		"B"	"+"	"B."				4
4	"A"				"A,B,+"		F	5
5						"(A + B),C,D,−,×"	T	6
6								2
2							T	3
3		"C,D"		"C,D."				4
4	"(A + B)"						T	3
3		"D"	"−"	"D."				4
4	"C"				"C,D,−"		F	5
5						"(A + B), (C − D), ×"	T	6
6								2
2							T	3
3		"(C − D)"	"×"	"(C − D)."				4
4	"(A + B)"				"(A + B), (C − D), ×"		F	5
5						"((A + B) × (C − D))"	T	6
6								2
2							F	

Note If POST has an initial value that is correctly represented, the F exit of box 6 will never be taken.

The trace table (Table 13·1) is included to help the reader follow the logic of Figure 13·17 for our example. As a further exercise, try some other postfix strings.

1. Draw a flowchart fragment that, when executed, will scan a string called TEXT, assumed to be in standard postfix representation, and place commas in the string to separate operands and operators and thus convert TEXT from standard to special postfix form.

2. Draw a flowchart fragment that, when executed, will remove all superfluous parentheses from a fully parenthesized infix form initially represented as a string assigned to TEXT.

Converting Strings to or from Integers

Occasionally, it will be useful to interpret certain strings of digits as numbers instead of as characters. Line B_h of Figure 13·1 is a case in point. In this problem, we are essentially asked to search for an instance of the pattern

"LESS□" || *n* || "□MINUTES"

If we find a match with this pattern and if we are allowed to assume that the discovered value is a string of n characters, all of which are digits, then, after assigning the unknown to X, our next steps are as follows.

Convert the digit string X to a new digit string, say, Y. This new string, interpreted as an integer, is to be 60 times the *integer interpretation* of the string X. The replacement phrase to be inserted in the text is of the form

"LESS□" || Y || "□SECONDS"

But how do we express the transformation from X to Y? We hesitate to use the expression

$60 \times X$

because it is not clear whether we are to think of the product as a string of characters or as an integer number. Suppose, instead, we imagine that two functions are available for *converting* from digit strings to integer representation and vice versa.

1. The function

stoi(X)

standing for *s*tring *to* *i*nteger, returns the *integer* value equivalent of the digit string argument X. (By a *digit string* we simply mean a string of digits.)

> stoi ("835") = 835

2. The function

> itos(i)

standing for *i*nteger *to* *s*tring, returns the digit *string* value equivalent of the integer argument i.

> itos (7) = "7"

Using these functions, Figure 13·18 shows the steps necessary to accomplish this minutes-to-seconds "editing."

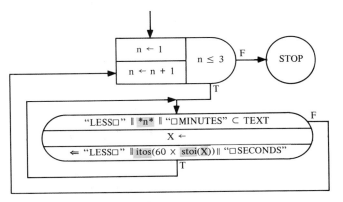

FIGURE 13·18
The minutes-to-seconds problem.

EXERCISES 13·6,
SET B

The following two exercises involve construction of a function and a procedure involving string variables. These exercises assume you have studied Chapter 9.

1. Construct a flowchart for the function LENSTR of Chapter 2 to determine the length (number of characters) of a string. The function LENSTR will have one parameter—a string variable. The function should return an integer, which is the number of characters in the string whose name is supplied as an argument.

Example application

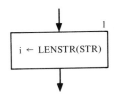

If the value of STR, *prior* to execution of box 1, was "THE□

NEW□MOON", then *after* execution of box 1, the value of i would be 12.

2. Construct a flowchart for a procedure called DELETE to delete from one given string *all* occurrences of *each* character contained in another given string. The two parameters of DELETE are as follows.

   (a) STR, the string from which the deletion(s) are to be made.
   (b) LIST, the string providing the characters whose occurrences in STR should be deleted. The matching argument for LIST may be either a string variable or a string constant.

Example application

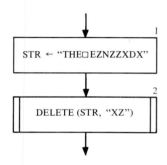

After execution of box 2,

$$STR = \text{"THE}\square\text{END"}$$

3. Using the functions EVAL (explained in Chapter 2), itos, and stoi, show how you would express the search of a string EXP, consisting of a very simple postfix expression such as "ab+", "cd−", or "pg/" and replace it with its value expressed as a character string numeral. For example, if the value of the variable a is 3 and the variable b is 4, then your flowchart should cause the value of EXP, initially "ab+" to be replaced by the value "7".

More Elaborate Patterns (Repeated Occurrence of the Same Unknown)

For further examples showing the use of unknowns in pattern matching, we will return to some of the editing requirements listed in Figure 13·1. Consider the problem suggested on line B_g of that figure. Any occurrence of "the sum a × b + a × c" can easily be recognized and transformed by a simple pattern search. One example is shown in Figure 13·19.

A more interesting but still not sufficiently challenging problem is one in which we are looking for expressions of the form

"a×" *something* "+a×" *something else*

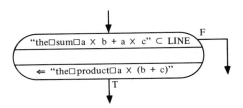

FIGURE 13·19

where the *somethings* are each one letter in length. Figure 13·20 illustrates a solution. Two possibly *different* unknowns, each one character in length, are needed in this pattern.

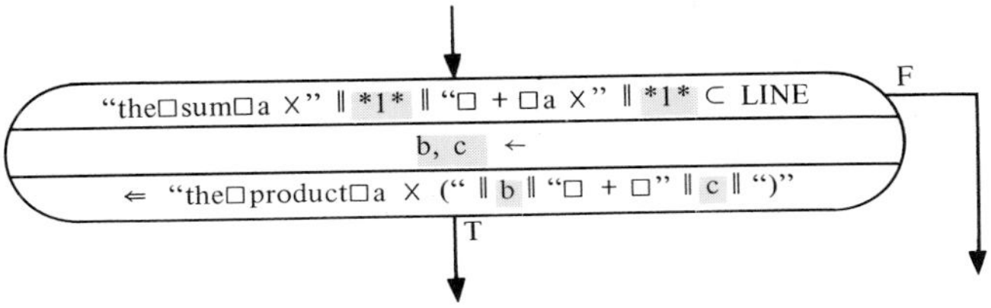

FIGURE 13·20
Two different unknowns in the same pattern.

However, there are two related problems of considerably greater interest that suggest themselves at this juncture and force the introduction of certain notational complications.

1. Suppose we wish to search for expressions of the form

    something "× b +" *same something* "×c"

which, if found, is to be transformed into the form

    something "× (b + c)"

For example,

    "y × b + y × c"

would be an instance of the above pattern but, of course,

    "y × b + z × c"

would not.

What kind of pattern expression would be applicable for this kind of search? Obviously the same unknown must be identified twice at specified points in the substring. We can visualize such a search as one where the first recognition of the unknown is regarded as *tentative*. The second recognition of the same unknown (if found at the right place) will then be regarded as *confirming* the value that was tentatively recognized before. Failure to find two occurrences, properly positioned, must be regarded as a failure.

So much for the idea of repeated occurrence of the same unknown. But how will we represent such an unknown in a pattern expression? Obviously, there must be some way to recognize that two arbitrary unknowns, previously denoted by "*1*", refer to the *same* unknown quantity. We will use the scheme of placing an identifying integer after the first "*" and following it with a "/" character. A suitable pattern match that can be expressed for this problem is shown in Figure 13·21.

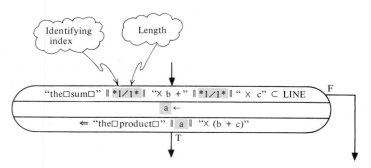

FIGURE 13·21

Here we see that if the match is successful, that is, after twice noting the same single character unknown at the right places in the matched substring, the unknown is then assigned to a. The replacement compartment indicates the desired form of the altered substring.

2.   We can generalize even further on this problem, and with fascinating results. Suppose, for example, we wish to search for *any* factorable arithmetic expression that has the form

$$a \times b + a \times c$$

where a, b, and c are each a single-letter unknown representing an arithmetic variable. A suitable pattern match to use for such a search is shown in Figure 13·22.

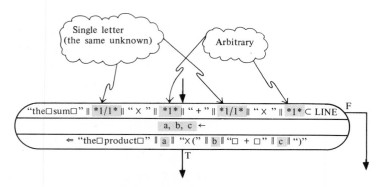

FIGURE 13·22

In the last part of Chapter 8 we examined the process of translating infix expressions to postfix form and discovered how fairly simple extensions of this process lead to the development of interpreters or compilers. We first discussed these algorithms assuming that the key variables INFIX, POST, and ST were structured as lists of single characters. Now, however, it will be illuminating to see how easy it is to detail the algorithms by representing these variables as strings and by expressing the detail using the string processing operations and notations already developed in this chapter.

The "power" of string processing operations lets us achieve nearly a one-to-one correspondence between flowchart boxes of the generalized algorithms and those of the detailed algorithms. For example, consider the flowchart given in Figure 8·8 for converting infix expressions to postfix form. If these expressions are considered to be character strings, and if we now assume that blanks separate and trail all infix characters, then Figure 13·23 is an equivalent algorithm expressed in string processing terms.

First, examine these two flowcharts for similarities of structure without concern for the details within the matching flowchart boxes. The two structures are almost identical, that is, *isomorphic*. With few exceptions, each box of the generalized flowchart (Figure 8·8) can therefore be regarded as an explanation of the code in the corresponding box of the detailed flowchart.

Discussion

We will consider in more detail a few of the boxes where the correspondence is not too obvious. First, consider box 4.

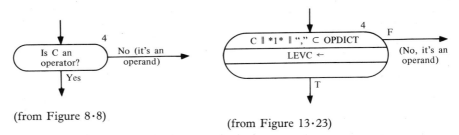

(from Figure 8·8)

(from Figure 13·23)

To determine whether the value of the scanned character C is an operator, one searches a dictionary of operators, OPDICT, wherein is recorded every operator symbol that can

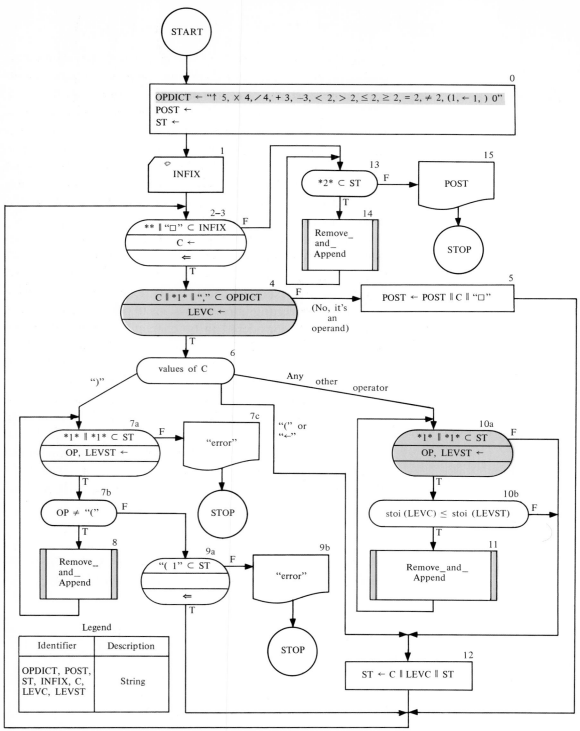

FIGURE 13·23
String processing version of
Figure 8·8. For details of
boxes 8, 11, and 14, see
Figure 13·24.

be anticipated in the infix expression. (See box 0 of Figure 13·23 for the *definition* of OPDICT.) Then, if a pattern match to locate an instance of the value of C in OPDICT fails, we know that C is *not* an operator. This is the approach taken in Figure 13·23.

Notice that by defining OPDICT as a list of pairs, each consisting of the operator symbol and its precedence level followed by a comma (rather than simply a list of the operator symbols alone), then when the match succeeds, the precedence level may be captured. So, box 4 in Figure 13·23, in fact, does extra "duty." Capturing the precedence level in LEVC facilitates the work involved in box 10b. To see why this is so, let us compare the loop structures of boxes 10 and 11 in each flowchart.

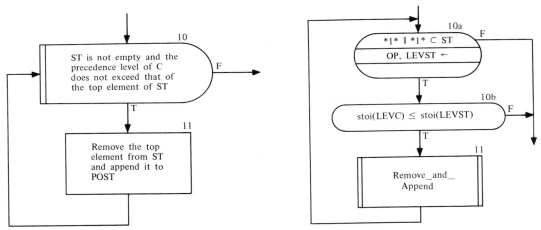

Both fragments amount to *while* loops (although box 10a of Figure 13·23 has greater power than an ordinary *while* box).

Note that we have not attempted to combine boxes 10a and 10b as

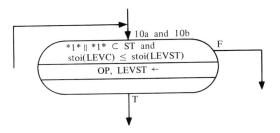

although no theoretical consideration prevents us from doing this. But to do so would overly burden the "clean" meaning so far ascribed to the hamburger box. We prefer instead to risk the awkward double exit from the loop in this one instance. By stacking *value pairs* (i.e., operator symbol, precedence level) instead of stacking operator symbols alone, the hamburger box version of box 10 again does double duty. The stack is not empty if at least one value pair is contained in it. Since each component of a value pair is a single character, the pattern expression *1* || *1* is applicable. Moreover, since the stack is represented as a character string whose *left* end corresponds to the *top* of the stack, the pattern match for a nonempty stack will not only succeed but can be followed by the capture of the topmost pair. The operator symbol is captured in OP and its precedence level value is captured in LEVST.

Now, the explanation of box 10b

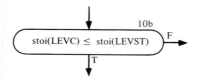

should be almost obvious. If the precedence levels of C and ST are to be compared, the values of LEVC and LEVST might first be converted from character representation to equivalent integer representation. [For many actual computer systems this extra conversion step is quite unnecessary when characters can be compared in the greater-than ($>$) sense just as integers can. Such computers "recognize" a lexical ordering of the characters of their alphabets. This lets the characters "0" through "9" have the same relative ordering as the corresponding integers 0 through 9. This, for example, was the case for SAMOS, as may be seen in Figure 1·27. Unfortunately, SAMOS had no *greater than* compare operation that could take advantage of this ordering.]

Finally, we consider how to map box 11 of Figure 8·8 into string operation terms. If boxes 8, 11, and 14 are all to be treated alike, then the detail for box 11, although perhaps somewhat repetitious, could be treated as shown in Figure 13·24. Since only the operator symbol is to be appended to POST, the precedence level is discarded at this point. A sufficient number of the details in Figure 13·23 have now been discussed to enable you to "fathom" the rest of it without difficulty.

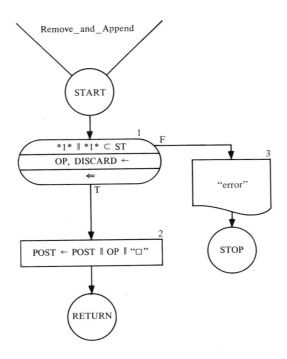

FIGURE 13·24
Details for
Remove_and_Append.

Converting the Infix-to-
Postfix Translator
into an Interpreter

Figure 8·10 showed a generalized approach for converting the infix-to-postfix translator into an Interpreter. Realizing that we intend to express the Interpreter algorithm in terms of string processing operations prompts us to arrive at a more succinct way of expressing Figure 8·10, still in generalized terms. This is seen in Figure 13·25.

By way of review, the idea behind the interpreting operation is now to treat POST as a *stack*. Whenever an operator would otherwise be appended to POST we now pulloff the topmost two items, which are either operands that are simple variables or are values that represent intermediate results on these variables. The new operation is carried out on these topmost two operands, and the new result is then placed on the top of the stack.

If you compare Figure 13·25 with Figure 8·10, you will see that a separate stack of temporary or intermediate numerical results (called TEMP) is no longer necessary. This is because when strings are used in place of lists of single characters, any intermediate result, no matter how large or how small, can be converted to an equivalent string of characters and appended to POST.

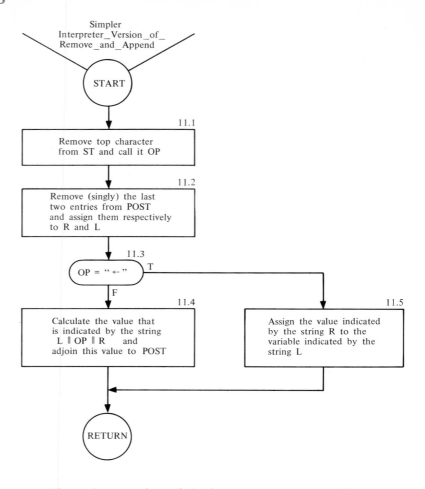

FIGURE 13·25
Simpler version of Figure
8·10. Interpreter Remove_and
_Append procedure assuming
string processing operations.

Now, the mapping of the interpreter version of Remove_
and_Append, from the new generalized expression of it (Figure
13·25) to the detailed level as seen in Figure 13·26, becomes
an almost trivial activity. A quick comparison of the two figures
shows their overall structure to be essentially identical, completely so, if we recognize that the F exits from boxes 12.1
and 12.2 of Figure 13·26 can never be taken in a correctly
executing infix evaluation.

The mapping of boxes 11.1, 11.2, and 11.3 should be
straightforward. However, note that POST, being a stack, is
now treated such that the "top" of POST is its *left end*. This
treatment facilitates string pattern matching when POST is the
subject of the search. What is of more interest is how boxes
11.4 and 11.5 have been mapped to the detail level. (Here we
use the word *adjoin* to mean *place at the left end*.)

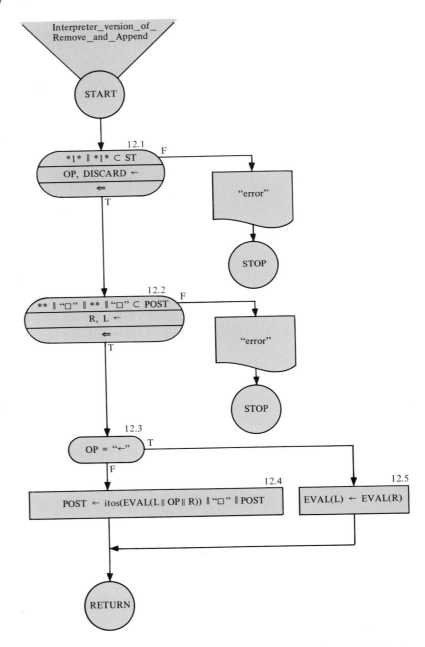

FIGURE 13·26
Details of Figure 13·25.
Simpler version of interpreter
Remove_and_Append
procedure.

To express box 11.4, repeated on top of page 730, in terms of string processing operations, we employ the EVAL function introduced in Chapter 2 to carry out the indicated arithmetic that the value of the string L ∥ OP ∥ R represents. For example, if the value of L ∥ OP ∥ R were "A × P", where A = 3 and P = 7, then EVAL ("A × P") would result in

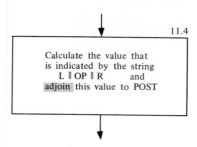

the integer value 21. This value is converted into the string "21" by employing the integer-to-string conversion function itos. This then explains how the expression

$$itos(EVAL(L \parallel OP \parallel R))$$

comes to be used in box 12.4 of Figure 13·26. Now, because the top of POST is the left end of the string, this value is adjoined to POST, using a blank character as a separator. The meaning of the resulting box 12.4,

is now clear.

The mapping of box 11.5

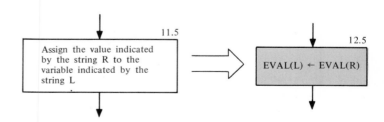

employing the EVAL function both on the right and on the left of the assignment arrow accomplishes our purpose. When executed, box 12.5 will assign to the variable that is the string value of L the value obtained by treating the string value of R as an expression. For example, if the value of L were "Q" and the value of R were "A" (and the value of A were 16)

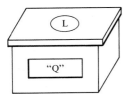 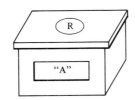 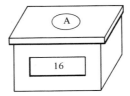 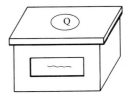

then execution of box 12.5

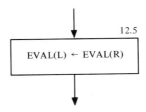

would assign 16 to Q.

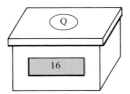

Two items, one rather important, remain to be attended to before we are ready to close out our discussion of the interpreter algorithm.

1. Since POST is treated as a stack whose top is its left end, then box 5 of the algorithm in Figure 13·23 must be altered. Box 5 should now be

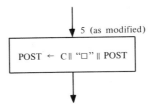

2. If the algorithm of Figure 13·23, as clarified by Figure 13·26, is to act as an interpreter of simple assignment statements, it must have access to the current values of the variables that appear in the right-hand side expression of each statement that is to be interpreted. How will this be brought about?

Clearly the algorithm seems incomplete as it now stands. For it to be useful, we must assume some kind of environment in which it is expected to function. For example, it can be regarded as a component of a larger algorithm or machine in which the values of the individual variables of the statement are assigned to the storage containers of those variables before interpretation of the statement is begun.

Actually, however, there is one context in which our algorithm is complete as it stands, provided we modify it to loop from box 15 back to box 0 instead of stopping. This is the case where the algorithm executes on a (small) computer that is intended to behave as a desk calculator. Imagine that the keyboard of the calculator contains keys as follows.

1. Keys for each letter of the alphabet, $\boxed{A}$, $\boxed{B}$, $\boxed{C}$, and so on, each corresponding to a variable of the same name.

2. Keys for each of the operator symbols, for example, $\boxed{\leftarrow}$, $\boxed{+}$, $\boxed{-}$, $\boxed{\times}$, $\boxed{/}$.

3. A special key called the *interpret* key, $\boxed{\text{Interpret}}$.

Turning on this calculator causes execution of the algorithm of Figure 13·23 to begin. When box 1 is reached, the execution stops and waits for the person sitting in front of it to key in an infix statement.

A statement consists of a series of key strokes ending with the striking of the interpret key. For example, the series of strokes

$\boxed{B}\ \boxed{\leftarrow}\ \boxed{4}\ \boxed{\text{Interpret}}$

would cause the value

"B ← 4"

to be assigned to INFIX, and the algorithm would then proceed with the interpretation of that statement. A careful trace of the algorithm will reveal, in this instance, that executing box 14 causes the value 4 to be assigned to the variable B, and then executing box 15 causes this value to be displayed.

As a result of entering this statement and causing its interpretation, B now has a value! You can probably guess the rest. Suppose the following four statements are then keyed into the calculator and interpreted in turn. (Remember, the algorithm now loops back to box 0, so each time it "goes" until it reaches box 1 and then waits for a person to key in a new statement):

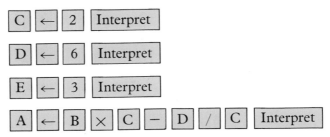

Et voilà! By the time the person is ready to input the last of these statements, the computer, behaving like a desk calculator, will have all the values of the variables needed to evaluate A, so the last statement is also completely interpretable!

EXERCISES 13·7, SET A

1. Develop a short sequence of key stroke statements for the desk calculator modeled in the foregoing text. Now trace our interpreter algorithm to verify that it behaves as a correctly working calculator when the input to the interpreter corresponds to a "proper" sequence of key stroke statements. Modify the algorithm so that it displays meaningful error messages at all appropriate places to provide helpful hints to the person sitting at the calculator as to how to correct his errors.

Converting the Infix-to-Postfix Translator into a Compiler

Figure 8·13 showed a generalized approach for converting the infix-to-postfix translater into a compiler. Figure 13·27 is a corresponding algorithm expressed in terms of string processing operations. An examination of Figure 8·13 and Figure 13·27 once again reveals the close structural similarity of the flowcharts. The reader should have almost no difficulty recognizing the equivalence of corresponding boxes.

However, before making these comparisons, a quick review of the compiler idea developed in Chapter 8 may be helpful. The postfix string is again thought of as a stack called POST. When an operator is about to be removed from the stack to be appended to POST, that operator together with two operands removed from the top of POST, are instead used to

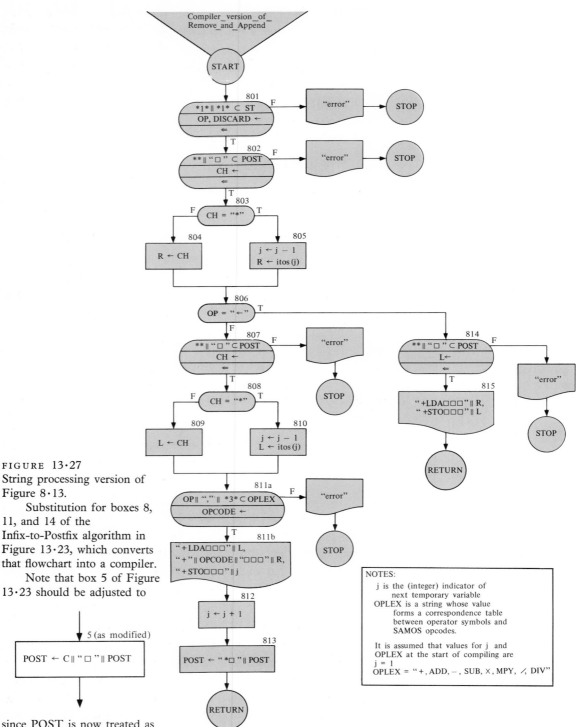

FIGURE 13·27
String processing version of Figure 8·13.

Substitution for boxes 8, 11, and 14 of the Infix-to-Postfix algorithm in Figure 13·23, which converts that flowchart into a compiler.

Note that box 5 of Figure 13·23 should be adjusted to

5 (as modified)

POST ← C ‖ " □ " ‖ POST

since POST is now treated as a stack whose top is at the left end.

generate a sequence of symbolic SAMOS (or SAMOS-like) instructions. These generated instructions, when eventually executed, will have the effect of computing and storing the result of the indicated operation (operand, operator, operand).

As a way of indicating the computation of this intermediate result, two things are done besides the generation (and printing out) of the symbolic SAMOS instructions.

1. A mark (the asterisk) is appended to POST as a place holder for the intermediate result.

2. Since that result, during execution of the generated instructions, is assigned to a temporary variable, a count, j, of such variables is incremented. The count j is decremented for each generated instruction that refers to a previous result.

Improving the Compiler Algorithm

The compiler developed thus far is, of course, limited to the handling of simple assignments statements only. A "full blown" compiler should handle an expanded set of statement types, such as conditional branching, input, output, and while statements. Moreover, subscripted variables and other types of data structures should also be dealt with. All of these extensions are in the nature of feasible refinements but are not of pressing interest to us. They are, however, the subjects of some concern to advanced students and professionals in the computer field.

Even if we are content to limit our view of the compiler to simple assignment statements, that is, no subscripts or functional references, there is, however, still room for a good deal of improvement. For example, it will be noted that each time the left operand represents the result of the preceding operation, the compiler generates a pair of superfluous instructions. Thus, for

$$A \leftarrow B + C + D$$

the compiler generates

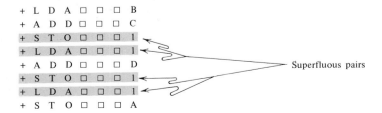

that is, eight instructions, of which four are not needed. In point of fact, there are actually two levels of refinement we can make to our algorithm; each eliminates unnecessary instructions.

First Level of Refinement

Have the compiler avoid generating STO, LDA instruction pairs, such as illustrated above, whenever the accumulator holds the left operand. That is, if, on a machine such as SAMOS, the result of an immediately preceding operation can be regarded as held over in the accumulator, then the next group of instructions that is generated can execute with the accumulator representing the left operand.

Second Level of Refinement

Have the compiler avoid generating extra STO, LDA instructions by switching roles for left and right operands whenever the right operand is represented by the accumulator and the operator being treated is commutative. The commutative operators are "+" and "×".

First and second levels of refinement are illustrated in Figure 13·28. The reader should study the cases illustrated in Figure 13·28 until he is convinced that the improvements suggested are indeed examples of the more general situations described in the two preceding paragraphs.

As a final remark, note that in Section 11·4 we learned that reducing the number of store operations can help to combat floating-point roundoff error. If the compiled instructions in Figure 13·28 involved floating-point operations, then eliminating extra store and load sequences not only improves the efficiency of the algorithm but may improve the quality of the results as well.

EXERCISES 13·7,
SET B

1. Study the cases illustrated in Figure 13·28. Based on these examples, prepare a similar table of compiler output for the following statements; that is, determine the improvement, if any, that would result from refinement at levels 1 and 2.

   (a) $T \leftarrow A + B - C + D - E$
   (b) $T \leftarrow A \times B - C \times D + E \times F$

2. One strategy for achieving the compiler refinements discussed in the text is to revise the compiler so it postpones the generation of instruc-

Part a
Statement is: $\quad A \leftarrow B \times C - D \times E$

Generated Instructions	Without Refinement	First Level of Refinement Only	Second Level of Refinement Also
1	+LDA␣␣␣B	+LDA␣␣␣B	
2	+MPY␣␣␣C	+MPY␣␣␣C	No further improvement possible because "−" is non-commutative
3	+STO␣␣␣1	+STO␣␣␣1	
4	+LDA␣␣␣D	+LDA␣␣␣D	
5	+MPY␣␣␣E	+MPY␣␣␣E	
6	+STO␣␣␣2	+STO␣␣␣2	
7	+LDA␣␣␣1	+LDA␣␣␣1	
8	+SUB␣␣␣2	+SUB␣␣␣2	
9	+STO␣␣␣1	+STO␣␣␣A	
10	+LDA␣␣␣1		
11	+STO␣␣␣A		

Part b
Statement is: $\quad A \leftarrow B \times C + D \times E$

1	+LDA␣␣␣B	+LDA␣␣␣B	+LDA␣␣␣B
2	+MPY␣␣␣C	+MPY␣␣␣C	+MPY␣␣␣C
3	+STO␣␣␣1	+STO␣␣␣1	+STO␣␣␣1
4	+LDA␣␣␣D	+LDA␣␣␣D	+LDA␣␣␣D
5	+MPY␣␣␣E	+MPY␣␣␣E	+MPY␣␣␣E
6	+STO␣␣␣2	+STO␣␣␣2	+ADD␣␣␣1
7	+LDA␣␣␣1	+LDA␣␣␣1	+STO␣␣␣A
8	+ADD␣␣␣2	+ADD␣␣␣2	
9	+STO␣␣␣1	+STO␣␣␣A	
10	+LDA␣␣␣1		
11	+STO␣␣␣A		

FIGURE 13·28
Examples of first and second levels of refinement of the compiler algorithm.

tions that store intermediate results until it can be determined that the next operation to be "compiled" cannot make use of the intermediate result (that is not yet stored) as either a left operand or, in the case of a commutative operator, as a right operand. Modify the flowcharts of Figures 13·23 and 13·27 as required to achieve these refinements.

To get you started, the following flowchart fragment is a generalized description of an approach that might be taken for modifying boxes 811 and 812 of Figure 13·27. Additional modifications may be needed. In any case, first express all proposed modifications at the generalized descriptive level and then map these changes into a description in terms of string processing operations.

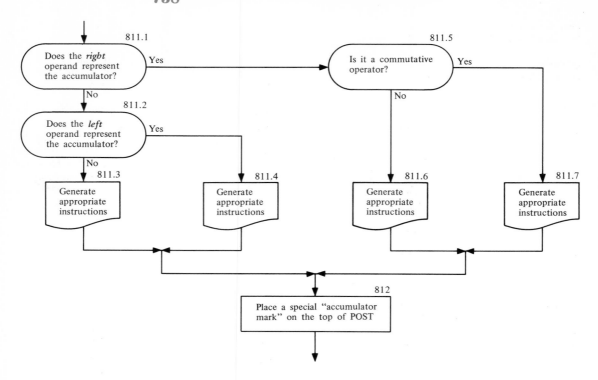

The Making of an Assembler

The last process we wish to consider, and only briefly at that, is the job of converting the symbolic SAMOS instructions generated by the compiler to actual 11-character SAMOS instructions. Figure 13·29 summarizes the problem for a specific case, and Figure 13·30 gives a generalized algorithm for this

Statement as input to
the refined compiler: $Z \leftarrow E + F + (A + B) \times (E + D)$

Input to the Assembler (Symbolic SAMOS)	Output from the Assembler 1 2 3 4 5 6 7 8 9 10 11
+LDA⬛⬛⬛E	+ L D A 0 0 0 1 0 0 1
+ADD⬛⬛⬛F	+ A D D 0 0 0 1 0 0 2
+STO⬛⬛⬛1	+ S T ⬜ 0 0 0 1 0 0 3
+LDA⬛⬛⬛A	+ L D A 0 0 0 1 0 0 4
+ADD⬛⬛⬛B	+ A D D 0 0 0 1 0 0 5
+STO⬛⬛⬛2	+ S T ⬜ 0 0 0 1 0 0 6
+LDA⬛⬛⬛E	+ L D A 0 0 0 1 0 0 1
+ADD⬛⬛⬛D	+ A D D 0 0 0 1 0 0 7
+MPY⬛⬛⬛2	+ M P Y 0 0 0 1 0 0 6
+ADD⬛⬛⬛1	+ A D D 0 0 0 1 0 0 3
+STO⬛⬛⬛Z	+ S T ⬜ 0 0 0 1 0 0 8

FIGURE 13·29
Showing conversion to actual SAMOS. *Assumptions.* Storage addresses are allotted to the variables beginning at 1001 on a first-come, first-served basis with no distinction made between types of variables.

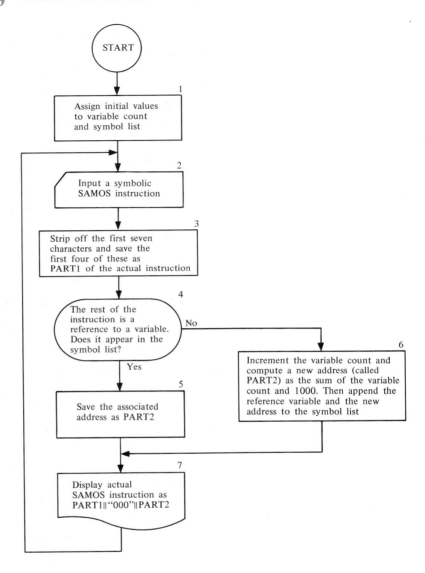

FIGURE 13·30
Generalized algorithm for a
simple *assembler*.

process. We choose to assume that the compiler that produces
the symbolic SAMOS instructions has been refined in the
manner discussed earlier—although this assumption is not essential for our discussion here.

An algorithm that converts symbolic instructions into
actual instructions is called an *assembler*. The object of an
assembler is to convert references to variables into references
to computer storage locations and to do this in a consistent
manner. Thus, when the same variable is referred to several
times in the sequence of symbolic instructions, the same stor-

age location should be used each time. Although temporary variables do not appear explicitly in the original assignment statement, if the compiler has decided that such variables are needed, then storage locations for these variables must also be allotted.

Some predetermined group of storage locations should be earmarked for the variables, so the "base" or beginning address of this *work area* of storage should be known to the assembler. In the Figure 13·30 algorithm this work area is assumed to begin just past location 1000. To do this job right, the assembler must establish a one-to-one correspondence between the distinct references to variables and the distinct addresses of the associated storage locations within the work area.

The correspondence can be achieved by developing a list of all the variable references (symbols) and their matching addresses in the work area. Each time another symbolic instruction is to be converted into an actual instruction, this *symbol list* must be searched to determine the appropriate address for that symbol (a type of table lookup operation that we have encountered in previous string processing applications.) If the symbol cannot be found in the list, it must be added to the list along with the storage address that is to represent that variable in this and any subsequent instructions that are to be processed by the assembler.

In the simplest approach we can think of, storage addresses can be allotted on a first-come, first-served basis. For example, when the assembler processes the symbolic instructions given in Figure 13·29, the new variable references, in their order of appearance, are

E, F, 1, A, B, 2, D, and Z.

Thus, if the base address of the work area is to be 1001, then storage addresses allotted to these references should be 1001 through 1008, respectively. The detailed flowcharting of the steps given in Figure 13·30, or in a more sophisticated assembler, are left as a set of exercises for the student.

EXERCISES 13·7, SET C

1. Assume that the symbol list mentioned in the assembler of Figure 13·30 is to be a character string consisting of a sequence of value pairs,

each of the form

(variable, computed address)

Develop a detailed flowchart for the algorithm described in Figure 13·30 expressed in terms of string processing operations.

2. Show what modifications, if any, are required to the flowchart you developed in Problem 1 so that the assembler can process a series of instruction sequences, each the result of compiling a separate assignment statement. For example, your assembler—or your assembler, suitably modified—must be able to process all the instructions produced by a compiler for the sequence of statements:

$$A \leftarrow 7$$
$$B \leftarrow 8$$
$$C \leftarrow 9$$
$$D \leftarrow A^2 + B^2 - C^2$$
$$E \leftarrow B^2 + C^2 - A^2$$
STOP

3. Show what additional changes, if any, would be required in your assembler, over and above any you found necessary in answering Problem 2, to handle a compiler's output for the sequence:

READ A, B, C
$$D \leftarrow A^2 + B^2 - C^2$$
$$E \leftarrow B^2 + C^2 - A^2$$
PRINT A, B, C, D, E
STOP

4. Show what additional changes, if any, would be required in your assembler, over and above any you found necessary in answering Problem 3, to handle a compiler's output for the sequence:

LINE 1 READ A, B, C
$$D \leftarrow A^2 + B^2 - C^2$$
$$E \leftarrow B^2 + C^2 - A^2$$
PRINT A, B, C, D, E
GO TO LINE 1

SAMOS has served throughout this book as a prototype computer whose organization is typical of a very large number of actual everyday computer systems. Although to our knowledge no one has ever built the SAMOS computer itself, it is relatively easy to simulate one computer on another. In fact, SAMOS has been simulated on many different computers and so, for all practical purposes, SAMOS exists.

A machine such as SAMOS can be simulated and the simulation used in place of the real thing because its functional characteristics and behavior can be completely specified. This appendix serves as such a specification. Here we complete the description of the SAMOS computer organization assuming, to start with, that you are familiar with the preliminary description found in the latter part of Chapter 1. (Later portions of this appendix are written for readers who have studied Chapters 4, 9, and 11.)

SAMOS may be thought of as an extendable machine. Although the introduction in Chapter 1 mentioned only 10 basic instruction types, we will see that these can be augmented with various other instructions, for example, with a set to carry out arithmetic operations on floating-point numbers. Each enrichment of the instruction set makes it easier to map from certain types of flowchart operations to an equivalent "machine language" instruction sequence. That is, although the basic set is sufficient in principle, in practice it is far easier to "code" or map flowcharts into computer programs when additional instruction types are added to the SAMOS repertoire. Of course, as in all engineering design, there is a trade-off here. Increasing the number of different instructions in a computer, each with its own rules for proper use, increases not only the training a programmer requires but also his chance of making a costly error in mapping a flowchart into a valid computer program should this mapping have to be performed manually.

A·1
Review

First, let us review briefly some of the features of SAMOS already discussed in Chapter 1. SAMOS is centered about a storage consisting of 10,000 separate cells, each identified by an integer address (from 0000 to 9999). Attached to this storage are an input device, an output device, and a processing unit. These are shown schematically in Figure A·1, which is similar

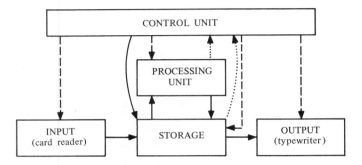

FIGURE A·1
Schematic diagram of
SAMOS.

to Figure 1·29. Exercising control over all four components (dashed lines) is a control unit that receives its instructions (dotted line) from storage in the following way. If the present instruction has come from storage address n, the next instruction will normally come from storage address n + 1. How this works can be seen by a quick glance inside the control unit where there are several special-purpose cells or *registers*. One register, the *operation register*, holds the three-character operation code (e.g., LDA). One register, the *address register*, holds the four-digit address part of the instruction being executed. Another register, the *instruction counter*, contains the four-digit address of the current instruction in storage.

The registers shown in Figure A·2 illustrate an instruction to load the accumulator with the contents of 1492; this instruction comes from storage address 0013. Of course, there

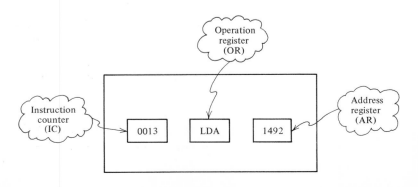

FIGURE A·2
Inside the control unit.

is much more in the control unit, including a device to increment the instruction counter by one when an instruction is completed, and a facility to sense the sign of the accumulator in the processing unit.

The normal execution cycle of an instruction can be described in terms of these registers.

1.   The instruction counter, IC, has some initial value that is sensed and used to establish a path from the specified storage cell to the control unit.

2.   A copy of the contents of the specified storage cell is transmitted over the established path, with the operation code entering the operation register, OR, and the address part entering the address register, AR.

3.   (a) The contents of the OR register is sensed and its value used to connect circuits to perform the indicated operation. (b) At the same time, the contents of the AR is sensed and used to establish a path between the specified storage cell and the processing unit (or the input or output unit).

4.   The instruction counter is incremented.

5.   The instruction, for which the circuits and paths have been established, is now performed and the cycle repeated.

We will see presently that a few instructions require alterations to this "normal execution cycle."

You know from Chapter 1 that the processing unit contains a special register called the accumulator, ACC. This register receives the result of each arithmetic operation (Figure A·3). There is provision for an extension to this register

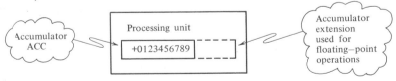

FIGURE A·3
Inside the processing unit.

(dashed portion) that is useful for floating-point operations, as discussed in Chapter 11. See Section A·9 for more details.

A·2
Getting things started

As yet we have said nothing about *how* a program is placed in storage or how the instruction sequence gets started. Somewhere on the machine are buttons to allow external control. One pair of buttons turns the electric power off or on. Another pair is labeled "STOP" and "START". Pressing STOP interrupts the instruction execution cycle, described above, just

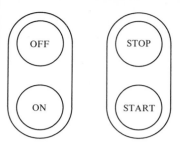

before step 1 (sensing the contents of the instruction counter). Nothing changes; the execution of instructions simply stops. Pressing the START button restarts the execution cycle again.

There is yet another button involved in the problem of getting started. It is called the "LOAD" button and, when you press LOAD, the computer reads a card and transfers what is punched in columns 1 to 11 to the storage cell with address

0000. It then reads another card and transfers the contents of columns 1 to 11 to address 0001. It continues to read cards, sending the contents of the first 11 columns to storage cells with successively higher addresses until it encounters a card on which the first 11 columns are blank. Upon finding such a card, the instruction counter, IC, is automatically set to value 0000 and the execution cycle begins.

Preparing and Loading a Program

The machine language instructions are punched, one to a card, in columns 1 to 11. Any required constant values are considered to be part of the program. They are punched on cards in the same way. The first column of a constant *must* be a sign. Thus zero is represented as

+ 0000000000

and is *not* a blank card. All cards are stacked in the card reader with the instructions first and a blank card placed at the very end.

Supplying Data

If data are to be read during the course of executing the program, cards punched with the data are placed in proper order *after* the blank card. When the LOAD button is pressed, the program's instructions and constants are loaded into storage and execution begins.

Note that the loading process assumes that for every program the first instruction to be executed is located in 0000. If the first instruction of your program is not in 0000, *you must place an unconditional branch instruction* (BRU) *there so that a branch to the first instruction of your program will occur immediately.* Some programmers like to place required constants or literal values at the beginning of the program. The locations of the literals are then known at the time one writes instructions that refer to these literals. Thus Figure A·4 shows how the Fibonacci sequence algorithm (Figure 1·33) could have been coded with literals placed ahead of instructions. A BRU instruction at location 0000 causes a skip around the literal values 0, 1, and 1000 when execution starts.

A·3
A review of the basic instruction set

In Chapter 1 we studied 10 basic instructions. These are sufficient to program many problems of interest and are reviewed in this section.

In explaining how a SAMOS instruction carries out its task, we will refer to a very particular storage cell (among the 10,000 available cells) or to an individual register of the control unit or processing unit. Storage cells are actually identified uniquely only by their numerical addresses, not by arbitrarily chosen pseudonyms. But let us adopt the convention that *one name for the number currently in a storage cell is its numerical address enclosed in parentheses.* Thus (0005) is a name for the number in the cell whose address is 0005. In a similar spirit we will give specific names to the contents of special registers.

Special Register	*Name* *for the Number Contained Therein*
Accumulator	(ACC)
Address register	(AR)
Instruction counter	(IC)
Operation register	(OR)

Notice that the parentheses are *part* of the name.

STORAGE LOCATION (Address)	± 1	OPERATION CODE 2 3 4	5 6 7	ADDRESS 8 9 10 11	REMARKS
0000		B R U	0 0 0	0 0 0 4	Skip around the literals
0001	+	0 0 0	0 0 0	0 0 0 0	zero ⎫
0002	+	0 0 0	0 0 0	0 0 0 1	1 ⎬ literals
0003	+	0 0 0	0 0 0	1 0 0 0	1000 ⎭
0004		L D A	0 0 0	0 0 0 1	1a NEXT ← 0
0005		S T O	0 0 0	0 1 0 0	
0006		L D A	0 0 0	0 0 0 2	1b LATEST ← 1
0007		S T O	0 0 0	0 1 0 1	
0008		L D A	0 0 0	0 1 0 1	2 SUM ← LATEST + NEXT
0009		A D D	0 0 0	0 1 0 0	
0010		S T O	0 0 0	0 1 0 2	
0011		L D A	0 0 0	0 0 0 3	3 SUM > 1000 T
0012		S U B	0 0 0	0 1 0 2	F
0013		B M I	0 0 0	0 0 1 9	
0014		L D A	0 0 0	0 1 0 1	4a NEXT ← LATEST
0015		S T O	0 0 0	0 1 0 0	
0016		L D A	0 0 0	0 1 0 2	4b LATEST ← SUM
0017		S T O	0 0 0	0 1 0 1	
0018		B R U	0 0 0	0 0 0 8	5 SUM
0019		W W D	0 0 0	0 1 0 2	
0020		H L T	0 0 0	0 0 0 0	STOP
0100					NEXT
0101					LATEST
0102					SUM

FIGURE A·4
The Fibonacci sequence algorithm (Figure 1·33) recoded to place the constants at the beginning of the program.

The concept of reading a value from one of these cells and assigning it to another is similar to the familiar one used in Chapter 1. For example, reading the value contained in cell 0005 and assigning it to the accumulator can be expressed as an ordinary assignment.

$$(ACC) \leftarrow (0005)$$

Occasionally, we would like to be able to speak of the assignment of a constant value. For example,

$$(IC) \leftarrow 0$$

means replace the value in the instruction counter by the constant value 0 (not the value contained in register 0). Similarly,

$$(IC) \leftarrow 1492$$

means replace the value in the instruction counter by the constant value 1492.

Every instruction in SAMOS has the following form.

1	2	3	4	5	6	7	8	9	10	11
S I G N	Operation to be performed			0	0	0	Storage address			

The instruction is composed of 10 characters plus a sign. If these characters are numbered from left to right, we have:

Position

1 — The sign has no meaning in the case of an instruction. We will either use + or leave it blank.

2, 3, 4 — Characters in these positions indicate the operation to be performed. For example, ADD for addition, DIV for division, etc.

5, 6, 7 — These positions are used for *indexing*, a concept to be explained later. For now we will assume that they are zero.

8, 9, 10, 11 — These characters form a four-digit number from 0000 to 9999, and they usually represent a storage address.

Now let us see how to move data to and from the accumulator.

Load

Example

| + | L | D | A | 0 | 0 | 0 | 1 | 4 | 9 | 2 |

Meaning   (ACC) ← (1492)

The value in the accumulator (thought of as a storage box) is replaced by (a copy of) the current value in storage address 1492. The contents of 1492 remain undisturbed.

The address 1492 is, of course, only one of 10,000 possible addresses that could be used in one of these instructions. Throughout the remaining discussions, we will select addresses for our examples essentially "at random." They are intended merely to be representative.

Store

Example

| + | S | T | O | 0 | 0 | 0 | 5 | 0 | 0 | 1 |

Meaning   (5001) ← (ACC)

The value in storage location 5001 is replaced by (a copy of) the current value of the accumulator. The value of the accumulator remains the same.

Integer arithmetic is done with the following four instructions.

Add

Example

| + | A | D | D | 0 | 0 | 0 | 7 | 2 | 2 | 2 |

Meaning   (ACC) ← (ACC) + (7222)

A copy of the integer stored in location 7222 is added to the current value of the accumulator and the result is assigned to the accumulator.

(If two 10-digit integers are added in this way, forming an 11-digit sum, the highest order, that is, the most significant digit, will be lost. Only the lowest-order 10 digits of the sum will be assigned to the accumulator, and at this point the machine will stop! This halting condition is referred to as *accumulator overflow*.)

Subtract

Example

Meaning $(\text{ACC}) \leftarrow (\text{ACC}) - (6218)$

A copy of the integer stored in 6218 is subtracted from the current value of the accumulator. The result is assigned to the accumulator. (Accumulator overflow can occur on subtracting a 10-digit integer from a 10-digit integer of unlike sign.)

Multiply

Example

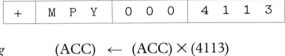

Meaning $(\text{ACC}) \leftarrow (\text{ACC}) \times (4113)$

A copy of the integer stored in the accumulator is multiplied by a copy of the integer in 4113. The product is developed and assigned to the accumulator. Since the number of digits in a product *can* equal the sum of the numbers of digits in the numbers that are multiplied, the programmer must be careful that the number of nonzero digits in the product never exceeds 10; otherwise the machine will stop on accumulator overflow.

Divide

Example

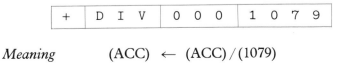

Meaning $(\text{ACC}) \leftarrow (\text{ACC}) / (1079)$

The integer value of the accumulator is divided by the integer value of (1079). The integer quotient is developed and assigned to the accumulator. *The remainder is lost!*

To compute a remainder, R, when dividing a numerator N by a denominator, D, it is necessary to utilize the relationship

$$R = N - D \times Q$$

where Q is the integer part of the quotient N/D. (See Section 2·4.) For example, if the numerator is stored at 0050, and if the denominator is stored at 0051, then the following sequence of SAMOS instructions will store the remainder at 0053 and the integral part of the quotient at 0052.

```
L D A    0 0 0    0 0 5 0
D I V    0 0 0    0 0 5 1
S T O    0 0 0    0 0 5 2
M P Y    0 0 0    0 0 5 1
S T O    0 0 0    0 0 6 0  ←  Location to hold an intermed-
L D A    0 0 0    0 0 5 0      iate value
S U B    0 0 0    0 0 6 0
S T O    0 0 0    0 0 5 3
```

Note that SAMOS will stop and print an error message if you try to add or subtract noninteger values. The same is true for multiplication or division.

Halt

Example

+	H L T	0 0 0	2 0 2 2

The machine stops. The effect is exactly the same as pressing the STOP button. If the START button in the operator's console is then pressed, the next instruction will be taken from 2022. This is the first instruction we have studied that changes the normal execution cycle. First, it stops the cycle. Second, upon resuming the execution cycle, the instruction counter is set to the *value* 2022. That is,

$$(IC) \leftarrow 2022$$

Branch Unconditionally

This very important instruction changes the sequence in which the instructions of a program are executed.

Example

Meaning (IC) ← 7777

This instruction directs SAMOS to "pick up" the next instruction from location 7777. No testing of the accumulator is required in this case.

Branch Conditionally

Some of the most important branching instructions are those that break the sequential execution of a program depending on the contents of the accumulator, for example, the "Branch on Minus" instruction.

Example

Meaning

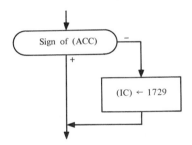

SAMOS is directed to "jump" to location 1729 for the next instruction if the sign of the accumulator is minus, that is, if the accumulator contains a negative number. If the sign of the accumulator is +, SAMOS will execute the next instruction in sequence. In SAMOS a zero will always be stored as +0000000000, never as −0000000000. Hence, the BMI instruction is logically equivalent to:

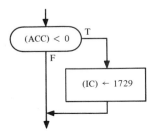

The following two basic instructions permit a program to input data and to output a result.

Read a Word

Example

+	R W D	0 0 0	3 3 4 6

Meaning   (3346) ← (first 11 columns of next data card)

This instruction causes SAMOS to take a card into the card reader and to assign the data value found in the first 11 columns of the card (10 digits plus sign) to location 3346. Data punched on the rest of the card are ignored, and the card itself drops into a stacker.

Results are printed on the typewriter by the "Write a Word" instruction.

Write a Word

Example

+	W W D	0 0 0	2 6 7 2

Meaning   (output medium) ← (2672)

This instruction causes SAMOS to return the typewriter carriage, advance to the next line, and type a copy of the information stored in location 2672 in the first 11 columns of the typewriter.

A·4 Some illustrative problems

Chapter 1 presented a SAMOS program for computing the terms in the Fibonacci sequence. Here, we consider several other programs in the language of SAMOS. The use of a printed coding form, as shown in Figure A·5, is a considerable convenience.

FIGURE A·5
Coding form for SAMOS showing five instructions, where each is located, and remarks on each.

LOCATION	+/-	OPER	INDEX REG.	ADDRESS	REMARKS
1	2 3 4	5 6 7	8 9 10 11	← CARD COL.
0 0 0 0		L D A	0 0 0	1 0 0 1	(ACC) ← (1001)
0 0 0 1		A D D	0 0 0	1 0 0 2	(ACC) ← (ACC) + (1002)
0 0 0 2		A D D	0 0 0	1 0 0 3	(ACC) ← (ACC) + (1003)
0 0 0 3		A D D	0 0 0	1 0 0 4	(ACC) ← (ACC) + (1004)
0 0 0 4		S T Ø	0 0 0	5 0 0 0	(5000) ← (ACC)

Suppose we want to type the information now punched in the first 11 columns of a large number of cards. This is usually referred to as "listing the cards." We can use the flowchart and program of Figure A·6.

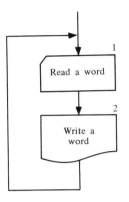

LOCATION	+/−	OPER.	INDEX REG.	ADDRESS	REMARKS
		1 2 3 4	5 6 7	8 9 10 11	← CARD COL.
0 0 0 0	+	R W D	0 0 0	0 0 0 3	BOX 1
0 0 0 1	+	W W D	0 0 0	0 0 0 3	BOX 2
0 0 0 2	+	B R U	0 0 0	0 0 0 0	REPEAT
0 0 0 3	+	0 0 0	0 0 0	0, 0 0 0	TEMPORARY

FIGURE A·6
Program to "list" the cards.

The program occupies four storage words. Location 0003 is used to hold momentarily the information read from each card. The "Branch Unconditionally" instruction returns the machine to location 0000, the beginning of the program. The machine will stop when it is unable to complete the execution of the RWD instruction, that is, when there are no more cards in the card reader.

To implement the flowchart of Figure A·7a, which replaces N by its absolute value, assume that the numerical value of N is stored in location 0500. Then the program in Figure A·7b does the trick. Notice that N, here synonymous with (0500), is loaded into the accumulator. Then we say, "branch to location 0003 if the accumulator is minus, otherwise go to

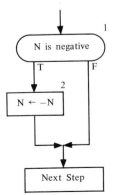

LOCATION	+/−	OPER.	INDEX REG.	ADDRESS	REMARKS
		1 2 3 4	5 6 7	8 9 10 11	← CARD COL.
0 0 0 0		L D A	0 0 0	0 5 0 0	(ACC) ← N
0 0 0 1		B M I	0 0 0	0 0 0 3	IF (ACC) < 0 GO TO LOCATION 0003
0 0 0 2		B R U	0 0 0	0 0 0 6	OTHERWISE GO DIRECTLY TO LOCATION 0006
0 0 0 3		S U B	0 0 0	0 5 0 0	(ACC) BECOMES 0
0 0 0 4		S U B	0 0 0	0 5 0 0	(ACC) BECOMES −N
0 0 0 5		S T 0	0 0 0	0 5 0 0	(0500) ← −N
0 0 0 6		NEXT STEP			

(b) Equivalent SAMOS code.

FIGURE A·7

(a) Flowchart.

the next instruction in sequence, that is, to 0002." The instructions located at 0003, 0004, and 0005 then generate −N by subtracting N from itself two times and storing the result in 0500. Eventually, the two branches merge at location 0006, since the instruction in 0005 is STO, a nonbranching instruction, and the instruction at 0002 was an unconditional branch to 0006.

We now see one way that SAMOS can be programmed to execute the unary minus operation. Simply load the value of the variable into the accumulator. Then subtract the same

FIGURE A·8
A way to achieve unary minus.

LOCATION	+/−	OPER	INDEX REG.	ADDRESS	REMARKS
		1 2 3 4	5 6 7	8 9 10 11	←CARD COL.
0 0 0 0		L D A	0 0 0	0 5 5 2	(ACC)←(0552)
0 0 0 1		S U B	0 0 0	0 5 5 2	(ACC)←(ACC)−(0552) MAKE (ACC)=0
0 0 0 2		S U B	0 0 0	0 5 5 2	(ACC)←(ACC)−(0552)

value two times. Figure A·8 shows the coding to achieve the assignment

$$(ACC) \leftarrow -(0552)$$

A·5
Shift instructions in real arithmetic and character manipulation

The *shift* instructions form another group of *orders* or *commands* for the SAMOS machine. These instructions are especially useful in performing arithmetic on nonintegers. To a lesser extent they are also useful in manipulating strings of characters.

Although the basic instruction set of SAMOS has instructions for integer arithmetic but none for floating-point arithmetic, it is still possible to perform a computation such as

$$8.25 \times 3.5 - 17.5 = 11.375$$

if we take advantage of the shift instructions. The integer numbers in SAMOS contain no decimal point, which means that the program must recognize where the decimal point should be. Let's treat each of the numbers in the computation above as an integer (i.e., 825, 35, and 175) and see how to insure a correct answer. First, we multiply 825 × 35 to get 28875. This we understand to mean 28.875, but SAMOS does not "know" that. From the product, 28875, we want to subtract 175 but that gives 28700, the wrong answer. What is the trouble? Remember that for addition or subtraction the decimal points of the two numbers must be *aligned*. We didn't want to subtract 175 but rather 17500 to give 11375 (interpreted as 11.375).

This example points up the need to be able to move (shift) a number two positions to the left in a word. Obviously, other examples would require shifts of different distances. To accomplish these shifts, SAMOS provides the following *shift left* instruction.

Shift Left

Example

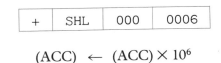

| + | SHL | 000 | 0006 |

Meaning

$$(ACC) \leftarrow (ACC) \times 10^6$$

This instruction shifts the contents of the accumulator six positions to the left. During the shifting process, the sign position remains unchanged, the leftmost six digits (or characters) are *lost*, and the rightmost six digits (or characters) are filled with zeros. For example, suppose the accumulator contains the number +0123456789.

ACC Before Execution of SHL Instruction

| + | 0 | 1 | 2 | 3 | 4 | 5 | 6 | 7 | 8 | 9 |

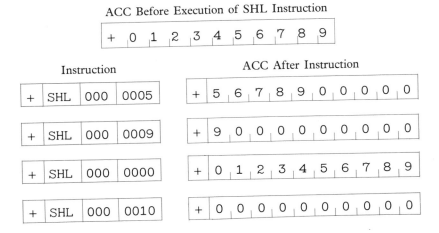

Instruction   ACC After Instruction

| + | SHL | 000 | 0005 | | + | 5 | 6 | 7 | 8 | 9 | 0 | 0 | 0 | 0 | 0 |

| + | SHL | 000 | 0009 | | + | 9 | 0 | 0 | 0 | 0 | 0 | 0 | 0 | 0 | 0 |

| + | SHL | 000 | 0000 | | + | 0 | 1 | 2 | 3 | 4 | 5 | 6 | 7 | 8 | 9 |

| + | SHL | 000 | 0010 | | + | 0 | 0 | 0 | 0 | 0 | 0 | 0 | 0 | 0 | 0 |

Similarly, suppose the accumulator contains the alphabetic characters "JOE SMITH".

ACC Before Instruction

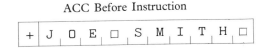

| + | J | O | E | □ | S | M | I | T | H | □ |

Instruction				ACC After Instruction										
+	SHL	000	0004	+	S	M	I	T	H	□	0	0	0	0
+	SHL	000	0007	+	T	H	□	0	0	0	0	0	0	0

It should be easy to convince yourself of the usefulness of the following complementary *shift right* instruction, which is also part of the SAMOS instruction set.

Shift Right

Example

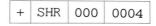

This is similar to the corresponding SHL, except that the contents of the accumulator are shifted four digits or characters to the *right*.

SHR Instruction

+	SHR	000	0006

ACC Before	ACC After

While the SHL and SHR instructions achieve a shifting of characters left or right, these instructions are not too useful for coding nonnumeric algorithmic processes. For example, how could we write SAMOS code for

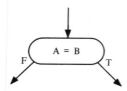

where values of A and B are character strings? The current SAMOS arithmetic unit is not able to perform arithmetic such as ADD and SUB on nonintegers. So it is not possible now to load the accumulator with the contents of A and subtract the contents of B for the purpose of determining whether this difference is zero. Merely having a special instruction such as BNZ (branch on zero) to test whether the accumulator is zero would not help. A new set of SAMOS instructions is needed to deal with problems of this type. (See Problem 2 below.)

EXERCISES A·5

1. Write SAMOS instructions to accomplish the calculation

$$8.25 \times 3.5 - 17.5$$

from integer inputs of 825, 35, and 175 assigned to (1001), (1002), and (1003), respectively.

2. Define additional SAMOS instructions that will be useful in coding the following types of flowchart steps

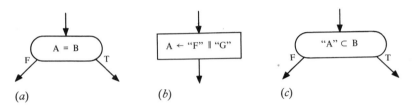

(a) (b) (c)

where A and B are string variables of 1 to 10 characters in length, and if fewer than 10, have trailing blanks. (The definition of each new instruction should amount to a functional specification using a style of description similar to what we have used in describing SAMOS instructions such as LOAD, SHIFT LEFT, and BRANCH ON MINUS.) Show how the new instructions you have designed would be used in coding flowchart steps *a*, *b*, and *c* and also the four decision steps given at the end of Section 3·5.

A·6
Index registers for looping on a counter variable

In this section we consider problems related to indexing and looping. Do not try to read all of this section until you have studied Section 4·1.

Suppose we are asked to write a program for summing 50 numbers. There are several ways to do this. If the numbers are already held in storage (say in addresses 1001 to 1050), and if the resulting sum is to be assigned to (5000), the flowchart and program of Figure A·9 will work. Can we include a loop? Certainly, one possible loop is to remove the assumption that the numbers are already in storage. Let the numbers be punched in 50 consecutive cards. Figure A·10 shows a flowchart and program to compute the sum. While this is a

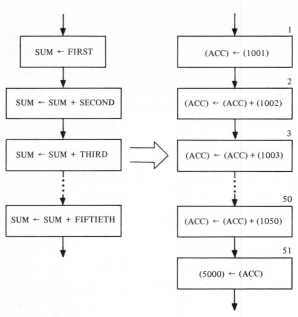

FIGURE A·9
One way to sum 50 numbers.

big improvement over the program in Figure A·9, there are still two reasons why we are not well pleased with the program of Figure A·10: (1) it provides no way to stop (other than by running out of cards) and no way to store or write the sum; and (2) it limits us to summing numbers punched on cards. Nevertheless, Figure A·10 uses only one ADD instruction to sum 50 (or really any number of) numbers.

Let's return to the assumption that the 50 numbers are held in storage but this time regard the 50 numbers as elements

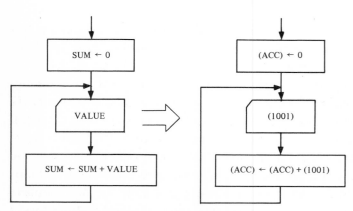

FIGURE A·10
Another way to sum.

of a *list variable*. A list variable can be represented in SAMOS storage simply by allocating a contiguous block of storage cells, one cell for each list element. For example, if the block of storage at addresses 1001 to 1050 is reserved for a list variable, named VALUE, then the cell at 1001 may be regarded as $VALUE_1$, 1002 as $VALUE_2$, . . . , and 1050 as $VALUE_{50}$. Now we want a way to apply a single ADD instruction to all 50 list elements.

Evidently, the *address part* of the ADD instruction must be changed before each use. Since the storage addresses of consecutive ADD instructions in Figure A·9 differ by one, we might start with what we can call the "base" ADD instruction.

ADD 000 1000

Then we can produce all the needed ADD instructions by adding the numbers 1, 2, 3, 4, . . . , 50 to (the address part of) the base instruction. For example, for the first instruction, we have

$$
\begin{array}{lr}
\text{"base"} & \text{ADD } 000 \; 1000 \\
& +\qquad 1 \\ \hline
\text{first inst.} & \text{ADD } 000 \; 1001
\end{array}
$$

In fact, we can generalize this process by saying that to obtain the ith ADD instruction, add i to the base instruction. Then, if i is called the "index," the 50 instructions are gener-

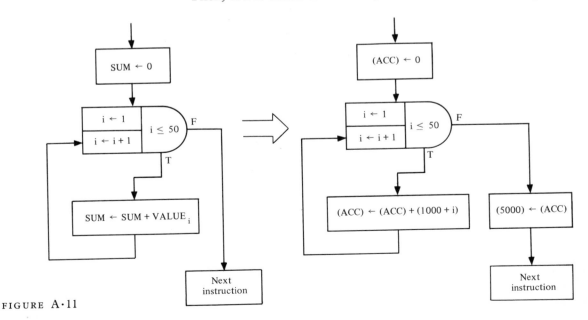

FIGURE A·11

ated by repeating the process, the index taking the values
$i = 1, 2, \ldots , 50$. This process is shown in flowchart form
in Figure A·11. Here we are using the symbol i as an integer
variable, but not as the name of an ordinary SAMOS storage
cell. For example, if the value of i is 4, the symbol $(1000 + i)$
is to be interpreted as a name for the contents of the cell whose
address is $1000 + 4$, that is, (1004). The variable i (as we will
see in the next section) will have its value stored in a special
register called an *index register,* which can be incremented (or
decremented) without disturbing the value in the accumulator.

Another way to obtain the same results is shown in Figure
A·12, where the index is started at 50 and decreased by 1 until
it is zero.

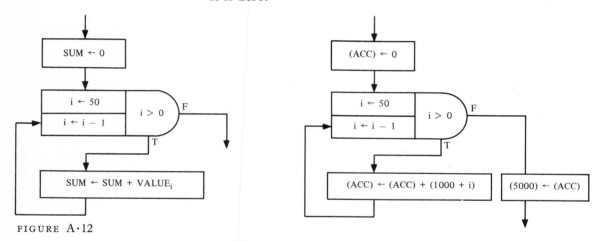

FIGURE A·12

Using *indexing instructions,* which we are about to introduce, it is easy to write programs equivalent to these flowcharts.

Indexing Instructions and
Their Use in Loops

SAMOS has three special index registers to be called R1, R2,
and R3. Each is capable of holding a four-digit address. These
registers can be thought of as part of the control unit shown
schematically in Figure A·13. Notice that there is no place
for a sign in an index register, so it cannot contain a negative
number.

How can index registers be used to alter instructions?
Recall that positions 5, 6, and 7 in each instruction have not
been used. They correspond to index registers 1, 2, and 3,
respectively. If position 5, 6, or 7 in the instruction contains
anything other than zero, the value of the corresponding index

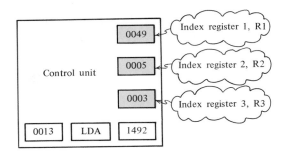

FIGURE A·13
More detail of the control unit.

register will be *added* to the address register before the instruction is performed. For example, with the index registers as shown in Figure A·13:

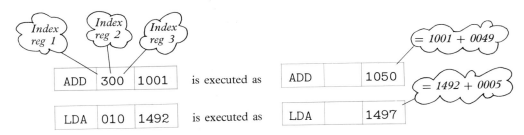

Thus, with index registers, the programmer can cause the address specified in an instruction to change before execution and *without changing the instruction as it appears in storage.*

Load index

The *load index* instruction enters a four-digit number into one of the index registers. There are three load index instructions: LI1, LI2, and LI3, one for each index register.

Example

| + | L I 2 | 0 0 0 | 1 7 4 1 |

Meaning $(R2) \leftarrow (1741)_{8-11}$

This instruction assigns to or "loads" index register 2 with a copy of the address part (positions 8, 9, 10 and 11) of the information stored at location 1741.

The instruction complementary to load index is the *store index* instruction. Here the four-digit number currently held in an index register is assigned to the address part (positions 8, 9, 10, and 11) of a designated storage cell.

Store index

There are three store index instructions: SI1, SI2, and SI3.

Example

| + | S I 3 | 0 0 0 | 2 2 2 9 |

Meaning $(2229)_{8-11} \leftarrow (R3)$

This instruction assigns, that is, stores, the value of index register 3 in the address part (positions 8, 9, 10, and 11) of location 2229. This operation will leave the sign and the next six positions of (2229) unchanged.

An index register can be decremented and tested by a *test index* instruction.

Test index

There are three test index instructions: TI1, TI2, and TI3.

Example

| + | T I 1 | 0 0 0 | 7 7 1 1 |

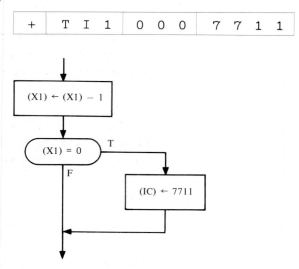

Meaning. Index register 1 is first decremented (reduced by 1). If the resulting value in the index register is zero, SAMOS then branches to location 7711 for the next instruction; otherwise, SAMOS continues in the normal instruction sequence.

Now we can return to the flowchart of Figure A·12, which sums 50 numbers to see how the index registers can help. To take advantage of the test index instruction, it is necessary to

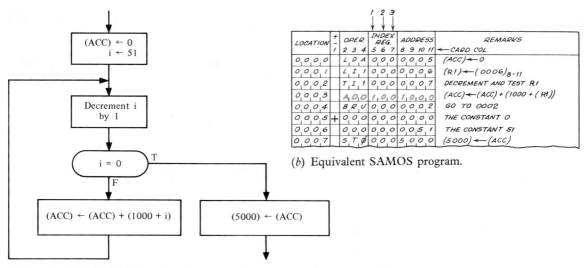

(b) Equivalent SAMOS program.

LOCATION	+/− 1	OPER. 2 3 4	INDEX REG. 5 6 7	ADDRESS 8 9 10 11	REMARKS ←CARD COL.
0 0 0 0		L D A	0 0 0	0 0 0 5	(ACC)←0
0 0 0 1		L I 1	0 0 0	0 0 0 6	(R1)←(0006)$_{8-11}$
0 0 0 2		T I 1	0 0 0	0 0 0 7	DECREMENT AND TEST R1
0 0 0 3		A D 1	0 0 1	0 0 0	(ACC)←(ACC)+(1000+(R1))
0 0 0 4		B R U	0 0 0	0 0 0 2	GO TO 0002
0 0 0 5	+	0 0 0	0 0 0	0 0 0 0	THE CONSTANT 0
0 0 0 6		0 0 0	0 0 0	0 0 5 1	THE CONSTANT 51
0 0 0 7		S T Ø	0 0 0	5 0 0 0	(5000)←(ACC)

(a) Logic of Figure A·12 modified to take advantage of the test index instruction.

FIGURE A·14
Summing with the use of an index register.

alter the loop logic by initially setting the index i to 51 instead of 50, to reflect the fact that the index register will always be decremented before it is tested. The altered flowchart logic of Figure A·12 is shown in Figure A·14a. The SAMOS program is shown in Figure A·14b. The program is remarkably compact: only six SAMOS instructions and two literals are required to do the addition, assuming the 50 numbers to be added are already in storage locations 1001 through 1050.

Notice that the program starts in location 0000, with locations 0005 and 0006 being used to store the constants 0 and 51, respectively. The instruction at 0000 loads the accumulator with a zero. At 0001 we "load index 1" with the address portion of (0006), as shown below.

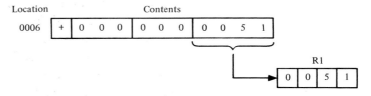

The instruction at 0002 does two things. First, it decreases (R1) by 1 (and makes it equal to 50 the first time around). Then it performs a test on the value of (R1). If the value is zero (i.e., if we have finished adding all the fifty numbers), SAMOS branches to location 0007 to store the sum in location 5000. Otherwise, SAMOS continues in sequence to 0003 where

Base Instruction: ADD 100 1000			
Time the instruction is executed	Contents of R1	Instruction actually executed	Effective address
first	0050	ADD 000 1050	1050
second	0049	ADD 000 1049	1049
third	0048	ADD 000 1048	1048
⋮	⋮	⋮	⋮
50th	0001	ADD 000 1001	1001

FIGURE A·15

the base instruction is located. This instruction is executed as shown in Figure A·15.

After each ADD instruction, it is necessary to return to location 0002 by means of the "branch unconditionally" instruction. The TI1 instruction in location 0002 again decreases the value of (R1) by 1, and tests whether or not (R1) is zero to choose between the ADD and the STO instructions. Eventually, after "going through the loop" 50 times, (R1) will be zero, the loop will terminate, and the results will be stored in location 5000.

EXERCISE A·6

Revise the program in Figure A·14 to *locate* the largest number among those being summed. The search for the largest can be conducted as part of the same loop in which the summing occurs. *Hint.* Since the *index* value of the largest number is what is wanted, it will be necessary to use a *store index* instruction to *save* the index value of the largest number.

A·7 Finding values in a table

Suppose we are given a table of integers from 0 and 1000 and their cube roots, as shown in Figure A·16.

We want to write a program that will "lookup" values of the cube root in this table for any given integer n between 0 and 1000 and will print this value on the typewriter. We will assume that the table of Figure A·16 has been punched in 1001 cards, each card containing the value of a cube root. The program should read the table into storage and then input from the card reader a value of n. SAMOS should print the value of n and its cube root, then read another value of n, and so on, until it runs out of data. Data sets should be separated with a blank line in the output.

n	$\sqrt[3]{n}$
0	0.000 000
1	1.000 000
2	1.259 921
3	1.442 250
4	1.587 401
⋮	⋮
999	9.996 666
1000	10.000 000

FIGURE A·16

A possible way to write the program is shown in Figure A·17. The instructions are in locations 0000 through 0005. The instruction at location 0003 has been printed in green to remind us that its address portion, 0008, is to be incremented by (R1).

LOCATION	+/−	OPER.	INDEX REG.	ADDRESS	REMARKS
1	2 3 4	5 6 7	8 9 10 11	←CARD COL.	
0 0 0 0		R W D	0 0 0	0 0 0 6	(0006) ← n
0 0 0 1		W W D	0 0 0	0 0 0 6	WRITE THE VALUE OF n ON TYPEWRITER
0 0 0 2		L I 1	0 0 0	0 0 0 6	LOAD R1 WITH VALUE OF n
0 0 0 3		W W D	1 0 0	0 0 0 8	WRITE (0008 + (R1)), THE $\sqrt[3]{n}$
0 0 0 4		W W D	0 0 0	0 0 0 7	WRITE A BLANK LINE FOR SPACING
0 0 0 5		B R U	0 0 0	0 0 0 0	BRANCH TO 0000 FOR ANOTHER VALUE [OF n
0 0 0 6	+	0 0 0	0 0 0	0 0 0 0	n
0 0 0 7	+				BLANK LINE FOR TYPEWRITER SPACING
0 0 0 8	+	0 0 0	0 0 0	0 0 0 0	$\sqrt[3]{0}$
0 0 0 9	+	0 1 0	0 0 0	0 0 0 0	$\sqrt[3]{1}$
0 0 1 0	+	0 1 2	5 9 9	2 1 0 5	$\sqrt[3]{2}$
0 0 1 1	+	0 1 4	4 2 2	4 9 5 7	$\sqrt[3]{3}$
0 0 1 2	+	0 1 5	8 7 4	0 1 0 5	$\sqrt[3]{4}$
⋮		⋮	⋮	⋮	⋮
1 0 0 7	+	0 9 9	9 6 6	6 5 5 6	$\sqrt[3]{999}$
1 0 0 8	+	1 0 0	0 0 0	0 0 0 0	$\sqrt[3]{1000}$
					BLANK CARD TO TRANSFER TO 0000

TABLE

FIGURE A·17

Location 0006 is used to store the value of n temporarily. Location 0007 is filled with blanks for separating data sets in the output. The table is placed in locations 0008 to 1008. When instructions and data are read in from cards they are stored in locations 0000 through 1008, a final blank card will cause a transfer of control to location 0000.

The program works as follows. The instructions in 0000 and 0001 read an integer data value into location 0006 and print this value on the typewriter. The instruction in 0002 loads R1 with the integer found in the address part of 0006. The next instruction prints on the typewriter the value found in 0008 + (R1). The address 0008 + (R1) is the place in the table where the desired cube root is stored. For example, you should trace out the steps and see that when the given integer is 1, the cube root is found in location 0009; when the integer is 1000, its cube root is found in 1008, and so on.

Notice also that the decimal point that appears in the table of Figure A·16 has been eliminated from the table stored in SAMOS. What we have done is to store each cube root as $\sqrt[3]{n} \times 10^8$, an integer, and we have kept in mind the fact that the decimal point is between the second and third digit from the left of the number. When the cube roots are printed as

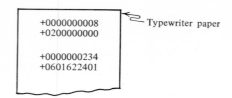

```
+0000000008
+0200000000

+0000000234
+0601622401
```
Typewriter paper

FIGURE A·18

shown in Figure A·18, the programmer must recall the location of the decimal point and possibly mark it with pencil or pen on the output (such as 02∧00000000).

After the cube root of the number has been printed, the instruction in location 0004 causes a blank line to be printed. Then the instruction in 0005 causes a branch back for another value of n. Notice that the blank line has been supplied by location 0007, and that a + sign was attached to it. This sign is necessary because a completely blank card in the input deck would transfer SAMOS to location 0000 before the table was read into storage. This transfer is accomplished by the blank card following the cube root table.

The output of this program is shown in Figure A·18 for the values of n = 8 and n = 234, respectively.

The program of Figure A·17 may be easily modified so that the output shown in Figure A·18 will have the decimal points of n and $\sqrt[3]{n}$ aligned. The output would then be

```
+0008000000
+0002000000

+0234000000
+0006016224
```

A·8
The use of subprograms

(This section should be read only after you have studied Chapter 9.) Functions and procedures can be programmed as independent sequences of instructions, often called subprograms or *subroutines* because they are used by other programs.

We will now show how the cube root program of the preceding section can be modified for use as a subroutine. In this example we want to compute

$$x = 2 + 3a^{1/3} + b^{1/3}$$

where a and b are positive integers not greater than 1000. We assume that pairs a and b have been punched into consecutive

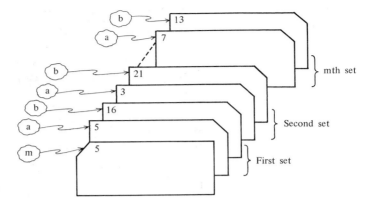

FIGURE A·19

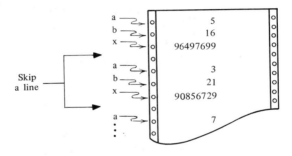

FIGURE A·20

cards, and that we want to compute x for m such pairs. An input deck is shown in Figure A·19. An output is shown in Figure A·20.

A Cube Root Subroutine

We first design a subroutine with the following specifications.

1. The subroutine will assume that the argument, an integer between 0 and 1000, inclusive, has been placed in the accumulator before control "passes" to it.

2. The *return address* is the address of the next instruction to be executed in the main program following the completion of the subroutine's task. This return address should be saved by storing it in some convenient register before entering the subroutine. We choose index register 2 for this purpose.

3. The subroutine should place the cube root in the accumulator before branching back, i.e., returning, to the main program.

LOCATION	+/−	OPER.	INDEX REG.	ADDRESS	REMARKS
	1	2 3 4	5 6 7	8 9 10 11	← CARD COL.
0 0 0 0					RESERVED FOR BRANCHING
0 0 0 1		S T 0	0 0 0	0 0 0 5	(0005) ← (ACC)
0 0 0 2		L I 1	0 0 0	0 0 0 5	LOAD R1 WITH THE VALUE OF n
0 0 0 3		L D A	1 0 0	0 0 0 6	(ACC) ← (0006 + (R1))
0 0 0 4		B R U	0 1 0	0 0 0 0	BRANCH TO ADDRESS IN (R2)
0 0 0 5			n		ARGUMENT
0 0 0 6	+	0 0 0	0 0 0	0 0 0 0	$\sqrt[3]{0}$
0 0 0 7	+	0 1 0	0 0 0	0 0 0 0	$\sqrt[3]{1}$
0 0 0 8	+	0 1 2	5 9 9	2 1 0 5	$\sqrt[3]{2}$
⋮		⋮	⋮	⋮	⋮ TABLE
⋮		⋮	⋮	⋮	⋮
1 0 0 5	+	0 9 9	9 6 6	6 5 5 6	$\sqrt[3]{999}$
1 0 0 6	+	1 0 0	0 0 0	0 0 0 0	$\sqrt[3]{1000}$

FIGURE A·21
Cube root subroutine.

The program of Figure A·21 follows these specifications. This is a slight modification of the program in Figure A·17. The table is stored in locations 0006 to 1006; location 0000 is reserved for branching to the main program. Whenever we want to use this subroutine, the following steps should be taken.

1. Place the argument in the accumulator.

2. Load the address of the next instruction following the call on the subroutine into index register 2.

3. Branch to location 0001.

The cube root will be available in the accumulator upon exit from the subroutine. Since R1 and R2 are used by the subroutine, R3 is the only index register available for use in the main program.

The Main Program

The main program is shown in Figure A·23 and it occupies locations 1007–1042. A general flowchart is shown in Figure A·22. This diagram does not show all the steps required to enter the subroutine or other machine language details that are important when the actual coding is done. These details are explained in the remark section of the coding form of Figure A·23.

The program makes use of index register 3 to count the number of sets of data. Index registers 1 and 2 are reserved for the subroutine. You should follow the program, step by step, paying special attention to the contents of the accumulator and the index registers.

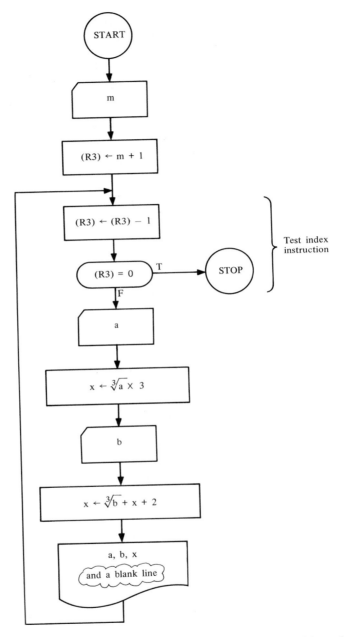

FIGURE A·22

Notice that the constants located in 1033 and 1034 are used to load R2 with the address to which the subroutine should return. Other constants are available at locations 1035 through 1037. Locations 1038 through 1042 are used to store the values m + 1, m, a, b, and x.

As before, the program will be executed by SAMOS if

LOCATION	+/−	OPER.	INDEX REG.	ADDRESS	REMARKS
	1	2 3 4	5 6 7	8 9 10 11	← CARD COL.
0000		BRU	000	1007	SUBROUTINE GOES IN PLACE OF HEAVY LINE
1007		RWD		1039	(1039) ← m
1008		LDA		1039	}
1009		ADD		1035	} m ← m+1
1010		STO		1038	
1011		LI3		1038	(R3) ← m+1
1012		TI3		1031	DECREMENT AND TEST (R3)
1013		RWD		1040	(1040) ← a
1014		LDA		1040	(ACC) ← a
1015		LI2		1033	(R2) ← RETURN ADDRESS [1017]
1016		BRU		0001	BRANCH TO SUBROUTINE
1017		MPY		1037	(ACC) ← 3 × (ACC)
1018		STO		1042	(1042) ← $3\sqrt[3]{a}$
1019		RWD		1041	(1041) ← b
1020		LDA		1041	(ACC) ← b
1021		LI2		1034	(R2) ← RETURN ADDRESS [1023]
1022		BRU		0001	BRANCH TO SUBROUTINE
1023		ADD		1042	(ACC) ← $\sqrt[3]{b} + 3\sqrt[3]{a}$
1024		ADD		1036	}
1025		STO		1042	} $x \leftarrow 2 + \sqrt[3]{b} + 3\sqrt[3]{a}$
1026		WWD		1040	PRINT a
1027		WWD		1041	PRINT b
1028		WWD		1042	PRINT x
1029		WWD		1032	PRINT A BLANK LINE
1030		BRU		1012	BRANCH BACK FOR ANOTHER SET
1031		HLT		1007	STOP.

CONSTANTS:

LOCATION	+/−	OPER.	INDEX REG.	ADDRESS	REMARKS
	1	2 3 4	5 6 7	8 9 10 11	← CARD COL.
1032	+				BLANKS FOR TYPEWRITER SKIPPING
1033	+	000	000	1017	FIRST SUBROUTINE RETURN ADDRESS
1034	+	000	000	1023	SECOND SUBROUTINE RETURN ADDRESS
1035	+	000	000	0001	+1
1036	+	020	000	0000	+2.00000000
1037	+	000	000	0003	+3
1038	+	000	000	0000	VALUE OF m+1
1039	+	000	000	0000	m
1040	+	000	000	0000	a
1041	+	000	000	0000	b
1042	+	000	000	0000	x
					BLANK TRANSFER CARD

FIGURE A·23

we place all the program cards in the card reader in order, followed by a blank card and by the data, and press the LOAD button. The instruction in 0000 branches to the start of the main program at location 1007 as soon as the blank card has been sensed.

A·9
Floating-point arithmetic

The SAMOS machine's repertoire of instructions can be further augmented with single and double precision floating-point instructions, as discussed in Chapter 11. Recall from that chapter that for single precision floating point, the SAMOS accumulator must be extended to double the number of precision digits of an ordinary SAMOS floating point number.

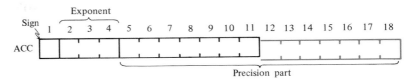

This extension will allow addition of two floating-point summands that differ by 7 in their exponents. (For further explanation of floating-point addition, see Section 11·1.)

The LDA instruction is insensitive to the type of value being loaded into the SAMOS accumulator; hence a floating-point number can be loaded into the accumulator by a LDA instruction. We can now reinterpret the LDA instruction with the aid of the following sample instruction.

LDA	000	0197

Meaning: clear the *entire* accumulator (including its extension in positions 12 through 18) and then place the contents of storage location 0197 into accumulator positions 1 through 11.

Suppose location 0197 contains a floating-point number. In that case, succeeding instructions may perform floating-point addition, subtraction, multiplication, or division by supplying the address of the second summand, the subtrahend, the multiplier, or the divisor, respectively, the first operand being the number held in the accumulator.

The actual execution of a floating-point add or subtract instruction involves the intermediate steps described in Section 11·1. If the operand referred to by the add (or subtract) instruction has a larger exponent than does the number currently in the accumulator, the two numbers (operands) are interchanged before the addition (or subtraction) takes place. Only in this way can accumulator positions 12 through 18 be properly utilized. (If one were to look "below the surface" of SAMOS one would find certain hidden registers that are used to carry out the compare and interchange substeps of floating-point add and subtract instructions.)

We will assume that the selected codes for the instructions are:

FLA   floating add
FLS   floating subtract
FLM   floating multiply
FLD   floating divide

Each operation leaves a floating-point result (sum, difference, product, or quotient in positions 1 through 11 of the accumulator). The result may then be stored using the multipurpose STO instruction that, like the LDA instruction, is insensitive to the type of value involved in the operation.

For example, code for the flowchart box

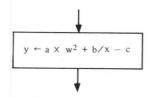

$$y \leftarrow a \times w^2 + b/x - c$$

might appear as shown in Figure A·24. Here it is assumed that values of each variable are real and are represented in floating point. As you can see, there is nothing especially difficult about coding floating-point operations.

LOCATION	± 1	OPER 2 3 4	INDEX REG 5 6 7	ADDRESS 8 9 10 11	REMARKS ← CARD COL
0200		L D A	0 0 0	0 3 5 0	Load a
0201		F L M	0 0 0	0 3 5 3	Multiply by w
0202		F L M	0 0 0	0 3 5 3	Multiply by w
0203		S T O	0 0 0	0 3 4 9	Store in temp
0204		L D A	0 0 0	0 3 5 1	Load b
0205		F L D	0 0 0	0 3 5 4	Divide by x
0206		F L A	0 0 0	0 3 4 9	Add aw^2
0207		F L S	0 0 0	0 3 5 2	Subtract c
0208		S T O	0 0 0	0 3 5 4	Store in y

FIGURE A·24
Illustrating the use of floating-point arithmetic operations.

SAMOS' ability to simulate the real numbers can be extended even further by providing for operations on double precision floating-point numbers. To see how this extension can be achieved, we first explain how values for variables and constants can be represented as SAMOS double precision floating-point numbers. Such numbers are stored in pairs of "adjacent" storage words. The first word is assumed to hold the sign, the exponent, and the first 7 precision digits, while the second word holds the remaining 10 precision digits. The sign of the second word matches the sign of the first word. If, for example, the variable x were treated as a double precision variable, and if its value were 1 / 3, then its appearance in SAMOS might be

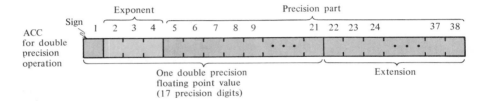

A further extension of the accumulator would be required, accommodating at least 17 precision digits but possibly as many as 34 such digits, to allow for multiplying two double precision numbers or adding two double precision floating-point summands that differ by as much as 17 in their exponents.

Some new operation codes would, of course, be required to load copies of a pair of adjacent storage words into the accumulator, to store from the accumulator *into* a pair of adjacent storage words, and to cause addition, subtraction, multiplication, and division involving a second double precision operand. New instructions for loading and storing might be

LDW   *l*oad *d*ouble *w*ord, and
SDW   *s*tore *d*ouble *w*ord

For example,

| LDW | 000 | 0200 |

would mean: clear the entire accumulator and load a copy of the contents of 0200 *and* 0201 (into positions 1 through 21 of the accumulator.

SDW	000 0500

would mean: store accumulator positions 1 through 21 containing the sign, exponent, and 17 precision digits into locations 0500 *and* 0501.

New instructions for double precision floating add, subtract, multiply, and divide might be:

FDA   *f*loating *d*ouble *a*dd,
FDS   *f*loating *d*ouble *s*ubtract,
FDM   *f*loating *d*ouble *m*ultiply, and
FDD   *f*loating *d*ouble *d*ivide

Thus the double precision coding for the flowchart step

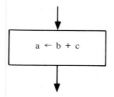

where a, b, and c are double length variables, might be

LDW   000   0200   beginning location of b
FDA   000   0202   beginning location of c
SDW   000   0204   beginning location of a

Many computers devoted to scientific computation have built-in floating-point instructions and some, usually the larger computers, also have built-in operations for double precision computations. Many of the computers that do not carry out these operations "in hardware" offer the programmer the equivalent capability via software subroutine "packages" that simulate the faster hardware capability.

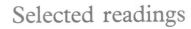

The reader of this book may find certain topics of special interest and wish to pursue the study of a particular area. We have selected, for each major topic or group of topics, several books, articles, or essays.

The reading list is by no means exhaustive. On the other hand, hardly any of these references requires extensive preparation in mathematics, physics, or other specialized technical areas. Some of the cited references can be read with ease any time after completing the chapter(s) under which they are listed, while others require the full course of study to be appreciated.

Two books are especially noteworthy, each a fine collection of articles and essays.

A. *Perspectives on the Computer Revolution,* edited by Z. B. Pylyshyn, Englewood Cliffs, N.J.: Prentice Hall, 1970, 540 pp.

B. *Computers and Computation,* Readings from *Scientific American,* with introductions by R. R. Fenichel and J. Weizenbaum. San Francisco: W. H. Freeman and Co., 1971, 283 pp.

A cited article in one of these collections has an abbreviated reference. For example:

"Computer Logic and Memory," by D. C. Evans, in B, pp. 17–27 refers to an article that appears in *Computers and Computation.*

Within each group of references, all articles precede all books and each category is listed alphabetically by title.

Chapter 1
General perspective:
Implications and Applications

"Educational Implications of the Computer Revolution," by G. E. Forsythe, in A, pp. 378–389.

"Intellectual Implications of the Computer Revolution," by R. W. Hamming, in A, pp. 370–377.

"Legal Safeguards to Insure Privacy in a Computer Society," by Alan F. Westin, in A, pp. 472–479.

"On the Impact of the Computer on Society," by J. Weizenbaum. *Science,* May 12, 1972, pp. 609–614.

"The Social Responsibilities of Computer People," by E. C. Berkeley, in A, pp. 461–471.

"Uses of Computers in Education," by P. A. Suppes, in B, pp. 249–260.

"Uses of Computers in Organizations," by M. Greenberger, in B, pp. 243–248.

"Uses of Computers in Science," by A. B. Oettinger, in B, pp. 261–269.

"Uses of Computers in Technology," by S. A. Coons, in B, pp. 231–242.

Computers, by J. M. Adams and D. H. Haden. New York: Wiley, 1973, 584 pp.

Computers and Society, by R. W. Hamming. New York: McGraw-Hill, 1972, 284 pp.

Computers and Society, by S. Rothman and C. Mosmann. Chicago: SRA, 1972, 337 pp.

Algorithms

"Algorithms and Automatic Computing Machines," by B. A. Traktenbrot, in A, pp. 69–86. Also Boston: D. C. Heath, 1963, 101 pp.

"The General and Logical Theory of Automata," by J. von Neumann, in A, pp. 87–113.

Computation: Finite and Infinite Machines, by M. L. Minsky. Englewood Cliffs, N.J.: Prentice-Hall, 1967, 317 pp.

Computers:
History, Logic, Storage,
Input and Output,
Architecture

"Computer Displays," by I. E. Sutherland, in B, pp. 53–69.

"Computer Inputs and Outputs," by I. E. Sutherland, in B, pp. 42–52.

"Computer Logic and Memory," by D. C. Evans, in B, pp. 17–27.

"Information," by J. McCarthy, in B, pp. 1–15.

"Integrated Computer Memories," by J. A. Rajchman, in B, pp. 28–41.

The Analytical Engine: Computers—Past, Present, and Future, by J. Bernstein. New York: Random House, 1963, 113 pp.

Digital Computer Fundamentals, 3rd ed., by T. C. Bartee. New York: McGraw-Hill, 1972, 467 pp.

Introduction to Computer Organization and Data Structures, by H. S. Stone. New York: McGraw-Hill, 1972, 321 pp.

Chapters 2, 3, and 4
Flowcharts

"Flowcharting with the ANSI Standard," by N. Chapin. *ACM Computing Surveys,* Vol. 2, No. 2, June 1970, pp. 119–146.

Fundamentals of Flow-Charting, by T. S. Shriber. New York: Wiley, 1969, 127 pp.

Programming Languages
(See also the programming
language supplements for
this book.)

Basic Programming, 2nd ed., by J. G. Kemeny and T. E. Kurtz. New York: Wiley, 1971, 150 pp.

Concepts of Programming Languages, by M. Elson. Chicago: SRA, 1973, 333 pp.

FORTRAN IV, by E. I. Organick and L. E. Meissner. Reading, Mass.: Addison-Wesley, 1974, 293 pp.

A Guide to COBOL Programming, by D. D. McCracken and V. Garbassi. New York: Wiley, 1970, 209 pp.

Introduction to Algol, by R. Baumann et al. Englewood Cliffs, N.J.: Prentice-Hall, 1964, 142 pp.

An Introduction to APL, by W. Prager. Boston: Allyn and Bacon, 1971, 133 pp.

Programming Languages: History and Fundamentals, by J. E. Sammet. Englewood Cliffs, N.J.: Prentice-Hall, 1969, 785 pp.

Structured Programming in PL/C, by G. Weinberg, N. Yasukawa, and R. Marcus. New York: Wiley, 1974, 220 pp.

*Supplementary Problems
and Methods*

"Sorting," by W. A. Martin, *ACM Computing Surveys,* Vol. 3, No. 4, December 1971, pp. 147–174.

A Collection of Programming Problems and Techniques, by H. A. Maurer and M. R. Williams. Englewood Cliffs, N.J.: Prentice-Hall, 1972, 256 pp.

Computer Science: Projects and Study Problems, by A. I. Forsythe, E. I. Organick, and R. P. Plummer. New York: Wiley, 1973, 292 pp.

Elementary Computer Applications, by I. Barrodale, F. D. K. Roberts, and B. L. Ehle. New York: Wiley, 1971, 254 pp.

Introduction to Computer Science Including 300 Solved Problems, by F. Scheid. Schaum's Outline Series. New York: McGraw-Hill, 1970, 281 pp.

Problems for Computer Solution, by F. Gruenberger and G. Jaffray. New York: Wiley, 1965, 401 pp.

Chapter 5
Problem Solving

"The Architecture of Complexity," by H. A. Simon, in *The Sciences of the Artificial.* Cambridge, Mass.: M.I.T. Press, 1969, pp. 84–118.

"Information-Processing in Computer and Man," by H. A. Simon and Allen Newell, in A, pp. 256–273.

How to Solve It, by G. Polya. Princeton, N.J.: Princeton University Press, 1957, 253 pp.

Programming: Methodology and Style

"Systems Analysis and Programming," by C. Strachey, in B, pp. 70–77.

ACM Computing Surveys, Vol. 6, No. 4, December 1974. (A collection of five papers on programming.)

The Elements of Programming Style, by B. W. Kernighan and P. J. Plauger. New York: McGraw-Hill, 1974, 147 pp.

An Introduction to Programming: A Structured Approach Using PL/I and PLC, by R. Conway and D. Gries. Cambridge, Mass.: Winthrop, 1973, 460 pp.

Systematic Programming: An Introduction, by N. Wirth. Englewood Cliffs, N.J.: Prentice-Hall, 1973, 169 pp.

Chapters 6 and 7
Games and Game Analysis

"Algorithms and Automatic Computing Machines," by B. A. Traktenbrot, in A, pp. 72–79.

"A Chess-Playing Machine," by Claude E. Shannon, in B, pp. 104–107.

"Computer v. Chess Player," by Alex Bernstein and M. de V. Roberts, in B, pp. 108–112.

"The Eight Queens Problem" and "Instant Insanity" in *Computer Science: Projects and Study Problems,* by A. I. Forsythe, E. I. Organick, and R. P. Plummer. New York: Wiley, 1973, pp. 15–25.

Chapter 8
Interpreting and Compiling

Anatomy of a Compiler, by J. A. N. Lee. New York: Reinhold, 1967, 275 pp.

Compiler Construction for Digital Computers, by D. Gries. New York: Wiley, 1971, 493 pp.

Programming Languages, Information Structures and Machine Organization, by P. Wegner. New York: McGraw-Hill, 1968, 401 pp.

Translation of Computer Languages, by F. W. Weingarten. San Francisco: Holden-Day, 180 pp.

Postfix Machines

HP-65 Owner's Manual, Cupertino, Calif.: Hewlett Packard Company, 1974, 107 pp.

A Narrative Description of the *B5500 Disk File Master Control Program.* Detroit: The Burroughs Corporation, Form No. 1023579, October 1969.

Chapter 9
Programming Language Semantics

"Ten Mini-Languages: A Study of Topical Issues in Programming Languages," by H. F. Ledgard, *ACM Computing Surveys,* Vol. 3, No. 3, September 1971, pp. 115–146.

Programming Languages, Information Structures and Machine Organization, by P. Wegner. New York: McGraw-Hill, 1968, 401 pp.

See also references to specific programming languages such as those cited under Chapter 2.

"Elements of Data Management Systems," by G. G. Dodd, *ACM Computing Surveys*, Vol. 1, No. 2, June 1969, pp. 117–133.

Chapter 10
Data Processing and Information Systems

"Evolution of Business System Analysis Techniques," by J. D. Couger. *ACM Computing Surveys*, Vol. 5, No. 3, September 1973, pp. 167–198.

"Hash Table Methods," by W. D. Maurer and T. G. Lewis. *ACM Computing Surveys*, Vol. 7, No. 1, March, 1975.

"Table Look-Up Techniques," by C. E. Price. *ACM Computing Surveys*, Vol. 3, No. 2, June 1971, pp. 49–65.

Computers: A Systems Approach, by Ned Chapin. New York: Van Nostrand Reinhold, 1971, 686 pp.

Management Information Systems: Conceptual Foundations, Structure and Development, by Gordon B. Davis. New York: McGraw-Hill, 482 pp.

Chapters 11 and 12
Numerical Computation

"Computations with Approximate Numbers," by D. B. DeLury. *The Mathematics Teacher*, Vol. 51, 1958, pp. 521–530.

"Pitfalls in Computation," by G. E. Forsythe. *American Mathematical Monthly*, Vol. 77, No. 11, November 1970, pp. 931–935.

"Solving a Quadratic Equation on a Computer," by G. E. Forsythe, pp. 138–152, in *The Mathematical Sciences: A Collection of Essays Edited by COSRIMS*. Cambridge, Mass.: The M.I.T. Press, 1969, 271 pp.

"A Survey of Error Analysis," by W. Kahan. *Information Processing 71*, Vol. 2, North Holland Publishing Co., 1972, pp. 1214–1239.

Experimentation and Measurement, by W. J. Youden. New York: Scholastic Book Services, 1962, 127 pp.

Floating Point Computation, by Pat Sterbenz. Englewood Cliffs, N.J.: Prentice-Hall, 1974, 316 pp.

Numerical Methods with Fortran IV Case Studies, by W. S. Dorn and D. D. McCracken. New York: Wiley, 1972, 447 pp. (See the annotated bibliography on pages 415–420 of this book for discussion of other texts that require less, the same, or more mathematical preparation than this one.)

Chapter 13

"On-line Text Editing: A Survey," by A. van Dam and D. E. Rice. *ACM Computing Surveys*, Vol. 3, No. 3, September 1971, pp. 94–114.

SNOBOL 3 Primer, by Allen Forte. Cambridge, Mass.: The M.I.T. Press, 1967, 107 pp.

A SNOBOL 4 Primer, by R. E. Griswold and M. T. Griswold. Englewood Cliffs, N.J.: Prentice-Hall, 1973, 184 pp.

Appendix

Answers to selected exercises

Chapter 1

EXERCISES 1·2

3. (a) Using the Fibonacci sequence of Table 1·1:

Month No.	$r = \dfrac{\text{No. Rabbits This Month}}{\text{No. Rabbits Last Month}}$	(Answer to part c) $\dfrac{1}{r}$
2	1.000	1.000
3	2.000	.500
4	1.500	.667
5	1.667	.600
6	1.600	.625
7	1.625	.615
8	1.615	.619
9	1.619	.618
10	1.618	.618
11	1.618	.618
12	1.618	.618

(b) The ratios seem to settle down to the constant value 1.618.
(c) See column 3 of the solution to part a.
(d) It looks as though the following relationship is true.

$$r - 1 = \frac{1}{r}$$

(e) Assuming $r \neq 0$, multiply the equation by r and subtract 1 from both sides. Then

$$r^2 - r - 1 = 0$$

By the quadratic formula,

$$r = \frac{1 \pm \sqrt{5}}{2}$$

Since each term of the r sequence in part a is greater than zero, we select the positive value of r $(1 + \sqrt{5})/2 \approx 1.618$. This value has been called the Golden Ratio.

EXERCISES 1·3

1. The effect of changing the order of the two assignment statements is that after the two are executed the values of SUM, LATEST, and NEXT will all be the same. Subsequent execution of the statement

$$\text{SUM} \leftarrow \text{LATEST} + \text{NEXT}$$

will assign to SUM twice its previous value. Thus the successive values of SUM will be 1, 2, 4, 8, 16, 32, 64, 128, 256, 512, and 1024.

EXERCISE 1·4

One solution to the problem is

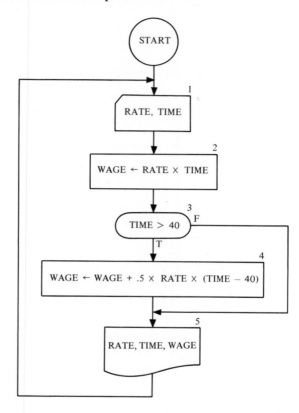

EXERCISES 1·6

1. Assuming the variables RATE, TIME, and WAGE are stored in locations 0100, 0101, and 0102, respectively, the following program is one solution.

STORAGE LOCATION (Address)	± 1	OPERATION CODE 2 3 4	5 6 7	ADDRESS 8 9 10 11	FLOWCHART EQUIVALENT ← Character Number
0 0 0 0		R W D		0 1 0 0	1: RATE, TIME
0 0 0 1		R W D		0 1 0 1	
0 0 0 2		L D A		0 1 0 0	2: WAGE ← RATE × TIME
0 0 0 3		M P Y		0 1 0 1	
0 0 0 4		S T O		0 1 0 2	
0 0 0 5		W W D		0 1 0 0	3: RATE, TIME, WAGE
0 0 0 6		W W D		0 1 0 1	
0 0 0 7		W W D		0 1 0 2	
0 0 0 8		B R U		0 0 0 0	Arrow from flowchart box 3 to box 1

2. (a) 0351
(b) 0018
(c) BMI
(d) HLT

4. (a) 5
(b) 2

5.   This solution is only one of many possible solutions.

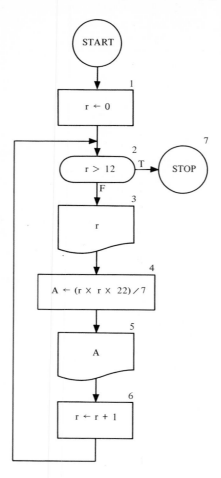

Suppose $r = 4$. SAMOS evaluates the expression $(22 / 7) \times r^2$ as $3 \times 4 \times 4 = 48$. (Remember, SAMOS has only integer division). However, SAMOS evaluates $(22 \times r^2) / 7$ as $(22 \times 16) / 7 = 352 / 7 = 50$. The second result is more accurate than the first, as you can see by doing the computation with real division. In the first evaluation, the error introduced by the integer division of 22 by 7 is magnified when the quotient is multiplied by r^2. In the second evaluation division is the last operation.

STORAGE LOCATION (Address)	± 1	OPERATION CODE 2 3 4	5 6 7	ADDRESS 8 9 10 11	FLOWCHART BOX EQUIVALENT
0 0 0 0	+	B R U	0 0 0	0 0 0 7	
0 0 0 1	+	0 0 0	0 0 0	0 0 2 2	Constant
0 0 0 2	+	0 0 0	0 0 0	0 0 0 7	Constant
0 0 0 3	+	0 0 0	0 0 0	0 0 0 0	Variable r
0 0 0 4	+	0 0 0	0 0 0	0 0 1 2	Constant
0 0 0 5	+	0 0 0	0 0 0	0 0 0 0	Variable A
0 0 0 6	+	0 0 0	0 0 0	0 0 0 1	Constant
0 0 0 7	+	L D A	0 0 0	0 0 0 4	⎫
0 0 0 8	+	S U B	0 0 0	0 0 0 3	⎬ Box 2
0 0 0 9	+	B M I	0 0 0	0 0 2 1	⎭
0 0 1 0	+	W W D	0 0 0	0 0 0 3	Box 3
0 0 1 1	+	L D A	0 0 0	0 0 0 3	⎫
0 0 1 2	+	M P Y	0 0 0	0 0 0 3	
0 0 1 3	+	M P Y	0 0 0	0 0 0 1	⎬ Box 4
0 0 1 4	+	D I V	0 0 0	0 0 0 2	
0 0 1 5	+	S T O	0 0 0	0 0 0 5	⎭
0 0 1 6	+	W W D	0 0 0	0 0 0 5	Box 5
0 0 1 7	+	L D A	0 0 0	0 0 0 3	⎫
0 0 1 8	+	A D D	0 0 0	0 0 0 6	⎬ Box 6
0 0 1 9	+	S T O	0 0 0	0 0 0 3	⎭
0 0 2 0	+	B R U	0 0 0	0 0 0 7	Arrow from box 6 to box 2
0 0 2 1	+	H L T	0 0 0	0 0 0 0	Box 7

SAMOS PROGRAM

Chapter 2

EXERCISES 2·1

3. (a) True.
   (b) True.
   (c) False. Box 2 would be executed only once.
   (d) Output 4.
   (e) False. Box 2 is executed only once if the input value of SWITCH is ≥ 1.
   (f) False. Any numeric value may be input for SWITCH. It makes more sense if these values are integers ≤ 1.

4. Sufficient criteria are:

(a) A variable that appears on the right side of one assignment does not also appear on the left side of the other assignment step.

(b) The left sides of the two assignment steps are different.

Thus the order of the steps is immaterial in parts a and e, but is important in parts b, c, and d.

EXERCISES 2·2,
SET A

3. (a) The output is:

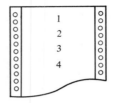

(b) 0009

(c) BRU 000 0003

4. (a) Correct: John, Betty, Bruce
Incorrect: Gwen, Max, Sarah, Kelley, Paul

(b) Gwen starts numbering output lines with 0.
Max's lines will not be numbered consecutively.
Sarah is caught in an endless loop after the first F exit.
Kelley stops after the first line of output.
Paul's lines will all be numbered 1.

(c)

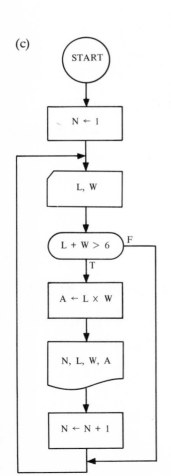

6.

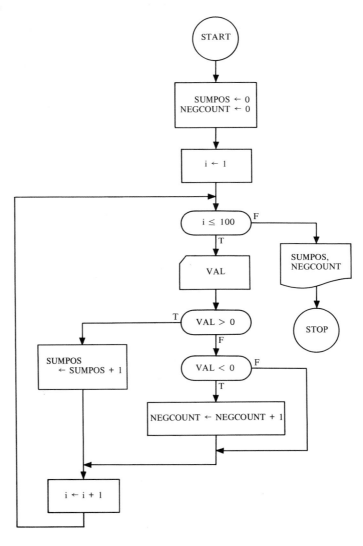

1.

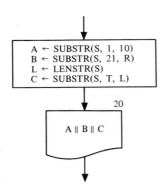

alternatively,

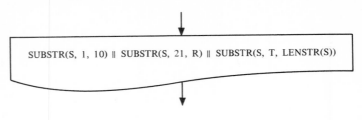

SUBSTR(S, 1, 10) ∥ SUBSTR(S, 21, R) ∥ SUBSTR(S, T, LENSTR(S))

3. (a)

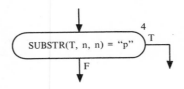

(b)

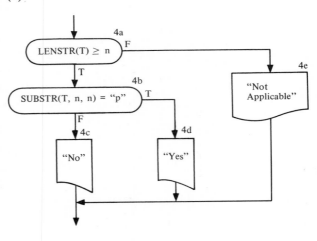

3.

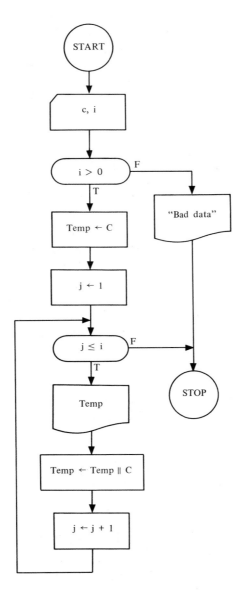

1. (a) ①, ②, ③, ⑤, ⑥, ⑦, ④, ⑧

   (b) ②, ⑦, ③, ④, ⑤, ①, ⑥

2. (4)

4. A divide-by-zero condition would be detected when executing box 4 for the first time, since Z is zero.

1. (a) True.

(c) Set(4).

(e) True. Box 2 serves as the test for escape from the outer loop under sentinel control.

(g) Locations 0006, 0007, and 0008.

(i) A location for the constant 1000 must be chosen. A possible location for 1000 would be 0029, assuming locations 0025 through 0028 are used to code box 9 and the loop back to box 4.

3. (a) $T = 0$
$P = 0$

(c) $-15, -13, 14, 14$
The effect of executing this flowchart fragment is to assign to X the greatest integer that is less than (or equal to) X, that is, [X].

5. (a) True (24 is less than 71).
False. The subexpression, $A < CHOP(E/D)$, corresponds to $16 < 1$, which is false.

7. (a) 2004   (d) 0   (e) 2022, 1

9. (a) 6823

14. No. of items = $CHOP(NBOY/9)$

Chapter 3

1.

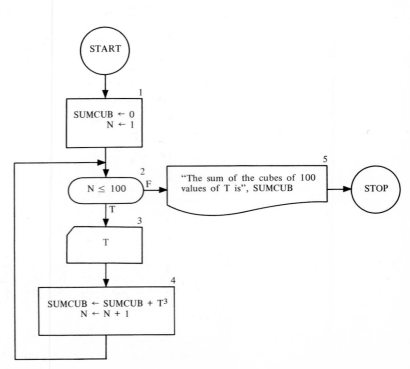

2.

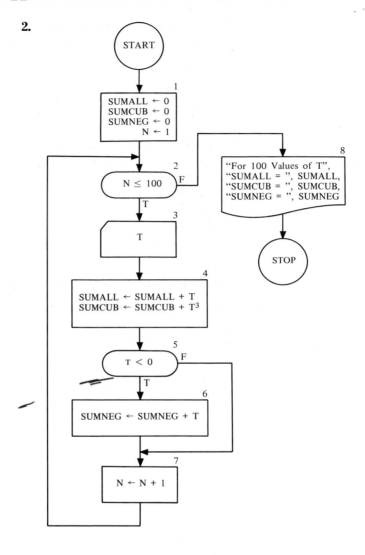

1. The given flowchart is *not* logically equivalent to the associated word statement. The following flowchart is equivalent.

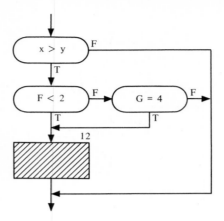

4. Flowcharts b and d are logically equivalent to the word statement.

7. Flowchart fragment b is logically equivalent to the word statement.

6.

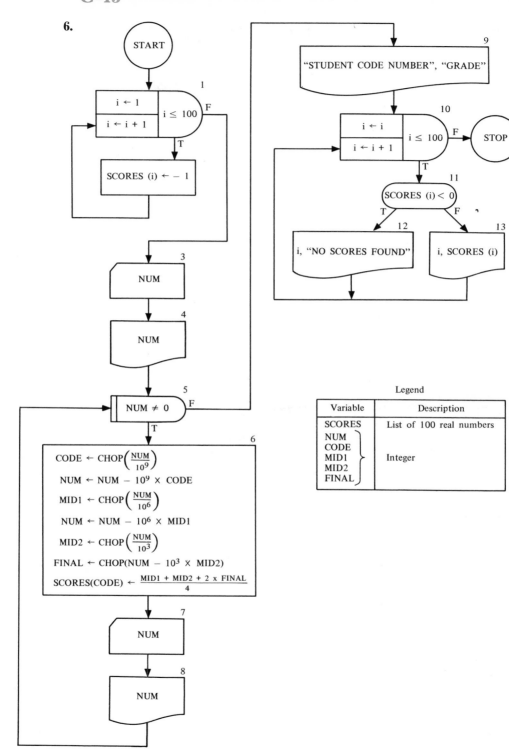

EXERCISES 3·6,   **1.** (a) 4 (input in box 1)
SET B   7, 2, −5, 4 (input in box 2)

Sequence	Box 3	4	5	6	7	8	Current Value of K
1	✓						1
2		✓					
3			✓				
4	✓						1
5		✓					
6				✓			2
7					✓		
8		✓					
9			✓				
10	✓						1
11		✓					
12			✓				
13	✓						1
14		✓					
15				✓			2
16					✓		
17		✓					
18				✓			3
19					✓		
20		✓					
21		✓					
22	✓						1
23		✓					
24				✓			2
25					✓		
26		✓					
27				✓			3
28					✓		
29		✓					
30				✓			4
31					✓		
32						✓	
Total	5	10	4	6	6	1	

Appearance of
Scratch pad memory for
the A list.

A

1	7̶	2̶	−5	
2	2̶	7̶	−5̶	2
3	−5̶	7̶	4	
4	4̶	7		

This much of the table is given to the student.

(c) 32 boxes are executed after the input steps and before (STOP).

(d) 10 times.

EXERCISES 3·6,
SET C

1. (a) The correct choice is (2) A: 1, 2, 3, 5
   B: 4, 6, 7, 8

(b) The correct choice is (1) 8, 7, 6, 5, 4, 3, 2, 1

5. (a) False.   (d) True.
   (b) False.   (e) True.
   (c) True.   (f) True.

Chapter 4

EXERCISES 4·1,
SET A

1.

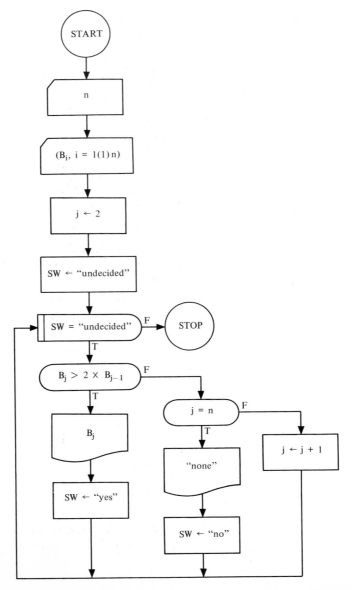

3. (a) No. The while loop will cycle endlessly for this set of data. Values of i cycle over 1, 5, 3, 7, 4, 8 without finding a case where $i = c_i$.

(b) Alter box 4 to read:

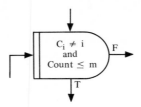

(c) Make changes as follows:

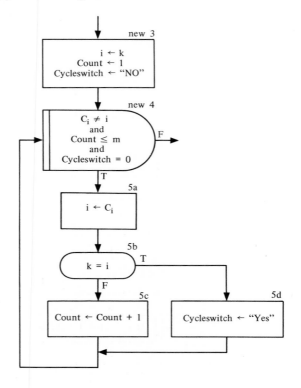

1.

3	2	1
6	5	4
9	8	7

3. Fragment 5.

6. If the value of K exceeds that of N, the cloud in sequence b will be executed, but the cloud in sequence a will not.

8. (a) Given a list of N elements called A, a new list, called B, is formed
and displayed (printed). Elements of B are the respective even-
valued elements of A.

(b) -4, 6, 6, 12

13.

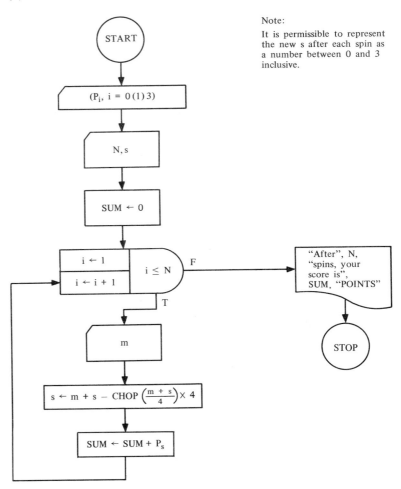

Note:

It is permissible to represent
the new s after each spin as
a number between 0 and 3
inclusive.

EXERCISES 4·1,
SET C

2. Alternative 2.

5.

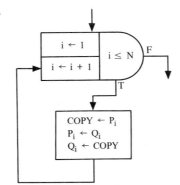

9.

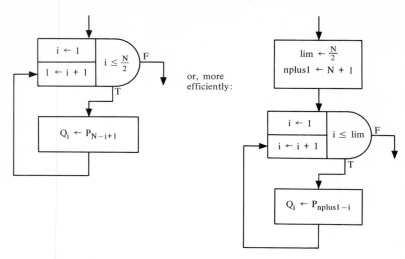

or, more efficiently:

13. (a) $N = 2, S = 3$
(b) 5 times
(c) 2 times
(d) 22

17.

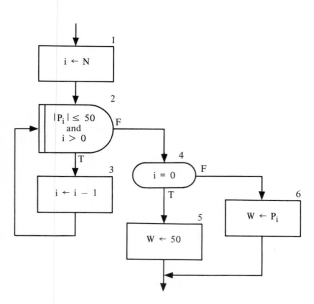

3. (a) Yes, they are equivalent in net effect.
Figure 4·17a evaluates a polynomial of the form:

$$A_0 + A_1 \times X + A_2 \times X^2 + A_3 \times X^3$$

while Figure 4·17b evaluates a polynomial of a similar form,

$$B_0 \times X^3 + B_1 \times X^2 + B_2 \times X + B_3$$

after it is reexpressed in the mathematically equivalent form:

$$((B_0 \times X + B_1) \times X + B_2) \times X + B_3$$

(b) It is only necessary to generalize box 1 of each flowchart, for example, for Figure 4·17a, box 1 should be changed to

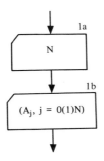

(c) The Sunday method (Figure 4·17b) is more efficient since on each transit of the loop, only one multiplication (and one addition) is required as compared with two multiplications (and one addition) required in the everyday method (Figure 4·17a).

EXERCISE 4·1,
SET E

1.

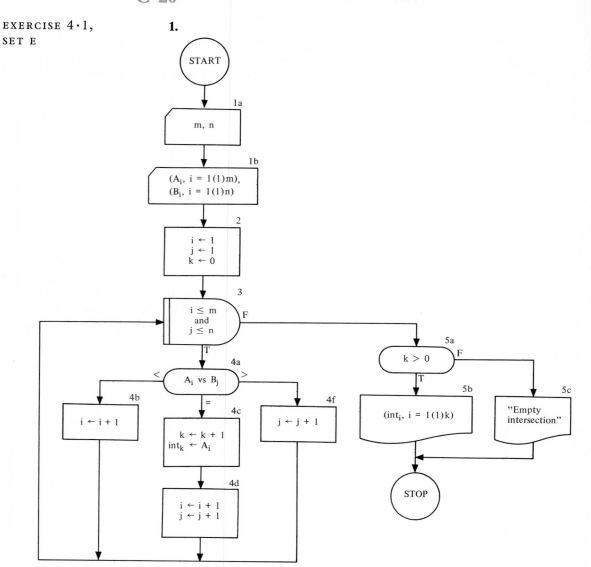

EXERCISES 4·3

1. (a) (4)
     (b) (2)
     (c) (4)

4. 46

6.

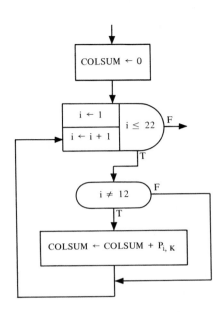

10. (a)

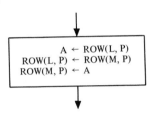

This solution assumes A is a list whose length is the same as the number of columns in the matrix P.

13. (c)

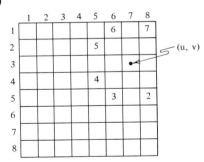

(d) The Knight.

16.

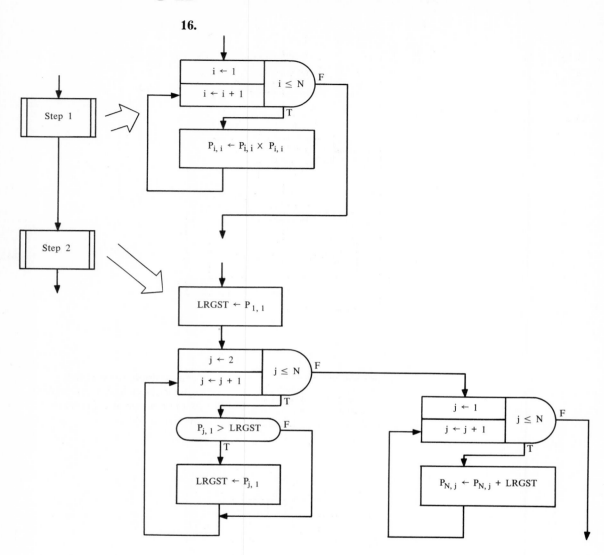

Chapter 5

EXERCISES 5·1,
SET A

1. Each time box 4 is executed, 8 multiplications are required, since H^3 is $H \times H \times H$, and so forth. Box 4 is executed $10 \times 10 \times 10$ times. Thus 8000 multiplications are required.

EXERCISES 5·1,
SET B

4.

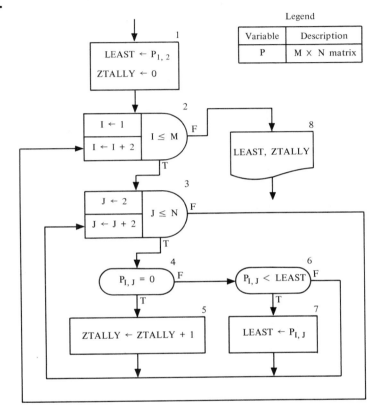

Check values: For the matrix $P = \begin{bmatrix} 2 & 3 & 0 \\ 0 & 7 & 9 \\ 12 & 10 & 19 \\ 18 & 16 & 12 \end{bmatrix}$

The output values are
LEAST = 3, ZTALLY = 0

2. (a) Solution without lists or arrays.

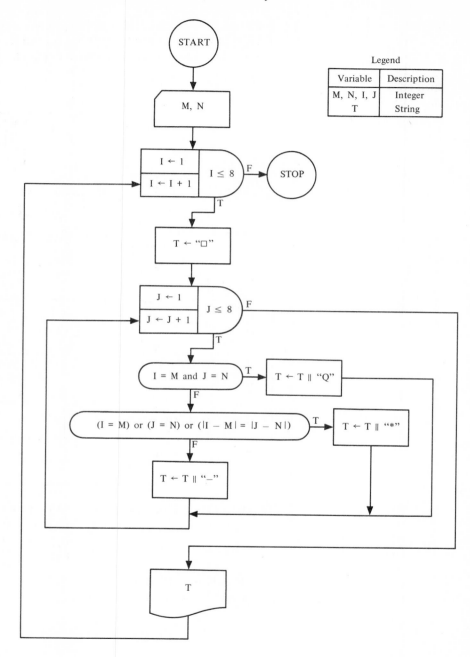

Legend	
Variable	Description
M, N, I, J	Integer
T	String

(b) Solution using a list.

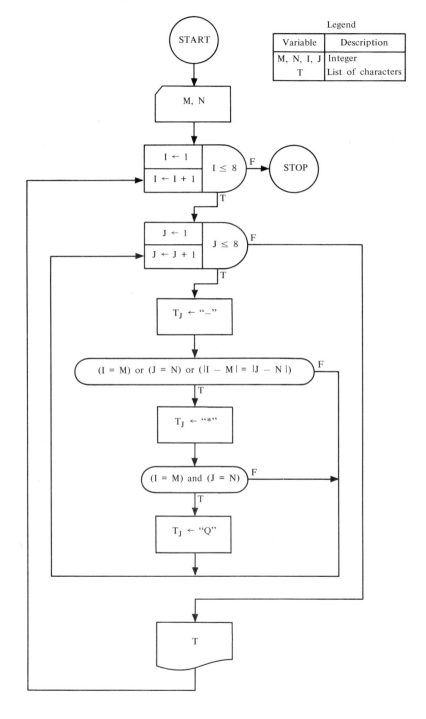

(c) Solution using an array.

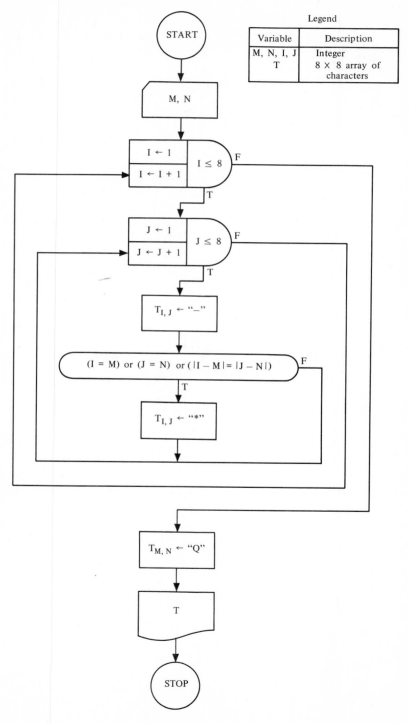

5. (a) If execution reaches box 5, n is an integer because box 5 lies on the true-path from box 2, that is, CHOP(n) = n.
    (b) 3, 5, 7, 9, 11, 13, 15, 17, 19, 21, 23, 25.
    (c) The same values as in part b.
    (d) 15, 25.
    (e) 3, 5, 7, 11, 13, 17, 19
    (f) The algorithm is generating all the primes less than or equal to n by a method called the Sieve of Eratosthenes. In box 4 the only even prime, 2, is output. Then, starting with 3, all the odd integers not greater than n are assigned to the corresponding positions in the array A, that is, $A_3 \leftarrow 3$, $A_5 \leftarrow 5$, and so forth. These components of A are then tested one at a time starting with 3. If the component is not zero, then it is a prime and this prime is output in box 9. Then all its odd multiples are set to zero because they are *composite* numbers. Since even multiples of odd integers are even, even multiples can be disregarded.
    (g) Initialize k to the current value of j, that is, $k \leftarrow j$ instead of $k \leftarrow 3$ in box 10.

EXERCISES 5·1,
SET E

1.

Legend

Variable	Description
Graph	60 × 132 array of characters

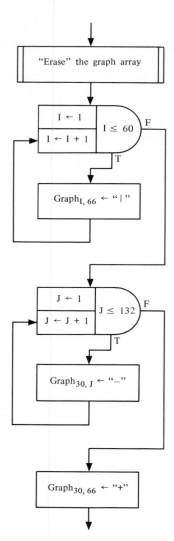

EXERCISES 5·2

3. (a) 5 times (box 2 is executed 3 times and box 3b3 is executed 2 times).

(b) 3 times (box 3 is executed 3 times and box 3b3 is not executed at all).

(c) 6 times (box 3 is executed 3 times and box 3b3 is also executed 3 times).

EXERCISES 5·4

1.

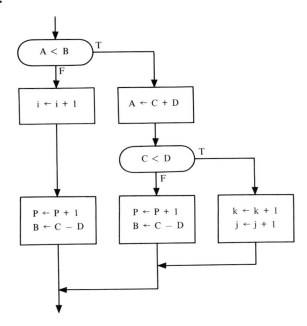

2.

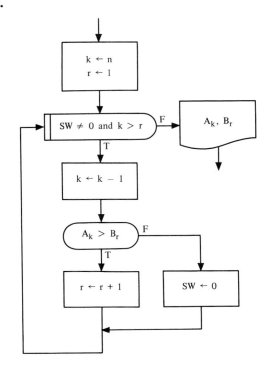

Chapter 6

3.

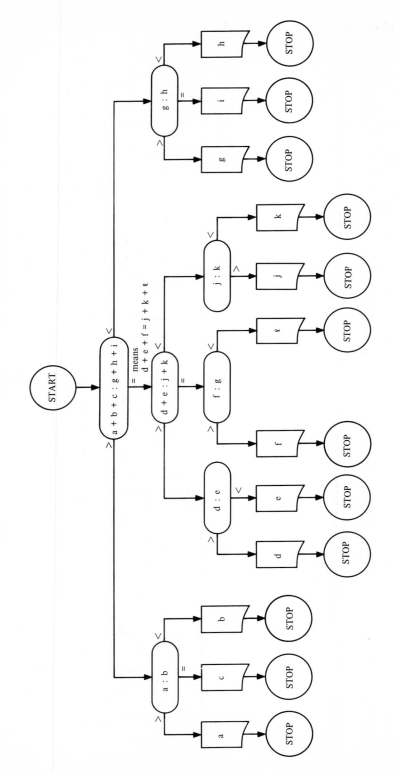

EXERCISE 6·1,
SET B

1. (a) One for each terminal point, or 32 games.

   (b) The answer is the product of the probabilities of the individual moves of this particular game which, in this case, is:

   $$\begin{array}{cccccc} \text{Player:} & A & B & A & B & A \\ \text{Value selected:} & 1 & 3 & 1 & 2 & 1 \end{array}$$

   $$\text{Probability:} \quad \frac{1}{3} \times \frac{1}{2} \times \frac{1}{2} \times \frac{1}{2} \times \frac{1}{2} = \frac{1}{48}$$

   (c) If in a like manner we compute the probabilities for each of the 12 paths that lead to wins for A and sum them, and divide this sum by the sum of the probabilities of all 32 games, we get 5/12 as the likelihood of a win for A by this random move selection approach to the game. This can be expressed as 41(2/3) chances out of 100.

   Comment The following is another way to sum probabilities. A game that is won at the root of the tree is given a weight of 1, and at successive levels the weights are 2, 4, 6, and 8. The sum of weights for terminals marked A is 40. The sum of weights for all terminals is 96, hence the ratio 5/12. This ratio, incidentally, differs only slightly from the ratio of A-win terminals to total terminals, which is 3/8.

EXERCISE 6·1,
SET C

3. Yes, there are two distinct feasible sets of five courses. The full tree is as follows.

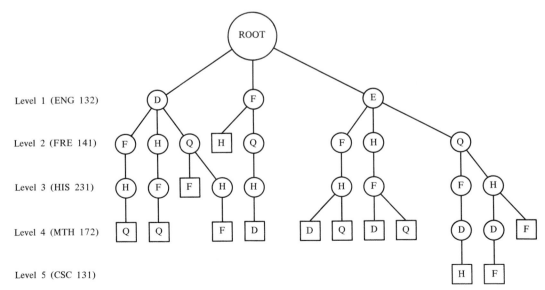

Time Table

Course	Letter Codes for Feasible Set				
	No. 1	No. 2	No. 3	No. 4	No. 5
ENG 132	E	E			
FRE 141	Q	Q			
HIS 231	F	H			
MTH 172	D	D			
CSC 131	H	F			

EXERCISES 6·1, SET D

1. (a) 0
(d) 65536

5. (a) $y\left(4 - 2 \times \dfrac{y}{3}\right) + y^2$

(b) This tree is equivalent to the given expression.

(c) $y\left[\left(\dfrac{4 - 2y}{3}\right) + y^2\right]$

7. (a) $q - \left[r^s / t - \left(u^v - \dfrac{w \times y}{z}\right)\right]$

9. b and c are false.

11. For $\boxed{D}$ the path list is (3, 1, 3).
For $\boxed{U}$ the path list is (3, 3, 1, 3).
For $\boxed{\uparrow}$ the path list is (3, 1, 1, 3, 2).

13.

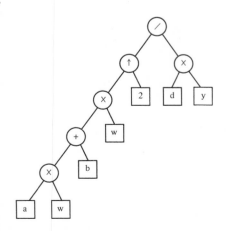

Chapter 7

EXERCISES 7·2,
SET A

1. The square node is number 7 in level-by-level tree search.

2. False. In the tree shown nodes X and X′ are at level 2 and node Y at level three (if we take the root node to be at level 1). In a

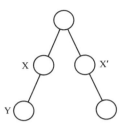

level-by-level tree search both X and X′ will be examined *before* Y. In a natural-order tree search X will be examined *before* Y, but X′ will be examined *after* Y.

EXERICSES 7·2,
SET B

2. (a) 10, 9, 8, 4, 6
   (b) 4. The algorithm prints the code numbers of those neighbors of the country coded 5 that appear below it in the diagram of the tree.

EXERCISES 7·3,
SET A

1. Color the root node to indicate a win for A.

2. The node marking rule is correct as stated: a node representing a player's turn to move can be marked as a *win* for that player, if at least one segment emanating from this node leads to a win for that player; otherwise the node should be marked as a win for the other player.

EXERCISES 7·3,
SET B

1. (a) B controls the game at node 3.
   (b) A controls the game at node 1.

2. (a) Answer 2 is correct; player B will always win.
   (b) Answer 3 is correct; 2, 8, 9, 10, 14, 15.

EXERCISES 7·3,
SET C

1. Move$_k$ was the last segment tried at level k (because it was admissible, it appears in the path list). In retreating one level we want to pick up the natural-order selection of segments where we left off. Thus the next segment to be tried, TMOVE, should be assigned the value, MOVE$_k$ + 1.

2. No, it is not necessary to reset MOVE$_k$ and/or MOVE$_{k-1}$ to zero in Retreat1 and Retreat2. Before these elements appear again on the right of an assignment statement, they will have been assigned new values by the Advance procedure.

Chapter 8

EXERCISES 8·2

1.

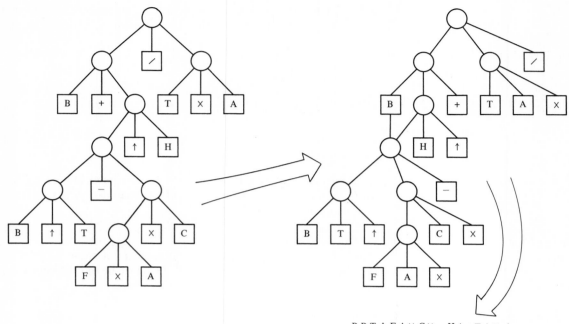

$$BBT\uparrow FA\times C\times -H\uparrow +TA\times/$$

6. (c)

10. (a) $\times y + / - 4 \times 2\,y\,3\uparrow y\,2$ expression in *pre*fix form

(b) $y \times 4 - 2 \times y / 3 + y\uparrow 2$ expression in unparenthesized *in*fix form

Note that the initial meaning has been lost because parentheses were not reinstated during the tree scan, but the fully parenthesized infix form:

(b') $(y \times (((4 + 2 \times y)) / 3) + (y\uparrow 2)))$

can be achieved if a left parenthesis is inserted upon encountering an operator for the first time and if a right parenthesis is inserted upon encountering an operator for the last time.

(c) $y\,4\,2\,y \times - 3 / y\,2\uparrow + \times$ expression in *post*fix form

EXERCISES 8·3, SET A

1. (a) 5

5. (a) Yes.
(b) Yes.

EXERCISES 8·3, SET B

1. Case a.   Stack   1001
                Stack   1002
                Add
                Stack   1003
                Add

> Stack   1004
> Add
> Stack   1005
> Add
> Store   1006

EXERCISES 8·4   **1.**

Character Scanned	Stack	Postfix Expression
(	(	
n	(	n
/	(/	n
2	(/	n2
)	(/	n2/
×	×	n2/
(	×(	n2/
2	×(	n2/2
×	×(×	n2/2
a	×(×	n2/2a
+	×(×+	n2/2a×
(	×(+(	n2/2a×
n	×(+(	n2/2a×n
−	×(+(−	n2/2a×n
1	×(+(−	n2/2a×n1
)	×(+(−	n2/2a×n1−
×	×(+×	n2/2a × n1 −
d	×(+×	n2/2a × n1 −d
)	×(+×	n2/2a × n1 − d × +
□	×	n2/2a × n1 − d × + ×

6. In no way whatsoever, except to recognize that the relational symbols can be treated as if they are operators whose precedence levels are lower than that of + and −.

EXERCISE 8·5   **1.** Assume a special mark is used to represent the end of the infix expression. One possible mark might be the blank character, (□). [Another might be a nonalphabetic mark such as the pound sign (#).] Then box 2 details would be

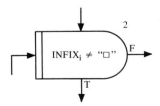

EXERCISE 8·6   **3.** (a) The sequence   +STO□□□1
                                         +LDA□□□1

is superfluous.

(b) To eliminate such superfluous instructions it is necessary to postpone generating store instructions (as done in box 811 of Figure 8·13) until they are known to be needed. The store and subsequent load instructions are not needed when the accumulator mark, "*", has been found at the next-to-top of the stack (T exit of box 808) and are not needed if the operator is commutative when the accumulator mark has been found at the top of the stack (T exit of box 803). Suppose switches are set on the T exits of boxes 803 and 808 to indicate whether left or right operands are held in the accumulator. Then box 811 can be replaced by a flowchart fragment that generates the wanted instructions based on the nature of the switch settings and on whether the operator is commutative. Details should be worked out by the student.

Chapter 9

EXERCISES 9·1

2. Something is wrong.

3. (a) Globals
(b)

43	12
3	7

(c)

INTDIV (N, D, Q, R)

START

$Q \leftarrow 0$

$N \geq D$ F → $R \leftarrow N$

T

$N \leftarrow N - D$
$Q \leftarrow Q + 1$

RETURN

Legend for INTDIV

Identifier	Treatment	Description
N, D, Q, R	Parameter	Integer

5.

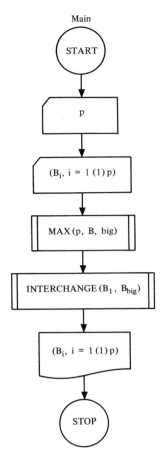

Main

START

p

$(B_i, i = 1\,(1)\,p)$

MAX (p, B, big)

INTERCHANGE (B_1, B_{big})

$(B_i, i = 1\,(1)\,p)$

STOP

Legend for Main

Identifier	Description
p, i, big	Integer
B	List of p reals

EXERCISES 9·2

2. (a) The procedure INTDIV will supply as return parameter values the remainder *and* the quotient of M divided by N. To use INTDIV as currently defined, we must supply a matching argument for *each* parameter (see Problem 1) including one to match the third parameter.

(b)

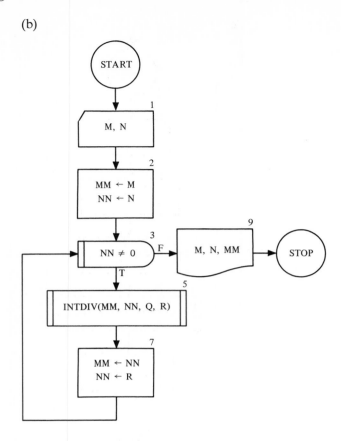

4. (a) No. A and B of INTERCHANGE must be called by reference so the interchange action can affect values of the matching arguments (which must be variables and not expressions).

    (b) The purpose of reference parameter k is to indicate, for the benefit of the caller of MAX, the index or position of the maximum value that MAX has "found." Changing k to a call-by-value parameter will prevent MAX's caller from accessing this information.

    (c) Yes. Letting parameter A be a call-by-value parameter simply means that a complete copy will be made of the matching list-valued argument. MAX would then search the copy of the list argument. The position k of the maximum value is the same in the copy as it is in the original.

7.

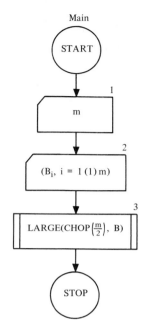

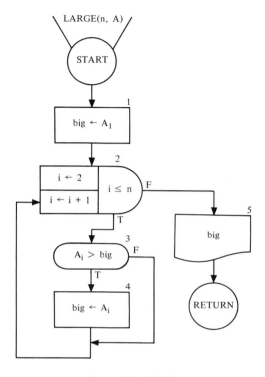

Legend for Main

Identifier	Description
m, i	Integer
B	List of m elements

Legend for LARGE

Identifier	Treatment	Description
n	Value	Integer
A	Reference	List
i	Local	Integer
big	Local	

Comments   Box 3 of Main shows a possible use of LARGE. The call in box 3 asks for the largest value in the first CHOP$(m/2)$ elements of B, to be displayed by LARGE. The legends leave unspecified the type of elements in B and the corresponding types for A and big, since this information was not supplied in the statement of the problem. In many programming languages it is necessary to specify a type, for example, integer or real, for each identifier in each program or procedure. Since no step in LARGE needs to alter n, this parameter is treated as call-by-value. To avoid copying the list B, the corresponding parameter A is treated as a reference parameter. This treatment is safe, since no step in LARGE now alters any element of A. If further changes are made to LARGE, however, care must be taken to prevent modifications that will have the effect of altering elements in A.

EXERCISES 9·3   **1.**

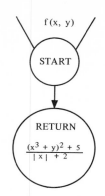

2.   (a)

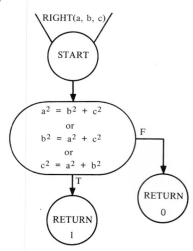

7.

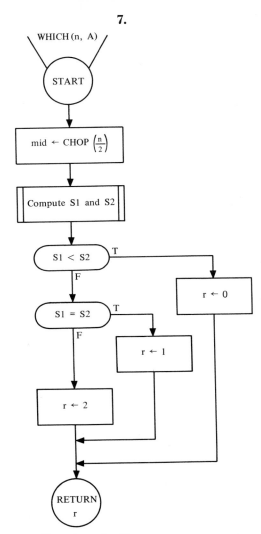

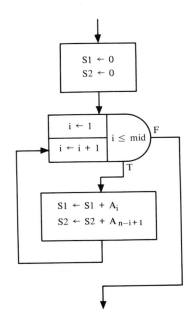

Legend for WHICH

Identifier	Treatment	Description
n	Value	Integer
A	Reference	List of n elements
i, mid, r	Local	Integer
S1, S2	Local	Same type as elements of A

Note when n is odd,
the sums S1 and S2 do not
include the middle term
which would have to be
considered excluded from
each sum or included in each
sum and in any case would
not contribute to the result
returned by WHICH.

EXERCISES 9·4,
SET A

2.

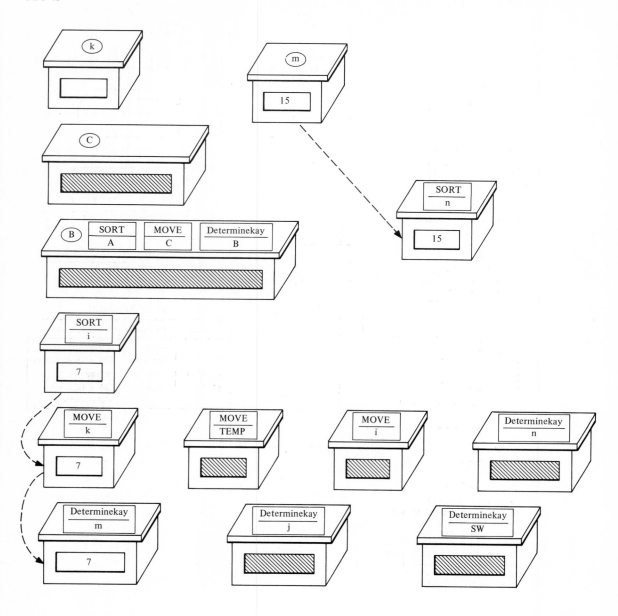

4. (a)

	Legend for SCALE	
Identifier	Treatment	Description
n	Value	Integer
C	Reference	List of n reals
code	Reference	Integer
lim	Value	Real
i	Local	Integer
T	Local	Real

	Legend for MAX	
Identifier	Treatment	Description
lim	Value	Integer
list	Reference	List of reals
L	Local	Real
i	Local	Integer

	Legend for NEG	
Identifier	Treatment	Description
n	Value	Integer
List	Reference	List of reals
sw, i	Local	Integer

(b)

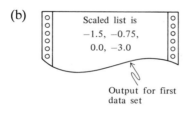

Output for first
data set

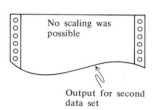

Output for second
data set

(c)

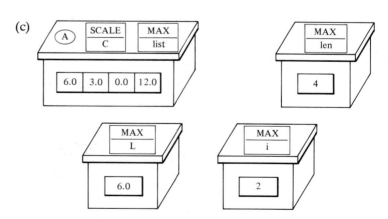

EXERCISE 9·5   2.   Trace Table

Name of Executing Procedure	Box	Action
Main	1	$r \leftarrow 7$
Main	2	$A \leftarrow (4, -5, 7, 9, -4, 8, 6)$
Main	3	
SUM	1	$i \leftarrow 1$
		$s \leftarrow 0$
SUM	2	
F1	RETURN	return 1
SUM	2	$1 \leq 7$ is true
SUM	3	$s \leftarrow 4$
		$i \leftarrow 2$
SUM	2	
F1	RETURN	return 2
SUM	2	$2 \leq 7$ is true
SUM	3	$s \leftarrow -1$
		$i \leftarrow 3$
⋮		
SUM	2	
F1	RETURN	return 8
SUM	2	$8 \leq 7$ is false
SUM	RETURN	return 25
Main	3	print out the value 25
Main	4	
SUM	1	$i \leftarrow 1$
		$s \leftarrow 0$
SUM	2	
F2	RETURN	return 1
SUM	2	$1 \leq 3$ is true
SUM	3	$s \leftarrow 4$
		$i \leftarrow 2$
SUM	2	
F2	RETURN	return 3
SUM	2	$3 \leq 3$ is true
SUM	3	$s \leftarrow 11$
		$i \leftarrow 3$
SUM	2	
F2	RETURN	return 5
SUM	2	$5 \leq 3$ is *false*
SUM	RETURN	return 11
Main	4	print out the value 11
Main	5	
SUM	1	$i \leftarrow 1$
		$s \leftarrow 0$
SUM	2	
F3	RETURN	return 1
SUM	2	$1 \leq 7$ is true
SUM	3	$s \leftarrow 4$
		$i \leftarrow 2$
SUM	2	
F3	RETURN	return 3
SUM	3	$3 \leq 7$ is true
SUM	3	$s \leftarrow 11$
		$i \leftarrow 3$

Trace Table (Continued)

Name of Executing Procedure	Box	Action
SUM	2	
F3	RETURN	return 6
SUM	2	$6 \leq 7$ is true
SUM	3	s ← 19
		i ← 4
SUM	2	
F3	RETURN	return 10
SUM	2	$10 \leq 7$ is *false*
SUM	RETURN	return 19
Main	5	print out the value 19
Main	STOP	

EXERCISE 9·6

4. (a) Output for the given data set is

(b) Changes are as follows:
for Main: box 3 should be:

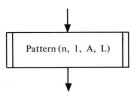

for Pattern: revise to:

Legend for Pattern

Identifier	Treatment	Description
i, n	Value	Integer
A, L	Reference	List

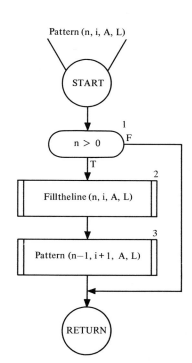

for Filltheline: revise funnel:

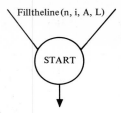

Filltheline(n, i, A, L)

Legend for Filltheline		
Identifier	Treatment	Description
i, n	Value	Integer
A, L	Reference	List
q	Local	Integer

EXERCISE 9·7,
SET A

1. (a)

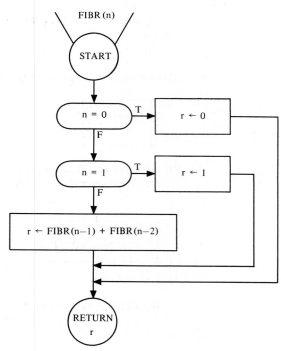

(b)

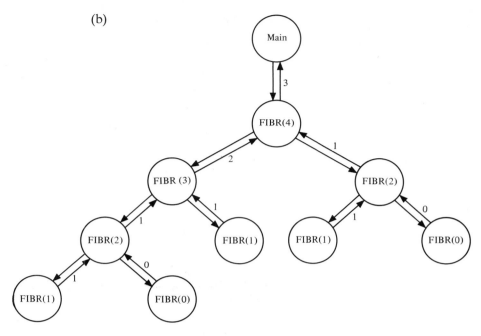

(c) The correct answer is 176.

Chapter 10

EXERCISES 10·4

1. If N is an *odd* power of 2, the output file will appear on Tape C. If N is an *even* power of 2, the output will appear on Tape A. For example, if $N = 1024 = 2^{10}$, the output will appear on Tape A.

2. After the file is split on to two tapes, Mergesort must be called $\log_2 N$ times. Each invocation of Mergesort results in the reading of N records. Hence, the work done using Mergesort is $N \times \log_2 N$.

EXERCISE 10·5, SET A

2. Changes required are in boxes 101 and 103 of MOVE and in box 203b of Determinekay, in the "funnels," and in the subprocedure references. The revised flowchart boxes are:

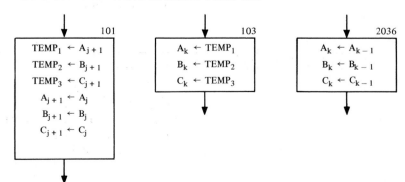

The new funnels are:

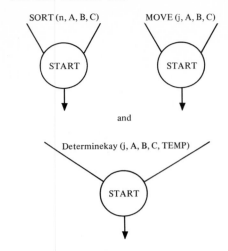

The new subprocedure references are box 3 in SORT and box 102 in MOVE:

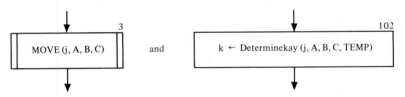

Legends for SORT, MOVE, and Determinkay must include entries for lists B and C. Also, entries for TEMP in the legends for MOVE and Determinkay must show TEMP as a list of three strings.

EXERCISES 10·5,
SET B

2. (a) Alternative 4 if empty spaces in B are not mapped to LIST. (Alternative 3 if empty spaces are mapped to LIST, as would be required if sorting with a list is attempted.)

(b) AL | 15 | 8 | 29 | 22 | 1 |

This answer assumes that alternative 3 is chosen in part a.

(c)

	1							8						15								22							29						
LIST	W	I	L	L				J	I	M	□	L	E	E	A	L	F	R	E	D			R	O	Y				M	A	C	K			

(d) With a six-element list, empty spaces could be eliminated in mapping from B to LIST, and adjacent values could be "differenced" to compute the actual length of each record including the last record. The computed record lengths along with the individual starting points could then be used to sort the variable-length records. With a sixth element in AL, LIST and AL could have the following values:

	1				5							12						18			21			
LIST	W	I	L	L	J	I	M	□	L	E	E	A	L	F	R	E	D	R	O	Y	M	A	C	K

AL | 1 | 5 | 12 | 18 | 21 | 25 |

3. (a) Alternative 3.
(b) Alternative 4.

4. (a) Alternative 3.

EXERCISES 10·6

2. The new procedure called Search will have five parameters, as explained in the legend. Its structure will be similar to that of Search-chain.

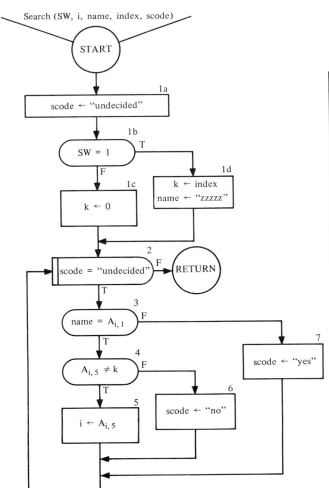

Search (SW, i, name, index, scode)

Legend for Search

Identifier	Treatment	Description	
SW	Value	Integer	1 if finding a predecessor index 0 if searching for a name
i	Reference	Integer	
name	Value	String	(dummy value supplied when finding a pre‑decessor index)
index	Value	Integer	(dummy value supplied when searching for a name)
scode	Reference	String	(dummy name supplied when finding a pre‑decessor index)
A	Global	Table of five columns	
k	Local	Integer	

Note The logic of boxes lb, lc, and ld ensures that for finding a predecessor index, box 3 is always true, while, for searching for a name, box 4 always amounts to a test for the existence of a successor chain element.

5. (a) The Findpredecessor procedure can be eliminated when each list
    entry contains a pointer to its predecessor.

Chapter 11

EXERCISES 11·1

1. The SAMOS floating-point representations of the given fractions are:

p, the approximation to $\frac{1}{3}$ . . . .

1	2	3	4	5	6	7	8	9	10	11
+	+	0	0	3	3	3	3	3	3	3

q, the approximation to $\frac{1}{7}$ . . . .

1	2	3	4	5	6	7	8	9	10	11
+	+	0	0	1	4	2	8	5	7	1

r, the approximation to $\frac{1}{21}$ . . .

1	2	3	4	5	6	7	8	9	10	11
+	−	0	1	4	7	6	1	9	0	4

The SAMOS floating-point product p × q is

1	2	3	4	5	6	7	8	9	10	11
+	−	0	1	4	7	6	1	9	0	2

which is *less* than r.

Let a, b $< 10^8$ be positive integers and let p and q be the
SAMOS approximations to $1/a$ and $1/b$. If p does not equal $1/a$
exactly, it can only be *less* than $1/a$ as a result of the chopping of
some least significant digits when the SAMOS approximation was
made. The same observation is of course true for q, i.e., $q \leq 1/b$.
The SAMOS approximation to $1/(a \times b)$ is r. The assertion
$p \times q \leq r$ says that for positive numbers, a and b, the product of
the chopped SAMOS approximations is less than or equal to the
chopped SAMOS approximation to the product. This is clearly true.

3. (a) If π^k is to be a SAMOS floating-point number, π^k must be less
    than 10^{99}, that is,

    $$k \log \pi < 99$$

    $$k < \frac{99}{\log \pi} \sim 199.135$$

    Thus 199 is the largest integral power of π that can be expressed
    as a SAMOS floating-point number.

    (b) $e^k > .1 \times 10^{-99}$

    $$k \log e > \log \frac{1}{10^{100}}$$

    $$k \log e > -100$$
    $$k > -230.2585 > -230$$

EXERCISES 11·2

1. $x = \pm.d_1d_2 \times 2^e, \quad -1 \leq e \leq 2$

The possible nonzero precision parts of the numbers, disregarding sign, are

$$.10_2 = \frac{1}{2}$$

$$.11_2 = \frac{1}{2} + \frac{1}{4} = \frac{3}{4}$$

(The first digit of any nonzero precision part is normalized to be nonzero.)

The exponent values can be -1, 0, 1, 2. Thus b^e can have the values $1/2$, 1, 2, and 4. This number system then contains, in addition to zero, the following 16 values:

$$\pm\frac{1}{4}, \pm\frac{3}{8}, \pm\frac{1}{2}, \pm\frac{3}{4}, \pm1, \pm\frac{3}{2}, \pm2, \pm3$$

The diagram of the system is:

2.   (a) Putting the numbers into base 2 notation and adding:

$$-\frac{3}{2} = -.11 \times 2^1$$

$$+1 = \frac{.10 \times 2^1}{-.01 \times 2^1}$$

This sum normalizes to $-.10 \times 2^0$ or $-\frac{1}{2}$, which is a number in the system.

(b) $\dfrac{3}{4} = .11 \times 2^0$

$\dfrac{3}{8} = .11 \times 2^{-1}$

Multiplying .11 by .11, we have .1001 which we chop to .10. Thus the result is $.10 \times 2^{-1}$, or $\frac{1}{4}$.

$$-\frac{3}{8} = -.11 \times 2^{-1}$$

$$\frac{3}{8} = \quad .11 \times 2^{-1}$$

Multiplying $.11 \times .11$ we again chop to .10. Thus the result is $-.10 \times 2^{-2}$ or $-\frac{1}{8}$.

(c)

No. of $\frac{3}{4}$'s Accumulated	Fractional Notation	Base 2 Decimal Notation	Scratch Pad	Chopped Result In Base 2 Decimal Notation
2	$\frac{3}{4} + \frac{3}{4}$	$.11 \times 2^0 + .11 \times 2^0$	$.11 \times 2^0$ $+.11 \times 2^0$ $\overline{1.10 \times 2^0}$	$= .11 \times 2^1$
3	$\frac{3}{2} + \frac{3}{4}$	$.11 \times 2^1 + .11 \times 2^0$	1.10×2^0 $+.11 \times 2^0$ $\overline{10.01 \times 2^0}$	$= .10 \times 2^2$
4	$2 + \frac{3}{4}$	$.10 \times 2^2 + .11 \times 2^0$	$.10 \quad \times 2^2$ $.0011 \times 2^2$ $\overline{.1011 \times 2^2}$	$= .10 \times 2^2$
5	$2 + \frac{3}{4}$	$.10 \times 2^2 + .11 \times 2^0$		$= .10 \times 2^2$

EXERCISES 11·3

(a) In the given floating-point system an infinite loop would occur. At some time the variable x would have the value 3.9 and the next value would be 4.2 but never exactly 4.00.

(b) The stopping condition 4.2 would be all right, but x $\leq$ 4.2 is safer.

EXERCISE 11·4,
SET B

1.

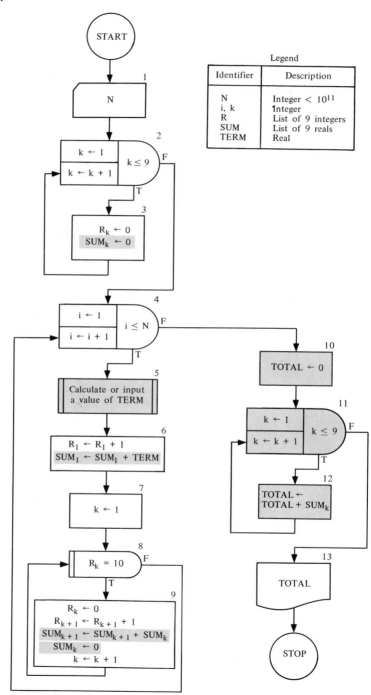

Legend

Identifier	Description
N	Integer $< 10^{11}$
i, k	1nteger
R	List of 9 integers
SUM	List of 9 reals
TERM	Real

EXERCISE 11·6   **1.**

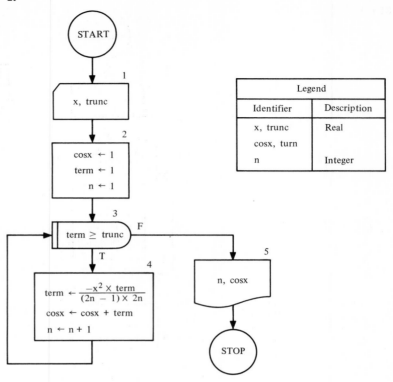

Legend	
Identifier	Description
x, trunc	Real
cosx, turn	
n	Integer

Chapter 12

EXERCISE 12·1,
SET B

1. Using four decimal precision arithmetic, and four steps for the method of bisection, we find that the root lies between 2.0625 and 2.125.

Step No.	x	$x^3 - 2x - 5$
Start	2	− 1
	3	14
1	2.5	5.625
2	2.25	3.1656
3	2.125	.3457
4	2.0625	− 0.03513

EXERCISES 12·2   **1.** (b) 42.850

5. (c) $n \cong 3000$

EXERCISES 12·3   **2.** (a) SUM is needed as an auxiliary variable if we are to preserve the conceptual separation of the summing process from the updating steps (boxes 3c·1, 3c·2, and 3c·3 from box 3c·4). SUM accumulates and holds the value to be used in updating MID. But before updating MID the current value of MID must be used in updating TRAP (first assignment step in box 3c·4).

(b) Box 3b·1 sets new values for n, w, and ERR for the next iteration when the number of intervals n is doubled, the interval width w is halved, and the new error estimate ERR is calculated for the trapezoid rule. Box 3c·4 updates values for TRAP, MID, and SIMP. Note that the new TRAP is computed as the mean of the old TRAP and MID. But the new SIMP is based on the new TRAP and the new MID.

5. Since the Simpson's rule result for n = 16384 is correct to eight digits, then the roundoff error is less than one part in the eighth place for all values of n less than 16384, since roundoff is probably less for smaller n.

(1) n	(2) Truncation Error = π − Simpson of Part B	(3) Cumulative Roundoff Error = Simpson Part B − Simpson Part A	(4) Sum of (2) and (3)
512	.00001402	.0000039	.0000179
1024	.00000496	.0000079	.0000129
2048	.00000175	.0000158	.0000176
4096	.00000062	.0000317	.0000323
8196	.00000022	.0000624	.0000626
16384	.00000008	.0001241	.0001242

A plot of $\log_2 n$ versus values in column 4 shows that minimum error for an eight-digit precision Simpson's rule calculation of π is obtained at about n = 890. At this point the cumulative roundoff error "overtakes" the truncation error.

EXERCISES 12·4

2. (a)

	Multiplications (Including Division)	Additions (Including Subtractions but Not Counting the Steps in Iteration Boxes)
NORMALIZE	$4 \times 6 = 24$	0
ELIMINATE	$4 \times 6 \times 4 = 96$	$4 \times 5 \times 4 = 80$
BACKSOLUTION	$1 + 2 + 3 = 6$	$1 + 2 + 3 = 6$
Total	126	86

4. (a) In PARTIALPIVOT

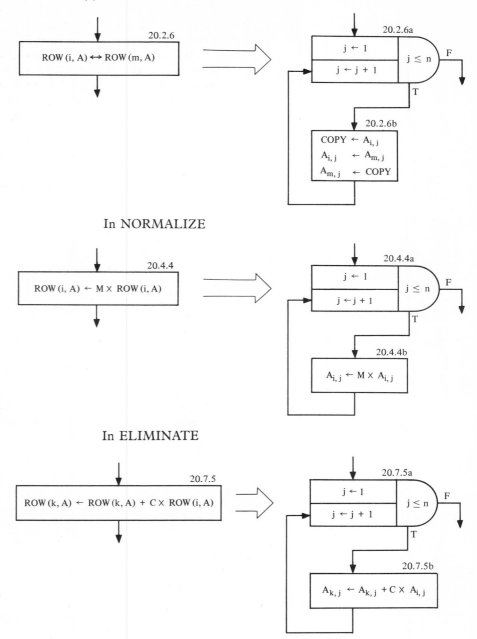

In NORMALIZE

In ELIMINATE

EXERCISE 12·5   **2.**

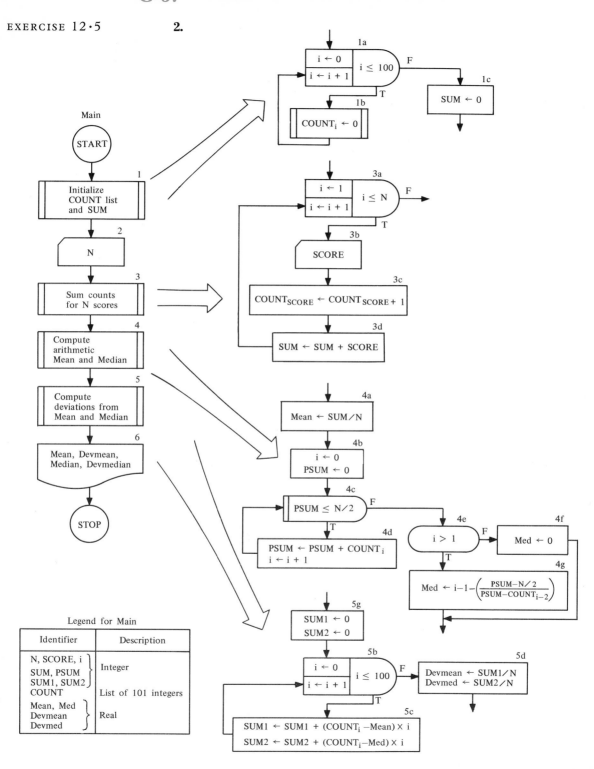

2. Recall that, in general, the root-mean-square deviation from the number $\bar{x}$ is given by

$$\sqrt{\frac{\sum_{k=1}^{N} (x_k - \bar{x})^2}{N}}$$

To minimize this deviation, we minimize

$$\sum_{k=1}^{N} (x_k - \bar{x})^2$$

To do this, we first expand out the squared expression, simplify, and complete the square:

$$\sum_{k=1}^{N} (x_k - \bar{x})^2 = \sum_{k=1}^{N} (\bar{x}^2 - 2x_k\bar{x} + x_k^2)$$

$$= \sum_{k=1}^{N} \bar{x}^2 + 2\sum_{k=1}^{N} x_k\bar{x} + \sum_{k=1}^{N} x_k^2$$

In this latest expression, notice that $\bar{x}$ and $\bar{x}^2$ do not depend on the value of k. Thus, when we add N constants, each of which has the value $\bar{x}^2$, we are simply calculating $N\bar{x}^2$. Similarly, since $\bar{x}$ does not depend on the value of k, it is a constant in every term of the second summation and so can be factored out of the sum. These facts lead us to restate the expression as follows:

$$\sum_{k=1}^{N} (x_k + \bar{x})^2 = N\bar{x}^2 - 2\bar{x}\sum_{k=1}^{N} x_k + \sum_{k=1}^{N} x_k^2$$

$$= N\left(\bar{x}^2 + 2\bar{x}\frac{\sum_{k=1}^{N} x_k}{N}\right) + \sum_{k=1}^{N} x_k^2$$

Before the step of completing the square, we note that this last expression can be simplified to

$$N(\bar{x}^2 - 2A\bar{x}) + S$$

where

$$A = \frac{\sum_{k=1}^{N} x_k}{N}$$

is the arithmetic mean of the data values and where

$$S = \sum_{k=1}^{N} x_k^2$$

is the sum of the squares of the data values. Now

$$\sum_{k=1}^{N} (x_k - \bar{x}^2) = N(\bar{x}^2 - 2A\bar{x}) + S$$

$$= N(\bar{x}^2 - 2A\bar{x} + A^2) - NA^2 + S$$
$$= N(\bar{x} - A)^2 - NA^2 + S$$

Chapter 13

EXERCISES 13·4

1. In TEXT, "APPLE" will be replaced by "APPLE□PIE" the first time box 1 is executed. Thereafter every execution will add another "PIE", and there is no stopping condition built into the loop. When you design a pattern match, think about whether it will terminate by itself or whether it will grow and grow like the "APPLE□PIE".

2. (d)

EXERCISES 13·5, SET A

1. (d)

2. TH BY FLL DWN

EXERCISE 13·5,
SET B

1. The correct answer is:
 (d) Box 7 prints "(DX)" and box 8 prints "( )".

EXERCISE 13·6,
SET A

1.

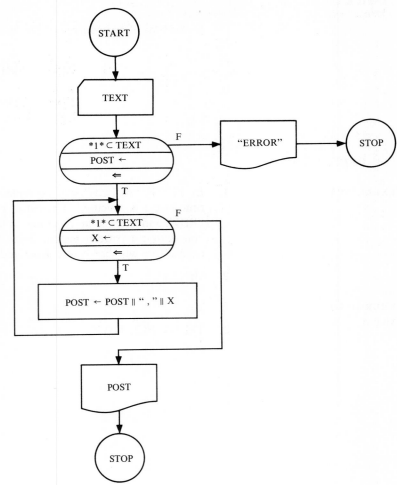

1. (a) The statement is T ← A + B − C + D − E

Generated Instructions	Without Refinement	With First Level Refinement	
1	+LDA A	+LDA A	
2	+ADD B	+ADD B	No further improvement is possible
3	+STO 1 ⎫	+SUB 1	
4	+LDA 1 ⎭	+ADD D	
5	+SUB C	+SUB E	
6	+STO 1 ⎫	+STO T	
7	+LDA 1 ⎭		
8	+ADD D		
9	+STO 1 ⎫		
10	+LDA 1 ⎭		
11	+SUB E		
12	+STO 1 ⎫		
13	+LDA 1 ⎭		
14	+STO T		

EXERCISES 13·7,
SET C

1.

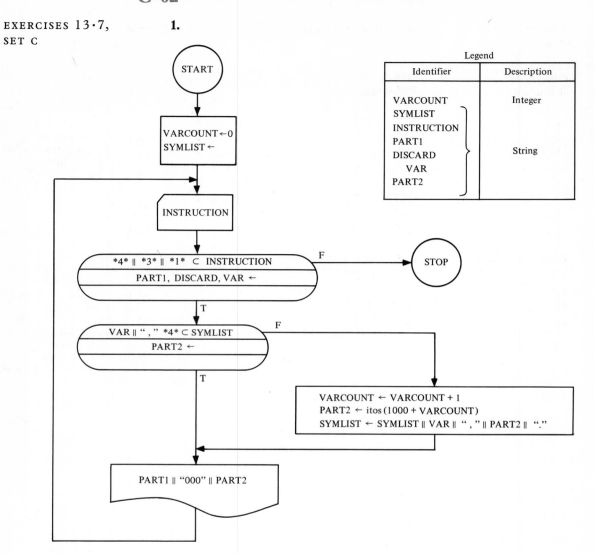